The Modern World

II

Realities

LITERATURE AND WESTERN CIVILIZATION

The Modern World

II

Realities

GENERAL EDITORS

David Daiches

Anthony Thorlby

ALDUS BOOKS · LONDON

Aldus Editor Kit Coppard

Copy Editor Maureen Cartwright

SBN 490 00244 7

© 1972 Aldus Books Limited, London

Printed in England by Unwin Brothers Limited, Woking

Contents

Preface

Literature discovered a new quality in human experience during the 19th century: the real. It brought a reality into focus that seemed not to have been there before. In part, what had been discovered was an unprecedented historical fact—urban industrial existence. In part, history was itself the fact: civilization as a cumulative, total achievement of mankind in the mass. But this discovery revealed something not only about the new land- and townscape in which other men lived; it revealed also something about the discoverer. The individual's situation seemed to be changing, and he felt himself to be alone and unsure of himself, as he looked on at an alien world. This feeling did not invariably lead to adverse moral judgment; although criticism of man's "alienated" condition in modern society inspired 19th-century writers from first to last, as we shall see, they were provoked to much self-inquiry besides, and even to enjoyment of their detached position. Literary inspiration began to roam more widely beyond the categories of moral understanding than it had done in previous centuries; indeed, society's traditional norms of behaviour and happiness revealed themselves as questionable.

What else could be looked for? Did politics, did science, did art point to a new way? Was a more direct encounter with the outer world required —or a more self-conscious grasp of the inner one? These are questions that will be raised again and again in the course of the following chapters. The search for the real strikes out in different directions in different countries, of course; history presented the task differently in America and in Finland, for instance, and differently again within the confines of Jewish life. Moreover, the writer found himself having to adjust to a new relationship with the outside world in a quite practical sense: his public, not merely his subject matter, was changing. Mass readership meant numberless, faceless readers with very dissimilar standards of literary expectation and even of literacy. How should the writer address them and what about? Again, the answers vary according to the writer's situation: that of Petőfi in Hungary is unlike that of Tennyson in England or of Baudelaire in Paris. And it will be different again from that of Joyce in Ireland and Brecht in Germany—and of both of these last in exile. In order to show some of the directions in which Western literature and civilization moved in the 19th century, it has been necessary to reach back into the 18th century and forward into the 20th, recapitulating themes from Volume IV in order to carry them further, and anticipating others that will be taken up again in Volume VI.

THE EDITORS

CHAPTER I

Writers and Cities in the 19th Century

Asa Briggs*

Already before the middle years of the 19th century a British writer had described the period in which he was living as "the age of great cities," and Benjamin Disraeli had advised his fellow-countrymen to visit Manchester, "the most wonderful city of modern times," if they wished to understand the way the world was moving.[1] Fifty years later, across the Atlantic, huge new cities, such as Chicago and Pittsburgh, had sprung into existence, gripping the imagination and sometimes provoking the alarm of natives, immigrants, and visitors alike. Their boosters called them "prodigies"; their critics, "cancers on the body politic." Yet, whatever the value judgments, an American commentator of a new generation and outlook was echoing the unanimous view that "the tendency towards concentration or agglomeration is all but universal in the Western world."[2]

Urbanization is only one of the great themes that are associated with the 19th century. Industrialization is another, and the commitment to "progress," never expressed unanimously or without qualification, a third. In England in 1800, there was no town with the the exception of London with a population of more than 100,000: in 1891 there were 23. In the United States in 1800 there were only 6 towns with a population of 8000 or more; in 1880 there were 286. The "urban fact" was related to the expansion of industrial, market economies, and was often—and in face of strong opposition—identified with the march of progress. It was difficult not to have views for or against the city.

The enormous mass of 19th-century writing about both particular cities and *the* city has been read and re-read during recent years in the light of changing 20th-century urban experience. The city remains as much a

* Professor of History and Vice-Chancellor, University of Sussex.

problem centre of modern civilization as it was during the 19th century, although in the meantime the pressures of industrialization and economic development have brought in new countries and taken new forms, and the trust in "progress" has been undermined in many parts of the world.

Taking 19th-century writing on its own terms, it is perhaps distinguished above all else by a strong sense of the particularity of place, a sense that survived not only the building of factories but also the building of railway stations and hotels. This sense, now for various reasons in danger of being lost,[3] emerges—often with direct force, sometimes obliquely—not only in diaries, travel notes, and lectures, but also in the pages of newspapers, rightly thought by the first "urban sociologists" on both sides of the Atlantic to catch the essence of city patterns of life and thought.[4] The newspapers dealt with the commonplaces and with the dramas of daily life in particular places, emphasizing the sense of local community. To think of *the* city (or to have it in mind when talking about a particular city) demanded an extension of such immediate preoccupations. To move from facts, good or bad, to symbols required a sense of perspective, an ability to recall and to relate, to compare and to contrast. Manchester, for example, had to be juxtaposed across the centuries, as Disraeli juxtaposed it, with Athens; Birmingham, priding itself on its "civic gospel," with Florence; Paris, with greater imagination than historical accuracy, with Babylon; the new cities of the century and the "ideal cities" that were never realized in brick or stone with the New Jerusalem. The sociological generalizations about cities came later, although there was a perpetual attempt throughout the century to formulate them.

As the relevant 19th-century writings, no less alarming in their size and complexity than the cities themselves, have been re-examined and reviewed, the facts of urban growth in different countries—and no two countries had the same chronology—have been subjected to increasingly systematic compilation, classification, and analysis.[5] They are facts that bear not only on particular cities or the relations between cities but also on what was happening to human relations inside cities—relations between individuals and between groups. Attention has also been paid to urban morphology—the forms of city organization and growth—and, most recently, to the sights, sounds, and (not least) smells that provoked considerations both of economics and of aesthetics,[6] and have in turn been modified by them.

It is plain from the writings that reactions were mixed—even at one moment of time or for one individual—toward both the growth in the size of existing cities, familiar or strange, and the increase in the number of big cities inside or outside one's native country. To appreciate the significance of what was happening, we need a dialectical theory of culture that concerns itself with pride and fear, with conflicts and contradictions. Compare what Carlyle and Disraeli have to say about Manchester, or the differences in mood within Carlyle himself. Or consider Kipling on Chicago:

> I have struck a city—a real city—and they call it Chicago. . . . This place is the first American city I have encountered. It holds rather more than a million people with bodies, and stands on the same sort of soil as Calcutta. Having seen it, I urgently desire never to see it again. . . . I went out into the streets, which are long and flat and without end. And verily it is not a good thing to live in our East for any length of time. Your ideas begin to clash with those held by every right-thinking white man. I looked down interminable vistas flanked with nine, ten, and fifteen storied houses, and crowded with men and women, and the show impressed me with a great horror. Except in London—and I had forgotten what London is like—I had never seen so many white people together, and never such a collection of miserables. There was no colour in the street and no beauty, only a maze of wire-ropes overhead and dirty stone flagging underfoot. . . . I spent ten hours in that huge wilderness. . . .[7]

It is possible to set alongside Kipling 100 clashing images of Chicago,[8] just as it is possible to anthologize almost indefinitely on London or New York.[9] Manchester and Chicago, however, were the real shock cities of the 1840s and 1890s respectively, both of them conspicuous for problems (of class and race respectively) and for bustling vitality, both pointing not to the past but to the future. As the journalist W. T. Stead put it in 1894, Chicago was "not laden down by any *damnosa hereditas* of the blunders and crimes of the past; her citizens are full of faith in the destiny of their city."[10] For Carlyle, Manchester in the 1840s had been "every whit as wonderful, as fearful, as unimaginable, as the oldest Salem or prophetic city."[11]

If the 19th-century reactions to the city were mixed, they were no different in this respect from most other 19th-century reactions to the phenomena of economic and social change: the railways and the steamboats, the furnaces and the forges, the mills and the banks. It remains difficult, indeed, even in retrospect, to separate reactions to what sociologists came to call "urbanization" from reactions to "industrialization" and "progress." Nor does the difficulty disappear when we recall, first, that many of the towns and cities that grew fastest during the 19th century were not really industrial cities at all; and second, that most of what we consider to be characteristic 19th-century "reactions" had been preceded by "anticipations" during the pre-industrial 18th century. Rousseau in *Émile* (1762) had warned that "the breath of man is fatal to his fellows. . . . Cities are the burial pit of the human species."[12] He was not speaking simply for himself or even for an *avant-garde* in his own generation, but with the weight of a substantial body of current opinion and a long tradition behind him. Voltaire, who extolled the benefits of "civilization," had an equally rich tradition behind what he had to say about the qualities of London as a capital city;[13] so, too, had Dr Johnson.

There are greater complexities. More than 100 years before Kipling, a traveller from the world's Far East, looked into the faces of the *misérables* in Chicago (to use Victor Hugo's word for the victims of urban society in Paris), William Blake, the home-based citizen, spelled out his own experiences in London:

> I wander thro' each charter'd street,
> Near where the charter'd Thames does flow,
> And mark in every face I meet
> Marks of weakness, marks of woe.[14]

When a student of the relationships between civilization and literature confronts passages of this kind from different historical periods, from different parts of the world and from different literary genres—there are similar passages about cities in Wordsworth's poetry and Dickens' novels—he is forced to take into account not merely a dialectical theory of 19th-century culture ("the long revolution," as Raymond Williams has called it) but also different dimensions of interpretation and criticism.[15] It was not merely that there were varieties of reaction to the 19th-century city but that there were different layers of response: immediate and contemplative, intuitive and ratiocinative, inherited and idiosyncratic. In turning to the symbols and in trying (to use a phrase of Northrop Frye's) to "crack symbolic codes," it is necessary to wend a devious critical path through literature itself, old and new.[16]

The literature of the United States provides the most easily accessible set of initial examples. During the 19th century the "virgin continent" was transformed into a modern society, although it was not until the 1880s, 50 years after Britain, that urbanization, dramatic urbanization, became a controlling factor in American national life. In one turbulent decade the number of towns of between 12,000 and 20,000 people increased from 76 to 107, the number of towns of between 20,000 and 40,000 people from 55 to 91, the number of cities of between 40,000 and 75,000 people from 21 to 35, and the number of still bigger cities from 23 to 39.[17] Not surprisingly,

14

popular writers made the most both of the new horizons of individual opportunity and of the new turmoil of social relationships. Yet what Henry Nash Smith has called "the myth of the garden," Richard Hofstadter "the agrarian myth," and Leo Marx "pastoralism" (popular and sentimentalized or private and subtle) survived the great transformation.[18] "The soft veil of nostalgia that hangs over our urbanized landscape," Marx writes, "is largely a vestige of the once dominant image of an undefiled, green republic, a quiet land of forests, villages, and farms dedicated to the pursuit of happiness."[19] There were many late-19th-century echoes of Thomas Jefferson's *Notes on Virginia* (1785)—"the mobs of great cities add just so much to the support of pure government, as sores do to the strength of the human body. It is the manners and spirit of a people which preserve a republic in vigour. A degeneracy in these is a canker which soon eats to the heart of its laws and constitution."[20]

To explain American pastoralism Marx returns *via* Emerson, Thoreau, Hawthorne, Jefferson, Wordsworth, Goldsmith, Thompson, and Shakespeare's *Tempest* to Virgil's *Eclogues*. Yet he notes a basic 19th-century twist. Taking as his starting-point Nathaniel Hawthorne's description in 1844 of a neighbourhood known as "Sleepy Hollow," he points to Hawthorne's intrusion of "the whistle of the locomotive," "a startling shriek" that "brings the noisy world into the midst of our slumbrous peace." The passage from Hawthorne, far from being unique, may be paralleled without difficulty in Thoreau's *Walden* (1854), Melville's *Moby Dick* (1851), and Mark Twain's *Huckleberry Finn* (1884), three of the classics of American literature.

What distinguished such passages from those in earlier pastoralist literature was the role of the locomotive whistle, "a little event" in a century of great events. "In the stock contrast between city and country," a contrast with ancient origins, "each had been assumed to occupy a more or less fixed location in space; the country here, the city there. But in 1844 the sound of a train in the Concord woods implies a radical change in the conventional pattern. Now the great world is invading the land, transforming the sensory texture of rural life—the way it looks and sounds— and threatening, in fact, to impose a new and more complete dominion over it. True, it may be said that agents of urban power had been ravaging the countryside throughout recorded history. After they had withdrawn, however, the character of rural life had remained essentially unchanged. But here the case is different; the distinctive attribute of the new order is its technological power, a power that does not remain confined to the traditional boundaries of the city. It is a centrifugal force that threatens to break down, once and for all, the conventional contrast between these two styles of life."[21]

As the American cities grew during the last decades of the 19th century, at a rate that would have surprised Hawthorne, the threat of the city was heightened. The fact that city boosters set out to enhance its lure and to extol its material power merely added to the feeling that within the American city, man had created a "wilderness" of his own—a term that, as we have seen, was used by Kipling and was to be used by many writers after him. Even Walt Whitman, who, on returning to New York in 1870, praised "the splendour, picturesqueness, and oceanic amplitude" of the great American cities, dreamed in his *Passage to India* (1868)—making Kipling's journey in reverse—of a primal return to the "gardens of Asia" where history began:

> ... the voyage of his mind's return,
> To reason's earthly paradise,
> Back, back to wisdom's birth, to innocent intuitions,
> Again with fair creation.[22]

Henry James, who also journeyed eastward (although no farther than Europe, which was his "new world"), found "a kind of sanctity" in London just because it was not a wilderness. "It is the single place in which most readers, most possible lovers, are gathered together; it is the most inclusive public and the largest social incarnation of the language, of the tradition."[23] It might not be a "pleasant, agreeable, or cheerful place" or "exempt from reproach": it was "only magnificent . . . the biggest aggregation of human life, the most complete compendium of the world."[24]

There was no single dominant city in America, no city that was both metropolis and capital, like London or Paris; and in turning from American to European reactions to the city, both London and Paris—and at a later date Berlin and Vienna—occupy a special place in the literature not only of their own countries but of the countries of visitors and exiles. Moreover, no European country could claim the pedigree of a virgin land, and in every case—not least in Papal Rome, "the oldest city"—there were so many layers of historical experience that reactions were bound to be complex. F. A. Vizetelly, the well-known translator into English of Émile Zola's *Paris* (1898), one of "a trilogy of the three cities" (along with *Lourdes* and *Rome*), quoted in his introduction some lines written about Paris by a very different writer from Zola, Lord Byron:

> I loved her from my boyhood; she to me
> Was as a fairy city of the heart.

He also quoted Victor Hugo:

> Before possessing its nation, Europe possesses its city [Paris]. The nation does not yet exist, but its capital is already here. . . . It is from three cities, Jerusalem, Athens, Rome, that the modern world has been evolved. They did the work. Of Jerusalem there now remains but a gibbet, Calvary; of Athens, a ruin, the Parthenon; of Rome, a phantom, its empire. Are these cities dead then? No, a broken eggshell does not necessarily imply that the egg has been destroyed; it rather signifies that the bird has come forth from it and lives. . . . From Rome has come power; from Athens, art; from Jerusalem, freedom; the great, the beautiful, the true. . . . And they live anew in Paris, which in one way has resuscitated Rome, in another Athens, and in another Jerusalem; for from the cry of Golgotha came the principle of the Rights of Man. And Paris also has its crucified; one that has been crucified for eighteen hundred years—the People. . . . But the function of Paris is to spread ideas. Its never-ending duty is to scatter truths over the world, a duty it incessantly discharges. Paris is a sower, sowing the darkness with sparks of light. It is Paris which, without a pause, stirs up the fires of progress. . . . It is like a ship sailing on through storms and whirlpools to unknown Atlantides, and ever towing the fleet of mankind in its wake.[25]

The most remarkable point about this grandiloquent passage is the total omission of London. Yet there were many English writers in the 19th century who would have taken issue with James and granted Paris the primacy, at least in the arts, even if, as has been claimed, many of them "learnt far less about France from all the works of Flaubert and Zola than from George Moore's slender *Confessions of a Young Man* (1888)."[26]

Hugo himself had written of mediaeval Paris, seeking to establish its identity, in his *Notre-Dame de Paris* (1831), a huge Gothic canvas, inspired by Scott, with rich tableaux, some grotesque, others sublime, very different in purpose and scale from any American writing about cities. The buildings are the heroes of the novel, some of them being compared fancifully with living or mythical animals. The Île de la Cité is a tortoise, the Louvre a hydra, and the Cathedral itself a sphinx, with its rose window resembling the eye of a cyclops. For contemporary Paris we have to turn to Eugène Sue's best-seller *Les mystères de Paris* (1842–3), which is significant also because it was imitated in many other countries, as well as translated: *The Mysteries of London*, by G. W. M. Reynolds, T. Miller, and E. L. Blanchard, was published between 1846 and 1850; *The Mysteries of Berlin* appeared in 1845; and E. Z. C. Judson's *The Mysteries and Miseries of New York* appeared in 1848.

This was the decade when, as we have seen, there was a new consciousness of living in "the age of great cities," and Sue, rightly labelled a social romantic, was anxious to reveal to his readers what a socially disturbed place the modern city really was:

> The only thing we can hope to do is to draw the attention of the intelligentsia and the more prosperous classes to the great deprivation and suffering in society, facts that can be deplored but not denied.[27]

Sue could be as theatrical as Hugo, but he interspersed statistics with his melodrama, drawing heavily on new data that were then available for the study of cities. In this connection, as in so many others, Paris was the right place to start, although already by the end of the 1830s the "statistical method"—arithmetical figures instead of figures of speech—was winning adherents everywhere.[28] The annual *Recherches statistiques sur la ville de Paris* had begun to appear in 1817, and 12 years later Parent-Duchâtelet and Villermé had launched their *Annales d'hygiène publique et de médecine légale,* the first regular journal in the world to concentrate on problems of public health—or what came to be called more comprehensively "the sanitary idea."[29] This "idea," which implied a battle against Fate, was to fascinate many of the greatest writers of the 19th century, notably George Eliot in England.[30]

Like many 19th-century writers after him—with a very different novelist, Dickens, outstanding amongst them—Sue was concerned with the horrors of poverty and disease and with the correlations between them, which had nothing to do, in his context, with the Industrial Revolution or the advance of steam technology. He was even more concerned, however, with the activities of the Parisian underworld and the colourful, often criminal, exploits of what were called (and not only in Paris) *les classes dangereuses.*[31] He knew that a large and respectable reading public could be entertained and titillated with details of the curiosities of city life. A percipient critic noted in the English liberal newspaper the *Daily News,* which for a brief time was edited by Dickens:

> The French novelists seem to set about . . . pictures [of vice] in a kind of jocular, half-credulous vein, which they communicate to their readers, and which inspires a feeling of half-reality, very consoling in horrors, and leaving full enjoyment of the comic gayer scenes. No Englishman could at all attempt that light *charlatanerie* of the French, and for us to rival it by taking such stories more *au sérieux* is equally hopeless.[32]

Similar documentation to that employed by Sue was to be used more seriously—and more memorably—in French by Hugo in his second long novel about Paris, *Les misérables,* not published until 1862, long after it was written.

There remains a great divide between Hugo, whom Zola attacked virulently, and Zola himself, although (as we have seen) Vizetelly cheerfully used the former to introduce the latter. In the meantime, there had been large-scale political changes influencing life in Paris and the relationship between the capital and the provinces of France. Paris remained, as it had been before the revolution of 1848, a city without large-scale industry and consequently without much of a proletariat, but it never lost its revolutionary propensities or its revolutionary reputation. Above all, it continued to grow, whatever the regime. It had doubled its size between 1800 and 1850—at a time when the population of France as a whole was growing far more slowly than that of any of its neighbours—and during the hustling Second Empire, when large parts of it were re-developed by Haussmann, it continued to expand, annexing many of its burgeoning suburbs in 1859. By 1881 it had more than two million people, and in 1900 it was still the largest city in Europe after London. Zola was as much impressed by its immensity as Henry James was with the "numerosity" of London; he also made much of its variety and of its contrasts.

Before the revolution of 1848 the exile Heinrich Heine—one of a large number of German refugees in Paris—had stated that Paris was "really France." "The latter," he went on, "is only the countryside round its capital. . . . Everything outstanding in the provinces soon makes its way to the capital, the focus of all light and brilliance."[33] During the Second Empire, when many Frenchmen, like Hugo, were in exile from their own country, Paris glittered in all its glory as a centre of fashion and display for the whole of Europe. And during the very different regime of the Third Republic, which seemed in domestic terms to be the regime of the provinces,[34] the city continued to attract writers and artists from all countries. "All good Americans," declared Thomas Appleton, "when they die, go to Paris."[35] "It boasts today," wrote the English essayist Frederick Harrison in 1894, "that it is the most brilliant, the most ordered, the most artistic city of men, and one of the most sanitary and convenient for civilised life. And no reasonable man can deny that the substantial part of this boast is just."[36]

For Zola, as for Balzac before him, interesting themes for the novelist could be found in the French provinces as well as in Paris. Yet he was always interested in big cities. In the novel *Paris*, the young Abbé Froment, who has arrived there *via* Rome and Lourdes, continues his personal quest. As in so many other novels about men in cities, the colour and mood of the place, even its weather, correspond closely to the hero's personal feelings. We begin in the first few pages with "the Paris of mystery, shrouded by clouds, buried as it were beneath the ashes of some disaster," and we end the novel with Paris bathed in rich evening sunlight.

> This was no longer the city of the sower, a chaos of roofs and edifices suggesting brown land turned up by some huge plough. . . . Nor was it the city whose divisions had one day seemed so plain to Pierre: eastward, the districts of toil, misty with the grey smoke of factories; southward, the districts of study, serene and quiet; westward, the districts of wealth, bright and open; and in the centre, the districts of trade with dark and busy streets. It now seemed as if one and the same crop had sprung up on every side, imparting harmony to everything, and making the entire expanse one sole, boundless field, rich from the same fruitfulness. . . . And Paris flared—Paris which the divine sun had sown with light, and where in glory waved the great future harvest of Truth and Justice.

We are not so far from Hugo after all, and it is not surprising that in the light of passages like this, heavy with symbolism, recent writers on Zola have dwelt less on his scientific aims, on his appeal to naturalism, and on his clinical methods, than on the mythic and poetic qualities of his work. Nonetheless, in two of the volumes in the novel cycle *Les Rougon-Macquart* (1871–93), Zola dealt realistically with a market and a department store, two of the great 19th-century city institutions. *Le ventre de Paris* (1873; The Belly of Paris) explores Les Halles: at the same time it gives Zola a chance to explore some of the conflicts of interest that influence the relationships between people in cities and people outside. The market-gardener, Mme François, has every reason for distrusting *ce diable de Paris*. *Au bonheur des dames* (1883) presents a department store that in the mechanism of its daily operations harnesses the same kind of ruthless drive as any factory in an industrial city. Both these novels about urban institutions could have been written only at that particular period in the evolution of Paris. They were of their time and for their time, continuing, in Zola's own estimate, the heritage of Stendhal and Balzac.[37]

There was one very different heritage in 19th-century France, which is represented in a new and distinctive set of attitudes toward Paris and the city. It is a heritage associated not with the novel—which, it has been claimed, is the distinctive literary genre of the city[38]—but with poetry. The key figure is Baudelaire, a link with the earlier romantic poets, to whom later generations of poets turned. Baudelaire was born in Paris, lived there for more than 40 years, and died there. He drew some of his most powerful poetry from the city that he knew so well, and about which he had no illusions:

Paris change, mais rien dans ma mélancholie
N'a bougé! Palais neufs, échafaudages, blocs,
Vieux faubourgs, tout pour moi devient allégorie,
Et mes chers souvenirs sont plus lourds que des rocs.[39]

(Paris changes, but nothing in my melancholy has moved! New
public buildings, scaffoldings, blocks, old suburbs, everything becomes
an allegory for me, and my dear memories are heavier than rocks.)

Zola saw the city as a challenge, an intricate institutional complex with a
past and a future, where individuals and groups, even when in conflict,
were held within the city's grip. Baudelaire saw the city as a place of
perpetual change, never still, where individuals pursued inner adventures
of the mind, prompted by the sensations of each fleeting moment—
moments that were linked through memories and pressed forward through
desire:

Fourmillante cité, cité pleine de rêves,
Où le spectre, en plein jour, raccroche le passant.[40]

(Swarming city, city full of dreams, where in broad daylight ghosts
accost a man in the street.)

There might be the same "dirty yellow fog" that we meet in Zola—or in
Dickens—but there were very different shapes in the fog. There might be
the same scorn for bourgeois values, but whereas Zola, like Balzac,
plotted the chart of bourgeois fortunes, Baudelaire affirmed contemptuous
counter-values, making a Bohemia out of the whole city. No writer was
more conscious of what Walter Pater called "the quickened multiple
consciousness" that the city made possible.[41] Baudelaire's quickened
consciousness encompassed the evil and the good, "multitude and solitude"
(terms that he wanted to make "equal and interchangeable"), boredom
and the "drunken spree of vitality."[42]

When Baudelaire wanted to get out of Paris, the idea of the "voyage"
returned in a different context; it was not of a "sleepy hollow" that he
was dreaming, but of exotic journeys of escape, which he well knew had
no real destination, but which lured his imagination into "the sinuous
folds of ancient capitals, where all things, even horrors, turn to magic."
In the last resort the alternative to life in the city was not escape from it,
but death.

Baudelaire's Romanticism was fundamental; his use of symbols stopped
far short of the symbolism in Verlaine, Mallarmé, and Rimbaud, all of
whom took Baudelaire's city for granted. Yet the fact that they could take
it for granted was due in part to the way in which Baudelaire had
begun to transform the nature of poetry under the pressure of modern

city life. Imagery acquired a new topography.[43] Thereafter, writers of other countries and of many cities persistently reverted to Baudelaire's images. Eliot's "Unreal City" in *The Waste Land* is London, but the phrase suggests Baudelaire's *cité pleine de rêves*: for Eliot, in the confusion of 20th-century war, the towers were everywhere falling: Jerusalem, Athens, Alexandria, Vienna, London. Joyce—who, as Harry Levin has pointed out, lived in as many cities as the author of the *Odyssey*, each more polyglot and more metropolitan than the last—depended for his unique sense of the city not only on his own experience, but on a rich texture of literary and historical association. Feelings of attraction and recoil, absorption and disengagement, are all expressed in his work, which is not only of immense imaginative power but of the most subtle complexity—as complex, indeed, as the 19th- and early 20th-century city itself.[44]

Through this second heritage we move far away from the simplicities of the 19th-century American deviation from pastoralism or from the kind of contrasts between city and countryside that we find in the verse of an English writer such as Matthew Arnold:

> Calm Soul of all things; make it mine
> To feel, amid the city's jar,
> That there abides a Peace of Thine
> Man did not make, and cannot mar.[45]

Not that all writers after Baudelaire placed the city beyond Good and Evil. The Flemish poet Émile Verhaeren, a socialist as well as a symbolist, thought of cities as scenes of nightmare, and in his *Les villes tentaculaires* (1895) described them as sucking the life-blood out of the countryside. Similarly Rilke—who, like other German writers (as we shall see), started with a different set of city perspectives—was oppressed by what he called "the guilt of cities," and generalized about their destructive power:

> Die Städte aber wollen nur das Ihre
> und reissen alles mit in ihren Lauf.
> Wie hohles Holz zerbrechen sie die Tiere
> und brauchen viele Völker brennend auf.[46]
>
> (But cities will only ends of their own and sweep up everything into their own running. They smash up animals like hollow wood and devour many peoples by burning.)

Germany, not united until 1871 and even after that not including all German-speaking peoples within its boundaries, was a country of many historic cities that had stood out in the Middle Ages as oases of freedom. In the 18th century some had been associated with court, others with middle-class rule. In the 19th century many of them became centres of "liberalism" until new forces began to emerge late in the century.[47] Yet there was no German equivalent of Paris, even after 1871. Berlin's population grew from less than 200,000 at the end of the Napoleonic Wars to just under 400,000 at the time of the revolution of 1848, and was approaching two million at the end of the century;[48] but with few exceptions—notably the novelist Fontane (1819–98)—the leading German writers lived in other places. Friedrich Hebbel (1813–63), the great German dramatist who hailed from Schleswig-Holstein, worked in many cities before settling in Vienna, which was the home of Austria's "national" playwright, Franz Grillparzer (1791–1872), and of what was probably the most lively German-speaking theatre anywhere. The Austrian novelist Adalbert Stifter (1805–68), on the other hand, spent the last 20 years of his life in Linz, after becoming disillusioned with the character of revolutionary politics in the capital during 1848. Although the Swiss novelist Gottfried Keller (1819–90) left the provincial confines of Zürich to study in Munich and Heidelberg, and then went on to Berlin, he returned to live in his native Switzerland; so, too, did the Swiss poet Conrad Ferdinand Meyer (1825–98), after spells in France and Italy. The great philosopher Hegel held a chair in Berlin until his death in 1831; but Burckhardt the historian refused a chair in Berlin with some virulence after Ranke had died. Germany meant not only Berlin, but also Munich, Leipzig, Frankfurt, Cologne, and Hamburg, not to speak of Zürich, Basel, and Vienna. Moreover, on the eve of unification 63·9 per cent of the inhabitants of the area that was to be unified lived in places with less than 2000 inhabitants. Even as late as 1910 the proportion was 39·9 per cent.[49] There was never any shortage of "village tales" in 19th-century Germany.

Mme de Stael had noted in *De l'Allemagne* (1810) that no single set of influences radiated outward from one centre throughout Germany; even at the end of the century, in the golden years of the Wilhelmine Empire, the remark would still have been true. There was more fear of the *Großstadt* in Germany than in any other country, and sociologists such as Ferdinand Tönnies made the most of the differences between the hectic and feverish life of the metropolis and the ordered existence of smaller, more conservative, more homogeneous, and more self-contained urban communities. It was in Germany, indeed, that the now-familiar sociological distinction between "face-to-face" communities and cities with a network of secondary relationships was first established.[50] The *Landstadt* (country town), it was maintained, was genuinely related to the countryside; even though it could not escape the changes of the 19th century, it had more the characteristics of the *Dorf* (village) than of the *Großstadt*.[51] Despite the growth of industry, particularly during the last decades of the century, and the emergence of busy new industrial towns in the Ruhr and Silesia (which were almost completely neglected by German writers), most writers looked backward rather than forward, and inward (particularly through the *Bildungsroman* and the *Novelle*) rather than outward.* It has been argued that "whereas it was not France and England and Russia which wrote the great novel of the 19th century, but Paris, London, and Petersburg plus Moscow, in Germany it was the *country* which wrote the *Novelle*, and the tiniest German country most of all, since Switzerland alone furnishes three of [the] five [specially identified leading] provincials. If the modern novel pictures the man of cosmopolis, or whatever it pictures from a window is cosmopolis, the German *Novelle* depicts man *before* cosmopolis and seen from inside. Hence the infinite variety of scenery, society, and oddity. It is the *ancien régime* of mankind."[52] Certainly, writers who did not conform to these patterns were rebels not only against cities—or history—but against everything.

Yet the comment is not entirely convincing. First, it is not countries or cities that write novels or *Novellen*, and the people who really wrote them in the 19th century had often seen enough of the outside world, as Keller had, to be critically aware of the forces of change and the personal dilemmas they posed. Second, the *Landstadt* was changing enough to encourage a different kind of speculation and response from towns and villages that remained settled in ancient ways. Keller's Zürich grew in his lifetime, for example, from a community of less than 30,000 to a city of over 150,000, and there was already much uprooting. Third, it is impossible to write of Germany at any period of its history—after the first legendary moves from the forests, which so interested 19th-century German historians— without taking towns and cities into the reckoning. Attitudes were set long before the 19th century began, and they influenced ways of thinking in the more mobile society that developed with industrialization.[53] A positive attitude toward the cities of the past and the values associated with them is well reflected in the writings of some members of the generation of "nationalists" during the early years of the century. This positive attitude is at least as clearly defined as the *völkisch*, anti-urban writing of a new generation at the end of the century.[54] According to Fichte,

* There are some notable exceptions in the work of Wilhelm Raabe (1831–1910), for instance *Pfisters Mühle* (1884; Pfister's Mill), where the idyllic waters of an old millstream are polluted by industrial effluvia; but in this, as in many other stories, the focus of contrast between past and present is in personal reminiscence and nostalgia. The nearest he came to social realism in depicting city life was in *Die Akten des Vogelsangs* (1896; The Vogelsang Documents), which describes an old-fashioned suburb becoming swallowed up by the metropolis.

for example, it was in the mediaeval cities that "every branch of cultural life" had quickly developed into "the fairest bloom." The mediaeval burghers had transmitted to Germans of a later time qualities that they most needed: "loyalty, uprightness (*Biederkeit*), honour, and simplicity." The age of the great mediaeval cities was "the nation's youthful dream of its future deeds . . . the prophecy of what it would become once it had perfected its strength."[55]

Obviously such writing was designed to assert a special German identity. The fact that unity, when it eventually came, was achieved not through the political revolutions of 1848 but through Bismarck's long-term policies of "blood and iron," encouraged writing about the past within an accepted set of traditions, and about the present in terms of the best way in which the individual German, who was often supposed to be essentially not a "political" creature in the Anglo-French sense of the word, could realize his full stature within a united Germany. Nor did it need Germans of Bismarck's Germany to dwell on the safe keeping of what was best in the German heritage. Stifter, after writing a number of early stories about life in Vienna, concentrated on individuals within small groups: nobility of soul was as natural as fresh air. The more people lived in cities, the more necessary it was to return to the country, not only to the domesticated countryside but to the primitive country of mountains and forests. Only there could the "wretched degeneration" of the times be adequately countered. *Der Nachsommer* (1857; The Indian Summer), written in the form of a *Bildungsroman*, was, in the words of a contemporary American critic, "an ideal portrait, just far enough removed from reality to make it idyllic."[56] Perhaps not surprisingly, his writing was compared at the time with Hawthorne's and comparisons were also made with Wordsworth.[57] Yet in Stifter's Arcadia there was no intimation of the kind of intruding "little event" that we noted in American "pastoralism." As Fuerst has pointed out, both the "elemental" Stifter and the "sentimental" Eichendorff used railways extensively, but "shrank from mentioning them in literature."[58] The first German writer to do so was the Naturalist Gerhart Hauptmann, in his short story *Bahnwärter Thiel* (1887; Railwayman Thiel), and it is significant that it is told from the point of view of a peasant-like railwayman in the country, a "real" human being unable to comprehend the impersonal, destructive force of the passing trains.

In the writings of Keller there is always a contrast, implicit or explicit, between nature and civilization. The rural landscape is bathed in golden light, whereas the towns and cities are darkened by intrigue and infamy. *Der grüne Heinrich* (1855 [revised version, 1878–80]; Green Heinrich) is a *Bildungsroman* that concentrates autobiographically on the tortuous inner development of the hero. What it says in its early chapters about life in the big—though scarcely very modern—city is segmented and unconvincing, but what it says about the country and the small town where Heinrich finally comes to terms with himself is moving, and in places profound. Keller was aware of the dialectic of his times and of the ambivalent influence of "progress" even on the small town itself—the intrigues and iniquities of bourgeois life in *Martin Salander* (1886) make this abundantly clear, and so do his satirical poems—but by preference he settled for the norms that he believed were everywhere being threatened, and his miniature world in Seldwyla, an imaginary little Swiss town, is a counter-world of the mind and the heart to the metropolis that he feared rather than understood.

Theodor Fontane remains something of an exception within the pattern. Although he was born on the North Sea coast of Prussia, wrote sensitively about the landscape and history of Brandenberg, and described Junker attitudes, past and present, with insight and understanding, he chose to make Berlin his home. His novels belong to the last years of his life, and the best of them concern Berlin itself and Berlin society. They were not the first 19th-century German novels to focus on Berlin or on the *bourgeoisie*. Wilhelm Raabe's *Die Chronik der Sperlingsgasse* (1857; The Chronicle of Sparrows Alley) had dealt with a small street in a big city, though in a lyrical, old-world manner, and there had been other writers willing to explore the metropolis.[59] Fontane, however, conceived of his Berlin novels as a cycle that would portray what life in Berlin was really like.[60] The novels were far removed from the *Bildungsroman* and the *Novelle*, for they dealt not with the inner development of heroes or with their "education" through different stages of experience (their *Bildungsweg*), but with the nexus of social relationships and the entanglement of individual fortunes within a changing social scene. *Irrungen, Wirrungen* (1888; Diversions, Confusions) and *Stine* (1890) explored aspects of class; *Frau Jenny Treibel* (1893) exposed bourgeois pretensions to "culture"; *Die Poggenpuhls* (1896) examined the effects of economic pressures on traditional class status; and *Der Stechlin* (1898), his testament, presented a broad cross-section of the Berlin world. Fontane does not so much depict as talk about the industrial working class itself, "the fourth estate," which formed a sizable proportion of the Berlin population even in 1848. But in his letters and fiction, particularly in his last novel, there are hints and references to the growth of this new class and of the Social Democrats who represented them.

26

The question that preoccupied Fontane, as it was to preoccupy his admirer Thomas Mann, was what would happen to the old Prussian values of a military aristocracy and an essentially "unbourgeois "*Bürgertum* in the very rapid social and economic transformation of Germany that was then taking place. The old black and white flag of Dubslav von Stechlin badly needs patching, but "if anything red is sewn onto it, it will surely tear to bits." The language is steeped in apprehension, as it is in the legend of the lake on von Stechlin's estate: the depths of the lake respond like a seismograph to disturbances in the wider world, and when these are very great a "red cockerel" is seen. Perhaps most relevant to Fontane's conception of the transformations within Berlin is his repeated use of a vantage point in the country outside (von Stechlin's dilapidated castle out on the Mecklenburg border), or of trips into the country (especially on the Spree), or of a little bit of country *within* the city (the market garden of *Irrungen, Wirrungen*). Fontane realized the inevitability of urban change, but was too ironical and too old a writer to be able to champion progressive ideas; he also regretted what was being lost. The dying Dubslav von Stechlin is told that despite the appearances of decadence and intellectual pretentiousness that he sees engulfing the age and, with it, his own son, the new and the old will be reconciled in a modified but unbroken tradition. It was doubtless Fontane's own wish, and easier to imagine aesthetically than politically. He was both exasperated and amused by the pretensions of the new Berlin and of its new middle classes, who had neither genuine aristocratic allegiances nor progressive ones. As a result, they may cut comic figures, like Kommerzienrat Treibel and his wife; but they may be guilty, too, of deceiving themselves and others about the real basis of their life, of keeping themselves emotionally in the childhood-garden world of *Effi Briest* (1895). Fontane could never fully break with it himself, in fact, believing on grounds of taste (which were for him inseparable from ethics) that the smaller values of life are the most important ones. His response to the monstrous challenge of the city was to take refuge in the humorous anecdote. His preference "for the anecdotal and the mannered . . . because if you can see what's behind the incidental details, they always show you the really human quality in events,"[61] is the secret of both his strength and his weakness as a writer. He has achieved less fame abroad than any writer of comparable stature, yet no novelist has caught more exactly the very accent and character of a city.

While Berlin was growing, Vienna—a more cosmopolitan city—was changing too in appearance and mood from the place that was thought of simply as the "real world" by Grillparzer's idealistic artist in *Der arme*

Spielmann (a tale begun in 1831) to the place that the satirist Karl Kraus (1874–1936) made into a symbolic capital of doomed empire. When the Café Griensteidl, where Viennese intellectuals and journalists chose to meet, was pulled down in 1897 for road improvements, Kraus wrote a pamphlet entitled *Die demolierte Literatur*, which began: "Vienna has been demolished into a big city." The city grew most rapidly between 1846 and 1857, but by 1890, when the suburbs were incorporated by law, in its extended form the whole complex had reached a population of over 1,300,000. The old inner city had been "ringed," and the old complex of churches and palaces complemented by parliamentary and administrative buildings, museums, theatres, and opera houses. There was—*pace* Kraus—less of a gulf between artists and *bourgeoisie* in imperial Vienna than there was in Paris. Some of the cafés, at least, belonged to both, and they often share the same faded photographs. As Carl Schorske has said, "The democratization of culture, viewed sociologically, meant the aristo-cratization of the middle classes. Increasingly, from the age of Grillparzer to the age of Hofmannsthal, poets, professors, and performing artists were valued guests, in fact, prize catches of the hosts and hostesses."[62] More-over, the different artistic and cultural circles criss-crossed. The musicians Mahler and Walter would meet and discuss Kant and Schopenhauer at the home of the Wittgensteins; the physicist and philosopher of science Boltzmann took music lessons from Bruckner.

Yet in Vienna—a crucible of many 20th-century ideas and prejudices—there were intimations of decay as well as of change. Ferdinand Saar (1833–1906), story writer and poet, recorded as early as the 1870s—for example in his history *Die Steinklopfer* (The Stone Breakers)—the helpless misery of one section of the Viennese working class; and in his poem "Proles" he dealt realistically with jerry-building in the new and poorer districts of the great city:

> Die ersten Häuser! Fast schon im Verfallen,
>   Obgleich man sie erst kürzlich aufgebaut!
> Aus hohen Schloten sah ich's düster wallen
>   Und hörte der Fabriken Arbeitslaut.
>
> O welche Luft, beklemmend und mephistisch,
>   Da schon mein Fuss die Gassen jetzt beschritt!
> Halbnackte Kinder, blutleer und rachitisch
>   Vor jeder Schwelle und bei jedem Tritt.[63]
>
> (The first houses! Almost beginning to fall down, although they have only just been built! I saw dark smoke pouring from the chimneys, and I heard the sound of the factories at work. What air, oppressive and mephitic, as I paced the streets! At every doorway and at every step, half-naked children, anaemic and suffering from rickets.)

In an elegy to Stifter he exclaimed, "I revere the memory of the poet who opened an Eden for me—an Eden which, alas, I have lost."[64]

This mood became increasingly familiar to the younger generation at the turn of the century. It can be felt, for example, in the early poetry of Hugo von Hofmannsthal (1874–1929), which evokes exquisite impressions of the unity of life, and of a cultural tradition, in a way that suggests, nonetheless, that disintegration is imminent. And it was: the breakdown of the poet's lyrical gifts—even, indeed, of his sense of language—is described in his famous Chandos letter (*Ein Brief*, 1902). The mood of cultural pessimism in most German-speaking poets of this generation was inspired by more, of course, than the mere size of cities. Nietzsche's apocalyptic prophecies of the doom of civilization were undoubtedly influential, for instance; though these were rarely directed at city life as such, of which Nietzsche had not had much experience. Nor had the Salzburg poet Georg Trakl (1887–1914), and yet demonic images of steel and stone and ghastly cities loom up on his visionary landscapes of transcendent suffering and longing:

> O, der Wahnsinn der grossen Stadt, da am Abend
> An schwarzer Mauer verkrüppelte Bäume starren,
> Aus silberner Maske der Geist des Bösen schaut. . . . [65]

> (O, the madness of the big city, when crippled trees stand by the black wall in the evening, and the spirit of evil stares out from a silver mask. . . .)

This imagery contrasts, as we might expect, with more serene—though scarcely more realistic—images of villages, parks, and gardens in Trakl's poetry.[66]

Carl Schorske, doubtless with Leo Marx's "Machine in the Garden" in mind, has argued that in Vienna, where there was a conscious effort to bring the garden into the heart of the city throughout the 19th century, life proved too big for art. The expressionist artist Oskar Kokoschka, who violently broke into the garden, was expelled from it. In a city that prided itself on its civilization—great though its social contrasts were in fact— Kokoschka acclaimed instinct; and a similar sense of elemental forces behind the false façade inspires much of Kraus's satire. It was in this city, which more than any other in Europe was to be dethroned from its glory by the cataclysms of 20th-century history, that Freud explored the deep-seated discontents of civilization itself, beginning with the family. Expressionism belongs as much to this setting and to this time as Impressionism belonged to late-19th-century Paris: as Schorske has pointed out, "in a rent society, with pent-up energies that could find no constructive outlet, prevailing culture seemed to a new generation not a creative illusion but a lie. In their prophetic explosion in the garden the Expressionists anticipated Europe's greater explosion, the new reality of world war and revolution."[67]

There has been much debate about what stylistic or thematic features may be said to be common to the many writers and painters throughout Germany (and beyond) who have been dubbed Expressionists. Even their "message," as interpreted by Kurt Pinthus in the famous anthology of their work, *Menschheitsdämmerung* (Berlin 1920), is ambiguous; it could mean the half light of a new dawn for mankind, or the twilight of its extinction. In the imaginations of many artists of the time, it meant both. Similarly, the ever-recurrent imagery of city life in the poems of Heym, Stadler, Becher, and Werfel wavers in mood between horror and hope, a sense of the depth of the change that was being wrought and an equally deep uncertainty as to where it would lead.

No one could have compared London with a garden in either the 19th or the 20th century, although Englishmen, more than any other people in the world, dreamed of "garden cities" combining "all the advantages of the most energetic and active town life with all the beauty and delight of the country."[68] In England, indeed, there were many cities besides London— as we have seen, Manchester was one—that stimulated the imagination of writers and carried with them the sense of the city. It was only during the last few decades of the century that London established its dominance not only as the national capital but as "the world city," and the English writing on cities of that period has much in common with parallel writing in other countries.

The size of London disturbed many Englishmen even during the early decades of the 19th century, when its population was less than one million, and William Cobbett's savage descriptions of the "great Wen," as nasty as it was noisy, were accepted by many people who would have spurned Cobbett's radicalism. Yet there were London poets (branded as "the Cockney School") who sang its praises, and the romantic Benjamin Haydon stated boldly that "so far from the smoke of London being offensive to me, it has always been to my imagination the sublime canopy that shrouds the City of the World."[69] Charles Lamb, an enthusiastic Londoner, catalogued its qualities impressionistically:

> Streets, streets, streets, markets, theatres, churches, Covent Gardens,
> shops sparkling with pretty faces of industrious milliners, neat
> seamstresses, ladies cheapening, gentlemen behind counters lying,

authors in the street with spectacles . . . lamps lit at night . . . noise
of coaches, drowsy cry of mechanic watchmen at night, with bucks
reeling home drunk; if you happen to wake at midnight, cries of Fire
and Stop Thief; inns of court, with their learned air, and halls, and
butteries, just like the Cambridge colleges; old bookstalls, Jeremy
Taylors, Burtons on Melancholy, and Religio Medicis on every stall.
These are thy pleasures, O London-with-the-many-sins.[70]

This is a good essay in associative imagery, but too "literary" in tone—
like much of the writing in *The London Magazine*, founded in 1820—to be
entirely convincing; it links the 18th- and 19th-century worlds of the
metropolis. For all its size, London was still "manageable," still a coherent
entity; and this feeling of manageability persisted in writings 30 to 40
years later in, for instance, *Figaro in London* (1831–6), which reached a
peak circulation of 70,000, and in *Punch*, which was founded in 1841.

As the 19th century went by, however, London became as unmanageable
as it was for long ungovernable, and the statistician as explorer had to
step in where the satirist had trodden before him. *Punch* made fun of
statistics, but when, like Dickens, it turned to such pressing urban issues
as public health, it could not itself dispense with the statistics. Even
Wordsworth, whose poems included vivid portraits of London, wrote to
H. S. Tremenheere, the prototype of the Victorian inspector, that "we
must not only have knowledge, but the means of wielding it, and that is
done infinitely more through the imaginative faculty assisting both in the
collection and application of facts than is generally believed."[71] Whereas
in 18th-century London poverty and riches had existed side by side,
during the 19th century different parts of the great city became increasingly segregated from each other in a society of "two nations,"
an image that recurs time and again before, as well as after, Disraeli used
it.[72] By the last decades of the century, West End and East End seemed
separated by an unbridgeable gulf. Although there was still poverty in the
West End, it was hidden from view: in the East End, it was open and
omnipresent. It was in an effort to discover the *terra incognita* of the
socially submerged districts of London that Charles Booth set about
his great survey of London life and labour in 1889, a survey that was to
be imitated at other times and in other places, but never with such a
strong sense of motivation.[73] Inevitably such a survey illuminated the
varieties of life in London, and equally inevitably it turned attention
away from the "curiosities" of a big city to the more massive inequalities
of social class. Some of the insights of Henry Mayhew's remarkable
London Labour and the London Poor (1851–62) were missing, but the range
and the power were formidable.[74]

The growth of the city turned attention throughout the whole of the century to the nature of change itself, to the tearing down and the building up, to the destruction and the construction, to the flux and the uncertainty of it all. By the last decades of the century there were vast areas of suburban London that were completely unknown to those Londoners who did not live there. Such was the combination of awareness of the spread of London and incapacity to explain its causes and its likely consequences, that the metaphors used to describe it were usually borrowed not from society but from nature. The words "flood" and "tide" were often employed, as they were in descriptions of the city crowds. "A city," wrote Arthur Sherwell in 1901, "is like a great hungry sea which flows on and on, filling up every creek, and then overspreads its borders, flooding the plains beyond."[75] Less familiar images were also used. Patrick Geddes, who was to exert a powerful intellectual and moral influence on Lewis Mumford, one of the best-known and most influential 20th-century writers on cities, thought of London as "a vast irregular growth without previous parallel in the world of life—perhaps likest to the spreading of a great coral reef."[76]

Yet given the sense both of contrast and of change, there was also every kind of mixture of pride and prejudice, much of it localized even within London itself. If there was never any shortage of writings about the shortcomings of London, neither was there any shortage of appreciation of its delights. Henry James preferred London because it was more sophisticated than the American cities, all of which seemed alike.[77] Booth was drawn to city life in general, however horrifying some of his disclosures were, not least to himself. London for him was a stage rather than a laboratory, and because New York also seemed like a stage he found it as exciting as London. One of his helpers, H. L. Smith, made the point very clearly. What was it, he asked, that brought so many people to London? "The contagion of numbers," was the answer, "the sense of something going on, the theatres and the music halls, the brightly lighted streets and the busy crowds—all, in short, that makes the difference between the Mile End Fair on a Saturday night and a dark and muddy country lane, with no glimmer of gas and with nothing to do. Who could wonder that men are drawn into such a vortex [note the metaphor again], even were the penalty heavier than it is?"[78]

It is helpful to take all these impressions and expressions into account in reading Dickens on London, and it is important in understanding what he had to say to pay full attention to his letters and speeches as well as to his novels. It is important also, of course, to remember that his position was not simply that of an observer: he himself was an element in the changing scene, and how he chose to describe it depended both on his shifting memories and moods (or "correspondences") and on his fleeting vantage point in time. He was well aware of the flux. "Scenes changed before his eyes, place succeeded place, and event followed event, in all the hurry of delirium,"[79] we read in the early *Pickwick Papers*, in which only very seldom can Mr Pickwick himself stand back from what he sees:

> Mr Pickwick stood in the principal street of this illustrious town, and gazed, with an air of curiosity, not unmixed with interest, on the objects around him.[80]

Dickens later jotted a note in his Memorandum Book about "representing London—or Paris, or any other great place—in the light of being actually unknown to all the people in the story, and only taking the colour of their fears and fancies and opinions. So getting a new aspect, and being unlike itself."[81] This approach seems not very far removed from Baudelaire's "bathing himself in the crowd";[82] and Hillis Miller, describing the role of the fog in the novel *Bleak House* (1853), draws a further pertinent comparison with Baudelaire: "for Dickens, as for Baudelaire, the disorder of the outward particulars of the city world corresponds to a human condition of hallucinatory incoherence."[83]

We should not turn to Dickens, therefore, for verbal photographs of London in Victorian times, although innumerable books have been written and continue to be written with titles such as "The London of Dickens."[84] We should rather seek to apprehend, even if we can never fully comprehend, the great city (which must be related to other great cities, and to clusters of symbols as well as of facts) through a welter of impressions interspersed with occasional set pieces.

First, we can apprehend the contrasts, including, in many virtuoso passages, chains of contrasts within contrasts:

> Midnight had come upon the crowded city. The palace, the night cellar, the jail, the madhouse: the chambers of birth and death, health and sickness, the rigid face of the corpse and the calm sleep of the child: midnight was upon them all.[85]

Then we can apprehend the mutabilities:

> There was no such place as Stagg's Gardens. It had vanished from the earth. Where the old rotten summer-houses had once stood, palaces now reared their heads, and granite columns of gigantic girth opened a vista to the railway world beyond. The miserable waste ground, where the refuse had been heaped of yore, was swallowed up and gone; and in its frowsy stead were tiers of warehouses crammed with rich goods and costly merchandise.[86]

C

The intrusion of the railway was not a "little event" to Dickens: it was a catastrophic agency of total transformation, at its harshest an agency of death. In *Dombey and Son*, as Kathleen Tillotson has pointed out, "its appearance on each of four carefully spaced and placed occasions is emphasized by a volcanic upsurge in the style, by description much overflowing its narrative function. In these descriptions may be discerned the fascination of the new as well as the horror of the strange; but the tone is mainly that of dread."[87]

Yet the city set-pieces in Dickens are by no means always laden with dread: some of them recapture the jollities of city life with immense gusto; others reflect Dickens' interest in the curious and the strange, an interest that was rooted in his childhood. Some deal with the old parts of the London of his youth, others with the extended London of his later years, far beyond Portland Place and Bryanston Square. In *Nicholas Nickleby* (1839) there is one superb description of a busy city scene, beginning with the water images we have already noted in other writers:

> Streams of people apparently without end poured on and on, jostling each other in the crowd and hurrying forward, scarcely seeming to notice the riches that surrounded them on every side; while vehicles of all shapes and makes, mingled up together in one moving mass like running water, lent their ceaseless roar to swell the noise and tumult....

The passage ends with the curiosities and contrasts of the city:

> Nor were there wanting objects in the crowd itself to give new point and purpose to the shifting scene. The rags of the squalid ballad-singer fluttered in the rich light that showed the goldsmith's treasures; pale and pinched-up faces hovered about the windows where there was tempting food; hungry eyes wandered over the profusion guarded by one thin sheet of brittle glass—an iron wall to them; half-naked shivering figures stopped to gaze at Chinese shawls and golden stuffs of India. There was a christening party at the largest coffin makers, and a funeral hatchment had stopped some great improvements in the bravest mansion. Life and death went hand in hand; wealth and poverty stood side by side; repletion and starvation laid them down together.[88]

For the outer suburbs there are different images:

> They were in a neighbourhood which looked like a toy neighbourhood taken in blocks out of a box by a child of particularly incoherent mind, and set up anyhow; here, one side of a new street, there, a large solitary public house facing nowhere; here, another unfinished street already in ruins; there a church; here, an immense new warehouse; there a dilapidated old country villa. . . . [89]

No other 19th-century writer could describe so well the indeterminate tracts of countryside that were neither urban nor rural, tracts that have become a characteristic feature of 20th-century landscapes:

> The neighbourhood in which it stands has as little of the country to recommend it, as it has of the town. It is neither town nor country. The former, like the giant in his riding boots, has made a stride and passed it, and has set his brick-and-mortar heel a long way in advance; but the intermediate space between the giant's feet, as yet, is only blighted country, and not town. . . . [90]

The real country meant different things to Dickens in different novels: a paradise of security in *Oliver Twist*, with its "jessamine honeysuckle"; a closeness to heaven that is, in the last resort, not close enough, in *Little Dorrit*. Arthur Clennam could feel "that sense of peace, and of being lightened of a weight of care, which country awakens in the breasts of dwellers in towns,"[91] but the only real escape from "the contradictions, vacillations, inconsistencies, the little peevish perplexities of this ignorant life" was the escape identified by Baudelaire—death. Then, however, there could be a transcendence.

> The beauties of the sunset had not faded from the long films of cloud that lay at peace on the horizon. From a radiant centre over the whole length and breadth of the tranquil firmament, great shoots of light streamed among the early stars, like signs of the blessed later covenant of peace and hope that changed the crown of thorns into a glory.[92]

There are so many facets of Dickens that it is difficult to turn easily from a passage of this kind to the practical writings and speeches about the immediate, urgent, and often intractable problems of the growing 19th-century city as it was, particularly the problem of public health in London, which he talked about with great strength of feeling. Yet the theme of public health, which to many other reformers was associated with "getting behind Fate" through the introduction of more effective machinery of social control,[93] was directly related by Dickens to the drama of individual retribution and redemption. In *Bleak House* the filth of Tom-all-Alone's affects everyone, rich and poor, devoted and indifferent alike:

> There is not an atom of Tom's slime, not a cubic inch of any pestilential gas in which he lives, not one obscenity or degradation about him, not an ignorance, not a wickedness, not a brutality of his committing, but shall work its retribution, through every order of society, up to the proudest of the proud and to the highest of the high. Verily, what with tainting, plundering, and spoiling, Tom has his revenge.[94]

This passage was written after the passing of the first English Public Health Act of 1848. One year after the publication of *Bleak House*, however, the General Board of Health set up under the Act was dissolved. Throughout Dickens' lifetime the health problems of London were never fully solved, and writers of a new generation, such as William Morris, following in the footsteps of John Ruskin, were to project their dreams of a clean London far outside the 19th century. It was in Utopia that Morris saw the London scene transformed:

> The soap-works with their smoke-vomiting chimneys were gone; the engineer's works gone; the lead works gone; and no sound of riveting and hammering came down the west wind. . . . Both shores had a line of very pretty houses and there was a continuous garden in front of them.[95]

Although Humphry House was right to point out that it was in London, the London of his own times, that the pulse of Dickens must be taken,[96] Dickens was nevertheless interested in other cities, too. When he visited Paris in 1847 he wrote of "wandering into hospitals, prisons [prisons were always a *must* in Dickens itineraries], dead-houses, operas, theatres, concert-rooms, burial grounds, palaces, and wine-shops . . . . Every description of gaudy and ghastly sight has been passing before me in rapid panorama."[97] When he visited the United States he wrote memorable accounts of each of the great cities he visited, sometimes finding the perfect phrases, as in his description of Washington:

> It is sometimes called a City of Magnificent Distances, but it might with greater propriety be called the City of Magnificent Intentions; for it is only on taking a bird's eye view of it from the top of the Capitol that one can at all comprehend the vast designs of its projector. . . .[98]

Finally, in *Hard Times* (1854), he painted a picture of a new industrial city, Coketown, with such powerful strokes of the brush that the name "Coketown" was chosen by Mumford as the symbolic name of all new 19th-century industrial cities, whatever the aliases behind which they masqueraded.[99]

> It was a town of red brick, or of brick that would have been red if the smoke and ashes had allowed it; but as matters stood it was a town of unnatural red and black like the painted face of a savage. It was a town of machinery and tall chimneys, out of which interminable serpents of smoke trailed themselves for ever and ever, and never got uncoiled. It had a black canal in it, and a river that ran purple with ill-smelling dye, and vast piles of buildings full of windows where there was a rattling and a trembling all day long, and

many small streets all very like one another, inhabited by people equally like one another, who all went in and out at the same hours, with the same sound upon the same pavements, to do the same work, and to whom every day was the same day as yesterday and tomorrow, and every year the counterpart of the last and next.[100]

Although Dickens thought of Coketown as "a triumph of fact," a critic writing from a 20th-century vantage point must regard his version of Coketown rather as a triumph of fancy. Dickens did not know this new kind of industrial community (described by a different writer as "a system of life constructed on a wholly new principle"[101]) as well as he knew London. Not long before writing *Hard Times* he had described a factory as "a grand machine in its organization" in which "the men, the fingers, and the iron and steel, all work together for one common end";[102] but in the novel itself he had to deal not with the common end but with the implications of industrial conflict. For all its strengths—and it has many—the novel is ultimately unconvincing, even though, as A. O. J. Cockshut has pointed out, it inaugurates "a new pastoral tradition . . . in which the Industrial Revolution can really share" in such passages as:

> They walked on across the fields and down the shady lanes, sometimes getting over a fragment of a fence so rotten that it dropped at a touch of the foot, sometimes passing near a wreck of bricks and beams overgrown with grass, marking the site of deserted works. They followed paths and tracks, however slight. Mounds where the grass was rank and high, and where brambles, dockweed, and such like vegetation, were confusedly heaped together, they always avoided: for dismal stories were told in that country of the old pits hidden beneath such indications.[103]

In some ways Mrs Gaskell understood more of the tang of the new industrial North, country and town, than Dickens did, but in novels such as *Mary Barton* (1848) and *North and South* (1855) it is clear that her understanding, if not her sympathy, was limited by the facts of her own social position. She could write skilfully about working-men, the new products of an industrial society, but she could not fully comprehend their thoughts and feelings. There are no outstanding 19th-century novels in Britain that deal with industrialization with a full sense of conviction from the inside, from the standpoint of the industrial worker himself; and, as Raymond Williams has perceptively written, even when sympathy was present, it was often transformed, "not into action, but into withdrawal."[104] For the *critique* of industrialism we have to turn to Ruskin and Morris and to the writers of socialist essays and poems during the late-Victorian revolt of the last decades of the century.

In the meantime, George Gissing and the young H. G. Wells made the most of London. Gissing was a great admirer of Dickens, about whom he wrote an extremely interesting biographical study, but he pointedly contrasted Dickens' desire to please as many of his readers as possible with his own unflinching determination to tell the truth whatever the cost. He collected as many facts about London as Zola collected about Paris, and wrote sensitively, often painfully, about both its inner core and its outer suburbs, where "bits of wayside hedges still shivered in fog and wind." Wells got nearer than any other British writer to having a "theory" of London. It was set out most fully in *Tono-Bungay* (1909), where George Ponderevo thinks he can discern "lines of an ordered structure" out of which the confusion of London has grown and can "detect a process that is something more than confusion of casual accidents, though indeed it may be no more than a process of disease."[105] At the end of what many of his contemporaries called "this wonderful century"[106] Wells was as critical of the course of past progress as Morris. In *The New Machiavelli* (1911) he dismissed the whole Victorian epoch as "a hasty trial experiment, a gigantic experiment of the most slovenly and wasteful kind." "Will any one, a hundred years from now," he asked, "consent to live in the houses the Victorians built, travel by their roads or railways, value the furnishings they made to live among or esteem, except for serious or historical reasons, their prevalent art and the clipped and limited literature which satisfied their souls?"[107]

By then there were many new voices, outside even more than inside Britain. In Britain itself D. H. Lawrence had almost the last word. "The English are town-birds through and through, today, as the inevitable result of their complete industrialization. Yet they don't know how to build a city, how to think of one, or how to live in one."[108] Henry James, by contrast, was for once invincibly matter-of-fact. "When a social product is so vast and various," he said of London, "it may be approached on a thousand different sides, and liked and disliked for a thousand different reasons."[109]

References

1. R. VAUGHAN, *The Age of Great Cities* (London 1843); BENJAMIN DISRAELI, *Coningsby* (London 1844).
2. A. F. WEBER, *The Growth of Cities* (New York 1899), p. 1.
3. See ASA BRIGGS, "The Sense of Place," in *The Fitness of Man's Environment*, Smithsonian Annual, II (Washington 1968).

4. See R. E. PARK, E. W. BURGESS, and R. D. MACKENZIE, *The City* (Chicago 1925); E. W. BURGESS (ed.), *The Urban Community* (Chicago 1926); D. READ, *Press and People* (London 1961).

5. K. DAVIS, "The Origin and Growth of Urbanization in the World," *American Journal of Sociology*, Vol. IX (Chicago 1955); P. HAUSER and L. SCHNORE (ed.), *The Study of Urbanization* (New York 1965).

6. See F. M. JONES, "The Aesthetic of the Nineteenth-Century Industrial Town," in H. J. DYOS (ed.), *The Study of Urban History* (London 1968); W. Z. HIRSCH (ed.), *Urban Life and Form* (New York 1967); K. LYNCH, *The Image of the City* (Cambridge, Mass. 1960); A. L. STRAUSS (ed.), *The American City, a Sourcebook of Urban Imagery* (London 1968), and *Images of the American City* (New York 1961).

7. RUDYARD KIPLING, "How I Struck Chicago and How Chicago Struck Me," *From Sea to Sea* (London 1914), pp. 230–48.

8. See B. L. PIERCE, *As Others See Chicago* (Chicago 1933).

9. For London see, for example, D. M. LOW (ed.), *London is London* (London 1949). For New York, see B. STILL, *Mirror for Gotham* (New York 1956).

10. Quoted in ASA BRIGGS, *Victorian Cities* (Harmondsworth 1968), p. 56.

11. *ibid.*, p. 93.

12. J. J. ROUSSEAU, *Émile ou de l'éducation* (1854 edn.), Boo I, p. 36.

13. See H. N. BRAILSFORD, *Voltaire* (London 1935).

14. WILLIAM BLAKE, *Songs of Experience* (1793).

15. RAYMOND WILLIAMS, *The Long Revolution* (London 1961). See also his earlier study, *Culture and Society* (Harmondsworth 1958).

16. NORTHROP FRYE, "The Critical Path. An essay on the Social Context of Literary Criticism," *Daedalus* (Middletown, Conn., and Columbus, Ohio 1969).

17. ARTHUR M. SCHLESINGER, *The Rise of the City* (New York 1933), pp. 76 and 79. See also his essay on "The City in American Civilization," in *Paths to the Present* (New York 1949); B. MCKELVEY, *The Urbanization of America* (New Brunswick, N.J. 1967); C. N. GLAAB (ed.), *The American City. A Documentary History* (Homewood, Ill. 1963).

18. H. N. SMITH, *Virgin Land* (Cambridge, Mass. 1950); R. HOFSTADTER, *The Age of Reform* (London 1962); LEO MARX, *The Machine in the Garden* (Oxford 1964).

19. MARX, *op. cit.*, p. 6.

20. Quoted in *ibid.*, p. 125. For the echoes, see BRIGGS, *Victorian Cities*, pp. 80 ff.

21. MARX, *op. cit.*, pp. 31 f.

22. WALT WHITMAN, *Passage to India*, VII, 171 ff. (published with *Leaves of Grass*, Washington 1871).

23. HENRY JAMES, *English Hours*, ed. by A. L. Lowe (London 1960), p. 10.

24. Quoted in ASA BRIGGS, *Victorian People* (London 1954), p. 76.

25. ÉMILE ZOLA, *Paris*, trans. by F. A. Vizetelly (1898), pp. xi and xiii f.

26. C. CAMPOS, *The View of France* (London 1965), p. 6.

27. *Journal des Débats* (Paris), 8 February 1843.
28. London Statistical Society, *Fourth Annual Report* (1838). Cf. the *Tenth Annual Report* (1844): "The pursuit of statistical enquiries has already made such progress . . . as henceforth to be a necessity of the age, and one of its most honourable characteristics."
29. For the background, see the Introduction by M. W. Flinn to his edition of *The Sanitary Condition of the Labouring Population of Great Britain* (London 1965).
30. See ASA BRIGGS, "Middlemarch and the Doctors," *Cambridge Journal*, Vol. I, No. 12 (Sept. 1948). Cf. CHARLES KINGSLEY, "Great Cities and their Influence for Good and Evil" (London 1857).
31. For the term and its historical significance, see L. CHEVALIER, *Classes laborieuses et classes dangereuses à Paris* (Paris 1958). A good contemporary account of the position of the parallel group in the United States is in C. L. BRACE, *The Dangerous Classes of New York* (New York 1872).
32. Quoted in L. JAMES, *Fiction for the Working Man* (London 1963), p. 143.
33. HEINRICH HEINE, *Französische Zustände* (1832).
34. J. NERÉ, "The French Republic," *The New Cambridge Modern History*, Vol. XI, ed. by F. H. Hinsley (Cambridge 1962), p. 322.
35. Oliver Wendell Holmes made the remark famous by quoting it in *The Autocrat of the Breakfast-Table* (London 1858), Ch. 6.
36. F. HARRISON, "Historic Paris," reprinted in *Thoughts and Memories* (London 1926), p. 331.
37. See GEORG LUKÁCS, *Studies in European Realism*, trans. by E. Bone (London 1950), p. 85.
38. See V. KLOTZ, *Die erzählte Stadt* (Munich 1969).
39. CHARLES-PIERRE BAUDELAIRE, "Le cygne" (1860).
40. CHARLES-PIERRE BAUDELAIRE, "Les sept vieillards" (1861).
41. C. F. SCHORSKE, "The Idea of the City in European Thought: Voltaire to Spengler," in O. HANDLIN and J. BURCHARD (ed.), *The Historian and the City* (Cambridge, Mass. 1963), p. 110.
42. MARTIN TURNELL, *Baudelaire, a Study in his Poetry* (London 1953), p. 193.
43. A. M. BOASE, *The Poetry of France*, Vol. III (London 1964), p. lxv.
44. See HARRY LEVIN, *James Joyce* (London 1960), p. 23.
45. MATTHEW ARNOLD, "Lines Written in Kensington Gardens" (1852). Arnold never referred to Baudelaire, although he professed himself interested in French literature.
46. RAINER MARIA RILKE, *Das Buch von der Armut und vom Tode* (1903). In his diatribe *Degeneration* (New York 1895), Max Nordau had written of cities robbing even the richest citizens of their "vital powers."
47. J. J. SHEEHAN, "Liberalism and the City in 19th-Century Germany," *Past and Present*, No. 51 (1971).
48. For population movements, see R. HEBERLE and R. MEYER, *Die*

Grossstädte im Strome der Binnenwanderung (Leipzig 1937), and R. HARTOG, *Stadterweiterungen im 19 Jahrhundert* (Stuttgart 1962).

49. H. HOLBORN, *A History of Modern Germany, 1840–1945* (London 1969), p. 370. See also T. S. HAMEROW, *The Social Foundations of German Unification* (Princeton 1969).

50. R. HEBERLE, "Ferdinand Tönnies' Contributions to the Sociology of Political Parties," *American Journal of Sociology*, Vol. LXI (1955); E. G. JACCOBY, "Ferdinand Tönnies: A Centennial Tribute," *Kyklos*, Vol. 8 (Basel 1955).

51. G. RÜMELIN, "Stadt und Land," *Reden und Aufsätze*, Vol. I (Tübingen 1875).

52. N. FUERST, *The Victorian Age of German Literature* (London 1966), p. 118.

53. See R. DAHRENDORF, *Society and Democracy in Germany* (London 1968).

54. For this writing, see G. L. MOSSE, *The Crisis of German Ideology* (London 1966).

55. J. G. FICHTE, *Reden an die deutsche Nation* (Jena 1921), pp. 125 ff.

56. Quoted in FUERST, *op. cit.*, p. 66.

57. *ibid.*, p. 65.

58. *ibid.*, p. 73.

59. See K. ZIEGLER, "Die Berliner Gesellschaft und die Literatur," in H. ROTHFELS (ed.), *Berlin in Vergangenheit und Gegenwart* (Tübingen 1961).

60. Letter of 9 May 1888 to his son Theodor.

61. *Frau Jenny Treibel*, Ch. VII.

62. C. SCHORSKE, "The Transformation of the Garden: Ideal and Society in Austrian Literature," *American Historical Review*, Vol. LXXII (New York 1967).

63. FERDINAND VON SAAR, *Gedichte* (Kassel 1904), p. 247.

64. FERDINAND VON SAAR, *Sämtliche Werke*, Vol. III (Vienna 1909), p. 77.

65. GEORG TRAKL, "An die Verstummten" (1913), *Dichtungen* (1917).

66. See, for example, "In der Heimat" (1913) and "Im Dorf" (1913).

67. SCHORSKE, *op. cit.*, *Amer. Hist. Rev.*

68. Quoted in BRIGGS, *Victorian Cities*, p. 75. London itself had a powerful influence on the international movement to create parks. See G. F. CHADWICK, *The Park and the Town* (London 1966).

69. Quoted in BRIGGS, *ibid.*, p. 311. For London, see Ch. 8 of this book *et passim*.

70. Letter to Thomas Manning, 28 November 1800, quoted in R. W. KING (ed.), *England from Wordsworth to Dickens* (London 1928), p. 151. See also Lamb's article for *The Londoner*, first published in 1802. "I was born, as you have heard, in a crowd. This has begot in me an entire affection for that way of life, amounting to an almost insurmountable aversion from solitude and rural scenes." "The very deformities of London," he went on, "which give distaste to others, from habit do not displease me." (Quoted in G. GORDON [ed.], *Charles Lamb* [Oxford 1921], pp. 75 f.)

71. See *I Was There, the Memoirs of H. S. Tremenheere* (Eton, Windsor 1965).

72. It was used, for example, by W. E. Channing, the Unitarian preacher, in Boston in 1841: "A Discourse on the Life and Character of the Rev. Joseph Tuckerman." For the expression of similar ideas in the city of Liverpool, the link city between Britain and the United States and Britain and Ireland, see M. B. SIMEY, *Charitable Effort in Liverpool in the Nineteenth Century* (Liverpool 1951).

73. CHARLES BOOTH, *Life and Labour of the People of London*, 17 vols. (London 1889–1903). See also T. S. and M. B. SIMEY, *Charles Booth* (Oxford 1960).

74. See E. P. THOMPSON and E. YEO, *The Unknown Mayhew* (London 1971), for a recent assessment.

75. Quoted in BRIGGS, *Victorian Cities*, p. 313.

76. *ibid.*, p. 12. For the various 19th-century influences on Mumford, see his bibliographies in *The Culture of Cities* (New York 1938) and *The City in History* (New York 1961).

77. The theme is developed in MORTON and LUCIA WHITE, *The Intellectual Versus the City: From Thomas Jefferson to Frank Lloyd Wright* (Cambridge, Mass. 1962), and in MORTON WHITE, "Two Stages in the Critique of the American City," in HANDLIN and BURCHARD, *op. cit.*, pp. 84 ff.

78. CHARLES BOOTH, *op. cit.*, Vol. III (1892), p. 75.

79. CHARLES DICKENS, *The Pickwick Papers* (1837), Ch. 21.

80. *ibid.*, Ch. 7.

81. CHARLES DICKENS, *Memorandum Book* (1855–65), quoted in J. HILLIS MILLER, *Charles Dickens, the World of His Novels* (Cambridge, Mass. 1958), p. xv.

82. See TURNELL, *op. cit.*, p. 193.

83. HILLIS MILLER, *op. cit.*, p. 163.

84. See H. HOUSE, *The Dickens World* (London 1941), pp. 12–4, 147.

85. CHARLES DICKENS, *Oliver Twist* (1838).

86. CHARLES DICKENS, *Our Mutual Friend* (1865), Ch. 15. Cf. *Household Words*, 11 October 1851 for the disappearance of "our school."

87. KATHLEEN TILLOTSON, *Novels of the Eighteen-Forties* (Oxford 1954), p. 200.

88. CHARLES DICKENS, *Nicholas Nickleby* (1839), Ch. 32.

89. CHARLES DICKENS, *Our Mutual Friend* (1865), Book II, Ch. 1.

90. CHARLES DICKENS, *Dombey and Son* (1848), Ch. 33.

91. CHARLES DICKENS, *Little Dorrit* (1857), Book I, Ch. 28. Note also in this novel the unforgettable account of a Sunday evening in London (Book I, Ch. 3). For a recent study of Dickens and the city that concentrates on "death" as a unifying theme, see A. WELSH, *The City of Dickens* (Oxford 1971).

92. *ibid.*, Book II, Ch. 31.

93. See, for example, B. W. RICHARDSON, *The Health of Nations*, 2 vols. (1897); also ASA BRIGGS, "Cholera and Society in the Nineteenth Century," *Past and Present*, No. 19 (London 1961), pp. 76–96.

94. CHARLES DICKENS, *Bleak House* (1853), Ch. 46. Throughout this novel Dickens emphasizes the sense of city characters of all types being trapped in an apparently impersonal system. For examples of his interest in public health outside his novels, see *All the Year Round*, Vol. IV (1860), pp. 29–31; Vol. V (1861), pp. 390–4, 423–7, 453–6, 470–3, and 486–9; also K. J. FIELDING (ed.), *The Speeches of Charles Dickens* (Oxford 1960), pp. 127–32; and HOUSE, *op. cit.*, pp. 194–9.

95. WILLIAM MORRIS, *News from Nowhere* (London 1891), Ch. 2.

96. HOUSE, *op. cit.*, p. 146.

97. See U. POPE-HENNESSY, *Charles Dickens* (London 1945), Ch. 22.

98. CHARLES DICKENS, *American Notes* (1842), Ch. 8.

99. LEWIS MUMFORD, *The Culture of Cities* (New York 1938).

100. CHARLES DICKENS, *Hard Times* (1854), Ch. V.

101. *Bentley's Miscellany*, Vol. VII (London 1840).

102. *Household Words*, 5 February 1853.

103. A. O. J. COCKSHUT, *The Imagination of Charles Dickens* (London 1961), pp. 141 f.

104. WILLIAMS, *Culture and Society*, p. 119.

105. See BRIGGS, *Victorian Cities*, pp. 343–55 for a fuller account of the significance of Gissing and Wells in this context.

106. See, for example, A. R. WALLACE, *The Wonderful Century* (Toronto 1898).

107. H. G. WELLS, *Experiment in Autobiography*, Vol. I (London 1934), p. 277.

108. D. H. LAWRENCE, "Nottingham and the Mining Countryside," *Adelphi* (June–August 1934); *Phoenix* (London 1936), p. 139.

109. HENRY JAMES, *op. cit.*, Ch. 1.

CHAPTER 2

Poetry and Ideology

István Eörsi*

Of all the arts, literature has the closest ties with ideology. Because language is the raw material of literature, ideology is immediately and inevitably present in it. This is particularly true of lyric poetry. Unlike the objective representation of epic and drama, where the richness of the realized world and the host of conflicting views may divert attention from the author's ideological attitude, lyric poetry, by virtue of its subjectivity, is attitude incarnate. The lyric poet does not set out to express facts, but rather his own relationship to them. This relationship, naturally, may be of various sorts; there may be no overt ideological commitment, or even a positive rejection of such commitment, but ideological elements may still infiltrate a work indirectly. When a Parnassian poet, striving apparently to achieve purely aesthetic effects, uses the word "multitude" in a poem without any obvious ideological message, the word unavoidably carries ideological overtones.

What makes the relationship of the lyric poet to the world immeasurably complex is the fact that lyrical poetry is always the product of a moment; Goethe called his own work in this style impromptu or "occasional" poetry. As a result, a poet may write poems that express quite contradictory views—poems, let us say, of revolutionary hope and poems of despair—during the same period of his life; each is the authentic expression of an emotion or mood. And because of its dependence on the mood of the moment, lyric poetry is also more likely than any other genre to reflect daily changes in political events and public feelings. Thus, generalization about the ideological significance of poetry produced by men in different countries, and at different times, is peculiarly difficult. We shall concentrate on a few examples here, rather than attempt to label every tendency and variant. These examples may serve to illustrate

* Poet and critic, Budapest.

several characteristic dilemmas that 19th-century poets encountered and some changes in their manner of reacting to them.

We shall choose our examples mainly from the period 1830–70. It was a period that saw great economic and political changes in Europe as a whole. Prior to 1830 the tendency of governments was conservative and reactionary. After the February revolution in France, more liberal governments found themselves caught between the interests of the manufacturing and mercantile class and the pressures of mass discontent and socialist agitation. The period is divided by the explosion of pent-up forces in the widespread revolutions of 1848–9, after which they subsided again or were suppressed until the Paris Commune of 1870. Against this chronological scheme, however, must be set another, geographically based one: economic and industrial advances spreading from England, or political ideology spreading from France, moved into countries that were socially still relatively retarded. The same is true of the movement of culture. Byron's Satanism was taken up and developed three decades after his death by Baudelaire, Carducci, and others, while in England aristocratic, intellectual-revolutionary attitudes of revolt declined. A similar timelag was to mark the influence abroad of, say, Rimbaud after 1870. The effect of situations upon ideas was perceived by the young Marx when he lamented that the German radicals of 1848 were thinking still in terms that, on the French calendar, belonged to 1789.[1]

No poet was more conscious of cultural change than Heinrich Heine, when, as a German exile in Paris, he wrote his memoirs (*Geständnisse*) around the middle of the century: "The old school of German lyrical poetry came to an end with me, and the new school, the modern German lyric, was also inaugurated by me."[2] The old school was that of Goethe with its distinctive classicism, rational objectivity, and philosophy of art. The new school was founded on subjectivity and irony, and constantly contrasted imagination and reality.* In Germany the first reaction against Goethean classicism in fact came from Romantics such as Novalis and Tieck, but Heine did not regard their work as "modern," partly because this would have weakened his claim to have been its inaugurator. In 1846, in the preface to his poem *Atta Troll*, he remarked:

> It was merely to amuse myself that I wrote this [poem] in the whimsical dream style of that Romantic school in which I passed the most agreeable years of my life, and ended by thrashing the schoolmaster.[3]

* This question is taken up again in Ch. 4, "Irrationalism."

46

The "new" that Heine stood for made a break not only with the cultural principles of the Goethean era but also with the romantic ideology of revolt against Weimar classicism.

Heine is remarkable for having understood a major cultural development of his time not merely *post factum* but while it was taking place. Already in 1828, in his criticism of a history of German literature by Wolfgang Menzel, he states:

> The principle of the Goethean era, the idea of art [as an ideal], is fading, and a new era based on a new principle is emerging. How strange, as Menzel's book makes clear, that it is emerging in the form of an insurrection against Goethe! Perhaps Goethe himself now feels that the beautiful objective world, which he brought into existence by word and example, has of necessity to collapse; that the ideal of art is beginning to lose its hold; and that new, fresh spirits are being forced to the fore, who are wrecking Goethe's civilized world like northern barbarians invading the south, and setting up in its place a realm of the most untamed subjectivity.[4]

Goethe's "beautiful objective world" was the product of a transitional period; it was achieved in a place that the tide of bourgeois development, the motive force of 19th-century history, had yet to reach. The small, enlightened class in the German towns and principalities, still spiritually on the defensive after the shocks of the peasant wars, developed no revolutionary ideology; it adapted itself to existing social forms, and reached various kinds of compromise with the nobility. The unprecedented flowering of the arts and philosophy in Germany had no practical effects. Goethe's spiritual horizon is immense, his inspiration towers in its pagan, atheistic beauty above the narrowly Christian norms of his country; yet his actual environment was a tiny princely court.

> This giant was a minister in a German pigmy state. He could never move naturally. It was said of the seated Jupiter of Phidias at Olympia that if he were suddenly to stand he would break the roof apart. This was exactly Goethe's position at Weimer; if he had suddenly leapt up from his seated quiet he would have broken through the top of the state, or, more likely, would have battered his own head against it.[5]

The harmonious coexistence of a small state and great inspiration could not last, however. The French Revolution, the Napoleonic wars, and the subsequent waves of reactionary patriotism dissipated the poetry of humanistic progress; indeed, progress of any kind became difficult to believe in.* The ideal proportions of, and relations between, man's

---

* This question is dealt with in detail in Vol. IV, "The Drama of Freedom."

spirit and man's surroundings that were symbolized concretely in Greek art became submerged beneath the shapeless, energetic prose of aspiring capitalism and the vociferous outpourings of nationalistic feeling. Some of the effects of this change can be felt in the second part of Goethe's *Faust*. The Hellenism of Keats and Shelley all but disappears from English poetry (returning only as erotic phantasy in Swinburne). In Russia, Pushkin alone achieved something approaching classical plasticity in his poetry, which is harmonious in its basic proportions despite its ragged finish. In general, we may say that bourgeois rule and political reaction put an end to the age that could conceive of art as commensurable with life. The cult of art for its own sake was a quite different phenomenon, as will be seen in a later chapter.

Heine's problem was how to preserve, despite the decay of concreteness in artistic expression, the humanistic values implicit in older styles of art, and how to develop these values further, in a manner acceptable to the times. As the transitory harmony symbolized by classicism passed away, subjectivity became an increasingly dominant principle in the arts. One of the ways in which it expressed itself was through ironical representation, where the individual delivers a verdict on the basis simply of his *own* supremacy. Heine was soon led to adopt this style, partly as a result of crucial experiences in his youth: the sight of Napoleon's rule on the Rhine, and the patriotic upheaval against it. For Heine, who was of Jewish origin, Napoleon heralded the emancipation of religious sects; whereas for those of bourgeois descent he heralded bourgeois emancipation, the abolition of feudal prerogatives. In the anti-Napoleonic reaction of the nobility, Heine could observe, even in his adolescence, many of the things that were later to inspire his satire: devastating narrow-mindedness, the devaluation of ideals, and a foisting of slogans onto the mass of the people, not in order to express the general interest, but rather to conceal it. "Patriotism was the order of the day, so we became patriots; for we do whatever our princes order."[6]

It was a paradoxical situation. The patriotism and propaganda for freedom, which Heine saw taking so reactionary a form, owed their original inspiration to the German Romantic school—the school that had also developed literary irony. The paradox is made more complex by the fact that Heine was a disciple of Hegel and used his master's philosophy of history in his struggle against Romanticism. Hegel, however, was a philosopher devoid of irony; his objective idealism makes him closer in kinship to Goethe, whom he admired. In his aesthetics, Hegel argues against the chief ideologists of Romanticism, the brothers Schlegel, and

48

shows how at the centre of ironic consciousness there stands an abstract Ego, imagining itself to be absolute, and conceiving of everything else as "a phenomenon it itself has made and may itself destroy."[7]

> Whoever adopts such a standpoint of divinely inspired genius, looks down aristocratically on the rest of mankind, who are declared to be dull and limited, inasmuch as for them law, morality, and the like are fixed, binding, and inherently valid.[8]

Hegel could be said, of course, to be resorting to irony here to condemn irony; but he sees the value of this attitude as compromised by the knights errant of Romanticism, and adopts it himself only as an aside. He contrasts it with the virtues of the comic, which is for him a distinct and positive form of vision. "The distinction between the ironic and the comic is basically that the *content* of what is destroyed is different in each case."[9] Hegel's distinction is somewhat arbitrary, in that he recognizes objective value only in the comic. But the trend of his argument is sound precisely because it associates value with objectivity in the realm of the comic. In the case of irony, too, where subjectivity comes to the fore, much still depends on what is objectively being attacked. Hence Heine could derive justification for irony from the anti-ironical Hegel.

In the preface to the 1831 volume of his *Reisebilder* (Travel Pictures), Heine comments on the Catholic romantic poet Ludwig Uhland:

> [He] used to sing songs of mediaeval love and faith so solemnly and prettily amidst the ruins of old castles and cloisters. These pious and chivalric sounds, these echoes of the Middle Ages, that were still to be heard everywhere in the recent period of nationalistic narrow-mindedness, are now, of course, dying away amidst the noise of a more modern struggle—the fight for freedom, and all the din of a general European movement toward a brotherhood of peoples; they are dying away before the shrill exultant cries of pain in those modern poems that fake no Catholic harmonies, but make rather a relentless, Jacobin assault on our feelings for the sake of truth.[10]

It is not difficult to guess that the modern poems Heine is referring to are his own. Romantic irony is characterized by escape from reality, but Heine's is characterized by the aspiration to enthrone again, with "Jacobin relentlessness," truth and reality as against illusions and castles in the air. Thus, Heine does achieve the objectivity that Hegel declared a prime virtue in art, despite his use of subjective irony in the romantic manner.

With Heine, to use Friedrich Engels' expression, "the sentimental enthusiasms of the *Bürger* [bourgeois reader] are deliberately jacked up in order just as deliberately to bring them down to earth again with a

D

bump."[11] The German philistine, enchanted by lime-trees and nightin-gales as well as by patriotic and religious processions, and still insisting on *eine zahlungsfähige Moral* (a solvent moral standard),[12] found himself listening in Heine's poetry to the discord between his situation and his sensibility, a discord that was glossed over in daily life. Sometimes the poet himself shared the illusions he exposed; even as an emigre he retained deep emotional ties with German culture and society. Heine's irony is consequently directed also at himself: his scornful laughter is mixed with rueful groans, and this mixture of voices supplies the accompanying music to the intellectual awareness of many of his poems.

Thus, we find that Heine uses not stylistic criteria—in the manner of much modern criticism—but ideological judgments to define Romanti-cism. He was not the only writer to do this, of course. Already in 1823 Manzoni had argued that the word "romantic" meant different things in Germany, France, England, and Italy.[13] It is easy to find a common denominator on purely literary grounds. If, for instance, we take as the chief characteristics of Romanticism its sentimental and escapist nostalgia for the past, its retreat into the realm of the imagination from a trivial, prosaic present, or its cultivation of musical and pictorial effects more lush than real, then it is easy to identify the German Romantics with, say, Shelley and Keats. But if we consider the direction of the escape, then we see that the German school wanted to conjure back the Middle Ages, whereas the author of *The Cenci* has recourse to the Middle Ages to discover there a frightening analogy with present despotism. Or again, the allegorical feminine characters of German romantic literature, its nymphs of wood and stream, beckon only into wonderland; whereas Hope, when she appears in *A Mask of Anarchy*, calls for a people's revolu-tion. Even in Shelley's poetry there is much worship of nature, senti-mentality, and wildness of imagination. But the reason in his case is that he lived in a more advanced country at a time when Europe was domi-nated by the Holy Alliance, and had become disgusted already by the prospect of bourgeois society. He had to resort to Utopian rhetoric, worked up by acts of willed emotion, to maintain his revolutionary perspective. Shelley, with his heightened passion, his musicality, his revolutionary reinterpretation of the Greek ideal of beauty, was in fact a Utopian rather than a Romantic. He looked to the future for escape from the present, whereas his German contemporaries looked to the past.

Ideologically, Heine stood nearer to Shelley, whom he may not have known at all, than to the German Romantics, but he could not indulge in the English poet's unambiguous rhetoric. The long, complex history of bourgeois evolution in England had led to social contradictions of a kind that in Germany could as yet be barely suspected. Germany was still in a pre-revolutionary state, but France, Heine's second homeland after 1830, underwent one revolutionary crisis after another. Heine was thus in a position to understand what kind of revolution he had to hope for in Germany, while being under no illusion that it would solve the problems of the German people. In his letters of 1830 he still hailed the events of July with joy, but nine years later he wrote:

> Since time immemorial the people have shed their blood and suffered, but for others, not for themselves. In July 1830 they won a victory for the bourgeoisie, a class as worthless as the aristocracy it replaced. . . .[14]

Heine never ceased to be deeply concerned with German problems, even while living in France. And, as befitted a disciple of Hegel, he accepted the necessity of real historical development by way of bourgeois capitalism, which he could not reject with the uninhibited enthusiasm of Shelley, because he saw that it alone would destroy German feudalism. Heine expressed his recognition of this fact in his own paradoxical way when he called Rothschild one of the greatest revolutionaries of the period, a founder of modern democracy.[15] At the same time, Heine's disenchanted view of bourgeois democracy can be seen in his reportage on French life (*Lutetia*, 1840–3, 1854), in which he observed that the rival political parties had, as in England, only one object in view: to obtain material benefit for themselves by being elected to power. The bourgeois class, he remarked, was instinctively afraid only of communism. For the rest, it was indifferent to which form of government might prevail, whether monarchical or republican; it was even willing to tolerate a bit of Robespierrism: "The bourgeoisie wants above all law and order to protect its existing property rights, and a republic can satisfy this need just as well as a monarchy."[16]

Heine's political clear-sightedness distinguishes him from his contemporary revolutionaries and revolutionary poets in Germany. He himself formulated the difference in his polemical treatise on Ludwig Börne (1840). He characterized Börne as a sincere and able revolutionary, but one who was prepared to sacrifice the full sensuous enjoyment of life on the altar of his ideals out of a short-sighted, ascetic Jacobinism. He accused Börne of "Nazarene" obtuseness, a word that embraced for Heine the spiritual outlook of both Judaism and Christianity, as opposed

51

to the "Hellenic" virtues of classical antiquity.* (This contrast was to become familiar in England from Matthew Arnold's use of it in *Culture and Monarchy*, 1869.) Heine interpreted the development of Western civilization in terms of a struggle between the Nazarene spirit of asceticism and the Hellenic cult of the senses. One pole was represented by the early Christians and the doctrinaire republicans, and the other by the Greeks, the Renaissance, Goethe, Hegel, and Heine himself. It would be easy to find fault with this theory from a historical point of view; but Heine did not mean it literally. It was his way of asking, in characteristically witty fashion, a serious question. What should the goals of the long-awaited German revolution be, and what should those of the more active revolutionary movement in France be? Was the austere Jacobinism of 1789 still valid, as opposed to the claims of a new hedonism that had emerged with the third estate? In his poetry and prose Heine never ceased to mock abstract revolutionary theory and that kind of senseless enthusiasm "which plunges, scornful of death, into a sea of generalities—reminding me always of the American sailor who so admired General Jackson he flung himself off the mast-head into the water, shouting: 'I die for General Jackson'."[17] Heine's best satire is rooted in the hard facts and plain thinking of his revolutionary poems, the "Zeitgedichte" (Topical Poems), and of his finest cycle of political poetry, *Deutschland, ein Wintermärchen* (1844; Germany, A Winter Fairy Tale). There is no nebulous phraseology, no ascetic morality, but instead a demand for immediate enjoyment of life:

> Wir wollen hier auf Erden schon
> Das Himmelreich errichten.[18]
>
> (We want to establish the kingdom of heaven on earth here and now.)

Heine arrived in Paris with Hegelian luggage; for him, Hegel was an atheist who disguised the fact out of tactical expediency, because his philosophy contained the seeds of revolution. Heine's poem "Doktrin" links his conception of Hegelianism with his demand for sensual enjoyment; it becomes a doctrine that can best be put into practice by beating the drum and kissing the canteen girl ("*und küsse die Marketenderin*"). The influence of France is clear, not least in acquainting Heine with French socialist thought, particularly that of Saint-Simon. There he learned to surpass Hegel's notion that the human spirit consummates its longings through an act of higher self-awareness. The spirit's self-realization had to be coupled with the body's self-realization. Heine develops

---

* A more exact account of the relationship between the two cultural influences is in Vol. I, "The Two Traditions: the Hebraic and the Hellenic."

Hegelian ideas in a socialist direction, by insisting that the progress of mankind cannot be conceived purely as a spiritual affair, that men have a right to be fed as well as a right to culture. In a preface to *Die romantische Schule* (1835) he emphatically asserted: "I do not belong with the materialists, who make the spirit a mere bodily thing; I rather give back to men's bodies their spirit—I permeate their bodies with spirit. I make them holy."[19] Here the Saint-Simonian influence is visible alongside a basically Hegelian conception of spiritual alienation overcome, and of subject and object at one. The spiritualization of the body is akin to the "paradization" of the earth, as expounded by Saint-Simon in his *Nouveau Christianisme, dialogues entre un novateur et un conservateur* (1825; New Christianity, dialogues between an innovator and a conservative), where the only way to eternal life is by labouring to increase human welfare. Heine expresses this view in a more radical, more this-wordly manner in the notorious stanza of "Deutschland":

> Ja, Zuckererbsen für jedermann;
> Sobald die Schoten platzen!
> Den Himmel überlassen wir
> Den Engeln und den Spatzen!

> (Yes, the best green peas for everyone, as soon as the pods have burst! Heaven we will leave to the angels and the sparrows.)

The poet strips socialism of its Christian cloak, and puts spirit to work for the attainment of sensual pleasure. (It is no accident that in the preface quoted above he contrasted spirit with body rather than with matter.) At the same time Heine said of the Saint-Simonians:

> They found themselves in an unfavourable situation, and the general atmosphere of materialism was oppressive to them, at least for a while. They were appreciated in Germany. For Germany is the country where pantheism flourishes: it is the religion of our greatest thinkers and of our best artists. . . . [There] deism long ago ceased to be an acceptable theory. . . . We are free and desire no thunderous tyrants. We have come of age and need no paternalistic care. Nor are we contraptions made by some mighty mechanic. Deism is a religion for underlings, children, citizens of Geneva, and clock-makers.[20]

Because pantheism is free of sectarian narrowness, Heine can hit out at deism and mechanical materialism at one and the same time. But the shortcomings of his own position are conspicuous too: his praise of pantheism scarcely harmonizes with his own atheism, so that one feels his opposition to deism is more formal than forthright. Moreover, his enmity toward asceticism had the effect not only of setting him against

53

the Church and latter-day Jacobins, but also of making him suspect and even reject the early socialist movements. He is right in recognizing the sectarian character of these movements, and their frequently comic conception of social reality; but he generalizes on an inadequate basis about all possible varieties of socialism and communism. His attitude toward the future is an ambiguous mixture of hope and aversion, as becomes particularly evident after the failure of the 1848 revolution. As Georg Lukács has pointed out in his seminal study of Heine, this most German of poets was bound to remain solitary, caught between the bourgeois revolutionaries on the one hand and the socialists on the other.[21] It was a most creative solitude at the centre of many contradictory forces: with the disappearance of the age of Goethe, Heine resorted to romantic irony in order to save Goethean Hellenism from Romanticism; he was a bourgeois revolutionary, who already saw with the eyes of a socialist; he despised capitalism and feared socialism—but as a German he longed for the revolution that would lead to it; he felt aversion from the people, yet he was a folk-poet in his aesthetics as well as in his political creed; the only thing he praised without reservation in Romanticism was its affinity with the common people. To embrace and express these contradictory attitudes, he had to create a dynamically individualistic mode of writing, and in so doing managed to depict a great deal of contemporary German reality. In Georg Lukács's words:

> It is precisely on account of his ironical subjectivism, which his critics condemn as "un-German," that Heine is the most thoroughly German poet of the 19th century. His problems of style reflect most completely, and with the finest artistic effect, the great turning point in the development of Germany before and after 1848.[22]

It was Heine, indeed, who closed the old German poetic school, and opened a new era in German poetry; it is not his fault that his initiative found no continuation in Germany until the end of the century.* The new poetic school developed elsewhere, however, after 1848. But before going on to analyse it, we must discuss the episode of 1848, and its effect upon the relationship of poetry to ideology.

Poetry, as we have said, is the art best suited to respond to the change and movement of events. But even political poetry—if it wants to remain art—must remain faithful also to aesthetic standards. This defence of artistic integrity does not necessarily lead to *l'art pour l'art*. It is not

---

* Some examples have been given in Ch.1, "Writers and Cities in the 19th Century," of the renewed response to German social growth among the Expressionist poets of Germany.

aestheticism that Heine is proposing when he declares: "I am for autonomy in art; art should not be the servant of either religion or politics, it is an end in itself, as the world also is." [23]

To be effective, political poetry must vitalize its message by bringing into play rich emotional and intellectual resources; every sung moment must be elevated to the level of language recognized by the age as "true poetry." The poet cannot simply rely on his message to indoctrinate the masses directly; he can at best hope to exert some kind of indirect moral influence.

It sometimes happens, however, that the demands of the historical moment and the demands of particular poetic talents coincide. At this point poetry may become a decisive factor in the life of a people, and even the day-to-day political events pass immediately into literature. Such historical conjunctions may widen the range of poetry to its advantage, although they may also be a sign of weakness in political practice. A nation may be forced to assemble its greatest talents under a single ideological or artistic banner when it is unable to solve the most urgent problems of its existence. At a time when there are no revolutions, philosophy may provide such a banner for the initiated few—thus Kant was Robespierre's contemporary in Germany—whereas at times of acute social and national conflict it is quite possible that poetry will assume the task of political leadership.

This is what happened in 1848 in Hungary with the lyrical poetry of Sándor Petőfi (1823–49). As early as 1847 Petőfi himself clearly saw the obligations to which he was committed, and gave them general expression in an image that he thought to be true for the "Poets of the 19th Century":

> Pusztában bujdosunk, mint hajdan
> Népével Mózes bujdosott,
> S követte, melyet isten külde
> Vezérül, a lángoszlopot.
> Ujabb időkben isten ilyen
> Lángoszlopoknak rendelé
> A költőket, hogy ők vezessék
> A népet Kánaán felé. [24]

> (We wander in the desert, as Moses wandered in days of yore with his people, following the column of fire sent by God to guide him. In modern times, God has destined the poets to be such columns of flame, to lead the people toward Canaan.)

One year later, history decreed that Petőfi should play precisely this role of leader. He led the radical group of Budapest youths who, on the Ides of March, 1848, sparked off the anti-Hapsburg revolt—a liberation movement with plainly bourgeois objectives. It was altogether in keeping that he should initiate these events with a poem, the "National Song." Petőfi could not, in fact, become a real leader of the people, because Hungary was still so backward and feudal a country that the social and ideological conditions necessary to implement his radical, socialistic Jacobinism were lacking. In a word, he lacked mass support. But, because the contradictions in which Hungary was trapped at that time admitted of only a lyrical "solution," and because Petőfi's genius was admirably suited to this task, he could behave as a popular leader. He became an embodiment of political and ethical ideals as the revolutionary pressure rose, and in his subjective, poetic way he continued to play this role until his death in battle in 1849. The emotions associated with popular leadership informed his everyday activities as well as his political actions (e.g. his opposition to the progressive gentry who dominated the war of independence, and to their leader, Lajos Kossuth). Kossuth organized national unity on a political basis, harmonizing the interests of the nobility and the people in the best way that conditions would allow. Petőfi's point of departure was the primacy of the people; he moved always with a deeply subjective—one might say lyrical—truth, viewed from the perspective of world history rather than from Hungary's national conditions. This feeling also informed his poetry, which carries a political significance hitherto unknown in Europe.

The Hungarian Revolution of 1848 was preceded by a period of reform, which has been discussed in an earlier chapter.* We saw there what motivated the aristocracy to lead the struggle for bourgeois progress: it needed reform (and capital) if it was to survive under Austrian domination, to which the nascent forces of Hungarian capitalism offered a chance of resistance. We may further recall that Mihály Vörösmarty (1800–55), the greatest poet of the age of reform, is generally classed as a Romantic—he once appeared at a national congress wearing full armour—and that his popular early epic *Zalan Futása* (1825) is an appeal to the aristocracy (by one of its own members) to be worthy of their ancestors. Later, under the influence of liberal ideology coming from western Europe, his poems acquired a more serious intellectual content. Hungarian mythology disappears, and praise of the past gives way to criticism of the present. His patriotism develops a keener social edge. His philosophic poem "Reflections in the library" (1844) illustrates the change:

* See Vol. IV, "Literature and National Consciousness: Hungary."

Országok rongya! könyvtár a neved,
De hát hol a könyv, mely célhoz vezet?
Hol a nagyobb rész boldogsága?—Ment-e
A könyvek által a világ elébb?

(Rag of countries, thy name is library, but where is the book that
leads to the goal? Where is the happiness of the majority? Was the
world advanced by books?)

The tension existing between culture and people is tragically heightened
in this poem, which is at once hopeful and fearful in tone. "A new
aspiration begins to stir," evoking the portrait of a united nation where
the divided interests can be united again:

. . . hogy a legalsó pór is kunyhójában
Mondhassa bizton: nem vagyok magam!
Testvérim vannak, számos milliók,
Én védem őket, ők megvédnek engem,
Nem félek tőled sors, bármit akarsz.

(. . . and that the last pauper in his hut should have the confidence
to say: I am not alone, I have brethren, numberless millions, I am
defending them, they are defending me, I do not fear thee, Fate,
whatever thine intentions.)

This is followed, however, by pictures of devastation that conclude with
broad general demands rather than any positive political programme:

Mi dolgunk a világon? küzdeni
Erőnk szerint a legnemesbekért.
Előttünk egy nemzetnek sorsa áll. . . .

(What is our duty in this world? To struggle, according to our
ability, for what is noblest. The fate of a nation is set before us. . . .)

It is not certain that there is hope; but one thing *is* certain: one ought to
act. Two years later this desperate optimism (or, rather, self-denying
pessimism) stiffens into a bitterness that points toward revolution in the
poem "The House of the Country" (1845), i.e. the Hungarian
Parliament:

A hazának nincsen háza,
Mert fiainak
Nem hazája. . . .
Neve: szolgálj és ne láss bért.
Neve: adj pénzt és ne tudd mért.
Neve: halj meg más javáért.
Neve szégyen, neve átok:
Ezzé lett magyar hazátok.

(The homeland has no House, because it is no homeland to its sons. . . .
Its name is: serve and see no wages. Its name is: give money without

> knowing what for. Its name is: die for the benefit of others. Its name
> is shame, its name is curse: that is what your Hungarian Homeland
> has become.)

When the new generation of poets made their appearance—first and
foremost Petőfi and János Arany (1817–82)—they had something to
associate themselves with, both poetically and ideologically. The age of
reform had created its own public, intense in its opinions even if somewhat
limited in its intellectual horizons. There was much activity in journalism
and publishing, and a poetic language had taken shape that was not
totally remote from popular speech. The best-known poets of the age of
reform had tried their hand at writing (or imitating) folk-songs. Besides,
liberal-revolutionary politics had permeated poetry, and patriotism began
to assume a new, popular meaning.

Vörösmarty also made a personal contribution to the renaissance of
Hungarian literature, in that he was one of the first to "discover" the
20-year-old Petőfi, acting as a fatherly friend and assisting him both
financially and morally.

There is undoubtedly a continuity of culture here; but there is no less
surely a break. Vörösmarty attacked his homeland for not being a homeland for the common people as well as for the nobility. His poetic language
became simpler and his virtuosity more puritan, and his poetry as a
whole, in its less heavily intellectual moments, was theoretically enjoyable
by the common people (though only theoretically, because the mass of
the people were not very literate). Petőfi, however, attacked not merely
the monopolizing of his homeland by the nobility but the very concept
of the nobility itself, with its privileges and constitution. He did not have
to try to keep the recently developed poetic language close to popular
idiom because popular poetry was his poetic mother tongue. When, in
1847, he read in manuscript the narrative poem *Toldi* by János Arany
(then an almost unknown village clerk) he praised it in these terms:

> Popular poetry is the only true poetry. We ought to endeavour to
> enthrone it! If the people control poetry, it will not be far from
> gaining control over politics too. This is the duty of our century, to
> achieve this is the aim of every noble heart who has grown sick of
> seeing millions martyred in order to secure a life of idleness and
> pleasure for a few thousands. To heaven with the people, to hell
> with aristocracy![25]

To which Arany replied:

> I passionately share your ideals concerning the people and its
> poetry. . . . If for no other reason, I must do so out of *egoism!*

> I cannot hope for a national poetry until a popular poetry has flourished.[26]

In their aesthetic programmes, then, the two poets are in agreement; but it is no accident that Petőfi emphasizes the political significance of popular poetry, whereas Arany still talks of national poetry. This agreement and difference is characteristic of the personal lives and poetic careers of the two poets. The principal character of Petőfi's first great work, *János Hero* (1844), is the traditional orphan of folklore; after a long series of adventures, both natural and supernatural, he becomes king of Fairyland and there attains his fair love, as though to compensate him for the lack of justice on earth. Petőfi distributes rewards and punishments with a simple, passionate sense of justice that is in every sense popular. János Hero's fairy kingdom marks the first step on a road that leads straight to the revolutionary slogan: "To heaven with the people, to hell with aristocracy!" Now, János Arany's first major work, *Toldi*, adapts an ancient Hungarian legend. Miklós Toldi is stripped of his rightful inheritance by his elder brother, who forces him to lead a peasant's life, while he himself lives as a courtier with the king. Miklós is driven to commit murder, whereupon his brother outlaws him; after years on the run, the hero regains his rightful place by winning a national tournament against a Czech who had worsted all Hungarian challengers till then. As a reward, the king receives Miklós into his court and grants him pardon. In spite of his aristocratic descent, Toldi is meant as a symbol of the people: he is a youngest son, brave, open, strong, his mother's favourite, and so on. Nevertheless, the two stories differ in their perspectives: János Hero becomes a king, whereas Toldi receives constitutional recognition and is reconciled with the *status quo*. As for style, Arany's poem is in no way inferior to Petőfi's in popular vigour and folk realism. It is a perfect demonstration of the truth of its author's self-characterization when he describes himself in a poem addressed to Petőfi:

> S mi vagyok én, kérded. Egy népi sarjadék,
> Ki törzsömnek élek, érette, általa;
> Sorsa az én sorsom s ha dalra olvadék,
> Otthonn leli magát ajakimon dala.

> (And what am I, thou askest. An offspring of the common people, with them are my roots, I live for them and by them, their fate is my fate, and when I melt into song, their song feels itself at home on my lips.)

This kind of simple identification with "the people" was still just possible in Hungary at that time, although the word was beginning to

be an anachronism in Europe at large.* In the more developed capitalist
countries, the significance of the word was beginning to change; it was
acquiring romantic, anti-bourgeois connotations of contrast with the
urbanized masses. This conception of "the people" was not unknown in
Hungary either, where it was sometimes used by the conservative-
reactionary nobility in opposition to the westward-looking tendencies of
bourgeois ideology. The sense in which Petőfi and Arany speak of the
people would also have been impossible earlier, before the plebeian
masses had become sufficiently organized to make their presence felt in
politics as well as in art. Petőfi and Arany wrote during that brief period
when the Hungarian bourgeoisie was still so underdeveloped that the
notion of "the people" could not be used against it from below; despite
obvious social differentiation, they could genuinely voice a revolutionary
programme in the name of a united people, urging both the abolition
of the nobility's privileges and national independence. "There is no
homeland where there are no rights; and the people are destitute of
rights,"[27] Petőfi writes in the summer of 1846, surpassing the radicalism
of Vörösmarty's poem, "The House of the Country," written in the same
year; for Petőfi presents the people as a force that has no home in the land.

The possibility of unpretentious identification with the people accounts
also for the fact that both epic and popular narrative could flourish in
Hungary as a single, coherent genre. During this period, the literary
genre dominant in the more developed Western countries was the novel;
prose fiction could give a detailed chronicle of daily life and also a
criticism of it. It described a world governed by the *rentier*'s principle that
"time is money;" therefore time was (and long remained) central to the
novelist's vision, which is concerned with the way people become rich or
impoverished, grow old, and change. This process develops "realistically"
—that is, according to visible lines of perspective. This visible perspective
explains why, even in backward Russia, the novel could become the dominant genre; in the last analysis even Pushkin's *Yevgeny Onegin* is not a poetic
narrative, still less an epic, but rather a novel in verse, the precursor of
Goncharov's *Oblomov*.[28] For Russian social history from the Decembrist
revolt up to 1917 did have a unified character, a perspective, within which
"gleams of light flashed in the kingdom of darkness."[29]

Hungary, too, was developing a sense of direction prior to 1848, and
it is significant that during that period the first critical-realistic novels

---

* Romantic notions of the people and the peasantry continued to be revived in many literatures throughout the century. The question is touched on repeatedly in the chapters that
follow.

on the western model began to appear. But the shortness of the period, and the numerous social contradictions already described, prevented the Hungarian novel from growing up along with a normal bourgeois way of life—for the simple reason that such bourgeois "normality" as yet scarely existed. Instead, the revolution with its ideology of the "people"— the lyrical triumph of the people in their homeland—made the popular epic the appropriate and favourite genre. The people—the peasant, or the warrior possessing peasant-like qualities—reappeared in literature: authentic characters, fresh and clear-cut, and invested with an air of timelessness. For in Hungary, especially in the peasant way of life, time was *not* money. These epic heroes do their daily work with Homeric nonchalance, but they also have the charm of ordinariness and good rustic common sense. The literary triumph of "the people" extended, moreover, beyond the epic genre. Petőfi did not merely imitate folk-song: he wrote a kind of popular song that the people adopted for themselves. In his landscape poems the Hungarian lowlands, the abode of "the people," take their place among the hitherto more romantic landscapes of poetry, lovingly idealized and yet still recognizable in their homely detail.

This literary triumph of the people gains poetic power from being linked with the broader issues of world history through Petőfi's enthusiasm for French Revolutionary Jacobinism and contemporary socialist ideology, which he understood in a realistic, unromantic way. He admired Marat, and had a deep knowledge of the history of the French Revolution. His interpretation of *égalité* was extraordinarily modern; for him it meant not merely equal rights, as it did for members of the aristocratic reform movement, but economic and spiritual equality, as we see in "The Poets of the 19th Century":

> Ha majd a bőség kosarából
> Mindenki egyaránt vehet,
> Ha majd a jognak asztalánál
> Mind egyaránt foglal helyet,
> Ha majd a szellem napvilága
> Ragyog minden ház ablakán:
> Akkor mondhatjuk, hogy megálljunk,
> Mert itt van már a Kánaán!

> (When everyone has an equal share in the basket of bounty, when everyone is equal at the table of Right, when the sunbeam of Spirit shines on the window of every house, then we may say: let us stop, for we have come to Canaan!)

This quality of universal aspiration makes itself felt in Petőfi's poetry almost regardless of subject-matter. In a love poem to his wife, "The Melancholy Autumn Wind Converses with the Trees," he declares:

> Egyik kezemben édes szendergőm
> Szelidden hullámzo kebele,
> Másik kezemben imakönyvem: a
> Szabadságháboruk története!
>
> (In one hand I hold my dozing love's softly heaving bosom, in the other my prayerbook: the history of the wars of liberation!)

With Petőfi, effortless identification with the people went hand in hand with the natural identification of revolution with love. Personal emotions and sentiments fused in the white heat of the poet's revolutionary temper. In this period—the 1840s—Petőfi's poetry, as well as Vörösmarty's and Arany's, would have stood in the forefront of Europe's literature but for the barrier of language. At the same time, it was possible to discern in it features that were to remove Hungarian poetry after 1848 from the mainstream of European writing. Identification with the people had meant, even before 1848, that problems that in the West were raised by urban life—the individual's isolation and withdrawal from mass society, his search for personal solutions, his more refined, more explicit, sometimes more perverted, eroticism—remained completely unknown to Hungarian poets. On the other hand, their simplicity could have seemed merely simple-minded, and their idealized popular modesty merely prudish.

The Hungarian nation itself, however, was thrown by history briefly and unexpectedly into the thick of revolutionary developments. There were few minds capable of responding adequately to this historical challenge, and the revolutionary faith of these few was kept alive partly by poetry, which became a way of avenging the failures of reality. Poetry was a form not of escape from, but of commitment to, life. Petőfi, conscious though he was of his own genius, confessed in a diary fragment:

> Posterity will possibly say that I was a bad poet, but it will have to admit that I was a man of righteous ethics, which amounts to saying a republican, for the chief slogan of the *respublica* is not "Down with the king!" but rather "Purity of ethics!" Not the shattered crown, but incorruptible character, solid honesty, is the foundation of the Republic. . . .[30]

It is a fascinating confession, but of what use would it have been to Petőfi, had he not been lucky enough to die in battle shortly before the defeat of the revolutionary campaign? He would have seen the *respublica* betraying its own ideals in France, and the bourgeois virtues perverted—in short, he would have become aware of all that Heine had already recognized during the reign of the bourgeois king: the contradiction between words and deeds, between ideals and life; the concept of "the people" debased; the sudden vanishing of the historic moment, never to return. These things cast a spell over Petőfi's earlier poetic achievements and made it impossible to continue them. Hungary was reduced once more to a futureless, hopeless country; the swelling female bosom ceased to inspire thoughts of liberty. The surviving Vörösmarty, on the verge of insanity, took leave of his art with a couple of grand, desperate, visionary poems. Although János Arany developed as a poet and translator of great skill and refinement, and enjoyed an admirable Indian summer blooming with late lyric flowers, he lamented for several decades the consequences of Hungary's dismissal to the periphery of history. Until 1848, Hungarian poetry had kept pace socially, politically, and aesthetically with the life of the country; now it found itself at a halt. The old feudal, patriarchal, and rustic norms became everywhere increasingly untenable, but there were as yet no others to replace them. *Il n'est plus actuel*, is what the ageing János Arany read in a review of his admirable *Toldi* in the 1860 annual of the *Revue des Deux Mondes*.[31] And, in fact, neither popular poetry, folk ethics, the Jacobin republican ideal, nor the rhetoric of popular justice was possible any more. After 1848 an entirely new kind of poetry came to the surface and finally dominated the literary scene, reversing the relationship between aesthetics and ideology.

The failure of the 1848 revolution did not affect the course of poetry immediately, or in equal measure, in all the countries of Europe. In Russia, for instance, there was no revolution; the debate continued about the right way to liberate the serfs, and about the rival merits of western progress and Slav traditions. In Nikolai Nekrasov, the greatest Russian poet of the period following Pushkin and Lermontov, we find a combination of European liberalism with the revolutionary ideals of a Russian peasant democracy. He depicts the harrowing condition of the serfs with a poetic realism that has its aesthetic and ideological roots in the era preceding 1848. In Italy, where in 1848 revolutionary republicanism survived for only a few weeks (in Rome) or even days (in Milan), the dominant issue remained the unification of Italy. For Carducci, who published sonnets in praise of the French Revolution (*Ça ira*, 1883), as for most of his contemporaries, the regeneration of Italy was primarily an expression of middle-class aspirations that were compatible even with monarchy (and later with Fascism: Mussolini is said to have admired Carducci). English poetry, too, was but little affected by the events of 1848. Here the social urgency of poetry declined after the deaths of Keats, Shelley, and Byron, which were followed shortly by the consolidation of the bourgeois order as a result of the electoral and parliamentary reforms of 1832, which made it possible to control social change to some extent by means of legislative enactment.

The predicament of the poet can be seen more clearly in countries where the revolution had been most decisively crushed, such as Hungary, Germany, and Austria. In Germany the "bears growling out their message" (*Tendenzbären*, as Heine called his contemporary political poets) no longer had much of a message left to growl. In Berlin and Munich, academicism and an imitative Goethe-cult ruled the day. Theodor Storm (1817–88) of Holstein, a poet of genuine gifts, retreated into a hermetic world of his own to escape a trivial, unpoetic present. Storm's poetry of modern solitude, with its delicate lyricism of atmosphere and intimately concentrated formalism, achieves power through resignation. It is a provincial example of the kind of modern poetry that elsewhere in Europe, and primarily in France, developed into *l'art pour l'art*. Both his style and his tormented state of mind are reminiscent—*mutatis mutandis*—of the later lyric poetry of his contemporary, János Arany.

The only German poet to react significantly to the poetic trend of the future after 1848 was Heinrich Heine. In his collection of poems *Romanzero* (1851), and in other later or posthumously published poems, we can see "the flowers of evil" beginning to bloom luxuriantly. It was the shameful defeat of the 1848 revolution in Germany, and its deterioration in France into Bonapartism, that brought an end to his revolutionary outlook, while at the same time his pagan love of life was forced to its knees by his gruesome illness. For the last eight years of his life he was confined to his "mattress-grave," half paralysed and blind, with repulsive wounds on his back, and was carried from one corner of his room to another by an old woman. Yet a deep spiritual (and financial) need kept him writing, and we can observe clearly the process of change that he underwent. There was, of course, the much-debated crisis of his religious conversion. In a postscript to *Romanzero*, he attributed his taking refuge in a personal God to his own misery.[32] But all this is expressed in a tone of irony that bears witness to a bad conscience. He rejects the idea that he has become converted to the literal tenets of any creed: "I have not played about with any symbolic significances, nor have I entirely renounced my reason."[33] Words such as "play about," and

64

particularly the adverb "entirely," carry Heine's idea of religion to the edge of heresy.

Heine is clear-sighted about the second source of his search for God, both in his *Geständnisse* (1854; Confessions) and in conversations with the visitors who came in such numbers to his bedside. In January 1850, he explained to Ludwig Kalisch that it was the brutal crushing of the workers' insurrection in June 1848 that had made him aware that his former pantheism was insufficient: to endure those horrors one needed a personal God.[34] This is how he defends himself to the atheist Meissner in January 1849:

> This is what one is brought to when one is ill, mortally ill and broken! Don't hold it against me as if it were a crime! If the German people are driven by necessity to accept the King of Prussia, why should not I accept a personal God?[35]

Heine's conversion was by no means a mere farce. It sprang ultimately from a rupture in his personality, which he described in September 1850 to Fanny Lewald and Adolf Stahr as follows: "In my mind I am convinced that our life comes to an end with death; but my feelings cannot grasp the fact."[36] Heine, the most rational of men, could respond to this division between his head and his heart only by irony, sarcasm, and a religiosity that was tinged with blasphemy. This ambiguity in his religious feeling helped to produce the "flowers of evil" in his poetry. The phrase, which Baudelaire was to make famous and which became virtually synonymous with the most modern trend in 19th-century poetry, was first used by Heine, who applied it to the poem "Lass die heil'gen Parabolen" (*Zum Lazarus*, 1853–4).[37] The poem puts the blame on God for the unbearable evils of this world. During this period, Heine wrote some pious poems as well as some that are utterly cynical. The duel between intellectual pride and physical helplessness marks Heine's poetry after 1848, showing itself in a fantastic wavering between emotional extremes.

In his Confessions Heine mentions other reasons for his conversion. He alleges that he was led to it by the alliance with communism of an increasingly vulgar atheism, "smelling of cheese, brandy, and tobacco."[38] He first expounded his objections to communism in a preface to the 1855 edition of *Lutetia*: with its prosaic utilitarianism, communism would exterminate beauty and culture—everything that he, Heine, had been living for. At the same time, Heine *does* look forward to communism, accepting that, if everybody has the right to eat, then the consequences of this should be faced too: let this old, unjust, exploiting world perish,

E

"fiat justitia, pereat mundus!"[39] Moreover, Heine welcomes communism on the grounds that it is capable of defeating his mortal foes, the German nationalists. Here was a second cause of dissension within himself: he both looked forward to and feared the same thing. This contradiction too is "evil," because insoluble, and it can yield nothing but "evil flowers." With Heine, then, not only was the old school of German poetry closed, and a new one opened, but in a far wider sense he had anticipated a poetic trend that was destined to flower most fully in France. The French cultural growth, with Baudelaire as its finest product, did not derive from Heine, of course, but took shape in complete independence from him. The French movement saw no need for wars of liberation or revolutions, and would have felt as alien such lines as these, in which Heine sums up his life:

> Verlorner Posten in dem Freiheitskriege,
> Hielt ich seit dreissig Jahren treulich aus.
> Ich kämpfe ohne Hoffnung, dass ich siege,
> Ich wusste, nie komm' ich gesund nach Haus.[40]

> (For thirty years I have held out in positions that were lost in the war of liberation. I fight without hope of winning, I knew I should never get home alive and well.)

There was only one great figure, a gigantic exception in contemporary French poetry, who would have responded positively to these lines of Heine's: Victor Hugo (1802–85). It may sound strange to call the leader of French Romanticism an exception, for as a poet, novelist, and dramatist he enjoyed the greatest influence and reputation throughout the century. It would perhaps be more appropriate to regard him as the "norm," in the sense that his feelings were more akin to the common vitality of men than those of his younger contemporaries. He established a literary school, set literary fashions, aroused public opinion; for decades the appearance of each new book by him was an event, even a scandal. Why the need, then, to see him now as an exception?

It was precisely Hugo's extraordinary normality that was abnormal in the period after 1848. To the end of his life Hugo remained the prototype of the liberal-revolutionary poet, still as an old man much as he had been in 1830, when he defined Romanticism as liberalism in literature (in the preface to *Hernani*). This is not to say that Hugo merely clung to this simple generalization all his life and wrote nothing but variations on this one idea. He began, after all, as a monarchist, and continued to react immediately and with great rhetorical skill to specific changes in events. We cannot here follow him through his long and varied career; we shall remark only that his liberal terminology, his world of liberal thoughts and sentiments, always achieved some happily concrete expression, owing to the fact that his poetic emotions were sensibly determined by current events. His poems against Napoleon III, vibrant with indignation, have as distinct an aura as those written in defence of the crushed Commune. There can be no doubt that his liberalism continued to absorb as many socialist elements as was possible without putting his life in danger. He is right when he says of himself, in a poem entitled "To Louis B." written in the 1870s:

> Non, je n'ai point changé. Tu te plains à tort, frère. . . .
> Je suis l'homme pensif que j'ai toujours été,
> Contemplant la nature, adorant la beauté. . . .
> Je veux les peuples grands, je veux les hommes libres.
>
> (No, I have not changed at all. You are wrong to complain, brother. . . . I am the thoughtful man I have always been, contemplating nature, adoring beauty. . . . I want to see great peoples, I want to see men free.)

What is outstanding in Victor Hugo's immense *oeuvre* is that, although he followed so keenly the course of events and adjusted his pathos to the demands of the moment, he maintained an inner integrity, avoiding those inner crises and transformations of the soul that made so many of the best poets of the century indifferent to politics. In his poems written to his grandchildren, the big ideals of Homeland, Steadfastness, Progress, and Fraternity still shine as luminously as they had shone half a century earlier. Hugo is unrestrained, unself-conscious, and for a 19th-century intellectual unusually direct and simple in his use of the vocabulary of liberalism. He used it *defiantly*—and suffered the consequences of defiance by being forced into exile. He was not deceived when contemporary politicians used similar slogans; he continued to use them, but in order to protest his opposition. Heine and Baudelaire were aware that liberalism was, in effect, emotional steam rising from the surface of the capitalist social system, and—being for various reasons unsympathetic to that system—they turned away, ironically or spitefully, from its liberal propaganda. Hugo could see as well as they could that the existing social system would not solve the social problems of the age, but he opposed his society with its own liberal rhetoric, hoping to use it more effectively. This may have been naive of him, ideologically as well as intellectually, but it did prove an effective source of poetic inspiration. Although his slogans sound abstract, his motivation was concrete. In his best poems his emotions crystallize clearly and substantially about the subject-matter, lending it weight and sensuous seriousness. In his plasticity of style the romantic Hugo recalls the artistic achievements of the Goethean era.

Although he remained a poet of the early 19th century in his ideals and emotions, Hugo's plasticity of imagination enabled him to develop modes of writing, and especially of seeing, that were to dominante French lyric poetry long afterwards. Everything turned into poetry in his hands, and he occasionally anticipated Impressionism, Verlaine's masterpieces of musicality, and even rural idylls of the kind that Francis Jammes (1868–1938) was to write. His mastery of atmosphere, his rich variety of subject-matter, and his verbal virtuosity were to affect more poets than have cared to acknowledge him. What no one has been able to recapture, however, is Hugo's confident expression of political ideology with lyric fervour, his ability, indeed, to treat ideology *as* poetry. Revolution and lyric poetry were to be drawn close to one another again at the beginning of the 20th century; by then, however, the inspiration was not Hugo's but that of the real or assumed ideology of a new class.

The normality of Hugo's way gradually became abnormal. Until 1848, he was swimming with the mainstream of development; moreover, he was the living symbol of that sudden effervescence that came into literature with the equation of Romanticism with liberalism. Baudelaire, recollecting those years, said of Hugo that "he exercised a veritable dictatorship in literary matters."[41] During the Empire period, however, different moods and sentiments dominated artistic life—the ideology of *l'art pour l'art*, various kinds of decadence, political nihilism, and what Baudelaire and his followers called "dandyism." For this generation, the outer world could *not* be seen in the resplendent colours shed on it by Hugo's rhetorical imagination. Small wonder, then, that Baudelaire should have grown more and more impatient with the ideals, and particularly the literary manner, that Hugo stood for. In Baudelaire's posthumous collection of fragments and aphorisms, *Mon cœur mis à nu* (My Heart Laid Bare), we find this comment on Hugo: "The man is so lacking in elegiac feeling,* so etherialized, that he would unnerve even a notary."[42] Baudelaire also admired Hugo, as some of his critical writing shows, but in the end it was just this prosaic quality that was unacceptable to Baudelaire the dandy. Hugo, too, was aware of their opposition and expressed it in a letter written to Baudelaire on 6 October 1859: "You are not wrong in foreseeing some discord between us. I understand the whole of your philosophy (for there is a philosopher in you as in every poet); I do more

* For a discussion of the elegiac feeling in the 19th century, see Ch. 5. "The Elegiac Note in Tennyson, Arnold, Pushkin, and Leopardi," and the conclusion of Ch. 4, "Irrationalism."

than understand it, I admit its truth; but I stick to my own. I have never said: art for art's sake; I have always said: art for the sake of progress."[43]

This letter, published as a preface to Baudelaire's study of Gautier, was wholly unsuccessful in persuading Baudelaire to be less resentful of his great contemporary. The word "progress" was for Baudelaire rather what holy water is for the devil. In the second, unpublished preface to *Les fleurs du mal* (1861), he wrote contemptuously:

> Despite the help and encouragement that several celebrated pedants have given to man's natural stupidity, I would never have believed our fatherland could have advanced so very rapidly in the way of progress. The world today has acquired so thick a layer of vulgarity that it gives to the contempt felt by a man of wit the violence of passion.[44]

Mon cœur mis à nu is full of similar invective against the "Americanizing" effects of industrial machinery, and against the bloody daydreams of progressive Utopians, together with contempt and hatred for the bourgeois who lives only for his money-bags. Elsewhere Baudelaire voices his loathing of utility, and of those he calls "useful people." He observes with bizarre wit: "If a poet demanded of the state the right to keep several bourgeois citizens in his stable, people would be very startled, whereas if a bourgeois asks for some roast poet it is thought quite natural."[45] Thus, although the word "progress" continued to have for Hugo the same power and significance that it had had before 1848, it inspired in Baudelaire only revulsion and scorn. It should not be forgotten, of course, that at the time of the revolution Baudelaire fought at the barricades, edited ephemeral journals, and took part in the general enthusiasm for democracy. We may regard this activity as sincere, although he himself later explained it as due to a thirst for revenge, the natural joy of destruction, and the influence of books. It was, however, no more than an incident in his life. His disgust at the crass materialism he saw everywhere was the expression of an artistocratic, isolated nature, rather than of any political belief. With tragic gloom and grotesque intensity of vision he meditated on the spectacle of universal rottenness, of which he created the most celebrated symbol in "Une charogne" (*c.* 1844; A Decaying Carcass), a poem ostensibly written for the woman he loved:

> Et pourtant vous serez semblable à cette ordure,
> À cette horrible infection,
> Étoile de mes yeux, soleil de ma nature,
> Vous, mon ange et ma passion.

> (And yet you will be like this filth, this horrible infection, star of my eyes, sun of my nature, you, my angel and my passion.)

The poem was probably inspired by some actual experience, and it would be an error to attribute to it an allegorical meaning; but it is undoubtedly characteristic of Baudelaire's entire spiritual attitude: behind the appearance of prosperity there is the truth of desolation, behind the appearance of virtue there is dishonesty, behind the slogans of progress there is a bestial reality—the herding together and mechanizing of people. Because the ethics of this world are deeply unethical, let the *mal* come with its flowers, let decay flourish.

Baudelaire's opposition to the capitalist society of his day was in a sense "romantic," not in Hugo's liberal definition of the word, but rather in the German manner; it emanates from his anti-capitalism and anti-bourgeois anger. There are considerable differences, of course. The German Romantics wanted to revive the Middle Ages in their fight against emergent capitalism. Baudelaire's disgust was aroused by the spectacle of a fully developed bourgeois society, and he turned not to the Middle Ages but to the Kingdom of Beauty, to Adventure, and to spiritual non-conformity. His guiding artistic principle is to expose the evil of an age that has surrounded itself with beautiful illusions. He tears them down to reveal the rotten truth, the carcass.

For this reason, the letter of Victor Hugo quoted above angered Baudelaire not only because of its commitment to "progress," but also because it alleged that Baudelaire was a partisan of art for art's sake. (He can scarcely have derived much consolation from Hugo's meaningless assertion that the principles of art for art's sake and art for the sake of progress are, after all, identical.) Baudelaire did not, in fact, profess to be a partisan of *l'art pour l'art*; it is a falsification of literary history to regard him as such. His remarks on the subject are contradictory and difficult to summarize, but we should note, for instance, how vehemently he rejected the theory of *l'art pour l'art* in his essay on Pierre Dupont in 1851: "The puerile Utopia of the school of art for art's sake was inevitably sterile, because it excluded morality and often even passion as well. It stood in flagrant opposition to the spirit of humanity."[46] Baudelaire is not, of course, talking about his own poetic practice here; but it is noteworthy that even in his study of Edgar Allan Poe, where he is most determined to reject all claims for the utility of art and its political or moral commitment, he makes a similarly powerful statement: "I do not mean to say that poetry may not have an ennobling effect on human conduct, or—and let there be no mistake about this—that its final result may not be to raise men above the level of vulgar concerns; to say any such thing would obviously be absurd. What I do say is that a poet weakens his poetic force if he pursues a moral aim, and it will be safe to bet that his work will be bad."[47] It is true that in this study he calls passion a disturbing, natural element from the point of view of art; but by denying any moral *aim*, he does not mean that art is an end in itself, but rather that it is independent of all vulgar aims and ends. It was in his very respectful study of Victor Hugo that he expressed this view most clearly, while defending the master, or perhaps in some degree attacking him while pretending to defend him:

> Here we have none of that moral preaching that can ruin the finest piece of poetry by pedantic aims and a didactic tone; here we have an inspired moral vision that has invisibly permeated the substance of the poetry, like those imponderable fluids that flow throughout the mechanism of the world. Morality here is not the deliberate aim of the poetry, but has become part of it, inherent in it as in life itself. The poet is a moralist without willing to be one, simply from the fullness and richness of his nature.[48]

I believe that the ideal formulated in this last quotation comes nearest to Baudelaire's poetic practice. Baudelaire expounds art as a high calling with obligations to life as a whole. He protests against adulterating poetry with merely useful things, as though it were a commodity in the public market. And he protests against the hypocrisy that, in the name of morality, condemns works of art as decadent or immoral. In *Mon cœur mis à nu* he describes the way a common whore reacts to the divine paintings and sculptures in the Louvre, covering her eyes again and again—in moral indignation! For Baudelaire, she symbolized all the stupidity of the bourgeois age about the relationship of art and morals.[49] He had good personal reasons for insisting on the absolute distinction between the purity of art and the rule of hypocritical morality reinforced by law: he himself had suffered in the courts for *Les fleurs du mal*. Baudelaire is, in fact, a moral writer; but the morality that permeates his work is that of the rebel. His escape into beauty, narcotic phantasies, and a world of sensations acquires a kind of moral force of its own; his Satanism is a way of refusing the aroma of sanctity that surrounds money. He takes the part of Cain against the world of the philistine, the money-grabbing Abels enjoying the protection of the law. And finally, in one of his greatest poems, "Le reniement de Saint Pierre," he contemptuously reveals the guilty secret of the world: Christ was more deeply wounded by remembering his days of lost triumph, when he whipped the *vils marchands* in the temple, than he was by the spear on Calvary. As for Baudelaire:

Certes, je sortirai, quant à moi, satisfait
D'un monde où l'action n'est pas la sœur du rêve;
Puisse-je user du glaive et périr par le glaive
Saint Pierre a renié Jésus . . . il a bien fait.[50]

(As for me, I shall certainly be satisfied to leave a world where action is not the sister of dreams; let me use the sword and perish by the sword. St Peter denied Jesus . . . he was right.)

This is far removed from the accepted norms of *l'art pour l'art*; it is certainly not impassive or impartial. On the other hand, it is equally far from the revolutionary attitude of Victor Hugo, the early Heine, Nekrasov, or Petőfi; far from that poetry in which a positive ideology provided an immediate well of inspiration. It is not the acceptance of beautiful ideals but the denial of ideals betrayed by an ugly reality that brings forth the flowers of evil; in this soil, poetry springs from the denial of political ideology, but there is, as I have tried to show, a positive moral and ideological implication in its twisted growth. Satanism, dandyism, and admiration for Cain (which Byron had first introduced into European literature) cease to be an aristocratic pose, a personal self-dramatization: they form the entrance to a self-contained world, an inner resistance movement. By making a new form of *value* out of the poetic contrast of disintegration and perfection, of "Spleen et Idéal," and a new ethics of denial and destruction, Baudelaire emerges as the founder and hero of modern poetry. Through the mediation of Rimbaud, and the derivative -isms of the turn of the century, he shaped the lyricism of the 20th century. With him, the formal devices of traditional lyric poetry are maintained with a self-conscious bravura. Yet despite his self-consciously ironical immorality, he achieves a perfection that is beyond the greatest of his successors.

References

1. KARL MARX, *Zur Kritik der Hegelschen Rechtsphilosophie: Einleitung*, *Marx-Engels, Werke* (Berlin 1957), Vol. I, p. 379.
2. HEINRICH HEINE, *Gesammelte Werke* (Berlin 1954–6), Vol. V, p. 542.
3. *ibid.*, I, p. 526.
4. *ibid.*, VI, p. 181.
5. *ibid.*, V, p. 318.
6. *ibid.*, V, p. 51.
7. G. W. F. HEGEL, *Aesthetik* (Berlin and Weimar 1965), Vol. I, p. 73.
8. *ibid.*, I, p. 74.
9. *ibid.*, I, p. 75.
10. HEINE, *op. cit.*, III, p. 602.

11. MARX-ENGELS, *Über Kunst und Literatur* (Berlin 1949), p. 248.
12. From the poem "Anno 1829," HEINE, *op. cit.*, I, p. 462.
13. ALESSANDRO MANZONI, *Sul romanticismo: Lettera al marchese Cesare d'Areglio* (written 1823, publ. 1846).
14. HEINE, *op. cit.*, V, p. 435.
15. *ibid.*, V, p. 403.
16. *ibid.*, IV, p. 548.
17. *ibid.*, I, p. 525.
18. "Deutschland," Song I.
19. HEINE, *op. cit.*, V, p. 26.
20. *ibid.*, V, pp. 265–6.
21. GEORG LUKÁCS, *Deutsche Realisten des 19. Jahrhunderts* (Berlin 1952) pp. 89–146 (especially pp. 95–6).
22. *ibid.*, p. 130.
23. HEINE, *op. cit.*, IV, p. 331.
24. SÁNDOR PETŐFI, "The Poets of the 19th Century" (1847).
25. PETŐFI and ARANY, *Correspondence* (Budapest 1949), p. 14.
26. *ibid.*, p. 16.
27. SÁNDOR PETŐFI, "The People."
28. See N. A. DOBROLYUBOV, "*What is Oblomovism?*" (in the periodical *Sovremmenik* [St Petersburg 1859]).
29. From Dobrolyubov's description of Ostrovsky's play *The Thunderstorm* (1859), *Sovremmenik* (St Petersburg 1860).
30. *Leaves from Sándor Petőfi's Diary. The Prose Works and Correspondences of Sándor Petőfi* (Budapest 1960), p. 413–4.
31. Quoted in DEZSŐ KERESZTURI, *And what am I . . . ?* (Budapest 1967), p. 181.
32. HEINE, *op. cit.*, II, pp. 259–60.
33. *ibid.*, II, p. 261.
34. H. H. HOUBEN, *Gespräche mit Heine* (Potsdam 1948), p. 274.
35. *ibid.*, p. 685.
36. *ibid.*, p. 801.
37. *ibid.*, p. 970.
38. HEINE, *op. cit.*, V, p. 583.
39. *ibid.*, IV, p. 674. Cf. the poem "Wanderratten" (Roving Rats).
40. HEINRICH HEINE, "Enfant perdu," *Romanzero* (1852).
41. CHARLES-PIERRE BAUDELAIRE, *Oeuvres complètes* (Paris 1968), p. 469.
42. *ibid.*, p. 629.
43. *ibid.*, p. 35.
44. *ibid.*, p. 127.
45. *ibid.*, p. 627.
46. *ibid.*, p. 292.
47. *ibid.*, p. 362.
48. *ibid.*, p. 472.
49. *ibid.*, p. 640.

CHAPTER 3

Peasant and Proletarian Roles in the Novel

John Bayley*

Not until late in the development of prose fiction does the novelist see himself as presiding over the whole society he describes, as the historian presides over his re-creation of the past. Almost all *theories* of the novel in the 19th century take as their premise that the novelist must be master of his subject, and that his subject will be society as a whole—the society that surrounds him. They assume that the novelist, like the scientist or historian, will take an essentially objective view; from the vantage point of experience and authority he will dominate his subject, and by dominating it interpret for us the society about which he is writing.

An aspect of this mastery and objectivity is the presentation of what is typical or characteristic of persons and communities: their trades, customs, social habits, and distinctions, and the peculiarities of region, class, and nationality. In order to achieve such a presentation the novelist must exercise not only the facilities of the creating and shaping imagination, but those of the sociologist, the journalist, the political and economic thinker.

All this reflects upon his status, and that of his work. During the 19th century the novelist became as important a public figure as these other spokesmen of the time. His views and verdicts were taken as seriously; his powers of interpreting the human community to itself were widely recognized and respected. In England the process could be illustrated by Dickens' insistence that what he wrote was TRUE (the capitals are his), and the London Library's decision to include on their shelves the novels of George Eliot, on the grounds that their seriousness and fidelity to life elevated them above the level of former fiction. The great novelist

* Fellow and Lecturer in English, New College, Oxford.

had become the master of reality, of a wide field of reality. The whole notion of realism,[1] in the critical exposition of the term by Georg Lukács, presupposes the novelist's power to distinguish what is real and significant in the phenomenal universe by discerning what is most *typical* of it, by drawing a clear distinction between Hegel's categories of the knower and the known. What can be known by the novelist and what can be made coherent by him is, and should be, the reality of things.

But what of the novelist himself? How is he related, as subject to object, to this world of typicality? We can see the novelist as surveying and ordering the external world, but we can also see him as part of it, constructing a world not out of its appearances to himself as external observer but out of his largely unconscious and involuntary vision of himself as a microcosmic parallel of all that is in it. The first stance of the novelist might be called realistic, the second symbolic. Both are of course an abstract and theoretical pose, enabling the critic to regard the novelist's relation to his material. Yet the basic distinction does help us in that it provides a means of understanding, and perhaps even judging, the complex questions and problems raised by 19th-century social fiction. On the one hand, we have the view that it is the novelist's task to discern the type, to describe it and to place it. On the other, we have the view that the novelist can manufacture his characters only from aspects of his own being, aspects of which he may not be fully conscious. To what extent, and in what ways, can the novelist be objective? When and how does the subject-object relationship cease to count?

It is obvious that the greatest novelists of the century—Dickens and Balzac are examples—are both observers and participators, who are capable both of seeing the world from outside and of transforming it by their vision, a transformation that—as Coleridge perceived when he said that "the genuine naturalist is a dramatic poet in his own line"—is also a continual process of self-transformation. We feel both the author and his characters changing under the stress of the creative process, and the author's world continually either contrasting or interpenetrating with the world of observed fact. But there are novelists of major stature—Zola, Giovanni Verga, Benito Pérez Galdós, and others—who adhere strictly to the doctrine that the novelist who writes about a whole human society must himself remain detached from it, for only by so doing can he maintain the accuracy and sobriety of fact and the precision of dispassionate recording. They are usually known as Naturalists, a term without any particular meaning except in relation to literary history and to the critical usage of the novelists themselves. In an age of science it seemed a more suitable descriptive term than Realism, a term inherited from the age and doctrine of Aquinas.

It is not my purpose in this essay to discuss 19th-century fiction in relation to these general concepts: the field is far too wide. But there is one aspect of it that has a particular bearing on the novelist's claim to be master of his material, on his mission to discern the typical, or on his tendency to find it in his own personal being and experience. The 19th century saw a great increase in the self-consciousness and the self-importance of novelists: it was also the age of general and ever-increasing class-consciousness. In no previous epoch or mode of literature had attention been concentrated on the poor, the low, and the ignorant for their own sake. Never before had they been objects of such solicitude and serious inquiry; objects who possessed for the writer a kind of irreducible mystery. At its crudest, Victorian fiction makes the poor into Noble Savages, receptacles into which ideas of virtue and sacrifice could be poured, but also beings who remained exotic, inalienably different. When the master becomes conscious of the slave as a different being, he cannot understand him by the same routine interchange, the same assumption of a common consciousness, that he takes for granted in dealing with his own kind and class: when Crusoe becomes really aware of Friday he cannot view him with the callous matter-of-factness that was natural to Defoe. By directing his attention onto the object below him the master does not close the gap between them, but reveals it.

The crucial paradox, therefore, is that while society was becoming more and more conscious of the alienation of one class from another, and while the social conscience concerned itself with the possibility of the reform and the education that would lead to greater social equality, the novelist's stance became more absolute and authoritative the more he needed to preside responsibly over the social field, to understand the masses through the representative characters he portrayed in his fiction, and to diagnose their plight. Realism, to be authoritative, must concentrate on the typical and relate it to the universal. But realism as a fictional technique looks down from the top; and if we examine its attitudes toward those at the bottom, and the ways in which it portrays them, we may obtain some insight into the achievement and the limitations of its attempt at objectivity: we may perceive its equivocal relation with the less deliberate, the more instinctive, creation of the subjective and symbolic novelist, who finds his world in himself rather than stretched out like a map at his feet.

I have said that a great novelist such as Dickens combines these two modes of apprehension, and a preliminary glance at the roles of his humble characters will show us how. Kit Nubbles the poor boy of *The Old Curiosity Shop* (1841), Jo the crossing sweeper in *Bleak House* (1853), Stephen Blackpool the workman in *Hard Times* (1854), and Joe Gargery the blacksmith in *Great Expectations* (1861), all have in common the characteristics that Dickens wishes and supposes—indeed, decrees—to be typical of their class and status in life. They are seen vividly and emotionally; seen with love, sympathy, or indignation; but they are seen from the outside. Dickens cannot compel his imagination to reveal to him what such persons feel like to themselves, on the inside. And when he puts his own experience and sense of himself in the position they occupy, the case is changed indeed. Oliver Twist, David Copperfield, Pip in *Great Expectations*—they are not representative children of the poor. They are consciousness classless and naked, forced by the pressures Dickens himself had undergone into the state in which many children of the poor existed, but which for them is a limbo to be escaped from, and from which they have a personal right to escape. About the nature of this right Dickens is not an observer of poverty, nor is he championing greater social equality; and it is emphasized that Oliver and David's sufferings are especially poignant and unjust because they are upper-class by origin. Pip is not, and yet Pip is never convincingly established as a true and typical member of the working class, precisely because Dickens identifies himself so strongly with him. As master and creator, the novelist can identify himself in his work with an *alter ego* in proletarian disguise, but not with a real and typical member of that class.

And yet, in conformity with Coleridge's perception that "the genuine naturalist is a dramatic poet in his own line," Dickens portrays the plight of the child who is hopelessly imprisoned by the conditioning of poverty far more movingly and convincingly through these unclassed figures drawn from his own experience than through his types of the real children of the poor whom he saw and sympathized with below him. Dickens' proletarian types are not essentially different from those of other serious and socially minded English novelists of his time. Stephen Blackpool is envisaged in just the same way as is John Barton, the father of Mary Barton in Mrs Gaskell's novel of that name, which appeared in 1848, six years before *Hard Times*; and the figure of Hetty Sorrel in George Eliot's *Adam Bede* (1859) is seen and controlled in very much the same way. With such characters their authors have every kind of sympathy except that of dramatic intuition and instinctive identification.

Dickens' vision and embodiment of the humble and the poor will be returned to later, but our theme must now be seen in the wider European perspective. The idea of the *typical* had of course entered fiction with the historical novel. Scott's imagination of the past had been in terms of its characteristic properties and picturesqueness, particularly that of the Scottish society that he loved; and he himself acknowledged a debt to Maria Edgeworth, who in her novels had isolated and dwelt on the peculiar typicalities of Irishness. The immense popularity of Scott spread the fashion and the emphasis to all European novelists, and Balzac—setting out to do for the contemporary scene in the *Comédie humaine* (collected edn 1842–8) what he felt had been done for the past in the *Waverley* series—is Scott's greatest legatee. But there is one historical novel that, although it follows Scott in point of plot and inspiration, is the first to introduce a dynamic social relation between its two major protagonists—an officer from the government establishment and a rebel from the masses kept in subjection below. That novel is Pushkin's *The Captain's Daughter* (1836), and its implication (for one can hardly speak of its message) was both original and prophetic, exercising—like all Pushkin's work—a profound effect upon the great Russian fiction that followed it during the next 60 years.

Pushkin is the first novelist with a historical subject to dispense with local colour, which he had conscientiously provided in his first (unfinished) novel, *The Negro of Peter the Great* (1827). In *The Captain's Daughter* he refrains from drawing the reader's attention in every paragraph to some characteristic and "interesting" aspect of his subject. Instead, he takes it all for granted; his spare, bald narrative covers a deceptive amount of ground, and tells us a great deal without seeming to. His narrator Grinev, a young army officer, becomes involved (like Scott's Waverley) in both sides of an uprising, and is also accused by his own side of having deserted to the other. But whereas Waverley's interest in what he experiences is concentrated, like that of his creator, on the picturesque and the typical, Grinev reflects Pushkin's unobtrusive emphasis on the psychology and drama of relationships. Grinev meets Pugachev, the peasant leader of the great Cossack revolt against Catharine the Great, and is profoundly impressed by him, though he scarcely realizes it. They have nothing in common, for Pugachev—a quite unsentimentalized portrait—is a brutal and ignorant peasant whose redeeming features are humour, energy, and a naive ambition: but by the end of the short novel Grinev's attitudes have undergone a considerable change. We have the impression that he will never be quite the same man again, and that this has been brought about by his contact with a son of the Russian soil.

It is the first of many occasions on which the hero of a 19th-century novel will be "converted" (though, again, this is to state overtly what Pushkin merely implies) by his contact with the people, the peasant or worker who is in some sense *dans le vrai* because he stirs the conscience of the privileged hero, deprives him of the confidence of class and conditioning, and makes him feel guilty. Tolstoy echoes this situation, far more emphatically, in *The Cossacks* (1854), where the hero fancies himself transforming—and having his own life transformed by—a peasant girl and an old Cossack, who in fact regard him with indifference as a mere curiosity and convenience. He treats the theme of master and peasant again, as we shall have occasion to notice later, in the relation between Pierre and Karataev in *War and Peace* (1864–9), and in the story *Master and Man* (1895), where the predicament of the servant, dying of exposure in a snow-storm, suddenly stirs the conscience of his rapacious and commercially minded master, who warms him with a fur coat at the cost of his own life, and before dying experiences a new and unfamiliar sense of peace and happiness. In *Resurrection* (1899) Tolstoy takes another hint from Pushkin, this time from the latter's unfinished play *Rusalka* (1836), which concerns a peasant girl, seduced by a prince, who drowns herself and becomes a "cold and powerful *rusalka*"—a malignant supernatural being who seeks revenge on the nobleman who has wronged her. In the naturalistic setting of *Resurrection*, Tolstoy's Maslova has her revenge on the penitent Prince Nekhlyudov.

In both cases the deprived victim becomes powerful, paralysing the will of the privileged man and racking him with guilt—a dramatic analogue of the social process that was to occur and recur throughout the century and into our own times. And one must again emphasize the importance of the word "dramatic." Tolstoy's success, like Pushkin's, lies in achieving a balanced and comparable reality between the master figure, who is often both hero and quasi-narrator, and the opposed figure of the serf, servant, peasant, or downtrodden victim. In the balance of reality they interrelate: neither is, fictionally speaking, the superior of the other, the protagonist whose consciousness is open to us while he comments on the closed consciousness of the unknown inferior. And this is the decisive development from the social and local interest of the historical novel, in which the peasant—like a figure in history—is seen as typical of his class and background.

In England the new novel of a complete cross-section of society, rich and poor alike, remained conservative: that is, it continued to employ all the time-honoured devices and techniques of the old novel of manners and intrigue. Scott, Dickens, and Hardy are all novelists of society in the widest sense, but they are largely untouched by those theories of fiction, and of the novelist's relation to his subject, that arose out of the novel's new paramountcy on the continent of Europe. The tradition that links them—the most enriching in the history of the English novel—can easily be illustrated. In *Oliver Twist* (1838) Dickens describes the underworld of London as Scott had described the peasantry of his own country. True, Dickens' purpose is a social one, but he is also fascinated by the extraordinary world he reveals and by its appeal to his own deepest instincts and most painful experiences. Yet he retains all the old conventions—coincidences, legacies, melodramatic villains—and develops them side by side with his social theme. He is defensive about this arrangement and defends it with an argument that should be better known than it is.[2] Ordinary life consists, he says (and this must have been particularly true to one of Dickens' volatile temperament), of a kaleidoscope of contrasting experiences, contrasting not merely in kind but in style, so that the novelist cannot be true to human experience by relying on the same approach and the same mode of narration throughout his work. For the novelist to observe people, he implies, is not enough: he must also get inside them, where he will find that the most melodramatic conventions of his craft have their counterpart in the dreams, obsessions, fears, and desires of ordinary people. Although Dickens did not know it, he had produced one of the most potent objections to the premise of social realism in the novel—the premise that society should be surveyed by the novelist as objectively and impartially as the objects of his inquiry are surveyed by the scientist.

We find Hardy doing very much the same thing in his Wessex novels. The *Zeitgeist* makes him much more aware than Dickens of the novelist's claims to be sociologist and thinker, and in his last novel, *Jude the Obscure* (1894), he approaches something very much like the objectivity of the continental realists. But he still maintains the earlier pattern of coincidence and melodrama, and it is significant that these do not mix so well with the delineation of obscure lives and struggles as they did in the earlier novels, of which *The Return of the Native* (1878) is a typical example. Diggory Venn pursues the ancient trade of "reddleman," an itinerant vendor of red dye to sheep farmers, and much is made by Hardy of the properties and way of life involved; yet we never see Venn pursuing his business or making a profit or loss on it. His other function is to overhear conversations and act as go-between in intrigues of passion and the heart, and he thus exists on two levels: as notional peasant and as classless instrument in a tale of tragic love (although we are told that his class position is betwixt and between, like that of Hardy himself).

As with Dickens, the mixed conventions of Hardy's plot and narrative may have come all the more naturally to him because his childhood was spent in a world from which he was separated not only by time, but by the circumstances of his life and education. Many of his characters exhibit a comparable duality between the natural background and the artificial plot. We have observed that Dickens' Pip is born in humble circumstances yet is always separated from the world of Joe Gargery, even before his education has begun. In *The Return of the Native* the characters are simultaneously persons living in and shaped by a real environment and swains in a contrived pastoral (the Christian name of one of them is Damon, a reminiscence of Marvell's mower), and this dualism is natural to the English tradition of regional and social fiction from Scott onward. Even George Eliot can use the same mode as if by instinct—though with her it is Wordsworth who is in the background—making of *Silas Marner* (1861) at once an objective study of a weaver's trade, with its peculiar effects on character and conditioning, and a kind of timeless fairy story or morality.

Although it has often been criticized by purists and intellectuals, this stubborn English fictional convention has the immense merit not only of universalizing in a large degree the characters concerned but also of removing them from the fixed frame in which we are invited to contemplate a class of society and its representatives. Fictional devices humanize the objects of fictional inquiry and by a paradox make them more "life-like," because they seem to be among us and kin to us instead of being contemplated from afar.

Such contemplation, can, of course, be of many different kinds—warm and humorous, or detached and scientific—but it is significant that the novel as it develops on the European mainland discards the old-fashioned apparatus of plot and melodrama techniques that lingered on in England (from a mixture of conservatism and innate prudishness) and that safeguarded the reader from being told "too much"—a mixture exasperating to Hardy, although he went along with it, but deeply fertilizing and congenial to Dickens. We should remember, too, that although the genius of Shakespeare had been so enthusiastically embraced on the continent, it was his power of liberation rather than his sense of decorum that influenced literature there. The English novel had him, as Jane Austen's Mr Crawford remarks, "in the blood," and it is for this reason that Dickens and Hardy can almost unconsciously follow—say—*Romeo and Juliet* in mingling the humorous and earthy tone of the common people with the high style of artificial amorous and tragic dialogue. For English writers Shakespeare underlined the *stylishness* of literature, whereas for writers abroad he seemed to give *carte blanche* for accuracy of social observation and free descriptive detail.

This accuracy appears in prophetic form in the stories of Prosper Mérimée, a great admirer of Pushkin (some of whose work he translated). Mérimée revered the Pushkinian dryness and simplicity of manner, but in imitating it he misunderstood it—not unnaturally, for the secret of Pushkin's art cannot be transmitted, least of all into another language. Whereas *The Captain's Daughter* is plain, organized, and orderly, *Colomba* (1840) and *Mateo Falcone* (1829) have a theatrical detachment that constantly draws the reader's attention to the lack of excitement the author is showing at these exotic goings-on, and to his calm command of peasant psychology and customs. This is really a throw-back to the Byronic pose and to the romantic appetite for strangeness, but the scientific manner of Mérimée was undoubtedly influential in the development of Naturalism. The static situation of *Mateo Falcone*, in which a Corsican father executes his son in cold blood for betraying a kinsman to the police, offers a miniature field for inquiry of the kind that Zola and Verga were to attempt on a far wider scale. Verga's best-known tale, *Cavalleria rusticana* (1880; Rustic Chivalry), has much in common with Mérimée's, being a demonstration of how Sicilian peasants defend their honour, to the death if need be, against each other. The son of a Sicilian land-owner, Verga began by writing novels about polite society, and then decided to change both his style and his subject-matter. He tells us that he came across the account of a voyage by a sea-captain—"short, without an unnecessary phrase"—and that this was a revelation to him. He began to write in a similar way about the peasantry he had known in his childhood, and in 1881 produced his masterpiece *I malavoglia* (The House by the Medlar Tree).

The example of Verga tells us so much about the ambitions and liabilities of 19th-century Naturalism that he is worth looking into in some detail; his comparatively small output offers the reader a clearer insight into the problems involved than do the vast and varied canvases of Balzac and Zola, from both of whom—and especially the latter—Verga had learnt a great deal. His ideal, as he tells a colleague at the beginning of one of his stories,[3] is "to write it as I picked it up in the lanes among the fields, more or less in the same simple and picturesque words of the people who told it me," the "naked honest fact" being better than having "to look for it between the lines of a book," or to see it through the author's lens." What matters is *what really happened*, "which modern analysis seeks to follow with scientific exactitude." In his translation of Verga's stories, D. H. Lawrence is contemptuous of this "Frenchy idea of self-effacement," pointing out with his usual shrewdness that when an author "starts putting his theories into practice and effacing himself, one is far more aware of his interference than when he just goes ahead"; and it is certainly a fact that the most compelling writers about man in society—Balzac, George Eliot, Tolstoy, Hardy, Lawrence himself, and even Kipling—are the most naturally and unrestrainedly chatty of personalities, continually giving us, in lectures, commentaries, and asides, their own views about human and social destiny and change.

Hardy's Tess Durbeyfield, for example, is put before us with a wealth of detailed observation and speculation, and there is no doubt but that the portrait is all the richer for it. Verga's *Nedda* (1874), a comparable novel about a Sicilian peasant girl, is a slighter affair not because Nedda is a less remarkable social phenomenon than Tess but because Verga's method insists with scrupulous accuracy on her presumed "non-consciousness," and thus makes it impossible for the reader to form any sympathetic relation to her predicament. Verga takes from Zola this rule of never exceeding in description the scope of a described character's own outlook, although in fact it had been less systematically practised for some time (by Grigorovich, for example, in tales such as *The Village* [1846], which influenced Turgenev, though he did not follow its method). The weakness of the method, too literally applied, is that it brings us too close for comprehension. We cannot in practice understand a fellow-creature except through a paradigm of our own consciousness, and to understand what is alien we need the author as middleman, with the entrepreneur's fluency that is a natural part of the authorial gift. While waiting for a bus, Zola is said to have noted automatically how the mean hero of *L'assommoir* (1877) would have described the waiting in a slang phrase: *je fais le poireau sur le trottoir*. The rule requires that the author learns to think as his characters would, and to record sensation in terms of their milieu. But Zola manages to lend a kind of gross and monumental Romanticism to the process—as in the remarkable chapter that is nothing but an account of the vast lunch the heroine, Gervaise, gives her friends during her brief prosperity. It contrives both to be soberly factual and to record the woman's *imagination* of opulence; and thus in a sense it looks forward to James Joyce's brilliant rendering in *Ulysses* (1922) of Gerty

McDowell in terms of her own novelettish imagination, or of "Lily the caretaker's daughter"[4] in terms of her meagre and slipshod utterance. The danger of the process is that it may repel us by its possessive virtuosity: one would rather a novelist played God than aped the clown, because the clown—almost by definition—is not capable of reading the novel or of understanding what is going on.

Zola is much too great a writer to be pinned down by the logic of his own theories; but the *veristi*, the Italian realists (and it is not without interest that Zola was himself half Italian), were held in them as in a vice. *Verismo* is more isolated and more self-conscious than Zola's Naturalism, less able to develop and transform itself into new perspectives, and the reason is the primitive and static nature of the Italian societies that form its subject. The huge social field that Zola surveys in the Rougon-Macquart series of novels has a swarming dynamism that bids fair to outrun the author's powers of observation and digestion: the Second Empire, of which Zola saw himself the literary dissector, came crashing down unexpectedly before he had finished chronicling it. Life caught up with art, and Lemaître maliciously observed that "Monsieur Zola is very nearly writing historical novels—just like Walter Scott." Yet Zola can portray a dynamically changing and developing class structure because he is describing the society of a particular time. The setting of Verga's *I malavoglia*, on the other hand, gives the impression of being almost timeless. The chronicle of the woes of a Sicilian peasant family has a kind of grand fixity very different from Hardy's Wessex or Zola's France. The distance that the technique sets between us and the characters—their "unavailability" to our consciousness—is here a positive advantage, for they become like the figures of a saga, who are known only by their actions and their sufferings and with whose *vie intérieure* we cannot in the nature of things be concerned.

These assets served Verga well when he wrote about the peasantry; but he wished to follow his masters in producing a much more ambitious survey of the whole of Italian provincial life, to be called *I vinti* (The Conquered). The series was to concern the human struggle for happiness in five contrasting social contexts. In *I malavoglia* the struggle is merely for existence: in its successor, *Mastro Don Gesualdo* (1889), for bourgeois prosperity. *La duchessa de Leyra* was to be concerned with the satisfaction of social vanity, a further projected novel with ambition; and the hero of the last, *Un uomo di lusso* (A Luxurious Man), was to combine "all these desires, all these vanities, all these ambitions." Only the first two of the series were written, and Verga's deserved reputation rests upon them.

For years he strove to continue with *La duchessa de Leyra,* but he finally abandoned it as a fragment and, except for a few more sketches that echo the earlier stories, Verga wrote no more for the rest of his life.

Verga could not continue the grandiose scheme of his series, as Balzac and Zola had pressed on with theirs, because he lacked their essentially Romantic powers of imagination: he was a better realist and Naturalist than they were. The peasantry of western Sicily remained his only subject because only with them could he exercise a total authority and knowledgeability. "Observation and recollection"—that was his own formula for what he had done, and when he had come to the end of these he could not draw on any further resources of creative vitality. His achievement shows how very much more than life-size, how Dickensian or even Shakespearean, are the figures of the great French realists, who held that they were describing unvarnished reality and dissecting the human animal as it was. Compared with the dry southern matter-of-factness of Verga, the persons and scenes of the French novels seem huge and phantasmal, almost as if seen through the distorting fogs and twilight of the north—the north of Ibsen and of Dickens. This is one characteristic that Verga shares with the Spanish novelist Pérez Galdós—in other respects a writer of far wider scope and achievement. (The Vergas were an ancient family of Spanish descent, and it is tempting to detect a common origin in the refusal of both writers to be, as it were, carried away by their characters, as Cervantes declined to be carried away by Don Quixote.) Both were bachelors, though they had plenty of discreet affairs; and both maintain an aloofness from the persons and scenes they describe that has nothing cold or ironic about it. It is difficult to think of any novelists, not even excluding the Russians, who are at once so at home with and yet so detached from the peasantry who figure in their books. The reason, again, must be the shared fatalism, and the absence of spiritual and mental alienation between the classes of an ancient hierarchy, that distinguish the societies of southern Europe.

Galdós, too, was greatly influenced by Balzac and Zola.* Prolific like most considerable Spanish authors, he produced over the years a gigantic series of historical novels, the 46-volume *Episodios nacionales,* that treat in detail almost a century of Spanish history between the Battle of Trafalgar and the 1880s. They are written with the objectivity that theory required, and with a consistent attempt to use only the language and the viewpoint of the *dramatis personae*; but they are of only local interest. Galdós's real achievement is his three or four long novels about Madrid,

* See Ch. 9, "Naturalism and the Spanish Novel."

of which *Fortunata y Jacinta* (1886–7) is the most remarkable. All objective studies of "a woman of the people" pale into insignificance beside the figure of Fortunata, mistress of a weak young upper-class *madrileño* who is married to Jacinta. And it is significant that Fortunata's husband, an ordinary artisan, is studied by Galdós not at all in terms of his class and station, but as a clinical portrait of neurosis, of a man who withdraws into himself and invents an eccentric religious philosophy in order to escape from the insignificance and humiliations of his position. It is true that Galdós has a tacit moral, as Zola declared he had in *L'assommoir*, which is to imply that the vital forces lay in the people—Jacinta, who is described with the same sympathy and perception as Fortunata, is symbolically childless—but there is never any suggestion that partisan lines are being drawn. Although the great novels of Galdós contain a catalogue of obsessed, extravagant, and peculiar people, and although everyone we meet is a "character," the author sees them and treats them quite differently from the way Dickens, Balzac, or even Zola treat theirs. However bizarre they may be, we never feel them to be the least different from what they must have been in life—in Galdós's observation of life. Galdós has no Pecksniffs or Micawbers, no Vautrins or Père Goriots, and certainly no admirable or pathetic lower-class characters such as Toodles, or Joe the crossing sweeper, or Hugo's petit Gavroche. When he is carried away it is not by indignation or on the wings of imaginative vision and pattern, but by his interest in the interminable dialogues of his characters and the all too realistically protracted procession of their desires and intrigues. Hence Galdós, despite all his great qualities, is sometimes rather boring for the outsider to read.

Nevertheless he is a universal novelist in a way that Verga is not—and is probably Spain's only one apart from Cervantes. He does not "own" a locality: all humanity seems to be his province. But the highly individualized localities of Spain were particularly suited to the prevailing post-Zola fashion for regional novels, novels whose *raison d'être* was to record the typical life—which in Spain was almost inevitably the life of the peasantry—in some province or community. Emilia Pardo Bazán wrote of Galicia, J. M. de Pereda of the Basque country, but (though excellent in their way) such novels smack of the guide book and what the Spanish call *costumbrismo*. A very different case, however, is *La barraca* (1898; The Cabin), a novel about the peasantry of the plain of Valencia by Vincente Blasco Ibáñez (whose novels after he obtained a European reputation cannot be compared with his earlier masterpieces). In his power of revealing the relation between a primitive community and the geographical and historical factors that have shaped it, Ibáñez rivals Verga, although he lacks Verga's ponderous solidity. A disciple of Maupassant, he works by a dramatic seizure of the relevant and revealing situation, and an aesthetic instinct for proportion and form that none the less appears to leave nothing out. *La barraca* and *Cañas y barro* (1902; Reeds and Mud), which is set among the fishermen of the lagoon, are not unlike more dynamic versions of Turgenev's early stories: they have the same ability to convey the life of a rustic community with obvious accuracy and yet with a style and elegance that, although completely the author's own, seem exactly adapted to the subject, neither condescending nor deliberately objective; and this naturalness is very different from the theories of authorial self-effacement of the Naturalist school.

But it is a rare thing. As a doctrine of style, Naturalism is caught between the incompatible aims of passive recording and scientific examination. Only writers of great natural power and personality can solve the problem by not seeming aware of it. And more often than not, in the 19th century, the narrow parochialism of peasant or regional life is echoed by the limited scope of those who made it their literary province. Such a localization is often a matter of language. Several German writers used a version of their native dialect: Fritz Reuter the *Plattdeutsch* of Mecklenburg, Otto Ludwig the speech of Thuringia, Ludwig Anzengruber that of the Austrian country districts. Whatever power their writing has is thus purely localized, even within the culture of the language, as the Scottish authors of the "Kailyard School" remained localized within the tradition of English literary culture. By contrast, the Border ballads and the songs of Burns were not written to exemplify the life and speech of a particular area: they speak unself-consciously to and from the whole of human experience.

But the lower class and its representatives all too often interested those who wrote about them because of the exemplary nature of their experience and its significance for society at large. This kind of interest was very prevalent in Germany, where writers and critics evolved a precise theory about where the reality of the people resided and how it should be described. The *Volk* in German are at once the working people and the nation at large, a dual meaning that English has never fully accommodated ("the people of England" still sounds artificial and semi-literary), and we might note, too, that the Russian word *narod* always signified the masses as opposed to the educated upper classes and the establishment of Church and state. The unity of the German word is partly wish-fulfilment (Germany was not politically united at the time of its first use), but it is with another significance that a character in Gustav Freytag's novel *Soll und Haben* (1855; Debit and Credit) remarks that "the novel should seek the people where it is to be found in its true and proper function—in its work." Work has become not only the great reality but also the great unifier, uniting all classes in a community of interest and purpose, a peculiarly German solution to problems of class alienation.

Balzac, too, had been interested in all forms of expertise and technical process, but he never attached Freytag's almost mystic significance to work as such. If we except the sociologists Durkheim and Weber—who may well have been influenced by the climate of Freytag's fiction in their theories of man at work as the proper unit for sociological study— Rudyard Kipling was the next writer to lay such an emphasis on occupations, and the pride taken in them, as the significant development in the consciousness of modern technological man. For Kipling the proletariat and the peasant were outmoded concepts that could and should be ignored. His soldiers, mechanics, engine-drivers, and plumbers were a new technocracy of labour that made nonsense of ancient class distinction: secure in the pride of their calling, they could converse as equals with officers, artists, or engineers, who would recognize freely in such an interchange that they were themselves only more advanced technicians in the same comradeship.

There is a crumb of truth in Kipling's notion—the new technology *did* produce an almost fanatical pride of work in its early servants—but in general it is as disingenuous and artificial as so much of the ideology exemplified in his art. Like the Tory slogan of "Young England" that Dickens had mercilessly mocked,[5] it seeks to perpetuate a caste system under the guise of a union of ideals and interests—although Kipling, unlike earlier Tories, believed in the ascendancy of officers rather than that of gentlemen. To take one example: the pride of the cockney Ortheris as a private soldier in Kipling's story "His Private Honour" is no more believable than is the pride of his Irishman Mulvaney in being a "good" Irishman who sees the point of the British Empire and resolutely sets his face against the Fenians and rebels of his own country. Compulsively readable though they still are, these stories embody phantasies whose existence is only in Kipling's desires and dreams. His down-to-earth, man-to-man creations can be seen with the lapse of time to have been concepts as idealistic and as unrelated to a real sympathy with the facts as are Dickens' Stephen Blackpool, or the many other pattern-plebeian figures of an earlier time.

Kipling's knowledge is never of the heart, and even his technical

89

detail is more showy than sound, but like Dickens he was at least involved emotionally in the world he imagined; whether he is in India, a Sussex cottage, or a ship's engine-room, he makes no claim to record objectively. The point may be worth making, for it is often assumed that what is wrong in these cases is a lack of understanding and information, the kind of knowledge that Verga and Hardy absorbed from their environment, and that other novelists, such as Zola and Charles Reade, acquired with toil and stored in documentary notebooks. The fact is that no amount of knowledge, however acquired, will guarantee the assent and agreement of the reader, unless the gap between author and subject has been some-how bridged. This the documentary form is unable to do, even in such a sympathetic and exhaustive form as Mayhew's *London Labour and the London Poor* (1851–62) and in the many similar documentaries of slum life in our own time. Whatever their predicament, human beings cannot be seen in this way without the fundamental need of fiction—to involve us not as tourists or philanthropists but as fellows in human possibility—remaining unfulfilled.

A tradition in art may be more effective in this context than indignant sympathy with the underdog or documentary exactness in recording his plight, both of which—although directly implying the need for action—emphasize the fundamental difference between "us" and "them," and thus perpetuate what can only be called the patronizing of the poor. It is significant that Scott, in spite of his knowledge and love of the Scottish folk and their ways, falls back on Shakespeare for two of his most memorable peasant creations, Meg Merrilies in *Guy Mannering* (1815) and Edie Ochiltree in *The Antiquary* (1816). Neither has any separated, documentary actuality: their characteristic humanity is generic and absolute, like that of Wordsworth's leech-gatherer and old Cumberland beggar; and the impressiveness of all these figures may make us wonder whether great art can ever afford to put specific class alienation in the forefront of its method, instead of its traditional assumptions of human unity.

Dickens at his best certainly does not think so. Nell's grandfather in *The Old Curiosity Shop* ("a harmless fond old man") specifically echoes the universality of King Lear (every old man, as Goethe said, is a Lear) as he does Lear's no less universal self-pity. Conversely, the scene of the novel that falls flattest is Miss Monflathers's denunciation of Nell for working in a wax-work show when she might have "the proud consciousness of assisting, to the extent of your infant powers, the manufactures of your country . . . and of earning a comfortable and independent subsistence of from two-and-ninepence to three shillings per week." The sarcasm is of course directed at contemporary apologists of child labour, but it temporarily deflates the imaginative vision of Nell, so vital to the reader's interest and participation, as a classless child whose sufferings and nobility are in no way connected with her station in life, and with whom readers from every station can thus identify.

But Dickens does not always have to declass his characters in order to give them intimate and universal appeal. The Marxist critic T. A. Jackson has pointed out* how many of his characters are shaped, flattened, distorted, or dehumanized by their environment and occupation, even though they may seem, like Bumble the beadle or the sick-nurse Mrs Gamp, to be primarily comic creations. That is certainly true, and the process is far more natural than the modern notion of environmental conditioning suggests. Mrs Gamp's speech reveals not only what she is but her own phantasy of herself in relation to the mythical Mrs Harris; the windowed grandmother whom Little Nell meets in the churchyard is described in terms of her own picture of how a poor widow should feel and behave in relation to the memory of her long-dead husband; and Biddy, in *Great Expectations*, gives an account of Mrs Joe Gargery's death that seems less like a "factual" account than what someone of Biddy's ideas and station would think such a death ought to be like. Dickens, in fact, contrives that such characters mime the universal joys and sorrows through the masque of their own class-conditioned response to them, so that we see both event and attitude simultaneously, in a revealing human alliance.

The phantasies of his men and women are dramatized and objectified by Dickens, and they have nothing to do with his own phantasy life and the obsessions of his own unconscious. Hence the extraordinary fidelity and delicacy of most of his portraits of the town and country poor. This might be contrasted with the scientific attitudes of the Naturalist authors—Zola in particular—who did not recognize the part played by such phantasies either in themselves or in the low life they studied. Yet in a penetrating essay on Zola, Havelock Ellis observed that his work will survive because it shows that there is "no such thing as realism, only a variety of idealisms."[6] No author, he implies, can confront the masses across the gap between what is familiar and taken for granted and what is strange and interesting, and still see them steadily and whole. Anatole

---

* *Charles Dickens: the Progress of a Radical* (London 1937).

France made a related judgment: "It is at Médan [Zola's home] that the last of the romantics lurks in hiding."

Both the psychologist and the satirist perceived what to us (since Freud) is a commonplace: the enormous vitality of such a writer as Zola springs from preoccupations of which he may be largely unconscious, and while he is dissecting society he is also revealing himself. Henry James, indeed, went so far as to hint that Zola's interest in the lowest strata of society was due to the distance that he wished to put between himself and the rest of the world, and that this form of Naturalism was really a kind of ivory tower.[7] James concluded that the generosity with which Zola flung himself into the Dreyfus case was a compensation for the withdrawal from life that the over-powering actuality of his novels really represented, and indeed demanded, from their author: no one could bury himself in so much *boue* on paper if he also had to get his feet into it in life. Certainly there is something in this, for Zola's apprehension of the great mass of the people and the immense blank anonymity and monotony of its toil required a discipline and dedication of approach comparable to that of James himself. Nothing could be less like a "slice of life" or a "loose baggy monster" than Zola's meticulous pursuit of the complex pattern of the Rougon-Macquart series, whose artifice is structured by Taine's and Michelet's pseudo-scientific theories of heredity and causal determination. As Verga, and to some extent Hardy too, could only present the lives of the common people through the ancient aristocratic medium of tragedy, so Zola had to image it in the modern convention and pattern of scientific determinism.

It is notable that in contrast with this European need to see the common people at an artificial remove and from an aesthetic viewpoint if they are to be seen at all, the great Russian writers—and especially Tolstoy—do not require an *idea* of the folk in art before they start to write about it. As we shall see, the Russian view of the peasant is tendentious, but it is always direct: starting so much later, on the threshold of the 19th century, the Russian novel seemed to have no need for the methods and conventions, both traditional and experimental, that mediated between the European reader and the actuality of the proletarian poor.

Yet Zola is not oppressed by his swarming subject-matter. His effort to depict it with scientific exactness is saved from claustrophobia by the fascination with which he contemplated these obscure lives: they did indeed liberate him into a kind of romance. For writers after him, including Kipling, the proletariat were participators in the new scientific dynamism; it was for Zola to emphasize their contemporary exploitation by it.

Zola's father had been a brilliant engineer who, but for his early death, might have been numbered with Brunel and de Lesseps, and for his son the horrors and abuses of industrial society still retained the glamour of the great men who had made it possible. The mine in *Germinal* (1885) is like some infernal deity, service at whose shrine both destroys the miners and imparts to them as its worshippers a diabolic energy and distinction. In *Nana* (1880) the very sordidness of the prostitute increases her fascination; she is drawn on the scale of a goddess, and filled even Flaubert with enthusiasm. *"Elle tourne au mythe, sans cesser d'être réelle,"* he wrote to the younger novelist. *"Cette création est Babylonienne"* (It has a mythic quality without ceasing to be real. This creation is Babylonian). To become a myth without ceasing to be real is indeed the justification and ambition of these ominous figures, who seem to represent not only the bourgeois gigantism of the period, but guilt and fear at the underground forces that capitalism had unloosed, and that now seemed likely to destroy it.

In his didactic gusto, his energy, and his frequent vulgarity, Zola is of course a disciple of Balzac, emulating his master but on a grosser and more grandiose scale; but there was an important difference between them, and Zola himself pointed it out. In a memorandum called "Differences between myself and Balzac," he speculated that his work would always be scientifically rather than socially engaged. "I do not wish to make decisions about human affairs, to be politician, philosopher, and moralist. I shall content myself with being a *savant.*" Balzac, the man of affairs, continually floating new schemes, continually on the verge of bankruptcy, represented in his own person both the struggles of the bourgeois and those of his working-class victim. He worked and suffered concurrently and spontaneously, and in the same mode as his characters. In his comments on the differences between them, Zola anticipated the distinction of Lukács between realism in the novel (which is a dynamic process, born of the constant engagement of the novelist in the struggles of the society he lives in and deals with) and Naturalism (which is static, externalized, and definitive).[8]

From the point of view of peasant and proletarian figures the importance of this distinction is that Naturalism, by what may seem a paradox, lends itself more readily than realism to *myths* about the working class. The explanation is precisely in its separateness—as theory—from the world it describes: Zola might not have agreed with Flaubert that *la vie est bête* (life is stupid), but his exhaustive researches, and portfolios of material from life, embody in themselves Mallarmé's dictum that the world exists

93

to end up in a book. Even at their most outsize, Balzac's characters remain real for us by their relation to other characters and to their society; but Zola's—and Flaubert's too—often appear incarnated in a supreme and, as it were, narcissistic pantheon, where they can be contemplated in and for themselves alone. Both Madame Bovary and Nana are more cult figures than human beings, and yet the background established by their creators is very far from mythic. The mean streets of *L'assommoir* and the crowds of *Germinal*, no less than the houses of Madame Bovary's Yonville and the boulevards of *L'éducation sentimentale* (1843–5), are milieus of the most meticulous and detailed social significance. Nana, Gervaise, and Emma Bovary may be mythic figures, but compared with Dickens' Nancy and Little Dorrit they are part of a symbolic landscape, a *paysage moralisée*.

This specific French mastery in making every aspect of a *petit-bourgeois* and peasant locale densely co-ordinated and interrelated is quite alien to the great Russian novelists. Russia of the 19th century did not lend itself to the kinds of integrated fictional survey possible in the West. Indeed, Tolstoy did not think that the novel, as the West understood it, was possible in Russia at all. He claimed that *War and Peace* (1864–9) was not a novel but a hybrid form *sui generis*: "what the author wished and was able to express in the form in which it is expressed." He even went so far as to say that from Gogol's *Dead Souls* (1834–52) to Dostoyevsky's *House of the Dead* (1862) there was no outstanding work in Russian that could properly be called a novel; and in a projected preface to *War and Peace* he asserted that he was not interested in "merchants, peasants, priests," whose lives were unknown and incomprehensible to him, but in the traditional life of his own class. Tolstoy reveals the gulf that separated the gentry from their inferiors in Russia; what European realist and follower of Balzac would have dared to write off the lower echelon of society in this way? And yet *War and Peace* gives us, or seems to give us, as spacious and detailed a panorama of a nation and people as Balzac and Zola were able to do in a whole series of volumes.

The remarkable illusion of comprehensiveness that Tolstoy achieves is due as much as anything to the fact that he alone of 19th-century novelists was able to effect a total reconciliation between the historical novel and the novel of present-day society. *War and Peace* is not amply and leisurely retrospective in tone, as are George Eliot's *The Mill on the Floss* (1860) and *Middlemarch* (1871–2): rather it contrives simultaneously to *be* the past and the present. Its portrayal of families and family life is so detailed and compelling that we are persuaded not only that these things are timeless and universal, but that they hold good for all classes and conditions of men.

Balzac and Dickens and Zola are not strong on family life, because they portray the bourgeois family as isolated by its egoism, its pretensions, and its money struggles from the society about it, and isolated by its own will: in this they are faithful to society as they saw it. Enclosed in themselves, Balzac and Zola's families suppurate in mutual suspicion and rivalry, microcosms of competitive capitalist society. Dickens' own recipe for portraying a popular happy family is by standardized jollification, eating, and drinking. Certainly there are no pleasures like the pleasures of the poor, but the poor—like the Nubbles family in *The Old Curiosity Shop*—will not come alive as individuals through Dickens' frenetic insistence on this. Yet, although he idealizes the family, Tolstoy does not strike us as sentimentalizing or misrepresenting it, and this may be because the huge and patriarchal establishment of a Russian aristocrat, containing all classes of servants and hangers-on, did indeed resemble in some sense the state of Russia as a whole. Instead of the complete society, Tolstoy offers us the complete family; and he distracts us from wondering too much about its credentials by opposing it in a dynamic antagonism to the Napoleonic organization and invasion, to other ways of life. It is significant that Tolstoy here has more in common with Galdós, in another backward country at the other end of Europe, than with any other European novelist. In *Fortunata y Jacinta* Galdós also portrays in the greatest depth and spaciousness family life that seems to comprehend an entire society, and the heroines of that novel can be justly compared to the feminine portraits of *War and Peace*.

Russian critical interest, as Tolstoy implies, was in the purpose of the novel, not in its form. And although Tolstoy himself was quite out of sympathy with the journalists who did so much to shape the thought and expectations of the Russian *intelligentsia*, all his work is related to theirs by devious links of scepticism, protest, and reaction. In one of its aspects *War and Peace* is a novel of special pleading, directed against the radicals who had rejected utterly the culture and way of life of the Russian land-owners. At the time of the abolition of serfdom Tolstoy implies that the serf-owning gentry at their best were and are the real Russia, and the idyll of family life, in the great hunting scene in *War and Peace* and the mowing with the peasants in *Anna Karenina* (1875–7), is intended to embrace the life of the peasants and the whole rural community. It is significant that Karataev, the peasant soldier of *War and Peace*, is looked upon by Pierre as a kind of brother; after Pierre's marriage to Natasha they often speak of him together, and Pierre assures Natasha that he would have understood and approved of their way of life. Indeed Pierre, Rostov, and Karataev are in some sense an ideal Russian family, standing for the Russian being and mentality that Dostoyevsky symbolized in darker hues in the four brothers Karamazov. If it is valid, such a comparison between the two great novels shows how different their mode of encompassing and portraying a society is from that of the European realists.

Dostoyevsky himself, most notably in *The Devils* (1872), attacks and satirizes the radical position and beliefs, and includes a venomous sketch of Turgenev. Turgenev produced *Fathers and Children* (1862) in answer to criticism that he had not portrayed a positive young Russian radical hero. In his reactionary novel *No Way Out* (1864), Leskov transparently lampooned the radical aristocrat Sleptsov. In fact after Pushkin and Gogol—and they too were drawn, posthumously, into the struggle— there is no great work of literature in Russian that is not either tendentious and partisan itself or that could not be used as ammunition by those who were; and this clash of attitude and creative vision—which has no parallel on the same scale in the West—is one of the principal reasons for the amazing richness and fertility of the Russian 19th-century novel and its enhancement by a continual process of self-contradiction. The peasant idyll of *War and Peace*, for instance, should be compared with the peasants of Nekrasov's lively verse tale *Who is Happy in Russia?* (1879) and with the appalling picture of gloom, tyranny and brutish stagnation in Saltykov-Shchedrin's *The Golovlyov Family* (1876) and *Old Years in Poshekhonie*, or with Bunin's later portrait of a Russian community, *The Village* (1910). The point is that we do not feel about these latter that only here is the truth, and that Tolstoy's picture is a superb feat of idealistic and misleading retrospection. The two visions complement each other, and indeed can coexist in the same author, for Tolstoy's "Russian family" is very different both in *The Cossacks* and in *Resurrection* (1899) from what it is in *War and Peace*. Realism and idealism in Tolstoy are not mutually hostile modes, the former succeeding and discrediting the latter; they are intertwined and interchangeable, each being necessary to the other.

One reason for this is the rapid development and telescoping, as it were, of Russian intellectuality and the literature that embodies it. Chernyshevsky and Dobrolyubov, disciples of the great radical critic Belinsky and the idols of the intelligentsia in mid-century, were stern idealists who saw literature in strictly utilitarian terms as the instrument of science and progress. The people were the repository of all the virtues, and those who sought to lead them—the *narodniki*—must cultivate saintly simplicity as well as the intellect. In *What to Do?* (1863) Chernyshevsky represented such a leader, Rakhmetov, who is as crude a propaganda figure as Godwin's Caleb Williams. Nekrasov, too, idealized the Russian people, but as an artist he also saw them clearly. Like *Little Dorrit, Who is Happy in Russia?* could almost be sub-titled *Nobody's Fault.* Nekrasov sees that the *pomeschiki* (landlords) are as much the victims of history as the peasants, and his comic portrait of a representative of the class lamenting the results of the abolition of serfdom is not unsympathetic. Far from being saintly, many of the peasants beat their wives and drink too much vodka (and who can blame them?); but many others do not, for they are as various as everyone else, and no class has a monopoly of vice or virtue. Nekrasov is an environmentalist in that he perceives the stupefying influence of centuries of servitude—he sketches a convict who continues to send the *barin* his dues from what he gets by begging in prison, "because it's better to be on the safe side"—but he is not methodically deterministic and he does not stand outside: he identifies his own sufferings and humiliations with those of the oppressed.

Only a decade or so later the ideals of the populists and the *pochvenniki* (autochthonists), who held that good literature must be a product of the national soil, were confronted with a very different kind of writer, some of whom—such as Pomyalovsky and Kushchevsky—had risen from that soil themselves. Gleb Uspensky, whose *Power of the Soil* (1882) shows a disillusionment with the ideal of the peasant, sank, like many of the divided intelligentsia, into depressive madness. The two plebeian novelists died young of drink after producing books of remarkable vividness and charm about their background, but—disappointingly for the intellectuals —without clear-cut ideological content. When the common people spoke it seemed to be with no particular awareness of their destined role in history, and it is significant that Russian critics have compared Kushchevsky's novel *The Happy Russian* (1871), which appeared in Nekrasov's magazine, to the family idyll of *War and Peace.*

But although the peasant and the proletarian began to be seen more as they really were and less as a solution, an inspiration, or an example, they did not cease to haunt the imagination of the nihilist and the "conscience-stricken nobleman" alike, perhaps because they represented a fixed point in a world of blinkered fanaticism or torturing self-doubt. They appealed as unconsciousness does to consciousness: their existence

G

itself was an act of faith, of which their betters could become suddenly and joyfully conscious, as Levin does in *Anna Karenina* after his talk with the peasant: "He says we must live for truth and God, and at the first hint I understand him. . . . I have discovered nothing. I have only perceived what it is that I know." Levin's joyful incredulity (which had been Tolstoy's own) is caused by his abruptly seeing the intellectual truth of something that the peasant had always taken for granted as the ground of existence. It is because the peasant is *dans le vrai* that Levin can formulate for himself what that truth is.

What is striking about this, in terms of our general argument, is the transposition almost into dramatic and spiritual terms of the 19th-century scientific discovery that individuals and classes are the products of environment. The faith of the peasant is quite simply a part of his way of life; it is no particular credit to him and he can do nothing about it, but just for this reason he can exercise a tremendous spiritual leverage on the man of the upper classes whose way of life has left him empty of faith, yearning and dissatisfied. In *The Death of Ivan Ilyich* (1884) the physical, uncomprehending presence of Tolstoy's young peasant Gerasim can help to save Ivan Ilyich from the fear of death. And in *War and Peace* Tolstoy dwells with repetitive verbal emphasis on those unconscious qualities of Karataev—his serenity, his smell, a kind of roundness that he embodies—that soothe and fascinate Pierre and help him to undergo hardship. But Tolstoy was a deeply divided man, and the genius of the great novels is to reveal and dramatize this division. Levin and Pierre want to draw spiritual certainty from outside, and yet they want to go on being themselves and leading their own way of life. The supreme aristocratic rapacity, the last word in class greed, could be said to be that of Tolstoy's heroes in taking from the peasant the faith they need— and then disposing of him, as Karataev is disposed of at the end of *War and Peace*.

This was certainly the view of the sardonic philosopher-critic Leon Shestov, whose two essays on Tolstoy are the most penetrating things ever written about him.[9] Shestov's comment about the end of *Anna Karenina* is that "the more Levin withdraws into the narrow sphere of his personal interests the more brazen he becomes in praise of 'the good.' " Princess Mary is a deeply and sincerely religious woman, but she unhesitatingly puts her home and children before any claims the sufferings of the people might make on her. In his novels, says Shestov, Tolstoy reconciled the ideal with the actual, the conscience about others with the claims of the ego. Although this profound perception of the "law of life" gives its ambiguous authority to the scope of his great novels, Tolstoy never came to terms with it himself—we should not revere him so much if he had—and the division within him finally drove him from his home and to his death. In *Resurrection* he had finally shown his sense of the dilemma of class guilt and its insolubility. Prince Nekhlyudov has seduced the peasant girl Masha, who becomes a prostitute in consequence, is involved in a murder, and is sent to Siberia. The prince follows her to Siberia, and does all he can to make restitution, but she receives his attempts with a cold malignancy and tells him that he is trying now to make use of her spiritually as he once made use of her body. This is a far cry from the relation of Grinev and Pugachev in *The Captain's Daughter*, where the underdog wins the sympathy of the officer but never arouses in him any agony of guilt: there the class war is one of simple conflict—desperation on one side meeting confidence and self-assurance on the other in a relation of kill or be killed.

In presenting the whole of a society and the antagonisms in it between rich and poor, haves and have-nots, the 19th-century novel did much to foment social guilt and social conscience, but there is no doubt that in some of the greatest novelists the awareness of these things is deeply—and, we must add, fruitfully—equivocal. Shestov goes as far as to say that Dostoyevsky's compassion for his follow convicts in *The House of the Dead* is made possible by the fact that he belonged to a different species—the short-term political prisoner who could expect to be paroled in a year or two to life in a free settlement—with the result that he could still study with detachment the psychology and type of the long-term convict. Had he really been one of them, and without hope, he could not have observed and felt as he did; for his capacity to survive as himself, and thus to have pity for them, depended on the maintenance of a barrier, of the power to say: "I won't be here forever, only for a few years."

The instinct to maintain this kind of barrier at all costs is deeply engrained in Dickens' creative psychology, as we have seen in *Oliver Twist* and in *David Copperfield* (1850). Oliver unconsciously, and David very consciously indeed, cling to the conviction that they are not in the milieu that they should be in; and both are rescued by almost magical means. Mr Dorrit, the "Father of the Marshalsea," becomes the character he is by refusing over many years to sink to the level of his fellow inmates: he patronizes them, and hence earns in the novel the status of epic ridiculousness through the obstinate maintenance of his class dignity. His daughter, little Dorrit, also fascinates and beguiles Dickens (as she did his original readers) by remaining untouched by the prison atmosphere and retaining as a part of her saintly poverty and humility the standards and demeanour of an ideal upper-class child. When Dickens himself worked at a blacking factory (the occasion that inspired the traumatic early experiences of David Copperfield) the boy who befriended him had the name Fagin; and it is significant that this name was transferred in *Oliver Twist* to the villain who wanted to keep the child in the slave world of the thief and the underdog, so preventing him from entering the gentleman's world of his birthright.

In all Dickens' works there is a striking difference between the tireless observer, crusader, and committee-man, and the fears and fascinations of a much deeper and less conscious relation with the Victorian underworld, a simultaneous and whole-hearted identification and rejection. He and the great Russians afford the most remarkable examples in the 19th-century novel of the social struggle being fought out in the life and imagination of the individual artist. Changed conditions and attitudes have, it may be argued, taken the heat out of this confrontation between author and society: the writer of today is alienated from his environment by its impersonality, and because he is not able to feel and fight within himself a struggle that both contains the wider social process and corresponds to it. He cannot confidently observe and encompass society—as Balzac and Galdós, Zola and Verga were able in their different ways to do—and he cannot reflect the scope and antagonisms of a society in himself and his own creations. Consider, for instance, the incapacity of the liberal novelist today to make anything creative out of the Negro problem: he cannot take it over, as Mrs Stowe did in *Uncle Tom's Cabin* (1852) and as Dickens himself did in a couple of telling scenes in *Martin Chuzzlewit* (1843–4), and he cannot find in himself any dynamism of participation or rejection. He can only follow the liberal line, as contemporary social realists of the Soviet Union follow the party line.

The absence of passion and of an inner assurance of his authority in the novelist leads here to something very like a revival of pastoralism—the observance of the typical and the careful maintenance of characters and situations inside a given role and an assumed psychology: the kind of pastoralism we find in its most robust and humane form in the social novels of George Eliot. In writing about a wide society, George Eliot needed to acquire confidence and authority over it, as she set out to acquire in the historical setting of *Romola* (1861–2). But there is evidence that this process, however good she was at it, went against the grain of her creative urge and failed to satisfy her. I have mentioned *Silas Marner*;

and it seems to me a much higher achievement than her most pastoral novel, *Adam Bede*, because of the strong element in it of poetic phantasy and fairy-story, as the realism of *Who is Happy in Russia?* is enclosed by the framework of a magical folk-tale. We have only to compare the main theme of *Adam Bede* with *Resurrection* to see the weakening effect of pastoral manipulation: Hetty Sorrel and Arthur Donnithorne are types exactly appropriate to their situation, and their relation is wholly lacking in that terrible individuality and unpredictability of response that distinguishes seducer and seduced in Tolstoy's novel. Similarly the idyll of the Poyser family, apparently so animated in its rustic perfection, becomes a wax-work beside any of Dickens' clan settings. Humour itself is used by George Eliot to soften and pastoralize the hard, analytic good-sense she brings to a class confrontation: the significance of the clash in *Middlemarch* between Mr Brooke and his impoverished tenant farmer is reduced to a certain artificiality by the fact that both—in a fashion appropriate to their background and status—are made winningly absurd.

George Eliot hankers, in fact, for a kind of creation that is not socially determined and sensibly predictable; she hankers for a classless figure whom there is no need to place and who can be seen with the eye of imagination for its visionary appeal. Indeed, she may well be the first novelist in English to examine fictionally the possibility of a classless hero—a hero of the type of Felix Holt, Ladislaw in *Middlemarch*, and Daniel Deronda. Such a quasi-international figure may come from a humble or an exotic background: the point is that there is no need for the author to place him specifically in relation to an environment or to a documented social class area. He is free both socially and mentally, as George Eliot would have wished to be free, and he can devote his energies to high-minded and humanitarian projects. That George Eliot is not very successful in her attempts to portray such a character (as Henry James was also not successful with his concept of Hyacinth Robinson in *The Princess Casamassima*) does not diminish the originality and importance of her pioneering vision.

Nor does it diminish the significance of the change. If George Eliot was weary of the socially enclosed and socially determined characters in whose portraiture she had excelled, did it not follow that the class at once most socially determined and most alienated from the writer's consciousness—the working class—was losing its lustre for the novelist and its invitingness as a field to attempt to master? After the sober Flemish realism of her earlier descriptions (George Eliot herself used the pictorial analogy) the international scene in *Daniel Deronda* (1876) is like an Impressionist painting laid on with dabs of crude colour, "brewed"—like the description of the gaming resort in the first chapter—"to a visible haze." A society is not catalogued and put in order but suggested, conjured into existence, as D. H. Lawrence was to suggest a society, 40 years on, in *Women in Love* (1921), which has something of the same relation to *Sons and Lovers* (1913) as *Daniel Deronda* has to *Middlemarch*. Lawrence, too, creates classless characters—Birkin in *Women in Love*, Mellors in *Lady Chatterley's Lover* (1928)—who are free enough to embody attitudes that can be explored and put forward by the author.

Another symptom of the change appears in the fact that Dickens' admirer and disciple, George Gissing, sees in the London scene nothing but hopeless bondage in "the weltering mass" for those who, like Oliver Twist or David Copperfield, were owed a superior position by their sense of themselves. *The Unclassed* (1884) and *Born in Exile* (1892) present the typical Gissing hero, "the imaginative person in low spirits," whose conscious alienation is the only thing that separates him from the apathetic and undifferentiated crowd. He shares their fate but is not one of them, and the point of the stories is precisely in this predicament: having no contact with the lower depths in which he is compelled to live. It makes Gissing's London a very different town from that in which Dickens' young heroes have their vivid nightmare confrontations. By contrast with Gissing's, the heroes of Arnold Bennett and H. G. Wells tend to be released into a viable world of fiction by methods not so very different from those of a picaresque novel. If—as was the case with Kipling—the mainspring of creative power resided in curiosity about people at work and a devouring interest in their professional and technological being, the portrayal of a whole society was no longer possible. Henry James thought at one time that Kipling might prove to be the "English Balzac," but the proportion and perspective of human beings in relation to their jobs and their other modes of being could no longer be held in a single imaginative vision. Kipling wrote no large novel; everything he touched becomes specialized to the point of exoticism and unreality. His powers are liberated only in technological and anthropomorphic phantasies—societies of animals, railway engines, parts of ships—so that, as James had later to observe gloomily, the human scene becomes converted by degrees into a purely mechanistic one.

Only Conrad, perhaps, is fully successful in adapting the microcosm of a technological world to the novel in which he can relate the rulers to the ruled. The ship is a hierarchy in which pastoralism is replaced by an unobtrusive professional authority, a knowledge as complete as that of Galdós or Verga. In *The Nigger of the "Narcissus"* (1897) the peasant figure, good or bad, is related once more to those in authority, a relation that reveals their essential natures to us and to each other. In *The Shadow-Line* (1917) the young captain is able to save his fever-striken ship by his unspoken partnership with the sailor Ransome. And in *Nostromo* (1904) Conrad attempts a much more complex creation of a human society, complete in itself and yet divorced from any actual place known to ourselves or to the author. In place of Verga's "observation and recollection" Conrad could draw on only the briefest acquaintance with a South American state, and sustaining his elaborate illusion made him feel—as he tells us—like a man with a laden wheelbarrow on a tightrope, who dare not for a moment shift his gaze or interrupt his onward movement. The virtuosity of Conrad's achievement may suggest to us that it was easier for a novelist of his period to secure objectivity in relation to an imaginary society than to an actual one: as the complete master of Costaguana, Conrad can exercise the omniscience of Balzac and Zola and the same mastery of social issues. The partnership of the intellectual politician Decoud and the masterful servant Nostromo in their enterprise to save the company's silver has something in common with the epic master-and-man relations in earlier novels we have mentioned, but it is manipulated into a pattern of much more deliberate significance. Decoud depends on the confidence of Nostromo, and when left alone he loses all sense of purpose and identity and shoots himself. Nostromo, on the other hand, loses in the crisis his unreflecting assurance that what he owes to himself—the standards of his own style and vanity— are harmonious with his loyalty to the company that employs him. Well before the silver is delivered into his hands, by the sequence of accident and coincidence, he has come to realize that he is being made use of. His fidelity and indispensability are taken for granted not by a human master but by a force of blind and impersonal avarice, a capitalist enterprise. Conrad wonderfully suggests the historical perspective here: a man such as Nostromo—"our man"—would have remained loyal to a feudal master or to a political ideal, because such a bond would have matched his own human qualities. But the company offers nothing but reward and profit. Having apprehended this, and having himself become a capitalist through the secret ownership of the silver, Nostromo becomes as isolated as Decoud himself. "Our man" is now his own man, but he has lost his *raison d'être* in the process.

Conrad's study of Nostromo is in a sense that of an international proletarian figure, corrupted by a system that he joins but cannot accept.

Its implications are far-reaching and it is written with great subtlety and insight. But the method may serve to underline the fact that, to study and command a society, the novelist perpetuated in his own person the situation of "the two nations." His stance is necessarily aristocratic, and Conrad's is no less so than that of Tolstoy, Galdós, and Verga. It may be that the imaginatively authoritative novel of man in society is possible only in a traditionally divided society, where the novelist unconsciously assumes the role of master. If he is not inspired by the dynamic of differentiation he must make use of various devices and stances of help-lessness and subjectivity, or (like James Joyce) he may adopt the role of exile, the role of *deus absconditus*, "paring his fingernails" in aesthetic detachment. His command of his material is no longer that of the master of realism, physically engrossed in actions and preoccupations that are counterparts of those he is putting down on paper, or that of the savant, the seeker after facts and compiler of documentary information. He does not so much order and control his material as will it into existence, making it one with the egocentric and dominating consciousness.

Dickens, as we have seen, depends on a graphic awareness of the great gulf between rich and poor, accentuating it the more he is compelled to cross and recross it in the vivid retrospect of his imagination; it is at its intensest that his genius needs the division most. In a letter to a friend he wrote: "I have great faith in the poor; to the best of my ability I always endeavour to present them in a favourable light to the rich."[10] One hundred years later Orwell virtually echoes this sentiment in *Nineteen Eighty-Four* (1949), but the rich are now Them, the Party, no longer concerned to amass individual wealth—for the whole resources of society are at their disposal—but as determined as the most corrupted capitalist to perpetuate their own power and privileges. Orwell also has faith in the poor, the "proles," for the bizarre reason that they are totally indifferent to the millennial fraud that has been enacted in their name. They are saved because they couldn't care less, and in his parable Orwell presents them to the idealist and the potential revolutionary as worthy, for this reason, of the faith of those who are utterly disenchanted with the communist system.

The uses of the underdog mythology die hard, and in the hypothetical society of Orwell—as in that of Yevgeny Zamyatin's *We* (1920)—a totally divided society is still an imaginative necessity to the writer who wishes above all to be realistic, to portray society as he sees it becoming, to command its true perspective from a position of independence. In these later 20th-century novels we can see the "freedom-bringing" motif of the peasant myth outlasting Naturalism's demand for scientifically based typicality. The people outside the establishment of power and possession, the proles and savages, paradoxically retain the original upper-class freedom of seeing society from an external vantage-point— hence their enduring fascination for the writer who must attempt to do the same. As the bourgeois achieved independence by authority and understanding, these peasants of the future are seen as achieving it by ignorance and non-cooperation.

H. G. Wells, in his millennial phantasy *The Time Machine* (1895), foresaw the top half of the two nations reduced to the status of well-cared-for cattle, farmed and devoured by their proletarian masters the Morlocks, who live in an industrial twilight below ground. Nothing could illustrate better the difference between the outlook of a science-inspired writer such as Wells and that of such a deeply engaged and concerned—though thwarted—novelist of society as Orwell. The latter must have felt, however unconsciously, that the role of the peasant or underdog figure was essential to the novelist's imagination of a human society, however nightmarish, that was still capable of change and development. Wells' vision is historically determined and without hope, and in the last resort it is the function of the underdog—in the imagination of the social novelist—to act as a protest against the vision of scientific determinism. He remains the reservoir of unpredictability. For Wells, the upper crust—the *Eloi*—had got no more than their historical deserts: they had become, irrevocably, the property of the productive class on whose labour they had lived for so long. For Orwell they would have been the heroes of the new society, the seemingly hopeless and impotent mass in which would be incubated new movements and revolts, new possibilities of freedom. Wells and Orwell may be equally misled, equally wide of the processes of humdrum reality, but there is no doubt which is closer both to the tradition and to the continuing possibility of the social novel, for Orwell's proles have been actualized and localized in the victims of Solzhenitsyn's novels. In the Soviet Union as he reveals it, the only dynamic society exists behind the wire of labour camps or in the wards of hospitals. Thus opted out, they become the equal of the establishment in human terms, instead of cogs in a co-ordinated state machine. However powerless they may be, and however empty of ideal and belief, they retain through servitude the capacity of real speech and real thought. With his own originality and his own powers of creative response, Solzhenitsyn carries on the great mythic tradition that those whom society rejects and despises must in the end be those who save it from itself.

References

1. Lukács's definition of realism is foreshadowed in his first major work, *Die Theorie des Romans* (Berlin 1920), and extended in *History and Class-Consciousness*, trans. by R. Livingstone (London 1971), and in his later works. In *The Historical Novel*, trans. by H. and S. Mitchell (paperback: Harmondsworth 1971), he emphasizes the notion of *typicality*, an idea that had already featured in the critical exchange between Marx, Engels, and Lassalle, and in much Marxist-orientated fiction.
2. *Oliver Twist*, opening of Ch. 17.
3. "Gramigna's Lover," in *Vita dei campi* (1880). Verga is addressing himself to a friend and fellow-writer, Salvatore Farina.
4. From "The Dead," in *Dubliners* (1914).
5. In the manuscript of Dickens' second Christmas book, *The Chimes* (1845). "Young Englanders" preferred to call the working class "the Order of the Peasantry."
6. From his essay on Zola in *Affirmations* (London 1898).
7. HENRY JAMES, *The Art of Fiction* (1884).
8. The distinction is made several times in GEORG LUKÁCS, *Studies in European Realism*, trans. by E. Bone (London 1950).
9. Shestov's two essays on the major novels of Tolstoy and on Dostoyevsky are *The Good in the Teaching of Tolstoy and Nietzsche* (1898) and *Dostoyevsky and Nietzsche: the Philosophy of Tragedy* (1903). Both have been published in English translation by Ohio University Press (Columbus 1968).
10. Letter to J. V. Staples, 3 April 1844.

CHAPTER 4

Irrationalism

Anthony Thorlby*

"There used to be Hegelians and now there are nihilists." The speaker is Pavel Kirsanov, the slightly faded champion of the old social order in Ivan Turgenev's novel *Fathers and Children* (1862). He believes in "principles taken on faith" and detests the modern attitudes of the young men who have just graduated from St Petersburg university and who "regard everything from the critical point of view." A quarter of a century earlier Pavel's brother had graduated there, and had been similarly touched by new currents of thought; Turgenev does not specify what these were, but they were probably of the sentimental liberal kind, made up of often rather diffuse feelings for art, progress, and humanity. Dostoyevsky also gives glimpses of that idealistic earlier generation—through his description of Versilov as a young man in *A Raw Youth* (1875), for instance, or of Stepan Verkhovensky in *The Possessed* (1872)—and he likewise notes the generation gap that separates their sentiments for the good, the beautiful, and the true from the more radical and dangerous attitudes of their children. By what process did the cultural and philosophical idealism, of which Germany had been the home and Hegel the last great exponent, change its character and decline into the nihilism that by the end of the century was associated with a thinker more forbidding than any conceived of by Turgenev, though remarkably akin to several characters portrayed by Dostoyevsky—namely, Friedrich Nietzsche? No more need be said here about the historical events of 1848 as a "cause" of this change; many writers throughout Europe were affected by those events and their aftermath—including Dostoyevsky, of course, and to a lesser extent Turgenev—but they reacted to them in very different ways. It is the differences that are interesting, and in particular the variant forms of one intellectual tendency that recurs in much 19th-century writing: the tendency toward irrationalism.

* Professor of Comparative Literature, University of Sussex.

Turgenev's young nihilist would certainly not have thought of himself as an irrationalist: he is a doctor and he believes in science; at first glance, therefore, the two terms appear to be polar opposites. Indeed, European civilization is commonly thought of as having progressed steadily toward rational and scientific goals for well over two centuries now, despite some occasional lapses into romantic, reactionary, or similarly irrational states of mind. What the study of literature and intellectual history may suggest, however, is that the opposition between these states of mind is of a peculiar sort. They seem gradually to have become inseparable; the more clearly one has emerged, the more strongly the other has been felt; they are opposites that posit each other. Turgenev presented this situation symbolically in the scene where his hero dies: he diagnoses his own fatal disease, and he fights to keep rational control of his consciousness—"to fix my thoughts on death, but nothing comes of it." His scientific materialism allows him none of the spiritual consolations of which his more simple-minded and essentially unself-conscious parents are capable. For Bazarov, death is accidental and senseless.

Some critics have seen this way of ending the novel as a weakness of plot, but it rings true both psychologically and symbolically. Life, too, was beginning to show itself as senseless for this exasperated scientist: love, friendship, family, even ordinary social existence offered no more than accidental sensations; to attach any "meaning" to them Bazarov considered to be poetic nonsense. Before the "red dogs" of delirium invade his mind, he has already felt irrational urges—the desire, for instance, to "smash people," and even to begin with his best friend. His refusal to recognize any "higher" human significance in love turns the emotion of love itself into a hateful compulsion to be resisted (or else, on another occasion, into a mere sensual impulse, which he can accept, but with quite senseless consequences). The woman in the book who would seem to be the ideal match for him, being highly intelligent like himself, is equally incapable of love. When, "under the influence of confused impulses," she is drawn toward Bazarov, she finds in her heart "sheer emptiness—or something hideous." Turgenev describes her feeling for him, which to the reader seems to be heavy with the alluring possibility of love, as one of profound fear—that kind of unidentifiable fear that is known to psychoanalysis and existentialist philosophy as *Angst:*

> While exchanging the simplest remarks with him, even when she
> joked with him, she was conscious of an embarrassed fear. Thus do
> people on a steamer at sea talk and laugh carelessly, for all the world
> as if they were on dry land; but the moment there is some hitch, if the

smallest sign appears of something unusual, there emerges at once on every face an expression of peculiar alarm, revealing the constant awareness of constant danger.[1]

This image of human existence, as being precariously suspended over an abyss, that rational understanding and civilized behaviour serve generally to hide from us, is almost identical with Schopenhauer's depiction of man afloat on the ocean of being or Kierkegaard's sense of lying over 70,000 fathoms of water. Similar images are produced a century later by Conrad's obsession with "the heart of darkness" and the "destructive element," or by T. S. Eliot when he writes about the moment

> . . . when an underground train, in the tube, stops too long between
>   stations
> And the conversation rises and slowly fades into silence
> And you see behind every face the mental emptiness deepen
> Leaving only the growing terror of nothing to think about.[2]

In order to appreciate the irrationalistic implications of Turgenev's image, however, it may be more illuminating to look rather further backward in time, and to compare the relationship between Bazarov and Anna Sergeyevna with that between Jane Austen's Emma and Mr Knightley. For one way of viewing this love story in *Fathers and Children* might be to see it as a rather conventional comedy about two people who are so clever that they don't realize who is in love with whom, even when it is themselves. Bazarov says:

> "And besides, love . . . surely it's an imaginary feeling."
> "Indeed? I am very pleased to hear that." Anna Sergeyevna expressed herself thus and so did Bazarov; they both thought they were speaking the truth. Was the truth, the whole truth, to be found in their words? They themselves did not know, much less could the author.[3]

Now, Jane Austen would not have written that last phrase, unless perhaps as a device to keep the reader in suspense. Turgenev means it. Both Bazarov and Anna Sergeyevna have reached a degree of *self-conscious* intelligence that makes it impossible to say what they really feel. This is not true of other characters in the novel; Katya and Arkady can make mistakes about their emotions and then find out what these really are. Some of the minor characters are also recognized for what they are, and the true state of their hearts and minds is diagnosed with the same moral assurance that "the whole truth" can be known as inspires Jane Austen's depiction of a Mrs Elton or a Harriet Smith. The difference is that, whereas this possibility of moral knowledge, and hence of right action, extends also to Emma herself, so that she can use her intelligence to recognize and act in harmony with her feelings, it does not extend to Turgenev's heroes. They are cut off from their fellow human beings, divided against themselves, and inhibited from that spontaneous participation in the life of the feelings, which they regard as mere "poetry." This divisive element in their make-up, moreover, stems from their greatest gift: their power of intelligence, their rational self-awareness. It is this tendency to see man's reason in a negative light that will be considered here as the primary characteristic of irrationalism. Its secondary characteristics consist in varying types of response to this division, the most common being the impulse to overcome it.

That the love story of Bazarov and Anna cannot be viewed in conventional terms of moral comedy is evident also on other grounds. Bazarov does in fact realize that he is in love and actually declares his feelings. But he does so not with "the sweet awe of the first declaration . . . [but with] a powerful, heavy passion not unlike fury and perhaps akin to it."[4] The contrast Turgenev draws here points to the heart of his inspiration as a writer. No writer has caught with more wistful charm the "sweet awe" of first love (*First Love* [1860] is among the most beautiful of Turgenev's short stories), and he makes the contrast to Bazarov's irrational fury felt throughout the novel by showing his younger friend and erstwhile disciple in nihilism enjoying all the "poetry" of that experience that Bazarov does not believe in and cannot achieve—except (ironically) for a brief moment, on his death-bed. If we ask why he cannot achieve or believe in the things that warmed Turgenev's imagination to its most lyrical effusions, we touch on a most difficult question. Bazarov himself in effect answers it in the language of social criticism: he is cut off from Anna Sergeyevna, from love and friendship, for reasons of class; living among the gentry makes him feel like "a fish out of water"; but the peasants are too primitive for him to feel at home among them either. Anna likewise could be said to have been damaged emotionally by the need to marry for money, and Bazarov to have died because of the backward state of life in the Russian provinces. Turgenev may have identified himself to some extent with Bazarov. Certainly, he was regarded as a leader of liberal opinion in the 1850s, after his first work, *A Sportsman's Sketches* (1847–51), had shown the peasants in a better light than their masters; the book, in connection with which Turgenev was briefly imprisoned and then banished to his estate, is even thought to have influenced the future Tsar Alexander II in his decision to emancipate the serfs. According to report, Turgenev's parading of his democratic sympathies irritated the young Tolstoy, and his belief in Western scientific progress was satirized by Dostoyevsky in the figure of Karmazinov in *The Possessed*. Finally, it seems significant that, just at the time when he was embarking on *Fathers and Children*, Turgenev should have visited the most famous Russian revolutionary, Aleksandr Herzen, who was then living in London.

Despite all this evidence, however, the light in which Bazarov has been presented remains somewhat enigmatic, and the novel was at once attacked by some of the very radicals who had previously supported Turgenev. Deeply hurt by this criticism, he left Russia and never returned; he settled in Paris, where he was more warmly appreciated by writers such as Flaubert and the Goncourts, who were concerned more with art than with social reform. In retrospect, Bazarov's death-scene reads like Turgenev's own farewell to his native land, whose old order he can admit at last that he loves—for its beauty. But he cannot live with it: like many an aesthete of the 19th century, he can enjoy the beautiful vision only in exile from the reality. Bazarov's death is matched by Pavel's equally self-sacrificing end, as he too goes into exile like this author; both men are cut off from life by their inability to love—one of them owing to his attachment to an idealized conception of the past, and the other to his entirely negative idea of it; between them stands a pretty peasant girl and her baby, a symbol of uncomplicated living.

The negative tone that pervades Turgenev's conception of Bazarov's life (and death), and that seems only to be in abeyance when he "loses himself" in his work—another trait that is as characteristic of a 19th-century writer as of a scientist—is not offset by Bazarov's positivistic and materialistic opinions. He still resembles the solitary and ineffectual idealist who had held the centre of interest in Turgenev's fiction from his early novel *Rudin* (1856) and the still earlier *Diary of a Superfluous Man* (1850). In his study of this type of figure, who inspired in Turgenev some interesting reflections on the comparable characters of Don Quixote and Hamlet, we discover what kind of mind is so sensitive to social questions. The mind of the poetic realist is an alien consciousness, so alien that we feel he could never become an effective revolutionary. Like his author, he is divided from society not so much by positive principles as by negative self-consciousness. His irredeemable alienation is contrasted in the opening scenes of the novel with the quite superficial nihilism that he has taught his young friend, Arkady. Arkady at first sees the *misère* of peasant existence on his family's estate, and is embarrassed by the sentimentality of his ineptly liberal father. But a mere change of mood is enough to make him feel at one again with the landscape of his childhood, which suddenly looks quite different in the spring sunshine, and he spontaneously kisses his father. Before long he will fall in love and espouse the traditional way of life. Not so Bazarov. He will draw close to no one, not even to the peasants whom he imagines that he understands but, as Turgenev ironically observes, in fact does not.

Two of the secondary characteristics of irrationalism are finely portrayed by Turgenev, one of them in a conversation between Bazarov and Arkady, where the connection with the primary characteristic of alienated intelligence is quite apparent. Bazarov says:

> "I'm thinking how happy life is for my parents! My father at the age of sixty can fuss around, chat about 'palliative measures,' heal people; he plays the magnanimous master with the peasants—has a gay time in fact; and my mother is happy too; her day is so crammed with all sorts of jobs, with sighs and groans, that she hasn't a moment to think about herself; while I . . ."
>
> "While you?"
>
> "While I *think*. Here I lie under a haystack . . . the tiny narrow space I occupy is so minutely small in comparison with the rest of space where I am not and which has nothing to do with me; and the portion of time in which it is my lot to live is so insignificant beside the eternity where I have not been and will not be. . . . And in this atom, in this mathematical point, the blood circulates, the brain works and wants something . . . how disgusting! how petty!"
>
> "Allow me to point out that what you say applies generally to everyone."
>
> "You're right," interrupted Bazarov. "I wanted to say that they, my parents I mean, are occupied and don't worry about their own nothingness; it doesn't sicken them . . . while I . . . I feel nothing but boredom and anger."[5]

Bazarov's intellectualized observations correspond to Anna Sergeyevna's sensation, noted earlier, of "sheer emptiness or something hideous." The emotions aroused in him by his purely self-orientated, self-conscious awareness of his position in the universe have the same demonic character as her *Angst:* they have no particular object, but assail every aspect of existence, and reduce the fact that human beings also exist in relationship to one another, in society, to a source of common delusion. For Bazarov, his parents (and other people generally) are play-acting, living roles that absorb them fully, but that appear, in the face of his own negative sense of infinitude, to be entirely false. This intuition of falsity in the mind's shared, or socially conventional, preoccupations and projects defines another of the secondary characteristics of 19th-century irrationalism that will be discussed more fully later (it does not engage much of Turgenev's attention). Its usual definition may be noted here in passing, however:

it has come to be known, through Ibsen and Shaw, as "the life-lie." The other secondary characteristic of irrationalism, which is of more fundamental concern to Turgenev and well evidenced by this novel, is the need to overcome the rift that mind causes in nature. It is a rift that death will put an end to, of course, as far as every individual is concerned. Bazarov resists this senseless end to the limit of his conscious power, holding the "red dogs" of delirium at bay as long as he can. On the last page of the book Turgenev tries to pass beyond this position of negative resistance, which seems also to be a form of insistence on the senselessness of the world. In a sentimental passage he reunites Bazarov with a more beneficent and beautiful order of nature, indeed the very opposite of the one this nihilist describes above, the order to which Arkady has "succumbed" through love, and from which his parents have never been separated:

> [They] start to pray again and cannot tear themselves away from that place where they seem to be nearer to their son, to their memories of him. . . . Can it be that their prayers and their tears are fruitless? Can it be that love, sacred devoted love, is not all powerful? Oh no! However passionate, sinful, or rebellious the heart hidden in the tomb, the flowers growing over it peep up at us serenely with their innocent eyes; they tell us not only of eternal peace, of that great peace of "indifferent" nature; they tell us also of eternal reconciliation and of life without end.[6]

Turgenev is usually regarded not as a "philosophical" writer but as one interested in people rather than in ideas. This eminently reasonable distinction between things in reality and the things of the mind cannot, however, be maintained in any very rigorous fashion with regard to literature. Admittedly, there are books in which more obviously philosophical matters are discussed than in others, but such discussion is necessarily put into the mouth of someone. Even if this someone is the author, the ideas in any work of imaginative literature will be expressed less in abstract than in concrete form, that is, one in which they have "grown together" (*concretum* is the past participle of *concrescere*) with an objective representation of the world. This ideal identity of subjective and objective experience could be said to be the goal of all art; and the power of art could be said to reside in the glimpse it affords us, albeit in fictional terms, of what the totality of experience, its objective and its subjective face, is like. In this view, the universality of art, which has always been recognized, comes to be seen less as a reflection, "like a picture," of a quality external to the mind, than as a fulfilment that is not complete until the creative mind has made up the whole. The development of aesthetic

H

theory before and during the Romantic period laid increasing stress on the subjective component in the artistic process, as regards both the spectator and the artist himself. Above all, the fusion of a spiritual with a material element, i.e. of form with content, acquired special significance: in a work of art man's inner life could be said to take on external reality at the same time as external reality is spiritualized by man's creative consciousness of it. The sense of totality that is symbolically represented in art opened the door to renewed metaphysical speculation about the totality present in life.

The greatest revival in European metaphysics since the Middle Ages, when conceptions of totality were based on religious intuitions (and had to be squared with rational knowledge of the world*), took place at the turn of the 18th and 19th centuries. It took place largely in Germany, in a period of wide national revival also in the arts, especially the lyric, dramatic, and musical arts, to which the new aesthetic theory, with its emphasis on the subjective component, applies more readily than it does to painting and architecture; and its conception of totality was much influenced by intuitions about the character of art and the creative process. These intuitions it endeavoured to formulate in a manner that would encompass the then rapidly increasing knowledge of nature and history; indeed, the analogy between nature and art became one of the great commonplaces of the time. "A work of art must be treated as a work of nature and a work of nature as a work of art," declared Goethe.[7] This intellectual tendency reached its apogee in the philosophy of Hegel, who treated all science and history in this way.

The influence of German idealist philosophy, and of Hegel in particular, was felt throughout Europe,† and it excited Turgenev when he was a student in Moscow and later in Berlin, the home of Hegelianism. His enthusiasm was typical of his generation; during the 1830s it was shared, for instance, by the Russian critic Vissarion Belinsky and the future anarchist Mikhail Bakunin. Moreover, like so many of those who were carried away by this particular kind of philosophical idealism, Turgenev was carried in a direction rather different from that taken by Hegel himself. The possibility of apparently endless changes of direction within a nevertheless recognizably homogeneous manner of thinking is one of the most striking and fruitful features of this intellectual tradition. The most famous example of the way Hegelian thinking could be reversed is seen

---

* See the discussion of this question in Vol. II, "Christian Thought."
† It is referred to, for instance in Vol. IV, "Literature and Ideology"; "Protestantism and Humanism in Scandinavian Literature"; and "Literature and National Consciousness: Hungary."

in the materialist direction taken by Feuerbach and Marx. No less striking, however, is the resistance put up by Kierkegaard from a quite
different, patently religious position; but it is equally clear that Kierkegaard would not have reached this position without Hegel's influence.
Yet another example is provided by Nietzsche, who would appear to be
an opponent not only of Hegel but also of socialism and Christianity.
Among Nietzsche's all-too-numerous contradictory remarks, however,
we find the following: "We Germans are Hegelians, even if there had
never been a Hegel, because (in contrast to all the Latins) we instinctively
ascribe to 'becoming' a deeper meaning and higher value than we ascribe
to 'what is'."[8] Nietzsche obviously could not foresee the extent to which
French writers would become interested in the inner process of consciousness with Bergson's philosophy, nor the fascination with Hegel's philosophy
that was to be widely experienced by French intellectuals, both existentialists and Marxists, in the 20th century. In pointing simply to the notion
of "becoming" as containing the secret of Germanic inspiration, Nietzsche
does not here throw much light on its dialectical implications, of which he
was nonetheless a master. His word does, however, hint at an irrationalistic potential in the idealist tradition that had made it liable, since its
inception by Kant, to produce ambiguous, indeed contradictory, variations. That their movement does in fact contain an irrational and even
demonic element only gradually becomes clear: for instance, in the way
Nietzsche re-interprets Schopenhauer's re-interpretation of Kant; or in
Schelling's development that is influenced both by Kant and by Fichte's
reaction to Kant. The movement away from Kantian idealism via Hegel
toward Marx claims to offer the one true path past the irrational abyss,
which has engulfed, in the Marxist view, almost all subsequent modes of
bourgeois thought. The various objections that have been raised to this
view tend to take the form of a counter-claim that Marxism, in both theory
and practice, remains dialectically linked with its opposite. Its tendency
toward totalitarian terror in politics is held to be the outcome in reality
of a theoretical distortion of the way in which reason relates to existence,
universals to particulars. (Its revolution in the name of the whole has to
keep taking a stand against the quite "irrational" counter-revolution by
individuals.) If this is so, then the origin of that distortion lies in Hegel's
intellectual procedures. German idealist philosophy may be likened, in
fact, to an ideological instrument having remarkable leverage: although it
seemed capable of moving mountains only in a speculative or metaphorical sense, there was always the possibility that the metaphor might be
taken literally.

In a famous passage at the close of the book that Heine wrote to explain the character of German intellectual culture to the French, he prophesies something resembling an apocalypse for Europe when the abstract revolution in German thought should find its "real" expression: "Kantians will one day come who are prepared to be absolutely radical also in the world of everyday experience, and to be ruthless . . . [in] destroying the past to its very roots. . . . The idealist philosopher of nature will become a terrible figure as a result of his having allied himself with the primitive powers of nature. . . . Then a drama will be enacted in Germany, by comparison with which the French Revolution will seem to have been a harmless idyll."[9] Heine's intuition is complementary to that of Turgenev, whose first revolutionary idealist, Rudin (in the novel of that name), cannot really live his new vision of the world. He can awaken in others the vision of "the interconnection of those ideas—of philosophy, art, science, life itself—the general laws of nature . . . nothing seemed any longer senseless or accidental; a wise inevitability and beauty seemed to prevail everywhere."[10] Rudin's weakness is quite explicitly described by Turgenev: although he can talk beautifully about the need for a binding faith and about the evils of scepticism, it is only beautiful talk: "Rudin seemed full of fire, courage and vitality, but spiritually he was cold and almost timid." "He himself achieves nothing, precisely because he has no character, no fire in the blood."[11] And finally, in words spoken by a woman to Rudin: "*Vous êtes un poète.*" The phrase is illuminating because it hints at the autobiographical element* in this characteristic Turgenev hero who suffers again from "apathy of feeling and will combined with the devouring activity of thought"—a quality that Belinsky praised Turgenev for having captured in one of his earliest poems ("Conversation"), and that he considered to be a disease of the age. It is illuminating also because it reminds us that there was an aesthetic element in this disease.

The sense of being divided from the world by a negative quality inherent in intelligence, which we have defined here as the starting-point for various kinds of irrationalism, may turn out to be the product of a crisis in man's aesthetic self-consciousness, his imaginative picture of himself and his world. In a word, he suspects that he does not truly experience the sentiments and ideas he imagines, cannot *be* the idealist he pretends, cannot *live* the poetic vision. He glimpses the beautiful totality at the expense of being excluded from it. The prospect that excited and—

---

* Another component of Rudin's character is probably taken from Bakunin, in admiration of whose real revolutionary courage Turgenev made Rudin die on the barricades in an epilogue to the novel added in 1860.

to judge from the style—also appalled Heine was what might happen if the self-conscious feeling of being the creator of a beautiful vision from which man is cut off in aesthetic contemplation were to be replaced by the impulse to seize and forge it in reality, to remake the world in its totality—to transform not merely material conditions but the spiritual quality of life as a whole.

One of the most striking factors in the development of German idealism at the close of the 18th century was that the Germans were spectators of a revolution in which they did not participate.* What was a matter of immediate politics in France could be regarded as an aesthetic spectacle from across the Rhine. For some (including Hegel), enthusiasm for the Jacobin cause cooled at the prospect of the Terror, but revived again at the still more splendid sight of Napoleon, who brought order and greatness to the explosive forces of the revolution. To Schiller, writing in 1798 the prologue for a play partly inspired by the figure of Napoleon and above all by the grandeur of contemporary events, it seemed that "reality itself is becoming poetry." Moreover, the crux of this tragic play, *Wallenstein*, concerns the difference between being a spectator and being an actor, between participating in history and standing outside it. Wallenstein is first seen by others as a hero, a man of action; but the play goes on to show him turning to look on at himself and at the world of events; instead of making simple, soldierly decisions, he becomes fatalistic and sentimental. His sense of values becomes increasingly aesthetic: what matters to him is the beauty or meanness of his rôle. He is self-conscious about his own greatness and tries to read the stars—an act that symbolizes the impossibility for any man to survey his own fate, except in retrospect. One way of reading the famous line from Wallenstein's longest soliloquy about history and heroism—

> Denn mich verklagt der Doppelsinn des Lebens
> (I stand accused by life's two-sided sense)[12]

—is to take the two "sides" or aspects of life as referring to the way it is in itself and the way it appears for others. For, once an individual reaches a high point of self-consciousness, he may come to see even his own life in this dual aspect: he will wonder whether he is to be identified with, and judged by, the deeds he is doing, or whether he is (like an onlooker) free in his mind, which remains always pure, no matter what happens to him as an objective person.

* See the discussion of this question in Vol. IV, "Leopardi, Hölderlin, and the Post-Revolutionary Crisis."

In his sense of double or divided vision, Wallenstein is rehearsing, in fact, one of the commonplaces of the literature of his period, the great period of German literature that embraces both a classical and a romantic mood, apart from its contributions to the intellectual culture of the 19th century—contributions that illumine and often determine much that was to be thought and written later in the century throughout Europe. The styles that German scholars distinguish as *Klassik* and *Romantik* are not totally unrelated, but are themselves part of a dialectical process of evolution, often within the career of one writer (as with Goethe and Schiller); they are divergent manners of exploiting the possibilities latent in the German situation and inspiration. Briefly, the awareness of subjective division from the world can be either intensified or overcome, either exploited for its dissonances or adjusted to produce balanced harmonies. Goethe declared the former, romantic, attitude to be sick, and the latter, or classical, ideal to be healthy. He was able to pontificate thus about contemporary literature because he had experienced both as phases in his own growth, a subject that fascinated his extraordinarily self-aware mind and makes his autobiography an inseparable part of his work. His work is a placing at a distance of his experience; his life develops then in the light of that aspect of his nature, indeed of himself as a part of nature, that he has mastered. He conceived of the whole as a process in which the mind realizes itself within a dynamic relationship—a kind of living dialectic—with nature. The mainspring of this process is a perpetual drawing apart of its constituent elements and their subsequent drawing together again. (Goethe developed from this insight a biological theory of diastole and systole.*) The work that records the presence within Goethe, until late in his life, of a deviant or divergent tendency is *Faust* (Pt I, 1808), and it is there that we find what is probably the best-known statement of the commonplace that was to be repeated in one form or another by so many voices besides that of Schiller's Wallenstein:

> Zwei Seelen wohnen, ach! in meiner Brust . . .
> (Two souls reside, alas! within my breast . . .).[13]

This line is as celebrated as "To be or not to be," or the many variants on "*O miracle d'amour!*"—"*O comble de misères!*" in 17th-century French drama. Like those of Shakespeare and Corneille, Goethe's line doubtless owes its fame to its symbolic resonance, which catches with memorable simplicity the essence of a particular situation, a particular way of looking

---

* Goethe's relationship to scientific thought is discussed in detail in Vol. IV, "Science and the Literary Imagination: Voltaire and Goethe."

at the world. Hamlet's choice between being and not being is stated in conventional religious terms, just as Corneille's tragic paradox is in conventional moral ones; but the dilemma of Goethe's Faust is not of this kind. He cannot choose between the two different modes of being toward which the two halves of his soul are drawn, because one cannot "choose" between consciousness and existence. He would be prepared to sell his soul entire to the Devil, if the Devil could bring the process of experience to a halt and Faust could achieve spiritual entirety:

> Werd' ich zum Augenblicke sagen
> Verweile doch! du bist so schōn!
>
> (If I should say to the passing moment: stay still! you are so beautiful).[14]

The immediately preceding lines make it clear that Faust does *not* want the customary kinds of enjoyment and satisfaction that the Christian Devil was supposed to provide. For Goethe, the crucial problem posed by life does not stem from a traditional sense of division between the flesh and the spirit, this world and the next. Such distinctions presuppose a moral and religious world view; but Goethe's view is essentially aesthetic. Although conflict and division appear to exist externally in the world, they are, in the total reality known to art, expressions of man's divided self. In *Die Wahlverwandtschaften* (1809; Elective Affinities) Goethe observes how a man's character and circumstances "constitute a whole." A truism, perhaps, but an aesthetic one. Any writer might say this of *other people*. What is different in Goethe's case, as in the case of the many writers who were subsequently to work in this mode of thought, is that he introduces this aesthetic perception into the experience of living as an educative or moral principle. (Like Schiller, he believed in the possibility of the aesthetic education of man, and loosely thought of this ideal as akin to that of the ancient Greeks.) The "moral" taught by the aesthetic view is this: the apparent discord in the world is really an essential phase of personal experience, which—looked at as a whole—contains and resolves it. The pangs of self-consciousness are thus both the expression *and the substance* of the world's pain—a kind of "necessary evil" in the process of life. The poetry of *Weltschmerz* (world-pain)—which began its career with a deeply Germanic colouring, and has remained a typical form of modern literary inspiration—transposes a theological idea about creation after the fall into a psychological idea about the character of subjective experience. Indeed, the German compound word blurs the distinction between objective and subjective evil: it allows them to be thought of as identical. Within this larger identity compounded of subject and object, which is "life"—again, there is no distinction in the German word *Leben* between "life" and "living"—self-consciousness comprehends both the principle of division and the possibility of a more fully realized unity. Returning now to the question of Faust's pact with the Devil, we see that the beautiful thing he wants is not really a thing at all. He conceives of beauty as though it were a moment; and what he wants is lasting possession of this moment, the power both to possess it in words, by *saying* it, and to *live* it in reality. He wants to grasp the totality of the two sides of his nature, as though he could be man and poet, spectator and actor, at once, and enjoy in actual life the timeless beauty of art.

An elaboration in philosophical terms of the spiritual situation symbolized by Faust's pact is to be found in the work of Hegel, who was much influenced by Goethe's writings. The cornerstones of Hegel's thought are such concepts as "being-for-others" (as opposed to being-in-itself); the disunity within being that is engendered by the "negativity" of the mind's effort to understand the world; and above all the concept of consciousness as a way of defining a new kind of reality, in which subject and object no longer stand related to one another by static rules of thought but are linked dialectically—that is, in a process of thinking that does not arrive *at* the truth but rather *is* the truth. The role of the mind ceases to be merely legislative with regard to what is received as reality (a proposition to which any idealist philosopher of the time would have assented and toward which the drift of much 18th-century philosophy could be said to have moved). With Hegel, the mind's role becomes creative in an absolute sense: its activity generates reality. Needless to say, reality has a singular meaning for Hegel; it means nothing less than the whole; that is, something more than either the empirical world of things or the ideal world of thought. Hegel imagined these two worlds as two aspects of the same reality, the external and internal aspect of being. Individual things or thoughts are real only in relationship to one another, and they achieve this relationship in the cumulative consciousness of mankind. The wholeness of reality is thus itself in process of becoming. Wholeness is not an absolute in the traditional sense of an immutable realm of transcendence existing for itself in infinitude, in the way God used to be imagined in the heavens. Infinitude can no more be separated from finitude than externality can from internality. The infinite is that aspect of the finite that may be seen as ceaselessly transcending any given state of itself, most obviously through the agency of human activity, in time.

This ceaselessly self-transcending process of life might seem necessarily to evade any final rational comprehension. The paradox of Hegel's system, however, is that he makes a form of equation between the rational and the real. This allows him to arrive at such formulae as: "The rational is the real and the real the rational." The mediating factor in this equation, which changes the meaning of the word "reason" quite as much as it changes the notion of the real, is evidently consciousness. Hegel defines reason as "the conscious certainty of being all reality." Consciousness enjoys a different mode of being from either being-in-itself or being-for-others; consciousness exists also for itself. Herein man may know himself and recognize the negativity of his own position; he realizes that he is not "at home" in the world precisely because of his critical intelligence. He is able then to turn his critical powers on his own reason—as Kant had tried to do, though not in a sufficiently consistent and thorough-going fashion, in Hegel's view—and to "negate the negation." In this celebrated culmination of Hegel's logic, the mind overcomes its alienated state of partial comprehension, and a new kind of "reason" is born that Hegel equates with the "self identity" of being.

> Consciousness, as consciousness of self, has a double object. The first it knows immediately as the object of sense certainty and perception, but for consciousness this carries the marks of negative knowledge. The second object of consciousness is itself [in its inward character of being conscious of its own activity]; this is its true essence and is initially present only in a contrary mode through its opposition to the first object [i.e. through negating the first negative]. Self-consciousness here realizes itself as a movement in the process of which this opposition is suppressed, a movement whereby being achieves identity [undivided sameness] with itself.[15]

The notorious difficulty of Hegel's system contrasts with a recurrent, almost obsessive, sameness in his intellectual method, that new type of dualistic thinking that goes under the name—also much altered in meaning from ancient usage—of "dialectic." This contrast stands out in the explicitly conservative conclusions to which Hegel meant his system to lead, on the one hand, and the potentially revolutionary consequences of his method, on the other. It may be illuminating to glance back here at Goethe's *Faust* in order to note a similar kind of ambiguity. Faust's method—which is to ally himself with a devilish spirit "who always negates," as he says—is not very likely to lead to that paradoxical goal of his, a lasting moment of bliss. Goethe should not, of course, be thought of as having failed to see this contradiction; his imagination could scarcely have grasped it more firmly as the essence of Faust's situation. The sort of mind that longs so passionately to possess life's beauty in this way is simply imagining the reverse of what it immediately knows: namely, the process of ceaseless striving, of failing to possess, of not being totally at home in the world either of the mind or of nature. Faust's is the quintessentially divided mind of modernity, in whose experience "everything contradicts itself," to paraphrase Hegel's spiritual rule—one which, as we have suggested, was to carry 19th-century thought on a career as dialectically varied, contradictory, and in some cases destructive, as Faust's own. The critical question concerning this dialectical type of thinking is this: is it inherently unstable, to the point where the value and meaning even of reason appear uncertain, and it starts to be dogged by a kind of demonic *alter ego* in the guise not of primitive unreason but of a sophisticated irrationalism?

For, it should be added here, one thing irrationalism is not: it is not a word for mere absence of thought, unthinking barbarism, mindless life. It is an *-ism*, an attitude of mind, that may admire primitive and even brutal phenomena, but precisely in its act of conscious admiration it stands apart from them. We may go even further, in fact, and deny the full application of the word to anyone who distinctly recognizes irrational behaviour for what it is; he is not yet, simply in the act of recognition, an irrationalist. Even if irrational elements seem to loom particularly large in his account of the world, he is still not necessarily to be regarded as an irrationalist. (One would not apply the word to Hobbes, Voltaire, or even Freud.) When a man goes on to admire the primitive, he certainly begins to qualify for the title, although the grounds for his admiration may vary considerably, as may its object and his manner of expressing it. Thus, there is little in common as regards either style or content between, say, de Sade's mannered pornography, Leconte de Lisle's impassive paganism, and Péguy's ardent mystique of peasant toil. The irrationalistic tendency of writings such as these can be assessed on a common scale only by referring them to the question raised above: to what extent do they also cast doubt upon the value of reason as a way of dealing with reality? It may be argued that the German development of dialectic finally reached, in the work of Nietzsche, an extreme point of uncertainty as to the meaning both of reality and of reason, as a result of assuming them to be ideally one and interdependent. Ironically, it is Hegel's seeming apotheosis of reason that marks the beginning of a process of unstable "dialectic"—a word having a quite different significance from any it possessed in former systems of philosophy. Since the early 19th century, the proudest claims ever made by the human spirit to be totally in control of its destiny—not only of the inner world of the mind, but of historical reality as well—have been accompanied by a sense that civilization has never stood nearer to the abyss. Nothing haunts the mind more vividly as a symbol of this situation than Goethe's depiction of the old, blind Faust, who believes that the ultimate problems are merely those of large-scale engineering, and that these are well in hand (so that permanent bliss on earth is about to be achieved); in fact, Goethe shows, the labourers of hell are digging his grave.

Goethe's *Faust*, for all its suggestive symbolism and protracted variations, gives little "explanation" of the spiritual situation it symbolizes. It pretends to adopt, or at least to adapt, the religious explanation of Faust's fate that is embodied in the original tale; but, as we have already seen, Goethe's point of view has little in common with a mediaeval or religious one. Perhaps the most significant insight in the book lies in its form, rather than in any part of its content: some of it is in the form of bourgeois realism, some romantic and melodramatic, and some balances on a knife-edge between playful doggerel and soulful dream-symbolism that anticipates the whole range of modern experiment in drama, from the symbolist theatre of Maeterlinck and Strindberg to the "alienated" realism of Brecht or Beckett. Immediately, with the opening two scenes—which were not written first, for Goethe only gradually took the measure of the essential problem posed by the play—our attention is drawn to the aesthetic question of what it is that we are looking at: one scene shows the play as a human contrivance, the next as a heavenly one. Now, the traditional conventions of the theatre, varied though these have been, have assumed that human affairs have definite and necessary shape when seen from outside. The actors, immersed in the action, may not know individually what this shape is, but the audience does; the audience enjoys a spectacle that, in life itself, only the gods enjoy. The unrealistic aspects of drama, from the earliest ritual chorus to no less ritualized modern forms of dialogue and plot, can all be accepted "on faith" as the way the world appears from the outside, though it never looks or sounds like this when we are situated within it. Because drama simulates so concretely a transcendent type of vision, it is a literary genre that is particularly sensitive to changes in world-view. The uncertain level of seriousness with which the audience is expected to take the enactment of Faust on stage—and Goethe's drama is so unwieldy that it can hardly be staged as a whole at all—is in keeping with the uncertain reality of Faust's own experiences. Indeed, the "world" of Faust has many of the characteristics of a lyrical poem, although it is cast in dramatic form. It begins to explore the varieties of aesthetic illusion possible in a world that has *no* necessary shape independent of the mind's experience of it; whatever gods or devils it contains are self-consciously realized to be part of the act of experience. Faust's fate is not decided by any external standard, whether of good or of evil, nor by external events; it stems from the psychology of knowledge, of creative self-consciousness. That is why he is damned and saved for the same "sin"—for restlessness of spirit, which divides itself from the world in the act of trying to take possession of it, of trying to "know" it.

Goethe's *Faust* begins to exemplify, in fact, a tendency that Hegel prophesied would become the hallmark of modern art altogether: "The subjectivity of the artist [will] cease to be governed by any fixed or necessary character in either the content or the form of his art; [it is he who will] govern them, enjoying complete freedom of choice as regards both the matter and the manner of his production."[16] Hegel's generalizations about world history and culture as a whole, and his conception of this whole as culminating in the unsurpassable wisdom of his own philosophy, have been rather easy targets for critics. Criticism of such generalized conceptions has certainly not prevented them from being used, however; nor do the many inversions—Hegelians would say "perversions"—of their use, of the kind we have already noted, alter their fundamental character. This character resides in the new kind of intellectual insight generated by Hegel's dialectic. The "logic" of Hegel's thinking has nothing to do with mathematical method, which has always tended to make philosophers believe that there must be an unchanging realm of truth above or beyond the flux of experience. Hegel's logic is grounded not in mathematics but in psychology, the process whereby the mind becomes aware of itself. For Hegel, this process does not take place merely subjectively; he identifies it with the process of world history, and this in turn ceases to be a record of individual events and becomes active in the present as an idea. Whatever credence we may or may not wish to give to Hegel's system, he is surely right in asserting that the step he takes here goes beyond any previous philosophical position.

The problem of how the mind forms its idea (which is spiritual) of the world (which is material and therefore unlike itself) had been at the centre of philosophical debate in Europe for well over a century. It was possible to adopt a sceptical solution, like that of David Hume, who thought that the workings of the mind offered only a "faint analogy" with the reality of the world; or it was possible to believe, with Leibniz, that special arrangements must have been made by God to get the truth about the world "across" into the human mind. But in either event, the world was assumed to have a reality of its own, independent of human reason though (hopefully) in harmony with it. When Kant took the decisive step of recognizing that the farthest human reason could go— and it might indeed go very far—was in a *practical* direction so that it must *make* of the world a thing in harmony with its own highest moral ideal, he nevertheless assumed that there remained still the world in itself, as God had created it, untouched and untouchable by man. To Hegel, this vestigial "world" beyond the reality man concretely knows was a mere phantom, a philosophical conception that reason might now surpass. So long as philosophers had remained under the influence of a religious world-view, they had imagined the problem of cognition in terms of an individual subject trying to penetrate the mere appearance of things in order to know a truth kindred to himself. This three-cornered relationship, of which God formed the apex, and the base line rested on a static logic of knowledge within the limits of particular subjects and objects, Hegel radically transformed. He conceived of it as a dialectical movement that manifests itself throughout the whole of Being, from the realm of physical phenomena to that of self-reflective consciousness. The only thinker who had ever attempted (in Christian Europe) to conflate spirit and matter in a single concept of being was Spinoza.* Hegel declared that Spinoza's work marked "a crucial point in modern philosophy," and he was undoubtedly influenced by the unorthodox Jewish-Dutch philosopher, just as Goethe had been. But although some of Spinoza's ideas were rather loosely invoked by Herder and lesser writers of the German *Sturm und Drang* generation in support of irrationalistic ideals of oneness with nature, and although the basic tendency of Spinoza's thought proved capable of almost as much ambiguous interpretation as Hegel's—Coleridge and Shelley regarded him as a pantheist, George Eliot and Renan as a scientific materialist—it lacked the dialectical potential of Hegel's method.

Hegel's philosophy is so important for an understanding of 19th-century cultural history partly because it spans, like a last bridge over a widening river, the divergent currents that were to run toward positivism on the one hand and idealism on the other. It is constructed on the principle of contradiction, but it is used in a new way: not in order to exclude the false, but in order to supersede the true. Hegel is here systemat-

* See Vol. III, "The Golden Age in Holland."

izing an attitude that has since become dominant in modern culture, an attitude of historical self-consciousness that makes the modern mind feel raised up by history above the past: the present is superior to the past not simply by virtue of more, or more scientific, knowledge, but because it has achieved a different level of understanding. Hegel's dialectical logic owes its peculiar effectiveness to its discovery of what is implied by seeing life as a historical whole, a totality moving in time. All the achievements of the past, whether in politics and society or in philosophy and religion, acquire a dual aspect: positive in that they are expressions of vital energy; negative in that they represent limitations of that energy. Hegel called this energy by various names, but what it "is" in fact ceases to be a relevant question, and this has made his dialectical method available as a prototype for quite divergent theories. The crucial point in Hegel's position lies in his vision of the whole as a process within which everything positive, from a material force to a philosophical proposition, affirms itself *to the limit*: that is, in terms of its opposite. (Force can be measured only in relation to resistance; the word "good" only has meaning relative to the word "bad.") Applied to actual phenomena in time, Hegel's view leads to the conclusion that "the highest maturity or stage which any something can reach is that in which it begins to perish." Negativity becomes for him the motive principle not only of thought but of life itself:

> Contradiction is the root of all movement and all living phenomena. . . . The abstract conception of self-identity does not correspond to anything in actual life; but the fact that the positive is in itself negativity means that the positive passes beyond itself and becomes involved in change. Thus, a thing is living to the extent that it encloses a contradiction and possesses the strength to embrace and maintain it. . . . Negativity is the immanent pulsation of autonomous, spontaneous, and living movement.[17]

The secret of Hegel's secular theodicy, as his system might be called, is that the spirit proceeds by way of the negative, that all positive states and statements involve their opposite. A vision of the whole can be achieved only by the break-up of a primal oneness into parts, followed by a further negation of the validity of these parts. If the first operation is associated with man's practical attempts at understanding the world, when he uses his reason in a quite functional manner to differentiate and control his environment, then the use of reason in the second stage, when he becomes self-aware and critical of his own understanding, has a clearly higher and more purely spiritual significance. It was the exercise of this faculty of "higher criticism" that had fascinated Turgenev as a young man, when (like his hero Rudin) he learned from his Hegelian teachers in Germany to see "a common bond uniting the concepts of philosophy, art, science, life itself." The negativity of his hero's insight into this unity, Turgenev characterized (as we saw) by likening him to an artist and denying him the ability to feel or to act upon this doubly negative truth. The ambiguous positive-negative effects of Hegel's "higher" use of reason have already been hinted at with regard to other kinds of writer, and a few more examples may now be given. The term "higher criticism," for instance, came to be used in the 19th century almost exclusively to describe theological writing in the manner of Feuerbach and David Friedrich Strauss. All such efforts to comprehend the "phenomenon" of religion—and not only the Christian religion, which was now increasingly regarded as only one manifestation of a religious spirit indwelling in man and manifesting itself throughout history*—are anticipated in Hegel's own early theological writings. Thus, he anticipates one of the most important ideas in Feuerbach's *Essence of Christianity* (1841) when he writes: "It is a reward reserved for our time to reclaim, at least in theory, the riches that have been squandered on the heavens; but what kind of century will it be that will have the strength to realize this claim in practice and really lay hold of its spiritual property?"[18] Hegel's doubt goes even beyond Feuerbach, and anticipates Marx's famous criticism of Feuerbach:

> Feuerbach starts out from the fact of religious self-alienation, the duplication of the world into a religious, imaginary world and a real one. His work consists in the dissolution of the religious world into its secular basis. He overlooks the fact that after completing this work, the chief thing still remains to be done. For the fact that the secular foundation detaches itself from itself and establishes itself in the clouds as an independent realm is only to be explained by the self-cleavage and self-contradictoriness of this secular basis. The latter must itself, therefore, first be understood in its contradiction, and then, by the removal of this contradiction, be revolutionized in practice.[19]

This passage perfectly exemplifies the way in which Hegel's dialectical manner of thinking operates, besides pointing to its weakness. Once positive religious creeds are recognized as the way the human spirit first learns to identify itself—i.e. by negating the world in order to realize its

* Christianity had been compared with other religions before, of course, but in the 18th century a much cruder common denominator was used, as may be seen in the discussion of this subject in Vol. IV, "Literature and Ideology." The different approach shows the basically undialectical nature of 18th-century thought, which aimed to disprove religion as a misrepresentation of objective fact due to scientific ignorance. Religious studies in the 19th century were "scientific" in a higher sense because the religion- and myth-making capacity of the mind was accepted as an equally important fact of human nature and history.

difference from it—then the mind necessarily "surpasses" its belief in them; it negates what it sees to have been a negation. And what will it then have achieved? Not yet anything in practice, declares Marx; the revolutionary possibility is there, as Heine and Turgenev also knew, but it is far from being realized. The impulse to realize some form of reunion with mankind's lost riches, to transcend the negativity of all former mis-understandings of the world, to recapture the promise and meaning of the whole beyond the divisiveness of the parts: this is one of the main-springs of modern culture. It is responsible for an intensification of desire, in such diverse realms as literature and politics, to achieve some absolute satisfaction; to possess totally, to have at man's total disposal, "the means of production" was to become the dream of aesthetes and revolutionaries alike as the 19th century progressed. Indeed, the psychological reaction to the century's material progress was, broadly speaking, ambivalent. A sense of being deprived of an expected inheritance or fulfilment was quite as strong as any feeling of secure possession; the discovery of a new kind of movement in the history of civilization, a movement governed apparently by man's ability to take the levers of power into his own hands, began to be accompanied by fears for, and renewed strivings after, stability and the end of the process. Hegel has been much mocked for having located the consummation of history in the *status quo* of conserva-tive Prussia in his day (and even more for having located the consumma-tion of human understanding in his own system). Yet his "mistake" is no less a prototype of modern thinking than the dialectic that leads to it. Marx and Engels both exploit the ambiguity inherent in Hegel's method. Engels translates the theory of negativity, for instance, into the following more material terms:

> With Hegel, evil is the form in which the motive force of historical development presents itself. This contains the twofold meaning that, on the one hand, each new advance necessarily appears as a sacrilege against things hallowed, as a rebellion against conditions, though old and crumbling, yet sanctified by custom; and that, on the other hand, it is precisely the wicked passions of men—greed and the lust for power—that, since the emergence of class antagonisms, serve as the levers of historical development—a fact of which the history of feudalism and of the bourgeoisie, for example, constitutes a continual proof.[20]

Evil is necessary, here, for the surpassing of inferior stages of civiliza-tion; and if this surpassing is not to become mere senseless "revolution" in the course of things, but to issue in "positive" revolution, which will seize the values of man's labour and return them to their rightful owners, then a state must be achieved where the negative principle—the motive power of history—will be abolished. What needs to be done, in order fully to *establish* the good, is to "negate the negation"—that is, to move the levers of history once more so that the division of man against man is finally eliminated. In their conception of an end, Marx and Engels follow the lead of Hegel's dialectic toward a final conclusion: "Once the earthly family is discovered to be the secret of the holy family, the former *must then itself* be theoretically criticized and radically changed in practice." This is the categorical imperative of a godless age that no longer felt disposed to leave the redemption of evil to that other world it could see reflected in the alienated visions of artists, saints, and philosophers. Mankind's historical self-awareness made the redemption of its pawned property an urgent and real possibility; the transcendence of the whole was realizable in time. Herein lies the appeal of the revolutionary call to pass beyond the "unhappy consciousness" of mankind's separation, endured during millennia of painful evolution, from the promised land of his imagination. The place of which individuals could only dream, because they had projected it outside themselves in their competitive striving with others, was to become the possession of all in a society of classless individuals. There may be good reasons why the problems most difficult to solve in the first 20th-century attempts at classless societies have concerned the degree of individualism, divisiveness, and further evolution that can be admitted.* For these problems arise at the point where socialist ideology betrays its metaphysical inner structure, which derives ultimately from Hegel. However it may be translated into more material terms, the dialectic of alienation, and transcendence of alienation, remains grounded in a fundamentally negative view of consciousness. Moreover, its association of this negative process—particularly in its "higher" form of a double or self-negating negative—with "the immanent pulsation of living movement" (the movement, that is, of nature and history in some mysteriously unified and total sense) is always exposed to the risk of leading to more or less irrationalistic conclusions.

One of the less irrationalistic repercussions of the Hegel-inspired higher criticism in England, where its effect was anyway rather muffled, can be observed in the writings of George Eliot. She had not merely read about German currents of thought, but had plunged into them as the first translator of Feuerbach's *Essence of Christianity* and Strauss's *Life of Jesus*;

* Aspects of this question are treated in Vol. VI, "Literature and Politics in a Post-capitalist Society," and "Literature and Revolution in Russia."

I

and she was mentally prepared for the experience by having previously immersed herself in Charles Hennell's *Inquiry Concerning the Origin of Christianity* (1838). This book undertook in a more straightforward 18th-century manner to give a natural history of religion in order to free it "as a system of elevated thought . . . from those fables, and those views of local or temporary interest, which hung about its origin."[21] Hennell lacked any insight into the dialectical implications of his position (he was a "heroic rationalizer" of the Enlightenment school); George Eliot came to understand it better. She was able to measure the value of knowledge against the value of "life," and to portray the utter disproportion between them. She portrays it most memorably in the relationship of Dorothea to Casaubon—who significantly has a mental block about the Germanic scholarship in his field that has surpassed his own—in *Middlemarch* (1871–2).

Right from the start of her fiction (*Scenes of Clerical Life*, 1857), an essential part of George Eliot's inspiration sprang from the feeling, indeed the sympathy, she had for the quality of a way of life that is superseded by "human advancement." She knew that only a reactionary obscurantist could consciously resist "the striving after something better" that characterized for her the age she lived in. Yet as a novelist she also exclaimed (in *The Mill on the Floss*, 1860): "Heaven knows where that striving might lead us, if our affections had not a trick of twining around those old inferior things—if the loves and sanctities of our life had no deep immovable roots in the memory."[22] George Eliot makes the problem of progress sound here like a psychological one, as though she were about to anticipate some sort of Proustian solution to the dilemma of the self that becomes alienated from everything it loves.* But she also knew the problem of alienation in its social-critical aspect: not as a form of negativity in all critical consciousness, but as a negativity in the conditions of society. "Amidst the conditions of an imperfect social state . . . great feelings will often take the aspect of error, and great faith the aspect of illusion."[23] George Eliot avoided the extremism of expecting total redemption, on either a spiritual or a material plane, from such alienation of man's desires and efforts. Regarding two great heroines of the past, one a heroine of the active life, one of the spiritual, she accepts the pessimistic theory: "the medium in which their ardent deeds took shape is for ever gone."[24] This cultural pessimism about a lost past, in which the spirit fulfilled itself totally in real life (the way it does in art), was one of

* Proust's aesthetic psychology is discussed in Vol. VI, "Literature and Psychology"; see also Ch. 16, "The Cult of Art."

the profoundest obsessions of the century, as we have seen—virtually an inverted kind of faith, in fact. It was often an aesthetic illusion induced by the distance of time and the growing fascination with history. George Eliot tried to penetrate it, not altogether successfully, in her historical novel about religion, *Romola* (1862–3).

Middlemarch ends on a note of more modest reconciliation, the kind of reconciliation that is possible between individuals and within each individual, when they accept their common bonds, common destiny, and common continuity of things much as they were before. It is a family reunion, no more—but also, George Eliot concludes, no less, because the "growing good of the world is partly dependent on unhistoric acts . . . [and on] the number who lived faithfully a hidden life, and rest in unvisited tombs."[25] Neither Lenin nor Proust would have agreed. George Eliot's "negation of the negation" involves compromise, restraint, and resignation rather than revolution or revelation. It can take place at the end simply because an "opinion did not cause a lasting alienation; and the way in which the family was made whole again was characteristic of all concerned."[26] The words "opinion" and "characteristic" in this sentence are more significant than they seem: they express George Eliot's view of the superior importance of character to mere ideas. The latter are so often, perhaps always, inadequate or false; but George Eliot did not lose faith in the moral value of the individual character that underlies opinions and appearances. We can see her struggling to maintain this faith as she bears the burden of the rôle of omniscient author, a god-like and already somewhat old-fashioned rôle that more nihilistic writers (such as Flaubert) had pretended to renounce in the name of a purer belief in art alone. The rôle is reminiscent of the conventions of the theatre, although the novelist's "rôle" is, of course, like that of the spectator rather than that of an actor. There is an element of comedy in the way the family is made whole again at the end, under the patronage of the same benevolent uncle from under whose roof it first dispersed. He is a man who believes in "letting things be," a man "of acquiescent temper, miscellaneous opinions, and uncertain vote," a man in whom "the hereditary strain of Puritan energy was clearly in abeyance." Mr Brooke is the antithesis of the heroine, his niece, and indeed of the author herself. He *is* the undivided man, and he incarnates the ideal balance of character and intelligence, the common norm of English steadiness, toward which heroine and authoress can only gaze with a mixture of affection and impatience. He is the outward and visible manifestation of the quality that it is so difficult to arrive at subjectively: common sense.

The path that each individual must travel to develop this sense of community with other people constitutes the psychological groundwork of the entire novel, and indeed of other novels by George Eliot besides *Middlemarch*. The greater the separation of a person from others—through arid intellect, wayward imagination, vanity, hypocrisy, or a host of other "reasons"—the greater is the crash of disillusion when it comes. George Eliot formulates this general principle in an analogy that might have been used by many another writer of her age, from Schopenhauer to Proust:

> Your pierglass or extensive surface of polished steel made to be rubbed by a housemaid, will be minutely and multitudinously scratched in all directions; but place now against it a lighted candle as a centre of illumination and lo! the scratches will seem to arrange themselves in a fine series of concentric circles round that little sun.[27]

George Eliot introduces this image as a "fact"; she also implies that it is typical of the way "the serene light of science" can dignify "even your ugly furniture"; and she concludes by insisting that "these things are a parable of egoism." The reader can scarcely overlook the contrast between "the serene light of science" and the "little sun" of egoism; and unless we are aware of the scratches as in reality multitudinous and not concentric, as in fact directionless, the parable would not have any meaning. But what, then, does it mean, as a parable? At one level its moral is obvious enough. George Eliot goes on to speak of the self-centredness of Rosamond Vincy, whose lovely appearance does not correspond to a lovable character. This is familiar ground for moral comedy, where "eyes of heavenly blue [are] deep enough to hold the most exquisite meanings an ingenious beholder could put into them, and deep enough to hide the meanings of the owner if these should happen to be less exquisite."[28] When the full truth is brought to light, it is painful enough to Rosamond—"What another nature felt in opposition to her own was being burnt and bitten into her consciousness"[29]—but not very disturbing to the reader, who feels there is some justice in her fate. Similarly, we do not take very seriously George Eliot's ironical observation concerning her brother's disappointment at having cadged less money than he had expected: "What can the fitness of things mean if not their fitness to a man's expectations? Failing this, absurdity and atheism gape behind him."[30] George Eliot still has firm enough moral ground under her feet to be able to risk this hint of another level of meaning that might be uncovered if Fred's "little sun" were to be extinguished. Even the climax of the novel—if that is what the exposure of the truth about Bulstrode is intended to be—does not break through to any profounder level of meaning, because the man has pretended to be righteous while in reality committing a crime. We can feel indignant here at the moral contradiction without being drawn into the demonic uncertainty about the motive or meaning of all living, including killing, into which a Dostoyevsky, for instance, will lure us.

George Eliot comes closest to passing beyond the rational middle ground of a common-sense morality in her depiction of love. After what Dorothea goes through, the experiences of Bulstrode or Lydgate seem almost superficial. Dorothea's tragedy does have a double level: first, we see that, instead of the initiation into truth that she hoped marriage would bring, she has in fact tied herself till death to a mere "lifeless embalmment of knowledge." But second, and more importantly, her disillusion takes on a symbolic significance: it symbolizes the "higher" truth that all knowledge is of this kind. This insight uncovers humanity's common fate in a much grimmer light, which reveals the shapeless "multitudinousness" of reality: an infinitude of marks without rhyme or reason. George Eliot writes in this connection sentences that might have come from the pen of an irrationalist writer such as Nietzsche or Lawrence:

> The element of tragedy, which lies in the very fact of frequency, has not yet wrought itself into the coarse emotion of mankind; and perhaps our frames could hardly bear much of it. If we had a keen vision and feeling of all ordinary human life, it would be like hearing the grass grow and the squirrel's heart beat, and we should die of that roar which lies on the other side of silence. As it is, the quickest of us walk about well wadded with stupidity.[31]

The lesson that Dorothea learns from her experience in a moral sense becomes deepened by the problem her author experienced in rendering it into the concrete form of art: the problem of knowing how important a modern tragedy is. Dorothea acquires for her husband "a pitying tenderness fed by the realities of his lot and not by her own dreams." This could be construed as regard for others, a morality of pity and selflessness that might still be justified on rational moral grounds. The manner in which she feels this new bond, however, suggests that it has an aesthetic or imaginative intensity that makes it resemble complete empathy rather than mere sympathy; her emotion has "that distinctness which is no longer reflection but feeling—an idea wrought back to the directness of sense, like the solidity of objects."[32] This return from the negativity of solitary reflection to the concreteness of actual existence resembles the movement of the spirit that Hegel tried so often to define:

the self-identity of being in and for itself. It is a "reaching forward of the whole consciousness towards the fullest truth, the least-partial good," as George Eliot calls it, and it may serve to remind us again of the extent to which 19th-century forms of idealism were based upon an aesthetic ideal of wholeness. Dorothea, like her author, has found that the medium in which the ardent deeds of past heroines took shape is gone for ever. She suffers from the cultural self-consciousness typical of her age, which felt itself cut off from the beautiful spiritual illusions, both artistic and religious, that other ages seemed to have possessed. Having awakened to the difference between dreams and reality, she longs to dream again, for this is "the current in which all her thought and feeling were apt sooner or later to flow." But it must now be a "higher" form of dreaming, a dreaming with eyes wide open to the "ugly furniture" of contemporary life. The latter's ugliness must be dignified by a new symbolic understanding of the little suns that once made it shine so beautifully. George Eliot achieved this understanding, which was a source of inspiration to so many realist writers of the century: for realism seizes upon the ugly furniture only as a dialectical step up, by way of the negative, to a higher conception of beauty in the whole. Whether Dorothea could have (or is convincingly shown to have) lived at this level—which is to say, whether George Eliot was right in supposing that such higher understanding could be of any moral use, let alone compatible with progressive moral values—is open to doubt. Nietzsche, for instance, who understood better the tragic implications of this dialectical situation, was scornful of George Eliot's moralism. The only common bond that he could see in the light of a supra-individual science—assuming that any man could reach such a superhuman position as art pretends to place us in—was that every kind of value would prove illusory to us all, and that all men in Western civilization stood on the brink of a universal nihilism.

"It seems as if people were worn out on the way to great thoughts and can never enjoy them because they are too tired."[33] This is another of George Eliot's commonsense comments on the relationship of thinking to living. Transposed into the major key of European philosophy it acquires the power of a metaphysical judgment, having potentially revolutionary consequences, instead of sounding (in the context of the odd scholar, Casaubon) merely like a moral remark on a not very common foible of human nature. Consider, for example, the force that this kind of insight had for Kierkegaard, who breached the walls of rational theology and let in a tide of existential doubt, when he wrote: "I cannot *think* myself into Abraham" (*Fear and Trembling*, 1843). Far more was challenged by this insight than the ability of higher criticism to comprehend the Bible from a superior historical point of view; the entire validity of knowledge, of any mental formulation, was being opposed by a new conception of lived experience. The irrationalistic tendency of this opposition is plain, and prompts the further question: from what point of view is Kierkegaard judging that knowledge is *not* experience? Again, as in the case of George Eliot, the perspective of the writer is being used to conjure up a vision of what is authentically "real" and what is mere onlooking. Kierkegaard himself thought (as he often declares) that he was reacting against the intellectual influence of Hegel (whereas in fact he remained under it, despite the twist he gave it). This intellectual influence, he believed, was misleading his age into a false and complacent faith in knowledge, as if it were possible finally to realize Hegel's ideal and synthesize reality and reason: *das Leben denken* (to think life). Again and again Kierkegaard insists that "all understanding comes after the fact," and makes sport of the superhuman System "with its inviting prospectus promising happiness to all mankind," to which he pretends he is eager to pay homage, only to be told that "we are still under construction and the System is not finished."[34] It can never be finished, Kierkegaard discovers, and not simply because a little more time is needed or a few more bricks of knowledge. The palace of human progress, to which Kierkegaard likens Hegel's philosophy, cannot be inhabited by any actual human being (and least of all by the university professor himself, whose personal existence is conducted in a narrow hut adjacent to the ideal home he is constructing for mankind). The reason is that "existence separates thought from being, and breaks up their ideal unity."[35] If this is not recognized, then the metaphysical idealism that underlay, in Kierkegaard's view, the optimism of his century must end by betraying it into the hands of the enemy.

> The philosophical principle of identity is precisely the opposite of what it seems to be; it is the expression for the fact that thought has deserted existence altogether, that it has emigrated to a sixth continent, where it is wholly sufficient to itself in the absolute identity of thought and being. We may finally reach the stage of identifying existence with evil, taken in a certain emasculated metaphysical sense; in the humorous sense, existence will become an extremely long dragging out of things, a ludicrous delay.[36]

The conception of existence that Kierkegaard himself reached, at least in his imagination (for his books are almost all written under pseudonyms to emphasize the fact that in writing at all one is never truly *being* one-self), is already coloured by a quite remarkable feeling for"emasculated" evil and "ludicrous" humour. It is this feeling for some essential absurdity in the human situation that was to cause him to be rediscovered a century later as the source of modern existentialism. What Kierkegaard knew, however—and what has come to be overlooked by less thoughtful literary impresarios of "the absurd"*—is that the irrationality of existence, whether malign or comic, lies in the eye of the beholder. Indeed, it is likely to present itself to the gaze particularly of any mind that thinks it can be sufficient unto itself. Kierkegaard's writing is as dialectical (and difficult) as that of Hegel, and he purposely puts human understanding into a negative light in order to stress the greater wisdom of God, and the greater value of each human existence, which both goes before and goes beyond any knowable truth. This is not to say—in the case, anyway, of Kierkegaard, who was a believer—that there is no such thing as truth or that the world as a whole is absurd. The distinctive character of Kierkegaard's existentialism comes out in a passage such as the following:

> An existential system cannot be formulated. Does this mean that no such system exists? By no means; nor is this implied in our assertion. Reality itself is a system—for God; but it cannot be a system for any existing spirit. System and finality correspond to one another, but existence is precisely the opposite of finality.[37]

Man's capacity to reflect upon and communicate his experience thus becomes for Kierkegaard a source of temptation and despair: he thinks to usurp the privileged knowledge of God, and is cast down accordingly. Kierkegaard wrote as an outsider, as though estranged from the creed he held, because he considered that the mind on its own can discover only negative evidences of the truth. He tried to communicate "indirectly," as he called it ("dialectically" is the word we have used here), the positive quality of faith by exhibiting the negative quality of mere writing about faith.

Kierkegaard's theology is a projection of his own experience of being a writer into the realm of real, and particularly religious, experience. The projection involves, however, a reversal or inversion. He asks what the reality is like that we come to know as a religious story (and then system-atize into religious knowledge): the story of Abraham, for instance, or of Adam, or of Jesus. And he concludes that it must be the reverse of anything we can say or know, it must be truly inconceivable. Kierkegaard

* "The Absurd Hero" is discussed in Vol. VI.

is therefore consistent when he declares himself unable to write about faith or sin in themselves; he can only describe the psychological predisposition to sin and faith, but the moment in which they take place is beyond telling—it is a "leap." The mark of absolute difference that Kierkegaard drives like an axe between the written or mental concept and the real—"constantly keeping the wound of the negative open," as he puts it[38]—stems from his love of writing rather than from his love of God. His first book, the masterly collection of aphorisms, essays, stories, and fictitious letters called *Either/Or* (1843), concentrates on the character of the aesthete, the man who wants to possess "the beautiful" in reality. (Kierkegaard was doubtless under the spell as much of Goethe as of Hegel here; and he shows, as Goethe does in *Faust*, that to possess a beautiful person sexually is not the same as to possess "the beautiful"; indeed, the real act destroys that elusive ideal.) The extraordinary exclamation in *Fear and Trembling* that "I cannot think myself into Abraham" betrays a similarly impossible desire to possess the holy in reality. Kierkegaard is not satisfied merely to understand the *moral* of the story as, say, a test of obedience or a lesson that Jehovah (unlike other gods) did not desire human sacrifice; he wants to grasp *Abraham*, and finds that he cannot.

The problem of possession that Kierkegaard poses in such uncompromising and dialectically destructive terms presents itself to him in his capacity as an artist rather than as a believer—two capacities that he tried to keep distinct, as we have seen, by his use of pseudonyms. The result of his taking the viewpoint of the poet as his model of the mind's relationship to the world was twofold. First, Kierkegaard discovered certain similarities between the aesthetical and religious categories (as he called them), the most important being an impatience with moral values. The title *Either/Or* expresses a strange coincidence between the outlook of the aesthete and that of the Christian: each of them regards the phrase as the touchstone of his spiritual life, the one to justify his amorality, the other to point beyond morality to the spirit in which choice is exercised—to the subjective psychology, rather than any objective or rational principles, of choice. The second consequence of Kierkegaard's position is to relate the individual negatively to the realm of nature, to his fellow-men, and even to his own personality. In so doing, he discovered a psychology of hitherto unknown or largely inscrutable impulses: dread, despair, self-hatred, enclosure in a private world (*Indesluttedhed*), and underlying all something Kierkegaard called "the demoniacal." This last may express itself through good actions or bad.

Its beginning lies in "the fact of being as an individual originally set outside the universal" (the "universal" being Kierkegaard's rather contemptuous word for the common lot of mankind subject to common moral rules). Kierkegaard judges the individual's plight not in terms that are universally true for all men—the terms for which rational philosophers in the West have been searching since the time of Socrates—but by analogy with the uniqueness we recognize in genius. It is above all the genius who "from the start is disorientated in relation to the universal . . . and either seeks a demoniacal reassurance . . . or religiously reassures himself by love to the Deity."

Scholars have discussed the extent of Kierkegaard's debt to an author both earlier and less famous than either Hegel or Goethe, namely, Johann Georg Hamann (1730–99), to whom much of the irrationalism of the Romantic movement, particularly in Germany, can perhaps also be traced. It is true that Hamann has much to say about science being the death of nature and neo-classical rules being the death of art. He throws out hints about the character of language (which is for revelation and prophecy and not for mere recording of fact) and about the value of primitive poetry and myth (where the spirit's voice is heard most clearly) that were to be developed more fully by Johann Gottfried Herder. Goethe himself was so impressed by Hamann's praise of the senses and the feelings as indispensable to a full appreciation of nature that he considered editing Hamann's work, about which he wrote:

> The principle to which all Hamann's statements lead back is this: "Everything a man does, whether in action, or word, or otherwise, must spring from the united power of all his faculties: everything isolated is to be rejected." A splendid maxim! but difficult to carry out. It is, no doubt, applicable in life and in art; but when it comes to transmitting something by the word, and if the word is not poetic, a great difficulty arises. For the word must detach itself and become isolated in order to say and to mean something. In speaking a man must, for the moment, be one-sided; there can be no communication, no teaching, without particularization.

This is a very curious passage, written by the mature Goethe when he was surveying his own life in Volume XII of *Dichtung und Wahrheit* (1811–31), the autobiographical work that is the antithesis of *Faust*, for (as the title itself suggests) it looks at life from the point of view of both poetry and truth, poetry and truth reconciled instead of divided, a common ideal of unity binding both—"it is, no doubt, applicable in life and in art." How can Goethe write "no doubt," when he goes on (in words) to say that a great difficulty arises when it comes to using language that is not poetic? Can one *live* in the poetic medium? Goethe knows to what extent living—and the kinds of "meaning" that go with it—takes place in a quite different context. Behind this passage loom the doubts and chimeras of *Faust*, and they remind us how close the undoubting Goethe comes here to being self-contradictory. Goethe comes close, in fact, to acknowledging that self-conscious men, the kind who reflect upon the meaning of their lives and try to communicate it, *exist* (as Kierkegaard would say) "in the moment"—but what other time do we have?—i.e. in a realm that is separate, "detached," from the ideal completeness of either art or life. It is this view of life, as something ideally comparable with art but, alas, divorced from it by the rationalistic paraphernalia of thinking and communicating, that opens the door to dizzy prospects of irrationalism. Kierkegaard knew this and ventured through the door— but only under the cloak of pseudonyms, so that he could slip safely back. Goethe remained enigmatically standing on the threshold, in majestic poise, as he contemplated an ideal of classical wholeness, his back resolutely turned on another country of the mind that he knew lay behind him. Hamann is worth mentioning in this context because, despite his disagreement with the rationale of the Enlightenment, his statement of his position is still in the unself-conscious language of the 18th century. In a sense, he does not know what he is talking about; there is a naivety to his pronouncements that makes him—like Christopher Smart or William Blake—seem less an irrationalist than a trifle mad.

The simple fact that Goethe could turn with such sympathy to Hamann's writings—whereas he reacted quite unsympathetically to the kind of irrationalism he sensed in various "Romantics," such as Hölderlin or Kleist or Beethoven, who in retrospect appear to us as true precursors of the modern—shows again that the *way* the irrational is conceived is what counts. Hamann still conceived of it as a manifestation of the divine; it was simply a mistake to ignore—in favour of rationalistic goals of science, behaviour, and society—the passionate-sensual side of art, religion, personality, and indeed nature "as a whole." At the Last Judgment the two sides will be forever united, and one-sided souls damned. It is tempting to conclude that Hamann's highly religious temperament saved him from the kind of demonic irrationalism to which Kierkegaard in his cloak of doubt was drawn and to which Nietzsche was apparently to succumb. For Hamann, the rightness of the whole existed in the presence of God. For Kierkegaard, the presence of God could be known to a mind in "existence" only as a total paradox, and could be believed only "by virtue of the absurd." It is, however, more in psychological than in religious terms that the difference in emphasis and point of view between Hamann and Kierkegaard is apparent. Kierkegaard had begun to ask from what point of view can man ever know anything, including himself, and above all the "wholeness" of experience or nature. And his answer was: only from a demoniacal position "outside nature," an unnatural position arrived at by a dialectic of self-consciousness that can never achieve certainty, a dialectic that is (as we have already suggested) inherently unstable.

It would be idle to speculate about whether Hamann is a more religious man than Kierkegaard. What can be observed is that the quality, or style, of their apprehension of the irrational is different. One might say that in Kierkegaard it has grown more intense, because dialectically involved with his own awareness of it. To take a more obvious example of this change in the psychological quality of a perception we may quote a sentence of Kafka's that in substance says no more than the quotation from Goethe given above. Kafka writes: "Truth is indivisible, hence it cannot recognize itself; anyone who wants to recognize it has to lie."[39] The exploration of this perception led Kafka, as everyone who has read him knows, into a nightmarish world that has nothing in common with Goethe's (though much with Kierkegaard's). Or one might take a less ponderous example from the story by Borges of a tribe that wanted to make a map of its country. The tribesmen could not agree on an appropriate scale, and finally decided that the only true way to represent the ground was to make a map that was the same size as, and so fitted over, the land exactly. Borges here graphically symbolizes the ultimate meaning of the doubts cast by Hume and Kant upon the use of reason in judging the design of the universe when they argue that there is no model to judge it by.

Several important features of 19th-century irrationalism can now be summed up that modify our initial definition. First, the dynamic, and often demonic, energy of this form of inspiration lies in the degree of tension that is felt to exist between the alienated mind and what it is held to be alien from. Second, this tension is increased by the mind's attempts to reflect self-consciously upon its own alienated state, as though it could step outside its situation and grasp this as a whole—seeing it, as it were, from above, and so transcending it. Third, the discovery of such a point of view motivated much of the high feeling that surrounded art on the one hand (particularly literature and music), and history on the other;

together they constituted a new current of modern "belief" that may on the surface appear to revive traditional values but that at a deeper level erodes or transforms them. If these features are taken as marking the dominant line of irrationalism, we can distinguish from it various unimportant variations. One of these, for instance, is the mediaevalizing Christian revivalism that is often considered to be a hallmark of the Romantic movement and is condemned by rationalists as a phantasy-flight from reality. In most cases, however, there was little profundity in this literary vogue, which may have been escapist, but was rather more naive, imitative, or trivial than seriously irrational. The confidence with which Friedrich Schlegel or Novalis assert that "the various systems of philosophic rationalism, mutually subversive as they are of each other, will fall to the ground,"[40] or that "anarchy is the element that gives birth to religion, [which] will raise its glorious head to found a new world from the destruction of all particularized science,"[41] shows only that they experienced a relatively low degree of tension between the aspirations of the spirit and the condition of existence. In a confused, fragmentary fashion writers such as these thought that the infinite lay within their grasp, that "the sciences must all now become poeticized," and that "the only thing lacking in physics now seems to be a mythological view of nature."[42] In their mood of mystical fervour, Schlegel and Novalis display a simple-minded optimism that is paradoxically similar to that of Feuerbach: where he believed that mankind could reintegrate into a material whole those spiritual capacities falsely attributed to the supernatural, they believed they could reintegrate into a spiritual whole scientific knowledge falsely referred to soulless matter. Marx and Engels are surely right in their impatience with such pure speculation; the reconciliation of man's spirit with the world, if it can be achieved at all, must involve a more revolutionary struggle than that.

It is not among Romantics such as these, for whom the real opens so readily into phantasy—not in Hoffmann, Nerval, or Poe—that we find a truly tense or deeply riven vision of existence. We find it rather in writers such as Hölderlin and Kleist, Schopenhauer and Büchner, all of whom came to be appreciated only half a century or more after they had written. They have acquired the stature now of prophets of the age ahead, men who intuited "dreadful" (in Kierkegaard's sense of that word) implications in the path its culture was to take, and expressed them at a time when the taste and outlook of the day was dominated by either conservative or revolutionary idealism. They are the avengers of that idealism, making us wonder whether it had been guilty of some fearful hubris. They seem to have drawn the punishment for it upon themselves, as though they had violated the secrets of a god: Hölderlin was mad by the age of 35; Kleist committed suicide at 34; Büchner died at 23; and Schopenhauer's inspiration flashed with such singular brilliance in his 20s that he remained for the rest of his life condemned to reiteration or silence, and to the bitterness of failure.

Friedrich Hölderlin enjoyed with his friend and fellow-student, Hegel, a common enthusiasm for nature, antiquity, and the French Revolution—and a dawning sense of deeper processes at work that separate man from his ideals. Whereas Hegel rationalized the logic of this process, Hölderlin symbolized it. And his symbols, particularly those of water and of rivers, bring home the tragic movement of life released, like a stream from icebound mountains, by the action on the earth of the godlike sun—"Der gefesselte Strom" (The Bound Torrent). This torrent plunges downward, dividing the solid earth, fructifying it; a source of beauty and civilization crossed by bridges of commerce, it reaches moments of fulfilment and containment, it is "content" in the earth—but then passes on to the all-embracing sea, symbol of primeval chaos ("Heidelberg," "Der Rhein"). In one of his most famous poems, "Hyperions Schicksalslied" (Hyperion's Song of Fate), Hölderlin depicts in images contrasting the state of gods and the state of man what is essentially the criticism Kierkegaard was to make of Hegel nearly 50 years later: namely, that thought and being, mindless nature and incorporeal meaning, may be identical and form an ideal whole—in the absolute, but not for men:

> Doch uns ist gegeben,
> Auf keiner Stätte zu ruhn,
> Es schwinden, es fallen
> Die leidenden Menschen
> Blindlings von einer
> Stunde zur andern,
> Wie Wasser von Klippe
> Zu Klippe geworfen,
> Jahrlang ins Ungewisse hinab.

(But it is allotted to us not to rest in any place; what happens to suffering men is that they fade, fall, blindly from one hour to the next, like water thrown from one cliff to another, down through the years into the unknown.)

More demonic by far than Hölderlin's glimpse of the darker implications in Hegel is the way Heinrich von Kleist's imagination responded to his (probably rather limited) knowledge of Kant and Fichte. In him, the "spectator complex"—the desire to compensate for being a late-comer and outsider in the cultural and political development of Europe that we have mentioned already in connection with Germany—was exacerbated by personal factors: he came of an old Prussian military family, but disliked army life; he thought to become an enlightened philosopher-scientist, only to have his faith in positive knowledge shattered and to discover instead a capacity for passionate lyricism. Under the stress of these temperamental and situational factors, which included a patriotic hatred of France, his intelligence and emotions were forced into an almost schizophrenic state of vision. What he "saw" was that every aspect of men's conscious and social existence was a fabrication that disguised from them the *mysterium tremendens* of life "as a whole." For Kleist, in moments of violent illumination, and for various of his characters in ways adapted to their situation, the fabric is torn or grows alarmingly transparent. What lies behind it? That must, in the nature of things, be literally beyond telling, for language itself is part of the fabric of consciousness. Kleist can only hint at that wholeness through symbols and situations that are themselves a fabrication, a distortion, perhaps a mere accident. The circumstances of his story *Das Erdbeben in Chili* (The Earthquake in Chile) make it appear that when a natural catastrophe breaks down the structures of moral and religious custom, people find themselves for a moment in paradise. Another story, *Michael Kohlhaas*, makes hidden agencies provide a wronged man with the emotional satisfaction for his grievances that all the efforts of church and state, law and military diplomacy, cannot achieve. Almost all Kleist's plays—particularly *Amphitryon* (1807), *Penthesilea* (1808), *Käthchen von Heilbronn* (1810), and even the more realistic *Prinz Friedrich von Homburg* (1810) and *Der zerbrochene Krug* (1808; The Broken Jug)—exploit the difference between rational comprehension of the world and intuitions of its real character. The difference can appear comic or tragic according to the contrivance of plot and style; but it is always here that the crisis of each play lies. As a result Kleist discovers moments of demonic experience and kinds of irrational motivation that have no place in conventional moral psychology but anticipate the spiritual categories described by Kierkegaard and by more modern existentialists. That is to say, the distinctively Kleistian experience or motive is not irrational in the way that jealousy, ambition, lust, and the like have always been regarded as opposed to reason: emotion, and especially the basic emotion of love, becomes demonic in Kleist for spiritual, indeed metaphysical, reasons—because of uncertainty about the order and meaning of existence, or because of conflicting certainties about what people are and above all who the self is. When a man's idea of the world becomes confused, then he will do irrational and perhaps terrible things. Kleist is an irrational writer because he is inspired by the thought that *all* ideas of the world may be confused and false, and that spiritual doubt (or pure faith) is the realm in which the real drama of human behaviour takes place.

Existential psychology, then—which was to unmask in so much of the "realism" of modern literature men's false ideas about the world, the life-lies (as they came to be called) that they cling to and drown without— was born of an act of cultural self-reflection. The literary imagination reflected upon its own activity and wondered whether all the poetry and heroism that adorned the past had not been merely imagined, invented, made up. Schiller's discovery of this artist's psychology will be taken up again as a starting-point for another chapter,* but it may be remarked here that he developed this critical insight by thinking about the nature of Goethe's creative talent and how it differed from his own. And Kleist's further development of this psychology can be seen in his essay *Über das Marionettentheater* (On the Puppet Theatre), where he applies it not simply to the way books are written but to the way people behave. The psychology of creative self-consciousness once applied to life in this way generates a new kind of aesthetic power, which is immediately recognizable in the literary style of a Kleist or a Büchner. Their imagery ceases to look like more or less ingenious analogies perceived between objective things and events, a mere extension of simile: it becomes an expression of an inner world that bears no comparison with any natural order, a symbol of the inexpressible, an illumination that is enveloped in a profounder darkness. In Georg Büchner's plays, *Dantons Tod* (1835; Danton's Death) and *Woyzeck* (1836), even the mimetic function of the plot—perhaps the oldest and most fundamental convention of drama is that it should imitate an action—begins to be replaced by an expressionistic one. The successive scenes resemble patches of light falling on a dark river of events that is itself vast, shapeless, and inexorable. Any point of focus is arbitrary, any sense of being in control of the fluid element of history is a delusion. Consequently, human character loses the kind of moral coherence that depends on its being seen to produce, and to be responsible for, certain actions. Büchner wrote: "I laugh not at what sort of human being a person is, but at the fact that he is a human being, about which he can do nothing, and so I laugh at myself too because I share his fate."[43] The sentence indicates the only dimension of spiritual freedom left open

* See Ch. 5, "The Elegiac Note in Tennyson, Arnold, Pushkin, and Leopardi."

in Büchner's fatalistic world: he can at least become conscious of his plight and laugh (albeit the humour of his greatest plays is grim). Thus, the most that his characters can achieve are levels of awareness in this same dimension, and the level is marked by the style in which they speak. It is the rationalists and theorizers who sound most foolish, perhaps, though the scale is a poetic, not an intellectual, one; Danton with all his intelligence and wit symbolizes no more intensely the hopelessness of the human condition than does Woyzeck with his broken phrases and intellectual incomprehension.

It may seem surprising at first glance that Büchner was himself a student of science and medicine, and also an active revolutionary in very real danger of arrest for publishing a political pamphlet. How can he have reconciled such progressive views with the irrationalistic and nihilistic vision of his imagination? Alas, he did not live to enlighten us. Turgenev may have grasped something of this psychological puzzle in the character of Bazarov, who, as we have seen, also combines positivism and nihilism within his idealistic and deeply divided soul. Moreover, as we have also observed, there seems sometimes to be a connection between attitudes to life during the 19th century that superficially sound quite antithetical: the revolutionary implications in Hegel could lead in an existentialist as much as in a materialist direction. Jean-Paul Sartre is the contemporary thinker most concerned to reconcile them.

This survey would not be complete without some consideration of the line of thought that turned the techniques of German idealist philosophy toward more obviously irrationalistic ends. In this context, Friedrich Schelling is a philosopher of some importance. He was a fellow-student of Hölderlin's and Hegel's at the theological seminary in Tübingen. In the first years of the 19th century he was probably the most brilliant of the Romantic writers at Jena (the period ended, however, in quarrels and the departure of Schelling for Würzburg with August Schlegel's wife). Goethe himself was favourably impressed by those aspects of Schelling's writing that justified a poetical treatment of fact, and the more dualistic and irrational side of his theories influenced the fiction and theory of E. T. A. Hoffmann. Schelling's position has been well described as one of religious atheism:[44] it rests upon a religious awareness that being possesses a dimension that transcends rational comprehension, at the same time as it aspires to place the resolution of this mystery within man's purely human grasp, primarily by means of his artistic imagination. Thus, a statement like the following is fundamental to Schelling's philosophy, although not in itself original (it is at least as old as Socrates, and merely says in more elaborate language what Büchner observes in the passage quoted above):

> Two entirely different things are involved in knowing what an existant is, *quid sit*, and that it is, *quod sit*. The answer to the question *what* it is, gives me insight into the kind of thing it is; it enables me to understand it in the sense of having a conceptual understanding of it.... The insight into the fact *that* it is, however, gives me more than a mere conceptual understanding of it; it goes to that which is beyond mere rational concept, namely, existence itself.[45]

Schelling is also not particularly original in concluding from this that the proper task of philosophy in the rationalist sense is to instruct us negatively in the limits of rational knowledge. Beyond these limits, however, Schelling believes that a higher form of knowing is possible, and this he defined in different ways at different stages of his career. Sometimes he describes it as a kind of "reason," in the special sense that the German word *Vernunft* had acquired in post-Kantian philosophy, as opposed to mere understanding (*Verstand*). Schelling separates these two kinds of reason absolutely, making it impossible to pass by any rational means from one to the other. "It is clear that reason (*Vernunft*) is not a thing that can be taught, and all attempts to teach it by scientific method are useless."[46] On the basis of this separation Schelling developed a distinction between what he called positive and negative knowledge. Positive knowledge must, he declares, "be an absolutely free knowledge, precisely because all other knowledge is not free; it is a knowledge to which no proofs, or conclusions, or conceptual mediation will lead; in fact, a direct contemplation [*ein Anschauen*]."[47] The word "contemplation" has, especially in the context of German idealist philosophy at this time, clear associations with art, and Schelling's influence and interest, both in his own time and in the annals of cultural history, have much to do with his discrimination against reason in favour of art. Art as the home-land for those who have lost confidence in the meaningfulness of reason as a key to life's inner doors is one of the more important features of the spiritual character of the 19th century.* Its social importance consists primarily in the fact that this combination of irrationalism and aestheticism has often lent itself to conservative attitudes in politics.

One interesting ambiguity in Schelling's formulation is his designation of *Anschauung* as not only "positive" but also "primary." Although he talks of this contemplating as an *ultimate* achievement of intellect, there

* This theme is discussed further in Ch. 16, "The Cult of Art."

is an implication that this state of mind is pre-intellectual, like artistic inspiration prior to concrete expression. Schelling's thoughts waver between a religious conception of the state where mind is re-united with the spiritual reality of the world, and an imaginative conception of a state *before* consciousness has divided us from the world—a state possessed by children, buried still in our subconscious, drawing us to nature, with which we are ideally pre-united. This state and its ambiguity are present in much Romantic thought. We meet them again in Schopenhauer's description of the lyrical poet, who is at one with the World-Will, and yet is also said to renounce the Will in his character as artist. Schelling does not commit himself so openly to aestheticism as to discover in the aesthetic faculty alone—by which he means the power to form concrete images, the "plastic imagination"—the supreme form of spiritual wisdom. The supreme *Anschauung* is non-sensuous, purely spiritual, and has as its "object" that mysterious identity of all things (including subject and object) that is truly unknowable, though not unimaginable. A secondary act of imagination is therefore necessary in order to "objectify" the purely inward, undifferentiated vision, which, because it is not a vision *of* anything, plays an altogether unclear and unsatisfactory role in Schelling's philosophy. Not so his conception of art, whose secondary position seems not to matter in view of assertions such as these:

> It [art] is the true and eternal instrument of philosophy, its chief document, which bears constant and ever-new testimony to that which philosophy cannot represent in external form, namely the non-conscious element in all activity and creativity and the original identity of this element with the conscious one. It is for this reason that art is of the highest value to the philosopher, because it opens up to him, as it were, the holy of holies, where as in a single flame there burns, in eternal and primal union, that which is asunder in nature and in history, that which in living and doing, just as in thinking, must forever draw apart.[48]

Such claims for art not only explain Schelling's prestige with his idealist contemporaries; they also illustrate again how central the idea of art was to idealism itself. That is why it provides the key to the instabilities and ambiguities inherent in this way of looking at the world. It may be added that one outcome was to make the rift between art and science seem ultimately unimportant, to the eyes anyway of higher criticism, which transcended it. In countries influenced by Germanic thought the study of literature has ranked as a science (*Literaturwissenschaft*)—different in this from the anti-scientific tendency of English "appreciative" criticism—and it is noticeable still today that the problem of the "two cultures" arouses little interest in Marxist countries.*

Even the brief quotation above reveals the characteristic tendency of Schelling's writing. We see his heavy stylistic dependency on the undefined relative, the "that which" (*was* in the sense *quid sit*: not any particular thing but the fact of existence itself), the primal oneness, that cannot be distinguished in any other way. Distinctions and distinct things exist only in the fragmented worlds of time and space, history and nature. Art, however, unites them again, or reveals how they are united; their union, or rather unification (*Vereinigung*), implies, in Schelling's phrase, a burning like a flame, a reconciling of opposites that is not neutral but intense, not indifferent but luminous. In other words, what we glimpse here is an implicit dialectical progression, a division of fundamental oneness that in fact enriches it, and a gathering together of the divided parts into what is therefore a higher unity; thus, the revelation of art becomes more meaningful than "that which" it ostensibly reveals. For in art particularity is combined manifestly with absoluteness, the concrete instance with totality of meaning, and (above all) the elusive element of non-conscious existence with conscious awareness. Art overcomes, then, the very rift in existence. It was this idea, couched in Schelling's often dazzling (rather than clear) style, that made him a leader of the Romantic school.

His role dwindled with the years, however, and the cause of aestheticism came to be represented by a philosopher in whom the irrationalistic undertones reverberate more profoundly: Arthur Schopenhauer. He published his *magnum opus* in 1819 (when he was 30 years old), but he was largely ignored, both as a writer and as a teacher, during the earlier part of his life. Only as an old man did he suddenly begin to enjoy some acclaim, although he had added no significant work to his first statement of his system in *Die Welt als Wille und Vorstellung* (The World as Will and Idea), but only some variations and amplifications of its central theme. The most obvious explanation for his latter-day success—which increased still further after his death, finding many echoes in the widespread European cult of art—lies in the changing social character of Europe, and particularly of Germany, by the middle of the century. The discoveries of science on the one hand, and the economic and social problems engendered by capitalist industry on the other, made it increasingly

---

* For this reason the discussion of literature and science in this volume (Chapter 15) focusses primarily on English literature. The question is taken up again in Vol. VI, "Literature and Science."

difficult to believe in traditional religious and moral values. No work shows the declining conviction of the old-fashioned bourgeois in the 1860s better than Thomas Mann's *Buddenbrooks* (1901). And it is no accident that the book that fascinates the last head of the Buddenbrook family, as he struggles without enthusiasm to maintain the family business, should be a copy of Schopenhauer's philosophy. Had Thomas Buddenbrook followed his natural inclinations, and not the requirements of his social class, he might have married a vigorous working-class girl, rather than a decadent heiress, and perhaps then he would not have wearied so fatally of life. Nor might his silly sister have fallen into two disastrous marriages if she had married the seaman's son with the revolutionary ideas, instead of stifling her better instincts with self-important notions of her family's status. But it would have taken a revolution indeed to make such marriages between classes possible; and the uprisings of 1848, in the aftermath of which this generation of Buddenbrooks reached maturity, had proved abortive. Schopenhauer's pessimism, which seemed to him only the more clearly validated by the mob violence of that revolution, found its public at last among the disillusioned intellectuals of the later 19th century.

Schopenhauer's philosophy has a systematic appearance, but it may be doubted whether it owes much of its power to the logic of its arguments, which have generally been recognized as faulty; nor does he himself grant much importance to systematic knowledge or logical explanation. Certainly, he does not add anything of substance in the philosophical realm to the ideas of either Kant or Plato, from whom he chiefly borrows, and sometimes combines, disparate thoughts in a rather confusing way (Kant was not a Platonist, and says so). What Schopenhauer added was poetry: vivid and illuminating images that persuade by their beauty of language. Their power is symbolic, and Schopenhauer's writing as a whole demonstrates by example, even if it does not prove systematically, that all meaning has a symbolic rather than a rational basis. The way in which his own work develops is by illumination from one central point of insight, rather as an artist brings ever-new subjects under the recognizably same spell of his personal style. For 40 years after he had discovered his style, his source of symbolic meaning, Schopenhauer applied it merely to ever-new instances. The relationship of reason to this kind of momentary inspiration is well described by Schopenhauer himself: "My trick is really this: to wait for a propitious hour and to freeze the most living sense-experience of the world or my deepest feeling for it, which that hour has brought me, suddenly and instantaneously with cold abstract reflection and thus to preserve it in a transfixed state."[49] It is important to notice that Schopenhauer's moment of vision is *also* a moment of "cold abstract reflection"; indeed, it is as much the product of this highly self-conscious intellectual act as of any deep or irrational communion with "living experience." We are reminded here again of the difficulty involved in using the concept "irrational." It is sometimes used as though it pointed toward the actual contents of the world in some objective sense; Schopenhauer himself appears to justify the use of the word in this way, as we shall see. The definition that we have proposed here, however, makes the word point primarily to a mental assumption about the *relationship* that is supposed to exist between the mind and the world—namely, one of fundamental antagonism or rift. Irrationalism is a mental attitude or activity; it is born from the highest degree of "cold abstract reflection" of the kind that Schopenhauer describes in the passage just quoted. The fact that irrationalism should first make its appearance among German Romantic philosophers—who were all working in an idealist tradition of thought, deriving from that most rationalistic of thinkers, Immanuel Kant—is thus no accident. For the idealist method focussed attention on the world of self-consciousness; the knowable world was conceived as a phenomenon of consciousness, owing its intelligibility to the activity of the knowing mind.

Schopenhauer's position is, quite simply, that reason does not reach the true nature of existence at all. And it is interesting to note that he arrived at this position from a detailed study of Kant. Schopenhauer follows Kant in restricting the comprehension of reason to phenomena as they appear to the knowing mind, as objects to subjects. Reason cannot be applied to the totality of the world considered in itself, but only to the relations between parts of the world. There can therefore be no rational proof of the existence of God, based on the intelligible laws of the universe, nor any rational metaphysics. Thus, we find Schopenhauer making the same distinction as regards the limits of knowledge as that made by Schelling:

> [A] natural law and the conditions under which it operates in time and space are all that scientific explanation makes known or can ever make known. The force itself that is being expressed, the inner being of the phenomena that occur according to such laws—this remains eternally a mystery, something alien and unknown. . . .[50]

Although this force cannot be known, however, it plays a fundamental role in Schopenhauer's philosophy; it provides a dark source of illumination that enables him to interpret the value of the world that can be known. "The world," he begins, "is my idea," and goes on to sum up his earlier findings as follows: "For me matter and intelligence are inseparable correlates, existing only for one another, and therefore only relatively . . . the two together constitute the world as idea, which is what Kant meant by *appearance*, and consequently they are something secondary."[51] Schopenhauer's world is idea in the sense of mental image, or *Vorstellung*—a word that suggests that it is a kind of projection or illusion, and that it is of quite *secondary* value. What then is primary? Schopenhauer's title for his book already supplies the answer, and he explains the concept Will as follows:

> The word 'Will,' which is to unlock for us like a magic word the innermost being of every thing in the natural world, is in no wise an unknown quantity, nor something that is arrived at by rational methods; it is something that we are aware of spontaneously and so intimately that we know and understand what Will is better than anything else, no matter what.—In the past, the concept Will has been subsumed under the concept force [*Kraft*]; I look at the question the other way round and shall interpret every natural force as Will.[52]

The effect of this interpretative principle, this magic formula, upon the world as we know it is devastating. No matter that in the first place Schopenhauer has said that the innermost being of things "remains eternally unknown," whereas now he says that we know it more "spontaneously and intimately" than anything else. This kind of contradiction in Schopenhauer's method becomes transformed, thanks to the poetic power of his writing, into a symbol of a basic contradiction in the world (consciousness is *toto genere* different from the reality of life; yet we *are* this living thing that is conscious). It is in the contradictory processes of Schopenhauer's mind that we find the model that he inflated into a metaphysical process to explain the world as a whole. He often acknowledges, in passing or without comment, the importance to his system of this basic analogy between the structuring of the world as a mental or imaginative idea, and a cosmic form of the same process, by which everything comes into being. What I am doing in my mind is what the World-Will is doing on a vaster, universal scale. There is no *logical* connection between these two conceptions, one psychological, the other cosmological. The connection that Schopenhauer establishes between the way the mind creates, and the way the world is created, is of the sort we find in poetry, a connection by analogy or metaphor—a carrying over of meaning, through an imaginative jump, from one sphere to another. The tendency to regard this analogy as some kind of identity was not confined to Schopenhauer alone, but permeates many Romantic doctrines—for instance, that of the poet as a god figure, or at least a priestly possessor of the life-giving power. Schopenhauer writes: "The Will is the innermost being of each individual as well as of the whole; it appears in every blindly operating natural force; and it appears also in the consciously considered action of men. The great difference between these two things consists not in the thing that is manifested in each case, but merely in the degree to which it is manifested."[53] Needless to say, it is the poet who achieves one of the highest degrees in cosmic manifestation, and he does so, moreover, in an artistically brilliant fashion: he shows his genius by grasping from above, by detaching himself from, and so negating, the logic of the whole system.

The devastating effects of Schopenhauer's interpretative principle are not hard to imagine. The Will—that innermost being that Schopenhauer brings into imaginative focus by his act of icy intellectual withdrawal—is life symbolized as blind incessant striving, as everything that the mind, in such a moment of pure abstraction, is not. What is the Will striving after? Merely after perpetuation of itself, after more and more life; thus, Schopenhauer naturally points to the satisfaction of hunger and the sexual instinct as prime manifestations of the Will. Even man's vaunted evolution to a higher level of intelligent social organization than that possessed by lower animals achieves nothing more than they do. Or rather: the more that is achieved (which is a higher degree of individuation, rising finally to a consciousness of self and the rationality that has for centuries been supposed to go with it) is worth nothing, metaphysically speaking. It implies an increase in the degree of manifestation but no difference in the quality, or meaning, of *what* is manifested, namely, the mere Will to live. The function of intelligence is no more than practical, the maintenance of the human species; if man is cleverer than the other animals, he is also more systematic, deliberate, and ingenious in the satisfaction of his needs. Schopenhauer exposes with the fervour of a prophet the dark underside of man's claim to be civilized: industry is based on exploitation, wealth on slavery, and even higher individual culture on increased isolation and suffering.

Now, the distinctive feature of Schopenhauer's pessimism is not that he sees these evils, which many men have lamented. He is distinct from a religious prophet, for instance, in that he does not see evil as a falling away from or loss of something. It is the thing itself, life in its totality, that is the ultimate source of evil in the world. It does not lie in the nature of this or that particular action or object (*quod sit*), but in that which is really not a thing at all: in the metaphysical mystery that life is there and continues (*quid sit*). Schopenhauer is speaking a kind of religious language, in fact, but he is speaking it negatively; and we may anticipate Schopenhauer's paradoxical conclusion by noting here that he aspires to a rejection not of particular evils in the world, but of the very principle of the world's existence, the Will itself, the mysterious *quid sit*. Schopenhauer's devaluation of the life process—together with his symbolic vision of the world as mere idea, which reduces everything in it to vain illusion, a mere "objectification," as Schopenhauer calls it, of the relentless Will within us—does not rest upon any physical ground of fact or description. Physically, the world seems to function not at all badly, even on Schopenhauer's own premises: the illusion works, and we strive. Schopenhauer is judging it, of course, metaphysically; and his concept of the Will, and hence of the quite "secondary" character of the world as idea, is a metaphysical concept. The main philosophical problem here is: how, within a world such as Schopenhauer posits, is it possible for such a negative judgment to arise? He makes graphically clear the problem that Hegel's formulation of it obscures: namely, what "the negation of the negation" can possibly mean. Where do such metaphysical insights spring from and where do they lead?

One way of answering this question is to observe how Schopenhauer evades it. He concentrates attention on the fact that men have manifested throughout history "the strongest impulse to philosophical reflection and metaphysical explanation of the world. . . . Temples and churches, pagodas and mosques, in all lands and in all ages, in splendour and vastness, testify to the metaphysical need of man, which, strong and ineradicable, follows close upon his physical need."[54] The two needs are evidently different, yet what source of energy—even spiritual—is there other than the universal Will, whose essentially senseless character we already know? Like Schelling before him, and many writers since—William James and Carl Jung, to name but two, who are dissimilar in other ways but comparable from our present point of view—Schopenhauer respects the splendour and vastness of all such psychic manifestations; he pretends not to say (but, of course, he implies) that they are merely splendid and vast delusions. He evades the issue by making a distinction (still descriptive) between two different kinds of metaphysics. One he calls a "metaphysics of the people," which is what religions are: a dressing-up of truth in allegorical disguises that the unintelligent masses can grasp. The other kind of metaphysical system "requires reflection, culture, and leisure for the recognition of their evidence; they can be accessible only to a very small number of men."[55] What, then, is this truth, and how is the evidence for it recognized? The evidence is the same for the vulgar as for the élite: the fact of suffering and death. The simple-minded religious man is convinced that "pain and death cannot lie in the eternal, original, and immutable order of things, in that which in every respect ought to be."[56] Schopenhauer himself can scarcely share this conviction, because for him it is precisely the painful, indeed lethal, striving of the Will that constitutes the immutable order of things. What other truth can he possibly recognize? The answer is that "it is the sight of suffering and wickedness in the world . . . that leads us to philosophize. Not merely *that* the world exists, but still more that it is such a wretched world, is the *punctum pruriens* of metaphysics, the problem that awakens in mankind an unrest that cannot be quieted."[57] In other words, Schopenhauer is recognizing the process of making metaphysics to be an all-important value in a world that metaphysically does not have any meaning. It is the *spectacle* of man's struggle to make sense of the world that moves him. The fact that it is, for him, a hopeless and senseless struggle does not destroy Schopenhauer's interest in the spectacle; it enhances it. For the spectacle then is a tragic one and aesthetically meaningful.

We see here the emergence of a position that has since become a cliché of irrationalistic thought: namely, that man is forced to make his own values in a valueless world. When the words "value" and "world" are used in this way they become very slippery. The world that is valueless is imagined as somehow utterly separate from the human activity of making values for it; and it is here, in this act of mental separation, that we find the crux of the irrationalist position. Abuse is heaped upon the "world" to dramatize the heroic virtue of value-making man. Moreover, the values that man makes are not to be regarded even then as really existing in the world, for then half the credit would be lost; it is the activity of *making* them that is alone virtuous. Thus, although the values are not to be taken literally, the creative activity of making them is to be admired; in existentialist terminology, it is "authentic." The existentialist term points clearly enough to the context from which it derives and the experience that it best describes: the context of art.

Already in Schopenhauer we see, then, how insight into the way the creative imagination works can become expanded into a total philosophy of life, with important ethical and social implications. Many 19th-century writers were to share Schopenhauer's and Schelling's belief in the privileged position of art and the artist. In a situation in which "there is not a creed which is not shaken, not an accredited dogma which is not shown to be questionable, not a received tradition which does not threaten to dissolve," the study of poetry seemed to offer "an ever surer and surer stay."[58] "The spontaneity of consciousness" that was Hellenism and "the strictness of conscience" that was Hebraism might both be lost, yet the sweetness and light of pure culture remained. When Schopenhauer speaks of a great mind, he is usually thinking of an artistic genius, whose creativity stems from neither knowledge nor dogma; he is above all uncommitted. "To require that a great mind—a Shakespeare, a Goethe—should make the dogmas of any religion . . . his own conviction, is to require that a giant should put on the shoe of a dwarf."[59] Similarly, with regard to ethics, Schopenhauer sees no more reason why a philosopher should be a saint, than that a saint should be a philosopher; it would be "extraordinary," he writes, "to require of a moralist that he should not recommend any virtue except those he himself possesses."[60] The direction of Schopenhauer's remarks is always the same, so that when he finally preaches pity as almost the only virtue to which he does commit himself (because founded on a sense of the one tormenting Will that makes all individuals suffer in the same way), the effect is not to awaken any very active concern for one's neighbour, but rather to evoke a mood of tragic sorrow at his plight, not unlike catharsis at a play. The recognition of a common pain prompts only more complete detachment: ascetic withdrawal, not charity, is the outcome of Schopenhauer's ethics. It seems scarcely necessary to add that Schopenhauer held conservative opinions in politics, and regarded the state as capable only of controlling some of the worst evils of man's metaphysically determined egoism, rapacity, and cruelty. To evolution, amelioration, or even any conception of progress he remained steadily opposed, blaming the prevalence of such idiocies most frequently on Hegel and his still-more-pernicious left-wing followers.

Schopenhauer's pessimistic philosophy enjoyed such a vogue toward the end of the century because it subtly suggested the possibility of doing two things at once. It resigns us to our rôle as servants of the Will: how easy it is to interpret Schopenhauer's words as a symbolic description of man's place in a competitive society dedicated to the production of more and more products at the expense of everyone concerned. Yet at the same time as his philosophy is telling us this, it is *pleasing* us with its symbolism, releasing in us a mood, and releasing us *into* a mood, of cultural contemplation, where we enjoy all the sublime poetry that man's plight has inspired. Schopenhauer first formulated the paradox on which the aestheticism of the 19th century was largely to rest: namely, that there is beauty in the *spectacle* of man's misery, in *les fleurs du mal*. Schopenhauer made this ideal sound like a religion (which it indeed became for many later aesthetes). Yet, as we have seen, this ideal of renunciation was not religiously binding in any doctrinal or even ethical sense. It was a way rather of possessing the world in complete detachment from it, a way of discovering symbolic meaning in all the panoply of existence. "To those in whom the Will has turned against and denied itself, this so-solid world of ours with all its suns and Milky Ways fades and is—Nothing."[61] It recalls a line from Shakespeare—a line that Shakespeare, however, clearly wrote about art, at the end of a beautiful play.

The paradoxes of irrationalistic thinking by no means reach their limit, however, in the formulations of Schopenhauer. In the work of Friedrich Nietzsche, irrationalism enters a final and more alarming phase that, toward the turn of the century, makes itself felt as one of the most significant factors in the cultural life not only of Germany but of Europe as a whole. Like Schopenhauer, Nietzsche was denied any personal fame until the very end of his life (by which time he was insane), but when at last recognition—not to say notoriety—came, it attained proportions that Schopenhauer's never achieved. Schopenhauer fascinated various intellectuals and writers, as dissimilar as Wilhelm Busch and Thomas Hardy, Sigmund Freud and D. H. Lawrence. Nietzsche, too, has had many distinguished names associated with him, but his ideas have also reached a vaster, nameless public. Special editions of *Also sprach Zarathustra* (1883–92) were produced for German soldiers to carry in their rucksacks during World War I; and, in the period that followed, the involvement of his ideas in Fascism and in the more overtly ideological propaganda of World War II has resulted in an interminable dispute among scholars as to whether Nietzschean thinking does not demonstrate conclusively that irrationalism must end in social and political catastrophe. The dispute is about what is really meant by "Nietzschean thinking," or more precisely, about what is the right way to interpret his work; for there is undoubtedly more than one way.

Nietzsche's "philosophy" is not systematic. Like Schopenhauer's, but to a still more pronounced degree, it springs from one obsessive centre of inspiration that can barely be touched conceptually with words. As a source of interpretative or symbolic meaning, capable of illumining vast areas of human knowledge and experience, this centre seems impossible to exhaust; yet one paragraph, even one aphoristic sentence, can give the impression of saying perfectly and profoundly all that Nietzsche sees there.

The success of Nietzsche's writing depends, then, on its deeply imaginative character, to a greater extent than is the case with Schopenhauer, who still concerned himself with a kind of Kantian categorization and analysis. Nietzsche's work begins with a tendentious defence of Greek tragedy, which he places in explicit opposition to the philosopher's ideal of theoretical knowledge. Later, he pretended to regret this youthful declaration of faith in art, and to have espoused the cause of a new and "gay" science. But what his mature work offers is scarcely knowledge in any scientific or rationalistic sense, unless an understanding of the way the imagination works, not in theory but in practice, can be called knowledge. The confusion and danger surrounding his books stem from the fact that they look like truth and are fiction. Which is not to say that they contain no truth whatsoever, but that they are misleading about what kind of truth it is. Nietzsche's gospel, which Zarathustra speaks in a biblically poetic style, is that there *is* only one kind of truth. Far from adopting the conventional distinction between art and science— which has become one of the cliché problems of modern education—he tried to assert that there is a point of view from which they are "essentially" the same. He has two names for this point of view, this mysterious centre of his thought: he sometimes calls it "the Dionysian," which expresses its artistic-mythological aspect; and he sometimes calls it "the Will to Power," a concept he took over from Schopenhauer but believed he had made more scientific through his qualification of it by a principle of power. He uses this principle to subsume all other kinds of force or energy, whether in physics, biology, psychology, or history. We have already heard Schopenhauer make similar use of the irrationalistic concept of the Will.

Now, we must be careful not to forget our point of departure, and must remind ourselves again that irrationalism is not based on the observable contents of this world: things contrary to reason have always been observed there. Irrationalism springs from the mind's response to them, from the methods and assumptions of the observing mind. Schopenhauer is a shade less irrationalistic than Nietzsche in that he admits his principle of the Will to be a metaphysical one; and although he says that it is known to us "spontaneously and immediately," the thing itself cannot actually be observed, and certainly cannot be equated with any of the laws that science demonstrates in its descriptions of phenomena. Nietzsche does not preserve even this degree of rationalism about the character of the concepts he is using. Schopenhauer was maintaining, in fact, a dualistic structure of thought, which he had inherited from Kant, although he transformed it by using his symbolism of the Will to expose the categories of our understanding as delusions. Nietzsche began his philosophical career by getting hold of this shaky system and discovering that it would easily come to pieces. He became obsessed with the idea that there were not really two worlds at all, one of appearances merely and the other possessing some more abiding kind of reality. This distinction, he insisted, must be seen for what it "actually" is: an invention of philosophers. The distinction itself should be interpreted according to the technique of symbolic evaluation that Schopenhauer himself had invented. He should have turned his invention against himself, and Nietzsche proceeded to undertake this task for him (describing the kind of philosophizing that resulted as one that made him "take sides against myself").

The question that Schopenhauer had failed to consider, in arriving at his ideal of renunciation and at his philosophy of art and saintliness as a denial of the world, was what his own will was doing, as he wrote his book. Was it not expressing itself in a passion of creative energy? And the artist who denied himself direct enjoyment of the world for the sake of his art—was he not, in fact, simply creating for himself the best possible conditions for his work? Similarly, the unworldly philosopher or the celibate priest is merely finding a way to express *his* will, hoping to perpetuate something more lasting even than his physical presence in the world—namely, his spiritual power over the world. Of course, these saintly men, these intellectuals and artists, have *called* their ideal dominion over things by high-falutin names, designed to impress lesser mortals who could possess such things only physically. The so-called cultural values of Western civilization all devalue the physical world at the expense of a "higher" one, which does not really exist. What does exist, as a result of this psychological manoeuvre by the men who invent values, is a social situation where the intellectuals have managed to gain power over other men of greater physical strength, the "natural" lords of the earth. The real meaning of those religious and moral codes—indeed, of all the elaborate superstructure that the spiritual élite has erected over existence in forms ranging from science to art—is not what they would have us believe. It is a way of gaining power just as much as any other; the technique is merely more sophisticated and subtle. Moreover, this refinement of the Will to Power into such devious ways of attaining its ends must be reckoned, on the single scale of vitality and health that Nietzsche claims to be using, as decadent and sick.

There is scarcely any need to explain why these doctrines of Nietzsche's are "dynamite," a word applied to his *Jenseits von Gut und Böse* (1886; Beyond Good and Evil) by a contemporary reviewer; Nietzsche told his friends about it with pride and came to adopt it himself to describe his own work. (It is not difficult to see why Nietzsche—a sick intellectual, if ever there was one—imagined that what intellectuals generally enjoy most is a sense of power.) From a philosophical point of view there are so many things "wrong" with Nietzsche's system that a critique of it has usually been considered irrelevant. Indeed, the distinctive feature of his writing, as we have said, is that it does *not* constitute a system, and that it discredits systematic thought as part of the false superstructure in which the mind thinks it has captured life; whereas the mind is actually the prisoner of its own structures, and of all the rules that it believes must regulate (life's) meaning: rules of logic and language, syntax and grammar.

What, then, are we to think of Nietzsche's mind and language; from what point of view is he pronouncing these anti-truths? When he takes sides not only against himself, but against the very basis of rational thought, does he not discredit his own words also? Just occasionally he does seem to admit this, as in the last paragraph of *Jenseits von Gut und Böse*, where he says that, by the time his thoughts have become articulate in language, they begin to look disturbingly like "truths," which is the last thing he wants them to become. Truths bore him. Such passages are significant, because they enable us to glimpse the essential character of Nietzsche's intellectual life. His starting-point, the centre of his Dionysian view of existence, is undoubtedly that which was known to him most "spontaneously and immediately," namely, a certain kind of intellectual excitement. It was what drove him to write; and according to the old-fashioned classification of human abilities into separate faculties, it might have been called "inspiration." The fact that Nietzsche called it the Will to Power has tremendous consequences, for he was making explicit a new type of psychology (implicit already in Schopenhauer) that breaks down the barriers between different kinds of human faculty and activity. He is saying, in effect, that this power known to him inwardly is the same power that does and creates all things, including the havoc and evil in the world. This is not at all the same thing as saying that genius and madness are "near allied"; that ancient dictum presents a quite rationalistic view of madness, which is regarded as a purely *mental* form of aberration, something a little more extreme, but not much more harmful, than eccentricity. Nietzsche wants us to believe that the great creations of the mind are allied not at all to madness in this sense, but to murder, violence, tyranny, and torture, of which they are rationalized versions. It is reason that appears to be the aberration from the blond and bestial norm. Time and again Nietzsche asserts that creative strength springs from the depths of evil.

How *can* Nietzsche have believed this, or have expected his readers to do so? We may leave aside for a moment the more general question of why Nazi propaganda, embodying a vulgar form of this belief—strength that shrinks from nothing, culture based on power—should have awakened enthusiasm in a civilized society; many conditions peculiar to the state of Germany in the 20th century are involved. If we concentrate rather on the intellectual structure of Nietzsche's belief, we may see that he is basically not distinguishing between an intuitive or imaginative awareness of something and the thing itself, between imagination and reality. A drama about murder and suffering is *not* the same thing as murder and suffering. Nietzsche, however, blurs the differences between the real and the literary experience already in his first book, *Die Geburt der Tragödie* (1872; The Birth of Tragedy). What really gives us pleasure, he declares, when we watch a tragedy, is "the destruction of the individual," and not all those mere secondary sentiments, such as pity, that neo-classical and superficial writers have tried to associate with this most primitive rite. Nietzsche's assertion is shocking and was meant to shock. His aim was to announce and evoke a new age, when we should again enjoy the tragic terror of existence. We who have seen the terror, and are less inclined to enjoy it tragically, find ourselves challenged to reply to Nietzsche's theory.

There are several objections that we can make. Nietzsche does not have any sound basis on which to account for the effect even of stylization on the Dionysian ritual, which did, he admits, "mask" the central horror, as the Athenian stage developed, and marked the difference between barbarism and civilization. What the dramatists had actually done and written, explicitly and consciously, to give to sheer destruction the shape and meaning of tragedy, Nietzsche deals with very inadequately: he tries to explain the play itself as a kind of reflex of the basic pleasure, a kind of escape from its annihilating intensity. In the end, however, Nietzsche answers (or betrays) himself. His cloudy ruminations on this crucial point of whether there must not after all be a duality at the heart of existence, as well as of art, evaporate suddenly when Nietzsche reveals what personal experience he is starting from. It is the experience of listening to Wagner's music, and in particular to the opera *Tristan und Isolde*. The individual whose destruction is the source of so much pleasure was evidently, in the first instance, Nietzsche himself; for Wagner's music gave him the immediate and spontaneous feeling of losing his (Nietzsche's) identity in some cosmic power. But even as he lost himself, he saw the dream-like action of other individuals, equally destroyed, upon the stage, and he "identified" with them. When Nietzsche came thoughtfully to reflect on this experience, at a time in his life when he was engaged in classical philological studies, he made an incredible leap to the conclusion that this must have been the way in which Greek tragedy had been "born." The action on the Greek stage was a kind of dream projection—outward into phantasy figures—of an experience going on in the Greek chorus, which was celebrating the rite of Dionysus's murder. And the chorus itself was a symbolic body, enacting outwardly the inward loss of identity in the collective audience. There, in the spectator, was the source of "the tragic"; but the relationship of this mystic power to the writer's creative intelligence, which is surely needed to produce an actual play, or even a single line of verse, is glossed over. The extent to which Nietzsche's aesthetic theory is spectator-based is made even more apparent in his account of the rôle played by Socrates; he was the spectator who would not lose himself, who would not even go to the theatre, and whose intellectual influence was so strong as a result that it destroyed the artistic culture and community of Greece.

Now, although Nietzsche renounced his youthful admiration of Wagner, and came to regard such musical ecstasies as decadent—which is to say also that he recognized his own intellectual kinship with Socrates and tried to establish common ground again between art and knowledge—Nietzsche's philosophical procedures continue to follow the same pattern. Thus, 15 years after *Die Geburt der Tragödie*, we find him explaining the "birth" and evolution of morality along similar lines. Individuals whose identities are in danger of being destroyed project moral phantasies onto the world to protect themselves; others, who have a chance to avenge some damage they have suffered, rationalize the pleasure that cruelty provides by calling it "punishment." Always the line between the primitive reality and the subsequent meaning is blurred. Nietzsche draws this line in a direction that makes it look historical, like a process in time; and the words he uses to describe it are metaphors of organic growth. We should not be deceived, however, into thinking that his ideas have any objectively verifiable foundation in history, biology, or any other of the sciences that he seems to be talking about. The only "science" he understands—and understands profoundly—is the science of interpretation, which he sometimes calls psychology but might just as well call rhetoric. "It is," he declared, "infinitely more important what names things are called by than what they actually are."[62] Here we witness the most drastic re-formulation, to the point of obliteration, of the metaphysical distinction between consciousness and reality with which we began. That which is infinitely more important than what things are is no longer the mystery *that* they are, but the *names* by which they are called. The mysterious "thereness" of the world, the aspect of existence that transcends all rational comprehension of what and how it exists (the *quid sit*), has lost its independent value. What remains of value in the world, indeed, the mystery itself of reality's existence, has been handed over into man's keeping, as man's poetic possession, to be interpreted to the limit of his powers. Hallowed be the name he gives it. *Fiat voluntas sua.*

The religious overtones in Nietzsche's work are unmistakable. He knew what challenge he had issued to the Graeco-Christian traditions of the West. Either the world may mean whatever man wills it to mean, or it may not, because it has a "real" presence with which man must come to terms. Nietzsche's Zarathustra proclaims: "On any metaphor you may reach any truth."[63] This is the latter-day equivalent, in terms designed to catch the inward-looking imagination of a modern intellectual, of the claims made by the Greek Sophists that man is the measure of things; and it bears some resemblance also to the offer, made by Satan in the Christian Gospels, of all the kingdoms of the earth. His claim that "there are no facts, only interpretations," may make sense in our dealings with literature, but leads to disaster in our dealings with life. Nietzsche's argument is invariably sophistical in that he does himself presume to know the facts behind the façade of civilization's false interpretations. (Indeed, it is not clear what the words "fact" and "interpretation" mean unless we can know the difference between them.)

Nietzsche believed he had found a cure for what he regarded as the sickness of his age, a sickness that had afflicted mankind for 2000 years, for so long as men had hungered for a truth, for contact with a reality, that he asserted is not there. The answers to such questions as Nietzsche raises can be grounded only in belief, both for Nietzsche and for whoever approaches his work; they were grounded in religious faith for Plato no less than for Christ. Yet even a mere onlooker at the pattern of Nietzsche's life and writing must be struck by the fact that the power he meant was the power of words, and that the health he praised and promised was the ideal of a physically very sick man. Did his words convert his sickness into health? It is a purely aesthetic judgment that says that they do, because his words sound so fine and powerful. Must not a rationalist, be he religious or not, insist that in fact Nietzsche simply ignored the reality of his human condition, both that aspect of it that he shared with all men (but tried to push off onto a lesser breed who were to be overcome by supermen), and that part of his own personal condition that was physiologically diseased? It was a disease that no poetry could possibly convert into health; the possibility of achieving either a medical cure or religious salvation must depend, in the general and in the particular case, on admitting (or attempting more realistically to identify) what is the matter. Nietzsche seems never to have admitted this, even to himself; his way of dealing with the problem of his own illness, which more rational minds must regard as sin or syphilis or both, was to call it a struggle for power. As a poetic answer, his writing *has* the power: the power of a Dostoyevsky novel, the power perhaps of the literary form that Nietzsche loved above all, the power of tragedy. But to mistake the nature of this power, to equate it with truth, not fiction, is surely madness. Unfortunately, there were madmen waiting in Nazi Germany ready to act out Nietzsche's imaginative tragedy; to push "interpretation" beyond the margins of any previous human experience of "fact."

Nietzsche once remarked that Dostoyevsky was the only writer from whom, had he known his work earlier, he might have learnt something. He does not say what the lesson would have been, but we may risk declaring what it *ought* to have been: namely, that an aesthetic world-view may be enjoyed in art but not in life. Taken literally—as a basis for action and not just for imaginative speculation and literature—the irrationalistic vision of such a philosophy is liable to become a dangerous influence in society. In the 20th century there were to be many examples of writers apparently espousing the cause of political irrationalism (as Bertrand Russell, for instance, came to believe D. H. Lawrence had done), or at least betraying a fascination with "the abyss," to use a favourite term of Thomas Mann's. Yet it is surely a misreading and a misuse of literature to allow its intuitions of a larger whole to destroy man's faith in the value of his reason. Reason may not be able to demonstrate its own value, or indeed spiritual values of any kind, and may ultimately stand in need of faith. The metaphysical trend of thought that we have analysed here and that, as we have seen, subsumed reason within ideas of a larger whole that were based on art, began by providing a higher form of "reason" to dispense with outmoded religion, and ended by undermining the security of rational consciousness altogether. To quote Turgenev's line again: "There used to be Hegelians and now there are nihilists."

No writer understood this destructive tendency better than Dostoyevsky, and it is interesting to consider why he satirized Turgenev in the figure of the foolishly pretentious writer Karmazinov (in *The Possessed*), thereby implying that Turgenev had not really understood it. Their political ideas differed, of course, and Dostoyevsky felt that "the great genius had lost touch with the fatherland"[64] as a result of living abroad; but their real point of difference comes out in their literary style. Dostoyevsky accuses Karmazinov of writing "solely with the object of self-display." Even when he is toying with advanced ideas—" 'There is no crime!' 'No,' I said through my tears, 'but if that is so, there are no righteous either' "—even when he is parading his lack of conventional beliefs, Karmazinov is a quite conventional writer. He is the omniscient author who sees it all: life truly mirrored in the individual's imagination; the writer whose word is his bond with the truth.*

For Dostoyevsky, the truth is essentially obscure. Every individual's consciousness of it differs. Indeed, truth is not imagined as a thing, an ultimately observable reality, but as a process, in which what the case is and what the case is thought to be interact dialectically. In a sketch for a preface to *The Possessed* Dostoyevsky wrote that the whole point of the novel lay in knowing what should be considered the truth. His taste for lurid French and English crime journalism and fiction is well known, but his quite original manner of presenting murder stories shows that he was not interested simply in mysteries where the facts alone are in doubt. What is in doubt is their meaning, to the point where Dostoyevsky comes close to exemplifying Nietzsche's dictum that "there are no facts but only interpretations." The reader can never finally be sure about what happens at the critical points in Dostoyevsky's novels, though he is plentifully supplied with evidence and explanations; the reality itself transcends all understanding of it. Who was responsible for Karamazov's murder? Or Shatov's? Or that of Nastasya Philipovna? What was written on the missing sheet of Stavrogin's confession? He says: "Nothing happened, I tell you, absolutely nothing," and then continues: "It was a moment of real terror."[65] Despite all Raskolnikov's plans before the event and meditations on it afterwards, he can still say that he does not know why he killed the old pawnbroker. Dostoyevsky's sense of a reality transcending anyone's idea of it is the source of one of his most powerful effects. He is uniquely gifted in evoking a demonic quality in events that drives his personages and his stories onward, with a kind of inexorable pressure: situations and people surge up with dreadful suddenness, coming into

---

* That Turgenev was, in fact, not like this, being well able to understand and depict characters who have come to the edge of nihilism, even if stylistically he followed another path, will perhaps have been made clear at the beginning of this chapter.

existence in unforeseen, uncontrollable ways, and passing into a past that is never finished. It is within this extraordinary narrative flow, sometimes moving with turbulent, confusing speed, sometimes strangely still and deep, that his profuse ideas are immersed. It is almost impossible to lift any of them out individually and decide whether they are Dostoyevsky's own— as though they might be trustworthy outside the context of his fiction— despite the fact that he himself tried to formulate his views theoretically in his *Diary of a Writer* (1873–4). Deprived there of the irrational depths suggested by his novels, they are for the most part rather lifeless and dull.

The point of view from which Dostoyevsky discovered his sense of a transcendent reality was not a religious one in the conventional sense of the word, even though it developed into a kind of Slavic Messianism. His inspiration emerges at first as the product of intense feelings of isolation from society and a brooding of the mind upon itself: the early story called *The Double* (1846) was always regarded by Dostoyevsky as particularly important, although critics generally have not shared his enthusiasm for it. The paranoia of a little bank clerk is doubtless not in itself very interesting, but the psychology of self-consciousness, of the mind's total otherness from existence, that this story sketches in still-undistinguished, sentimental language, was to provide Dostoyevsky with his greatest literary effects. The culminating scene in the life of his last intellectual hero, whose thoughts retrace much of the ground we have described here, comes when Ivan Karamazov sees his own "double" in the guise of the devil. But before he could achieve that climactic vision, Dostoyevsky's genius had to be schooled in the quite unsentimental implications of his point of view. The hardest, but probably decisive, lesson came with his years of political imprisonment in Siberia. What he learned there may be judged from his fictionalized account of his experiences in *The House of the Dead* (1862), where two themes are stressed. First, the hero is separated for reasons not only of class but also of education and intelligence from the common people (mainly serfs, of course, but also from other people whom he observes). And second, the hero comes to understand in depth what for Karmazinov-Turgenev is a mere idea, namely, "that there is no crime." Dostoyevsky writes: "Crimes cannot be compared even approximately . . . the variations in the same crime are infinitely numerous. There are as many shades of difference as there are characters."[66] This perception strikes at the superficial fabric that the mind habitually recognizes as reality, and tears it to reveal the infinite variety and depth of existence beneath. It is in itself a paradoxical perception, because it both affirms and negates the possibility of expressing existence in words; indeed, the phrase "the same crime" does not make sense if the perception is true, and yet the perception cannot be stated without it. This ambiguity was to remain typical not only of Dostoyevsky's writing but of existential thought generally: does it promise liberation from the tyranny of received opinion or justify the creation of a new order of truth by force of the will? Here, Dostoyevsky goes on to plead the humanitarian cause of creating a nobler "image" of the criminal, who (he believes) will then live up to it, instead of being repressively beaten down in a way that produces no remorse but merely a self-protective shell of toughness and phantasy. Nietzsche, too, has this humanitarian side, though (as we have seen) it is practically impossible to disentangle it from the demonic and menacing aspect of his thought. It is, not surprisingly, impossible to separate the positive and negative aspects of an aesthetic philosophy, of life seen "as a whole." If we imagine life in this total manner, then individual statements and points of view, together with the activities of reason that enable individuals to share a conventional view of experience, are liable to be exposed as inadequate and arbitrary. But we can, precisely, only imagine this, not live it. Reason will protest that there is an irreducible paradox in the idea of the falsity of all ideas.

Paradox, however, is not necessarily a flaw in a work of the imagination: it may be a source of profundity and strength. If we allow this to be true of Dostoyevsky's fiction, it follows that none of the multiple views expressed in his novels, not even that of the narrator, is to be regarded as "true" by itself. Whatever truth the novels contain they represent as a whole. There are patches of greater spiritual light, moments of insight, within this whole, but they do not last and are not identical with it. Thus, Raskolnikov has moments of horror and repentance at the thought of murder, but they do not stop him from committing murder, or from relapsing into quite different thoughts of unrepentant "freedom and power." True, the book ends during a phase of religious conversion more radical than anything that has gone before, but not even the last sentence of all should be read as saying that Raskolnikov has found "the" truth. Dostoyevsky writes simply: "That might be the subject of a new story—our present story is ended."

How well Dostoyevsky knew himself, and the character of truth for all modern intellectuals like himself, who are conscious of experience primarily as an inner process of self-reflection that is more important than its "objective" content, i.e. its conventional meaning. All his novels contain characters in whom self-consciousness is developed to a greater or lesser degree. This provides the dimension of depth, obscurity, and spiritual tension that transforms old-fashioned psychological notions of motive and feeling—love, jealousy, greed, hatred, and so on—almost beyond recognition. In addition to the action, the novels show a new kind of psychological reaction that takes place between individuals and within individuals as a result of what they think and know. Where traditional psychology deals in terms of physical objects, Dostoyevsky's psychology deals in metaphysical terms of knowledge and ignorance, certainty and illusion, faith and doubt. There is a scene in *Crime and Punishment* (1866) where this psychological order is represented pictorially to the point of appearing schematic. It occurs when Raskolnikov is trying to make Sonya understand that he has committed the murder. Dostoyevsky tells us, in italics, that *"the idea* never entered her head."[67] Sonya sees only that Raskolnikov is deeply unhappy; her spontaneous heart is all of a piece with her selfless consciousness and simplicity of mind. At the same time, on the other side of a thin partition wall, there stands an eavesdropper, a monster of cynical intelligence, Svidrigaylov. His mind is utterly divided from human feeling, as his physical situation at this moment seems to symbolize. What he hears, he understands with the immoral interest of a blackmailer. Later, he tells Raskolnikov that the two of them are very alike, and tries to make the hero participate in his own perverse views and projects. Sonya and Svidrigaylov represent the two poles of spontaneous faith and intellectual doubt, oneness of heart and mind as opposed to near-schizophrenia, between which Raskolnikov wavers and tries vainly to choose.

Dostoyevsky put his finger here on the critical question for the growth of modern civilization: how far does man have the power to make of the world and of himself what he will? And what ultimately governs his will and intelligence? That there *is* a question of great profundity here, which casts the character and aims of the will into doubt, distinguishes 19th-century culture gradually more and more from that of the Enlightenment, which in spite of all its varieties of scepticism and free-thinking generally lacked any notion of *consciousness*—not at all the same thing as reason—as an unstable medium that refracts reality and destroys sanity. Dostoyevsky experienced this instability personally, not only in the spiritual isolation of the prison camp, but also through illness—his epilepsy, in which the body sprang into mindless convulsions after a moment of extreme mental illumination—and in some of his reactions to love and gambling. With regard to the latter, for instance, he discovered that the gambler is not interested simply in making money. He may have what he considers a rational system for winning, but he does not stick to it; the gambling passion lies in the risk, an irrational desire both to win and to lose. In this, Dostoyevsky observed, "he is a poet in his own way, but ashamed of this poetry because he is conscious that it is unworthy, although the element of risk redeems him in his own eyes."[68]

This psychological insight certainly redeems Dostoyevsky's novel *The Gambler* (1866), whatever its faults in conventional literary terms. Dostoyevsky sees his hero not only as "a poet," but also as typical of a new, modern generation: "a man who has lost all faith but dare not disbelieve, rebelling against authority but also afraid of it."[69] Here is the origin of an irrational fascination, which goes beyond every effort of the "rational" soul to conquer it, and which obsesses most of Dostoyevsky's heroes—just as it was the obsession that made him a greater writer. In actual life it lured a man on to disaster and evil, as Dostoyevsky well knew; but in literature, disaster and evil are indispensable to the imagination, being the ingredients of "tragedy" in a "higher" sense. It is, above all, Dostoyevsky's experience of writing, of self-consciously reflecting on life and refracting it as an idea, that provided him with his psychological model for understanding the existence of the irrational. And it also, of course, made many of his heroes resemble—inwardly, if not outwardly—himself and one another. There are even hints that Dostoyevsky felt that in projecting this irrational obsession outward into literature he was casting out a devil—it is to the casting out of a devil that the title of *The Possessed* refers—and that the effect upon the world of letting loose demonic ideas would be the same as that which destroyed the Gadarene swine. The book is about the way ideas that derive from the vague Hegelian speculations of an older generation are put into bloody, senseless practice by the young.

The depth of Dostoyevsky's fiction derives, then, from a relationship rather like that of the gambler to the gambling table; a relationship between idea and event, between consciousness and existence, between sophistication and spontaneity. The relationship may result in a bloody confrontation or a spiritual conversion; but it is always more or less irrational and demonic. (As Kierkegaard repeatedly says of it, in order to show that Hegel described it incorrectly, "it cannot be mediated" by reason; literature may symbolize it, and only faith perhaps transcend it.) All Dostoyevsky's intellectual heroes share Prince Myshkin's intuition when he gazed at the universe and felt:

> Every blade of grass grew and was happy. Everything knew its path and loved it, went forth with a song and returned with a song; only he knew nothing, understood nothing, neither men nor words, nor any of nature's voices; he was a stranger and an outcast.[70]

Although Dostoyevsky's "alienated men" interpret their situation in very different ways, they are all drawn by similarly ambivalent emotions toward the world from which they feel cut off, as well as toward deeper layers of the self. Sexual impulses provide the most common pull, and yet how strangely distorted these appear in the context of Dostoyevsky's metaphysical preoccupations: not like the love of one person for another so much as the longing of individuals for salvation. Thus, Raskolnikov subconsciously decides to confess his murder to Sonya before he has committed it, and when he has been told only about her utter humility. Or again, Prince Myshkin falls in love with Nastasya when he first sees her in humiliating circumstances. Across the abyss that separates these strange lovers, feelings are generated of a desperate, irrational kind, beside which conventional notions of love and marriage count for nothing. Dostoyevsky is usually supposed to have learnt from his own tormented love affair with Appolinaria Suslova about the "character" of women like Nastasya, or Pauline (in *The Gambler*), or Lizaveta (in *The Possessed*). But it is not so much a type of woman who causes ambivalent relationships of the kind so frequent in Dostoyevsky's fiction, where hate and love, fear and longing, contempt and respect are inextricably interwoven: they are caused rather by a type of situation. This situation is the product less of anyone's character or deeds in an objective, moral sense, than of the ambience in which Dostoyevsky's personages meet one another, an irrational atmosphere for which the author is responsible. This responsibility for a disastrously divided view of human relations is disguised in the first great archetype of the situations where an intellectual meets a simple woman: the scenes with Lisa in *Notes from Underground* (1864). There the intellectual himself is the "author" of the notes, but the whole mode of seeing is unmistakably Dostoyevsky's, and the irrational behaviour and character of the anti-hero (as he describes himself) is no less clearly the product of his self-reflectiveness as a writer.

Dostoyevsky leaves his reader in no doubt about how dangerous and destructive the alienated, self-reflective mind can be. Looking down from its state of heightened consciousness onto the surface of events, which is illumined by little points of thought, small as spots of sunshine on the sea, it knows that "beneath it is all dark, it is all spreading, it is unfathomably deep."[71] (The phrase is not Dostoyevsky's, but Virginia Woolf's; similar, equally suitable images might be taken from many modern writers who have explored the irrational depths known to the creative imagination— from Paul Valéry, for example, who calls such spots of light "idols.")[72] Men live and love by the light of their ideas, in which they are extremely vulnerable and likely to be misled. They are most likely to be misled by attempting to take a superior view, that shows up conventional ideas against a background of nothingness. But is this not what Dostoyevsky himself is doing? And are his novels not, therefore, imaginative projections of what his own idea of the world would mean in reality? There are two aspects to this question that must be considered here. The first is Dostoyevsky's obsession with the theme of the suffering and corrupting of children. Svidrigaylov is guilty of it and haunted by a vision of it. So is Stavrogin, who has caused a little girl to commit suicide because what he has done makes her feel she "has killed God." For both these men, who are otherwise without a belief in the world, the image of corrupted innocence is the only value that impresses them—like Raskolnikov's dream of the beaten animal, or his memories of the childlike woman he butchered. (The "victim" of Prince Myshkin's saintliness, for that in effect is what Nastasya is, also seems "like a child" to him.) That this theme had wider implications for Dostoyevsky is suggested also by the fact that he linked a dream of how mankind had lost its "sylvan paradise," and had become estranged from the natural happiness of its origins, with Stavrogin's obsessive hallucination in which little Matryosha appears to him. Dostoyevsky described exactly the same dream of a lost paradise in another novel, *A Raw Youth* (1875), where the dreamer has once again been involved in obscurely scandalous relations with a young girl. The dream ends differently in the second instance, however; the dreamer awakens to see "the setting sun of the last day of civilization. One seemed to hear the death knell ringing over Europe in those days."[73] The days in question are those of 1848, and passages such as these, lifted out of context, have sometimes been read as statements of Dostoyevsky's own political views. Although Dostoyevsky did base some political views on his metaphysical psychology, just as Nietzsche also did, the "truth" of his ideas lies in the spectacle of a tragic flaw in civilization itself that both these writers contemplated in the depths of their own creative experience, rather than in any possibility of a solution to the problem. For both men derived their inspiration as writers from an insight into the negative rôle of the mind.

If the destruction of innocence and of its naive faith in goodness and truth is one major theme in Dostoyevsky's fiction, the destruction and inadequacy of intelligence is the other. There are moments when the bright-eyed love of a child seems to conquer the despair of nihilism and death: when Polya kisses Raskolnikov, for instance, or (in the closing chapter of *The Brothers Karamazov*, 1879–80) when Ilyusha's death becomes for his comrades a positive and religious bond. That "blood is the cement you want to bind your groups together"[74] is Stavrogin's statement of the "same" truth in nihilistic and murderous terms—terms that have since become brutally familiar in the revolutionary politics of Europe. What is the difference between the positive and negative forms of this statement? It is the difference that runs like a rift through the middle of Dostoyevsky's world, like the wall that separates Svidrigaylov from Sonya: it is the barrier that intelligence imagines as standing between itself and life, once it becomes self-conscious and tries to comprehend the mind's character from outside. Literature lends itself to this act of imagination; indeed, art altogether provided the original model for the philosophical elaboration of this viewpoint, as we noted at the outset.

Another recurrent theme in Dostoyevsky, that of blackmail, reflects his preoccupation with this problem in symbolic form: for blackmail depends upon the altered value of the truth once it is known to someone on the outside. Dostoyevsky's greatest representation of the problem of the intellectual and writer, as of the problem of what ideas mean in an unself-conscious as opposed to a self-conscious context, comes with his depiction of Ivan Karamazov. Ivan's essay on the church might have come from the pen of Nietzsche, with just the same ambiguity of presentation that leaves the reader in doubt as to whether to accept this view of how religion has protected mankind from the truth. The doubt remains in the case of Nietzsche's work, but Ivan's ideas are encompassed by the larger framework of Dostoyevsky's novel. And in the reality established by the novel he goes mad. The scene, moreover, in which he goes mad enacts the very process we have been considering here: the process of imagining the negative limitations of the mind and of attempting to transcend them. Imagination ceases then to be the instrument of fellow-feeling between man and man, and takes on the appearance of the devil. The devil of Ivan's imagination inverts the ancient, humanistic tag that expressed the kinship of all mankind, and declares: "*Satan sum et nihil humanum a me alienum puto.*"[75] Nietzsche had said of the imagination that it enabled man "to ride to any truth." Dostoyevsky shows that this image of the mind leads in the end to evil, delusion, and madness.

Ivan's devil is a symbolic representative of the modern mind talking to itself about its own spiritual nature. "By some primordial decree," he begins, "I was appointed to 'negate,' while as a matter of fact I'm genuinely kindhearted and not at all good at 'negation.'" The devil declares he would gladly accept "annihilation for myself," but that thinking men cannot do without the negative spirit of criticism. "If everything on earth were rational, nothing would happen . . . there would be no events. . . . I serve so that there should be events and perform what is irrational by order." (By order, be it noted, of the modern mind striving after understanding of itself and of the world.) As a result men suffer, but after all, he concludes, "they live a real and not an illusory life; for suffering is life. Without suffering, what pleasure would they derive from it? Everything would be transformed into an endless religious service: it would be holy, but a little dull." Before he disappears, the devil mocks Ivan's efforts to transcend this negative wisdom and make of it a positive doctrine to the effect that "everything is permitted" for the emancipated man-god of the future. The devil puts his finger on the illogicality of Ivan's ideas when he remarks: "All this is very charming; only, if you want to lead a life of crime, what do you want the sanction of truth for?" Ivan keeps on asserting that everything the devil says—with the one exception of the Latin tag quoted above, which does surprise him—is what he himself has thought, so that he can believe there is no devil, no objective evil, there at all. He argues against this *alter ego*, as Nietzsche does in his own philosophizing, in an effort to maintain rational control of his thoughts. But, like Nietzsche, he fails and goes mad. Dostoyevsky is able to understand and represent this madness so vividly because it closely resembles an act of the creative imagination. Ivan *lives* a moment of imaginative creativity to the extent that he cannot tell whether the figment is literally there. Dostoyevsky thus makes us see what the world would be like if it were fashioned totally in the image of man's creative will: man would be totally unable to tell the difference between illusion and reality, between subjective imaginings and objective fact. There is no difference between them in art, nor indeed in dreams, and this enables Dostoyevsky to point out the psychological connection between dreams and art:

> In dreams and particularly in nightmares, caused by indigestion or whatever you like, a man sometimes sees such artistic things, such a complex and actual reality, such events or even a whole world of events, woven into such a plot, full of such astonishing details, beginning with the most exalted manifestations of the human spirit to the last button of a shirt front that, I assure you, not even Leo Tolstoy could have invented it.[76]

It is the devil who speaks these words, and he is describing a state of consciousness in which the separateness of the mind from reality is overcome. Hegel was the thinker chiefly responsible for letting loose upon the modern world the beguiling thought that man's rational understanding is in some way alienated and that it lies within his power to overcome that negative state. There have been many variations since in the way this basic situation has been formulated, as we have seen. Freud was to bring the inner realm described by Ivan's devil to the light of science under the name of the unconscious, while Nietzsche was defining it independently in these years as the "Dionysian" strain. The devil here claims that it is his realm, "where everything is a sort of indeterminate equation." He even tells Ivan that "I love your earthly realism. With you everything is drawn in clear outlines, here everything is a formula, here everything is geometry."[77] This contrast between an ultimate indeterminacy in the character of existence and the artificial patterns imposed on it by thought was increasingly to provide the inspiration for the major achievements of modern European culture. Dostoyevsky fixes the point where the proud bid of reason to comprehend itself, its most exalted reaching after freedom and power, its idealism that would identify the world with the will of the human spirit, conjures up a mocking phantom of unreason and nihilism. Meanwhile, in the society outside Ivan's study, a bastard, the illegitimate offspring of the Karamazov spirit and a mindless creature of nature, has taken Ivan's nihilism literally and committed a murder.

In conclusion, we should remind ourselves that we have brought together manifold ideas and attitudes, and defined them as constituting a unified state of mind, called irrationalism, simply because irrationalistic tendencies were its most menacing outcome where European society and the inherited values of Western civilization have been concerned. The question whether the events of modern history have in fact shown Europe to be more in the grip of "the irrational" cannot, of course, be answered factually; it is precisely when one tries to use a cultural criterion of this kind that one comes to the conclusion that "there are no facts, only interpretations." Similarly, it is impossible to answer on any factual basis questions regarding the cause of irrationalism. This is not to deny that one may interpret certain factual features in the historical situation as encouraging this outlook. Because the historical and social situation varied from country to country, however, quite as much as the individual styles of expressing it, there can be no question of finding a total explanation—or solution—for even the most noxious ideas. (The only "total" solution, doubtless, would be to suppress the creative and self-conscious imagination altogether, in some act of "real" solidarity with some final wholeness; for it must be admitted that individual genius does seem to thrive in literature on negative, tragic, and similarly irrational intuitions.) Thus, we may observe that Russia was, and has long remained, a country in which a particularly acute confrontation was inevitable between rational, progressive ideas and a primitively "natural" way of life. A sense of self-consciousness and alienation from the people—and from their often equally simple-minded masters—provoked a crisis of some sort in almost every Russian intellectual of the 19th century. The major dispute in Russian political thought during this period was between those who believed Russian society must be Westernized as quickly as possible, and those who saw in the very backwardness of Russia a unique opportunity to take a different path and avoid the evils of Western progress. The political "reason" for the murder of Shatov in *The Possessed* is that he has gone back on his progressive views, and believes now that "to be cut off from the peasantry is to be cut off from God."[78] Dostoyevsky's profundity lies in his vision of how this reason becomes blurred in practice; a far more demonic irrationality is let loose by those who "correct" his reactionary step. Stavrogin (for inner reasons of his own) has the strength to control the murderous impulses that well up in him against Shatov. But in the less-inward members of the revolutionary party the murder serves to establish not a progressive idea but a hierarchy of power and a reign of terror.

Dostoyevsky was not the only Russian writer to depict the psychological tensions within intellectuals in Russia, as we have seen in our opening account of Turgenev. Other examples and comparisons might equally well have been given; not all of them would have the political and religious accent stressed by Dostoyevsky and Turgenev, but most would show a similar psychological predicament in self-consciousness. One of the most famous is known by the name of Goncharov's hero Oblomov, and "Oblomovism" has been regarded sometimes as a national characteristic of Russian life. Goncharov himself was brought up in family circumstances that enabled him to see the old traditions at their best—the securely unchanging, pleasantly indolent aspects of the feudal estate, patriarchal rather than tyrannical—and yet also to witness the forces of bourgeois change. He was educated in the same intellectual atmosphere as Turgenev, but remained an onlooker on the fringe of the new ideas. Goncharov's first novel, *A Common Story* (1847), tells of the conflict between the old and new social orders that recalls Turgenev's *Fathers and Children*, except that both orders, between which the hero's life vacillates, prove equally corrupting in the end. In *Oblomov* (1859), Goncharov separated the two worlds in a psychologically more disturbing manner: the old becomes perfect by being turned into a dream, an endless daydream of an idyllic past, a place where, with obvious symbolism, "the sky seems to come nearer to the earth."[79] (Goncharov actually wrote *Oblomov's Dream* as a separate short work and then included it in the larger novel.) The contemplation of this ideal form of existence, where the heart feels forever at home, totally destroys Oblomov's ability to live or love or do anything. He is incapacitated by the very strength of his imaginative idealism, which vanquishes his mind and will with a far deeper, irrational power. Liberal critics saw in the book an indictment of the squirearchy, which was ruined morally by the very system that sustained it economically. But the psychological law that destroys Oblomov has its roots in the way the imagination, rather than the economy, works. Oblomovism survived the abolition of the social system, as may be seen in Konstantin Fedin's novel *Cities and Years* (1924), or in the following remarks of Lenin himself:

> We are indeed in the position, and it must be said that it is a very absurd position, of people sitting endlessly at meetings, setting up commissions, and drawing up plans without end. There was a character who typified Russian life—Oblomov. He was always lolling on his bed and mentally drawing up schemes. . . . Russia has experienced these revolutions, but the Oblomovs have survived.[80]

A comparable state of mind may be detected in the mournful note so dear to Victorian poets, and readers, in England.* How often we find English poets of the 19th century confronting the irrational mystery of the world from a position of lofty and self-conscious loneliness. The mood is associated with Tennyson, above all, watching "the stately ships go on/ To their haven under the hill,"[81] and with the Lady of Shalott in her tower, able to survive only if she looked at the world in her private mirror, symbol of the poet's self-reflectiveness. We catch the tone again in many of Arnold's poems, as he stands *looking on* at Oxford, or Rugby chapel, or Dover Beach; it was the surest stance for letting in the "eternal note of sadness" that was felt to be the quintessence of serious poetry. If we ask why this was felt to be the case in England (and look beyond the poets' need to escape from industrial capitalism), we may discover an explanation by going back to Keats, the originator of this poetic mode—who, in fact, barely refers to his historical or social environment. What he *was* acutely aware of, however, was his cultural situation. It was Chapman's Homer that brought him to that silent peak. The fear of death was made more harrowing by the thought that he might not have time to write

* This theme is taken up again in Ch. 5, "The Elegiac Note in Tennyson, Arnold, Pushkin, and Leopardi."

poetry as beautiful as Spenser's or Shakespeare's. Keats struck that archetypal attitude of standing on the shore of the wide world and *thinking* when the idea of death made him realize in what way the poet who comes late in a tradition is already outside it, excluded. His profoundest insights into the psychology of art are inspired by a question that indicates great cultural self-consciousness. Like Faust, he wants to know whether life is *really* beautiful, whether in his imagination he wakes or dreams. And he finds that it is beautiful only to the outsider, the onlooker who sees the whole:

> . . . watching, with eternal lids apart,
>   Like nature's patient, sleepless Eremite,
> The moving waters at their priest-like task
>   Of pure ablution round earth's human shores. . . .[82]

One final factor, which undoubtedly contributed more to the formation of the *Weltanschauung* of the 19th century than can be properly investigated here, is worth mentioning again in connection with this question of cultural self-consciousness: it is the role played by the study of history. There is no doubt not only that this increased from the early 18th century onward, but also that its methods and presuppositions changed. Most scholarly discussion of this subject has focussed on overt problems of ideological tendency (whether a given historian was progressive or conservative in his views) or of presentation and technique (whether a historian pretends scientifically to stick to fact or is aware of imaginative and evaluative aspects of his task). May not the effect of historical thinking have been psychologically decisive in a direction that is quite distinct from, even opposed to, the "lessons" that reason was supposedly learning from the past? In a word, did historiography as a whole contribute to that sense of alienation from the world? Certainly, the spectacle of history "as a whole" encouraged in some thinkers not only irrationalistic conceptions of events as manifestations of a single, organic force, but also ideas of some metaphysical connection between the workings of the world-organism and the workings of the poetic imagination. The most striking examples of such ideas are found among the most "poetic" historians, such as Michelet and Carlyle. Their style of writing, and also their importance, were summed up by Taine as follows:

> They see a notion *in its entirety*; they perceive the powers which organize it; they reproduce it by divination. . . . They think only by sudden concentration of vehement ideas, they are revealers or poets. Michelet amongst the French is the best example of this form of intellect, and Carlyle is an English Michelet.[83]

Taine is describing, in effect, the intellectual procedure that Schopenhauer called his "trick": the freezing of the vital flow of existence in a
static image. Whether this is truly what the mind does in its confrontation
with reality cannot, as a matter of fact, be known; what the nature of this
relationship truly is remains finally a question of faith. But as we have
tried to show here, many modern European minds have come to see
human consciousness as fulfilling some such negative or oppositional role
vis-à-vis the "thing itself." Hence, Michelet interprets the events and
personalities of the French Revolution as an eruption of primordial elements, like fire and water, blood and sap, which have to be contained
within limits, gradually solidifying into forms that are then dead and
decay. His own mission he felt to be a resurrection of that entire process
through his writing, in which the past would be fulfilled and all its
striving immortalized. As with Nietzsche, the distinction faded from his
mind between the reality of the world as fact and its rebirth in his mind
as creative interpretation. Without any of the symptoms of physical illness,
Michelet experienced ecstatic moments of identification with the whole
of history, similar to those that marked Nietzsche's madness. Such visions
of absolute unity, in which consciousness and being are finally at one,
express a deep desire, indeed a spiritual need, to overcome a sense of
dichotomy that at the outset we posited as fundamental to the irrationalism
of the age: the assumption that reason and reality are essentially divided.
Used in this dualistic fashion, the terms "reason" and "real" become
unstable. To the creative imagination the overcoming of this instability
has proved an inspiring adventure and challenge. But in politics and
personal experience the price of stability readily escalates into totali-
tarianism, while that of instability just as quickly falls into anarchy and
decadence.

References

1. IVAN TURGENEV, *Fathers and Children* and *Rudin*, trans. by R. Hare
   (London 1947), p. 151.
2. T. S. ELIOT, "East Coker," III (1940); published in *Four Quartets*
   (London 1944).
3. TURGENEV, *Fathers and Children*, p. 150.
4. *ibid.*, p. 91.
5. *ibid.*, pp. 109–10.
6. *ibid.*, p. 176.

7. JOHANN WOLFGANG VON GOETHE, "Kampagne in Frankreich" (1792). *Sämtliche Werke*, ed. by E. von der Hellen (Stuttgart 1902–7), Vol. XXVII, p. 122.
8. Quoted in KARL LÖWITH, *From Hegel to Nietzsche* (London 1964), p. 180.
9. HEINRICH HEINE, *Zur Geschichte der Religion und Philosophie in Deutschland* (Paris 1835), Bk III.
10. TURGENEV, *Rudin*, pp. 226–7.
11. *ibid.*, p. 269.
12. FRIEDRICH SCHILLER, *Wallenstein* (1799), Part II, Act I, Scene iv.
13. GOETHE, *Faust*, Part I (1806), "Vor dem Tor."
14. *ibid.*, "Studierzimmer."
15. GEORG WILHELM FRIEDRICH HEGEL, *Phänomenologie des Geistes* (1807), Bk IV, Jubiläumsausgabe (Stuttgart 1927–40), II, p. 141.
16. HEGEL, *Vorlesungen über die Aesthetik* (1820–6), *op. cit.*, XIII, p. 228.
17. HEGEL, *Wissenschaft der Logik* (1816), *op. cit.*, IV, pp. 546 f.
18. HEGEL, *Theologische Jugendschriften*, ed. by H. Nohl (Tübingen 1907), p. 225.
19. KARL MARX, *Theses on Feuerbach* (1845), in KARL MARX and FREDERICK ENGELS, *Selected Works* (Moscow 1955), Vol. II, p. 404.
20. FREDERICK ENGELS, *Ludwig Feuerbach and the End of Classical German Philosophy* (1888), in MARX and ENGELS, *op. cit.*, Vol. II, p. 387.
21. CHARLES HENNELL, *Inquiry Concerning the Origin of Christianity* (London 1838), p. viii.
22. GEORGE ELIOT, *The Mill on the Floss* (1860), Bk II, Ch. 1.
23. GEORGE ELIOT, *Middlemarch* (1872), Ch. 85, "Finale."
24. *ibid.*
25. *ibid.*
26. *ibid.*
27. *ibid.*, Ch. 27.
28. *ibid.*, Ch. 12.
29. *ibid.*, Ch. 78.
30. *ibid.*, Ch. 14.
31. *ibid.*, Ch. 20.
32. *ibid.*, Ch. 21.
33. *ibid.*, Ch. 30.
34. SØREN KIERKEGAARD, *Concluding Unscientific Postscript* (Copenhagen 1846), trans. by D. F. Swenson and W. Lowrie (Princeton 1941), p. 98.
35. *ibid.*, p. 294.
36. *ibid.*, p. 295.
37. *ibid.*, p. 107.
38. *ibid.*, p. 78.
39. FRANZ KAFKA, "Aphorism 80," in *Wedding Preparations in the Country and Other Posthumous Prose Writings*, ed. by M. Brod (London 1954), p. 47.

40. FRIEDRICH SCHLEGEL, *Philosophie der Geschichte* (Vienna 1828), Vorlesung (lecture) 18.

41. NOVALIS (Friedrich von Hardenberg), *Die Christenheit oder Europa* (1799).

42. FRIEDRICH SCHLEGEL, *Gespräch über die Poesie* (1799).

43. GEORG BÜCHNER, Letter to his family, March 1834.

44. See GEORG LUKÁCS, *Die Zerstörung der Vernunft*, Gesamtausgabe (Neuwied, Berlin 1962 ff.), IX.

45. F. W. J. VON SCHELLING, *Sämtliche Werke* (Stuttgart 1856–8), Vol. II, iii, p. 57.

46. *ibid.*, Vol. I, iv, p. 361.

47. *ibid.*, Vol. I, iii, p. 369.

48. *ibid.*, Vol. I, iii, p. 627.

49. Quoted and translated by J. P. STERN, *Re-interpretations* (London 1964), pp. 165–6.

50. ARTHUR SCHOPENHAUER, *Sämtliche Werke* (Wiesbaden 1949), Vol. II, p. 116.

51. *ibid.*, Vol. III, p. 19.

52. *ibid.*, Vol. II, p. 133.

53. *ibid.*, Vol. II, p. 131.

54. *ibid.*, Vol. III, pp. 176–7.

55. *ibid.*, Vol. III, pp. 180–1.

56. *ibid.*, Vol. III, pp. 187–8.

57. *ibid.*, Vol. III, p. 190.

58. MATTHEW ARNOLD, "The Study of Poetry" (Introduction to *The English Poets*, ed. by T. H. Ward [London 1880]); the phrases immediately following are taken from Arnold's *Culture and Anarchy* (1869).

59. SCHOPENHAUER, *op. cit.*, Vol. III, pp. 185–6.

60. *ibid.*, Vol. II, pp. 437 f.

61. *ibid.*, Vol. II, p. 487.

62. FRIEDRICH NIETZSCHE, *Werke*, Musarionausgabe (Munich 1922), Vol. XII, p. 92.

63. *ibid.*, Vol. XIII, p. 236.

64. FYODOR DOSTOYEVSKY, *The Possessed* (1871–2), trans. by Constance Garnett (London 1914), p. 432.

65. "Stavrogin's Confession," trans. by R. Lord in *Dostoyevsky, Essays and Perspectives* (London 1970), p. 121.

66. FYODOR DOSTOYEVSKY, *Notes from the House of the Dead* (1860–2), trans. by Constance Garnett (London 1915), p. 46.

67. FYODOR DOSTOYEVSKY, *Crime and Punishment* (1866), trans. by David Magarshack (paperback: Harmondsworth 1951), p. 345.

68. FYODOR DOSTOYEVSKY, letter to N. N. Strakhov, 18 September 1863.

69. *ibid.*

70. FYODOR DOSTOYEVSKY, *The Idiot* (1868–9), trans. by E. M. Martin (London 1914; repr. 1963), p. 408.

71. VIRGINIA WOOLF, *To the Lighthouse* (London 1927), Part I, Ch. 11.

72. In his poem "Le cimetière marin" (1920).
73. FYODOR DOSTOYEVSKY, *A Raw Youth* (1875), trans. by Constance Garnett (London 1916), p. 462.
74. DOSTOYEVSKY, *The Possessed*, p. 376.
75. "I am the devil and nothing human, I think, is alien to me" (*Homo sum: humani nil a me alienum puto*: Terence, *The Self-Tormentor*, Act I, Scene I).
76. FYODOR DOSTOYEVSKY, *The Brothers Karamazov* (1879–80), trans. by David Magarshack (paperback: Harmondsworth 1958), Vol. II, p. 755.
77. *ibid.*, Vol. II, p. 750.
78. DOSTOYEVSKY, *The Possessed*, p. 31.
79. IVAN ALEXANDROVICH GONCHAROV, *Oblomov* (1859), trans. by David Magarshack (London 1954).
80. Lenin's speech to a meeting of the Communist Group at the All-Russia Congress of Metalworkers, 6 March 1922, in V. I. LENIN, *Collected Works* (Moscow 1966), Vol. XXXIII, pp. 223–4.
81. ALFRED LORD TENNYSON, "Break, Break, Break" (1834).
82. JOHN KEATS, "Bright Star!" (1819).
83. HIPPOLYTE ADOLPHE TAINE, *History of English Literature*, trans. by H. van Laun (London 1920).

CHAPTER 5

The Elegiac Note in Tennyson, Arnold, Pushkin, and Leopardi

John Holloway*

In this essay I attempt to throw light on an area of English poetry by a comparison with the work of two poets writing in other languages. The critical work that seems to give the best clue to these poets collectively is one in a fourth language: Schiller's *Über naive und sentimentalische Dichtung* (1795). The essay is doubtless too widely known for its title to mislead, but I had better point out that Schiller does not use either *naiv* or *sentimentalisch* in a condemnatory sense. While he fairly clearly prefers the first to the second, by *naiv* he means something akin to what folk-song enthusiasts mean by "ethnic"; and *sentimentalisch* one may equate variously with "literary" or "sophisticated" or even—in terms of the latter part of Schiller's essay—"idealistic." The "sentimental" poet (in Schiller's special sense) is one who, far from being a simple piece of Nature, *wird sie suchen* (will be a seeker after Nature). He is so, because he is one for whom unity of being (*ungeteilte sinnliche Einheit; ein harmonierendes Ganze*) is not a sensuous fact of life but a moral ideal: something that is not realized in fact, but toward which the poet must strive. Schiller goes on to say that the sentimental poet turns of necessity to one or other of two modes: the *satiric*, or the *elegiac*.

Schiller's ideas call to mind several English poems of the mid-19th century, notably Tennyson's "The Lotus Eaters" (1833). Some may recall only the elegiac note of this poem—the "eternal note of sadness," to use Arnold's phrase in "Dover Beach"—and think that what most characterizes the poem is the "music that gentlier on the spirit lies/Than tired eyelids upon tired eyes"; or lines such as:

* Reader in Modern English Literature and Fellow of Queens' College, Cambridge.

> Why are we weigh'd upon with heaviness,
> And utterly consumed with sharp distress,
> While all things else have rest from weariness?
> All things have rest: why should we toil alone,
> We only toil, who are the first of things,
> And make perpetual moan. . . .

Yet such an impression would be incomplete. The idleness of the lotus eaters is an idleness "like Gods together." Its antithesis is not the activeness of their previous life but its disorganization:

> Rolled to starboard, rolled to larboard, when the surge
> was seething free.

This is one with the disorganization left behind at home, which they doubt if they could put right even if they tried:

> Is there confusion in the little isle?
> . . . The Gods are hard to reconcile.
> 'Tis hard to settle order once again,
> There is confusion worse than death. . . .

The sirens' music answers the mariners' questioning; and it offers a harmony wider than that of music. But to whom does it bring this harmony? The whole of Section VI of the poem, from which the above lines are taken, makes this clear. It speaks of "our wedded lives," of the "island princes" who have "eat our substance." Only when it is clear who these lotus eaters are is the almost explosive force of the first line revealed:

> "Courage!" he said, and pointed toward the land. . . .

Clearly, the speaker is none other than Ulysses himself; or rather, it is an anti-Ulysses who transvalues Ulysses' values, and finds the goal of his journeying and striving in the very place where Homer's hero refused to seek it.

Once one recognizes that "The Lotus Eaters" is a poem offering solution and "harmony" to seeking and striving, then something is also explained about the poem "Ulysses," which is a kind of companion-piece to it. Here the elegiac quality, the "eternal note of sadness," is not dominant but it is certainly prominent; and many readers of the poem have seen this simply as betraying the fact that Tennyson's romantic sensibility clashed with his epic intention. This is to forget that, thanks to Virgil (the poet he most admired), Tennyson believed that the note of *lacrimae rerum* was itself at the very heart of epic. If Ulysses is indeed a hero and an incomparably travelled man, it is in the nature of things that he travels "with a hungry heart"; that he can say "all times I have enjoyed/Greatly, have suffered greatly"; that he proposes to sail the "broad dark seas" and to go "beyond the sunset." The one poem is counterpart to the other. If courage and wandering, seeking and striving, are background to the "mild-eyed melancholy Lotus eaters" in the first poem, then naturally, in the other, to "drink life to the lees" through unresting heroic endeavour will bring with it no extrovert immersion in a plethora of transient gaieties, but a brooding sense that

> . . . all experience is an arch wherethro'
> Gleams that untravell'd world, whose margin fades
> Forever and forever when I move.

We are reminded of how Schiller describes the *sentimentalisch* character in its most general terms: "The sentimental mind has no character except a restless spirit of speculation that is impatient at every limited act of understanding, and presses forward toward the absolute."

Once it is clear that the heroic seafaring of these poems claims attention for the spiritual seeking it represents, there is no surprise in finding affinities with poems of a non-heroic kind. Arnold said to his Scholar Gypsy (my italics here, and also below):

> Thou waitest for the *spark from heaven!*

The metaphor, and its underlying meaning, is comparable with Ulysses' rainbow arch. In each case, the goal is that "more-than-experience," by virtue of which the mind, *sentimentalisch* but not sentimental, augments and significates experience. There may seem to be a contrast between Ulysses' "equal temper of heroic hearts," and the Scholar Gypsy who trails his fingers idly in the stripling Thames, who sits "leaning backward in a pensive dream" (lotus-eater-like) with his plucked flowers in his lap, or who is seen "hanging on a gate" watching the threshers. But although he is reticent and passive, it is his own powers, not those of the people he contrasts with, that are "firm to the mark." It is he who is "still nursing the unconquerable hope"; a Ulysses wise enough to have divined that, in a world of bustlers, it is the waiter or the seemingly idle wanderer who is most meaningfully the seeker.

Nor, by the same token, need one be surprised that in Arnold's "Thyrsis" (1866) a walk up the hills of Oxfordshire simply to find a tree warrants comparison with Ulysses' heroic intentions:

> Who, if not I, for *questing* here hath power?

Arnold exclaims, as he thinks again of the "fugitive and gracious light" that the Scholar Gypsy, Clough (who is the subject of the poem), and he himself, all "seek" ("light" and "seek" both bring one back to Schiller). Finally, Clough's closing message to Arnold runs:

> Why faintest thou? I wandered till I died.
> Roam on! The light we sought is shining still.

His also was no idle wandering. Thyrsis does not wish to "smite/The sounding furrows" like Ulysses; but his withdrawn and elusive seeking is just as real a striving, just as intent a pursuit of the ideal. In "The Lotus Eaters" and in "Ulysses," too, Tennyson seems only to be reviewing the *possibility* of a certain poetic enterprise. One of these poems is about renouncing a voyage, and the other is about preparing for one. Arnold's elegiac poems frequently do just what Tennyson's poems leave undone. "Haworth Churchyard," "Obermann," "Obermann Once More," "Heine's Grave," and indeed "Thyrsis" itself, are more than elegies about people: each is a meditation on the occasion of *concluding* a pilgrimage. So, too, is "Stanzas from the Grande Chartreuse," in which the recurrent purpose of all these pilgrimages is made explicit. Arnold exclaims, as the Alpine climb concludes

> Approach, for what we seek is here!

And what is it that the poet seeks? "Take me," he writes

> . . . and fence me round
> Till I possess my soul again.

If there is an elegiac note, an "eternal note of sadness," in these poems, it is there in the first place because something is lost, or at least is wanted and not possessed. It is there also because, in view of what this thing is, it has to be sought in gentleness and quiet. But it is there above all because for these poets the essential nature of the quest seems to unite deprivation with loneliness. What is sought—to possess one's soul again—is exactly what, in the nature of the case, the social and communal cannot give. Moreover, this makes its way most intimately into several of Arnold's poems, controlling the smallest details of setting, situation, and incident, and contributing powerfully to the emotional quality and resonance of the poems.

In "Haworth Churchyard," for example, it is surely the overriding weight of the personal question ("Unquiet souls! . . . ye shall find yourselves again," the poem ends) that explains the distant, unaware quality of Arnold's reference to the Yorkshire miners:

> Where, behind Keighley . . .
> . . . a rough, grimed race have their homes—
> There on its slope is built
> The moorland town.

The most generic word he could find—"race"—expresses Arnold's sense that the miners and their town are irrelevant. "But," the poem significantly goes on:

> . . . the church
> Stands on the crest of the hill,
> Lonely and bleak.

If "but" means anything here that "and" would not mean, it is to stress the "lonely and bleak" that is the poem's concern—a concern in which the social would be only a distraction.

Arnold's sense that the "seeking" is inner and personal, that the social can have nothing to say to it, comes out also, in a remarkable way, in what he has to say about Wordsworth in "Memorial Verses":

> He laid us as we lay at birth
> On the cool flowery lap of earth. . . .
> Our youth returned; for there was shed
> On spirits that had long been dead,
> Spirits dried up and closely furl'd,
> The freshness of the early world.

If one thinks of "Resolution and Independence," "Salisbury Plain," "Peter Bell," many of the most important passages in "The Prelude," or the "still sad music of humanity" that Wordsworth so stresses in "Tintern Abbey," it becomes clear that Arnold's insight is very partial. He must simply not have seen Wordsworth the poet of deep human affections, of the archaic simplicity and reality of the social bond. What he sees is the Wordsworth of "I wandered lonely as a cloud."

It is mistaken to think of "The Scholar Gypsy" (1853) and "Thyrsis" as escapist pieces without grasp of everyday reality. Everyday reality then was not what it is now. The detail of both these poems is full and rich; not a literary imitation—from Shakespeare, say—but an intimate and genuine extract from mid-19th-century English rural life on the fringes of the West Country.

> Shepherds had met him on the Hurst in spring
>   At some lone alehouse in the Berkshire moors
>   On the warm ingle-bench, the smock-frocked boors,
> Had found him seated at their entering. . .

185

> For most, I know, thou lov'st retired ground!
>   Thee at the ferry Oxford riders blithe,
>   Returning home on summer-nights, have met
> Crossing the stripling Thames at Bab-lock-hithe,
>   Trailing in the cool streams thy fingers wet,
>   As the punt's rope chops round. . . .
>
> And then they land, and thou art seen no more!
>   Maidens, who from the distant hamlets come
>   To dance around the Fyfield elm in May,
> Oft through the darkening fields have seen thee roam
>   Or cross a stile into the public way.

Arnold's description, real as it may be, is intensely selective. The "smock-frocked boors" in the "lone alehouse" on the Berkshire Downs often *met* the Scholar Gypsy "on the warm ingle-bench . . . at their entering"; but "mid their drink and clatter, he would fly." The "riders blithe" *meet him* sitting solitary in the ferry-punt at Bablock hythe. The country girls have *seen him*, a solitary figure, as they come to their dances around the "Fyfield elm." Similarly, in other stanzas, the Scholar Gypsy hangs on a gate "to *watch* the threshers." The children "have known thee *eying* . . . the springing pastures," as they gather cresses, and *watch* him "move slow away." The poet himself "once . . . passed thee" battling against a snowstorm, and turning to *watch* the "line of festal light in Christ-Church hall." Details in "Thyrsis" belong here too: the boatman's girl unmoors the skiff in which Thyrsis and the poet journey away; the mowers suspend their scythes to watch them pass; the lights come out in the scattered farms; the poet is left in the darkness with his journey uncompleted. Every time, it is *removal* from the social group and its communal activities (whether labour or otherwise is unimportant) that receives the stress. Often, that communal activity seems to be deliberately suspended in order that the poignantly personal moment can open before us and fill our minds. It is in this "suspension" of the communal, for the sake of the inner, that the elegiac note, the note of sadness, is to be heard.

Pushkin is a poet altogether more intricate and subtle than Arnold. The unwary might proceed to study the elegiac note in *Yevgeny Onegin* (1833), and perhaps see—more or less as Bottom puts it in *A Midsummer Night's Dream*—only an ass's head of their own. For example, the "verses full of lovers' nonsense" that Lensky composes before the duet, come as near as anything in the poem to plain if gentle burlesque of the whole romantic-elegiac mode. Yet even here, Pushkin in the end remains enigmatic in his own attitude to the lines. It is no more possible to see

Yevgeny Onegin as out-and-out burlesque of the melancholy and elegiac than it is possible to see Shakespeare's early comedy as out-and-out burlesque of being in love and of putting love into poetry. Yet to look in detail at what creates the elegiac note in the poem is to find something that in general is wholly different from Arnold.

The striking fact is that it is not Pushkin's major characters and their inner life that provide the note of sadness (the beautiful lines on the moment of Lensky's death are an exception). What really brings the pang, the eternal note of sadness, is the sudden intrusion into the private and personal story of man's continuing common life. In Chapter I there is a deeply evocative picture of the river Neva at night. But although Yevgeny himself stands "pensively" by the riverside wall, the elegiac pensiveness of the scene is evoked for the reader by the sentries who call to each other, and are scarcely heard in the dark and distance; by the rattle of a droshky in a far-off street; by the rowing-boat the oarsman sends gliding down the sleeping river; by the sound of a distant watchman's or boatman's horn; by the sound of someone singing. It is these touches of ordinary humans at their ordinary affairs that, in the poet's own words, "held us enchanted." This is not common life introduced to surround the protagonists, watch them, and turn them into a cynosure. It is common life significant in its own right.

In Chapter III, Tatyana tells her old nurse that she is in love. But the pathos and sadness of this celebrated incident in no way arise through Tatyana herself. "I've fallen in love," she whispers "sorrowfully"—and the old nurse answers, "my dearest one, you must be ill." It is an old joke, and it does not fail here. But the note of sadness came earlier on (Ch. III, stanza 17), when the nurse lamented that she had forgotten the stories she once could tell:

> А нынче всё мне тёмно, Таня:
> Что знала, то забыла. Да,
> Пришла худая череда!
> Зашибло. . . .

> (But now everything is dark to me, Tanya; I have forgotten what I knew. Yes, a bad turn of things has come! It's gone confused. . . .)

This too has a familiar ring. But the parallels are other ones. "We have seen the best of our time"; "and these same crosses spoil me." In idea, and in poignant simplicity of style, this is not Romantic cult of sensibility, but a truly Shakespearean vision of the common lot. And it is through the nurse, not Tatyana, that Pushkin invites us to look most deeply into the nature of youth, girlhood, virginity. In the next stanza the old woman recalls her own early forced marriage:

Я горько плакала со страха,
Мне с плачем косу расплели,
Да с пеньем в церковь повели.

(I bitterly wept with fear, and the others in tears unbraided my hair, and then sang as they led me to the church.)

To this whole range of experience, Pushkin's mind naturally turns. Thinking of the mists, the falling leaves, the geese heading south in autumn, his mind passes to the tilled fields empty of labourers, the shepherd and his horn and his sheep, the girl at the spinning wheel, the noise of children skating (IV, 40–2). Morning in the city makes him think of the pedlar on his rounds, the smoke rising from the chimneys, the baker at his work (I, 35). When he depicts Lensky's neglected grave, he comes to reflect on how, now that Olga visits it no more, the old country shepherd has returned once more to sit there and plait his sandals as he used to do. In the poignant sequence in which Tatyana wanders through Yevgeny's house with the old housekeeper, while the untranslatable Russian diminutives thicken on the page, deepening the emotional resonance, it is once again the feelings not of the principal character (though these, of course, we infer), but of the housekeeper, that are explicit:

... "А вот камин;
Здесь барин сиживал один.

... Вот это барский кабинет;
Здесь почивал он, кофий кушал,
Приказчика доклади слушал
И книжку поутру читал ...
И старый барин здесь живал;
Со мной, бывало, в воскреоенье,
Здесь под окном, надев очки,
Играть изволил в дурачки.
Дай Бог душе его спасенье,
А косточкам его покой
В могиле, в мать-земле сырой!"

("There's the fireplace; that's where the master always sat alone. ... And here's the master's study; he used to sleep here, drink his coffee, listen to the steward's reports, and in the mornings he read a book. ... And the old master, this was his place too; and sometimes on Sundays he would put on his glasses and be so good as to play cards with me, here by the window. May God rest his soul, and grant peace to his dear little bones in the grave, in damp mother earth!")

For a moment, Onegin and Tatyana are both forgotten, and what fill our minds and make the moment one of elegy and sorrow are the days of old and their universal rhythms of life: the days that, in the scene mentioned earlier, Tatyana had asked her old nurse to tell her about.

To some extent, one could say that, while Arnold fits Schiller's definition of the *sentimentalisch* poet, Pushkin fits what he says of the *naiv* one. The suggestion could be pushed too far; but when Schiller speaks of Homer's "dry fidelity to the fact," or says that *naiv* poetry is "the offspring of life itself, into which it leads us back," or speaks of the "calm spirit of observation" of the *naiv* character, or likens the *naiv* poet to the "realist," each time he seems to point toward Pushkin and to part of what impresses us in *Yevgeny Onegin*.

Nor is it surprising that Schiller's essay should throw light on the English poets, and also the Russian one. A younger contemporary of Herder, Schiller like him was conscious of the distinctive national past and background of the German culture that was so much his concern, and aware at the same time of developments that were bringing about a more sophisticated and less direct relation between the writer and his society. Schiller stood near a watershed: although he was a member of an advanced intellectual society, he could still look backward and be conscious of the more archaic patterns of the traditional world of northern Europe. (The great folk collection *Das Knaben Wunderhorn* [1805–8] was published within a very few years of Schiller's essay.)

The point is that Pushkin's position was of very much the same kind as Schiller's. In one sense, the Russian poet was a more sophisticated writer than either Tennyson or Arnold; certainly more than the former, who had no awareness of Pushkin as Pushkin had, say, of Byron. Moreover, Pushkin also had a kind of archaic strength that would have been almost impossible for the English Victorians. The Russian upper-class intellectual may have been alive to French culture and German speculation, but he was also a member of a society that belonged to an earlier world: Pushkin died in 1837, only four years after the death of St Seraphim, the last great Russian mediaeval mystic. Outside the two capitals, Pushkin's Russia was still an archaic country. If it was no longer the kind of society that (to recall Schiller's reference) Homer knew, it was still in large part a society centred upon a simple, traditional, exclusive distinction between landlord and serf. Moreover, the inner quality of Russian peasant life at that time is something we can partly gauge. Tolstoy's novel *Childhood* (1852), with its evocation of the tragic grandeur of Grusha the wandering eremite—a familiar figure of the author's early years in the Russian countryside—is set in the period when Pushkin was writing *Yevgeny Onegin*. In so far as Pushkin's attention to rural Russia was not focused on the gentry, it came inevitably to rest on an archaic and traditional order of society, where life was still poignant, sacralized, and charged with feelings that could make it a symbol of the permanent human lot. Turgenev's *A Sportsman's Sketches* (1847) are set in almost exactly the time of Pushkin's poem; and in these the old peasant Cassian, who reproaches the "Sportsman" for shedding the blood that is so precious to God, and the boys on "Byezhin Prairie" with their dreams of the supernatural, are near enough to the world of Justice Shallow and Justice Silence for one to re-affirm the Shakespearean comparison.

Hence, perhaps, the unexpected impression one immediately forms on turning from *Yevgeny Onegin* to Tennyson's *Maud* (1855): that Tennyson is less interested in society and in ordinary people than Pushkin was (as we saw, Tennyson's interest is individualized and inward-turning), yet, for all that, the social structure hinted at in passing in his poem is altogether the more articulated and dynamic of the two. There is no surprise in this: it follows inevitably from the nature of Tennyson's own more advanced and differentiated society. "A Monodrama" may be *Maud*'s subtitle, but it is a monodrama set against a panorama; and the panorama, though it emerges only in outline, hint, and suggestion, is comprehensive and deeply impressive.

In saying this, I am thinking not of the reference to the war, or of the observations about trade and fighting—which are no more than trivial and regrettable appendages to the poem at its beginning and end—but of the panorama of Victorian society that emerges through the central *fiction* of the poem. We begin with a hint of Victorian commercial England: the protagonist's father walking through his own woodlands, half-crazed, "for a great speculation had failed." The son lives on in the old house, set now in only a vestige of the old estate. Below is the village with its ale-house and gossip, its scandal and high-Church Victorian parson. Up the hill—

> Workmen up at the Hall!—They are coming back from
> abroad. . . .

"They," who like so many rich Victorians go on tours to Florence and Rome, are the family that profited by the speculative disaster. The father, with his brand-new peerage, doubtless a bought one, is always up in town; so, for his own pleasures rather than for the family wealth, is the son. Maud is courted by the "new-made lord" with his mock-Gothic castle and new plantations, all based on what his grandfather made from his coalmines. Elsewhere we glimpse the radical "Little Englander"; the Manchester-School orator making a speech at the local market-town; the grand political dinner to maintain the Tory interest; the venality of political life; and the sensational press.

In spite of all this, of course, *Maud* is almost the opposite of a realist, "slice-of-life" poem; and although it is not a poem in which the elegiac note is predominant, it is permeated by something related to that elegiac note:

> Living alone in an empty house . . .
> Till a morbid hate and horror have grown
> Of a world in which I have hardly mixed
> And . . .
> . . . a heart half-turn'd to stone. [I, 6, 8]

This is not the chosen withdrawal of Ulysses or the lotus-eater mariners, nor the other kind of chosen withdrawal of the Scholar Gypsy or of Arnold himself at the Grande Chartreuse. But it is a related situation. The individual is involuntarily separated from his fellows, weighed upon by unhappy emotions ("I have neither hope nor trust," the protagonist says), and seeking, although in the end unsuccessfully, to re-establish contact with those from whom he is separated. This is why Tennyson had to establish the social landscape from which the protagonist is alienated. In one context after another, we encounter the speaker's aloneness, and his half-hearted or abortive attempts at ending it. He is out walking; Maud is

> Over the dark moor land
> Rapidly riding far away. [I, 9]

She waves once to him and, with her two companions, is gone in a moment. Onegin's Tatyana, after wandering about the house "like a shadow," and feeling heartbroken, also goes for a long solitary walk. But Pushkin immediately develops the scene in his usual objective manner: the fisherman's fire on the river-bank, and the village dancers going home. There is a sharp contrast here with Arnold's country-dancing maidens in "The Scholar Gypsy." The latter help to *isolate* Arnold's protagonist: Pushkin's dancers are simply about their own gregarious affairs. Tennyson's hero, and Arnold's, are left solitary: Tatyana's walk brings her to Onegin's house and the kindly old housekeeper.

Again, in *Maud*, the speaker wanders into Maud's garden, and stands outside the sleeping house. (I, 14, 4). After Maud has been "made my

Maud by that long loving kiss," and later on has gone home, the protagonist sits by himself, in the darkness, under the great cedar tree, and
thinks of the "lonely Hell" out of which he has at least partly come. As
he does so, he listens to the sea, rather like Arnold in "Dover Beach":

> Is that enchanted moan only the swell
> Of the long waves, that roll in yonder bay?

He senses, even now, some "dark undercurrent woe" that still troubles.
Later, he is "at the gate alone" in the rose garden at dawn, and this
time Maud is coming: but the course of events takes an unexpected turn,
and in the scenes that follow he is alone on the hillside, thinking of the
fatal duel; he is alone, "a shipwreck'd man," on the French coast; he is
alone, full of remorse, in London; and, in the splendid phantasy that
closes Part II of the poem, the alienation is finally confirmed as he
imagines himself a *felo-da-se*, buried at a city crossroads, cursed with the
eternal noise of his fellow humans all round him, both dead and alive,
in the ground and above, but now forever cut off.

The London daybreak scene in *Maud* (II, 4, 9) calls to mind Section 7
of *In Memoriam* (1850):

> . . . far away
> The noise of life begins again,
> And ghastly through the drizzling rain
> On the bald street breaks the blank day.

Day breaks like this as the poet is standing disconsolately outside the
"park house" where Hallam once lived. In fact, it soon becomes clear
that although in *Maud* the protagonist's unhappiness takes in part the
form of anger and rancour, while in *In Memoriam* this is not so, all the
same there is something of a sustained resemblance as to situation. In
Section 11, the grief-stricken Tennyson looks across over the "high
wold" and the plain of Lincolnshire, but his thoughts are far away, with
Hallam's body brought home on the ship. He is in the condition of
"abstractedness and quiet" that Schiller attributes to the *sentimentalisch*
poet. In Section 23, he wanders alone through an imaginary landscape
to where he and Hallam had had to part company. The once gay scene
is now mournful, but the real point is where Tennyson says he is "in
my sorrow *shut*." What is it to be "in . . . sorrow shut"?* This becomes

---

* This notion of "shut-up-ness" was, for Kierkegaard, one of the most serious forms of demoniacal
dread: "dread of the good," as he calls it in *The Concept of Dread* (1844). See the discussion
of this point in Ch. 4, "Irrationalism."

clear in Section 108, by which point *In Memoriam* has entered the restorative phase of experience:

> I will not shut me from my kind
> And lest I stiffen into stone
> I will not eat my heart alone. . . .

It is easy to infer from this simply that Tennyson, when writing *Maud*, drew again on the experience he had passed through over Hallam's death, and to conclude that this poem also has a marked autobiographical interest. But there is another point of interest: Tennyson, like Arnold, was entering one of the recurrent psychic experiences of his age, and in recording this imaginatively he was expressing the typical 19th-century myth of the individual cut off, isolated. To think of William Crimsworth in Charlotte Brontë's *The Professor*, of Henchard on the bridge in *The Mayor of Casterbridge*, of Gissing's *Henry Ryecroft*, of Iden in Jefferies' *Amaryllis at the Fair*, of George Eliot's *Theophrastus Such*, of Arthur Clennam or Silas Marner, of Hopkins' last sonnets, or of Arnold's poem beginning "Yes, in the sea of life enisl'd/We mortal millions live alone . . .", is to call to mind things that certainly cannot all be seen as one and the same, but that have a real kinship. Nevertheless, this is more than simply a phenomenon of 19th-century England. The literature that created a name for this mythical figure is Pushkin's. In *Maud*, Tennyson is giving his version of the general type that Dostoyevsky depicted in *Notes from Underground* (1864), or that Turgenev depicted in Chulkaturin: the "superfluous man."

It is less clear whether one should see Tennyson's "Oenone" and "Tithonus" as also within this same general range; whether, in short, they disguise a myth-type of the 19th century in myth-tales of classical Greece. But, in each case, the poet has chosen characters who can soliloquize because they have the leisure of loneliness and isolation and are outside the normal pattern of social life. In each case it is these patterns that led to grief, to the "eternal note of sadness." And, in each case, what interests the poet is to enter into the mood of his characters, to depict it from within, to grasp it in as whole a way as he can.

It is at this point that it is illuminating to look at Leopardi.* One of his shorter but most famous poems, "A se stesso" (1833; To himself), could fairly easily be slipped into *Maud* at the moment when the protagonist's embitterment and despair are at their deepest, and he cries:

---

* One useful collection is *Poems from Giacomo Leopardi*, trans. by John Heath-Stubbs (London 1946).

> . . . strike dead the whole weak race of venomous worms
> That sting each other here in the dust. . . . [II, 1, 2]

I am not claiming an identity of feeling; but this could easily have been followed by

> Or poserai per sempre
> Stanco mio cor. . . .
> . . . Non val cosa nessuna
> I moti tuoi, ne di sospiri è degna
> La terra. Amaro e noia
> La vita, altro mai nulla; e fango è il mondo.

> (Now you shall rest forever, my weary heart. . . . Nothing is worth your feeling so deeply, nor is the earth worthy of your sighs. Bitter and tedious [is] life, it is never anything else; and the world is mud.)

The moods of Tennyson and Leopardi are obviously similar. Yet what makes this assimilation possible is that it concerns an extreme point in the work of each poet. "A se stesso" was written at a time when Leopardi was in a quite special state of despair and humiliation, and it has a quite special note of personal preoccupation. One is reminded of the "desperate egoism" that Pushkin found in Byron. "A se stesso" is not typical of Leopardi: its overtly psychological resonance characterizes few of his other poems. But the passage in *Maud* to which I related it comes when the inner struggle of the protagonist reaches a nadir at which it flows into something that is other than personal and is more than personal: something, that is, more like the essential Leopardi.

The two poets arrived at this point of resemblance, however, from opposite directions. A similar line of thought applies to Arnold's poem "Dover Beach." Metrically, this is in a form that makes one wonder if it was written under the influence of Leopardi's verse. Certainly, Arnold seems in the earlier part of the poem not to concentrate on the psychic state of his speaker, but rather to meditate upon the world itself. So one could say that "Dover Beach" brings Arnold nearer than usual to Leopardi's mode of composition—except in the last stanza, beginning

> Ah, love, let us be true
> To one another!

Then, at last, we see Arnold's underlying preoccupation, a preoccupation with release from psychic isolation, transpiring through the seemingly meditative surface.

In Leopardi there is a remarkable contrast between the writer's personal life and his creativity. His family difficulties, his enforced isolation at Recanati, his misfortunes in love—one cannot but see these things as powerfully contributing to form the sort of poetry that he wrote. But if these are largely the *occasion* of his writings and of the note of unhappiness in them, they are, to a small degree only, the actual *substance* of those writings. Leopardi is a most striking example of what one might call the objectification of feelings into convictions. To see, in his work, what such a process is like, is to see how far Arnold and Tennyson were from it, not because they were poor poets, but owing to a radical difference of intent.

In Leopardi's earlier poems, such as "All' Italia" (1818) and "Sopra il monumento di Dante" (On Dante's monument), the objectivity is historical and patriotic. Leopardi laments the past greatness of Italy and its present helplessness before a tyrannical foreign invader. His patriotic lamentations over a *povera patria* that was once great not only in arms but also in the arts—"the divine works" produced by "the inspired Italians"—had been a theme in Italian poetry since even before Petrarch's *canzone* "Italia mia . . . ," which Leopardi's "All' Italia" clearly recalls. To this one should doubtless relate Leopardi's reference to the beauty of the Italian language as spoken by the common people where he lived; his admiration for "this our sovereign tongue, immense, omnipotent"; and, indeed, the whole body of his philological and classical studies.

But what most deserves stress is that this historical dimension of awareness, although less prominent in Leopardi's later work, is by no means absent from it. Almost his last important poem, "La ginestra" (The broom), sees the ruined cities on the side of Mount Vesuvius as "famed," and recalls how the broom that now grows about them also grows outside another and greater city, Rome itself, also fallen from greatness. Similar sentiments are expressed in "La sera del dì di festa" (1820; The evening of the fete day). The idea of a fall from ancient greatness to "new commonness" underlies Leopardi's two satirical epistles on the present age, "Al conte Carlo Pepoli" and the "Palinodia al marchese Gino Capponi." Again: "To weep is not my real inclination . . . but a necessity of the age," is how Leopardi put the matter in the 1820 Dedication to his poems. The two key terms—"*noia*" and "*fango*"—in the passage quoted above from "A se stesso," both appear in the early poem "Ad Angelo Mai," where the historical-patriotic theme is inescapable: the first term in the context of Italy's lost greatness, the second in the phrase "this age of mud," fit only to recover itself or to stand ashamed.

In what way does all this make a contrast, or the first part of a contrast, with the English poets? There is a good deal in Tennyson's verse (*Maud* itself, "Locksley Hall," the "Ode on the Death of the Duke of Wellington," and elsewhere) about the contemporary scene; but it is less rich in detail, and more fragmentary and confused or even self-contradictory, than what one finds in Leopardi, or at least what one finds if the satirical poems are borne in mind. But Tennyson's opinions about his own time were quite unrelated to any sense of English history as a whole, or of the values that could be located in it. This is a large subject, and requires an extended separate discussion; but a reading of Tennyson's historical dramas, along with, say, the poem "Sir John Oldcastle," shows a truly astonishing lack of historical perspective—of a sense of how, in his own time, what was good or bad was involved with, and a reflection of, what was good and what was evil in English history.

In his verse, Arnold simply does not touch on the history of his own country. It is Arnold's prose, and his prose alone, that offers something to set against the richly detailed picture of what we should now call a consumer-oriented, communications-obsessed, never-had-it-so-good world of Leopardi's "Palinodia." Here Arnold's poem "Stanzas from the Grande Chartreuse" is much to the point. A superficial reading might leave the impression that this was a diagnosis of Arnold's own time. On the surface it is about a period

    ... between two worlds, one dead,
    The other powerless to be born. ...

From this, it seems to look forward in cautious hope:

    Years hence, perhaps, may dawn an age
    More fortunate, alas! than we. ...

But the impression is illusory. The poem is concerned with an individually realized spiritual condition. From this particular standpoint, it is another *Maud*. Arnold says that this individual condition exists in response to the objective one, the historical situation: but what this latter is, the poem barely hints at. Set it beside the "Palinodia" or "Sopra il monumento di Dante," and this is transparently clear. The public world was a simple *donnée* for Arnold: it merely set up the conditions for individual psychic realities; and these were his concern. If there is objectivity in Arnold or in Tennyson, it is very much the objectivity of transforming psychic tension into psychic exploration. It has virtually no public dimension.

The poem that finally confirms this is among Arnold's best: "A Southern Night," written at Sete on the death of his brother William.

Arnold sets his poem at night: the evidences of society surrounding the poet serve, by a paradox, only to stress individualization and isolation. All around the poet are the fields and vineyards and olive trees; the scene is typical of the agriculture and productivity of southern France. But in the moonlight the olive trees look like ghosts. Sete itself is asleep; no people, nothing but a curve of "glistering houses white." Once before, the poem says, Arnold employed (in another poem) such a night to "deplore" his "own vexed heart."

But what was the pretext for this mood? William Arnold had had a remarkable career. Invalided home once from India as a soldier, he had returned at the invitation of John Lawrence to organize public education in the Punjab and had continued this work throughout the 1857 Mutiny. His wife died in the Punjab in 1858; and it was after this that William had been invalided home a second time, only to die on the journey. His death, and one poem, were contemporaneous with Arnold's Inaugural Lecture at Oxford, *On the Modern Element in Poetry*, in which his main idea is that great poetry emerges from, and registers, what is fine and great in the civilization of its time. Did William Arnold point to nothing of this kind in Arnold's own civilization? To me, he did; but Arnold was apparently not of the same mind. His brother's public career comes in a single line. He was

> at last fordone
> With public toil and private teen.

So much for this *magnanimo campion*. The phrase is from Leopardi's "A un vincitore nel pallone" (To a victor in the ball-game), another poem in which the author's main concerns are patriotic, historical, and public. William Arnold was a *vincitore* of a more impressive kind.

Here, in one respect, there is a danger of misunderstanding: of thinking that because Tennyson and Arnold, in many of their poems, had the individual and not society as their main field of interest, they were out of sympathy with their society, whereas Leopardi, who concerned himself with it more, was not. Rather the reverse is true. The relation in which both Tennyson and Arnold stood to Victorian England was not quite what it at first appears. True enough, both of them were critics of society and alive to some of its defects. But at the same time, both were upper-middle-class members of a society in which, on the whole, their class was dominant. Despite their criticism, both at bottom accepted membership and endorsed what they were members of: Tennyson in his traditionalism and loyalism, Arnold in his public service and (from at least 1853) in his more general participation in the problems and controversies of the time. The inner tensions that they felt and tried to resolve were, in the last analysis, the strains of belonging. Leopardi's involvement with society was greater only in the sense that his rejection was emphatic, considered, and radical. He saw the presence of the Austrians and the advance of commercialism from the standpoint of the decayed provincial upper class. It was no wonder that—in circumstances of family decline, long isolation in the depths of provincialism, and the very marked absence, over most of his life, of intellectual companionship—he should have more or less turned his back on his own age, and have found his most abiding stimulation and solace in the family library and in the long national past with which it gave him contact. At the same time it is easy to see how his patrician background, and his roots in traditional society, made it possible for him to have a consciousness of peasant humanity that sometimes calls Pushkin to mind.

For this, beyond question, is what one finds. Most of Leopardi's greatest poems are unlike those I have discussed: but neither are they concerned with subjective, psychic explorations. On the contrary, they are not public and historical because they are more generalized, more philosophical, and thus more objective even than the historical. Arnold himself, in his essay on Byron, noticed Leopardi's "grave fulness of knowledge," his superiority in "philosophic thought." There is a passage (1 July 1820) in Leopardi's *Zibaldone* (Notebooks) in which he records this transition from the historical to the general and philosophical:

> The total transformation within me occurred in effect within a year, the year 1819 to be precise, when I began to reflect profoundly about things (in these meditations I have written about matters concerning above all our human nature, different in this from earlier thinkers, who were almost all literary intellectuals), to become a philosopher by profession, and to feel the real unhappiness of the world. . . .

Not, the point is, his own unhappiness; but the world's.

Leopardi's treatment of his subject, however, is not abstract and speculative. Often it is richly perceptive of man's common traditional life, and it is largely this that gives his verse its power. Consider "La quiete dopo la tempesta" (The quiet after the storm) and "Il sabato del villaggio" (1829; Saturday in the village). They take us back at once to a close interest in the simplest things of everyday life seen in themselves and for their own sake. The first thing, after the storm, is that the chickens come out from shelter, and re-appear on the road again. The common noises (*rumorio*) of life and work begin again.

Immediately, one is back in the "realist" world of *Yevgeny Onegin:* even some of the details are the same, such as the sound of the distant carriage in a faraway street, which was one of Pushkin's evocative details in his picture of St Petersburg at night. Some details in "Il sabato del villaggio" also recall Pushkin. There is the *donzelletta* with the burden on her shoulder, which calls to mind the milkmaid (Pushkin also uses the diminutive) in the St Petersburg morning scene. There is the *vecchierella*, the little old woman, who is "telling tales of her good years," quite different from Arnold's housewife darning at her homestead door in the Cumber hills, who merely decorated one of the settings in which the Scholar Gypsy had "been seen."

Each of these two poems by Leopardi is something of a test case, in that each records a scene of apparent repose, fulfilment, and happiness. Life (as the first poem says) seems "sweet" and "welcome." If, even here, Leopardi could find reasons for seeing the human condition as he was prone to see it, he had surely established his case. "La quiete dopo la tempesta" seeks to do this by argument. If it is an outstanding felicity (the poem asks) simply to have emerged from trouble—

> Uscir di pena
> È diletto per noi
>
> (To come out of pain is a pleasure for us)—

then what is the obvious implication for the human lot generally? "Il sabato del villaggio" is more interesting in that it achieves its aim not by argument but by ironical presentation. Look twice at the scene of peace, it seems to say, and what do you find? Hence the juxtaposition of the *donzelletta* and the soon-to-fade "roses and violets" she had plucked; as also of the young girl and the old woman who recalls her own lost youth. The irony of the poem is continuous. When we read

> Or la squilla dà segno
> Della festa che viene
>
> (Now the evening bell announces the fete that is beginning)

it is not only the brief rest of Sunday that the single bell calls to mind. In an earlier poem on a very similar subject, "La sera del dì di festa," Leopardi thought of how

> per la via
> Odo non lunge il solitario canto
> Dell' artigian, che riede a tarda notte.
>
> (Down the road I hear not far away the lonely song of the workman who is going home late at night.)

Simply, the "workman," singing to himself as he goes home. In "Il sabato del villaggio," a workman again goes home (*riede*) from his day's work; and if he is not singing, he is doing the nearest thing: he is whistling (*fischiando*). But this time he is not simply a workman. He is a *digger* (*zappatore*), like, one may add, the sexton; and he is thinking "of the day of his rest," as he goes home to "his sparse table." It is really impossible to deny the irony in all this, any more than one can deny irony in the next stanza, where what one hears, late in the darkness of the Saturday night, is the hammering of the carpenter (*legnaiuolo*), who has to finish what he is making by dawn. What Carpenter's work, inevitably, does this bring to mind?

All this is to say that, in this poem, Leopardi is looking more deeply even than usual at the general tenor of ordinary life—looking (as I said) not once but twice; and it is this profound and considered scrutiny of the human condition, down to its inner and hidden quality, that normally comprises the substance of Leopardi's verse, and not his personal psychological predicament at all. The English poets are poets of another kind. Their "note of sadness" is by no means always directly "personal." Sometimes it is dramatic, and if behind the dramatic setting we detect the poet's own predicament, so do we also behind the *filosofo* in Leopardi. But it was an "eternal" note, for Tennyson and Arnold, in the psychological sense. One might use for it a phrase of Macbeth's: a "rooted sorrow," one peculiarly difficult to dislodge because it was part of the very structure of the psyche. It was the confrontation and exploration of such a psyche, in its different varieties and moments, that they undertook. The enterprise was intrinsically less demanding and ambitious than those—different as they were—undertaken by Pushkin and Leopardi: but it was no mere esoteric obsession. It was a psychic condition, clearly, that meant much to their age—as it does to the 20th century also; or so, at least, works such as "Prufrock" and *L'etranger* and Kafka's *The Burrow*, in their very different ways, lead one to suppose.

Only one English poem of this period seems of the same kind as *Yevgeny Onegin*: far less good, far less of a poem, but still one of the finest verse works of its period. The author was "Thyrsis" himself: what I have in mind is Clough's "Amours de voyage" (1849). Arnold read this poem in 1853 and said that it did not "suit" him. His elegy in effect ignores it; and although the poem was serialized in the *Atlantic Monthly* in 1858, it did not appear in England until some years after Clough's death. In "Amours de voyage," quite objectively, and in a wholly dramatized form, Clough shows that he comprehends life on the social plane as well as on the personal and inner one. The "life," the "society" objectively seen, is not simply that of Rome itself at the time when the poem is set—the brief republican period of 1849. Memorable as the war scenes are, incisive as is the insight they display, they belong to the background. Clough was an English poet, not a Roman one. He had an objective understanding of the life of his little group of English in Italy—half-resident, half-tourist as they all were. He had seen the rootless isolation of their restless but cultivated existence. With beautiful tact, he allows all this to emerge from nothing but what they themselves say. At the end, when the *amour de voyage* has been dissipated in the uncertainty and half-heartedness of their whole mode of existence, something a little like the note of elegy is heard:

> Rome is fallen; and fallen, or falling, heroical Venice. . . .

and

> He has not come as yet; and now I must hardly expect it.

The tone is so muted—almost wooden—that one can easily be tempted into seeing "Amours de voyage" as an unpoetical poem. I myself find that its artistry and poignancy impress me more at each reading: it is certainly the most unblemished longer English poem of its period.

It would be easy enough to argue that Clough's more objective treatment sprang from a greater social involvement, which had caused him to migrate from the seclusion of Oxford to the new University of London. But this argument is superficial. Objectivity and realism in writing about a little expatriate group of the kind depicted in Clough's poem cannot very convincingly be related, either in general to the conditions of mid-19th-century social and intellectual life in England, or in particular to the religious restrictions attached to holding a Fellowship at Oxford that exercised so much influence on Clough's career. Clough's handling of his tale seems more localized in its meaning, and more aesthetic in its implications. Perhaps this is the point at which the interrelation between literature and society, if it does not break down, at least loses its sharpness and cogency. If so, that would serve only to add to the variegated picture of social background, artistic intent, and literary substance that this discussion has set before the reader.

CHAPTER 6

The Bourgeois Imagination

Literature and Class Prejudice in Mid-19th-Century England

Laurence Lerner*

With varying degrees of consciousness, the Victorian bourgeoisie had an ideology.

> "We have shown the example of a nation," said Palmerston, "in which every class in society accepts with cheerfulness the lot which Providence has assigned to it; while at the same time every individual of each class is constantly striving to raise himself in the social scale—not by injustice and wrong, not by violence and illegality, but by persevering good conduct, and by the steady and energetic execution of the moral and intellectual faculties with which his Creator endowed him."[1]

Palmerston may sometimes look like the rugged survivor of an earlier age, but here he is speaking for the middle classes of 1850. Society is a struggle between individuals, a total but not too unpleasant struggle, in which self-help, virtue, and initiative lead to success. The fittest survive.

This picture of English society can be matched from a thousand sources. Beatrice Webb's mother believed that "it was the bounden duty of every citizen to better his social status; to ignore those beneath him, and to aim steadily at the top rung of the ladder."[2] A biographer wrote of Ebenezer Elliott that "free trade was his religion, and heaven was paved with cheap bread and rich mozaics of golden untaxed grain."[3] Cobden delighted in telling his fellow-Britons "that nobody can help them until they are determined to help themselves."[4] Between self-help, moral improvement, *laissez-faire*, struggle for survival, and progress there is sufficient resemblance for us to see them as a single complex of ideas;

* Professor of English, University of Sussex.

because of the glow of approval that suffuses them we can call them an ideology; and there is no doubt which class they served the interests of. This ideology turns up in expected and unexpected places. Darwin's theory of natural selection has many resemblances to it; and in a famous passage in his autobiography he tells how he got the germ of his theory from reading Malthus's *Essay on the Principle of Population* in 1838—an admission that Marx and Engels did not fail to pounce on: ". . . nothing discredits modern bourgeois development so much as the fact that it has not yet succeeded in getting beyond the economic forms of the animal world."[5] In discussions of the history of ideas, too, we find a belief in the survival of the fittest—not, as it happens, in Mill, who believed that the best ideas could be defeated in the struggle, that truth unaided might lose to falsehood; but in, for instance, Robert Owen:

> Let truth unaccompanied with error be placed before them; give them time to examine it and to see that it is in unison with all previous ascertained truths, and conviction and acknowledgment of it will follow of course.[6]

To find a name for this ideology we can turn to George Eliot. "If you are weary of English unrest," she wrote from Weimar, "of that society of 'eels in a jar,' where each is trying to get its head above the other, the somewhat stupid 'bien-être' of the Weimarians will not be an unwelcome contrast."[7] Eels in a jar: there, in a moment of irritation—or detachment—George Eliot has characterized the bourgeois ideal. The irked, acerb flavour of the phrase makes it all the more useful as a name: this is the acerbity that sees shrewdly, but without total hostility. George Eliot is not wholly unsympathetic to bourgeois self-help, but she is not taken in by it. For more complete hostility, we can look to those critics whose very style rejects the comfortable assumptions around them, Carlyle and Ruskin. Carlyle respected—or was prepared to respect—the captains of industry, but only in so far as they renounced "eels in a jar" for a traditional pre-bourgeois conception of service and responsibility: "Enlightened Egoism, never so luminous, is not the rule by which man's life can be led . . . 'laissez-faire,' 'Supply-and-demand,' 'Cash-payment for the sole nexus,' and so forth were not, are not, and will never be, a practicable Law of Union for a Society of Men."[8]

The eccentric Germanizing of Carlyle's language enacts the rejection that such a passage announces: it has individuality, but not the individuality his bourgeois readers expected. Carlyle's individuality is wholly a matter of style. He loves writing metaphysics about the absolute, but in this swamp where so many Victorians drowned formlessly he is continually giving vigorous linguistic kicks. He "reaches forth into the void deep," he is "alone with the Universe," but in the very act of telling us to look on man's soul instead of his appearance, he lays that appearance in front of us, dressed in pure Carlylese:

> Shall we tremble before clothwebs and cobwebs, whether woven in Arkwright looms, or by the silent Arachnes that weave unrestingly in our Imagination?[9]

The result is a strange mixture of perversity and insight, the one impossible without the other. Was it perversity or insight that eccentrically claimed in 1843 that advertising was a natural consequence of *laissez-faire* supply-and-demand, and that treated advertising as a cultural, and not merely as a commercial, phenomenon?

> Consider, for example, that great Hat seven-feet high, which now perambulates London streets; which my Friend Sauerteig regarded justly as one of our English notabilities; "the topmost point as yet," said he, "would it were your culminating and returning point, to which English Puffery has been observed to reach."[10]

Sauerteig, the comic, learned German who is wiser than the serious English, is of course an echo of Teufelsdröckh, professor of Allerlei-Wissenschaft at the University of Weissnichtwo, the grotesque hero of *Sartor Resartus* (1835). Teufelsdröckh is a perfect persona for the comments that Carlyle offers in this book: he is created from the author's awareness that his own style is grotesque, comic, and indispensable. He is a true persona, for Carlyle is both detached from him and deeply identified with him: Teufelsdröckh is ridiculous but profound, the licensed fool who sees through the pretensions of English society. We can see the brilliance of this conception if we compare it with Matthew Arnold's pallid imitation in *Friendship's Garland* (1871), which presents a similar attack on "eels in a jar" through the comments of the author's German friend Arminius. Is a self-administering community an ideal, Arminius asks himself. "That depends entirely on what the self-administering community is like. If it has 'Geist,' and faith in 'Geist,' yes; if it has not, no."[11] Now if we replace "Geist" by "culture," this has the exact shape and tone of a sentence from *Culture and Anarchy*: Arnold has used a German word, but he has continued to talk in his own urbane, judicious, slightly self-satisfied voice, quite unlike the thin intense scream of Teufelsdröckh's brilliant grotesquerie. Arnold does not need the persona as Carlyle does, and therefore cannot use it so effectively.

The other great critic of bourgeois ideology is Ruskin. "Your ideal of human life," he told the bourgeoisie of Bradford, "is that it should be passed in a pleasant undulating world with iron and coal everywhere underneath it." He then went on to analyse what he called the Goddess of Getting-on. " 'Nay,' you say, 'they have all their chance.' Yes, so has every one in a lottery, but there must always be the same number of blanks."[12] It is not easy to decide whether to call Carlyle and Ruskin reactionary or radical. Bourgeois ideology may be measured—and rejected—in comparison with the past or with the future. "Insisting on the need for government and speaking with scorn of liberty" could sound like an old Tory or a new Socialist. The famous controversy on progress between Southey and Macaulay[13] is similarly ambivalent. Southey writes as a very old Tory indeed (the social comments of his *Colloquies* are delivered by the ghost of Sir Thomas More), yet his rejection of industrialism because it is ugly reads like a first crude sketch of the view of William Morris, and his trust in "the intermeddling of Mr Southey's idol, the omniscient and omnipotent State," would have been denounced as socialism two generations later. There is nothing misleading about this ambivalence: it is a reminder that the best way to analyse mid-19th-century social attitudes is not—as Victorians such as Trollope assumed—by a two-fold division into conservative and liberal, but by a three-fold scheme such as Dicey's.[14] Analysing the relation between law and public opinion in England, Dicey divided the 19th century into three periods: a paternalist period in which the state was thought of as bearing social responsibilities; the (surprisingly brief) heyday of *laissez-faire*, in which the state was reduced to a night-watchman; and the beginnings of modern collectivism, in which the state once more extends its functions. It is easy to see how the first and last phases resemble each other in contrast to the individualism of the middle one; and it should not surprise us, therefore, to find Marx and Engels sympathetic to the "reactionary" Carlyle, or to see the close resemblance between Ruskin's critique of Victorian England and that of Marx. "The labourer is brought face to face with the intellectual potencies of the material process of production, as the property of another":[15] this is not very different from the analysis of the "degradation of the operative into a machine," the complaint that "it is not, truly speaking, the labour that is divided; but the men."[16] When Morris divides society into three classes—"a class which does not even pretend to work, a class which pretends to work but which produces nothing, and a class which works, but is compelled by the other two classes to do work which is often unproductive"[17]—it is not easy to be sure if this is the disciple of Ruskin or of Marx that we are hearing. One conclusion that might flow from this will not be altogether palatable to the Marxist: that the brilliant analysis of "the separation of the labourer from his means of production," which comes in the first volume of *Capital*, is an analysis not of the effects of capitalism, but of industrialism itself.

Two brief examples will show the presence of "eels in a jar" in the Victorian novel. Mark Rutherford's *Catherine Furze* contains some very shrewd analyses of social prejudices in a market town, and of the friction as one class rubs against the jagged edge of another. Old Mr Furze, the ironmonger, loses his shop in a fire, and is never the same man again; when his business re-opens, it is really held together by his young assistant Tom—clever, helpful, and the very model of the industrious prentice, 19th-century style, for he has mechanical ingenuity and the business sense of an *entrepreneur*. Tom's great enemy is Mrs Furze, who considers him pushing, and urges her husband to discharge him. There is no doubt that Mark Rutherford prefers Tom's enterprise to Mrs Furze's snobbery, but what is more interesting than his preference, and shows his sensitivity to social forces, is his awareness of Tom's power. Because he knows how to run a business unsentimentally, and Mr Furze no longer does, Tom is indispensable, and the haughty contempt of Mrs Furze ("send him about his business at once, before he . . . gets hold of your connexion")[18] is the anger of a class whose status has outlived its function. Tom is not pushing, but his personal modesty cannot undo the effect of his expertise, and as customers notice that he is the one who understands the business, he will inevitably get hold of the connection—or would have, if the novelist had not taken over from the social historian and given the plot a twist.

Catherine Furze, set in the 1840s, was not published till 1893. But the early Victorian decades did not need to wait two generations for analysis: they were very well aware of themselves. Elizabeth Gaskell, for all her old-world charm, was a remarkably up-to-date writer; and her mixture of old and new appears very strikingly in one of her most vivid characters, Ebenezer Holman, the farmer and Congregationalist minister in *Cousin Phillis* (1865). This sad (and grossly neglected) little story is told by a young apprentice engineer who visits the Holman family, relatives of his mother, and watches a love affair ripen between their daughter Phillis and his attractive, ambitious boss, Holford. This love story is the main theme of *Cousin Phillis*, but quite as interesting is the undercurrent that shows us that four of the characters (Paul, the narrator; his father; Holford; and Ebenezer Holman, who is really the hero) share a bond: they are all at home with the Industrial Revolution. Holman, deeply conservative in his moral values, is very talented mechanically, and in one gay little scene he listens attentively while Paul's father demonstrates how a turnip-cutter could be improved, and scrawls his points in charcoal on poor Mrs Holman's immaculate dresser. When Paul's ignorance of humanistic learning is first exposed he feels an aggrieved wish to defend himself to Phillis (" 'She shall see I know something worth knowing, though it mayn't be her dead-and-gone languages,' thought I"); this is childish enough to be rather attractive, but later we realize that he has been inarticulately confessing his allegiance to another and newer culture, the culture of (say) John Thornton, the hero of *North and South* (1855), the practical manufacturer who understands the classics because he understands life, who explains to the scholarly Mr Hale "the magnificent power, yet delicate adjustment of the might of the steam-hammer, which recalled to Mr Hale some of the wonderful stories of subservient genii in the Arabian Nights."[19]

Such, in unavoidable brevity, is a possible sketch of the bourgeois ideology, as seen by its defenders, its critics, and its novelists. It was often the novelists who saw more clearly than anyone that self-help and *laissez-faire* were the doctrines of an industrial culture, and that the real cultural revolutionaries, the men who were subverting traditional social assumptions, were those who were inventive mechanically. They might be conservative in many of their opinions, but their allegiance to the new skills led to an acceptance of new forms of organization, and made them, rather than those of advanced political views, the true plotters for the future.

If this complex of ideas was truly an ideology, then it must have shaped perception of social realities, and so have influenced the version of these that appears in Victorian literature. Let us therefore take a single social reality that could be perceived in very different ways. When the Victorian bourgeoisie looked at their social world, the one thing they constantly saw, and yet in a sense never saw, was the working classes. Here is one crucial application of the ideology, which will now form the subject of this essay. What did middle-class Englishmen think of the "operatives," as they called them? And what were the literary consequences of their attitude?

It was rare and difficult for a respectable middle-class Victorian fully to understand the working classes. Examples of this difficulty litter the well-meaning exhortations of clergy, governments, and newspapers. Throughout the early 19th century, a stream of pamphlets—conservative,

Whig, pro-capitalist, pro-government—gushed over the English prole-tariat, and dropped away unheeded and unread. The working classes found them unacceptable not only in doctrine but also in style: this is neatly illustrated in a letter of Francis Place, writing about an article on Trade Unions in the *Companion to the Newspaper,* a publication of the very middle-class Society for the Diffusion of Useful Knowledge. Place is a good man to consider here, because he was a believer in Political Economy, and a friend of working-men. He was thus sympathetic to the content of an article that urged labourers to save money and then withdraw from the market in order to raise the price of unskilled labour, and he is angry because he recognizes in the article's style a cultural gulf that the author had not the imagination to bridge:

> Not a working-man will read it without condemning it, and looking upon the writer as his enemy; he will see that . . . he is treated as an irrational creature and he will be more than ever confirmed in his false notions.[20]

This complaint, that middle-class writers were incapable of treating the working classes as true equals, can be made of many in the 19th century: it has been made of Place himself. It can certainly be made of Lord Brougham, the great champion of education for the working-man, the moving spirit behind the Mechanics' Institutes of the 1820s and 1830s. The bourgeoisie was divided about these institutes. The Tory view was usually that they were dangerous and would encourage working-men to forget their station and organize in discontent; the Liberal view was that education was a protection against revolution and would lead working-men to an acceptance of the social order. The controversy has obvious parallels in the 20th century, and it is very difficult, looking back, to decide who was right. What the institutes were aiming to do was to find a middle course between the open paternalism of traditional Toryism, which felt that an operative had no need of science or politics, and what seemed the revolutionary alternative of working-class organiza-tion for working-class ideals. Tories felt that if working-men were given opportunities they would use them in their own way, not in Lord Brougham's. In one way, both sides were wrong: the institutes had little impact on the working classes and (like the modern W.E.A.) they were more and more used by the bourgeoisie.[21]

As a contrast, let us look at a movement that genuinely belonged to the working class. There were three such movements in early Victorian times, all subversive, all interconnected: the Anti-Poor-Law Movement, the agitation for the Ten-Hours Act, and Chartism. There is an odd sense in which the opponents of the Mechanics' Institutes treated working-men as responsible adults: they believed that if they were offered opportunities, they would take them on their own terms. The opponents of the Ten-Hours Movement certainly believed this, and explicitly claimed it. Tooke, Chadwick, and Southwood Smith, the three Benthamites who formed the Royal Commission of 1833, opposed the Ten-Hours Movement because they objected to interfering with the freedom of contract between capital and labour. They saw very shrewdly that the adult operatives denounced the exploitation of children so that they could hide their own case behind this even stronger one; and they pointed out that the responsibility for child labour often lay with the working-class parents:

> Sometimes the sole consideration by which parents are influenced in making choice of a person under whom to place their children is the amount of wages, not the mode of treatment to be secured to them.[22]

It is easy for us to see nowadays that the commission's concern for freedom of contract was nonsense, and nonsense of a kind very useful to the masters: the working-man who worked 14 hours a day set no store by the freedom to make, if he wished, a contract that economic pressure had in any case forced on him. Nonetheless it is interesting that opponents of the movement use the rhetoric of responsibility, and use it both shrewdly and sincerely. Among the friends of the working class it does not survive so easily.

There is less patronage and condescension, however, among the friends of the Ten-Hours Movement than among those of the Mechanics' Institutes, and the reason is clear: the former was a movement of the proletariat, the latter a movement for them. Even the aristocratic Shaftesbury, with his 18th-century political views and his devout 19th-century religious views, was not a self-appointed leader like Brougham: he served what Marx and Engels enthusiastically hailed as a genuine proletarian movement, a step toward the workers' revolution in England. There is nothing in Brougham's career that corresponds to the "astonishment, doubt, and terror" of Ashley (as Lord Shaftesbury was in 1832) when G. S. Bull, on behalf of the workers' delegates, asked him to represent their movement in Parliament.[23] Shaftesbury obviously belonged to another world from that of the operatives, but he was their servant and not their patronizing adviser. Oastler, Bull, and Stephens, the grass-roots leaders, were not working-men either, but they thought and wrote like

the men they represented. Oastler, with true popular gusto, threatened
the mill-owners who broke the law in their factories that he would

> teach every factory child in the kingdom how to use a needle among
> the machinery. Oh yes, I'll do for them. I'm taking lessons how to
> teach little children how to do more harm than good.

The middle class answered, in the columns of the *Manchester Guardian*,
that

> a man who can use language like this—who can talk of teaching
> children to destroy the property of their employers—may if he
> please call himself a Christian and a philanthropist, but he is either
> a madman or a most hardened and despicable villain.[24]

The typical "friend" of the working class in the 19th century was not
Oastler but Brougham, or Brougham's henchman Charles Knight, the
secretary of the Society for the Diffusion of Useful Knowledge. Knight
was a modest and pleasant man who believed that one should not con-
descend to the working class, but he did not have either the ferociousness
or the common touch of Oastler.[25] And when working-men's clubs found
their way into literature they were seen through the eyes of Knight and
Brougham, not through radical or Chartist eyes. "The Philosophers," the
group of working-men with clay pipes and a look of concentrated intelligence who meet in Chapter 42 of *Daniel Deronda* (1876), are shown as a
spontaneous band of seekers and friends, but they say nothing that the
most timid politician or mill-owner need be afraid of. They are seen
from above, not from within.

Was the bourgeoisie applying or betraying its ideology when it held
aloof from full imaginative understanding of the working class? The creed
of self-help clearly held radical potentialities: whether they were realized
depended on which way you leaned. Most Victorians did not lean too
hard when the implications looked alarming. Self-help always remained
a doggedly middle-class creed, because it was individual self-help. "Much
as I want to see workmen escape from their slavish position," wrote
William Morris, "I don't at all want to see a few individuals more creep
out of their class into the middle class; this will only make the poor
poorer still."[26] Whether Morris is right or wrong economically, he is
certainly right ideologically. The great inarticulate alternative to "eels in
a jar" was class solidarity: inarticulate because the British working class
did not know that Marx had stated it for them. Indeed, the "working
class," in the sense I have been using the phrase, was still numerically
small by the mid-century. Most working-men were artisans whose modest

employer may have worked beside them at the bench: but those whose factory experience had shown them the experience of alienation and led them to trade union organization, though few, were the men of the future. And these few—the politically conscious—did not, for the most part, want to take middle-class advice and save:

> . . . your happiness, your position in life, will depend neither on the franchise nor the charter, neither on what parliament does, nor on what your employer neglects to do; but simply and solely upon the use you make of the fifteen or thirty shillings which you earn each week, and upon the circumstances whether you marry at twenty or at twenty-eight, and whether you marry a sluggard and a slattern or a prudent and industrious woman.[27]

The "objective" aim of exhortations like this is to urge self-help as an *alternative* to working-class organization. John Barton the Chartist—the passage above comes from the *Edinburgh Review*'s attack on *Mary Barton* (1848)—has "to thank himself for most of his sorrows and misfortunes." Why? Because he spent his time and money on trade unions instead of prudently saving it. He behaved, in other words, like a man in whom class-consciousness had superseded Samuel Smiles. Articulate working-men wanted to form trade unions and to demand the Charter—which *they* had drawn up—not to have the Corn Laws repealed, which the masters had told them was in their interests. And, meanwhile, with that unconscious cunning that the ideology of a class so often displays, self-help was pressed to the shape of greatest usefulness to the bourgeoisie. If the operatives helped themselves collectively by demanding political and economic rights, they were urged not to set class against class; if they helped themselves individually by "duly husbanding" wages instead of squandering them on subscriptions, they were given cosy ideological pats of approval.

It is something like this point that Dickens makes in *Our Mutual Friend* (1865) through the character of Betty Higden; and, as so often, he offers us the opportunity to draw a more complex conclusion than he intended. Betty Higden represents self-help run mad: she is an eel who doesn't mind going to the bottom of the jar. Her one fixed aim in life is to refuse charity. At the suggestion that the sick child Johnny should be removed "to where he can be taken better care of," she picks him up "with blazing eyes" and tries to run away: and when she herself is homeless and dying she will do anything—lie, starve, give away her money—rather than go on the parish. "Patiently to earn a spare bare living and quietly to die, untouched by workhouse hands—this was her highest sublunary hope."

Now Dickens' point is that charity has been so callously used to degrade the recipient, that to a pauper the Good Samaritan now looks like a pursuing Fury, whom she flees "with the wings of raging Despair": he does not say outright that Betty's refusal to be a burden on the rates is exactly that form of self-help most convenient to the rich, but he clearly suggests it. Ladies in carriages who buy from her persuade themselves that she is well-to-do in the world. "As making a comfortable provision for its subject which costs nobody anything, this class of fable has long been popular."

It is the same point as that made by Engels in *The Condition of the Working Class in England* in 1844: "Can anyone wonder that the poor decline to accept public relief under these conditions? That they starve rather than enter these bastilles?" Dickens' brilliance lies in seeing the grotesque result both in its own weird individuality, and as the product of social forces. Now, for the full power of this effect to be felt, the grotesque element is essential. Betty Higden is obsessed, and her independence is irrational, even crazy: it is a story that needs Dickens' grisly humour. When he pauses to rebuke "my lords and gentlemen and honourable boards" in solemnly moral language, he loses some of his power; when he ceases to regard the old woman as obsessed, the result is worse still:

> "I understand too well. I know too much about it, sir. I've run from
> it too many a year. No! Never for me, nor for the child, while there's
> water enough in England to cover us."

When a Dickens character uses language like this, a red light shines in the reader's response. This is not the ruthless morality of Dickens the comic, it is the cant of Dickens the sentimentalist, the writer of melodrama. We sense now that unbearable note of moral approbation that other Victorian novelists could handle, but that Dickens seldom or never could. Moral approbation is a fatal attitude for the novelist to apply to Betty Higden, for in asking us to admire what she has become, it suggests that her reaction of sturdy independence is not only courageous but wise. When he suggests this, Dickens has become like the lords and gentlemen he claims to be mocking. The brilliance of his creation of Betty Higden lies in the way it shows us that her courage is crazy, that her independence will destroy her. Over this brilliance Dickens spreads an attitude of respectable approbation that seems to find her behaviour rational. The brilliance shows her rejecting real charity as well as false, so complete a victim of an inhuman doctrine that she loves the Big

Brother of bourgeois ideology: the reassurances show her as martyr as well as victim, undo the suggestion that her independence destroys her, and smooth away the subversive edges.[28]

Why did the bourgeois ideology get twisted as it did? Why were sincere and intelligent Victorians able to mould it to the shape of class interest, while hardly noticing what they were doing? There may be no simple answer: partly, this is what always happens to ideologies. But one answer is obvious: the middle classes were afraid. Fear of mob violence and of insurrection was widespread and deep from 1789 until 1848. It ended almost suddenly: the Chartist hordes of the 1840s gave place, in the middle-class imagination, to the respectable working-man, coming up to London by special train with his family to see the Great Exhibition in 1851. In so far as fear of the drunken and violent poor persisted after this, it was no longer primarily political, as in the 18th century it was not political. It is hard to decide how far the fear of insurrection in the earlier 19th century was justified: what is beyond doubt, however, is that it existed. Honest men believed (and spread) incredible scurrilities about Tom Paine; practical men offered impossible advice to the poor; intelligent men believed that poverty was the result of improvidence.

How could a middle-class Victorian find his way out of the prison of prejudice? How could he learn to listen, to stretch his imagination, to see the working classes as they were? I can see three possible ways. First, by personal contact: to live among working-men and to serve them; to do, not what you wished to do for them, but what they wished you to do; to breathe their air and think their thoughts without a constant moral nag—in this way it was possible for a dedicated few to speak with an accent completely acceptable to the operatives (whom they would not, of course, call operatives). The two prime examples of this were William Cobbett and Richard Oastler; and both, significantly, began as Tories. Cobbett is the less significant here, because his aggressiveness was personal and eccentric, and because his contacts were with the rural rather than the urban poor: indeed, his picture of society is largely pre-industrial, and his greatest hatred is not for the capitalists but for the "tax-eaters," the recipients of government help. For Oastler, however, the great enemy was clearly the mill-owners: he opposed the Reform Bill, because he could not bear the thought of the country being in the hands of the £10 householders. In the Huddersfield by-election in 1837, Oastler actually ran as a combined Radical and Tory candidate, and a shrewd document by the local Radical Committee explained why they supported a man "who designated himself as an Ultra Tory." As well as points of specific agreement (anti-Poor Law, Ten-Hours agitation, "equal rights and equal laws"), they said, there was the fact that:

> He is our neighbour, and acquainted with the wants and wishes of the great majority of the inhabitants of the borough, and his previous conduct is to us a sufficient guarantee that he would do his duty.

No Whig or Philosophic Radical earned this kind of trust from the working-men, or was called "neighbour."[29]

The second way is by complete integrity: not just ordinary honesty, but the ability to free one's mind from the pressures of class assumptions and conventional attitudes. The creed of self-help, we have seen, could be radical if you took it seriously: but such seriousness needed a rare integrity. If any man in the 19th century had a free mind, it was John Stuart Mill: he knew what responsibility meant, and he knew that

> The working classes have taken their interests into their own hands, and are perpetually showing that they think the interests of their employers are not identical with their own, but opposite to them. . . . The poor have come out of leading strings, and cannot any longer be governed or treated like children. To their own qualities must be commended the care of their destiny.[30]

Mill's excursion into practical politics is often considered a failure; but his account in the *Autobiography* (1873) offers nothing that is at odds with this passage. He relates with special pride the occasion when he was asked at a meeting containing working-men whether he had written a passage saying that the working classes were generally liars.

> I at once answered "I did." Scarcely were these two words out of my mouth, when vehement applause resounded through the whole meeting. It was evident that the working people were so accustomed to expect equivocation and evasion from those who sought their suffrages, that when they found instead of that, a direct avowal of what was likely to be disagreeable to them, instead of being affronted, they concluded at once that this was a person whom they could trust.[31]

Why does this, in spite of the elaborate subordinate clauses in which Mill wraps all narrative, ring out with a note almost of its own? It is surely because we have here the voice of Chadwick and Southwood Smith, telling the working-men that if they are adults they must be told home truths; and the voice, for once, is not being used to promote someone else's interests at their own expense. A "friend" of the working class has become a friend.

But of all ways to emerge from the limitations of one's ideology, it is the third that most concerns us: for that is the way of the imagination. The one body of men who, by their very function, are able to transcend class limitations are the writers: for the act of literary creation *is* the entering into a human situation that is not altogether one's own. Of course the writer must find in his own emotional life the starting-point for understanding; but if he never goes beyond that life he will be a writer of so narrow a range that even the expression of his own life may fail for want of ballast.

Let us start with a very minor writer. Elizabeth Barrett Browning has lost her once handsome reputation, and the high esteem in which the Victorians held her poetry now seems astonishing. In one of her lyrics she was moved to write about labour conditions, and for the most part it is a sloppy and indifferent lyric:

> "For oh," say the children, "we are weary,
>   And we cannot run or leap. . . ."

This compassion is too near the easy romantic sob for the health of the poem; yet in two stanzas toward the end it does stiffen into something more interesting. After describing God's love ("We know no other words except 'Our Father' "),

> "But no!" say the children, weeping faster,
>   "He is speechless as a stone,
> And they tell us, of His image is the master
>   Who commands us to work on. . . ."

Did the poet realize how subversive a point this was? The children look up to Heaven and see only "dark wheel-like turning clouds": Heaven is the image of industrial society. And then, in a flash of subversion, or through the necessities of rhyme, she endorses the children:

> Do ye hear the children weeping and *disproving*,
>   Oh my brothers, what ye preach?
> For God's possible is taught by this World's loving,
>   And the children doubt of each.

Mrs Browning may have meant only to shed a gracious, rhythmical tear in passing, but her poem turns, for a moment, into something really disquieting.[32]

For a more sustained and profound example, we can turn to Blake. Blake's response to his society is in one sense obscure, as all his poetry is obscure; in another sense it is vivid, compelling, and direct. The simpler poems are often the most memorable.

London

I wander tho' each charter'd street,
Near where the charter'd Thames does flow,
And mark in every face I meet
Marks of weakness, marks of woe.

In every cry of every Man,
In every Infant's cry of fear,
In every voice, in every ban,
The mind-forg'd manacles I hear.

How the Chimney-sweeper's cry
Every black'ning Church appalls;
And the hapless Soldier's sigh
Runs in blood down Palace walls.

But most thro' midnight streets I hear
How the youthful Harlot's curse
Blasts the new born Infant's tear,
And blights with plagues the Marriage hearse.[33]

Blake combines directness of passion with verbal subtlety in a way one would have thought hardly possible. Look, for instance, at "charter'd." It burns with indignation: yet what it means is strangely complex. There is, first of all, the ambiguity between a charter as a stuffy old document that grants privileges and restrictions, and a charter as offering freedom. This gives alternative readings (they can hardly be combined). The former is perhaps the more obvious, but as we get to know the poem it tends to be replaced by the latter. But that, in its turn, is rendered ironic by the repetition. Political freedom—what charters grant—is a mockery in a land such as England, and the rights on which the English pride themselves were granted with a casual stroke of the pen to the whole city—streets and river and all—and therefore to no one.

The third stanza is the subtlest, subtle almost beyond analysis. The cry "appalls" the church, i.e. it both shocks it and casts a pall over it. "The church" is both the institution and a building. "Black'ning" can be active or passive: as an institution, the church blackens the moral scene; as a building, it grows blacker, from the soot shed by the chimney-sweeper. The two lines dodge with great skill between these two readings: the physical reading seems dominant in "black'ning," the institutional in "appalls." But neither of them interferes with the other. There is a rather different ambiguity in the next lines, depending on whether the soldier is a deserter being shot or (a subtler reading, surely) a reluctant trooper crushing a riot.

In Blake's vast, unwieldy, and ambitious prophetic books there are few (if any) passages as concentrated, or as successful, as this lyric, but there is a similar angry response to social injustice:

> They mock at the Labourer's limbs; they mock at his starv'd
>   Children:
> They bury his Daughters that they may have power to sell his sons:
> They compell the Poor to live upon a crust of bread by soft mild arts:
> They reduce the Man to want, then give with pomp and ceremony.[34]

Most of the indictment of Marx and Engels, of the Chartists, of Arnold and Morris, is sketched out here: even the idea of alienation is present, for the labourer's limbs are mocked—he is estranged from his species-being. Blake's angry vision of the labourer, however, is more often about exploitation than about industrialism. Vala, compelled to labour among the brick-kilns, complains

> We are made to turn the wheel for water,
> To carry the heavy basket on our scorched shoulders.

This pre-industrial imagery renders some effects impossible, but permits others. The climax of Vala's complaint reads

> Our beauty is covered over with clay and ashes, and our backs
> Furrow'd with ships, and our flesh bruised with the heavy baskets.[35]

Many of the complaints in *Vala* are merely repetitive, but this one ("our backs Furrow'd with ships") reaches a true climax, as the exploited workers are suddenly seen as the Earth itself.

These quotations, like all others in an essay of this sort, have been wrenched out of context; but in the case of Blake the context is such that we cannot be sure that the wrenching really matters. Even Blake scholars are not certain what story *The Four Zoas* is telling, what mythological or psychological reality is represented by Jerusalem, what points Blake is making by these analogies from work. These passages, and many others like them, illustrate a purpose that is obscure to us; and since they are so vivid and powerful in themselves, the reader seems justified in reversing the author's intention, and regarding the design of the poem as a means to achieving these brilliant local effects, and claiming that their true subject is not their actual subject—not Vala's night but the state of England. This is a sleight of interpretation that we do not need to carry out for the *Songs of Experience*.

My third example of the insight that creation brings is once again from a minor writer. A poor and pious widow with a 13-year-old son is visited by missionaries, who leave behind a few tracts, in which the lad reads of "pacific coral islands and volcanoes, coconut groves and bananas, graceful savages with paint and feathers"; and he lies in bed dreaming of how he will convert the Tahitians and the New Zealanders:

> And one day, I recollect it well, in the little, dingy, foul, reeking, twelve foot square back-yard, where huge smoky party-walls shut out every breath of air and almost all the light of heaven, I had climbed up between the water-butt and the angle of the wall for the purpose of fishing out of the dirty fluid which lay there, crusted with soot and alive with insects, to be renewed only three times in the seven days, some of the great larvae and kicking monsters which made up a large item in my list of wonders: all of a sudden the horror of the place came over me; those grim prison-walls above, with their canopy of lurid smoke; the dreary, sloppy, broken pavement; the horrible stench of the stagnant cesspools; the utter want of form, colour, life, in the whole place, crushed me down, without my being able to analyse my feelings as I can now; and then came over me that dream of Pacific Islands, and the free, open sea; and I slid down from my perch, and bursting into tears threw myself upon my knees in the court, and prayed aloud to God to let me be a missionary.[36]

If the Rev. Charles Kingsley had been told that religion was the opium of the people, and that romantic poetry was the quickest way out of a London slum, he would have turned in distaste from these clever, cynical ideas: yet what else is he telling us here? The intensity of the boy's longing for romance is a reaction from the grim prison walls; his spurious religious zeal has a ring of dreadful authenticity. More than that: Kingsley has built toward the violent irony of the last line with a skill that is usually far beyond him. The dreary, sloppy, broken pavement has to be as real as possible, to engender that final cry; and so there is a ring of hard fact, a blunt quality of mere ineluctable *existence*, about that 12-foot-square back-yard that frees it for an exhilarating instant from the shrouds of rhetoric and compassion. The imaginative excitement of the creative act has driven a moral man and ponderous writer out of his kind and into a new power.

Such are the possibilities of imagination; I turn now to its deflections. This discussion unfortunately has to be longer and more complicated: there is always more to say about the mixed cases, in which we are trying to perceive both the insights that imagination has brought and the failure that has come from not being able to sustain such insight.

For the first example, we can continue with *Alton Locke* (1850). Chapter X of this book is called "How Folk turn Chartist," and was intended—as was a good deal else in the novel—to make respectable readers uncomfortable. Poverty and exploitation roused Kingsley to generous anger, and he wrote his novel—as he had written his Parson Lot articles—to arouse sympathy for the oppressed. Every now and then there is a gleam of the strange, intense sensibility that enabled him to write the passage about the water butt and the missionaries: Alton's speech to his mother against religion (nobody believes in it, he claims, except "good kind people . . . who must needs have some reason to account for their goodness"), or Crossthwaite's comment on the M.P. who shook his head and told the workmen about the iron laws of political economy ("he may have been a wise man. I only know that he was a rich one"). A reader half-way through *Alton Locke* might think it was a genuinely subversive novel: but as he read on to the end he would find that his fears (or his hopes) were unfounded. Almost everything that really disturbs complacency in this book is eventually retracted. The very plot is an account of how Alton acquired and then shed his Chartist views. His speech against religion is immediately followed by "I had hardly spoken the words, when I would have given worlds to recall them—but it was to be—and it was." The account of why folk turn Chartists is followed by the "confession" that with him, "and I am afraid with many, many more, the means become, by the frailty of poor human nature, an end, an idol in itself." The chapter is, it turns out, ambiguously titled. It is not an account of the arguments for the Charter, offered for our inspection and possible acceptance, but an excuse, an explanation of how people are misled. "Folk" means other folk. Writing under his pen name of Parson Lot, Kingsley had complained that the Charter did not go "far enough"; as we read the end of *Alton Locke* we see just what he meant by saying that the Charter had become an end in itself or did not go far enough. He means that the Charter was political, and should not have been.

We can find an exact parallel to this in a far greater novel. George Eliot's Felix Holt is a radical who wants to get to deeper roots than his fellow-demagogues: "I want to be a demagogue of a new sort." Now the only important character in *Felix Holt* (1866) who seems to hold genuinely radical views is the Rev. Rufus Lyon, with whom Felix argues a good deal; and the only times when Felix advances opinions that are specifically political are when he makes a speech on nomination day—warning the workers (who have no vote, so hardly need the warning) that power can mean power to do mischief, that

all the schemes about voting, and districts, and annual Parliaments
and the rest, are engines, and the water or steam—the force that is
to work them—must come out of human nature—out of men's passions, feelings, desires;[37]

—or when he tells Mr Lyon ("being in a perverse mood") that "universal
suffrage would be equally agreeable to the devil." "Perverse" Felix no
doubt was that day; but it is difficult to regard the author's parenthesis
with much conviction when there is no trace of Felix's unperverseness—
that is, his ordinary radicalism—anywhere in the novel. There is no sign
that he has ever read Tom Paine or William Cobbett; nothing but the
slightest of hints that he does not believe in God. His radicalism "of a
newer sort" is not radical at all, for when we look at its content we see
that it consists of a mistrust of politics, a belief that the reform of institutions will achieve little without a change of heart. A generation earlier,
Sidney Smith had seen that the change-of-heart doctrine could, in a
political context, be a convenient way of blocking improvement. "Instead
of reforming the State, the constitution, and everything that is most
excellent," runs the conclusion of his Noodle's oration, "let each man
reform himself! Let him look at home, he will find there is enough to do,
without looking abroad, and aiming at what is out of his power."

A year or so after finishing *Felix Holt*, George Eliot wrote an article for
Blackwood's magazine, on the occasion of the Second Reform Act, that
she called "Address to the Working Men, by Felix Holt."[38] It is a deeply
conservative document, full of praise of "the wonderful slow-growing
system of things made up of our laws, our commerce and our stores of
all sorts," and warning against hurrying on political change. It should
not surprise us that the article is so conservative and that its title should
perhaps offend us. The great point about Felix in the novel is that he
is a working-man: the contrast with Harold Transom, the gentleman
who holds more radical opinions more superficially, is clear and effective.
But the article, removed from the context of fiction, contains the views
of Marian Evans, who was not a working-man, so that the use of Felix
as a persona is actually misleading. There is so much profound political
understanding in *Felix Holt* (the trade-union man whose speech Felix
answers is a figure almost unique in 19th-century fiction), that this need
the author felt to draw back, in the end, from politics, is a particularly
significant deflection.[39]

This discussion has assumed that what makes *Alton Locke* and *Felix
Holt* subversive is what makes them good novels: that as they draw
back from their subversive insights, they withdraw into the merely

conventional. I think this is true, but it seems an alarming yardstick to use: are radical novels good, and conservative novels bad?

Of course there are bad radical novels. Ernest Jones the Chartist, for instance, wrote a number; and in *Woman's Wrongs* (1855) we can see how lack of talent can impose the wrong moral on a book. John Haspen, the bullying husband, is shown as a mere brute when at home; he squanders his money on drink, beats his wife, and is condemned with all the clichés of sobriety, kindness, and thrift. At the factory, however, he offers heroic resistance to the bad employer who lowers wages and offers his workers the "freedom" to starve instead of working for him: here Haspen is praised with the clichés of radicalism. So easily has Jones fallen into each set of clichés that he does not notice that they are inconsistent with each other: Margaret Haspen rebukes her husband in the language of the *Edinburgh Review*, but Jones keeps that in one pigeon-hole, and the factory scenes in another; or rather he ought to, but they eventually mingle in some confusion.

No, it is not because radicalism is a virtue in any novelist that I have discussed Kingsley and George Eliot as I have: it is because they set out to describe politically conscious working-men to a bourgeois audience. Such an audience was very ready to underestimate the subversive and truly radical posture of these men. In so far as these novels aim to present the unfamiliar truthfully, then, they will be successful in proportion to their subversive understanding: imaginative withdrawal will be a retreat into the familiar ideology. For good literary reasons, a political yardstick can here become an aesthetic one.

For a more extended example, I turn to Dickens. What is the social point of *Hard Times* (1854)? "It's a' a muddle," says Stephen Blackpool to Bounderby; and if ever a system cried out for mending, it is the one that put Bounderby in charge and sent Stephen tumbling down a mineshaft; that built the tall chimneys, out of which "interminable serpents of smoke trailed themselves for ever and ever, and never got uncoiled." Now there are two characters in the book who are trying very hard to improve the system, and they correspond to the two main attempts historically, one from the centre, one from below. These two are Gradgrind and Slackbridge, and their efforts get small sympathy from Dickens. What is Gradgrind doing, among his army of blue-books, or travelling up to London to sit in Parliament, the national dust-heap? "Proving that the Good Samaritan was a Bad Economist," Dickens tells us, and of course he is right, for the Utilitarians designed the New Poor Law, justly loathed by its "beneficiaries." Yet he does not realize how radical a thing this is for Gradgrind to prove. Charity supports, it does not overthrow, the social structure: the manufacturers had nothing to fear from the Good Samaritan. If Gradgrind was a typical Utilitarian, he spent his time in the national dust-heap trying to get dangerous machinery fenced in, or to improve the sanitation of Coketown, not simply serving the interests of the masters. It was not really fair of Dickens to make him a friend of Bounderby.

Slackbridge's answer to the muddle is that the workers should organize and so make their power felt. It is a doctrine that could be held in all sobriety by a thoughtful working-man, but Slackbridge the demagogue is neither thoughtful nor a real working-man. Dickens has disdained no tricks to make him vulgar:

> An ill-made, high-shouldered man, with lowering brows, and his features crushed into an habitually sour expression, he contrasted most unfavourably, even in his mongrel dress, with the great body of his hearers in their plain working clothes.[40]

In the mouth of such a man, what can the trade union be but part of the organizer's rhetoric, what effect can it have but to oppress the well-meaning working-man who stands out? Whatever solution to the muddle lay here, Dickens has simply dismissed it.

There are two comments to be made on Slackbridge, one external, one internal. As a portrait of the typical trade union organizer of the time, he is a calumny, and Dickens knew that he was a calumny: for Dickens had been to Preston to gather material when he was planning *Hard Times*, and had attended a trade union meeting. There he had heard a demagogue, whom he names Gruffshaw, and had seen how, when Gruffshaw tried to push oratory and politics in the way of practical business, he was firmly put down. "My friends," the chairman said, "these are hard words of my friend Gruffshaw, and this is not the business."[41] This scrupulousness of the reporter was laid aside when the novelist took over.

The internal comment concerns the implausibility of the whole trade union episode. The satire on Slackbridge is Dickens at his crudest: he knits his brows, he sets his teeth, he pounds with his arms. When he speaks, his rhetoric is too broad to be worth seeing through. Yet though he makes so easy a target, Dickens will not let well alone; and the chapter is crammed with anxious authorial commentary, telling us over and over again that he was below the level of his audience. The novelist did not even take over here, the reporter changed sides. Even more implausible is Stephen's involvement. Slackbridge, to show his blackness, must victimize the hero, and therefore the hero must refuse to join the union. We are never told why: certainly it is not through loyalty to Bounderby. Stephen uses some utterly vague phrases ("I mun go the way as lays afore me") and refers to a promise he made to Rachel, which turns out to be even vaguer (if, as seeems possible, it was a promise to keep out of trouble, he can hardly be said to have acted on it). Finally, against all probability, Stephen is dismissed: for no particular reason, and in a sense for not joining the union. In this episode Dickens betrayed the truth and made a mess of his novel. It is tempting to see the two—the external and the internal flaw—as connected.[42]

Everyone agrees that *Hard Times* is unusual among Dickens' novels: it lacks some of his faults and many of his merits, and its opinions are, for Dickens, freakish. Certainly it suggests a violently anti-bourgeois writer, who could look like a radical if he had not taken such pains not to do so. Is this the real Dickens we are glimpsing? Was he at the deepest level naturally hostile to the bourgeois ideology? The sensibility shown in his novels is more complicated and shifting than the technique, and it is not easy to know what his deepest attitudes on social questions were. I have already cited that paragon of irrational self-help, Betty Higden; but he was also able to see self-help as an assertion of working-class independence. One of the sketches in *The Uncommercial Traveller* (1861) describes the "self-supporting COOKING DEPOT for the Working Classes." "Whatever is done for the comfort and advancement of the working-man," Dickens asserts, "must be so far done by himself as that it is maintained by himself. And there must be in it no touch of condescension, no shadow of patronage." He is in favour of the Cooking Depot because the staff are adequately paid, the food is good, and the books are properly kept; his only objection is that no beer is served because this shows a distrust of the working-man. It is an institution almost exactly similar to the canteen opened by the men of John Thornton's factory, which he is so careful not to interfere with, and where he is invited, as an equal, to sit down and take a snack on hot-pot days:

> If they had not asked me, I would no more have intruded on them
> than I'd have gone to the mess at the barracks without invitation.[43]

Self-help here is not, or not obviously, a doctrine convenient to the middle class, and it is not altogether surprising to find Dickens saying "there are in Birmingham at this moment many working-men infinitely better versed in Shakespeare and Milton than the average of fine gentlemen in the days of bought-and-sold dedications and dear books."[44] Here middle class and working class are one: they both, in their sturdy independence, contrast with the "fine gentlemen." And often Dickens' sympathy for the working class ran deeper than this: he liked them for what set them apart from the bourgeoisie as well, and dismissed patronage in favour not of sturdy self-help but of entertainment—that is, what the working-men actually wanted. In his essay "Two Views of a Cheap Theatre,"[45] for instance, he shows the sympathy we should expect for the project of Sunday-night prayer-meetings in the Britannia Theatre, Hoxton, yet he is not altogether satisfied with the preacher who condescended, who kept calling his audience fellow-sinners, and above all who set himself "in antagonism to the natural inborn desire of the mass of mankind to recreate themselves and be entertained."

Dickens (as this last sentence should suggest) is the greatest philistine in English literature. His ideal of the good life was cosy: Christmas at Dingley Dell; Traddles playing Puss-in-the-Corner in his chambers with his innumerable jolly sisters-in-law and his Sophy, who had "a loving cheerful fireside quality in her bright looks";[46] Esther the domestic paragon, settled in a Bleak House that turns out not to be bleak at all, but "quite a rustic cottage of dolls' rooms" set in "a pretty little orchard, where the cherries were nestling among the green leaves."[47] It is not quite the ideal of any one class. Sometimes it seems to emphasize the nuclear family: Wemmick at Walworth, with the Aged Parent making buttered toast and Miss Skiffins brewing tea behind the security of the raised drawbridge, in a home arranged around the traditional metaphor that an Englishman's home is his castle.[48] Sometimes it emphasizes the wider unit of popular culture: the party at Todgers' Boarding House, which included a gentleman of a sporting turn, a gentleman of a theatrical turn, a gentleman of a debating turn, and a table groaning beneath the weight of "boiled beef, roast veal, bacon, pies, and abundance of such heavy vegetables as are favourably known to housekeepers for their satisfying qualities."[49] The arts, the intellect, and the religious life are almost totally absent from Dickens' conception of happiness.

Victorian fiction has two great satiric portraits of philistines, by its two great novelists: Mr Bult in *Daniel Deronda* and Mr Podsnap in *Our Mutual Friend*, both minor characters, yet both, somehow, complete. The contrast between them is the contrast between George Eliot and Dickens. Mr Bult is completely credible: he had "the general solidity and suffusive pinkness of a healthy Briton on the central tableland of life"; he "was amiably confident, and had no idea that his insensibility to counterpoint could ever be reckoned against him."[50] Mr Podsnap is gloriously incredible. When introduced to a foreign gentleman (Podsnap believes "the whole European continent to be in mortal alliance against the young person") he asks " 'How do you like London?' as if he were administering something in the nature of a powder or potion to the deaf child; 'London, Londres, London?' "

> "The Constitution Britannique," Mr Podsnap explained, as if he were teaching at an infant school; "We say British. But you say Britannique, you know" (forgivingly, as if that were not his fault). "The Constitution, Sir."[51]

And now comes a paradox. We might expect that the caricature would come from the author who was looking from the outside, the realistic portrait from the author who felt close to what he was showing and so subtly attacking. Yet the opposite is true. George Eliot, the European traveller, the polyglot, the ex-editor of the *Westminster Review*, is genuinely free of all temptation to be Bult; Dickens, the laureate of fireside slippers and home-made punch, the *entrepreneur* who made £30,000 a year from his readings, the novelist who could portray an artistic poseur such as Henry Gowan but never, in all his books, a true artist—Dickens had a smack of Podsnap, all right. From which we must conclude that his brilliant caricature is drawn from a wholly external vantage-point to which Dickens had to retreat for safety; whereas the calmly brilliant sober portrait is the work of the writer who knew she could come very close without catching anything.

Dickens' ideal of personal relations, then, is balanced between the culture of two classes, inclining now to one, now to the other, and always to the solid centre of each. What of his picture of society as a whole? To answer this we must distinguish, even more clearly than criticism usually needs to, between the man and the writer. Dickens the man was a busy and practical reformer, eager to help in a thousand schemes, never much doubting that they were worth-while: in spite of all the coyness with which he handles sex, and the melodrama with which he shows vice, he must have known exactly what prostitutes were like, especially after the help he gave with Miss Coutts's home for fallen women. Dickens the novelist often set out to work for Dickens the man, and to expose abuses in society so that they could be reformed: the law's delay, imprisonment for debt, transportation, civil-service muddle. We know now that he was cautious about this, and that the abuses he noticed were those that most people had already noticed; but this strengthens rather than weakens the case that his purpose in writing was a reforming one.[52]

But what we have seen in *Hard Times* is not an isolated case. Dickens attacks abuses, but he does not really believe that they can be cured. The evil in *Bleak House* and *Little Dorrit* is inescapable. The fog that opens the former is a social abuse turned into a natural phenomenon, and so made permanent; the powerful descriptions of Tom-All-Alone's, the tenement that may even be the property in Jarndyce and Jarndyce, are sadly contemptuous of attempts to put it right ("There is not a drop of Tom's corrupted blood but propagates infection and contagion some-where"); even the death of Jo, nicely balanced between the restrained and the over-eloquent, owes its artistic success to its refusal to be explicitly reformist, to suggest remedies. The view of society in *Little Dorrit* is just as black. Because all society is a prison, the only possibility of happiness is in a pastoral retreat: Mr Meagles' residence at Twickenham, or Bleeding Heart Yard. And because these are not quite safe—Bleeding Heart Yard belongs to the extortionate Casby, Twickenham lets Henry Gowan in and he captures Pet—the best retreat is behind the walls of the Marshalsea. There the Circumlocution Office can do no damage, nor can Merdle break through and steal. And the world outside? Dickens originally intended to call the novel *Nobody's Fault*. It is a good reformer's title, if it is ironic; but is it? Merdle, who ruined thousands, is seen as the most pathetic victim of all; young Barnacle, when we finally get inside the Circumlocution Office, turns out to be rather likable, and as helpless as anyone else. On the deepest level Dickens seems to have believed that it really was nobody's fault.

Dickens has the opinions of a reformer, but the imagination of despair. The opinions found their way into his books, and were prominent in his life, and they urged that something must be done; the creative imagination shut its ears, knowing that nothing could be done, that society was a fog, a prison, a muddle; that those who wanted change were helpless before the Establishment.

We can now explain the anomaly of *Hard Times* and its attack upon industrialism. When Dickens died, Ruskin wrote that he had been "a pure modernist—a leader of the steamwhistle party *par excellence*. . . . His hero is essentially an ironmaster."[53] This is true of *Bleak House*; in *Dombey and Son* the railway is on the whole benevolent; and like any good modernist, Dickens loved to make fun of the Wisdom of our Ancestors ("Dirt, Ignorance, Superstition and Disease"). Why did he change sides in *Hard Times*? Clearly because *Hard Times* is set entirely in Coketown, a town that belongs to the ironmasters. Dickens feared and hated authority; he saw the community as groaning under the inevitable yoke of whatever powers may be. When industrialism is an independent force, a ray of light in the fog, an inventor defying the Circumlocution Office, he is all for it; but when industrialism has become the Establishment, fear and hatred are the only possible reaction.

Elizabeth Gaskell is a less complex writer than Dickens, and the deflections of the creative imagination in her work can be discussed more briefly. It will be simplest to take the earlier and less powerful of her two industrial novels, *Mary Barton* (1847), which was written to take the side of the working-man. That, at any rate, is what she *thought* she had done, and she even felt uneasy at the charge that she had given a one-sided picture, at the thought that "people at a distance should be misled and prejudiced against the masters, and that class be estranged from class."[54] "Some say the masters are very sore," she says in another letter, "but I'm sure I *believe* I wrote truth."[55] This apologetic tone is revealing. Is it present in the book itself? Is *Mary Barton* less whole-heartedly on the side of the workers than the author thought? The answer is surely Yes. There is a great deal of compassion in the novel, and some very honest and realistic description of poverty in Manchester; but it is deeply committed to, and at the end explicitly states, the doctrine of harmony of interests between classes, which (as we have seen) was a middle-class doctrine. The book's change of title is revealing. Originally it was to be called *John Barton*, for "he was my hero, *the* person with whom all my sympathies went, with whom I tried to identify myself at the time."[56] But John Barton is not, in the end, a very prominent character, for as the book grew, it turned into something more conventional: daughter displaced father, and love displaced politics. One crucial detail in the plot betrays this deflection: Jem Wilson's trial, the climax of the book, is for murder, and the concluding action is all concerned with this "violation of the eternal laws of God." But by turning her Chartist into a murderer, Mrs Gaskell shifted from the laws of men to those of God (a less dangerous subject), replaced a political by a criminal trial, and shirked the true challenge of working-class radicalism. And she spoiled her novel: for John Barton, external and cursory as his final treatment is, remains the most impressive character in the book.[57]

In her industrial novels Mrs Gaskell handled material she could not altogether control. Her imagination led her to an understanding of working-class attitudes, but she could not sustain this when its implications were too disturbing. Something like the opposite is true of Disraeli. He has appeared to some to be the great adventurer of Victorian politics, but it is as a novelist, rather than as a statesman, that he showed a really bracing irresponsibility. Disraeli's handling of human relationships is almost always stagey and unconvincing; but *Sybil* (1845) has an interest rare among his novels because of its taste for the lurid. *Sybil* comes to life best when Disraeli is describing scenes he knew nothing about: riot at the tommy-shop; the career of Devilsdust, the clever and impudent foundling; the naked brutality of life in Wodgate:

> There are no landlords, head lessees, main-masters, or butties in Wodgate. No church there has yet raised its spire. . . . The streets are never cleaned; every man lights his own house; nor does any one know anything except his business. The most usual stimulus to increase exertion, is to pull an apprentice's ears till they run with blood.[58]

It does not matter—though the fact is interesting—that Disraeli got the material for these scenes from blue-books. It is clear that these documentary accounts of the "other nation" took his fancy. The representation of the unfamiliar exploited a sense he had of the dangerous forces in society, and when writing out of bravado he showed a social intelligence far greater than his powers as a novelist. Again, George Eliot provides a contrast. The riot in *Felix Holt* is described scrupulously and at length; that in *Sybil* is wilder, more colourful, more entertaining. Disraeli's was the imagination that was titillated by danger.

The fear from which Mrs Gaskell's imagination fled was faced calmly by George Eliot, and set the adventurous fancy of Disraeli racing. Let us turn now to a novel written primarily out of fear, where riot is not incidental, nor a thrilling climax, but is the central theme of the book. Whatever else *Barnaby Rudge* (1841) is about, it is certainly about riot—a riot that turns into pure irrational violence, as irresistible as fire or flood. Dickens' intention was undoubtedly to rebuke the rioters, and to express his sense of shock at their savagery. Yet once again achievement did not square with intention: for as Dickens takes us through the streets of burning London, showing by the vivid light of the flames the crazy crowd looting, burning, drinking, dying, he is led to identify himself deeply with what he set out to deplore:

> There were men there, who danced and trampled on the beds of flowers as though they trod down human enemies, and wrenched them from the stalks, like savages who twisted human necks. There were men who cast their lighted torches in the air, and suffered

them to fall upon their heads and faces, blistering the skin with deep unseemly burns. There were men who rushed up to the fire, and paddled in it with their hands as if in water; and others who were restrained by force from plunging in, to gratify their deadly longing. On the skull of one drunken lad—not twenty by his looks— who lay upon the ground with a bottle to his mouth, the lead from the roof came streaming down in a shower of liquid fire, white hot; melting his head like wax. When the scattered parties were collected, men—living yet, but singed as with hot irons—were plucked out of the cellars, and carried off upon the shoulders of others, who strove to wake them as they went along, with ribald jokes, and left them, dead in the passages of hospitals. But of all the howling throng not one learnt mercy from, or sickened at, these sights, nor was the fierce, besotted, senseless rage of one man glutted.[59]

Any reader must feel the heavy thump of that last moralizing sentence; and must realize by contrast how vivid the rest of the paragraph was, how all detachment is swept away, all disapproval overwhelmed, by the sheer intensity of fascination. The men paddling as if in water, the ribald jokes to wake the dead: these are details that testify to the writer's eye being on the object and not on his own moralizing. And when the rioters reach Newgate and burn it, something in Dickens seems to have stood up and cheered at the power and ingenuity of pure violence, destroying the hated institutions of authority.

No discussion of literature can ignore the fact that it is literature. To perceive which attitudes are really present and operative in a novel, and which are merely aspired to, presupposes an awareness of artistic success and failure: the historian of ideology needs to be a literary critic too. Now, if we try to relate the two studies, and ask how artistic success is related to particular moral and social attitudes, it is clear that there is no simple answer. No ideology has the convenient consequence of making a novelist of you; no opinion precludes the imaginative realization of its consequence. Nonetheless it is worth asking whether the emotional conflicts we have looked at are artistically fruitful or artistically damaging. There seem to be two answers.

For we have found two separate consequences of the novelist's fear: it can distort, and it can make vivid. Because Kingsley was frightened, he drew back from the consequences of his own novel, and set out to undo his achievement; because Mrs Gaskell was frightened of political crime, she shunted John Barton's murder onto the merely personal level, or turned the troubles at Thornton's mill into an episode in a love affair. Fear has done artistic damage there. But the reason why the mob of *Barnaby Rudge* is so much more powerful than the mob of *The Old Curiosity*

Shop is that Dickens is now more involved and, if not more afraid, is certainly more uncomfortable, more disturbed—disturbed, perhaps, at his own involvement. In *Hard Times*, too, the industrial landscape is an uncomfortable one. "The piston of the steam-engine worked monotonously up and down, like the head of an elephant in a state of melancholy madness." That is comic, but it brings a giggle, not a laugh: it is frightening too. Fear has been artistically fruitful here.

How can fear have such opposite effects on different novelists? The reason, of course, is that we are applying two different criteria of excellence: power and truth. Fear spoiled the work of Mrs Gaskell because it distorted the truth; it improved the work of Dickens because it made vivid the tongue that spoke. There is not really any reason why these two criteria should not conflict. We could place all novels on a pair of axes, according as they are weak or powerful in their impact, true or distorted in their vision of social and personal relationships. No work of any merit will appear in the weak-distorted segment; but perhaps, too, no great work will stand equally near the positive extremes of truth and power. Among 19th-century novels, *Middlemarch*, *Anna Karenina*, and *Le rouge et le noir* stand high on the scale of truth; *Little Dorrit*, *Crime and Punishment*, and *The Scarlet Letter* far along that of power.

Now in saying this I have said nothing very new. These two criteria correspond to the well-known contrast between the realistic and the romantic. The realist allows his imagination to take the shape of observed reality; his concern is to check his fiction against his ability to watch, to listen, to deduce. The romantic's observation is shaped more by his own wishes, dissatisfactions, ideals, and fears: his world is more directly a projection of his emotional life. Of course, the two merge; but for describing many writers the distinction is useful, and corresponds to the observation of readers. Mrs Gaskell and George Eliot were clearly realists. Their genius was for observation and understanding, and although they drew on their own emotional life, they disciplined it with care; whenever they abandoned realism they fell into the commonplace. This is especially clear with Mrs Gaskell, because she had a fondness for romance: all her stories of bandits, murders, and concealment are mere cliché. She is sometimes praised for the honesty she showed in introducing Esther, the heroine's prostitute aunt, into *Mary Barton*. But although she was honest enough to admit Esther's existence, honesty collapsed when it came to her portrayal. Embarrassment, perhaps even ignorance, hindered truth-telling, and Mrs Gaskell had to fall back on her phantasies, which turn out to be utterly commonplace.

The case is less clear with George Eliot, because what she fell into was less obviously cliché. But the dream-like journey of Romola in the little boat to the plague-stricken village, for instance, cannot compare with the marvellous realism of Hetty's journey to Windsor and back; nor the obvious symbolism of Eppie's golden curls with the brilliant psychological realism of Gwendolen deciding when to wear which of her no doubt symbolic jewels. Both these women—like most women writers—had an imagination that was essentially realistic.

And Dickens? We must now conclude that in spite of his claims to be a realist, he was nothing of the sort. Of course the forms into which his phantasies distorted the world were not arbitrary, but strike an echo in the emotional life of his readers: such is the difference between the great writer of romance, and the merely fanciful. What weird truths we learn from the grotesqueries of Quilp, from the vision of a London mob led by a half-wit, a bastard, and a hangman, from the mutterings of that unending law-suit, and even from the spontaneous combustion of Krook! But they are not the truths of George Eliot, for they feed on the distortions of fear and longing.

In conclusion, I return to the social attitudes from which we began. Must we take our picture of Victorian society entirely from the bourgeoisie, or is there an alternative vision? Must we, in spite of our adjustments of the middle-class imagination, accept it as the only imaginative vision of that world available to us, or did working-class culture produce its own literature, with its own (different) version of human relationships— "eels in a jar" seen from below?

The answer, on the whole, is No. The literature of the Victorian bourgeoisie is one of the world's supreme artistic achievements; it is unreasonable to expect a less articulate, far less educated section of the community to have produced anything to compare with it. Yet lack of education, although it obviously incapacitates a class from producing a complex literature, has certain small advantages; and though there is no real proletarian literature in the 19th century, there may at least be a proletarian voice, whose sound can help us to correct the limitations of the bourgeois imagination.

Where can we look? First, and most obviously, to the memoirs of working-men, such as William Lovett, Thomas Cooper, and Samuel Bamford.[60] These three were remarkable men and their books are fascinating, but if we look in them for a true subculture, we may be disappointed. Samuel Bamford, the weaver-poet and radical leader (whom

I suspect to have been the original of Felix Holt), belonged to two worlds. On the one hand, he is continually slipping into genteel language. Describing the Blanketeers setting off to London in 1817, he writes of "a youth . . . waving his hand to a damsel pale and tremulous with alarm";[61] meeting a couple on a walk, he falls into conversation, and talks of "the noble and exalted pleasures of true affection, and . . . the sickening pangs of love betrayed, and the unhappiness which must eventually haunt the betrayer, whether man or woman."[62] If this is the style to which the self-educated aspired, the advantages of illiteracy were greater than one realized.

But Bamford also belongs to a world of Lancashire superstition and plant-lore, of fights and dialect and quack-doctors. He was in a splendid position to describe, for example, the incident when his friend Healey pulled two teeth instead of one and knocked over a jug of cream—and then had to haggle with the patient's mother over who owed money to whom. As we read Bamford's account of this episode,[63] we can see that he both does and does not belong to the world he is describing. He was Healey's friend, and like him was on the run from the law; yet he seems to see the whole adventure with a touch of the outsider's amusement. We have here something of the mixture of irony and love that Hardy brought to his Wessex peasants.

Like Hardy, Bamford is showing us a world that may belong in the 19th century if we count heads, but not if we measure the direction of change: it is an old, a static, a pre-industrial, even a pre-Reformation world. For this reason, Bamford cannot show us the industrial bourgeoisie from below.

Bamford, who was present at Peterloo, was too old to be a Chartist. Although he lived till 1872, he felt that working-class politics had passed him by, and he urged the Chartists to "turn from the precipice whither you have been led blindfold." Yet he was the same kind of man as they were: his great belief was in do-it-yourself. This was a doctrine, as we have seen, that the propertied and voting classes found it hard to accept. Carlyle was no friend of the bourgeoisie, yet he was quite as unable as they were to understand Chartism. What is the meaning of the Charter, he asked:

> What are all popular commotions and maddest bellowings, from Peterloo to the Place-de-Grève itself? Bellowings, inarticulate cries as of a dumb creature in rage and pain; to the ear of wisdom they are inarticulate prayers: "Guide me, govern me! I am mad and miserable, and cannot guide myself!"[64]

233

Now if there is any one thing that the Chartists did not want, it was this. "What is our present relation to you as a section of the middle class?" the Sunderland Chartists said to the Anti-Corn-Law League in 1840. "It is one of violent opposition. You are the holders of power, participation in which you refuse us."[65] That the sympathetic Carlyle could so misinterpret Chartist aims is a clear sign of a vast cultural gulf. Chartism was not a plea for guidance, it was an emphatic repudiation of guidance, an assertion by the working class that they would run their own affairs—and, if possible, the country too. The assertion can sometimes have an attractive breeziness. "Well done, Thornton," said Feargus O'Connor after one William Thornton had opened a Chartist meeting with a prayer. "When we get the Charter I will see that you are made the Archbishop of York."[66]

It was not only politics that the Chartist leaders felt the working class should do for themselves. Thomas Cooper urged working-men to "join hands and heads to create a library of your own. Your own prose and your own poetry: you ought to be resolved to create these."[67] This programme did not succeed, for the lure of bourgeois culture, like the lure of bourgeois ideology, was too strong. The English working class may never have felt enthusiastic about "eels in a jar," but they have never really rejected it, never told the Edinburgh Reviewers that they would have none of them, never really followed the call of Marx and Morris and Ernest Jones. Scholarships have tamed a thousand Coopers.

So there is no working-class culture as a presence in Victorian literature, there is only a working-class voice. It is a blunt voice that hates cant and is cynical about high-minded professions. It is the voice of not wanting to be helped. "Heaven preserve us from kind masters," it says. "Duty to your employer? Your duty is to have no employer at all," it says.[68] It must have heckled a thousand anti-Corn-Law speakers, a thousand Gladstonian Liberals, but it has usually (thank God? alas?) been content to heckle.

And to hear it, we do best to open the bourgeois authors. "I want an end of these liberties took with my place," said the workman to Mrs Pardiggle:

> An't my place dirty? Yes, it is dirty—it's nat'rally dirty, and it's nat'rally onwholesome; and we had five dirty and onwholesome children, as is all dead infants, and so much the better for them, and for us besides. Have I read the little book wot you left? No, I an't read the little book wot you left. There an't nobody here as knows how to read it; and if there wos, it wouldn't be suitable to

me. It's a book fit for a babby, and I'm not a babby. If you was to leave me a doll, I shouldn't nuss it.[69]

A workman said it, but it took Dickens to hear it. Mrs Gaskell, Kingsley, George Eliot, Dickens, all heard and captured this voice; then, some-where or other, in the same book, they anxiously retracted what they had made it say. One function of the literary critic, reading their work today, is to guard these moments of insight against the inevitable withdrawal symptoms: moralizings, authorial reassurances, contrived happy endings. It is not necessary to argue that this working-class voice is truer or wiser than the more complex voice of the bourgeoisie: the total impact of *Bleak House* is more profound than the impact of Mrs Pardiggle's workman. All we need to argue is that the voice is worth hearing. All voices are worth hearing: to the lover of literature this must be an article of faith. And at times there are voices that are especially worth hearing. The voice of working-class resentment is especially valuable when authority is being sanctimonious. This is neither rare nor confined to the 19th century. "Methinks I could not die anywhere so contented as in the king's com-pany," said Henry V before Agincourt, comfortable in the knowledge of his little joke, and the fact that he had archbishops to keep his conscience clear, "his cause being just and his quarrel honourable." "That's more than we know," growled this same sullen voice in reply.[70]

References

1. Lord Palmerston in the Dan Pacifico debate in the Commons (1850). Quoted in ASA BRIGGS, "The Language of 'Class' in Early Nineteenth Century England," in ASA BRIGGS and J. SAVILLE (ed.), *Essays in Labour History* (London 1960).
2. BEATRICE WEBB, *My Apprenticeship* (London 1926), Ch. 1.
3. "JANUARY SEARLE," *The Life of Ebenezer Elliott* (1850).
4. To Mr Hargreaves, 5 April 1863; quoted in JOHN MORLEY, *Life of Cobden* (London 1881), Ch. 34.
5. Frederick Engels to Albert Lange, 29 March 1865. Cf. GERTRUDE HIMMELFARB, *Darwin and the Darwinian Revolution* (London 1959).
6. ROBERT OWEN, *A New View of Society* (1813).
7. GEORGE ELIOT, "Three Months in Weimar," *Fraser's Magazine* LI, (June 1855).
8. THOMAS CARLYLE, *Past and Present* (1843), Bk I, Ch. 6.

9. THOMAS CARLYLE, *Sartor Resartus* (1831), Bk I, Ch. 10.
10. CARLYLE, *Past and Present*, Bk III, Ch. 1.
11. MATTHEW ARNOLD, *Friendship's Garland* (1871), Letter 2.
12. JOHN RUSKIN, *The Crown of Wild Olive* (1866), Lecture II: Traffic.
13. ROBERT SOUTHEY, *Sir Thomas More, or Colloquies on the Progress and Prospects of Society* (1829); LORD MACAULAY, "Southey's Colloquies," *Edinburgh Review* (January 1830).
14. A. V. DICEY, *Lectures on the Relation between Law and Public Opinion in England during the 19th Century* (London 1905).
15. KARL MARX, *Capital* (1867), Vol. I, Part IV, Ch. 14.
16. JOHN RUSKIN, "The Nature of Gothic," Section 16, in *The Stones of Venice*, Vol. II (1851).
17. WILLIAM MORRIS, *Useful Work Versus Useless Toil* (1885).
18. MARK RUTHERFORD, *Catherine Furze* (1893), Ch. 11.
19. ELIZABETH GASKELL, *North and South* (1855), Ch. 10.
20. Francis Place to Joseph Parkes, 7 December 1833; quoted in R. K. WEBB, *The British Working Class Reader, 1790–1848* (London 1955), Ch. 7.
21. Cf. RICHARD D. ALTICK, *The English Common Reader* (Chicago 1957), esp. Ch. 9.
22. *Report of Commissioners on the Employment of Children in Factories* (1833); quoted in G. M. YOUNG and W. D. HANDCOCK (ed.), *English Historical Documents* (London 1956), No. 250 f.
23. EDWIN HODDER, *The Life and Work of the 7th Earl of Shaftesbury, K.G.* (London 1886), Vol. I, p. 148.
24. RICHARD OASTLER, *The Law and the Needle* (1836); the *Manchester Guardian*, 24 September 1836.
25. Cf. CHARLES KNIGHT, *Passages of a Working Life* (1864–5).
26. William Morris to Mrs Burne-Jones, 1 June 1884; quoted in ASA BRIGGS (ed.), *William Morris: Selected Writings and Designs* (Harmondsworth 1962), p. 149.
27. Review of *Mary Barton* by W. R. Greg in the *Edinburgh Review* LXXXIX (April 1849).
28. *Our Mutual Friend* (1865), Bk I, Ch. 16; Bk II, Ch. 9 and 14; Bk III, Ch. 8.
29. CECIL DRIVER, *Tory Radical: the Life of Richard Oastler* (New York 1946), Ch. 25, Section 3.
30. J. S. MILL, *Principles of Political Economy* (1848); quoted in WEBB, *op. cit.*
31. J. S. MILL, *Autobiography* (1873), Ch. 7.
32. E. B. BROWNING, "The Cry of the Children" (1844).
33. WILLIAM BLAKE, "London," in *Songs of Experience* (1794).
34. WILLIAM BLAKE, *Jerusalem* (1804–20), Section 30.
35. WILLIAM BLAKE, *Vala, or The Four Zoas* (1797), Night the Seventh (a).
36. CHARLES KINGSLEY, *Alton Locke* (1850), Ch. 1.
37. GEORGE ELIOT, *Felix Holt* (1866), Ch. 30.
38. "Address to the Working Men, by Felix Holt," *Blackwood's* CIII (January 1868).

39. Cf. DAVID CRAIG, "Fiction and the Rising Industrial Classes," *Essays in Criticism* XVII (January 1967); ARNOLD KETTLE, "Felix Holt the Radical," *Critical Essays on George Eliot*, ed. by Barbara Hardy (London 1970).

40. *Hard Times* (1854), Bk II, Ch. 4.

41. "On Strike," *Household Words* VIII (11 February 1854).

42. Cf. GEOFFREY CARNALL, "Dickens, Mrs Gaskell, and the Preston Strike," *Victorian Studies* VIII (September 1964); also GEORGE ORWELL, "Charles Dickens" (1939), in *Critical Essays* (London 1946).

43. GASKELL, *op. cit.*, Ch. 42.

44. Speech in Birmingham, 6 January 1853; Collected Papers II, 400–6.

45. *The Uncommercial Traveller* (1861), Section 4.

46. *David Copperfield* (1850), Ch. 59.

47. *Bleak House* (1853), Ch. 64.

48. *Great Expectations* (1861), Ch. 25, 37, and 55.

49. *Martin Chuzzlewit* (1844), Ch. 9.

50. GEORGE ELIOT, *Daniel Deronda* (1876), Ch. 22.

51. *Our Mutual Friend* (1865), Bk I, Ch. 11.

52. Cf. HUMPHREY HOUSE, *The Dickens World* (London 1941); EDGAR JOHNSON, *Charles Dickens: His Tragedy and Triumph* (New York 1952); PHILIP COLLINS, *Dickens and Crime* (London 1962) and *Dickens and Education* (London 1963).

53. John Ruskin to Charles Eliot Norham, 19 June 1870.

54. J. A. V. CHAPPLE and A. POLLARD (ed.), *The Letters of Mrs Gaskell* (Manchester 1966), No. 42: Elizabeth Gaskell to Mrs Gregg, 1849.

55. *ibid.*, No. 35; Elizabeth Gaskell to Catherine Winkworth, 23 December 1848.

56. *ibid.*, No. 42.

57. Cf. JOHN LUCAS, "Mrs Gaskell and Brotherhood," in D. HOWARD, J. LUCAS, and J. GOODE (ed.), *Tradition and Tolerance in 19th-Century Fiction* (London 1966), Ch. 4.

58. BENJAMIN DISRAELI, *Sybil* (1845), Bk III, Ch. 4.

59. *Barnaby Rudge* (1841), Ch. 55.

60. SAMUEL BAMFORD, *Passages in the Life of a Radical* (1844); *Early Days* (1849); THOMAS COOPER, *The Life of Thomas Cooper* (1872); WILLIAM LOVETT, *Life and Struggles in Pursuit of Bread, Knowledge, and Freedom* (1876).

61. BAMFORD, *op. cit.* (1844), Ch. 6.

62. *ibid.*, Ch. 72.

63. *ibid.*, Ch. 9.

64. THOMAS CARLYLE, *Chartism* (1839), Ch. 6.

65. Quoted in MARK HOVELL, *The Chartist Movement* (Manchester 1904), Ch. 13. Cf. LUCY BROWN, "The Chartists and the Anti-Corn-Law League," in ASA BRIGGS (ed.), *Chartist Studies* (London 1959).

66. BENJAMIN WILSON, *The Struggles of an Old Chartist* (1887); quoted in J. F. C. HARRISON (ed.), *Society and Politics in England, 1780–1960* (New York 1965).

67. Quoted in ALTICK, *op. cit.*, Ch. 9, Section IV.
68. ERNEST JONES, *The People's Paper* (13 November 1852); quoted in
    G. D. H. COLE and A. W. FILSON (ed.), *British Working Class Movements:
    Selected Documents, 1789–1875* (London 1951), Ch. 15, No. 16.
69. *Bleak House* (1853), Ch. 8.
70. WILLIAM SHAKESPEARE, *Henry V*, Act IV, Scene 1.

Author's note: I thank my colleagues John Rosselli and Barry Supple, who read and annotated an earlier draft of this essay.

CHAPTER 7

Balzac and Dickens

Arnold Kettle[*]

Balzac (1799–1850) and Dickens (1812–70) are in many respects so different as novelists that the bringing of them together may not seem likely to be useful. They are roughly though not exactly contemporary, but in any case the developments of modern France and England are far from identical. Nor can one glibly assume that one is simply contrasting the two outstanding novelists of the time, for although Dickens's pre-eminence among his compatriots is now fairly generally agreed, it is less obvious that Balzac, as opposed to Stendhal (1783–1842), can be singled out as the indisputable master of the French novel of the first half of the 19th century.

Yet to bring the two writers together, in full recognition of their differences, is not to pursue a purely arbitrary comparison. They *are* linked, and not casually, these two giant figures whom subsequent purists have often tried, but without much success, to reduce in size. And they are linked, in the end, not by the more formal discussion of "schools" and "tendencies" and "influences," but by the richer history of the development of human society and human consciousness itself. What ultimately makes it rewarding, and even inevitable, to bring Balzac and Dickens together is the relationship of each—by no means identical but suggestively comparable—with the emergence of the 19th-century bourgeois world. Stendhal, of course, reacts quite as profoundly to this same phenomenon, but his reaction is in a basic way different: not less intense, not less critical, but different; and this is a matter not merely of opinions and ideas but, in the fullest possible sense, of artistic form and achievement. Perhaps the contrast can best be suggested by the introduction of a word that is often found in the discussion of Balzac or of Dickens but that scarcely anyone would use in relation to Stendhal: the word "vulgar."

The word itself is used in somewhat different senses about the two

* Professor of Literature, The Open University.

young writers. Dickens's vulgarity is associated above all with the milieu within which he operates; Balzac's is more often linked with his personal style and taste. But in both cases what is involved is a quality of sensibility directly related to the writer's position and attitude within 19th-century society. It is not, in the more abstract sense, an ideological matter, although it has ideological ramifications. Rather, what one would stress is the sense in which Balzac and Dickens participate in, and *belong* to, the very society they so relentlessly expose, so that acceptance and rejection are almost inextricably compounded, the depth of the criticism emerges out of the intensity of the participation, and the vulgarity is strength.

Balzac and Dickens were both involved in their respective societies (whose common aspects were at least as important as their differences) in a way that most later novelists (say, Flaubert or James) were not. One does not imply, of course, that the later writers were ignorant about, or indifferent to, what was happening in the world in which they lived, but rather that their view of the artist and his role was different. This is not primarily a biographical matter, reflected in the actual life and opinions of the writers concerned, though the biographical evidence is relevant. It is significant that Balzac and Dickens were both—in a sense one could not think of in relation to their successors—public men, engaged not only in the public disputes and debates of their time, but in activity as well. This makes their "commitment," in so far as the 20th-century word fits them at all, rather strikingly different from that of the "engaged" modern writer, whose commitment is generally to an idea about reality rather than to reality itself. Dickens, more than Balzac, was a practical man: his commitment was essentially to the exposure and improvement of social reality. But Balzac, too, with his passion for projects that reminds one of Defoe, saw life from a standpoint more closely associated with the examination and solution of actual problems than has become usual for a literary man. He seriously considered standing for parliament in 1831 (getting to the point of investigating his chances in three constituencies), and in 1848 was invited by one of the revolutionary clubs to stand for the Constituent Assembly. Dickens, too, was several times invited to become a parliamentary candidate, and his refusal, based on a life-long contempt for Parliament acquired through his early experience as a reporter, did not reflect any general unwillingness to assume the responsibilities of public life. The editorship of *Household Words* was only one of many ways by which he established for himself an active role in his relations with his vast public. He was an indefatigable lecturer, after-dinner speaker, public performer, and pronouncer upon the issues of the day. This was partly due to financial reasons, but the very absorption of both Dickens and Balzac in the financial aspects of the production of literature is itself significant. Taine's famous sentence, *Balzac fut un homme d'affaires, et un homme d'affaires endetté*[1] (Balzac was a businessman, and a businessman in debt), may not be the last word on a great writer, but it exposes an essential strand between the novelist and his times.

Balzac wrote so much and so compulsively that it is extraordinary that he had time to spare for anything else; but his bizarre donning of a monastic robe for the hectic activity of artistic creation does not imply a withdrawal from the world. He shut himself up to participate the more fully. And this sense of participation—the opposite of a standing aside, of a search for a vantage-point removed from heat and sweat—is expressed in the very fibre of the writing of both Balzac and Dickens. Each is prepared in the midst of a novel to relate the fictional situation he is concerned with to the actual problems and developments of the outside world, and on occasion to offer opinions and advice as to what should be done in actual France or England. Balzac has no compunction about discussing agricultural policy or the social role of the Catholic Church in the midst of a novel. In his prefaces and postscripts he writes of his fictional world as though it were the real world, discussing the development of his books not in terms of some artistic necessity but always in terms of the actual life and trends and needs of France. Of *Eugénie Grandet* (1833) he wrote:

> There is no invention here. This story is the imperfect translation of a few pages from the great book of the world. . . . It demanded patience rather than art.[2]

Dickens also, without any sense of incongruity, will step out of his role of omniscient narrator to appeal to the right reverends and wrong reverends to take more seriously their responsibilities toward the outcasts of the London slums. Nor did he scorn to change the conception of his books in response to pressures and suggestions from outside that struck him as reasonable. He was extremely sensitive not only to circulation figures but to advice from his readers. When a dwarf complained that the presentation of Miss Mowcher was in effect unfair to dwarfs, he modified the presentation in later instalments of *David Copperfield* (1850). The introduction of a good Jew, Riah, into *Our Mutual Friend* (1865) was deliberately done to counteract the fear that the figure of Fagin might suggest anti-Semitism. The point here is, of course, the contrast between such attitudes—which imply a view of the work of the artist as public, socially effective, and therefore morally responsible in a straightforward down-to-earth way, like any other activity—and more individualist views that see the artist's integrity in terms of his own isolated selfhood or of some ideal conception of autonomous art.

This rejection of any conception of "pure" or autonomous art is no doubt one of the causes of the reservations of modern readers in their attitudes to both Dickens and Balzac. This is connected with the accusation, especially where Balzac is concerned, of a rather gross materialism. Henry James, in an essay that is by no means unappreciative of Balzac's greatness, puts the point characteristically when he speaks of "all that, right and left, he causes to assail us, almost to suffocation, under the general rubric of *things*," and adds:

> The general money question so loads him up and weighs him down that he moves through the human comedy, from beginning to end, very much in the fashion of a camel, the ship of the desert, surmounted with a cargo. "Things" for him are francs and centimes more than any others, and I give up as inscrutable, unfathomable, the nature, the peculiar avidity of his interest in them. . . . His universe goes on expressing itself for him, to its furthest reaches, on its finest sides, in the terms of the market.[3]

It is the distinction of James that, shocked as he is by Balzac's failure "to make us forget that anything so odious [as money] exists," he should recognize that the very obsession he finds so distasteful lies also at the root of Balzac's incomparable strength and "gives him his place apart, makes him, among the novelists, the largest, weightiest presence."

James's comments, in this remarkably interesting essay, have a more than personal relevance. It is not just a matter of one immensely intelligent writer of a different school paying his ambiguous yet admiring tribute to a *confrère*. The intelligentsia of the bourgeois world, in its changing nature and emphasis, is speaking. It has become vulgar to see that world, as Balzac sees it, "in terms of the market." The retreat from the sort of realism that Balzac and Dickens supremely exemplify is revealed.

> I am quite simply a bourgeois living a retired life in the country, occupying myself with literature and demanding nothing of other people.[4]

Flaubert could write thus, and the contrast in attitude with that of a Balzac or a Dickens is striking. Again, what is involved is neither simply a way of life (significant as that is) nor a theory of art (though that is there too). What distinguishes a James or a Flaubert from a Dickens or a

Balzac is a quality of sensibility that reflects a new relationship with social reality. Between the artist and the world he is dealing with, some new factor seems to arise. It is not easy to define the new factor, and a too crude attempt to do so does not get us far—as H. G. Wells was to find when he was unwise enough to tackle Henry James on that subject. Distance has something to do with it, the sense of being and producing something separate from the ordinary stuff of existence—an inability to share, though not necessarily an unawareness of, the eternal reciprocity of tears and laughter. Flaubert hates the bourgeois world, but somehow seems to shield himself from it by an attitude of superiority. James marvellously explores the havoc wreaked by the money Balzac is indelicate enough to mention so often. The bourgeois intellectual puts up his defences. It is not that he is smug or uncritical or imperceptive; but he is not, like a Dickens or a Balzac, in the thick of things, and so he sees them differently. Material reality has somehow or other to be kept at a certain distance. To grant it a basic importance seems to be denying the claim of a deeper reality. "It were, in our opinion, an offence against humanity to place Mr Dickens among the greatest novelists," writes Henry James, "for we are convinced that it is one of the conditions of his genius not to see beneath the surface of things."[5]

The assumption that "realism," in either the Balzacian or the Dickensian sense, involves primarily a concern with "the surface of things" is common to much 20th-century criticism. It is an assumption highly misleading yet not implausible; for while it reflects a fatal under-estimation of the depth and seriousness of the two writers, it does at the same time guide us toward the nature of that depth and seriousness. For what brings Balzac and Dickens together and distinguishes them from so many of their successors is their unqualified respect for material reality.

The construction of most of Balzac's novels, especially the longer ones, is relatively simple. About one third of each novel consists of an "exposition," the statement, so to speak, of a situation from which we start. The drama follows, usually centred upon one protagonist and most often concerned with his downfall. Such a description, however, with its overtone of classical tragedy, can be misleading, apart from the fact that there are many stories to which it does not apply at all. In the first place, the distinction between introduction and what follows is not at all obvious, and if Balzac did not tend to point it out most readers would probably miss it. In the second place, few of the stories have a wholly dominant single protagonist, even when the title (e.g. *La rabouilleuse* [1842]) leads one to expect it. It is basic to Balzac's whole vision—a vision gradually more and more self-consciously organized and articulated—that nothing can ever be isolated or understood except in relation to everything else. The more you examine a beginning the more you see that it is not a beginning, and the more you concentrate on one character the more you are forced to discuss others. Hence his emphasis on *milieu* such as the description of the Maison Vauquer at the beginning of *Le père Goriot* (1834), or the "Dutch" interior of *La maison du chat qui pélote* (1830; At the Sign of the Cat and Racket), or the house near Tours in *La grenadière* (1832), and his need to develop always a number of central characters whose fates and motives are intertwined. Even in a very short and simple story such as *La messe de l'athée* (1836; The Atheist's Mass), centring upon a single action by a single character, Desplein, the point can be made only through the development of a full portrait of Bourgeat the water-carrier, with the whole story refracted through the consciousness of Bianchon: yet this is a tale that might appear to be the simplest, least evocative of moral fables.

Hence, too, the device about which Balzac himself quite rightly became so excited: the idea of recurring characters who appear in several novels. Like all technical devices this cannot, of course, be adequately considered in terms of technique. Percy Lubbock has argued that "the laborious interweaving of his books into a single scheme" has little to do with the effects he achieves, and that "in general a book of Balzac's suffers, rather than gains, by the recurrence of the old names that he has used already elsewhere"[6]; but this is surely to reveal a predisposition to see each book as autonomous, peculiarly separate and artistically self-contained. Balzac's point is precisely that life is not like that, as the whole conception of *La comédie humaine* testifies, and as Henry James recognized when he remarked: "The way to judge him is to try to walk all round him —on which we see how remarkably far we have to go."[7] The recurring characters in *La comédie humaine* are Balzac's prime defence against abstraction and isolation: the abstraction of ideas, the isolation of people. As an artistic device it serves much the same purpose (though on a more ambitious scale) as Dickens's complex plots, which with their interwoven strands serve to suggest the complexity, the chances, and the intangible logic of life itself. Even when a Balzacian character may surprise us by a certain inconsistency—as in the part played by Doctor Bianchon, normally a bulwark of respectable good sense, in *La muse du département* (1843; The Muse of the Department)—the effect is primarily to make us recognize the many-sidedness of the individual human being, a feature of life that Balzac's normal method of presentation perhaps does not sufficiently indicate. If we were to meet Rastignac in only one book we should get a very incomplete idea not only of what he does but of what, as a man, he is like. Development or change within the individual character is, in the Balzacian universe, often a longer-term phenomenon than a single novel can convey.

The recurring appearance of a person in different novels has, then, the tendency to counteract Balzac's normal method of presentation of character, which emphasizes type characteristics rather than the changing nature of the individual. In his *Avant-propos* to *La comédie humaine* Balzac outlines the theory on which his presentation of characters is based:

> Does not society modify man, according to the conditions in which he lives and acts, into men as manifold as the species in zoology? The differences between a soldier, a worker, a civil servant, a lawyer, an idler, a scholar, a statesman, a merchant, a sailor, a poet, a pauper, and a priest are as great, though not as easy to define, as those between the wolf, the lion, the ass, the crow, the shark, the seal, the sheep, etc. Thus social species, like zoological species, have always existed and will always exist.[8]

It is the various "social species" (endowed, it is worth noting, with the indefinite, as opposed to the definite, article) that form the basis of the two or three thousand "conspicuous types of a period" that act out the human comedy.

Put like this, Balzac's theory of character presentation may appear to be almost absurdly mechanistic, and there is indeed in the *theory* a strong element of mechanism, occasionally reinforced in the novels themselves. Sometimes he appears to accept something like the mediaeval physiology of the comedy of humours. He can say of Cousin Pons that *D'un tempérament sanguinbilieux, la bile passa dans le sang, il fut pris par une violente hepatite*[9] (He was of a sanguine-bilious temperament, the bile passed into his blood, and a violent liver attack was the result). But it is never wise to make fun of Balzac's apparently crude and characteristically French physio-psychological theories, for in practice he shows an unparalleled apprehension of the interrelations between physical and mental states. And his presentation of his individuals as social types does not in fact make them any less convincing as individuals. Philippe Bridau may have been conceived as a soldier to contrast with his brother the artist, but this in no way limits his authenticity as a unique character. On the contrary, as Georg Lukács has put it:

> The realism of Balzac rests on a uniformly complete rendering of
> the particular individual traits of each of his characters on the one
> hand and the traits that are typical of them as members of a class
> on the other. But he goes even further than this: he also throws
> light on the traits that different groups within bourgeois society have
> in common . . . clearly demonstrating the intrinsic unity of the
> social evolutionary process, the objective social bond between
> apparently quite dissimilar types.[10]

In other words he is able to convince us that Lisbeth Fischer, the cousin
Bette of that novel, is what she becomes because she has been an Alsatian
peasant and has developed the emotions, the qualities, the sensibilities that
an Alsatian peasant-woman would understandably develop if she were
subjected to the particular pressures and choices she has had to meet.
Although Lisbeth is presented with a number of insistent personal
emphases—on her complexion, her eyebrows, her odd clothes, her
frugality—that may at first seem limiting, these qualities that Balzac
reiterates and plays on are so firmly established within a specific social
situation that they bear any amount of probing. In this way the alliance
between Bette (the austere, self-disciplined, plain, virginal, hard-working
peasant) and Madame Marneffe (the luxurious, frivolous, self-indulgent,
pretty, unscrupulous, petit-bourgeois *poule de luxe*) becomes entirely
convincing, and the reader takes in his stride Balzac's more provocative
asides about the relation between celibacy and fanaticism. Balzac can
assure us that "Virginity, like all monstrosities, has its special riches, its
overwhelming splendours."[11] He has already long convinced us that on
the question of monstrosities he is a supreme authority.

Lukács, who has written with great insight on Balzac, has observed:

> The central category and criterion of realist literature is the type,
> a peculiar synthesis that organically binds together the general and
> the particular both in characters and situations. What makes a type
> a type is not its average quality, nor its mere individual being,
> however profoundly conceived; what makes it a type is that in it
> all the humanly and socially essential determinants are present on
> their highest level of development, in the ultimate unfolding of the
> possibilities latent in them, in extreme presentation of their extremes,
> rendering concrete the peaks and limits of men and epochs.[12]

Such an emphasis, which suggests how a writer like Balzac can be at the
same time "extreme" and yet typical, may suggest a somewhat abstract
approach, and Balzac does indeed seem, in comparison with Dickens or
almost any English writer, to have set considerable store on his "scientific"
credentials. But the effect of a Balzac novel is very seldom abstract, and

when the novelist does offer his readers a few sentences of moralistic generalization, the result—like the moralizing couplets at the end of *Doctor Faustus* or *Don Giovanni*—seems to belong to the necessary conventions of the form and time. Three quarters of the way through *La cousine Bette* (1846), Balzac writes:

> This sketch gives innocent souls some idea of the various havocs that the Madame Marneffes of this world may wreak in families, and by what means they can strike at poor virtuous wives, apparently so far beyond their reach. But if we consider how such evils may affect the highest level of society, around the throne itself, we realize the price paid for kings' mistresses and can estimate the debt a people owes its sovereigns when they set an example in moral conduct and family life.[13]

The sort of reaction such a passage evokes is typical of Balzac's strategy. Like Dickens, he risks extremes of banality that would engulf another writer, and turns them to his own purposes. Much of the time his method might be described as knowing how to go a little too far, and this does not apply merely to the more obviously "extreme" figures such as old Grandet. His account in *Le père Goriot* of Madame Vauquer's relationship with the bogus Countess of l'Ambermesnil is an example:

> After a good deal of serious consideration the two widows went together to the Palais-Royal where they bought a feathered hat and a bonnet in the Galeries de Bois. The Countess next took her friend to *La Petite Jeannette*, where they chose a dress and a scarf. With these weapons in use and the widow well armed she looked exactly like the creature on the signboard of the *Boeuf à la Mode*; yet in her own eyes she was so changed for the better that she felt she owed the Countess something and, though not generous by nature, begged her to accept a hat costing twenty francs. The fact was that she intended asking the Countess for further services, to sound Goriot and present Madame Vauquer to him in a favourable light. Madame de l'Ambermesnil lent herself very amiably to this plot. She laid siege to the old vermicelli-maker and succeeded in obtaining an interview with him. But when she found that her overtures, prompted by her private desire to secure him for herself, were received with embarrassment, not to say repulsion, she gave up, revolted by his coarseness.[14]

The achievement here is to dramatize the actions of the unspeakable women by contriving a sense of battle in which no quarter is given because the depths of insincerity and unscrupulousness on both sides, though funny (for they are harming only each other), are limitless. This sense of the limitlessness of bourgeois cupidity and self-deception, whether

247

seen comically or with a tragic irony, is what makes Balzac so marvellously witty a writer. Whereas others present the extremes of human conduct as funny or repulsive because they are abnormal, Balzac reveals the normal through making us grasp the significance of the extremes, so that the extremes become part of normality. The situations that most arouse his wit are the most outrageous, and his method is to add always one more sentence to allow for one more turn of the screw of remorseless egoism. Because the extremities are inherent in the normal actions and reactions of the characters, there is no clear and consoling line between the ordinary and the monstrous. Vautrin is one of his great inspirations because he personifies the very outrageousness that Balzac needs to complete his picture of a society of bottomless corruption. The minor Vautrins—such as Lousteau or even (though his malice is apparently more verbal than real) Bixiou—all play the part, as far as the formal aspect of the books is concerned, of Mephistopheles. They are licensed advocates in devilishness; but the evil they revel in is not metaphysical.

We should not underestimate the importance of Balzac's "scientific" aim, which he sketches so frankly in the *Avant-propos*. What makes it significant is not so much the validity of the philosophical points expounded—the judgments on Cuvier, Geoffroi de Saint-Hilaire, and the rest—as the temper and attitude that they express. What he is claiming is not only an unprecedented comprehensiveness—to range *systematically* over a whole society—but the wherewithal, the theoretical equipment, to conduct such an enterprise. And the truth is that a less exalted ambition would inevitably have produced a less impressive result. The purpose of his philosophy was to give him the courage, the range, and the equipment to turn himself from a writer of tales into the creator of *La comédie humaine*.

His range, though it has its limitations, is probably greater than that of Dickens. It does not really encompass the working class, despite the occasional proletarian, such as the joiner Jacques Brigaut and the potter Jean-François Tascheron, who are presented with sympathy but, by Balzacian standards, without much stuffing. But over the rest of French, especially provincial, society he moves with extraordinary confidence, though his upper-class parvenus are as a whole more successful than the representatives of the old aristocracy. And what emerges is an *oeuvre* very different from what the reader coming to Balzac by way of the *Avant-propos* or subsequent introductions stressing the sociological achievement must surely anticipate. What impresses above all is the intensity of the passion, the moral force, the combination of encyclopaedic knowledge and passionate intensity embodied in the whole performance.

La comédie humaine is at once a shattering examination of human egoism and an incredibly well-documented chronicle of French life in the first half of the 19th century, and neither aspect could achieve its full effect without the other. The documentation does at times, it is true, reach the point of absurdity: we cannot follow one of the characters into a room with pictures on the wall without being subjected to long disquisitions on the history of art; German music cannot be mentioned without Balzac feeling the need to assure us that he knows the name of every eminent, or even ephemeral, German musician. But even such excesses have the effect of assuring us of the sort of reality that interests Balzac, and of providing a setting of a solidity adequate to receive his more monstrous creations. How else to provide a milieu that could *contain* his Grandets and Séchard senior, his Balthazar Claës and Baron Hulot and Madame Cibot? The exaggerated documentation—the lists, the bills, the interminable financial calculations—would count for nothing were they not part of an achieved whole in which extremity is absorbed into, and illumines, a basically convincing scene. Thus the physical sufferings of Pierrette Lorrain form an acceptable artistic counterpart to the intrigues and inhumanities of the Rogrons only because the scene and society of Provins, with its fatal relationship to Paris, has been presented with such complete authenticity. Dickens does not always manage this. Too often he lifts his babes-in-the-wood out of their milieu—be it that of realism or of phantasy—and exhibits their sufferings under an isolating spotlight. That is why he can scarcely get away with the death of Little Nell, whereas Pierrette's death is absorbed into a novel that, although not one of Balzac's greatest, is a successful achievement.

The point of Engels' famous remarks about Balzac[15] is a double one. He insists that what is in the end important in *La comédie humaine* is not the author's political philosophy—his expressed determination to serve Church and monarchy—but the objective revelation of social conflict and change in the novels themselves. Balzac's integrity as an artist grappling with the actual stuff of reality, he argues, defeats the rather provincial limitations of his private opinions, so that he is forced by his demon of honesty to produce books whose living truth may often contradict the personal prejudices of the writer. The justice of this view is demonstrated by an analysis of such a novel as *Les paysans* (1844; Sons of the Soil) or even *Le curé de village* (1840), in which the tragic situation of Véronique Graslin in the first part of the book is artistically far more strongly and convincingly presented than the didactic and utopian developments of the second part, in which the author's own political and social views are embodied. Up to this point, however, Engels' comments might be (and too often have been) seen primarily as indicating Balzac's extraordinary value to the social historian—a point already attested by Marx in his tribute in the third volume of *Capital* (1894). The more significant aspect—to the literary critic, that is—lies in Engels' adjacent point, where he refers to Balzac as "a far greater master of realism than all the Zolas past, present, and future," because, as he puts it, "he *saw* the necessity of the downfall of his favourite nobles and described them as people deserving no better fate; . . . he *saw* the real men of the future where, for the time being, they alone were to be found—that I consider one of the greatest triumphs of realism, and one of the greatest features in old Balzac." This is not the moment to become involved in a discussion of realism (though we may note that what Engels is approaching, in his point about Balzac's revealing the men of the future, is a resolution of Aristotle's contrast between history and poetry). The immediate point of Engels' remarks is that they can help us to find the link between Balzac's artistic achievement and his social insight. The artistic achievement—the extraordinary intensity of his books—cannot be fully explained in terms of his more or less scientific, sociological understanding or his role (as he himself put it) of "secretary." A lesser writer might excel him there. For an analysis of his art, therefore, we need a somewhat different approach: the significant word in Engels' letter is the reiterated and emphasized "saw," implying something other than a rationalized awareness of a general phenomenon. If we can define the sense in which Balzac "saw" what was happening to France between 1816 and 1848, and expressed that vision in *La comédie humaine*, we shall be a little nearer to knowing why he is one of the greatest of novelists.

The key word, I would suggest—and one that Balzac himself often uses—is "egoism." *La comédie humaine* is an expression of the nature, the ramifications, and the horror of egoism. It is his apprehension of this horror that gives Balzac's creations their intensity, and determines the style and structure of his stories. It is the key to the character of the over-generous Goriot no less than to those of his terrible grasping daughters or of Rastignac or of the arch-egoist Vautrin. For Goriot is, in his way, a monster scarcely less shocking than Vautrin, and the piling-on of such epithets as "the good old man" soon achieves the effect of irony, and is seen to be another device of Balzac's in his attempts to find ways of expressing a vision that is, within the accepted social norms of language, almost inexpressible.

The horror of Balzac's monsters, like Shakespeare's, is that they are at the same time monstrous, unique, and typical. This is true even of the more amiable of them, such as César Birotteau or Cousin Pons, and also of the most virtuous. The good Adeline Hulot is as monstrous as the wicked Josépha and a good deal less human. Indeed, it is one of the striking things about *La comédie humaine* that the people who in moral terms come out of it best are on the whole the least firmly characterized. For Balzac had the true historian's instinct for worrying at the figures who were going to offer him most. Among novelists, only Proust rivals him in this, as in so much else. And Balzac, like Proust, was perfectly well aware that most people were not much like his main characters, any more than they were much like himself, and that the world—not least France—was not populated by monsters at all.

Although the depiction of egoism is the essence of *La comédie humaine*, the depiction is not moralistic. This does not mean that Balzac does not want his readers to draw any conclusions: obviously he does. Quite often, as we have already seen, he offers us a moral in a way that might lead us to think that he is one of those novelists whom Lawrence accused of not taking their finger out of the pan. But this should not mislead us. Balzac consistently uses adjectives that betray his own judgments of his characters, but this rarely prevents him from giving them their head. As has been said, he *loves* his Madame Marneffes, even when he most unambiguously disapproves of them. The egoism that obsesses Balzac, and that wreaks such appalling havoc among the characters of *La comédie humaine*, is never presented in the abstract or as an inflexible quality of the human condition as such. The egosim that is seen poisoning almost every human relationship in the novels is always associated with specific forms of social conduct, and especially with the central preoccupation of bourgeois existence, the accumulation of money. "*La finance,*" says the shrewd Doctor Bianchon, "*n'est autre chose que l'égoisme solidifié*"[16] (Finance is simply egoism solidified). This is the occupation that provides the unity between the various areas of French society revealed in the *Comédie*.

> *Each for himself, each on his own*, these two terrible phrases, along with *What's in it for me?* form the holy trinity of bourgeois wisdom and of that of the petit bourgeois. This egoism is the result of the vices of our civil legislation, carried through too precipitately and now consecrated by the July Revolution.[17]

It is Gobseck the banker who states the theme with terrifying clarity:

> Only one single true, natural feeling remains with us: the instinct of self-preservation. In your European societies this instinct is called

> *personal interests.* If you had lived as I have you would know that there's only one single material thing whose value is sufficiently certain for it to be worth a man's while to give it his attention. That thing is GOLD. Gold represents the whole of human strength.[18]

Humanity, in Balzac, is never an abstraction: it is a quality always seen historically.

This, if we look back over the way the novel has changed, can now be seen to be the great contribution of Stendhal and Balzac to its development. With them, everything is seen in terms of history. They see not only the past but also their own present society historically. Their characters are, above all, characters in history, made what they are by the forces that make and alter human society. Living through one of the most momentous periods of modern history—the aftermath of the French Revolution of 1789, the Napoleonic Empire, the restoration of the Bourbons, and the bourgeois monarchy of Louis Philippe—they absorbed into their very blood a sense of the significance of social change, so that they could no longer see men and women as figures manipulated for ever against an unchanging backcloth or as representatives of a human nature set and bounded by immutable laws.

Of course, many strands of unhistorical and metaphysical thinking remain in Balzac's outlook. But they are not really important, or if they are it is as a means of helping him to overcome the mechanistic limitations of so much contemporary scientific thinking. The really important thing is the remarkable pervasiveness of his sense of history, which emerges in many ways. It is most obvious, of course, in a book such as *Les chouans* (1829), a historical novel in the more conventional sense. But to see Balzac's historical sense as operating simply on the raw material of the past is to miss the main point. Dickens—who, as we shall see, did not share this vivid sense of permeating social change—produced the figure of Beau Turveydrop, the superannuated Regency dandy complete in every detail; but he is presented purely as an anachronism, a grotesque. He is a monster, but a peculiarly Dickensian one. He is not imagined historically at all: he is not allowed to absorb or radiate pressures that make him a significant force in the movement of *Bleak House* (1853). His selfishness, which all but destroys his children, is not functionally related to his "period." Any other anachronistic obsession would have served Dickens just as well.

With Balzac it is different. Even his descriptions of clothes tell their tale. It is worth comparing the presentation of Beau Turveydrop with the description of Cousin Pons.

> In maintaining in certain details of his get-up so deep a fidelity to the fashions of the year 1806, this passer-by succeeded in recalling the modes of the Empire without becoming merely a caricature. For the outside observer a flair of this kind is extremely precious, but accuracy of detail of this sort demands the expert analysis of the connoisseur; merely to raise a distant laugh the passer-by has only to offer one of those eccentricities that hits you in the eye, so to speak, like an actor who knows how to make a success of his entrances. This old man, thin and withered, wore a nut-brown spencer over a greenish coat with white metal buttons! . . . A man in a spencer in 1844! It was as though Napoleon had elected to come to life again for a couple of hours.[19]

Balzac's comment on how *not* to appreciate to the full an eccentric might well be applied to Dickens himself, so very much the actor who knew how to make a success of his entrances. But the point about Pons is that he has not been produced as part of a bag of tricks. His eccentricity is far more than a stage joke. He *belongs* to the Empire, which has made him the kind of person he is. The streets he walks along, the food he eats, the music he likes, are not the more or less casual attributes of a character presented simply in the terms of his own idiosyncrasy. And it is of course not merely the clothes and fashions and more superficial "period" gestures that one refers to when one speaks of Balzac's historical method. Other novelists are equally concerned that their characters should act out their drama against a clearly defined background. What is remarkable in Balzac is his sense not simply of the atmosphere but also of the forces of history. When he tellls us[20] that Joséphine Claës's character was a combination of Spanish pride and Flemish domestic submissiveness, he is not just illustrating her character but enriching our comprehension of it by calling in history. Victorin Hulot, he tell us,

> was a perfect type of the kind of young man produced by the 1830 revolution; with a mind absorbed in politics, taking his ambitions very seriously and containing them behind a solemn mask, very envious of established reputations, uttering sententious phrases instead of the incisive sallies that are the diamonds of French conversation, but with a self-possessed correctness, mistaking arrogance for dignity. Such men are walking coffins containing the Frenchmen of an older France. This Frenchman stirs at times and kicks out against his English envelope, but ambition checks him and he consents to stifle in it. These coffins are always draped in black cloth.[21]

This way of describing people is not just a convenience, a short cut to vividness, playing on the obvious associations of the contemporary reader: it is intrinsic to Balzac's vision of life. Without the history that has made them what they are, Balzac's characters are literally inconceivable. Even when one of them finds himself by accident divorced from this historical context (for instance, Colonel Chabert, a Napoleonic hero abandoned as dead on the battlefield, who returns to a world that has passed him by), there is nothing for him to do but die.

This all-pervading sense of historical development enables Balzac to treat all the phenomena of his age with a unifying eye. A novel such as *Les illusions perdues* (1837–43; Lost Illusions), one of his masterpieces, is at once a devastating critique of provincial and Parisian society and their relationship, an examination of Romanticism in its many colourings, and an altogether remarkable study of the effects of the development of capitalism on every aspect of the creation and production of literature. These themes are bound together in the poignant personal history of three people—David, Eve, and Lucien—who discover in the course of their loves, their work, and their relations with each other and with the outside world, the bitter contrast between the illusions, without which Lucien cannot live, and the reality of French bourgeois society. Lucien the poet is the son of a chemist of L'Houmeau, the newer, commercial section of Angoulême. As with several of Balzac's provincial towns, the very geography of Angoulême is significant, visually and socially: the old town, picturesque, feudal, and spiritually decayed, perched on the hill, and the ugly bourgeois suburb below, drawing its power from the river that separates it (by a gulf that is also social) from the old town. The treatment of the home of Mme de Bargeton, great lady of Angoulême, is typical of Balzac's method. It is Mme de Bargeton who "takes up" Lucien.

> Being given to exaggeration, she set an exaggerated value upon her person. Madame de Bargeton looked upon herself as a sovereign lady, a Beatrice, a Laura. She enthroned herself, like a mediaeval lady upon a daïs, looking down upon the tourney of literature, and Lucien would have to win her by his prowess at arms. He must eclipse the *wonderful boy* and Lamartine and Scott and Byron. The noble creature regarded her love as a creative power: the desire she kindled in Lucien would bring glory to him. This feminine quixotry is a sentiment that seeks to consecrate love, to use it, increase it, honour it. Madame de Bargeton, having made up her mind to play the part of Dulcinea in Lucien's life for seven or eight years, desired, like many provincial ladies, to give herself as a reward of a kind of service, a trial of constancy which would permit her to judge her lover.[22]

The literary references here are not literary in the narrow, damaging sense.

On the contrary, each of them enriches the implications of the passage and helps establish precisely both the quality of Mme de Bargeton's view of herself and its basis in the milieu over which she presides. The mediaeval images are not there for show or for ornament: the set-up at Angoulême *is* feudal, and Mme de Bargeton's illusions are linked in a thousand subtle ways with her social role. Because the pressure of the historical situation and the whole paraphernalia of Romanticism on Mme de Bargeton is revealed through her feelings, there is nothing abstract about the passage.

One of the most obvious differences between Balzac and Dickens is the former's much deeper intellectual grasp—it is part of his rich sense of history—of the ideological developments of his time, and of their relation to other developments. Despite his lack of elegance and his penchant for mysticism, Balzac is a child of the Enlightenment, feeling the need to grasp and explain intellectually the significance of the changing structure of feeling of his day. Some of the stories of *La comédie humaine* scarcely fit at all into the usual picture of a Balzac novel. *Mémoires de deux jeunes mariées* (1841–2; Memoirs of Two Young Married Women), for example, with its epistolary form and sophisticated surface, is a remarkably 18th-century production. It is formally in the direct line of Richardson and Rousseau, and this alignment is emphasized by the recurring references to *Clarissa* and *La nouvelle Héloïse*. The subject of *Mémoires* is the contrast between romantic and realistic conceptions of marriage and the report of the romantic Louise de Chaulieu is not only impressive in its remorseless revelation of the egoism at the basis of the high-falutin claims of the romantic lover who, while apparently standing out for the ideal relationship, in fact destroys the loved one, sucking the life out of two ideal husbands; equally interesting is the setting of this situation within the full context of the 18th-century battle of the sexes. "You are taking Clarissa Harlow for Figaro!"[23] exclaims Louise at one point, with sophisticated indignation. Richardson, Beaumarchais, Mozart—the link between Lovelace and Don Juan is indicated—the connections here make *Mémoires*, with its extraordinary, sometimes almost ludicrous, intensity of self-awareness, another example of how Balzac is able, by his continuous "placing" of people and situations, to provide them with reverberations that give a changed significance to all they experience.

Mémoires is obviously an achievement quite beyond the range of Dickens, whose affinities with the 18th century are of another sort (Fielding and Smollett, rather than Richardson and Rousseau) and who is perhaps the least intellectual of all great writers. Nor is Dickens—notwithstanding historical novels such as *Barnaby Rudge* (1841) and *A Tale of*

Two Cities (1859)—distinguished by any deep historical sense. Characteristically, he admired Scott (whom Balzac regarded as his most important
master) more for his success (before *The Pickwick Papers* [1837], *Waverley*
had been the classic best-seller) than for his example.

Balzac's philosophy has its eccentricities, but Dickens' is even more of
a hodgepodge. Unlike Balzac, he did not really see the point of having
a philosophy at all: in this, as in so much else, he partakes deeply of that
mixture of empiricism and philistinism so characteristic of British bourgeois
culture, and epitomized unforgettably by Mr Podsnap, for whom foreign
countries, though he had done very nicely out of them, were "a mistake."
It is perhaps worth suggesting that the contrast between the French and
British writer here, as elsewhere, has itself to be seen historically. The
British bourgeois revolution had, after all, reached its decisive stage a
century and a half before Dickens was born. Whereas Balzac's father
lived half his life under the old regime, Dickens was born into a society
that, despite conservative fears that events abroad might cause a new
revolutionary upsurge, could look back to its glorious revolution with a
certain complacency. One of the characteristic British convictions as the
19th century progressed was that Britain was "different," and the
especial difference consisted in its not being subject to revolutions.
Another way of expressing this difference is to recall that the British
bourgeoisie had been more successful than any other, and that the
Industrial Revolution was farther advanced. Material success is a great
antidote to philosophical speculation: British empiricism was to a considerable extent the product of this success.

The contrast between the "philosophical" preoccupations of Balzac
and the practical ones of Dickens is basic: it determines the very nature
of their art. Both are vulgar, and the vulgarity has a similar source but
operates through different channels. The source is their shared sense of
the breakdown of aristocratic society and the emergence of the bourgeois
world with all its horrors and its promises: the horrors of industrial
capitalism, the promise of democratic advance. Neither writer—it should
go without saying—formulated his view of the world in anything like
such terms: but we cannot explain or even fully understand the significance of the two men unless *we* do. They expressed their sense of what
was happening in the world through their art, not through their ideas.
And they expressed it differently because they were different people
looking at the world from different points of view.

The difference in point of view is, of course, as significant in its way
as the shared source of power. With Balzac the horror of the egoism

released by bourgeois power is the dominant factor. It is therefore not difficult to explain why his books are sombre; it is more difficult (especially in view of his scepticism about any developments that could even broadly be described as "democratic") to explain why they are not depressing to the spirit. For this, I think, we have to turn to the vitality engendered by his pleasure in the sheer physical nature of existence, his indignation at the suppression of the potentialities of human beings, and that abundant sense of history that allows him to see everything in terms of change and growth and decay. As old Goriot dies, science goes on, learning from his sufferings. It matters scarcely at all that so many of his characters are defeated, and go down before wickedness. In the very openness of a Rastignac before corruption there is a kind of challenge.

Balzac's vulgarity is the physical vulgarity of the participator who is not afraid of joining in the game or the battle, the vulgarity of the glutton, of the sensual man who does not know when he has had enough until he has had too much, but also knows that to fear excess is to fear fulfilment. Balzac's sense of the promises within the bourgeois world is not expressed through any overt feeling for the democratic forces within that world, let alone for the new potentialities opening up for the working class. He is not, in that sense, a popular writer. What he has triumphantly to offer is an extension of fearlessness before reality, a respect for reality, for science, for human resilience and toughnesss, for the revolutionary nature of the historical process itself.

Dickens is quite different. He *is*, in the most obvious and least ambiguous sense of the word, a popular writer, consciously drawing strength from his identity with, and confidence in, the traditions and aspirations of the common people of his time. He does not need a more or less scientific theory of the unity of man and nature to back his confidence in the future of man, nor a theory of history to tell him which side he is on in the social and political struggles of the day. His political position, as he recorded it in the last year of his life, is straightforward:

> My faith in the people governing, is, on the whole, infinitesimal;
> my faith in the people governed, is, on the whole, illimitable.[24]

This is not a philosophical position or, indeed, an analytical one. Dickens's radicalism has little consistent political theory behind it, and it is interesting that, even as far as the practical politics of his day were concerned, he seems to have had little sense of the meaning of either Chartism or trade unionism. But the expression of his broad class position is nonetheless

R

fundamental to his role as novelist, for it reflects that deep and un-intellectual yet sincere and consistent alignment with the people, as opposed to the ruling class, that grew stronger the longer he lived. I am not suggesting, it must be stressed, that Dickens' popular sympathies implied a class-consciousness of a Marxist sort: he had very little feeling for the industrial working class as such. Yet the tradition that he developed is by no possible definition bourgeois or even *petit-bourgeois*. The basis of his creative sensibility is his plebeian way of looking at the life around him from below.

It is also what determines the form and technique of a Dickens novel. His method, in contrast to Balzac's, is popular and theatrical. He draws continually on the traditions of folk culture, the urbanized folk culture of London especially, with its music-halls and melodramas, its broad-sheets and street songs and penny dreadfuls, as well as the older fairy-tales and nursery rhymes. Dickens' absorption of this tradition is shown by his apparently effortless ability to add to it, to create new figures, such as Oliver Twist and Uriah Heep and Mrs Gamp, who have taken their place alongside the older representatives of popular mythology.

Dickens is an almost wholly urban writer. Living, for him, is urban living. When Little Nell and her grandfather are forced out of their home and wander into the country, the first thing that strikes them is that "the houses were very few and scattered at long intervals," and imme-diately Dickens' prose softens up into a rather feeble attempt at the pastoral. But his observation thrives on closeness. There are innumerable houses in the novels, and most of them are very close together indeed—not only in the slums, but in highly respectable quarters such as Harley Street, with its "opposing rows of houses" looking "very grim with one another." The contrast between his attitude to London and Balzac's view of Paris is instructive. Compare the long passage on Paris at the beginning of *La fille aux yeux d'or* (1834–5; The Girl with the Golden Eyes) with the opening of *Bleak House*, or the description of the district around the rue du Doyenné in *La cousine Bette* with that of Tom-All-Alone's. The contrast is not primarily one of immediate contrasting personal responses. Balzac is as shocked as Dickens by the atrocious conditions of life, and the cry *Extirpez ces verrues de ma face!*[25] (Strike these excrescences from my face!) has a Dickensian quality to it. But the moral indignation of the Balzac passages is more general and intellectualized than Dickens'. Paris, as one would expect, is seen historically: it outrages Balzac's national pride, as well as his humanity, that such hovels should exist, especially so near the Louvre. Dickens' humanitarian feelings are more intimately involved. It would not be quite true to say that he describes Tom-All-Alone's from the point of view of its inmates, for to Dickens, too, these people are beyond the pale. What he is particularly keen to draw are the lines of connection between them and the rest of society: the landlords, the speculators, the Court of Chancery, all seen not historically but here and now. The sense of the corruption that the slum spreads is specific (described primarily, of course, in terms of disease, the disease that Jo is to carry to Bleak House) so that in so far as Tom-All-Alone's comes to have a symbolic significance in the novel, the symbolism is not a matter of "standing for" something but of actually representing in specific visual terms an area of reality that has repercussions beyond itself.

Dickens does not accept Tom-All-Alone's, but he accepts London in a way that Balzac scarcely accepts Paris, which remains for him the "wicked city." Balzac's attitude to Paris remains, indeed, very close to that of Rastignac at the end of *Le père Goriot* when, surveying the city from Père-Lachaise, he cries defiantly:

> "It's war between us now!" And as his first act of defiance against society Rastignac went to dine with Madame de Nucingen.[26]

Again, one has only to compare Balzac's excellent description of the Flicoteaux restaurant in the second part of *Les illusions perdues* with Dickens' superb evocation of the "slap-bang dining house"[27] that Guppy and Smallweed frequent to be aware of the contrasting attitudes of the two writers. Both are splendid passages; but whereas the description of the restaurant in the Quartier Latin involves an intellectualization of the scene that is only partly due to the fact that the clientele at Flicoteaux is itself largely intellectual, Dickens's enjoyment of his city restaurant in all its noisy squalor is unreserved.

Dickens' acceptance of urban life, however, is not uncritical or without its ambiguities. His London is even more monstrous than Balzac's Paris, not only because it is bigger and dirtier, but because it is seen from the inside. The constant images of filth and corruption—the dustheaps, the prisons, the slums, the stench of prostitution and sweated labour, the bureaucratic organization of power, and, omnipresent, the polluted Thames itself—impose themselves so deeply on the imagination because the moral judgments they imply are not imported from a different sphere or mode of perception, but are embedded in the very world that Dickens evokes. He is tremendously good at conveying, for instance, the appalling loneliness of big-city life, the isolation of people within a crowded city.

Almost all his characters build up phantasy worlds, and often little areas of actual existence—such as Boffin's bower or Mr Venus's shop—within which they try to express the needs that London frustrates. A particularly clear example is the double life of Wemmick, the lawyer's clerk in *Great Expectations* (1861), who escapes from the inhumanity of the life and language of his calling into a world that incomparably illuminates the gap (spanned only by a drawbridge) between public and private existence in modern capitalist society. Wemmick's home *is* his castle, and one sees exactly why and what it involves, including the inevitable tendency to try to counteract an inhuman public reality by a cozily sentimental domestic dream-world.

Wemmick's castle gives us an insight, too, into Dickens's characteristic method, which is to work, as a rule—in a way that contrasts with Balzac—from the particular to the general. His characters, it is true, are also envisaged as "types," as members of a specific class or grouping, and often first presented in this role in order to establish their place in the wider pattern of the book. But Balzac, one feels (without attempting an analysis of his creative processes), begins with his general overall sense of the movements and patterns of human existence and pounces upon certain characters and situations that he instinctively recognizes as particularly relevant to those patterns. Dickens, on the other hand, comes upon the more general insight through his exploration of some specific oddity that has appealed to his theatrical imagination. Obviously with both writers the process is more complex, and more dialectical, than one has space to explore here, but the contrast is nevertheless there. Old Dorrit, like Wemmick, has made his home his castle, and the fact that it happens to be in the Marshalsea prison merely means that his capacity for rationalizing phantasy must take different directions. When his child is born he retains enough of a link with the outside, "normal" world to feel a pang of regret that his daughter should start life in a prison. "Bah, bah, sir, what does it signify?" responds the doctor consolingly,

> "A little more elbow-room is all we want here. We are quiet here; we don't get badgered here; there's no knocker here, sir, to be hammered at by creditors and bring a man's heart into his mouth. Nobody comes here to ask if a man's at home, and to say he'll stand on the doormat till he is. Nobody writes threatening letters about money in this place. It's freedom, sir, it's freedom! . . . Elsewhere people are restless, worried, hurried about, anxious respecting one thing, anxious respecting another. Nothing of the kind here, sir. We have done all that—we know the worst of it; we have got to the bottom, we can't fall, and what have we found? Peace. That's the word for it. Peace."[28]

The first thing that strikes one about this passage is that in the context it is very funny, contributing grotesquely but richly to the total scene. But the more important function of the doctor's words is to throw light on a whole situation that is limited neither to a pathological self-deceiver such as Dorrit nor to the enclosed world of the Marshalsea. The nature of freedom is the subject of the doctor's chatter, and Dickens is forcing his reader to think about freedom even as he laughs at the grotesque absurdity of the scene.

Dickens often does this sort of thing. In *Bleak House,* as the respectable group of John Jarndyce's wards and hangers-on comes downstairs after visiting poor mad Miss Flite in her attic, they catch sight of Krook, the repulsive old rag-and-bone man, surrounded by his junk, teaching himself to read and write. Kindly enough, Jarndyce suggests that it might be easier if he were to get someone else to teach him.

> "Aye, but they might teach me wrong!" returned the old man, with a wonderfully suspicious flash of his eye.[29]

Again, it is a splendidly funny retort, and full of that Dickensian sense of grotesque "character." But the whole point really is that Krook's answer has a kind of crazy justness about it that chimes in with the central preoccupations and insights of *Bleak House* about the Law and its place in British society. Why shouldn't "they" teach him wrong, they who have never given Krook cause to suppose they could ever teach him anything right? And we have come to know only too well through this book that the language of the Court of Chancery—with which Krook is throughout paradoxically linked—is indeed the language not of clarity but of mystification and deception. What Dickens is doing is to expose the depths of incongruity and ultimately of alienation that lie behind this particular little scene.

From such examples of his method two qualities emerge that are worth stressing: Dickens' art, compared with Balzac's, is more verbal, and it is more theatrical.

The verbal texture of any novel is in an important sense always the essential thing about it, for the writer has ultimately nothing but words to offer his reader. But some novelists—of whom I think Balzac is one—depend less than others on the precise organization of the words they use. One has to be very careful in saying this, although the general point emerges from the fact that some writers are notoriously more difficult to translate than others, and that what we call poetry, which cannot be discussed in purely formal terms and obviously overlaps into the novel, invites an attention to words that seems to be qualitatively different from the way we look at what isn't poetry. The verbal effects of a Balzac novel are, by and large, non-poetic. This is not to say that they are unimportant. But when Balzac produces a list of objects in his work, for instance, the effect is simply to call into the reader's mind those objects, related only minimally to one another. The effect or significance inheres essentially in the things behind the words, and the words do a minimum of work in evoking them: it would not matter much if the words were in a different order. With a list in a Dickens novel,* however, the words, by virtue of their ambiguities and suggestiveness and the attention they compel, are likely to play a different role. Balzac's characters often have their idiosyncrasies of speech, but these tend to come from the subject-matter of their talk, rather than from its tone. Most often the important thing is what they talk about, rather than what they actually say. But Dickens works on an altogether different level. His characters expose themselves by the actual way they say something. Each has his own rhetoric, which arises out of his own particular life and his way of perceiving the world. So superb is this rhetoric, in the most successful examples, that it creates a whole new dimension of freedom within which the author (and therefore the character) is able to operate. This can occasionally be disastrous— we all know the moments when Dickens's characters get out of hand—but in general it is perhaps his greatest and unique achievement.

The way Dickens uses language is bound up with his role of entertainer, which is conceived very largely in theatrical terms. Balzac sees himself as a sort of glorified historian, extending and humanizing the production of history, whereas Dickens sees himself as a kind of universal circus-master presiding over an entertainment of boundless possibilities. Both writers are enormously, staggeringly professional, with a technical self-confidence that sometimes permits them to indulge their virtuosity for its own sake. How else can we regard *The Chimes* (1845)? How else can we explain how Balzac gets away with a piece as structurally ill-conceived as *La maison Nucingen* (1838; Nucingen and Company)?

The theatrical quality of Dickens's imagination is important because, unless we recognize it, we are likely to complain that his books are not "serious," when in fact they are serious in a very individual way. His theatricality is closely linked, by way of his enthusiasm for the drama and the music-hall, with the element in his work that we have recognized as "popular," and is most clearly evident when we realize that the best

* E.g. the list of names of Miss Flite's captive birds in *Bleak House*.

possible way with his books is to read them aloud. This is his true level of communication. Read aloud, his humour, which in the silence of private reading can seem a bit repetitive and heavy-handed, works triumphantly, and his wit flowers.

Because of his theatrical mode and comic tone it is not easy to define the sort of seriousness that Dickens achieves without seeming to step rather far away from the novels themselves. His critique of Victorian society, which became sharper with the years, is in fact no less devastating than Balzac's vision of the effects of the revolution of 1830. The world of Dombey is perceived with as much sharpness as that of Gobseck or Nucingen.

> The earth was made for Dombey and Son to trade in, and the sun and moon were made to give them light. Rivers and seas were formed to float their ships; rainbows gave them promise of fair weather; winds blew for or against their enterprises; stars and planets circled in their orbits, to preserve inviolate a system of which they were the centre.[30]

There is of course documentation in plenty in Dickens' novels; like Balzac's, they are a mine for the social historian. If you want to know about the Gravesend packet, or how a pawnbroker conducted his trade, or what happened in a wine-bottling warehouse, you can find out from Dickens. You can get a vivid description of what happened both on the stage and in the auditorium at Astley's, a sort of combined circus-cum-music-hall on the Waterloo Road. You can collect an immense amount of detailed information about the habits of watermen, pedlars, jailers, thieves, and lodging-house keepers. We know, for instance, that Mr Bob Sawyer's landlady was not prepared to work herself to death for someone "who never thinks of paying his rent, nor even the very money laid out for the fresh butter and lump sugar that's bought for his breakfast, and the very milk that's took in at the street door"[31]; clearly a valuable sentence for any historian of the development of retail trades in mid-Victorian London.

But to overstress the importance of this kind of documentation in Dickens is even more misguided than in the case of Balzac, for although the Frenchman does indeed rely rather heavily on the sheer solidity of his evocation of social fact, Dickens gets his effects by other means. He will, it is true, take a good deal of trouble over his description of certain material objects, such as the plate on the Podsnaps' dinner table in *Our Mutual Friend*:

> Hideous solidity was the characteristic of the Podsnap plate. Everything was made to look as heavy as it could, and to take up as much room as possible. Everything said boastfully, "Here you have as much of me in my ugliness as if I were only lead; but I am so many ounces of precious metal worth so much an ounce;—wouldn't you like to melt me down?" A corpulent straggling épergne, blotched all over as though it had broken out in an eruption rather than been ornamented, delivered this address from an unsightly silver platform in the centre of the table. Four silver wine-coolers, each furnished with four staring heads, each head obtrusively carrying a big silver ring in each of its ears, conveyed the sentiment up and down the table, and handed it on to the pot-bellied silver salt-cellars. All the big silver spoons and forks widened the mouths of the company expressly for the purpose of thrusting the sentiment down their throats with every morsel they ate.[32]

The interesting question here is why so persistent a concern with detail, with the upholstery of a scene, does not become heavy and tiresome. Clearly there is a danger that so much emphasis on material detail may lead to a rather tedious stress on the surface of things—the sort of thing Henry James was to complain of in his review of the book. What prevents this is not some kind of Dickensian whimsicality, but the novelist's instinct for relationships. He does not see his *minutiae* in isolation or as units in a list. The heavy pieces of plate on the Podsnaps' table (not unrelated to the heavy pieces of humanity that surround them) are linked together and given interest—one might almost say vitality—by the vulgar acquisitiveness they express. So the wine-coolers and salt-cellars and the rest amount almost to a criticism of life, certainly to a criticism of their owner: and the description of the table-furniture becomes not an inventory, but something more like a metaphor, contributing to the total image of Podsnapery that is the subject of the chapter. It is true that in the course of the paragraph we get a vivid impression of what a prosperous Victorian dinner-table looked like, but that is the lesser half of the effect. The surface reflects a more interesting, more critical reality, just as the Podsnaps' plate reflects (but distortingly) the faces of the company that uses it.

Dickens' relation with his public was a complex one. On the one hand, as we have seen, he was prepared to consider very seriously its demands and criticisms. In his *Avant-propos* Balzac had remarked of Scott that,

> obliged as he was to conform to the ideas of an essentially hypocritical nation, Walter Scott was false to humanity in his picture of woman.[33]

And obviously he would have felt much the same about Dickens' handling of sexual matters. But it would be false to proceed from this recognition of his relation to his environment to the assumption that Dickens was primarily concerned, for economic or other reasons, with circulation figures. The constant radical, and sometimes revolutionary, criticism of contemporary society that permeates his novels, especially the later ones, precludes any such conclusion. That is why it is important in using the word "popular" in relation to Dickens to avoid—despite his own immense commercial success—the mercenary overtones that the word has come to bear. It is true that there are plenty of aspects of his work that can be seen as concessions to the complacencies and limitations of his public; but to put it that way can be misleading too, for it is clear that Dickens himself did not think in such terms any more than Shakespeare had done. He did not think of himself as having some abstract message, ideological or aesthetic, that had then to be accommodated to the prejudices of his readers, although no doubt there were moments when such considerations arose. Fundamentally, it is through his treatment of specific situations, such as the extraordinary "spontaneous combustion" episode in *Bleak House*, that his radical feelings express themselves, and it is through tone and imagery, rather than more didactic methods, that he achieves the greater part of his effects.

Balzac and Dickens are realist novelists in the sense that they continuously concentrate their attention outward, upon the object (including of course the psychology of their characters and the moral values inherent in the conflicts they present), rather than inward, upon their own subjective impressions and reactions. But this is not to imply either that their own subjective attitudes are unimportant (how could they be?) or that they have a naive concern with the mere surface of things. The important point, perhaps, is that because they see themselves as part and parcel of the real world—Balzac above all through his deep sense of history, Dickens through his conscious identification with the common people—they have no temptation either to oversimplify or to play down the determining importance of an objective reality.

References

Note. All page numbers cited in Balzac's novels (except Ref. no. 2) refer to Gallimard's "Bibliothèque de la Pléiade" edition (Paris 1951–9); all page numbers cited in Dickens' novels refer to the Oxford University Press "New Oxford Illustrated Dickens" (London 1949–53).

1. HIPPOLYTE ADOLPHE TAINE, *Nouveaux essais de critique et d'histoire* (Paris 1896), p. 51.

2. Epilogue supprimé, *Eugénie Grandet*, ed. by P. G. Castex (Paris 1965), p. 265.

3. HENRY JAMES, "Honoré de Balzac," Introduction to English translation of *Mémoires de deux jeunes mariées* (London 1904), pp. xvii ff.

4. Quoted in M. TURNELL, *The Novel in France* (London 1950), p. 253.

5. HENRY JAMES, Review of *Our Mutual Friend* in *The Nation* (21 December 1865); reprinted in L. EDEL (ed.), *The House of Fiction* (London 1957), p. 257.

6. PERCY LUBBOCK, *The Craft of Fiction* (London 1921), p. 207.

7. JAMES, "Honoré de Balzac," *op. cit.*, p. xviii.

8. *La comédie humaine*, Vol. I, p. 4.

9. *ibid.*, Vol. VI, p. 609.

10. GEORG LUKÁCS, *Studies in European Realism*, trans. by E. Bone (London 1950), p. 43.

11. *La comédie humaine*, Vol. VI, p. 230.

12. LUKÁCS, *op. cit.*, p. 6.

13. *La comédie humaine*, Vol. VI, p. 370.

14. *ibid.*, Vol. II, p. 864.

15. Letter to Margaret Harkness, April 1888; reprinted in KARL MARX and FREDERICK ENGELS, *Literature and Art* (New York 1947), p. 42.

16. *La comédie humaine*, Vol. VI, p. 501.

17. *ibid.*, Vol. VIII, p. 710.

18. *ibid.*, Vol. II, p. 629.

19. *ibid.*, Vol. VI, p. 525.

20. *ibid.*, Vol. IX, p. 499.

21. *ibid.*, Vol. VI, p. 176.

22. *ibid.*, Vol. IV, p. 576.

23. *ibid.*, Vol. I, p. 222.

24. K. J. FIELDING (ed.), *The Speeches of Charles Dickens* (Oxford 1960), p. 407.

25. *La comédie humaine*, Vol. VI, p. 179.

26. *ibid.*, Vol. II, p. 1085.

27. *Bleak House*, pp. 275 ff.

28. *Little Dorrit*, p. 63.

29. *Bleak House*, p. 201.

30. *Dombey and Son*, p. 2.

31. *The Pickwick Papers*, p. 436.

32. *Our Mutual Friend*, p. 131.

33. *La comédie humaine*, Vol. I, p. 11.

CHAPTER 8

Literature and Society in Germany

George L. Mosse[*]

During the 19th century Germany became estranged from many of the traditions of the Enlightenment and the French Revolution that had found a home in other Western nations. The basic fact about German history since the 18th century has been the failure of the Enlightenment to take root.[1] Instead Germany looked inward, to its own supposed traditions of the past, obsessed with the problem of national unification. But this is not the whole of the German story. Toward the end of the century Germany was emerging as one of the most important industrial nations: growing and self-confident. Moreover, the German working classes had been organized into the strongest socialist party in Europe. Historians have long sought to analyse the complicated factors that formed German attitudes in the second half of the 19th century and that were to cast their shadow into our own time. The thought and attitudes current in Germany seemed to reject the liberalism that emerged in other industrial nations, and to stultify the rise of a bourgeoisie wedded to ideals of freedom and equality.[2]

Literature can be of the utmost significance in determining peculiarly German attitudes in an age of rapid industrialization and rising self-confidence. The relationship between literature and life is necessarily a complex one, but for Germany the kind of literature that was admired was deeply involved in the German quest for identity. The revolution of 1848 stands at the beginning of our analysis. That revolution seemed at first to have given liberalism a place in German life, and the radical uprisings that accompanied the revolution could have given Germany a vital revolutionary tradition of its own. Writers responded to both these

[*] John C. Bascom Professor of History, University of Wisconsin.

impulses, especially those of "Young Germany," and those associated with the ideas of Karl Marx. Perhaps a literary tradition both liberal and revolutionary could have helped to form German attitudes, the more so when a strong socialist party came into being after Germany was unified. But this was not to occur, and the literature that triumphed was that which fed upon a nationalist mystique as well as upon the ideals of German bourgeois society. The major part of this essay will be concerned with such literature, which was to form the attitudes of those who lived in German-speaking lands. But in order to see why nationalist and bourgeois literature triumphed, it is crucial to examine the failure of the impetus that sprang from the revolution of 1848: why Germany, in the second half of the 19th century, was barren of a tradition of letters that might have called for liberty and equality against the inherited inequalities of life.

Before and during the revolution of 1848 a group of writers known as "Young Germany" vociferously opposed the social reality of Germany, wanting to bring about greater freedom within the society that they knew. These men were liberals whose call to freedom and revolt, in the tradition of the Enlightenment, had a certain abstract quality: they were more interested in moral than in social questions. Moreover, in the face of a growing hostility from authority they retreated into an attitude of resignation, not untainted by cynicism.[3] When such literature was revived toward the end of the century, in the form of Expressionism or naturalism, it had a similar cynical and abstract quality: the revolutionary action it invoked had nothing to do with barricades but was concerned with literary sensitivity, which at best could lead to changes in manners and morals. To be sure, there are exceptions to this lack of a revolutionary literary tradition. Germany was, after all, the country of Marx and Engels, and they did arouse the enthusiasm of some writers and poets. The only creative artist with whom both revolutionary leaders were satisfied was Georg Weerth (1822–56), one of the writers to attempt a realistic portrait of the working-man. Yet his works are, for the most part, satires on the existing order, and do not fuse literature with revolutionary dialectic. Engels praised him above Goethe for his capacity to express a natural sensuousness.[4] Two other, more important writers also enjoyed the friendship and support of Marx and Engels, although never wholly or consistently. Georg Herwegh and Ferdinand Freiligrath were revolutionary poets, but both, characteristically, were aroused by the radical impetus of the revolution of 1848 rather than by any specifically Marxist experience.

Georg Herwegh (1817–75) provides perhaps the most important example of a writer and poet who continued his commitment to revolution through 1848 and on to his death in 1875. Herwegh clung to the concept of freedom, and saw that this must encompass the workers as well as the middle classes. Freedom for him was more concrete than it had been for the "Young Germans," and it included a sharp and bitter critique of capitalism. Significantly, the editor of his works, writing in the 1890s, failed to understand how this commitment could outlast the fact of German unity and lead to a bitter criticism of the new *Reich*. This commitment to freedom and democracy (Herwegh, like Marx, had supported the democratic uprising in Baden in 1848) was permissible in 1848, but was regarded as subversive once the *Reich* had come into being[5]—an indication of the changing atmosphere in Germany to which most writers succumbed.

Herwegh carried on, exclaiming in a poem that unity was an empty shell, and so was the law, if the oppression of men continued. Capitalism and the complacency of the liberals were to blame, and he composed poems on this theme after 1870, just as he had written some of the most famous poems on the need for revolution before and during 1848. His friend Ferdinand Lassalle (1825–64), with some justice, described Herwegh as *un nouveau Mirabeau*,[6] but a Mirabeau who worked in lonely eminence without penetrating the establishment or gathering a revolutionary following. Lassalle's own themes centred upon national heroes such as Franz von Sickingen, whose drive for freedom Lassalle endowed with a decidedly romantic appeal. Herwegh was not interested in past German examples but in the overthrow of the existing order.

Ferdinand Freiligrath (1810–76) wrote some of the most stirring poems of 1848; eventually he joined the editorial staff of Karl Marx's *Neue Rheinische Zeitung* and the League of Communists as well. His poems, which had praised humanity in general and were not devoid of melodramatic effects (e.g. *Ça Ira!* 1846), later became imbued with a vision of proletarian misery and the longing for a true equality. A poem such as "Die Toten an die Lebenden" (1848; The Martyred Dead Speak to the Living) is replete with revolutionary fervour, a call for an uprising that would fly the red flag over the barricades. Freiligrath followed Marx into exile in 1851, but in London he underwent a change that was to last until his return to Germany and his death. He drifted away from the circle of Marx and Engels, asserting a love of freedom and equality that, like that of the earlier "Young Germans," was based on a moral impetus rather than on sustained social analysis. Love for humanity in general, and for the republican form of government in particular, took the place of the call for revolution against the existing order. Finally, Freiligrath found that he could no longer deny the progress made by Germany under Prussian leadership. The national mystique threatened to displace the cry for change and even the exaltation of humanity.[7]

The "Young Germans" and these revolutionary poets had believed that literature should play a vital role in the formation of a new society. However, their emotionalism and moral impetus had left the solid ground of social reality far behind. Even Herwegh refused to submit to the discipline of a social movement and, in spite of his sympathy for it, never joined the League of Communists. Marx and Engels failed to create a literary movement that might accompany their quest for social justice. Yet, later in the century, the Naturalist movement seemed to give a second chance to the creation of a revolutionary literary tradition in Germany. By that time the socialists had united, and the strong social democratic party might have taken advantage of this literary genre to construct a socialist literature where earlier efforts had failed. For the Naturalists were better able to penetrate reality than the enthusiastic heralders of revolution of an earlier day.

Gerhart Hauptmann (1862–1946) made his name by portraying realistically the misery of the Silesian weavers and the reaction of the ordinary people to their plight. *Die Weber* (1892; The Weavers) stressed the importance of the environment in which they lived and worked. But this very stress upon the environment demonstrated the difficulty of fusing such Naturalism with a revolutionary tradition. The movement tended to become an environmentalism that alerted society to the fate that awaited many of its members. It could be used to inspire action in order to change that society, but Naturalism tended to ignore the idealism that might point to a better future and that was vital to a socialist and revolutionary impetus. Man became a cipher, dehumanized by his industrial environment, and showed little potential for improving his station in life. Eventually many Naturalists themselves sought an ideal, and most of them found it not in socialism, but within a romantic sentimentality fortified by the national mystique.[8] Gerhart Hauptmann himself trod this path, showing once more the force of a German literary tradition that could stifle all attempts to use literature as an instrument of fundamental social and political change.

Socialist critics rightly chided Hauptmann for failing to show how the weavers could escape their lot. And although Social Democrats acclaimed him as the principal representative of modern art, their chief critic, Franz

Mehring, added at once that "modern art is not great art."[9] Socialists could find no rapport with the modern art of their time and thus had no model upon which to build a contemporary socialist literature. Their way out was to stress the German classics: Goethe, Schiller, and even Mörike. Such a turning back into history was not likely to forge a link between socialists and the creative artists of the times, a link that Marx had thought important for the founding of a revolutionary tradition. Eduard Bernstein summed up the socialist dilemma: in the struggle toward the socialist goal, discipline and organization must prevail, and in this respect the artist was an outsider. Once the socialist society had come into being, there would be a great artistic flourishing.[10]

The creation of socialist literature was in the "future."[11] But what literature were the people to read and hear in the meantime? An effort was made to found a theatre that would rouse the masses against the injustices of the times. The *Freie Bühne* (Free Theatre), 1889, concentrated upon naturalist themes, presenting plays by Hauptmann, Ibsen, and Strindberg. Its successor, the *Freie Volksbühne* (Free People's Theatre), 1890, was eventually taken over by the trade union movement, but it continued to produce plays that the bourgeoisie also enjoyed. To be sure, the workers had their own plays, which were performed by amateurs, but these plays were didactic, and the plots tended to be swamped by the educational message. The doctrine of surplus value had to be explained at some length from the stage, and sentiment was handicapped by the moral that true love was possible only between Socialist Party members.[12] Apart from such plays, attempts at a radical theatre merely transmitted the predominant bourgeois culture to the working classes.

Even when self-conscious proletarians such as Max Kretzer wrote novels and poetry, their work seldom rose above the level of descriptions of the *triste milieu*; or, as in the case of Karl Henkel, it merely echoed Nietzsche's call to arms against the bourgeoisie. Minna Kautsky (1837–1912), mother of the socialist theoretician Karl Kautsky, wrote novels that advocated the ideals of social democracy and glorified the fighting spirit of proletarians who refused to be robbed of their humanity. Although she succeeded in picturing the awakening of class consciousness and the corruption of the upper classes, her friend Engels was right when he criticized her sentimentality and her simplistic notions of the social struggle.[13] A working-class, even a socialist, literature did exist during the *Reich* but it was sporadic at best and only a very few writers attempted to link their creative talents to the goals of the workers' movement.

To summarize, then, we can say that, by the end of the 19th century, all attempts to create a German literature founded on revolutionary principles and on the rhetoric of equality and freedom for all peoples, had been swept aside by the growth of a national mystique and by the ideals of bourgeois society. Characteristic of the preoccupation with nationalism was the search for a new religion that would cement German unity—a theme that evoked a more powerful response in the minds of Germans than ideas of radical change in the social structure. As we come to the mainstream of German literature during the second half of the century we must proceed by examples, ignoring many important writers and their works. But we shall see the emergence of a pattern that, together with the failure of a revolutionary tradition of freedom and equality, can help to explain many of the attitudes that have formed the German politics of our time.

Wilhelm Jordan (1819–1904) is forgotten today, but in the 1860s he travelled up and down Germany reading his version of the *Nibelungen* saga to large, enthusiastic audiences. Jordan was one of several writers who wanted to create a Germanic religion to supersede the "sterile Semitism" of traditional Christianity. Like his more famous contemporary, Paul de Lagarde, Jordan used the tradition of German idealism and a reviving national consciousness in order to create a faith based upon a return to ancient German sources of inspiration. His initial enthusiasm for the revolution of 1848 was forgotten in the effort to prove, through a recreation of Germanic sagas, that the *Volk* were endowed with a spiritual revelation, a creative instinct more vital than that of other peoples.

The practical result of the Germanic faith was to be a "reverential duty and unceasing work," as Jordan put it,[14] an attitude toward the world that contrasts markedly with that of Herwegh, but that most of his fellow-writers shared, even though it was not usually expressed in German epic verse. However, Jordan was no racist. His argument concerned religion and the nation: everyone born in Germany could participate. Like many others of his generation, Jordan was influenced by the Greek heritage, and in a rather confused way he connected this with the Germanic tradition. When writing about the Greeks, however, he repeats his main thesis: the Semitic religion had penetrated into Greece and prevented the Greeks from transforming the Homeric ideal into reality. Jordan's ideas and goals may sound strange, but he had a wide audience in a literary genre that attained some popularity.

Wilhelm Jordan demonstrates the euphoria of national unity in which writers and artists joined so whole-heartedly after 1871. Their revolution was that which Bismarck had brought about, and the stress upon unity meant that all dissension must cease. Social problems and the maladjustment of a nation forging ahead to world power could be overcome through the creation of a spiritual unity among all inhabitants. To be sure, poverty existed and so did the toiling masses, but such problems would vanish if the ruling classes treated them with sympathy and if the lower classes responded with good will. Men like Jordan and most national liberals were at one in this view of society, and much contemporary German literature echoed this "idealistic" emphasis.

One example of this is the growing number of writers who reached back into the German past in order to prophesy the national future. The historical novel was not confined to Germany, of course; at this time it achieved immense popularity throughout all Western Europe. But after 1848 the craving for national unity came to predominate within the German variant of this literary genre. Victor von Scheffel's *Ekkehard* (1855) maintained its popularity for the rest of the century. The preface to this work states explicitly that the historical novel should assume the role that had been taken by the epic poem during the youth of the *Volk*: the artistic interpreter (not to say myth-maker) of national history. The novel centres on the monk Ekkehard and his life in monastery and castle almost a thousand years ago. This was a time of "naive, yet vital" conditions of life, and strong beliefs that not even our "rationalistic fury" can deny.[15] Ekkehard demonstrates a virile courage against the enemies of the *Reich* (the Huns), a *Reich* that was unfortunately fragmented after the death of Charlemagne. Here nothing is small and petty; everything has a transcendent greatness. The native landscape of the Bodensee (Lake Constance) area forms a vital part of the plot. Scheffel built the national mystique into a skilfully constructed novel, and his view of true Germanism stresses the virility and immediacy of all personal relationships. Here, as we shall see, he is close to the themes of the peasant novel and the adventure stories of Karl May.

The Königsberg historian Felix Dahn (1834–1912) followed in these footsteps. His *Der Kampf um Rom* (1867; The Fight for Rome) rivalled *Ekkehard* in popularity, and Bismarck himself confessed that this was the only book he had read twice.[16] Dahn had intended to write a didactic novel, although the struggle of the Goths against Byzantium for the control of Italy was also a good adventure story. The hero of Dahn's book is a people: the Goths, ancestors of the Germans and endowed with the primeval virtues that give them strength and confidence in their

S

mission. They are defeated not so much by Italian and Byzantine cunning as by the influence of the southern environment. Italian luxury, rationality, and love for intrigue sap Gothic strength and will.

Dahn paints the Germanic ideal in strong colours: honesty, loyalty, and an absence of guile characterizes the whole nation. These qualities of character were also praised by Jordan in his version of the *Nibelungenlied*. Side by side with these virtues stood the love of freedom and representative institutions. Dahn, like many historians before and after him, resurrected the Germanic tribal organization (*Comitatus*) as the true origin of democracy and contrasted this with Byzantine despotism. The tribal assembly, with its free debate, was an integral part of the national ethos, and the German longing for national unity was closely linked to this political ideal. Typically, Dahn belonged to the progressive wing of the National Liberal party, and only after a personal conversation with his hero Bismarck, in the 1870s, did he move further to the political right.

Throughout the novel the Goths represent virtue and strength; the body mirrors the soul. The concept of beauty that informs such fiction (and not fiction alone) borrows from a Greek ideal and from Germanic mythology intermixed with romantic preconceptions. The blond and blue-eyed Goths echo a Germanic myth that is based upon those Germans whom Tacitus described so favourably. The emphasis on the right proportions of body and face, the athletic and sinewy build, all go back to the Greek examples. A particular ideal of beauty is found throughout Dahn's pages, and this ideal became an integral part of the German self-image. If we add to this ideal the virtues of the Goths, we have put together the "Aryan type" that was to play an increasingly important part in German literature from 1848 onward,[17] and was to reflect ever more sinister attitudes in the 20th century.

The noble woman is part of this image, and here Dahn adopted the motif of Sir Walter Scott's *Ivanhoe*. The beautiful Jewess Miriam is in love with the future king of the Goths, Totila. This love serves to ennoble Miriam (and her father), but it has no effect on her brother, who in the end betrays the Goths to their adversaries. Moreover, this Jewish youth mirrors in his outward appearance the evil that resides within his soul: he is small, puny, and in all ways unattractive. Dahn uses this Jewish stereotype, which had already emerged into popular consciousness and which became the foil to the Germanic ideal of beauty. Yet Dahn was not consciously a racist; Miriam and her father show that Jewishness can be redeemed through a true assimilation to the Germanic ideal.[18]

Dahn's other works never approached the popularity of this novel. He wrote stories and poetry about the Germanic gods that preached patriotism and involvement with the past of the people. Not surprisingly, he abandoned Christianity in favour of a pantheism that stressed the unique religious experience of every *Volk*. Dahn, like Jordan and many others, was preoccupied with the creation of a Germanic religion that would cement the new nation. But this cement, instead of leading to a Byzantine despotism, was to include an ideal of free political discussion. There was nothing in this Germanic image that threatened German bourgeois society and its ideals. The virtues we have outlined were aspired to by the German middle classes, and the ideal of beauty could easily be accepted as part of these virtues. The ideal of strength and of the "honest fight" (such as the Goths waged against Byzantium) was integrated with social Darwinism, nationalism, and the idea of progress, reflecting the restraints that German bourgeois liberalism imposed upon itself.

Germany's newly found self-confidence resulted in a strong emphasis on the inevitability of progress. Viewed in national terms this progress meant the retention of the *status quo* in a society that seemed already designed to make such progress possible. This *status quo* was not defined solely in terms of national unity, but also through an emphasis on the individual standing outside the sphere of direct political involvement and yet within a society that allowed him to unfold his own unique potential. The works of many German writers said, in effect: "Here in the nation that we have at long last created is a society that is rooted in tradition and yet allows you to develop your own creativity and worth. There is no need to concern yourself with politics or the social structure; instead you must look inward to develop your individuality within this world." A character in a novel by Paul Heyse put it succinctly: "the possible, the useful, the purposeful, and the necessary are and remain relative goals; it must be the task of the statesman to educate the public to a respect for law so that as many free individuals as possible may live harmoniously together."[19]

Whereas Felix Dahn's novel symbolically depicted the growth and direction of German nationalism, Gustav Freytag's *Soll und Haben* (1855; Debit and Credit) symbolized the ideal of German bourgeois existence. This novel attained an even greater popularity than *Der Kampf um Rom*. The hero is not the Germanic people but a Germanic merchant house, its "heroic" qualities residing in the fact that it is old and established, devoted to "honest work" within the limits of the small town in which it operates. At one level an aristocrat, Rothsattel, provides the contrast;

he is a spendthrift and prone to luxury, but his fortune is saved by the merchant house of Schröter, and he departs to settle on his eastern estates. Gustav Freytag (1816–95) did not want to abolish the nobility; on the contrary, he believed that every class had its place in the nation. It is a mistake for the Count of Rothsattel to dabble in finance, which is the business of the "honest bourgeoisie." His role is to recapture his strength and sense of mission by colonizing among the slaves. The real contrast in this novel, however, is between the house of Schröter and the Jewish house of Ehrenthal: the contrast between Christian honesty and stability and Jewish nervousness and false dealing. This contrast includes those who belong to both houses, and the stereotypes are the same as those Dahn was to draw later. The whole way of life of the two households is involved: Schröter's establishment is old, solid, clean, and comfortable; Ehrenthal's is dirty, small, and cramped. At the Schröters', all is *Gemütlichkeit*; at the Ehrenthals', hatred and rootlessness predominate. The quality of family life is central to this contrast, for at the Ehrenthals' there are quarrels and opposition between parents and children, whereas the Schröters lead a happy and settled existence. Given the importance of the family as the basis of the bourgeois ideal (a topic to which we shall return), this contrast is of the utmost importance. Wilhelm Jordan wrote that all ideals culminate in Germanism, but singled out for praise the "sacredness" of the family group.[20]

The ending of Freytag's novel mirrors once more the ideal he has set forth. The nervous, unsettled, Jewish youth, Veitel Itzig, drowns in a dirty river, but the Christian apprentice marries the Schröters' daughter and enters fully into the settled life of the ancient, honourable merchant house. Everyone gets his just deserts and the didactic nature of the novel is fully revealed.

Like Dahn, Freytag was no racist. He advocated the complete assimilation of Jews, and the thrust of his portrayal is directed against Jews as members of a foreign culture and civilization. He lived in Breslau, close to the masses of East European Jewry (as Dahn lived in Königsberg in the same frontier region), and his view of these Jews dominates the stereotype. This contrast between Jew and German was to fascinate many later writers, though none in the 19th century was as popular as Freytag or Dahn.[21] Yet the roots of the racist anti-Semitism of the 20th century were laid in this popular literature, even if Germany did not stand alone in emphasizing the contrast. East European Jewry *did* form a separate culture and civilization in Europe,* and as this was highly

* See Ch. 12, "The Emergence of Modern Hebrew Literature."

visible (partly because of the emigration of Jews into the west), it also provided the most exposed target against which to measure national differences.

Freytag wrote other works that emphasized the historical connection between past and present. He liked to trace back each of his subjects to its historical roots in order to discover an organic principle relevant to national concerns. The middle classes became such a concern in Germany, which was very slow to shed its feudal structure—and, indeed, never did so entirely during the 19th century. Typically the middle classes were regarded as a restless and disruptive element within a nation that prized organic development, especially after the revolution of 1848. Freytag's "settled" merchant house, firmly rooted in its locality, provided the ideal of bourgeois existence. The hero of *Soll und Haben* mentions that the Poles do not possess such a settled middle class, whereupon his friend replies: "This means that they are devoid of culture."[22] The limited horizons of this bourgeois ideal involved a very restricted definition of culture, and a dread of change.

Friedrich Wilhelm von Hackländer's novel *Handel und Wandel* (1850; Trade and Change) was one of the few earlier novels that, like *Soll und Haben*, centred on a bourgeois milieu. Here also speculation and risk-taking are derided in favour of "honest work." Life, even commercial endeavour, should be bound to one locality—the truth of this maxim being established when the hero is driven insane by the twin evils of foreign travel and reckless commercial speculation. Freytag himself ceased all correspondence with foreigners toward the end of his life.[23]

Such works reflect the reality of social values in Germany during the period of industrialization. Here the old patriarchal value structure existed side by side with the industrial process. In Germany, as Ralf Dahrendorf has remarked, the process of rapid industrialization produced social effects quite different from those in England and France. For one thing, Germany maintained a class structure that dated back to the pre-industrial age;[24] the liberalism that exerted so strong a hold on the French and English bourgeoisie had little following in Germany—though Freytag thought of himself as a liberal, and Dahn came from a liberal background. The shift away from a revolutionary tradition in German letters, which we have observed, is connected not only with a concern for national unity but also with the value system and structure of the German bourgeoisie.

The emphasis on rootedness, on the small provincial town rather than on the big city, pervaded the country and its literature at the very time when cities were growing and the working classes increasing in power and restlessness. Novels, even those of great popularity, fought a rearguard action against this development. *Die Chronik der Sperlingsgasse* (1857; The Chronicle of Sparrows Alley), by Wilhelm Raabe (1831–1916), centres upon the loneliness of the individual within the metropolis. The book is drenched with the pessimism of "evil times." The central character clings to life within the small street in which he lives, a microcosm of the urban scene behind which the great world looms as in a dream. Strobel, the diarist of the *Sperlingsgasse*, is an introspective individualist, and typifies the "characters" that many German writers offered their readers during this period. Friedrich Theodor Vischer (1807–87) continued this tradition with *Auch Einer* (1879; Also a Person), which presents an individualist who flouts the community of men and goes his own unorthodox way.

But such individualism is always circumscribed. Vischer's lonely hero praises the nation and affirms his love for his *Volk*. Raabe's Strobel clings not only to his alley but also to a belief in a mystical creative power (a belief evidently derived from the writings of Schopenhauer).* The necessary parallel of the particular and the universal preoccupied such men. Berthold Auerbach (1812–82), the founder of the German peasant novel, summarized this feeling in 1846: the more freely the individual is able to develop his potential, the greater the feeling of community that is released within his soul.[25] Such idealism was held to resolve the conflict between individuality and an organic view of life, between the ideal of freedom and the desirability of rootedness and order. These ideas were put into a framework of historical development, a nostalgia for the life of the past that had furthered this combination of freedom and ordered existence.

The harmony that comes with a settled existence also provides the theme for many of the novels of Theodor Fontane (1819–98). Prussia dominates his works—not the militaristic Prussia, which he abhorred, but Prussia as the "middling state of affairs" that typifies the values that lie at the root of Fontane's outlook on the world. Moderation is at the centre of these values: "Brandeburg was the one country that never produced any saints, but where, on the other hand, no heretics were ever burned either."[26] Man must make peace with his fate and his society, for ultimate happiness will always elude him. The tragedy of *Effi Briest* (1895) lies in her unwillingness to come to terms with her

* See Ch. 4, "Irrationalism."

fate and in a lack of personal stability that leads her into adultery. For Fontane, moderation means not only adjustment to reality, but also common sense as opposed to blind adherence to principles. The actions of Effi Briest's jealous husband are inspired by abstract principles, so that, when he kills her lover in a duel, he is incapable of the satisfaction of feeling true human passion toward his enemy.[27]

Moderation allied to sobriety, incorruptibility, honesty, and dedication to duty are the virtues that distinguish the citizens of Brandeburg-Prussia. To be sure, these are bourgeois virtues, but Fontane, like other writers discussed in these pages, believed that those who possessed them formed a true nobility regardless of class; and, unlike other writers (such as Paul Heyse), Fontane did not confuse the good life with opulence: modesty and simplicity are integral to the virtues he praised so highly.

The protagonist of *Frau Jenny Treibel* (1893) lacks both these virtues. Through her marriage she has risen from low birth into the upper ranks of bourgeois society. As the wife of a prosperous merchant, her newly found class consciousness corrupts her judgment. Jenny Treibel's chief characteristic is possessiveness: she not only clings to her station in life but also tries to rule everyone around her. In face of her attempted manipulation of his daughter's life, a kindly academic is forced to exclaim, "If I were not a Professor I would become a social democrat." Fontane, in this novel, contrasts the classical ideal ("become what you truly are yourself") with the false ideals of Jenny Treibel.[28] There is nothing wrong with rising out of your social class, provided that this enlarges your horizon rather than constricting it. Fontane is not attacking the virtues the bourgeoisie exalted, but castigating the selfish possessiveness that governs Jenny Treibel's outlook upon her new world. His ideal embraces those qualities that all writers in the mainstream of German letters had also praised, but he goes beyond them in emphasizing that adjustment to society also means gaining distance from the hurly-burly that society represents.

Fontane's heroes are pessimists who manage to overcome this pessimism and to gain harmony in their personal lives. Prussian virtues are central to this harmony, but a firm connection with Prussian history helps toward their attainment. Dubslav, the principal character of *Der Stechlin* (1898), or the evangelical sisters in *Wanderungen durch die Mark Brandenburg* (1862–82; Ramblings through the Mark Brandenburg) have their roots in the Prussian past. Although Fontane denied the usefulness of a hereditary nobility, his stress upon the Prussian past inevitably makes most of his heroes a part (or at least a reflection) of the Junker class and its values.

His definition of the Prussian heritage is bound up with the landscape within which it was formed, and works such as the *Wanderungen* attempt to combine Prussian history and the Prussian landscape into one indissoluble whole. This idea was not new. Many of the historical novels that we have discussed attempted this kind of fusion. The German ideal of rootedness, of the foundations for a settled society, included a wished-for harmony between those families that had long shared the fate of the nation, and the landscape that had helped to shape their destinies.

In the historical novel, as in the peasant novel, this concept of harmony tended to narrow the range of vision and promote an intolerant nationalism. In Fontane's work, however, the author's sense of history gives "distance" to his characters, enabling them to rise above society and to come to terms with their fate. In *Stechlin*, Dubslav typifies Fontane's harmonious man: not only does he possess the Prussian virtues, but he is opposed to narrow definitions of class and culture, and inveighs against a one-sided pride of nationality. Dubslav is tolerant because he is at one with his fate as well as with the history and landscape of his native soil. Fontane reached back into the past not in order to prophesy the national future, but to use the past to encourage virtues far removed from the exuberant nationalism or bourgeois acquisitiveness of his time.

Nothing in Fontane conflicts with the ideals of the bourgeois world of which he himself was sceptical; no call to revolt is sounded in his pages. He shared Raabe's pessimism about his own times; in his case, too, this pessimism led to a concentration on the individual rather than on society. His characters seem to withdraw from the world, because "quiet is better than noise."[29] But the emphasis is always on the effort to overcome this pessimism in one's own personal life and to emerge settled, harmonious, and with that larger view of man and his struggles that characterized the Prussian imagination. However large this view, it was still circumscribed by its connection with Prussian history and the Prussian landscape, and by an emphasis upon virtues that give Fontane's works their singularly old-fashioned character.

The limited horizons of German letters led to a change in the attainable ideal that many writers presented to their readers. German unity had for long provided such an ideal, but after it was attained in 1870, writers increasingly began to praise the good and the beautiful as a goal of life that stood outside any concern with society or politics. The *status quo* would include a Utopia that everyone could share. The work of Paul Heyse (1830–1914), the most celebrated and admired novelist of the Wilhelmine era, illustrates these ideals.

280

Heyse had supported the revolution of 1848 in his youth, and had even cheered the democratic uprising in Baden. After the failure of revolution, however, he shed his revolutionary fervour and began to recommend the quiet and orderly development of society.[30] He was called to Munich by King Ludwig II of Bavaria, and became, for a time, a member of the court's "round table," where literary matters were discussed and papers presented. Heyse's patron at Munich was the poet Emmanuel Geibel (1815–84), who had also repudiated his initial enthusiasm for the ideals of 1848 in order to become the "herald of German nationality." Geibel's poem "The Death of Tiberius," for example, presents symbolically the transfer of the Empire from Romans to Germans. Tiberius, dying, drops his sceptre out of the window, and it is caught by a German legionnaire who has seen Christ die on the cross. Geibel was much admired as the high priest of poetry, a reputation he himself did much to encourage. Heyse became something of a high priest as well, though his work was never as portentous and heavy-handed as Geibel's.

Heyse (and indeed the whole Munich group) has been accused of avoiding the darker aspects of life in favour of an emphasis upon beauty and form.[31] There is some truth in this criticism, but it ignores the fact that the quest for beauty was only part of a world view that Heyse projects in his novels.[32] In his most famous novel, *Kinder der Welt* (1873; Children of This World), he emphasizes the need to come to terms with the reality of life; he advises the new generation not to withdraw either into a rejection of the world for the sake of religion, or into martydom for the sake of a cause, and asserts that individual worth will improve the quality of life on earth. What is needed is the good will of all men. A master craftsman who wants to reform the world and suffers many disappointments is advised to remain within the limited circle of his profession and his small town: if he tills his own soil and works honestly at his craft, he will create a better society than those who theorize about social conditions and politics.[33] Heyse typically praises the "golden mediocrity" of some, provided it is not hedged about with pretentiousness.[34]

Individualism stands in the foreground of the novel: man must trust in his own worth, and neither the state nor religion should practise intolerance. These liberal maxims are combined with the contention that the individual can best unfold his personality within his own milieu, and develop an appreciation of the beauty contained in this world through pride in himself. This beauty is defined in Wilhelmine terms; Heyse's novels abound in descriptions of paintings and furniture that are judged through the conventional taste of the time. As for the working classes, the hero of *Kinder der Welt* founds a working-class cultural club and praises a capitalist who lets his workers buy shares in his firm. It is interesting to note that during the revolution of 1848 such workers' "cultural" clubs (*Arbeiterbildungsvereine*) had the political purpose of spreading democratic ideas. Heyse's club has no such purpose; it unites workers and the bourgeois leadership, who attend lectures on natural science that demonstrate the falseness of organized religion. The lower classes (Heyse wrote in one of his short stories) must be encouraged to attain bourgeois consciousness.[35]

Although Heyse was strongly opposed to the idea of nationalism in terms of an all-powerful state, his liberalism was essentially negative in quality; he praised individualism—but only the kind of individualism that renounced any political participation; above all, the harmony of the existing social order must be preserved. The revolutionary in *Kinder der Welt* gives way to a hero who believes in a settled life that will culminate not in social or political change, but in the appreciation of the good that life has to offer. It is not surprising that Heyse was so highly regarded in his day. His novels echoed the German bourgeois ideal, and it must have been comforting to read such works in a Europe that was neither quiet nor settled in its political and social order.

Paul Heyse had a host of followers, and his ideas appeared in many other novels of the time. Georg Hermann's very popular *Jettchen Gebert* (1906) is of special interest in this connection. Georg Hermann (the pen-name of Georg H. Borchardt, 1871–1943) set his novel in a Jewish milieu, and so it throws light on contemporary ideas about the assimilation of German Jews into bourgeois society. The Jewish element is merely superimposed on an idealization of the bourgeois way of life that Heyse and others had prized; it consists mostly in the names of characters and in certain religious holidays that are observed with bourgeois opulence. To be sure, the heroine Jettchen suffers an unhappy love affair and finally commits suicide—her lover being deemed "unsuitable" because he is both a Gentile and a penurious intellectual. But here, as elsewhere, Hermann is making a general plea for tolerance and damning the worship of wealth. The life led by the Geberts is in other respects praised, because it is a settled life where (as one character puts it) not much attention is paid either to a quest for the so-called higher things of life or to the changeable, drunken, and fleeting aspects of existence. Life within its own prescribed limits is the ideal for Hermann, as it was for Heyse: "life," so Hermann writes in a preface to his novel, "is a game and we must not take it too seriously." "Everything comes as it well must" is Hermann's fatalistic view of the world—a view that contrasts with Heyse's optimism. For both writers, however, a settled bourgeois life provides the best way of coping with the joys and disappointments of human existence.

Georg Hermann's own fate was tragic: the writer who so lovingly described the bourgeois milieu of Berlin perished at Auschwitz. Stefan Zweig was correct when he wrote to Georg Hermann, after the Nazis came to power, that ". . . it will one day be noticed as a peculiar sign [of the times] that it was precisely the Jews who painted the most lasting portrait of Germany at the turn of the century and after the war."[36] Nevertheless the German bourgeoisie had expelled the Jewish bourgeoisie from their midst, accepting the Jewish stereotype that Dahn and Freytag (among many others) had drawn in such stark colours. Hermann had praised the limited horizons entailed in the way of life of his characters; but they had become too limited to contain those whom he thought to be such prime examples of this way of life.

Paul Heyse linked his idealization of the bourgeoisie to excellent literary form, intimately connected with the past traditions of poetry and society. The Naturalists advocated an unlimited idealism that could lead only to anarchy.[37] Felix Dahn criticized the Naturalists in a similar manner. They acted wildly, as if nature were ugly and mean, whereas in reality "beautiful truths" and "beautiful human nature" exist on earth.[38] Heyse himself linked literary form to a life of work and duty culminating in the vision of a world of beauty and light. When such beauty is attached to an idealization of existing society, literary form becomes part of tradition and the *status quo*.

The primacy of personal relationships over any larger concerns is implied or expressed in all works written by the most admired Wilhelmine writers. But these personal relationships were not anarchic; they were given literary form through their connection with the settled and traditional order, which was expressed in these works by family relationships. Heyse's *Kinder der Welt* is filled with sentimental attachments of husband to wife, or with the love that exists between brothers. Jettchen Gebert suffered, at least in part, because she was in danger of destroying the fabric of her family. The family symbolized the very essence of the bourgeois way of life, and this symbol reached its greatest prominence in the work of some novelists at the very moment when the family structure came under attack by naturalist and expressionist writers. A whole world separates the solid families of writers such as Heyse from the cruel and despairing parents in Frank Wedekind's *Frühlings Erwachen* (1891;

Spring's Awakening), in which the family is the victim of strife between generations. The significant point here, of course, is that writers such as Heyse (who clung to tradition) and writers such as Wedekind (who explored the "pathology" of traditional bourgeois values) both started from the assumption that the family structure is the true microcosm of society at large.

The works we have discussed were widely read by middle-class readers, and they demonstrate the general direction of German literature in the second half of the 19th century. However, the world views held by these writers infiltrated the population at large from works that attained mass circulation through cheap editions or lending libraries. However slight the literary merits of such fictions, we should not underestimate the extent to which they may confirm and sharpen—even if they do not create—ideas about the value systems in society.

At first glance the highly successful books of Marlitt (the pen-name of Eugenie John, 1825–86) are sentimental love stories. But if we look closer we discover the same value system that the other, more critically appreciated writers had advocated. Marlitt's ideal was an "even-tempered, harmonious family life." Here children must obey their parents and man must assume authority over woman, for woman is destined "to found a happy family and not to fill her head with facts and figures."[39] Society depends on a social hierarchy, though not one founded on inherited privilege; sentimentality and refinement are the criteria of true social status. Marlitt's definition of sentimentality includes compassion toward the poor, a paternalism that will alleviate their present misery.

Within her novels men and women rise in the social scale only by accepting bourgeois manners and morals, including the ideal of "honest work." (In fact many of her characters move upward in the social scale through marriage rather than through their own endeavours.) It has been observed, with justice, that German literature lacks its Horatio Algers, and this serves to remind us of the realities of the German class structure, and especially of the dominance of pre-industrial attitudes within the industrial nation. Small wonder that Marlitt inveighs against the social climber, the pusher, and those who threaten the organic fabric of life: no unfettered individual effort is allowed in her world. Perhaps Marlitt's ideal can best be summed up in her own words: "There is something very beautiful about [this] ancient bourgeois order . . . everything stands or lies in its accustomed place . . . one is immediately at home."[40]

"To be at home" was another definition of the limited horizons necessary for a good and beautiful life. Within the limits of such rootedness, however, Marlitt emphasized her optimism about man's potential and individual worth. The worst crime society can commit is the degrading of man to the level of a machine, making him serve others and deny his own will. Marlitt enthusiastically supported Bismarck's fight against the Catholic Church, which she believed to be oppressive, and instead she advocated a pantheism brimming with Christian sentimentality. Individual freedom plays a part in her novels, as it did in Dahn's *Der Kampf um Rom*, but it is circumscribed by the narrow bourgeois ideal that she advocated. Marlitt was no strident nationalist; although she was loyal to Bismarck's state, her characters do not stress their Germanism. However, the environment in which they live, their roots in the locality, accentuate the provincialism that fills her novels, and that at the same time restricted the vision of her fellow-writers.

Marlitt was the favourite author of the *Gartenlaube* (Gazebo), a journal that, at its height, had the unparalleled circulation of half a million copies. This journal attempted to perpetuate the tradition of 1848, praising Voltaire and Rousseau as champions of freedom, and eulogizing Kant for attempting to exalt reason as the basis of society and economics.[41] However, the further the revolution of 1848 receded into the distance, the greater the stress it laid not only upon Voltaire and Rousseau, but also upon the need for order and social hierarchy. Bourgeois manners and morals provided the foundations for a better and settled life, and nothing must be allowed to challenge this tradition.[42]

The vision of life that we have discussed was not solely confined to novels in a bourgeois setting. The peasant novel had a long tradition in Germany, and Berthold Auerbach, who had popularized this type of work, was still alive in the decades following the revolution of 1848. His novels of village life idealized the simple peasant and the upright village priest. Ludwig Ganghofer (1855–1921) proved to be the most successful practitioner of this genre within the unified *Reich*. He was on the best-seller list of 1900, side by side with Tolstoy; even in 1957 he was still greatly admired, many Germans putting him in the company of such men as Gustav Freytag, Thomas Mann, and Ernest Hemingway.[43]

The peasant was used to symbolize a strength and virility not yet sapped by the all-pervasive modernity. Ganghofer's peasants are "examples of men within whom the primeval forces, the healthy instincts, and the force of life have not changed into the unhealthy, restricted, and average."[44] Moreover, Ganghofer's characters were drawn with sufficient realism for his readers to regard them as a reflection of life itself. His peasants tend to be superstitious, even mean and quarrelsome; but this, after all, is life: men should be recognized for what they are, and the reader should learn how to build a better future out of such a recognition. Ganghofer was an optimist; for him the genius of human existence, with all its secret recesses, will lead men to the light, if only they can break out of the fetters of culture (by which he meant urbanism and modernity). Life is hard, but it has potential if it will be guided by the inspiration of nature. Interestingly enough, in his youth Ganghofer had admired the cynical and worldly Heinrich Heine. However, by the 1880s he had repudiated his former hero, and he called this repudiation "a step toward health." That step had begun with his discovery of the mountains, the "sacred landscape" that symbolized for him the unspoiled force of nature.[45] At the same time Ganghofer turned from cynicism to optimism: men will find the force to break the fetters of artificial culture.

He constructed an elaborate Utopia in which every person would have his own land, and where euthanasia would be the lot of the congenitally sick. Such concepts are uneasily combined with traditional liberal virtues. Laws, not men, must rule in this state. There must be freedom of religion and for the creative artist. Above all, every man must know the joys of home and hearth, which so many peasants actually possess: the family would be safeguarded, and bachelors would pay most of the expenses of the state.[46] We are back with the praise of bourgeois virtues, of a German bourgeois Utopia, that Marlitt had typified at another level.

The German peasant novel never expanded into a true glorification of the primitive, after the manner of Gauguin and many French writers.[47] Instead, the tradition of the German peasant novel stressed an approach to nature that deprived it of that wild primitivism that threatened all forms of civilized life. Marlitt was also fascinated by nature, but her nature becomes a friendly landscape where the contours of the mountains are "soft and glowing."[48] Ganghofer's nature is more wild and rugged, yet in the last resort it also is tamed through the peasant's feeling of belonging, of identification with the land.

Human nature is tamed through providing a home for man: we are back with Marlitt's ideal of a society where everything lies in its accustomed place. Unlike the characters in Marlitt and the previous writers discussed, however, Ganghofer's peasants are involved with the struggle for life, where the qualities of shrewdness and cleverness can bring success. Such an emphasis upon struggle comes close to a glorification of force. Ganghofer was too sentimental to take this step, but Hermann Löns (1866–1914), his successor in popular esteem in this genre, combines the glorification of primitivism with an equal emphasis on the naked force necessary to protect this way of life from the corruption of modernity.

Stories of adventure in foreign lands could also be used didactically, and this combination brought enormous success to Karl May (1842–1912). May overshadowed even Marlitt and Ganghofer in popularity; indeed he may well be called the most popular German writer of modern times. Adolf Hitler once said that Karl May had opened his eyes to the world,[49] and he certainly opened the eyes of generations of readers during the first half of the 20th century. Between 1892 and 1913 over one and a half million copies of his collected works were published, and by 1938 this total had risen to nearly seven and a half million.[50] May's novels centred on the Orient or the American West. Both Kara Ben Nemsi in the Orient and the trapper Old Shatterhand march through dangers in strange lands, and emerge victorious over the evil that confronts them. Both master life—a life filled with persecution, mysterious secrets, and labyrinthine intrigues. These are the anxieties of modern urban existence transposed to the deserts of the Orient or the North American plains. Perhaps it is the fairy-tale element in May's works, coupled with the lure of adventure, that accounts for his great popularity. He himself stressed the didactic nature of his works, but, like many of the writings discussed in this essay, they could be read without embracing the author's world view.[51] Yet, even if we grant the complexity of the relationship between an author's world view and his readership, the close integration of world view and plot must have had an impact on the attitudes of those who read and enjoyed such works.

Kara Ben Nemsi and Old Shatterhand typify the morality that inevitably wins its battles, for as May himself tells us: "along the paths which Winnetou and Old Shatterhand rode, no mean actions were tolerated."[52] Evil is always punished. The hero combines kindness, and even sentimentality, with strong and decisive action, in order that virtue shall triumph everywhere. May glorifies the virtues that other novelists had also praised; but he surrounds them with a fighting spirit directed against those who would destroy them. The confrontation between good and evil is direct and simple. For Karl May, king, fatherland, and law are necessary institutions that give roots to man. Such roots help man to rise above the purely material plane to the highest ideal on earth: that of becoming a noble soul (*Edelmensch*). May's Utopia offers "a symphony of liberating thought"—the strong and noble souls whose wills are directed toward uprooting lawlessness and the evil instincts of man.[53]

May thus connects heroism with both Germanism and Christianity.

"You Germans," says one of his characters, "are a peculiar people, sentimental and yet when necessary you stand and fight."[54] The school reformer and *völkisch* thinker Ludwig Gurlitt described one of May's American Indian heroines thus: "she is modest and strict with herself . . . yet tender and of a deep soulfulness, filled with true femininity like Kriemhilde: an Indian woman with a German heart."[55] Karl May believed that Germany was the true repository of the virtues he praised, and that no German could do much wrong either on the North American plains or in the deserts of the Orient. But he never lapses into a strident nationalism: for him the American Indians are nobler souls than the whites who try to destroy them. His Germans in foreign lands fit themselves into the customs of other peoples; they tend to be Germans and men of the world at the same time. May's heroes also emphasize their Christianity, and as missionaries among primitive peoples they teach love and good manners not only by personal example but also through the use of force.

The hero dominates each of the novels, and becomes the personification of authority, a man who through his true nobility exemplifies the triumph of courage, love, and compassion in the wide confines of nature, following out God's plan for the world. The pantheism that surrounds and, in a sense, guides May's heroes toward the light, also suffuses the ideal society that Marlitt sets before us. For both, this is an inner piety that disdains any outward effect. Such inner piety supported the "pure heart" that would make a new and better life possible on earth. God's spirit and the inspiration of a "natural heart" will lead men out of the jungles of the city toward a genuine society where bourgeois virtues will reign. Neither for Marlitt's hierarchical society nor for May's hero is political freedom an essential part of this Utopian longing. Force plays its part, but it is dedicated to defeating evil—in the guise of all that is morally deficient, and lacking in compassion, sense of family, or the will to protect noble souls.

The tendency to view the world in moral terms predominated among such writers. The specific moral pattern that accompanied the rise of bourgeois society provided the foundations and the cement for the ideal commonwealth of men. Sobriety, hard work, and an emphasis on action play a large role in these novels, but virtue is also defined as including good manners, the "respectability" that contemporaries associated so closely with middle-class virtue. Morality and good manners were an integral part of the concern for society: the conventions society had produced also served to define it.

Those writers who rebelled against these literary norms took the view that conventional respectability merely served to distort the realities of life, and that the acceptance of bourgeois virtues deflected the individual from his search for personal integrity. The Expressionists revolted against the bourgeois image of society, but their revolution, in large part, centred upon the individual in his relationship to the conventions that surround him. Max Brod's *Schloss Nornepygge* (1908; Nornepygge Castle), which came early in the expressionist revolt, lamented the ability of the hero to "pierce through" the fool's paradise in which most people lived, for such insight transformed him into an outsider, naked and defenceless. Mozart's *Don Giovanni* provides the theme of the book, and Don Giovanni himself appears in order to demonstrate how such heroes can lead mankind toward liberation. Nevertheless the book's hero (or rather anti-hero) remains in his indifferent isolation. The rejection of the "home" that so many writers had helped to build for their readers left Expressionists with a feeling of isolation. As a result many expressionist writers longed to be fully and irresponsibly alive, and this marked a personal vitalism that saw man as a self-contained unity. "Am I not alive—am I not life?" cries a character in one of Georg Kaiser's earliest plays.[56]

The influence of Nietzsche, himself in revolt against the predominant patterns of social life, is unmistakable in such vitalism. This was a revolution, but not on the pattern of 1848, for society and politics were rejected in favour of individual perception and ecstasy. Nietzsche's phrase, "society puts the passions asleep,"[57] characterizes the attitude of many Expressionists toward the realities and miseries of life. The bourgeois writers had turned the vision of a better life toward "beauty and goodness" attainable within the framework of existing social reality. The expressionist writers rejected this reality, drifting off into a vitalism that encompassed, at one and the same time, a Nietzschean ecstasy and a pessimism about life itself. The "new" expressionist man believed in acting out the demands of his own chaotic soul. Sincerity to oneself did not mean settling into a home where everything had its appointed place; it meant hurling onself against the conventions of society. In Wedekind's *Frühlings Erwachen* the schoolboys face repression and punishment because they embrace what is only natural—sex—and society punishes men for such acts.

With the approach and the beginning of World War I, however, many Expressionists were moved to adopt more overtly political positions. The central character of Georg Kaiser's *Die Bürger von Calais* (1914; The Burghers of Calais) challenges traditional patriotism; he commits

T

suicide in order to persuade his fellow-citizens to give hostages to the English and accept defeat, rather than condemn the city and all its inhabitants to death. The preservation of man, not his destruction, must be the goal of politics. Action must be guided by reason in the cause of the love of mankind.

However, the love of man and the pacifism that inspired expressionist writing during and after the war were based more upon emotion than upon social analysis: the attempts of Expressionists to improve society "floated, as it were, in a sea that swept towards a shore of infinite promise."[58] It is not surprising that so many Expressionists ended up in the arms of nationalism and bourgeois society. Max Brod became a Zionist; Hans Johst, a prominent early Expressionist, went on to make his name as a Nazi writer. Gottfried Benn's poetry, before and after World War I, was filled with visions of disease, decadence, and death; he also wrote Dionysian hymns to the human ego. But by 1933 he was praising the logic of history as the absolute value to which man had to relate himself, and making speeches exalting the "new man" of the Third Reich.[59] Expressionism had proved to be an ineffectual and disappointing revolution. The new literary forms of the movement and its considerable artistic freedom provided no compensation for those who had wanted no less than to change the minds of men. German bourgeois society had survived in such strength that it eventually absorbed the very men who had attempted to storm its ramparts. A Nietzschean revolt led by creative artists was clearly not an effective way to accomplish a revolutionary task. Their frame of reference proved both too vague and too limited: the conventions they hated were merely symptoms, not the cause, of the sickness that they discerned in the society of their time.

The German bourgeoisie, however, discerned no such sickness before World War I. It rejoiced in a *status quo* that combined a supposed dedication to individualism with an emphasis on traditional manners and morals, and the national mystique. The mainstream of German letters followed this path. Liberal attitudes were undermined by the longing for a settled and ordered existence that would not threaten the Establishment. Nevertheless, as the new century opened, one powerful voice protested against the course that liberalism had taken in Germany.

Heinrich Mann attempted to link German liberalism with the tradition of the French Enlightenment. Mann had passed through nationalism and Expressionism in his early youth, and now he exalted the rationalism of the French tradition, castigating the romantic and irrational attitudes prevalent in German society. His novel *Schlaraffenland* (1900; Land of

Cockaigne) exposed the hypocrisy of the German *haute bourgeoisie*: millionaires applaud plays showing the misery of the working classes, but then go about their business as usual; life is regarded as a game where appearances are more important than reality, and where corruption has eaten into the very fabric of society. The exclamation of the book's chief character—"feeling is all that matters"—goes to the heart of Mann's condemnation of Wilhelmine Germany, because feeling is opposed to those rational attitudes that alone can produce a democratic society where freedom and justice reign.

For Mann, the ruling classes use their power in order to corrupt man's rational faculties: his ability to grasp what is true, good, and right. The anti-hero of his novel *Der Untertan* (1918; The Man of Straw) worships ". . . the power that rules over us and whose feet we kiss."[60] This power is exercised in the name of an ordered and settled existence, and it ruins those whom it cannot manipulate. Within the novel this power triumphs, even if not for ever; the kindly socialist who is deprived of his office and livelihood continues to praise the "spirit of humanity" that will eventually triumph; for power that cannot spread goodness and kindness throughout the world is not destined to last.[61]

Mann saw the outbreak of World War I as the natural consequence of the use of power for irrational and tyrannical purposes. His famous essay *Zola* (1915) was one more attempt to recall Germany to the sanity of the French rational tradition—a true liberalism that would defeat the irrationalism that had led the nation into militarism and oppression. Mann fully shared the optimism characteristic of the French Enlightenment: the people have the ability to construct a democratic society; it is the misuse of power by a "dried-up" establishment that stands in the way of the inevitable perfection of humanity.[62] With singular courage Mann looked forward to the defeat of Germany, for only such a catastrophe would open the way for the abolition of militarism and capitalism in favour of the "ideal republic of the future."[63]

The defeat of Germany and the revolution of 1918 failed to establish the ideal republic, however, and Heinrich Mann now called for a "dictatorship of reason," exhorting the hapless President of the Republic to exercise absolute power until the people could be freed from the yoke of "darkness and madness" that Wilhelmine rule had thrust upon them. Once again he reaffirmed his faith in the "rational spirit": it alone could bring democracy.[64] The economic problems that Germany faced were secondary, mechanical difficulties that could be tackled successfully provided the right spirit was present. This belief in the primacy of the spirit links Mann to that German idealism he hated so much, and to the abstract longing for freedom of the Young Germans; it is small wonder that he never joined any of the existing socialist parties. His novels are filled with the spirit of rationalism and humanism, but they are devoid of any Marxist social analysis and have no direct place in the movement to create a socialist literature.

In spite of this, Heinrich Mann did attempt to change the course of German letters. He was not interested in the Expressionists' chaotic search for freedom or in Nietzschean cries of revolt. As he wrote in 1917, "Why should the beautiful preference of the mature 18th century for goodness and the recognition of human equality not be recaptured?"[65] His books were widely read: *Schlaraffenland* had sold 100,000 copies by 1929, and *Der Untertan* sold 150,000 copies shortly after its appearance in 1918.[66] Nevertheless, it was too late to re-establish the influence of French rationalism over the German mind; that opportunity had been missed with the failure of the revolution of 1848. Instead, the mainstream of German letters continued to reflect the rejection of this particular liberal and revolutionary tradition.

Thomas Mann's reply to his brother's essay on Zola was rooted in a deeper and more abiding stream of German thought. *Betrachtungen eines Unpolitischen* (1918; Reflections of an Unpolitical Man) summarizes many attitudes that we have already discussed. Whereas Heinrich Mann had seen in the self-satisfied German bourgeoisie an obstacle to the realization of the ideal republic, Thomas Mann praises bourgeois existence as *the* truly German life-style, summarizing this way of life as *Ordnung, Folge, Ruhe* (order, progression, quiet).[67] Thomas Mann stresses order and ordered progress, concepts that his brother had condemned as serving to disguise the misuse of power. The bourgeois virtues that Thomas Mann exalts in other works also inform his idealization of this style of life: hard work, devotion to duty, and good manners.[68] So it is not surprising that he also praises the patriarchal relationship between employer and labourer.[69] He recalls Theodor Fontane in his attitude to the quiet and ordered life, but his emphasis on patriotism and on the metaphysical depth of the German soul further restricts his vision.

Heinrich Mann had also praised the bourgeois virtues of duty, punctuality, and moderation,[70] but he equated bourgeois democracy with French democracy, whereas his brother believed that middle-class life was the logical outgrowth of German idealism. Thomas Mann's pessimism about the political potential of the people led him to an acceptance that, in the political realm, might makes right. His brother, in contrast, asked: ". . . what is power if it is not justice?" Thomas Mann combines praise of the bourgeois way of life with cynicism about the possibilities inherent in human government. The ideal republic of his brother's dreams was nothing more than a phantasy, which was irrelevant to the reality of German life.

In the *Betrachtungen* the outward forms of government are dismissed as unworthy of serious consideration; this follows from the distinction he makes between culture and civilization. The "rich inner life of the soul," which determines individual development, is what makes for true culture, whereas civilization is a matter of mere outward forms, a superficial preoccupation with the here and now. Thomas Mann castigates the "love for demonstration and manifestos" as a shallow rationalism that merely encourages a generalized love for humanity.[71] The *Betrachtungen* is filled with confessions of faith in humanism, but this humanism turns out to be a hidden substance residing within the soul of the *Volk*. All that is truly "genuine" must be inner-directed; it expresses itself outwardly solely through the life-style of the bourgeoisie. For Thomas Mann a cultured bourgeois is a "romantic individualist,"[72] but in reality he himself romanticizes the whole bourgeois way of life, with its settled tradition and its rootedness where, in Marlitt's phrase, "one is immediately at home."

For all that, the unpolitical man turns political in time of war. Then the bourgeois is "at his place" in the national struggle and no questions are asked. War is the cement of national culture, the antidote to the cancer of civilization that threatens to dissolve society. Thomas Mann was deeply influenced by Nietzsche, although he does not echo Nietzsche's cry of revolt against the bourgeoisie. Instead he emphasized the philosopher's opposition to democracy, his "anti-radicalism," as he calls it. But it is to Nietzsche that we can trace his exaltation of primitivism—his belief that in war such primitivism is an outburst of the *Volk* soul with which the German artist must keep in touch.[73]

The *Betrachtungen* was written under the influence of a war experience that engulfed many Germans in a wave of Nietzschean ecstasy, but it is free of the harsh polemics against Germany's enemies that had become fashionable among so many of his fellow-writers. The tone, with some exceptions, is moderate; the arguments are advanced with an air of judicious restraint. To be sure, there is little in the book to foreshadow Mann's conversion to democracy only three years later (although, even after this conversion, he remained withdrawn from the world, preferring a quiet life among his own immediate circle).[74] Yet it is the *Betrachtungen*, rather than the works of his brother, that is in the mainstream of the

German literary tradition, for it summarizes many attitudes that dominated Wilhelmine society.

The works of overtly *völkisch* and nationalist writers never attained the popularity of the books considered in these pages.[75] Although the former were hostile to the bourgeoisie, they rejected a true change in the social structure in favour of a "change of attitudes." Their writings were in the process of becoming racist, whereas overtly racist views were absent from the popular works that have concerned us here.

German literature reflected a quest for identity within a new nation undergoing rapid industrialization. The foundations were laid for the future in the rejection of Western liberalism and in the failure to combine creative art and literature with revolutionary theory. During World War I, Thomas Mann's attacks upon enlightenment and rationalism were in the tradition of this 19th-century rejection. By the time Mann repudiated his own views, during the years of the Weimar Republic, it was already too late, and a national socialist revolution that none of these writers would have desired was about to engulf bourgeois and socialist alike.

References

1. GEORGE LICHTHEIM, *The Concept of Ideology* (New York 1967), p. 242.
2. RALF DAHRENDORF, *Society and Democracy in Germany* (New York 1967).
3. See JOST HERMAND (ed.), *Das junge Deutschland* (Stuttgart 1966).
4. See GEORG WEERTH, *Gedichte, Prosa* (Berlin 1960), and *Fragmente eines Romans*, ed. by Siegfried Unseld (Frankfurt 1965), p. 14.
5. GEORG HERWEGH, *Werke*, ed. by Herman Tardel (Berlin 1909), Vol. 1, p. c.
6. *ibid.*, p. xciii.
7. PETER DEMETZ, *Marx, Engels, und die Dichter* (Stuttgart 1959), pp. 122 ff.
8. See ERICH RUPRECHT, *Literarische Manifeste des Naturalismus 1880–1892* (Stuttgart 1962).
9. SUSANNE MILLER, "Critique littéraire de la social-democratie allemande à la fin du siècle dernier," *Le Mouvement Socialiste* 59 (Paris, April–June 1967), p. 55 *et passim*.
10. *ibid.*, p. 58.
11. See KARL KAUTSKY, *The Class Struggle*, trans. by W. E. Bohn (Chicago 1910), p. 159.
12. See URSULA MÜNCHOW (ed.), *Aus den Anfängen der sozialistischen Dramatik* (Berlin 1964).

13. ALFRED KLEINBERG, *Die deutsche Dichtung* (Berlin 1927), p. 371; MINNA KAUTSKY, *Auswahl aus ihrem Werk* (Berlin 1965), *passim*.

14. K. SCHIFFNER, *Wilhelm Jordan* (Frankfurt-am-Main 1889), p. 138.

15. JOSEF VICTOR VON SCHEFFEL, *Ekkehard* (Berlin 1855), pp. 14–5.

16. FELIX DAHN, *Erinnerungen* (Leipzig 1895), Vol. IV, Section II, p. 649.

17. GEORGE L. MOSSE, *The Crisis of German Ideology* (New York 1964), Ch. 4 and 11.

18. GEORGE L. MOSSE, "The Image of the Jews in German Popular Culture: Felix Dahn and Gustav Freytag," *Germans and Jews* (New York 1968), pp. 61–77.

19. Quoted in JOST HERMAND, "Zur Literatur der Gründerzeit," *Deutsche Vierteljahrsschrift für Literaturwissenschaft und Geistesgeschichte* (Halle 1967), Vol. 41, No. 2, p. 2208.

20. SCHIFFNER, *op. cit.*, p. 129.

21. See WILHELM STOFFERS, *Juden und Ghetto in der deutschen Literatur bis zum Ausgang des Weltkrieges* (Nymwegen 1939).

22. Quoted in EDUART ROTHFUCHS, *Der selbstbiographische Gehalt in Gustav Freytags Werken* (Münster 1929), p. 69.

23. JULIUS D. ECKARDT, *Lebenserinnerungen* (Leipzig 1910), Vol. I, pp. 48 and 67.

24. DAHRENDORF, *op. cit.*, pp. 36 ff. and 46.

25. BERTHOLD AUERBACH, *Schrift und Volk* (Leipzig 1846), p. 58.

26. Quoted in JOACHIM REMAK, *The Gentle Critic, Theodor Fontane and German Politics, 1848–1898* (Syracuse 1964), p. 57

27. Fontane calls him a "Prinzipienreiter," *Effi Briest* (Vienna 1942), pp. 219 and 244.

28. THEODOR FONTANE, *Frau Jenny Treibel* (Berlin 1893), pp. 285 and 320.

29. FONTANE, *Effi Briest*, p. 262.

30. PAUL HEYSE, *Jugenderinnerungen und Bekenntnisse* (Stuttgart and Berlin 1912), Vol. 1, pp. 99 and 191.

31. For example, ADOLF BARTELS, "Die Alten und die Jungen," *Grenzboten*, Vol. 55 (Leipzig 1869), p. 277.

32. PAUL HEYSE, *Kinder der Welt* (Berlin 1884), Vol. II, p. 61.

33. *ibid.*, pp. 262 f.

34. *ibid.*, pp. 78 and 189.

35. PAUL HEYSE, "Andrea Delfin," in *Die Reise nach dem Glück* (Stuttgart 1959), p. 392.

36. GEORG HERMANN, *Jettchen Geberts Geschichte* (Berlin 1912), Vol. 1; Letter from Stefan Zweig to Georg Hermann, 20 October 1935 (in Georg Hermann archive, Leo Baeck Institute, New York).

37. HEYSE, *Jugenderinnerungen und Bekenntnisse*, Vol. 1, p. 239.

38. DAHN, *op. cit.*, Vol. III, p. 305.

39. E. MARLITT, *Im Hause des Kommerzienrates* (Leipzig 1877), pp. 218 and 369.

40. *ibid.*, p. 41.

41. HERMANN ZANG, *Die Gartenlaube als politisches Organ* (Coburg 1935),

pp. 14 and 17. See also *Die Gartenlaube* 19 (Leipzig 1881), pp. 308–14.

42. RUTH HOROVITZ, *Vom Roman des Jungen Deutschland zum Roman der Gartenlaube* (Breslau 1937), p. 71.

43. EVA BECKER, "Literarische Zeitkommunikation 1860–1914," mimeographed MS, Proceedings of the Working Party "Deutsche Literaturwissenschaft" of the Fritz Thyssen Foundation (1965), p. 20; for 1957, see *Der Spiegel*, Vol. 11, No. 30 (Hamburg, 24 July 1957), p. 37.

44. LUDWIG GANGHOFER, *Der Dorfapostel* (Stuttgart 1902), p. 114.

45. HANS SCHWERTE, "Ganghofers gesundung," mimeographed MS, Proceedings of the Working Party "Deutsche Literaturwissenschaft" of the Fritz Thyssen Foundation (1965), pp. 95–128.

46. LUDWIG GANGHOFER, *Lebenslauf eines Optimisten: Buch der Jugend* (Stuttgart 1930), *passim*.

47. ROBERT MINDER, *Dichter in der Gesellschaft, Erfahrungen mit deutscher und französischer Literatur* (Frankfurt-am-Main 1966), p. 277.

48. *ibid.*, p. 278.

49. ADOLF HITLER, *Hitler's Secret Conversations*, trans. by N. Cameron and R. H. Stevens (New York 1953), p. 257.

50. VIKTOR BÖHM, *Karl May* (Vienna 1955), p. 3.

51. Note the stress on Karl May as a genial writer of fairy-tales, whose nationalism and Christianity can be discounted, in the novel *Die Aula* by Hermann Kant (Munich 1966), which was written in the German Democratic Republic. The view of May as a writer of fairy-tales is expanded in ERNST BLOCH, *Das Prinzip Hoffnung*, Vol. I (Frankfurt 1954), pp. 409 ff.

52. Quoted in BÖHM, *op. cit.*, p. 74.

53. KARL MAY, *Mein Leben und Streben* (Dresden 1910), pp. 74–5, 135, and 150.

54. Quoted in BÖHM, *op. cit.*, p. 101.

55. LUDWIG GURLITT, *Gerichtigkeit für Karl May!* (Dresden 1919), p. 140.

56. Quoted in WALTER SOKEL, *The Writer in Extremis* (New York 1964), p. 88. The play is *Rektor Kleist* (1905).

57. FRIEDRICH NIETZSCHE, "Die fröhliche Wissenschaft," *Nietzsches Werke* (Leipzig 1900), Vol. V, Section I, p. 41.

58. SOKEL, *op. cit.*, p. 182.

59. MOSSE, "Fascism and the Intellectuals," *Germans and Jews*, pp. 144–71.

60. HEINRICH MANN, *Der Untertan* (Leipzig 1918), p. 454.

61. *ibid.*, p. 490.

62. HEINRICH MANN, "Zola," *Essays*, Vol. I (Berlin 1954), pp. 156–236 (especially pp. 166 and 168).

63. *ibid.*, pp. 189 and 198.

64. HEINRICH MANN, *Diktatur der Vernunft* (Berlin 1923), *passim*.

65. ALFRED KANTOROWICZ, *Heinrich und Thomas Mann* (Berlin 1956), p. 24.

66. LORENZ WINTER, *Heinrich Mann und sein Publikum* (Cologne 1965), pp. 32 and 35 f.

67. THOMAS MANN, *Betrachtungen eines Unpolitischen* (Berlin 1918), p. 71.

68. *ibid.*, p. 246.

69. *ibid.*, p. 109.
70. ALFRED KANTOROWICZ, *Deutsches Tagebuch*, Vol. II (Munich 1961), p. 100.
71. THOMAS MANN, *op. cit.*, pp. 81, 92 ff.
72. *ibid.*, p. 106.
73. *ibid.*, pp. 47, 84, and 123.
74. THEODOR W. ADORNO, *Noten zur Literatur*, Vol. III (Frankfurt-am-Main 1967), p. 23.
75. See MOSSE, *The Crisis of German Ideology*.

CHAPTER 9

Naturalism and the Spanish Novel

Walter T. Pattison[*]

Émile Zola, whose name to Spaniards is synonymous with Naturalism, was not, of course, a completely isolated inventor of new, never-before-conceived ideas and literary attitudes. Many trends, social as well as literary, contributed to the formation of the new school and its chief propagandist. The growth of bourgeois society, along with the industrial and commercial revolution of the 19th century, brought with it an insistence on material values. Philosophy became positivistic, concentrating on natural laws, and hence impinging on science. Efforts to explain the broad lines of man's history through natural law resulted in Comte's three stages of human history; to analyse man's personality, Taine proposed his triad of *race, moment, et milieu* (race, historical moment, and environment). Literary men began to give prominence to the material detail; observation of reality was taking precedence over the imagination. Before Zola's first naturalistic novel, the Goncourt brothers had already brought together all the essential naturalistic threads of thought and of literary technique in *Germinie Lacerteux* (1865).

The chief problem for the naturalistic author was how to organize the details of observed reality. The infinite variety of possible details was limited by the emotional tone that the writer wanted to give to his novel, and the tone itself depended on the author's attitude toward the society he was describing, a topic to which we shall return in a moment. First, let us consider the problem of organization.

In the preface to *La fortune des Rougon* (1871; The Rise of the Rougons) Zola expressed his faith in science, and particularly in the laws of heredity and environment:

[*] Professor Emeritus, University of Minnesota.

> I shall try to find and follow the thread that leads mathematically
> from one man to another by solving the double question of the effect
> of temperament and of environment.

But, knowing the complexity and diversity of results of heredity, Zola
was in fact not bound at all by the hereditary principles of his so-called
"scientific method." He could introduce into the Rougon-Macquart
series such an unblemished figure as Doctor Pascal, and still claim that
heredity was operative even in the absence of the noxious family influence.
Environmental determinism was a much stronger factor.

In practice Zola generally took only a segment of society, either a
place (a mine, an apartment house, the Paris markets) or an occupation
(the politician, the artist, the laundress, the actress). Of course, these
two aspects of life impinge on each other, and sometimes they are so
intertwined that it is impossible to say which one predominates. But
the effect of the "division of labour" in society is to reduce the number of factors that influence a given person to a somewhat more
manageable size, and to restrict the milieu in which his story must take
place.

Although heredity does have some importance in the organization of
the Rougon-Macquart novels, much of Zola's observation is organized
in terms of poetic metaphor and analogy, which often follow a recognizable
pattern: environments, such as buildings, workshops, or farm land, are
like monstrous living creatures that resemble machines. To illustrate: the
department store (*Au bonheur des dames*, 1883) is a monster[1] through which
goods pass as through an alimentary canal,[2] but it also operates with a
fonctionnement mécanique (mechanically), disgorging the swallowed mer-
chandise after it has passed *à travers les engrenages des comptoirs*[3] (through the
cogs of the counters). This last mixed metaphor, combining the beast and
the machine, also epitomizes Zola's feeling that environment works with
an ineluctable force.[4]

Sometimes only two parts of the metaphor are equated: the mine
raises its chimney like a threatening horn, its pump gives out a sound
like breathing, the buildings crouch like an evil beast digesting human
flesh.[5] The distilling apparatus of the dram shop becomes a living monster.[6]
The Paris market was *comme un grand organe central battant furieusement,
jetant le sang de la vie dans toutes les veines*[7] (like a great internal organ
beating furiously, forcing the life blood into every vein). The Stock
Exchange beats like an enormous heart or rumbles like a steam engine
at work.[8]

Thus, Zola's conceptualization of the various features of environment is not in itself scientific. Pressing his figurative thinking even further, he turns metaphors into symbols. The garden of Le Paradou with its Tree of Life in *La faute de l'abbé Mouret* (1875; The Sin of Abbé Mouret), the hot, humid, and passionate conservatory in *La curée* (1874; The Quarry), and the immense, always unfinished painting in *L'oeuvre* (1886; The Masterpiece) are no longer just things. Zola "observes" them with his imagination, like a poet.[9]

How do people figure against this background? Here we must take up the question of Zola's emotive attitude toward the society he depicted. He saw the world, and collected details from reality, according to his temperament.[10] He hated the Second Empire, the historical period that he took as his subject and that, paradoxically, inspired his poetic imagination so profoundly. His artistic idealism was of a kind thatl would have made him hate any society, and it led him to paint a most urid picture of the epoch he had just lived through, as unscrupulous and depraved. Although Zola's Naturalism is usually associated (as a result of his own remarks on the subject) with science and, later, with socialism, both his art and his attitudes have obvious points of affinity with the aestheticism that is so characteristic of late-19th-century literature.* His vision of reality is fiercely pessimistic; his selection of details from the infinite mass available is dictated by his emotional posture.

Yet his indignation at human corruption is really the other side of his idealism.[11] At heart he was a reformer, a dreamer enamoured of the perfection for which he secretly strove. Although human beings are also "machines," the impressions they receive through their senses[12] can be converted into knowledge, judgment, and emotive drives that, in their turn, can become productive, useful work. This is Doctor Pascal's dream, and the doctor is undoubtedly speaking for Zola.[13] So, ultimately, both the doctor and Zola affirm their confidence in human perfectibility, or more generally their *foi ardente en la vie* (ardent faith in life). Pascal meditates:

> Seen from a great height, humanity looked like a vast piece of machinery, forever at work and engaged in making itself.[14]

There is even hope for the debased Rougon-Macquart family, which after all is also a symbol, *une humanité en raccourci* (an epitome of humanity).[15] As Pascal reviews the family history, he concludes that he was wrong to exult at the idea of not being part of it, and that the monsters in the family, not he, are the exceptions:

* See Ch. 16, "The Cult of Art."

> And to be a member of his family, my God! In the end this seemed
> to him just as good and fine a thing as to be a member of some other
> family—for weren't they all alike, was not humanity the same every-
> where, with the same sum total of good and evil?[16]

The doctor sees the spectacle of human life as Zola the artist does—
from a point of superior detachment. His idealism and optimism are
inspired by the *total* spectacle, by the process of life as a whole, by
humanity *en raccourci* (in epitome). The human figure who stands opposite
to him, and seems to represent symbolically man at his most environ-
mentally enclosed, is the miner,

> crushed by a routine of work that reduced him a little more each day
> to the status of a machine;[17]

or again,

> the miner lived in the mine like a brute beast, like a machine for
> extracting coal. . . .[18]

The underlying pattern of metaphor, with its deeper symbolic implications, is again apparent here. But we should not forget the standpoint
from which Zola observes man so apparently sunk in the earth of his
environment. The individual recedes to a position of relatively less
importance in his novels, and one of Zola's most impressive abilities is
to depict men in groups or crowds.

Benito Pérez Galdós (1843–1920), the greatest Spanish author to be
affected by Naturalism, offers many contrasts with Zola. In the first
place, by the time he took over, in mitigated form, the methodology of
the Frenchman, Galdós had given up the satirical criticism of Spanish
life and religion that characterized some of his earlier novels.[19] Although
his early life in the Canary Islands had given him an outsider's view of
Madrid (an attitude that is reflected in his early works), by the 1880s
he felt at one with the society he depicted. It had faults, to be sure, but
they were foibles rather than vices. They were faults that the author
himself shared, and that he regarded with good humour. Consider, for
example, a typical bourgeois problem, the marrying-off of a family of
girls. Isabel Cordero de Arnáiz has seven daughters, but her husband is
confident that she can find seven "first-class husbands." As they all take
their Sunday walk, dressed in their finest, the neighbouring shopkeepers
say: "There goes Doña Isabel with her samples."[20] The humorous tone
is struck and maintained. Zola, on the other hand, treats a similar

situation as a source of family conflict and bitterness, behind which his disdain for the middle class is clearly visible.[21]

Contrary to Zola, Galdós does not divide society into discrete segments. His novels are usually organized around a limited number of principal characters, often coming from very different classes and milieux. In his masterpiece, *Fortunata y Jacinta* (1886–7), the lowest class of Madrid is represented by Fortunata, and the idle well-to-do bourgeoisie by Juanito Santa Cruz. This novel contains a dissertation on the breakdown of class stratification, with the result that rich and poor, high and low, are often related to one another.[22] If there is a limitation in the size of Galdós's canvas, it is the near-elimination of the aristocracy. He concerned himself primarily with the bourgeoisie,[23] to a lesser degree with the proletariat, and only incidentally with the nobles.

The common people, Galdós observes, are the quarry of Spanish virtues. Of course they need polishing, and in his later years he thought that intermarriage between upper and lower classes would bring about the ideal combination of rough virtues and refinement. During his naturalistic period, he likened Fortunata to a well-endowed animal that needed only domestication to be perfect.[24] He seemed to hope that all Spaniards would ultimately be absorbed into the bourgeoisie. His attitude toward the middle class is in sharp contrast to Zola's: Galdós feels that it could become, in time, a synthesis of the best qualities of the upper and lower classes.[25]

One reason why Galdós focussed on the middle class was its relative novelty. The Industrial Revolution, from which the bourgeoisie sprang, was delayed in Spain by the Napoleonic invasion (1808–14) and the first Carlist War (1833–40). The chaos of war checked industrial growth. Galdós describes the cloth trade of Madrid in the early 1880s as divided into many small family shops, whereas Zola's picture of the same trade centres on the vast department store that drives the small shops to the wall. In short, industry and commerce were not nearly as advanced in Spain as in France. Galdós sees the bourgeoisie as an evolving new class, whereas for Zola it was already well established.

Galdós does not adopt Zola's savage attitude toward the society in which he lived; he recognizes that, if people are determined by natural laws, they must follow their natures and we must accept them as they are.[26] We can at most suggest to them that they should better understand nature and themselves. Above all, they should not lose contact with reality and let themselves drift into an illusory dream world. Galdós treats this tendency, at first, as the principal fault of the Spanish personality, but, later on, as the source of its greatest virtues. Much as in the case of Don Quixote, the attempt to force the real world into the pattern of one's ideals begins by appearing a foolish disaster but, in later works, appears as evidence of a noble spirit.

Galdós's first naturalistic novel, *La desheredada* (1881; The Disinherited Woman), is an account of the decline and fall of an unbalanced young woman, Isidora Rufete, who is striving to prove herself a relation of a noble family.[27] Her illusion, fostered by her insane father, leads her to reject proposals of marriage by respectable middle-class suitors but to accept a liaison with a worthless aristocrat. Galdós does not hesitate to state the moral: "If you yearn to reach a difficult, craggy peak, don't trust artificial wings"—the kind of moral comment that Zola would avoid in the name of objectivity. Galdós still feels that the spiritual quality of a person's life depends on a moral choice, and that he must warn his compatriots against the dangers of drifting into a world of illusions.

The same message, less obviously stated, reappears in all Galdós's naturalistic novels. In the 1890s, when Naturalism as such was dead (although its descriptive techniques and slum backgrounds still persisted), Galdós's attitude toward illusion changed. In *Nazarín* (1895), a priest who sets out to live as much like Jesus as possible is striving to impose an ideal on the real world. In this he manifests similarities to Don Quixote, and—as we might expect—he is judged insane. In *Misericordia* (1897; Compassion), an old serving maid is the incarnation of charity, and her spiritual force transforms much of the reality with which she comes into contact. Galdós now shows the dream triumphant, not of course over all society but in a limited sphere. In an earlier novel, one of his characters says: "Nature is the great mother and teacher who rectifies the errors of her deluded children,"[28] but now he shows the deluded children triumphing over nature's laws, and the spiritual forces of good overcoming natural egotism.

It seems that the fundamental contrast between Zola's and Galdós's attitude toward society lies in their concept of environment. Zola regarded the milieu as essentially bad, and the people formed by it as usually corrupt. For Galdós, environment is more complex. Although it is a powerful formative influence, its results are not always bad; and, even if bad, at times they result only in mediocrity or peccadilloes. The human spirit must be reckoned with: it can triumph even over baser drives.

Now let us see how Naturalism came to Spain and what was the condition of the Spanish novel at the time of its arrival.

When in 1877 the *succès de scandale* of *L'assommoir* catapulted Émile Zola from an insignificant position, little better than that of a literary hack, to a prominence such as Sir Walter Scott and Charles Dickens had enjoyed earlier, Zola's name began to appear in Spanish periodicals. By 1879,

> some realistic breezes were blowing, similar to the puffs of warm air that, on February or March afternoons, announce the germinating season. People were still not talking about Naturalism, although some novels of Zola were already circulating as a scandalous curiosity, as a lewd picture circulates. . . .[29]

The following year (1880) saw the publication of three Zola novels— *Une page d'amour*, *L'assommoir*, and *Nana*—in Spanish translations. The first original Spanish novel to show the influence of Zola appeared in the same year. Naturalism had definitely gained a foothold in Spain; it was to enjoy an increasing vogue for six or seven years, followed by a waning prestige, but it is not without influence even in the 20th century.

The naturalistic innovators were furiously opposed. An integral and important aspect of the quarrel was the opposing notions held by the older and younger generations as to the nature and purpose of the novel. The youthful Naturalists proclaimed that the novel was a serious study:

> . . . the novel has ceased to be a mere pastime, a means of whiling away pleasantly a few hours, and is rising to the level of a social, psychological, or historical study, but, above all, a study.[30]

Most important, it was to give a true picture of life; consequently, the writer must be an observer, a recorder of things seen, not one who imagines what things are like. The "idealistic novel" of the preceding generation was anathema to them. To see the new novel in perspective required viewing it against the background of the past.

The novel, in Spain as elsewhere, was the key genre of popular consumption. It was an opiate, an escape from dull reality for the seamstress and the clerk. To convert it into a serious study without losing its reading public was an almost unrealizable dream. After all, the novelist had to sell enough books to make a living, and the publisher did not want his warehouse crammed with unsold stock. The taste—or lack of taste—of the public had to be considered, even if an author felt that a serious study would benefit the reader more than escapist literature.

As we look back over the history of the Spanish novel in the 19th century, certain facts stand out clearly. First, the reading public expanded considerably, due to the much higher level of literacy: about 94 per cent

U

of Spaniards were illiterate at the beginning of the century, as opposed to 66 per cent at the end. Furthermore the population grew from some 10·5 million to 18·5 million, so that the potential reading public was greatly increased. Women, in particular, became addicted to the reading of escapist novels. A much higher percentage of the population lived in cities, where their working day, although long and usually boring, did not always leave them as exhausted as farm workers. At evening gatherings of urban dwellers, or even during the working day in a dressmaking establishment, it was not unusual for some better-educated member of the group to read aloud the current instalment of a serial novel.* Even some of the illiterate were thus part of the "reading" public.

With the build-up of the demand for escapist literature, the publication of novels became good business. Publishers could become rich, and to this end they controlled the nature and quality of the novels they published according to their judgment of what would sell. The advent of Naturalism was, in part, a rebellion of authors against norms imposed by the publishers, and against pandering to an uneducated public.

Early in the century, the control exercised by publishers went hand in hand with the low esteem in which authors themselves held the novel. For the author, during the first half of the century, the novel was simply a means of gaining a sum, never large enough to live on for more than a few months, by dashing off a manuscript in the briefest possible time. In 1834 Manuel Delgado, one of the publishers who made a fortune by exploiting writers, signed a contract with José Espronceda on 5 February, by which the author agreed to deliver four volumes of his *Sancho Saldaña* by 31 March. The following year Mariano José de Larra contracted to produce four volumes in two months. It is clear that these writers, who certainly thought highly of their own essays and poetry, attached little worth to their novels. Payment for this hack work varied from 1000 to 1500 *reales vellón* (about £20 to £30) per volume.

Quite obviously, writers could not live on the income from their novels. Translation was more profitable, simply because it was quicker. Spain was inundated with translations from French. Walter Scott's work, for example, came to Madrid by way of Paris. Very few of these Spanish versions were made by men of literary distinction. Reputable authors usually found employment in government offices or in journalism.

The periodical press grew with the increase in literacy and the urbanization of the populace. Although the first periodical in Spain goes

---

* These developments in Spain may be compared with the more extensive discussion of this topic in Vol. IV, "The Sociology of the Novel."

back to 1661, there was no great or consistent growth of journalism until the 19th century. Particularly noteworthy was the increase in Madrid from 6 periodicals in 1830 to 302 in 1870. The space given to literature in these publications was considerable.

About 1840, newspapers began to offer novels to their readers in daily instalments—the *feuilletons*, which were usually translations from the French. The cheap newspaper reached a public that could not afford to buy novels. Soon the idea of issuing novels in instalments—*novelas por entregas*—to be delivered once a week to subscribers, grew out of the popularity of the *feuilletons*. Each instalment consisted of 48 pages, for which the author usually received 40 *duros*, which averaged out at 5–6 *duros* a day. By dictating to a stenographer the author could increase his earnings to 15–18 *duros* a day, besides leaving himself some free time to devote to journalism. By producing four or five long novels a year— novels filled with unexpected incidents, innocent heroines, menacing villains, and noble heroes—these authors could support themselves. They were the first in Spain to live solely on their literary production.

The symbiosis of publisher, author, and public was, then, responsible for the sub-literary novel, a genre that thrived throughout the last two thirds of the 19th century and was a constant competitor of the "serious" novel. Writers such as Fernández y González are said to have kept four or five serial adventure stories going simultaneously. Others, such as Ayguals de Izco, took Eugène Sue as their model and indulged in lachrymose humanitarianism. An early article by Galdós speaks ironically of such authors:

> Let them paint passions for us with brilliant strokes, with graphic details that make us start from our seat. We want to see described with sure hand the most atrocious peripeteias that any imagination can conceive; let us be told, especially, about the most abominable crimes; . . . we want to see the suicide, the adulterous woman, the prostitute; . . . if there is a hospital, better; if there is a regenerating tuberculosis, wonderful! . . . if there is a gallows, superb! . . . Thus the superficial readers would exclaim, readers who receive under their doors a monthly or weekly ration of literature cooked up in the brains of certain novelists.[31]

Galdós was a champion of the serious novel: at first, he supported the realistic work of his friend J. M. de Pereda;[32] then, when the younger writers adopted Naturalism, he was the only established author to follow the new trend. Other writers of the older generation reacted in horror against the "immorality" of naturalistic themes and descriptions. Alarcón exclaimed indignantly:

> Let these French realists and Naturalists write another half dozen
> novels and they will have buried in their own filth that sad school
> which I shan't call exactly the *black hand* but I shall call the *dirty hand*
> of literature![33]

Pereda reacted irately against a critic who included him in the
naturalistic school:

> . . . if with such a classification one wishes to enrol me [as has
> already been done, and even as praise] under the banners, now
> triumphant across the Pyrenees, of a fetid Naturalism that paints
> in crude detail the ravages of alcohol, the filth of laundries, and
> the obscenities of brothels, I protest against the implied insult. There
> exist, nonetheless, people who have seen *poetry* and *beauty* in the
> depths of these literary latrines. What won't certain lynxes of
> criticism be capable of seeing?[34]

The tone of these two quotations is perhaps a little more violent than
that adopted by many less-known literary men of the time, but the
reaction is essentially the same. Especially after Emilia Pardo Bazán
brought out her *Cuestión palpitante* (The Burning Question)—first as a series
of newspaper articles in *La Epoca*, from November 1882 to April 1883,
then in book form in 1883—polemics raged between her opponents and
her champions. The division between the two camps corresponded exactly
with the line between the traditionalists and the liberals, a division in the
Spanish body politic that runs through the whole 19th century and
continues today. The partisans of tradition, essentially backward-looking
people who sighed for the institutions in force under Philip II, were of
course opposed to new currents in science and philosophy. They were able
to marshal the great power of the Church, and (when they were in
control) the agencies of the government, such as the office of censorship,
against free-thinking writers or professors. On two occasions the traditionalists obtained the dismissal of liberal professors from their university
chairs.

Despite these attacks on academic freedom, the Universidad Central
at Madrid was for a few years (about 1866–75) the focal point of new
ideas. But most frequently the university and up-to-date intellectual
activity had nothing in common. The philosophy taught in the class-
room was that of St Thomas Aquinas; the natural sciences were admitted
into the curriculum only with great reluctance and in a heavily censored
form. But in the brief period just mentioned, when Julián Sanz del Río
was Professor of Philosophy and, for a couple of years, Rector of the
university, the investigation of all subjects was encouraged. Coincidentally,

the abolition of censorship of imported books after the revolution of 1868 allowed Spaniards to become acquainted with the science of Darwin and the philosophy of Comte and Spencer. After the second "separation" of the liberal professors from their university chairs at the time of the Bourbon restoration (1875), the progressives found outlets elsewhere: in the Ateneo (where the most diverse ideas could find a forum) and in the Institución Libre de Enseñanza (a school for boys in which the liberals hoped to train a new, progressively oriented generation). The founder of the Institución, Francisco Giner de los Ríos, one of the "separated" professors, was Spain's most tolerant (in the best sense of the word) and enlightened educator of the 19th century. It was in the spirit, and in many cases under the direct influence, of such men as Sanz del Río and Giner de los Ríos that the young liberals who were later to be the vanguard of the naturalistic novelists grew up.

Sanz del Río had studied at Heidelberg and returned to Spain much influenced by the philosophical system of Karl Christian Friedrich Krause, a system that found little support outside Belgium and Spain. For our purposes we need only note that Krausism saw some good and some truth in all philosophies and religions; it advocated the use of reason for the critical examination of all dogmas or theories; it fostered, as a consequence, tolerance of all points of view, and particularly the abandonment of those immutable doctrines dear to the hearts of the traditionalists.

The very tolerance of Krausism caused its rapid downfall. Spaniards began to examine other systems. The positivism of Auguste Comte gained partisans about 1875. Five years later—that is, just when Naturalism was taking hold in Spain—the younger generation had become fascinated by Herbert Spencer.

> The evolutionary system of Herbert Spencer is very well received, especially by those dedicated to the study of natural sciences. While the scholastic doctrine is dominant in the sphere of official learning, evolutionism is penetrating and taking root in many young minds. Scholasticism is what appears on the surface; but the idea of evolution gives breath and life to the underlying essence, and either we are very mistaken, or the future belongs to it.[35]

This scientific philosophy was welcomed by youthful Spaniards in the same years that they became aware of Zola's scientific novels. They saw an identity of aims and methods in the two, and they dreamed of writing fictional works that would reveal the truth with all the precision of a scientific demonstration. As Emilia Pardo Bazán wrote:

> What is at the bottom of the question is an admirable idea about
> which I have always dreamed: the unity of method in science and
> art. That's no small thing! The arbitrary division has disappeared,
> and observation and experimentation are applied just as they are to
> anatomical studies.[36]

In the same way that science had discovered the laws of planetary motion, so the novelists would reveal the laws of human nature. And as science had triumphed again and again before 1880, so the authors of the serious novel would go from triumph to triumph in the future.

A literary trend had also helped to lay the groundwork for the new movement, namely, *costumbrismo* (the observation of local customs and manners). It found expression in the literary form of the essay (remotely foreshadowed by Addison and Steele; more directly by Jouy in his collection of political essays, *L'ermite de la chaussée d'Antin*). During the Romantic period the *cuadro de costumbres* (pictures of local colour) flourished, seeking to grasp essentially national qualities as shown in *types* (often chosen from among the lower classes, such as the innkeeper, the water seller, the barber) and in *scenes* (such as a local fair, a religious procession, a wedding banquet). The diversified nature of the realism (in the general sense) of Spanish life implied picturesqueness, and set the romantic *cuadro de costumbres* apart from Realism (in the special sense). But as the urban middle class developed, and recruited immigrants from the strongly differentiated provinces, it abandoned the picturesque regional costumes and local dialects. *Costumbrismo*, still with an eye to the picturesque, fled the city. On the northern coast of Spain it found a worthy companion in José María de Pereda, although the *costumbrismo* he practised differed sharply from that of the Romantics.

Pereda's most important collections of *cuadros de costumbres* (*Escenas montañesas* [1864; Scenes from La Montaña] and *Tipos y paisajes* [1871; Types and Scenes]) antedate both Spanish Naturalism and the vogue of Zola in France, yet Pereda was labelled "naturalistic" as soon as Spanish critics became aware of Zola's theories. Pereda is in fact the first Spanish writer to be associated with the movement, much to his disgust. We must ask what could be found in his *costumbrismo* to give rise to the critics' classification. The first new element is close and accurate observation, which necessarily individualizes the characters described. Pereda's observation becomes almost one with Zola's documentation: dialect peculiarities of local pronunciation are imitated and details of regional agricultural methods or of the fishermen's way of life are portrayed; and Pereda never hesitated to insist on the sordidness of much of the life in his province. Even his ardent defender against the accusation of Naturalism has to admit that his subject-matter is often identical with that of the Naturalists.

> That Pereda uses naturalistic procedures is undeniable; that he always seeks out the individual and concrete trait is also correct; that, enamoured of details, he always pursues them and treats them as the principal part of his art is visible to anyone who opens his books; that he is better in description and dialogue than in invention and composition is the necessary consequence of his artistic temperament; that he does not flee the depiction of anything true and human, and, finally, that he has invigorated his language with the language of the common people is also true and should be said in his honour.[37]

Thus spoke Menéndez Pelayo, the implacable enemy of Naturalism's determinism and obscenity. But in another passage he admits:

> Pereda does not flee from crude details nor the graphic and picturesque word, nor is he afraid of sordid poverty, nor does he fear entering the tavern and touching rags and sores. . . .[38]

Pereda was, then, the culmination of new trends in *costumbrismo*—purely Spanish trends that had been little by little modifying the "picturesque realism" of the Romantic writers, giving it a direct and accurate observation of a reality now regarded as sordid rather than picturesque. To pass from his formula to that of Zola it is necessary to add determinism and a slightly broader range of permissible subject-matter, including particularly scenes of sexual immorality. Pereda's writing was a factor favourable to the introduction of Naturalism, no matter how much it displeased him to be numbered among its adherents.

We have said that when Naturalism entered Spain in 1880 it was welcomed by the younger generation. Ortega Munilla, novelist and critic for *El Imparcial*, was 24 years old; the Catalan naturalistic novelist Narcís Oller was 34; Emilia Pardo Bazán, Leopoldo Alas, and José Yxart were all 28; Armando Palacio Valdés was 27. Against them were ranged all the other literary figures of Spain, with the single exception of Benito Pérez Galdós. Although Galdós could not be considered an old man (he was 37 in 1880), he was the well-established, widely read author of 26 novels. His *La desheredada* was hailed by the younger writers as the first good naturalistic novel. A series of eulogies of the author appeared in the periodical press; and when the young Naturalists founded a magazine as an organ of their ideas, Galdós's name headed the list of contributors, although in fact he never published anything in it. This magazine, *Arte y Letras*, lasted only from July 1882 to November 1883;

perhaps the brevity of its existence indicated the very slight impression that Naturalism was making on a reading public still devouring with avidity the adventure stories of Fernández y González and Pérez Escrich.

The same young group used to get together for their *apéritif* in the Cervecería Escocesa. Their habit of condemning the older literary generation caused them to be dubbed the *Bilis-Club* (Gall Club). When they were celebrating the première of Eugenio Sellés' play *Las esculturas de carne* (Statues of Flesh) in February 1882—a play by which they hoped that Naturalism would win over the theatre—someone proposed the idea of a banquet as a homage to Galdós. Contemporary documents show clearly that the intention was to celebrate not just Galdós's personal triumphs but also the triumph of Naturalism; yet when the banquet finally did take place (over a year later, on 26 March 1883) the tributes were not to the school but to the man. The 230 guests represented all shades of literary and political opinion. If the Naturalists hoped that the honoured guest would defend their school in his speech of thanks, they were disappointed. Galdós, in fact, did not speak: overcome with emotion, he handed out a printed copy of the remarks he was too timid to pronounce.

Although, in one sense, Galdós was a leader lost to the Naturalists, in another sense he was above the conflict. The Krausist philosophy of the university circle had been fundamental in his intellectual formation; it taught that a rational harmony could and should be established between conflicting parts. Thus the novel, split into the idealistic and naturalistic schools, could be re-established as a harmonious whole if both segments realized that they were interrelated. The material fact, says Galdós, is an exemplification of a higher law. Thus, idealism and materialism interplay: one does not exist without the other. This attitude was already present in Galdós's *El amigo Manso* (1882; Friend Manso),[39] and was to be reinforced by his reading of *War and Peace* in the French translation of 1884.

The discovery of Russian literature was for Spaniards the discovery of a spiritual Naturalism. They found in Tolstoy the precise amalgam of idealism and Naturalism that most of them had been seeking. Galdós, probably among the first of his countrymen to read *War and Peace*, was to give the title *Naturalismo espiritual* to one section of his next work, *Fortunata y Jacinta* (1886–7). While Galdós's novel was still in the process of composition, Emilia Pardo Bazán gave a series of lectures in the Ateneo, soon published in book form, called *La revolución y la novela en Rusia*. She declared: "*el elemento espiritualista de la novela rusa para mí es uno de sus méritos más singulares*" (the spiritual element of the Russian novel is for me one of its outstanding merits). Citing Vogüé, the French popularizer of Russian literature, on whom she leaned more heavily than she admitted, she continued:

> The French realists do not know the best part of humanity, which is the spirit. . . . For some time I have been thinking and writing that realism, to carry out fully its programme, must include matter and spirit, earth and heaven, admitting both the human and super-human elements.[40]

The impact of Russian literature in Spain was the beginning of the end of Naturalism. Although it lingered on for a few years, and left a heritage that is still visible, it was already on the decline. Zola himself hastened its end by the publication of *La terre* (1877; The Earth), which turned many former devotees away from the cult. Ortega Munilla wrote in sad disillusionment:

> It is necessary to make clear that Naturalism has found few adepts in Spain. . . . A few of us have been those who, against all obstacles and fighting against public opinion, have defended the theories of that master, and the rest have gone to seek in *Nana* and *L'assommoir* strong sensations, the vision of sensual love. . . . Today is a day of discouragement for that small number of Naturalists. *La terre*, a novel that has not yet appeared in book form, of which only the translation in *La Iberia* is known in Spain, is causing general indignation. It is said that it is an ensemble of filth, a manure heap on which a few human figures give themselves over to the most repulsive excesses.[41]

It is true that Munilla goes on to say that all Naturalism should not be condemned because of the bad taste of one of its proponents. He contrasts Spanish Naturalism with the French, and finds that his compatriots have produced a dozen books equal to, or even better than, the best of the French. But in spite of this whistling in the dark, he sees the eclipse of Zola's school. Several other critics joined him in saying that Naturalism had not taken root in Spain. By 1890, when Zola brought out *La bête humaine* (The Human Animal), Munilla and others expressed dissatisfaction with the work and disaffection with the author. One year later Emilia Pardo Bazán could say:

> . . . French Naturalism can be considered today a closed cycle. . . . [Naturalism had] its paladins in France: the new cycle, which we can call idealistic realism, found them in Russia.[42]

A new wave of piety was inundating much of Europe. Brunetière had declared the bankruptcy of science in 1887; the vacuum left by the disappearance of this blind faith was filled by religion. At the same time in France, Paul Bourget, the chief enemy of Zola, popularized the psychological novel: *Le disciple* (1889) is clearly an attack on deterministic philosophy. Although never widely read in Spain, Bourget's work was translated and received much favourable mention from the more enlightened critics. Caesar Lombroso and Max Nordau, who had a brief vogue, also focussed attention on the psychological study of mankind, particularly the nature of the genius. Finally Ibsen's plays, with their emphasis on psychological analysis, began to be influential in Spain in 1892. The Norwegian's popularity was immense; his influence is visible in the plays of Galdós and the youthful Jacinto Benavente.

All these trends culminated in novels that retain the detailed descriptions of slum *milieux*, but that reveal character not through direct statements by the author, but rather through dialogue and deeds, according to the system advocated by Bourget. The acts of the characters are not entirely determined by environment and heredity: at least some of them spring from the spirit. Thus, Benina, the servant who is the protagonist of Galdós's *Misericordia*, has charity for all, but this is certainly not a virtue that she owes either to her slum environment or to her ancestors. *Nazarín* portrays Galdós's ideal priest, who is judged insane simply because he aspires to imitate Christ in every way. Again, there is nothing in his background to account "scientifically" for his acts.

Although 1887 saw the beginning of the end of Naturalism in Spain, some writers still attempted to infuse it with new vitality. López Bago and Alejandro Sawa, for instance, combined Zolaism with the sentimental humanitarianism of Eugène Sue and Hugo's *Les misérables*. Their novels contain violent attacks on the aristocracy and the clergy, the corrupt oppressors of the virtuous common people. López Bago went to America about 1890, and Sawa left Madrid for Paris shortly before; their careers as novelists were brief and uninfluential.

Other, better-known novelists seem to have combined naturalistic techniques with Bourget's objective method of depicting psychology. These writers all have a common theme, the satirizing of aristocratic society, a topic common to most of Bourget's fiction. Pereda in *La Montálvez* (1888; The Montálvez Woman), the Jesuit Luis Coloma in his widely discussed *Pequeñeces* (1890–1; Pettiness), and Palacio Valdés in *La espuma* (1891; Foam) all retain Zola's doctrine of the objectivity of the writer and of determinism as the motivating force of the characters, but they bring in new ideas from the technique of Bourget.

Finally, Blasco Ibáñez, who began his literary life as a secretary to Fernández y González, and even produced novels, little known today, in the style of the *novela por entregas* (instalment novel), became the last of the Spaniards who can be called naturalistic. From 1895, in *Flor de mayo* (Mayflower), to 1902, in *Cañas y barro* (Reeds and Mud), Ibáñez chose his subjects from his native Valencian region and treated them with a mixture of *costumbrismo* and Naturalism. His descriptions of the ways of peasants and fishermen alternate with a pessimistic vision of the crushing effect of ambience. His is a Naturalism not of the mind but of the emotions.

So Naturalism as a clearly defined movement comes to an end in Spain. Its heritage in our century is revealed primarily in the greater freedom of modern authors to choose subjects and employ vocabulary formerly prohibited either by social pressures or by governmental censorship. Its attempts to create a serious novel were at least partially successful. The writers who were to form the "Generation of '98"—Unamuno, Baroja, Azorín, and others—were to profit from the efforts of the very generation they disowned and repudiated.

References

NOTE: The page numbers cited in Zola's works refer to the standard French edition, *Les oeuvres complètes*, ed. by Eugène Fasquelle, 50 vols (Paris 1927–9).

1. ZOLA, *Au bonheur des dames* (1883), pp. 17, 23, and 55.
2. *ibid.*, p. 41.
3. *ibid.*, p. 46. The store is called a "machine" on pp. 55, 64, 74, and 96.
4. *L'importance du milieu dans un roman de Zola ne saurait être trop soulignée.... C'est le milieu qui détermine le personnage....* (The importance of environment in a novel by Zola could scarcely be exaggerated. . . . It is environment that determines each character. . . .)—J. H. MATTHEWS, *Les deux Zola* (Geneva 1957), p. 43.
5. ZOLA, *Germinal* (1885), Ch. I.
6. ZOLA, *L'assommoir* (1877), Ch. II.
7. ZOLA, *Le ventre de Paris* (1873), Vol. I, p. 47.
8. ZOLA, *L'argent* (1891), Ch. I.
9. See MATTHEWS, *op. cit.*, pp. 82 ff.
10. We recall his well-known definition of art as *un coin de la nature vu à travers un tempérament* (a corner of nature seen through the medium of a temperament).
11. *La haine est sainte. Elle est l'indignation des coeurs forts et puissants, le dédain militant de ceux qui fâchent la médiocrité et la sottise. Haïr c'est*

aimer, c'est sentir son âme chaude et généreuse. . . . (Hatred is holy. It is the indignation felt by tough and powerful souls, a militant scorn from the hearts of those who are angered by mediocrity and stupidity. To hate is to love, to feel warmth and generosity of spirit.)—ZOLA, *Mes haines* (1866; My Hates), p. 1.

12. Zola believed that everything we know comes through the senses, an idea he owes ultimately to Condorcet.

13. ZOLA, *Le docteur Pascal* (1893), pp. 313 and 336.

14. *ibid.*, p. 377.

15. *ibid.*, p. 388.

16. *ibid.*, p. 319.

17. ZOLA, *Germinal*, p. 147.

18. *ibid.*, pp. 177–8.

19. For example, *Doña Perfecta* (1876), *Gloria* (1877), and *La familia de León Roch* (1878).

20. *Fortunata y Jacinta*, Vol. I, Pt I, Ch. II, Section 6.

21. ZOLA, *Pot-bouille* (1882), pp. 25 and 42.

22. *Fortunata y Jacinta*, Vol. I, Pt I, Ch. VI, Sections 1 and 2.

23. See his early article, "Observaciones sobre la novela contemporánea en España," *Revista de España* XV (Madrid 1870), pp. 162–8; and another recognition of the importance of the middle class in *Los apostólicos*, in *Obras completas* (Madrid 1950), Vol. II, p. 111.

24. *Fortunata y Jacinta*, Vol. I, Pt II, Ch. IV, Section 8.

25. It is true that when the middle class gave itself over to sterile, uncreative, bureaucratic politics it incurred Galdós's scorn. See v. LLORÉNS, "Galdós y la burguesía," *Anales Galdosianos* (Pittsburgh, Pa. 1968), Vol. III, pp. 51–9.

26. *El amigo Manso*, Ch. XXXIX.

27. Notice that Zola's Nana, who has few points of resemblance to Galdós's heroine, has no drives that partake of idealism, whereas Isidora's incentive is a perverted ideal.

28. *Fortunata y Jacinta*, Vol. I, Pt IV, Ch. II, Section 16.

29. EMILIA PARDO BAZÁN, *Apuntes biográficos*, published as the prologue in the first edition of *Los pazos de Ulloa* (1886; The Manor House of Ulloa).

30. EMILIA PARDO BAZÁN, prologue of *Un viaje de novios* (1881; A Honeymoon Trip).

31. BENITO PÉREZ GALDÓS, review of *Cantares* by M. Palau; originally published in 1866, republished in GALDÓS, *Crónica de Madrid* (1933; Madrid Chronicle), pp. 184–5.

32. BENITO PÉREZ GALDÓS, preface to J. M. DE PEREDA, *El sabor de la tierruca* (1882; The Flavour of the Homeland).

33. P. A. DE ALARCÓN, *Juicios literarios y artísticos* (Madrid 1883), p. 78.

34. J. M. DE PEREDA, prologue of *De tal palo* (1880; Chip Off the Old Block).

35. E. SANZ Y ESCARTÍN, *Revista de España* LXXXIII (Madrid 1881), p. 394.

36. Cited by C. BRAVO VILLASANTE, *Vida y obra de Emilia Pardo Bazán* (Madrid 1962), p. 91.
37. M. MENÉNDEZ PELAYO, prologue of *Los hombres de pro* (Men of Worth), in J. M. DE PEREDA, *Obras completas* (Madrid 1884), Vol. I.
38. *La Ilustración Española y Americana* XXIV (Madrid, 8 April 1880), p. 226.
39. See *Anales Galdosianos* (Pittsburgh, Pa. 1967), Vol. II, p. 148.
40. EMILIA PARDO BAZÁN, *Obras completas* (Madrid 1891–1926), Vol. XXXIII, p. 439.
41. J. ORTEGA MUNILLA, *El Imparcial* (Madrid, 27 September 1887).
42. In *La España Moderna* (Madrid, March 1891), pp. 68–9.

Bibliography

H. CHONON BERKOWITZ, *Pérez Galdós, Spanish Liberal Crusader* (Madison 1948).

CARMEN BRAVO VILLASANTE, *Vida y obra de Emilia Pardo Bazán* (Madrid 1962).

H. GUILLEMIN, *Zola: légende et vérité* (Paris 1960).

EUGENIO HARTZENBUSCH, *Apuntes para un catálogo de periódicos madrileños desde el año 1661 al 1870* (Madrid 1894).

F. W. J. HEMMINGS, *Émile Zola*, 2nd edn (Oxford 1966).

JUAN LOPEZ-MORILLAS, *El krausismo español* (Mexico 1956).

J. H. MATTHEWS, *Les deux Zola* (Geneva 1957).

LUIS MONGUIO, "Crematística de los novelistas españoles," *Estudios sobre literatura hispanoamericana y española* (Mexico 1958), pp. 143–67; originally published in *Revista Hispánica Moderna* XVII (New York 1951).

JOSÉ F. MONTESINOS, *Introducción a una historia de la novela en España en el siglo XIX* (Valencia 1955); *Costumbrismo y novela* (Berkeley 1960).

WALTER T. PATTISON, *El naturalismo español: historia externa de un movimiento literario* (Madrid 1966); *Emilia Pardo Bazán* (New York 1971).

GUY ROBERT, *Émile Zola: principes et caractères généraux de son oeuvre* (Paris 1952).

M. UCELAY DA CAL, *Los españoles pintados por sí mismos* (Mexico 1951).

CHAPTER 10

Realism in Scandinavian Fiction

Niels L. Jensen[*]

In the famous introductory chapter to the first volume of his *Main Currents in European Literature During the First Half of the Nineteenth Century* (1872–90), Georg Brandes calls for a new realist literature in Scandinavia that will debate the problems of life and society. Of the Danish literature of the previous decades Brandes uses the sweeping generalization: "It is not about our life, but about our dreams."

If Brandes' frequently quoted remark were to be believed, one would be hard put to it to find much in Scandinavian fiction that threw light on the social and cultural life of the 19th century. However, Brandes' words were written as part of a polemical manifesto that called for a radicalization of Danish intellectual life; they cannot be regarded as a fair account of the facts.

Danish literature of the first two decades of the 19th century was dominated by poetry and plays and romances with themes from the Nordic heroic age or the Middle Ages. From about 1824 onward, however, there is a clearly detectable interest in prose fiction and in descriptions of contemporary life and people. The reasons for this change in taste are, of course, complex. Apart from the perennial desire for novelty, which influences both the artist's choice of subject-matter and the interest of the reading public, there was also the emergence of a new middle-class reading public with preferences that differed from those of the highly limited circle of academics who read and bought the works of the early Romantics. The taste for prose fiction was whetted by the great popularity of Walter Scott's novels, which in Denmark (as elsewhere) helped to launch both national historical novels and fiction about contemporary life on their way. Some of the writers of the early school of Romanticism, for example Carsten Hauch (whose poetry expressed lofty scorn of the favours of the reading public), tried unsuccessfully to catch up with the

[*] Lecturer in Scandinavian Literature, University of Aarhus.

new trend; but new and greater talents emerged to cater to the change in taste. The most gifted of these was undoubtedly Steen Steensen Blicher (1782–1848). Unlike his contemporaries, who were mainly influenced by German romantic writers, this Jutland parson was well versed in 18th-century English fiction (he translated the *Vicar of Wakefield*); and, like his contemporary Pushkin, he was also indebted to writers of the German light-weight novella literature, such as Heinrich Zschokke. Blicher introduces a new psychological realism into his stories, with strong Jutland local colour, and he displays an unfailing ear for natural speech, particularly in his peasant characters. But his plot schemes are romantic, concentrating on abductions, *mésalliance*, highwaymen, and exotic, mysterious characters in a homely environment. In addition his stories, like Pushkin's, tend to be set in the past, the late 18th century or earlier. So, although Blicher's novellas, with their psychological realism and tragic vision of life, remain perhaps the greatest achievement of 19th-century Scandinavian fiction, one would hardly go to Blicher to find the bourgeois world of the early 19th century depicted. For this, we may turn to the work of Thomasine Gyllembourg (1773–1856). Mrs Gyllembourg began to write after her son, J. L. Heiberg (1791–1860), had achieved some success in the 1820s with his domestic comedies. Her *Hverdagshistorier* (Stories of Everyday Life), published between 1827 and 1845, explored the domestic life of the Danish middle class, and were praised by Kierkegaard. The setting of these stories is usually the Copenhagen home of a civil servant or merchant (though the occupation of the head of the household is, as a rule, only vaguely defined); alternatives are the rural vicarage and the manor house that feature so prominently in Scandinavian fiction throughout the 19th century.

The dominant theme in Mrs Gyllembourg's stories is marriage, as suggested by such titles as *Aegtestand* (1835; The Married State) and *Mésalliance* (1833). She writes with compassion about the young girl of good family, but without means, who in anguish awaits an honest suitor; or suggests the unutterable disgrace of the girl let down by a faithless fiancé. But beside such familiar themes she tackles subjects that belong to the darker side of bourgeois life. In one story she writes about a situation rarely mentioned but quite common in an age of class prejudice and double morality: the man of means and position who keeps a mistress and their illegitimate children in a secret ménage. In a story about the married state, Mrs Gyllembourg—a divorcée herself—lets a woman character convincingly defend the right of a woman to break the bond of a loveless and intolerable marriage.

In Mrs Gyllembourg's world, class distinctions are unquestioned, although snobbery of rank is frowned upon. There is unswerving loyalty to the absolute monarchy, and the patronage of aristocrats is accepted as a blessing. Mrs Gyllembourg pays much critical attention to domestic life: tidiness and cleanliness are cardinal virtues, and her young heroines are always paragons in this respect; their snowy white linen and homely industry go with their angelic spiritual qualities and appearance. Conversely, the slatterns and idlers, however beautiful, come to no good.

Mrs Gyllembourg's picture of bourgeois life and its values has much in common with that of her contemporary, the Swedish writer Frederika Bremer, in *Teckningar ur vardagslivet* (1828; Sketches from Everyday Life) and *Grannarne* (1837; Neighbours). Life in these books is idyllic and complacent: financial worries sometimes arise, but there is no grumbling about the state of society. Poverty and want among the lower orders are simply matters for charity and philanthropy, which are praised as supreme virtues. Social attitudes of this kind are characteristic of much Scandinavian fiction of this period. Even in the novels of H. C. Andersen—the only Scandinavian writer of his day to come from the poorest stratum of the working class—there is no criticism of the social or political system, although the traumas of poverty occur sporadically in his work. Meïr Aron Goldschmidt (1819–87) did not fully belong within the Biedermeier world* of the bourgeoisie, either, but apart from the novel *En jøde* (1845; A Jew), where he gives expression to his indignation over the prejudice faced by the Jew attempting to adjust to Danish middle-class society, his works of fiction show little concern with social and political problems that, as a maverick observer, he dealt with in his journalism.

Although the writers so far mentioned cannot be described as orthodox Christian, their works contain no attack on the Church or questioning of dogma. Free-thinkers do occur—as in Mrs Gyllembourg's *Montanus the Younger* (1837), Hans Christian Andersen's *At vaere eller ikke vaere* (1857; To be or not to be), and Goldschmidt's three-volume *Hjemløs* (1853–57; Homeless)—but invariably regain a measure of faith in immortality.

If one were briefly to characterize the human ideal of Scandinavian bourgeois or Biedermeier realism, one would point to its blend of 18th-century humanism, the romantic worship of nature and poetry, and a gentle, undemanding Lutheran Christianity. It is not so remote from the kind of harmonization Kierkegaard described with apparent approval

---

* A term originally applied to middle-class culture and life-style in Germany during the period 1815–48, suggesting complacement, pedestrian prosperity. In Scandinavian criticism the term implies, less disparagingly, a spirit of social optimism and idealism.

in his famous essay "Equilibrium" in *Either-Or*, Part II (1843)—but which he savagely denounced in his later writings.

Although Scandinavian fiction of the first half of the 19th century shows on the whole a picture of social and cultural harmony, there are also isolated, but significant, dissenting voices. J. L. Almquist's novel *Det går an* (1839; It Will Do) introduces us to a lower stratum of the middle class than is common in the Scandinavian fiction of the time. An Army sergeant picks up a young woman on a steamship voyage. He hopes for an affair and does in fact, in all propriety, spend the night with her in a room in an inn. She confesses to him that her childhood impression of her parents' unhappy relationship has made her reject the idea of conventional marriage. Instead she favours a free union of a man and a woman living under the same roof, bound only by mutual love and understanding. Not surprisingly, the author, who was in holy orders, came under heavy attack from the press and the Church authorities. Another early novel speaking out against convention is Camilla Collett's *Amtmandens døttre* (1855; The Sheriff's Daughters), which describes the plight of middle-class women who, debarred from any useful education, must look to marriage as their only livelihood. Miss Collett's fervour and indignation lends life to a work that, as fiction, is technically weak. The theme was later treated with consummate realist art in Jonas Lie's *Familjen paa Gilje* (1883; The Family at Gilje).

In mid-century Danish literature there are two works of considerable literary standing that take a devastatingly critical view of Danish middle-class society and its values. They are H. E. Schack's *Phantasterne* (1857; The Dreamers) and F. Paludan-Müller's verse novel *Adam Homo* (1842–9). *Phantasterne*, which appeared in the same year as *Madame Bovary*, is a study of daydreaming and its consequences. In a sense it is a comic novel indebted to Cervantes and Holberg, but it is also an unusually bold and penetrating analysis of the erotic daydreams of adolescence, exploring more or less the whole gumut of perversions. The novel describes the hero caught in his self-made Venusberg, and his hard and prolonged struggle to get control over his phantasies. He succeeds, and with a sobered outlook on life he obtains a useful position in society. In contrast, his friend and fellow phantast remains stuck in the megalomaniac dream-world of their boyhood.

The social criticism of the novel lies in its denunciation of the high value Romanticism has put on dreams and imagination in education. Bourgeois culture has, in the name of idealism, taught people to falsify reality, as is demonstrated in the way two women in the novel convert their frustrated sexuality into religious exaltation. In addition the phantasies of the boys, involving a worship of Napoleon, enables the author to expose this fad of hero worship and the jingoist nationalism with which it was connected. Not the least entertaining of their phantasies are the parodies on contemporary fiction, with demonic heroes and angelic heroines (both Blicher and Mrs Gyllembourg are among the targets here), and the superb skits on the political journalism and oratory of the day. *Phantasterne* made a greater impact on Scandinavian literature than most works of fiction: Ibsen, Strindberg, and Jacobsen were all deeply influenced by it.

Paludan-Müller's verse novel *Adam Homo* is modelled on Byron's *Don Juan*, both in its metrical form and in its ironic narrative tone. It follows the career of a Danish middle-class Everyman from cradle to grave. The first cantos are devoted to an account of the hero's childhood, striking a poetic note in descriptions of the child's discovery of the world in his father's vicarage, and a satirical one in its description of members of the local clergy. The first part of the work goes on to describe the hero's progress as an undergraduate in the capital, his mixed success as a tutor in big houses, his entry into café-society, and his involvement with a demonic homosexual dandy, who leaves him destitute in a *ménage* with two prostitutes. He eventually falls ill and is nursed back to health by his mother. He now completes his studies, and falls in love with a girl of humble origins but of exceptional feminine grace and spiritual depth. Adam seems set for a happy life, but after leaving his betrothed on a journey home before their marriage, he lingers on as a house-guest on a baronial estate. Here he tastes the pride, the thin cultural veneer, and the blasé depravity of the aristocratic way of life. When he arrives at his father's vicarage, he decides to give up his fiancée in order to marry a local countess, an affected, empty-headed feminist who is fond of dressing up in men's clothes in the manner of George Sand. The marriage is barren and loveless, but thanks to the society he now enters, Adam makes a splendid career. He has nothing to offer except eloquence, but he, who has so persistently compromised and betrayed in his personal life, can speak so loftily about the ideal in morals, art, and politics that he attains to the highest posts and honours in society.

Only in the hour of death does the emptiness of his existence become clear to him, and before the judgment of heaven he stands utterly condemned. He is redeemed, however, through the intercession of the girl he abandoned: in a saintly life of renunciation, works of charity, and religious contemplation, she has conquered her disappointment and remained faithful to her love—an outcome that reminds one of the sentimental faith of the "eternal feminine" in *Per Gynt*. It also shows the point of view from which Paludan-Müller judges the Danish society of his day. He is no social reformer or political rebel. His rejection of the values of Danish culture is determined by his religious ideal of renunciation of the world. This does not, however, make *Adam Homo*'s broad picture of the life of its author's own day any less trenchant, witty, or scornful. In this respect it recalls Kierkegaard's sketches from bourgeois life in the journal *Øjeblikket* (The Moment); and it is odd that the two writers should have had little understanding of or liking for each other. The importance of *Adam Homo* for Ibsen is well known.

Whatever the justice of Brandes' strictures of Scandinavian fiction, his appeal for a new realism criticizing the political, social, and ecclesiastical institutions of society and openly discussing relations between sexes did not remain unanswered. His critical writings played a major part in the rise of a school of realism in fiction in Scandinavia of an exceptional vitality and talent. The emergence of a new realist movement more or less coincided with the belated breakthrough of industrialism in Scandinavia. During the 1870s industrial and commercial expansion, on a hitherto unknown scale, was led by a middle-class of markedly conservative political and religious ideals.

Within the new school of realism there were two distinct trends. One, represented by J. P. Jacobsen (1847–85), looked less to the French school of Naturalism and realism, with its social indignation and political radicalism, than to the Russian school of realists, particularly Turgenev with his lyrical mood and his interest in introspective heroes and feminine psychology. Jacobsen, unquestionably the greatest talent of the new school in Denmark, was a faithful follower of the radical movement, and was influenced in his personal view of life by the ideas of Darwin and Feuerbach. He refused, however, to allow his works of fiction to become contributions to a debate. His novels and stories focus almost entirely on the psychology of individual characters and their erotic and religious problems. Society at large, and its social and political development, hardly enter his work at all.

There were, however, several other writers who took it as their task to record the changes in modern society, and engaged themselves in critical analysis of its problems. Prominent among them were the Norwegian novelists Jonas Lie (1833–1908) and Alexander Kjelland (1851–1906). In his novel *Garman and Worse* (1880), Kjelland centres his picture of the life of a provincial town upon a firm of shipping merchants in its

transition from an old fashioned trading-house, where human relationships count, to a modern, impersonal, and morally unsqueamish business
enterprise. In *Jacob* (1891), Kjelland describes with passionate disapproval
a representative of the new business class—an upstart tycoon who uses
any means to get control over the commercial and financial life of an
area, ruining anyone who resists his progress.

Both Kjelland and Lie—the latter especially in *En maelstrøm* (1884;
Whirlpool) and *Onde magter* (1890; Evil Powers)—reflected a widespread
tendency among writers of the Left to sense something unhealthy and
corrupt at the core of the new prosperity. In *Fortuna* (1884), Kjelland
shows how a dubious industrial enterprise, based on credit and juggling
with bills of exchange and shares, brings ruin to an entire community.
With a keen understanding of the power structure of society, Kjelland
observes how the collapse of the business mainly does harm to the workers.
For the responsible managers there is always a way. They do not stop
wearing decent clothes or go hungry as a result of their failure and crime.
The feeling of the rottenness of modern industrial society behind a
glittering façade is taken to extremes in Strindberg's novel, *Röda rummet*
(1879; The Red Room), and his pamphlet, *Det nya riket* (1882; The New
Kingdom), in which grotesque caricature transcends (and, for some
readers, obliterates) their critical purpose.

It is something of a paradox that almost all modern writers should take
such a gloomy view of industrialization and urbanization. For it is not
only the ills of the capitalist system that come under attack: not unlike
his romantic forbears, the artist feels an outsider in the new bourgeois
world, turning from it in despair and aesthetic disapproval. An early
example of this attitude can be found in Herman Bang's *Stuk* (1887;
Stucco), but it is of course important in Scandinavian fiction well into
the 20th century.

Among Scandinavian realists the writer who gave the widest and most
many-sided picture of his society and nation in the latter half of the 19th
century was the Danish novelist Henrik Pontoppidan (1857–1943). In
his early work in the 1880s he wrote with indignation about the wretched
conditions of the agricultural workers, who had been abandoned by the
middle-class farmers in their struggle for political influence and power.
During this period Pontoppidan also dealt with the effects of Denmark's
bitter constitutional battles on society and human relationships. Pontoppidan describes with savage irony the well-mannered brutality and
insolence with which the educated class of civil servants and professional
men treat the common people they are supposed to serve, and the social

ostracism that is the fate of members of the middle class who show sympathy with ideas of progress. But he is also scornful of the liberal leaders in politics, who appear to lack any real passion for the ideal of political freedom. Ultimately Pontoppidan questions the love of freedom and sense of reality in the Danes as a race. Centuries of Christianity and a penchant for lyrical reverie, nurtured by the very scenery of the country, have turned them into a nation of passive dreamers, children of twilight fearing the light of day. Pontoppidan's verdict on his countrymen reminds one of Mrs Alving's denunciation of her own generation in Ibsen's *Ghosts*.

Pontoppidan's most monumental works about the Danish society of the late 19th century are the two novels *Det forjaettede land* (1891–5; The Promised Land) and the eight-volume *Lykke-Per* (1898–1904). The first paints a wide canvas of the movement championing the ideas of religious revival, popular education in folk high-schools, political liberalism, and co-operative enterprise that left such a decisive mark on the life of Danish rural society in the second half of the century. Pontoppidan, who had first-hand knowledge of his subject, writes as a critical and ironic observer. He has a keen eye for the affectation, hypocrisy, and sheer muddle-headedness in its enthusiastic followers and leaders. His irony becomes particularly deadly when describing members of the Copenhagen bourgeoisie trying to emulate the folksy ways of the movement. Yet Pontoppidan is too sober a realist, and has too much affection for the people he writes about, to lapse into caricature. His descriptions of the large gatherings, lasting for days, where followers of the movement met to obtain spiritual uplift and moral support for their convictions, give a generally accurate picture of what actually took place. It also adds to the value of his novel as a chronicle of an era that Pontoppidan introduces human figures that are only slightly disguised portraits of actual people.

This feature is also found in *Lykke-Per*, whose theme is the rise of the radical movement in Danish intellectual life and politics. The novel follows the career of the hero who, like Adam Homo, has his origin in a Danish vicarage. Per, however, is in rebellion against his home background. Instead of theology he takes up the study of engineering (as did the author himself). While a student in Copenhagen, he enters radical intellectual circles, from which he gains access to the world of the Copenhagen bourgeoisie where radical intellectuals are beginning to find favour. Particularly interesting is his description of a liberalized Jewish household, whose hospitality and delight in tasteful, expensive decor and good living stand in sharp contrast to the self-denying austerity of Per's home background. To improve his fortune, Per becomes engaged to the daughter of the house, Jacobe—a free, strong, passionate personality such as Per can never be. But his Danish blood and Lutheran upbringing prove too strong: he leaves Jacobe and the circles where life and material success are grasped without scruple. At the end Per dies, a stoical hermit in a remote part of Jutland, where he has pursued his ideal of self-denial and has pondered the ultimate questions of existence. This ending reflects the pessimism that gradually takes the place, in Pontoppidan's later work, of the earlier militant radicalism—a development common to most of the Scandinavian realists. As they fought for intellectual freedom and for social and political justice, they also read and were influenced by the pessimistic, life-denying works of Schopenhauer and Eduard von Hartmann; and as the writers grew older, this influence proved the stronger. Both Ibsen and Strindberg are cases in point.

The life of the Danish nation, particularly the middle class, is described by Herman Bang (1857–1912) as faithfully as by Pontoppidan, and with a realist art that places him in the same high rank as a writer. Bang's realism was without any political engagement: he was first and foremost an artist relentlessly refining his realist technique. He began as an orthodox pupil of the French realists—about whom he wrote with considerable critical insight and acumen in *Realisme og realister* (1879; Realism and Realists—and went on to develop his own highly original impressionist style of writing. This he applied both to the hectic, decadent life of the metropolis and to the quiet provincial town. Like no one else he describes the frustrations and silent tragedies of middle-class life: the loneliness of spinsters and the alienated artist, the economic misery of those keeping up social pretences, and the dullness of provincial life. In his work the brutal and callous prosper while the sensitive and compassionate suffer in silence. Yet, for all the sadness pervading his work, he is, perhaps, the greatest comic writer in Scandinavian realist fiction. He has an unmatched gift for depicting people in groups; through a mosaic of banal utterances and seemingly casual remarks (put into ironic relief by the author's discreetly interposed comments), he unfolds the sad, grotesque comedy of their lives.

Bang's fiction, and especially his highly individual dialogue, does not lend itself readily to translation. Only one of his novels, *Ludvigsbakke* (1896), is available in English (translated by A. G. Chater [New York and London 1928]). Probably his greatest work is the short novel *Ved vejen* (By the Roadside), which was originally published with some short stories in *Stille existenser* (1886; Quiet Lives).

To conclude, it need hardly be said that this brief essay has had to be highly selective. Moreover, the exclusion of drama from consideration may give the impression that Scandinavian literature treats less variously of bourgeois reality than is actually the case. The works discussed, however, are representative of some of the major trends of the period, and are of a quality that entitles them to be considered in the context of European literature as a whole.

Bibliography

G. AHLSTRÖM, *Det moderna genomnrottet i nordens litteratur* (Stockholm 1947).

GUSTAV ALBECK, OLUF FRIIS, and PETER P. ROHDE, *Dansk litteratur historie*, Bind 2: fra Oehlenschläger til Kierkegaard (Copenhagen 1966).

VILHELM ANDERSEN, *Illustreret dansk litteraturhistorie*, Vol. III and IV (Copenhagen 1925).

HAKON STRANGERUP and F. J. BILLESKOV JANSEN, *Dansk litteratur historie*, Bind 3: fra Georg Brandes til Johannes V. Jensen (Copenhagen 1966).

SEVEN MØLLER KRISTENSEN, *Digteren og samfundet*, Vol. I and II (Copenhagen 1942).

CHAPTER 11

A Nation in Search of Identity

Finnish Literature 1830–1917

Irma Rantavaara*

> . . . it seems that it is the deliberate striving towards this rational self-awareness that calls forth the innermost spiritual strength of a nation. History shows that at the very time when a nation learns to express its own essence in words, it also becomes capable of promoting the development of the whole of mankind, in short, of taking its place among civilized nations.[1]

It is a paradox that, although few nations have as meagre a store of early written literature, few can rival Finland in the riches of her oral tradition. When the first edition (32 cantos) of the *Kalevala*, the national epic of the Finns compiled by Elias Lönnrot from the runic poems he had collected in eastern Karelia,[2] was published in 1835 by the society that had been established to promote Finnish literature, the chairman of the society voiced the general feeling of educated Finns when he said: "With these cantos in her possession, Finland can with a heightened feeling of self-confidence learn to understand her own past as well as her future development properly. She can say to herself: 'I, too, have a history.' " The second and enlarged edition of the *Kalevala*, containing 50 cantos (22,795 lines), appeared in 1849. Only 500 copies had been printed, and this printing lasted 14 years, which shows that the reading public at home was at first decidedly limited (even considering Finland's population, which in 1850 was 1,624,000). But the intelligentsia fully understood its value, and it had already begun to attract attention abroad. The 9th edition in 1904 brought the total printing up to 32,000 copies; by that time the Finnish population had grown by one million since the 1850s.

In 1840–1 appeared a collection of lyrical folk poetry, 652 poems, called *Kanteletar* (the *kantele*, Finland's national instrument, is a kind of zither;

* Professor of Comparative Literature and Aesthetics, University of Helsinki.

in the *Kalevala*, the sage Väinämöinen, the son of the water-goddess, cast a spell upon his audience by singing and playing on the kantele that he had made out of the jaw-bone of a pike). *Suomen kansan satuja ja tarinoita*—folk tales and legends of the Finnish people—appeared in 1852–66; *Suomen kansan vanhat runot*, the definitive compilation of the ancient poems published between 1908 and 1944, contains 1,270,000 lines in 33 volumes. Today the Finnish Folklore Archives are the largest of their kind in the world.

To understand the need for self-confidence, and hence the momentous importance of the *Kalevala* and *Kanteletar* for the Finns, a glance at Finland's history is necessary here as an introduction. The interest in folk poetry in Finland coincided with, and was to nourish, her national awakening. Elsewhere, the connection between folk poetry and the Romantic movement was often a matter of fashion, as it were, of bringing something new to existing forms of literature. In Finland, it led to the first great literary achievement, which has with justification been called the cornerstone on which "a young nation, emerging from the backwoods and for the first time taking her place among civilized nations, had to erect her culture."[3]

For over 600 years Finland had been united with Sweden. The first Bishop of Turku (Åbo) was the English-born Bishop of Uppsala, St Henry, who according to legend was killed in about 1160 by a Finnish peasant, Lalli.[4] At the Reformation, Finland turned Lutheran, and Latin, hitherto the language of church and school, was superseded by Swedish and Finnish. Bishop Mikael Agricola published a language primer in Finnish in 1544 and a translation of the New Testament in 1548. With them the history of written Finnish began, although for the time being Finnish was used mainly for religious purposes.

After the war of 1808–9, Sweden was forced to cede Finland to Russia, and Finland was granted internal autonomy as a Russian Grand-Duchy. Finns were allowed to retain their own laws and religion, and to use and develop their two languages, of which Swedish was spoken by the educated classes and, mainly in coastal areas, by the lower classes as well. (Today about eight per cent of the population is Swedish-speaking.) The promise of relative independence created optimism and acted as a stimulus to national cultural achievements.

At the beginning of the 19th century, Finland was still a sparsely populated agricultural country with pressing economic problems, which were felt to be the layman's as well as the specialist's concern. Henrik Gabriel Porthan (1739–1804), Professor of Rhetoric at Åbo Akademi, was, like many of his colleagues, ready to devote time to practical matters also. Porthan's importance lies elsewhere, however—in the fields of history and literature. His doctoral thesis *De poesi fennica* (1766–78), a series of studies of Finnish poetry, was the first to apply scholarly methods to the study of the oral folklore tradition. It has justly been called the work that laid the foundation of Finnish culture. Porthan studied the old forms of magic and incantations as well as the origins of the Finno-Ugrian languages and their dialects; he also paid attention to the problems of the Lapps. At his instigation and under his guidance national themes were taken up as subjects of academic research: rural community histories, the vicissitudes of the Finnish people, and their national characteristics were studied in learned dissertations. Not for nothing has Porthan been called "the father of Finnish history."

The starting-point of Finnish literature as an art-form has generally been linked with the Romantic movement, which reached Finland in the 1830s. The roots are, however, to be found in the soil tilled by Åbo Akademi at the beginning of the century, although it was with Elias Lönnrot (1802–84), Johan Vilhelm Snellman (1806–81),[5] Johan Ludvig Runeberg (1804–77), Zachris Topelius (1818–98), and Fredrik Cygnaeus (1807–81), that the plant was to burst into flower. The growing national consciousness gave stimulus to poetry especially in the 1830s and 1840s.

Relations with Tsarist Russia, which had at least begun hopefully, began to suffer setbacks: the Estates were not summoned, as promised, to discuss national questions, the censorship of printed matter began in 1829, and by 1850 no publications in Finnish were allowed except those on religious and economic topics. There was, however, some latitude in the field that the Romantic movement considered essential—that is, in matters concerning national development. A Chair of Finnish Linguistics had been established at the State University; in 1827 it was transferred to Helsinki after a great fire in Turku, but the Russian authorities decided what was to be taught and how. Adolf Ivar Arwidsson (1791–1858), a docent (reader) in history, inspired by German and Swedish Romantic poetry, was compelled to resign in 1822 from his office at Åbo Akademi and was expelled from Finland for publicly criticizing the authorities and the prevailing conditions. (It was Arwidsson who gave the Finns the slogan "Swedes we are not, Russians we cannot become, we must therefore be Finns.") In 1837 Snellman, then a young docent, was forbidden to deliver his planned lecture-series at the university on—ironically enough—"the real nature of academic freedom." He published his lectures in book form, however, in Stockholm in 1840. For the time being

331

he had lost any chance of getting a professorship, and in 1844 he settled in the small country town of Kuopio as headmaster of a school. There he started publication of the newspaper *Saima* (in Swedish), which became the main organ of, and stimulus for, Finnish national feelings. It was suppressed—as was to be expected—after three years of extremely influential existence.

In 1846 Snellman published, in three successive numbers of *Saima*, a survey of recent literature in Finland, including an analysis of what literature means to a nation. He pointed out that the awakened self-consciousness of the individual could be the springboard for higher intellectual activity, just as the spiritual energy of a nation should be based on the consciousness of its own nationality. It is in literature, Snellman emphasized, that a nation learns to look at itself, to know its own thoughts, its own way of discovering the essence of things, its own institutions, its manners, its history, its whole existence. Thus the importance of the *Kalevala* and *Kanteletar* could not be over-estimated:

> Like a gift from the gods, the *Kalevala* and *Kanteletar* came to light in order to give the hard-tried nation a potential foundation for rebuilding its disintegrating national consciousness. Without them, what indeed would at this moment be the future of Finnish literature? And with them, what riches our literature has to offer both to scholarly research and to the sense of beauty.[6]

Snellman's *Saima*, with its radical "Finnification" programme, had a stimulating effect on young intellectuals. Even those people who ordinarily spoke Swedish at home were inspired by it. The older generation were left wondering whether it would be really advantageous to replace an old cultural medium by a language that was still undeveloped. But generally they, too, came to accept the view that Finland was moving toward the hegemony of the Finnish language. They believed, however, that such a development would take its inevitable course and needed no artificial hastening. Finnish became accepted as an official language of administration in 1863, but higher education was still given only in Swedish. Aleksis Kivi, for instance, a village tailor's son from a rural commune some 35 miles from Helsinki, went to a Finnish elementary school, but in his more advanced studies had to struggle with a strange language in order to matriculate for the university.

"Cultural strength is the only salvation of our people," Snellman wrote to Cygnaeus in 1840. The February Revolution in France in 1848 gave new hope for patriotic optimism. In 1846 Runeberg had written *Vårt land* (Our Land), which was to become the Finnish national anthem, sung in both languages on ceremonial occasions. Set to music, its first performance took place on 13 May, 1848, at the University students' traditional spring festival, which that year developed into a great national celebration inspired by the prophetic words of Runeberg's poem. A new wave of optimism reached its climax on that day. This was the heyday of patriotic idealism. The February Revolution had shown small nations the way toward independence, even though it might take years of struggle to achieve. In Finland, particularly, these dreams had to remain hidden for the time being, but hope gave impetus to fresh activity in intellectual and cultural fields.

Increasing Russian pressure characterized the period between 1899 and 1905, between the so-called February Manifesto—a decree issued by Tsar Nicholas II whereby Russian laws were to be applied in Finland, contrary to what had been promised when autonomy was granted to the Finnish Grand-Duchy—and the general strike of civil servants in 1905, organized as a demonstration against Russian measures. (One encouraging result of the strike was that the Tsar repealed his February Manifesto.) Several attempts by the Tsarist government to intensify Russification took place during these so-called "frost-years": forced conscription of Finns into the Russian army, severe censorship, and banishment of leading nationalists to Siberia or to foreign countries. This was the age of Governor-General Bobrikov, who was assassinated by Eugen Schauman on 17 June 1904 on the steps of the Senate building in Helsinki (Schauman then shot himself). During these years, anguish, sorrow, and despair could be expressed only in more or less thinly veiled allegories. Juhani Aho (1861–1921) voiced the general feeling in the sketches he called *Lastuja* (Shavings): "Spring frosts first, then autumn frosts—between the two many of our best hopes have been squeezed and frozen, many of our most courageous dreams fallen like dead leaves." *Kansani kansallisuutemme* (My People—Tough and Strong like Juniper), which was included in the first collection of *Lastuja* in 1891, became a symbol and a household word. Aho's sketches were read throughout the country and quoted as encouragement and consolation during the worst "frost" years:

> We can listen to the winds around us as calmly as a juniper on a rocky hillside. Lightning can strike and splinter a spruce in the backwoods, but against a juniper copse it can do nothing, falling to the ground powerless. Horses can charge over the copse and guns can rumble over it, flattening it to the ground. But a juniper does not break. There is no bloody wound or a broken bone. When the tumult is over, the small bush straightens its sinewy stem and one twig whispers to another: "You grow in that direction, I will turn this

> way." And it does not take long before the tracks of feet and the ruts
> made by vehicles have been covered by new saplings. And tomorrow,
> when the ravager tries to find his earlier track, there is none to be
> seen. The saplings have grown and the copse appears intact again.

The first decades of the new century were characterized by important
social developments: the birth of a new political party, the Social Democrats, and the first parliamentary elections in 1907, the four-chamber
Estates having been replaced by a unicameral parliament based on
universal suffrage (women had been granted the vote in 1906). More
than 70 per cent of the voters went to the polls. Finland was heading
toward complete independence as a state, which was achieved in 1917,
helped by the great upheaval in Russia.

Finland's geographical position between East and West has politically
been a burden in many ways, but culturally it has had its advantages as
well. The constant pull and push of contrasting forces have often compelled the nation to action and reaction, to weighing gains and losses,
to beneficial soul-searching, in its search for national identity. These
processes have naturally been reflected in Finland's literature.

The turbulent political and cultural cross-currents in the 1840s and
1850s are graphically mirrored in Juhani Aho's novel *Kevät ja takatalvi*
(1906; Spring and Late Frost). The battle for human souls was waged
during those decades on ideological as well as religious fronts. The
impact of Lönnrot's and Snellman's work, the whole stormy transition
period with its enthusiasms, disappointments, and social changes, is
submitted to critical analysis. The novel is especially valuable as a study
of Pietism in Finland, with the truly monumental personality of Paavo
Ruotsalainen as its central force. The book is a *Bildungsroman*, of a nation
as well as of individuals. Antero Hagman, son of a pietistic clergyman
but early orphaned, is a fiery Snellmanite at the beginning. In the end
he finds his happiness and peace of mind in the religious beliefs of his
dead father. As a newly graduated youngster, he dreams of a wonderful
future for Finland, of a Finnish Renaissance, with the *Kalevala* and the
Bible as a common foundation for a Finnish brand of humanism. His
naive idealism is constantly under attack from a close friend, who derives
his inspiration from rationalism and history: "The culture of Finland
can as little be founded on the *Kalevala* as that of any other nation can
on their own mythology, however beautiful and original it may be.
The cornerstone of culture, its real foundation, is the history of the people,
what it really *knows* of itself. It must be built piece by piece, stone by

stone. Only after that has been done can the erection of the edifice be started. Stone by stone, based on what has been done before." This is Aho himself speaking, level-headed despite his romantic leanings.

Antero Hagman's mental development leads him from an urban milieu to settle down finally in a far-off country parsonage. His is the path of a romantic idealist in the middle of the century. Arvid Järnefelt's *Isänmaa* (1893; Fatherland) describes a contrary movement, from rural to urban surroundings, more typical of its day than Antero Hagman's progress. Heikki Vuorela, who has grown up on his home farm and is expected to take possession of it after his father, comes to Helsinki to study at the university. He absorbs whole-heartedly the Snellman-directed national awakening. He is one of the undergraduates of whom Järnefelt (1861-1932) gives an undoubtedly true-to-life picture, however sentimental it sounds now:

> And those Finnish peasant newcomers in academic life, those reticent boys with yet undeveloped features, their eyes aglow with the love of truth, their whole personality brimming over with a potentiality, still dim and groping, of an intellectual and emotional development—they understood thoroughly what Snellman had meant. Snellman himself could hardly have foreseen the full force of the influence that his thoughts had had on students of peasant stock. Snellman had said that the practical realization of his ideas called for the willingness of the intelligentsia to approach the "people" and to become integrated with it. The theorists preferred to speak about "nationality" and its "hegemony"; others understood "people" to mean the state. But young people did not delve deeply into the meaning of the concept. It was enough for them that when the word "people" was mentioned, the delightful, sunny picture of a familiar landscape came to their minds with the customary background of friends, ploughs, cattle, pastures. They had chosen the academic career in order to serve the people. Culture was for the people; people were not only to be confronted but properly understood. Young people interpreted Snellman's credo literally: it was an exacting and magnificent order to abandon all action inspired by vanity, social ambition, power, riches, personal happiness, and to consider the interests of the people to be the only stimulus for action, sacrificing oneself with one's whole heart, all one's hopes and aims, to the native folk, "to love and to cherish till death us do part."

The pathos expressed in the passage was genuine enough in the middle of the 19th century. But Heikki Vuorela's later development also reflects an actual trend. Youthful idealism gave way to "advanced" ideas:

> Fatherland had long since been a forgotten concept in Heikki's world. Nay—it was even something more than mere forgetting. That concept must not be remembered, it had been deliberately discarded from the mind. For when remembered, it brought a kind

of heartache with it. Although Heikki had long since learnt to consider patriotic declamations and pseudo-heroisms ridiculous and had admitted that cosmopolitanism was the only natural and rational attitude—even so, a fleeting image of a shimmering green landscape with its groves, pastures, cattle, rose in Heikki's mind bringing with it memories of home and creating a peculiar warmth in his heart and reminding him of the cold atmosphere around him now—and then vanished, leaving a painful longing in the mind.

Järnefelt himself had passed through all that: idealism giving way to disillusionment, nationalism developing into radical internationalism, his final stage of maturity being illuminated by the piece of simple wisdom that life's happiness lies in being needed. Happiness is the ability to love and to make sacrifices. This was to be the theme of his best novel, *Greeta ja hänen herransa* (1923; Greta and her Master). Arvid Järnefelt, together with his mother Elisabeth Järnefelt (1839–1929),[7] had become converted to Tolstoyism (Tolstoy's influence—brief or abiding—can be traced in most of the leading Finnish writers).[8]

In the 1860s new continental ideas were penetrating the North. Lively discussions were conducted in private and in public throughout the next two decades. The 1880s were particularly marked by ideological ferment. The names of Darwin, Spencer, John Stuart Mill, Marx, Taine, Comte, Zola, and the other contemporary prophets, were sure to come up in discussions. Scandinavian authors, through whom the new doctrines were mostly received, were eagerly read, to the extent—according to a report by a Helsinki newspaper in 1891—that one third of the literary output published in Sweden in the 1880s found a market in Finland. Even greater attention was given to Norwegian authors: Ibsen, Bjørnson, Kjelland, Garborg, Lie. Norwegian, it is said, came to be *the* language of culture, "as dear to our hearts as our own Finnish," in the words of Juhani Aho. Bjørnstierne Bjørnson, Gustav af Geijerstam, Herman Bang, and (above all) Georg Brandes paid visits to Helsinki, where large crowds thronged the University Hall to hear their public lectures. Outside Scandinavia, Paris became the headquarters of Finnish artists. From there they imported the latest trends: realism and impressionism in the 1880s, and symbolism in the 1890s. Painters and writers were in close contact with each other in Paris and drew inspiration from the same sources. Albert Edelfelt, in his recollections of encounters with Zola, describes how he read *L'assommoir* in one night to be able to discuss it with his fellow-artists. Axel Gallén-Kallela and Strindberg resolved artistic and other problems during intense discussions. Juhani Aho spent nine months in Paris in 1889–90; Maupassant, Daudet, and Bourget seem to have been his main sources of influence. Kasimir Leino, poet, critic, and scholar, studied there to prepare his doctoral thesis on Prosper Merimée. From Moscow, where he was studying in 1886–8, Arvid Järnefelt sent letters to literary magazines at home.

While the ideological battles were raging, Aleksis Kivi (1834–72) sat at his desk in Farjunkars, a rural community not far from Helsinki, and produced within a single decade a number of highly original works that in his own day were understood and appreciated by only a few, and condemned by those who insisted on accepted conventions in writing. He was financially supported by an elderly woman who, being Swedish-speaking, could not even understand what her protégé was writing. Appropriately enough, the *Kalevala* gave the theme for Kivi's first Finnish tragedy: *Kullervo*, written in 1860, when it won a prize in a drama competition, was published in 1864, when he also published a comedy, *Nummisuutarit* (The Cobblers of the Heath). In the short period that Kivi attended Helsinki University, he was influenced by Cygnaeus's lectures on the tragic element in the *Kalevala* (published in 1853 under the title *Det tragiska elementet i Kalevala*, in which the epic is analysed in the light of Shakespearean tragedy[9]). Shakespeare's influence is obvious in *Kullervo* as well as in *Karkurit* (1867; The Fugitives) and *Canzio* (1868).

Kivi's comedies, *Nummisuutarit* and *Kihlaus* (1866; The Betrothal), have rustic settings, simple plots, and scintillating humour. Finns never get tired of seeing the obstinate Esko strutting on the stage, ridiculous and—to them—lovable, a Finn to the core. *Seitsemän veljestä* (1870; Seven Brothers) can be said to reflect a seven-faceted Finn, struggling from the primitive backwoods toward a civilized mode of life through a hard-won victory over the ABC Book and other burdens that culture imposes on citizens. The seven brothers are for Finns as immortal as the figure of Don Quixote is immortal. Many people believe that *Seitsemän veljestä*, although it has been translated into other languages, is fundamentally untranslatable —but that is what everyone feels about great books. Its language is amusingly archaic, yet flexible and rich in nuances. It has the freshness of woods and the sensitiveness of delicate poetry. Realistic narrative is combined with lyrical passages of almost poetic prose. Every utterance of the brothers seems to have a special aptness, now spiced with humour, now lit with a sense of natural beauty inherent in one who lives so near to nature that his daily life is absorbed in the everlasting process around him. Kivi's mastery is further shown in his lyrical poetry, collected in *Kanervala* (1866; Heathland). It has taken 100 years for his poetry to be fully appreciated in all its verbal and thematic originality.

Kivi was an early realist: the general breakthrough of realism in Finland took place as late as 1885, with three works in different fields: Minna Canth's play *Työmiehen vaimo* (The Labourer's Wife), Juhani Aho's novel *Papin tytär* (The Parson's Daughter), and Axel Gallén-Kallela's naturalistic painting *Akka ja kissa* (Old Woman with Cat). But the peasant realism pioneered by Kivi has remained a permanent feature, most often mixed with humour. Classic examples are some of the novels of Ilmari Kianto (1874–1970): *Punainen viiva* (1909; The Red Stroke) is a humorous account of the coming of electoral agitators to the backwoods to rouse people from their political ignorance and to persuade them to go and draw their important red stroke, their voting mark, although these people only dimly understand what it is all about; *Ryysyrannan Jooseppi* (1924; Joseph of the "Ragshore") gives a graphic description of illicit distilling activities in the prohibition period. *Putkinotko* (1920), by Joel Lehtonen (1881–1934), a mixture of Naturalism and burlesque, is an experiment in the use of inner monologue, the duration of the narrative being one day.

Juhani Aho started his career with realistic sketches also dealing with the people of the backwoods: humorously in *Rautatie* (1884; The Railroad), in which an old couple, Matti and Liisa, go to see the latest wonder, the newly built railway; tragically in stories describing peasants who died of starvation and overwork in trying to win a living from the barren soil. In *Helsinkiin* (1884; To Helsinki), with its contrast between the initiation of young students into Helsinki life and their sheltered home life in the country, Aho introduces a naturalistic note. But on the whole Naturalism in its extreme form remained short-lived, despite the fact that there were plenty of targets for the social criticism implicit in it.

The work of Minna Canth (1844–97) is the purest example of Finnish Naturalism, showing a keen awareness of both literary and social problems. Minna Canth was a factory worker's daughter. Her intellectual development is an example of what natural talents, an open mind, and a strong will can achieve even when social circumstances are not propitious. Her education at a teachers' college was cut short by marriage, but she acquired some training in writing while helping her husband to edit a local paper. When she was widowed at the age of 35, and with seven children to support, she established a small shop in Kuopio—the country town where Snellman had been a headmaster, where Juhani Aho and his brothers went to school, and where Governor Järnefelt was to move with his family in 1884. Working there as journalists in 1887–9, the Ahos joined the circle of intellectuals who met at Minna Canth's home to discuss and debate. While looking after her shop Minna Canth read extensively and began to write short stories and plays—to which the opening of the Finnish National Theatre in 1872 was a further stimulus. The social problems that moved her may have lost something of their sting by now, but the dramatic force of her plays, her skill in dialogue —not the strong point of Finnish dramatists in general—and her psychological insight can still hold a wide range of audiences.

Minna Canth's letters are interesting documents, because they reveal the course of her reading. A parcel of books, often from abroad, arrived every week at her home. She read works by social and literary theorists as well as by classical and modern authors, in the original as well as in Swedish and Finnish translations. On 18 January 1885 she wrote: "I am not any longer wavering between *the old* and *the new*. I am entirely on the side of *the new*." On 26 June 1886 she wrote enthusiastically of Zola's *L'oeuvre* and declared herself a positivist—but retained Thomas à Kempis as bedside reading. She fought against all kinds of prejudice, and accused the clergy of reactionary attitudes and the institutions of the Church, school, marriage, and the law of hypocrisy. It is natural that the representatives of those institutions should have hit back hard. But it did not prevent her from being fearlessly on the side of the underdog. After reading Henry George, she wrote: "Socialism, pure socialism. It is the best that I have read on those questions." Her own socialism was George-inspired, on a Christian basis—she prophesied the amalgamation of religious and scientific thinking—but her radical independence in action owed more to her individual temperament and judgment.

For her plays and stories she took material from contemporary reality. *Työmiehen vaimo* was based on what she had seen in her childhood milieu in Tampere; *Köyhää kansaa* (Poor Folk), short stories published in 1886, and the play *Kovan onnen lapsia* (1888; Children with Hard Luck), drew on documentary evidence to reveal the hardships of the poor in those days. In her later plays she turned to the analysis of emotional conflicts: in *Papin perhe* (1881; The Clergyman's Family), the struggle between the old and the young, parents and children; in *Sylvi* (1893), adultery and murder; in *Anna-Liisa* (1895), an infanticide, with an obvious reference to her interest in Tolstoy.

Positivism and religious (though unorthodox) thought enjoyed peaceful coexistence in Minna Canth, despite her attacks against the Church as an institution and against the clergy, in whom she saw too much lip-service and lack of truly Christian feelings. Juhani Aho, son of a clergyman but himself an agnostic, was attracted to a study of the role religion has played in Finnish culture, especially in its more rigorous form. In a collection of 10 stories called *Heränneitä* (1894; Pietists), for which he made a thorough study through documents and interviews in the regions where the movement had been most enduring and tenacious, he illustrated the fact that Pietism in Finland meant an individual struggle not only against one's sinful nature, but also, in those days, against the ruling classes, against red tape in general, and against a bureaucratic, worldly clergy in particular. Fennomania, the national liberation movement, gained a great deal of support from the Pietists—an alliance that was to be the main theme in Aho's later novel *Kevät ja takatalvi.*

In *Panu* (1897), Aho illustrates another, earlier struggle for souls: on one side was the old pagan way of life, on the other, emerging Christianity. The research Aho did for this novel concentrated on literary sources dealing with old beliefs, magical rites, and shamanism. The central theme is based on a study by two well-known folklorists, Julius and Kaarle Krohn, of the old pagan modes of worship, describing how St Stephen was sent from Moscow to convert the Perms around 1600. In *Panu*, the parson Martti is sent from Turku to Kontojärvi to spread Christianity in Karelia. The atmosphere of the ancient world of the *Kalevala* is strongly evoked: the songs sung by Jorma and Kari, who represent the old culture, are in fact from the *Kalevala* and *Kanteletar*; the bear-hunting rites and other examples of hunting magic, and the various forms of worship, come from the works of folklorists.

Panu is a tribal chieftain, the chief shaman in North Karelia, who has to give way to Christianity. The farmers Jorma and Kari represent simple nature worship, gentle humanism, and tolerance. Neither Panu and his followers nor the representatives of Christianity are blameless in their dealings with each other, and both use treachery and violence. The aged Jorma, who worships the old (*Kalevala*) culture in which man and nature are still a unity, stands for humanism, but he has to retreat further into the woods to make way for the new culture. But although humanism is not, after all, enough, Jorma also reflects Aho's belief in the power of the mind. No doctrine, Christian or pagan, can ultimately help—only one's strong will and spirit. Kari, the young farmer, is an illustration of that, and he provides the link between the old forms of life and the new, bridging the past and the present.

In the 1880s Charcot was experimenting with hypnosis at La Salpêtrière, and reports of what he was doing were discussed also in Finnish newspapers. Aho himself wrote an article on hypnotism, which was of particular interest to him because he had always been convinced that many nervous complaints could be cured by the power of word and will. In *Panu* a lame girl is at first cured by Panu's incantations, but the parson's "exorcism" reduces her to her former state of lameness. Panu as a shaman is anxious to find the magic formula that he believes to be the basis of the parson's power. Aho, a rationalist, could not believe in miracles, but he did believe in what seemed like miracles, although they were sure to have a rational explanation. Throughout his writing career Aho, in spite of all his obvious romantic leanings, aimed at making people see things as they are, without self-deception and false beliefs.

The disillusionment and growth of sophistication brought about by the infiltration of rationalism into philosophy and realism into literature make an interesting and complex blend in Finnish writing and thought. Aho is in many ways a seismograph registering what was happening in the cultural and intellectual atmosphere, and in him combine several characteristics of the Finnish climate. There is something of the same dichotomy in him as there is in so much of Finnish mental make-up and culture: a reactionary tendency to retire to the old and the well-known, and to the solitude of the backwoods, yet at the same time an attraction to radical thought and extreme modernism, as can for instance be seen in Finnish architecture and design and in the originality of the literary idiom in the best of Finnish writings—for instance of Aleksis Kivi, Juhani Aho, Eino Leino, Volter Kilpi, Joel Lehtonen, Otto Manninen, Aaro Hellaakoski, F. E. Sillanpää, Toivo Pekkanen, P. Mustapää, Helvi Juvonen, and Lauri Viita.

Aho was a devoted artist, a skilled craftsman, and a close observer of what was happening around him and elsewhere. It is typical of his attitude to art that in his interpretation of the magic mill (the Sampo) in the *Kalevala*, he explains the forging of this magic object to be a symbol of artistic creation in general. In the same way that the Sampo grinds happiness for all mankind, the arts are invaluable; without them the life of a human being would be as dark as the world without sun. Ilmarinen, the smith, is a thorough worker, and the products of his forge do not easily pass the test of his severe criticism: again and again he pushes them back into the fire, and they are acceptable to him only after he has called the winds and other elements of nature to help him in his work. Aho, too, wrote and rewrote, polished and weighed expressions, images, and moods to create a successful whole. He began more and more to be concerned about promoting the development of written Finnish toward a synthesis of modern idiom with the rich spoken variants and vocabulary of the rural areas. His work as a member of a committee engaged on a new translation of the Bible was invaluable also to his own art.

In 1885 Aho published an extensive article on realistic writers that was

341

undoubtedly intended as a kind of credo; in fact, he never returned to pure Naturalism. His primary interest lay with the workings of the mind and emotions of an individual as well as of a nation, especially at the time of great changes caused by emotional, religious, or cultural upheavals, as in *Heränneitä, Kevät ja takatalvi, Helsinkiin*, and *Panu*. Aho is basically an interpreter of moods, as he himself recognized in a letter (1891) to Werner Söderhjelm from St Petersburg, where he spent some time with his wife, the painter Wenny Soldan:

> As to my "favourite authors," I do not really know whose influence on my own writing to "blame." Kivi and Runeberg above all, naturally, and particularly Kivi who *woke me up*. Then at one time I did nothing but read Shakespeare, before I learnt to know the new Norwegian literature. I admired Kjelland especially. But—much though I wanted—they could not make me an ideological writer, everything melted into "moods." And that was due, I think, to the Russian writers whom I read in translation and discussed with the Järnefelts, who interpreted them to me. . . .[10]

The depiction of moods and states of mind remains Aho's forte, but he knows how to combine subjective lyricism with analysis of the general cultural atmosphere and dominant attitudes of the middle classes. Thus his novels of the transition period from realism toward symbolism around 1890—*Papin tytär*, (1883; The Parson's Daughter), its sequel *Papin rouva* (1893; The Parson's Wife), and between them *Yksin* (1890; Alone)— are not only documents of his own sensitive imagination, which comprehends the emotions of both heroine and hero; they are also studies of different ways of life and changing attitudes. Aho has the eyes of the cosmopolitan outsider who views critically the safe but stagnant life of the educated classes, especially in the country; yet he passionately longs for much that is included in it—especially peace and solitude. He was never so happy as during his yearly spells of trout fishing in the rapids or hunting in the woods. He felt that without such respite he could not stand his hectic life in the centre of intellectual activity in Helsinki.

The protagonist of the two first-named novels, Elli, growing up—like Aho himself—in a lonely country vicarage, is an imaginative and adventurous child, fond of climbing trees and high roofs in order to gaze at sweeping views over lake and forest. Her native high spirits are subdued, however, mainly by her mother, who is nevertheless secretly in sympathy with her and remembers her own childish and youthful dreams, long since suppressed. As a result, Elli changes gradually into a sullen and obstinate adolescent. Compared with the daughter of some visiting

Helsinki sophisticates she shows herself to great disadvantage and feels humiliated. But the visit has some seemingly fortunate results, too: Elli is sent to school in the neighbouring town. Her initial happiness at school soon changes into loneliness and an intense longing for home. Her rare outbursts of high spirits make her an object of ridicule, and her attempts at making friends result in heartache. Elli is a being of extremes, wavering between apathy and exultation. From the start, life has had a damping and disillusioning effect on her. Back at the vicarage after leaving school, her early wounds are shown, through flashbacks, to be still unhealed. The atmosphere at home is depressing, because her mother has become a Pietist, who sings gloomy hymns with her friends in the kitchen. Elli and her father, who has retained at least something of his intellectual interests, discuss the poetry of Runeberg and Tegnér in the sitting-room. Elli has her books, her secret dreams, and her love of nature to keep her alive emotionally. One day a young parson arrives to help the ageing vicar, accompanied by a young Helsinki intellectual, Olavi Kalm, who is to stay for a few days before going to Paris to study. Elli inevitably falls in love with Olavi; equally inevitably, she marries the young parson out of sheer exasperation after months of silent pressure from her parents, who can think only of her financial security. She no longer has either the courage or the strength to fight against her fate. Like Minna Canth's *Hanna*, *Papin tytär* was an artistic contribution to the topical discussion of woman's role and education (Ibsen's *The Doll's House* had appeared on the Finnish stage in 1880).

Papin rouva—completed in Italy, where Aho spent the year 1893—was planned originally to appear together with the first part, but it remained unfinished for seven years. By now, Aho had shed the trappings of determinism and Naturalism—to the benefit of his gift for creating characters. Both Elli and Olavi are completely realized characters and are analyzed with masterly insight. Elli, still a sensitive, emotional being, also shows strength of mind; Olavi, though an egocentric man of the world, is capable of being touched by another's suffering. Six years have passed since they last met. Olavi arrives to finish off, in the quiet of the country parsonage, his doctoral thesis on "Woman in the Novels of French Realists"—a suitable theme for discussion with a view to furthering an incipient love-affair. Olavi is pleased and touched to notice that Elli is in love with him, and probably has been all the time he has been away. For a while he, too, is inclined to dream—though conscious all the time of the instability of his emotions—that he has at last found his ideal woman: sensitive, capable of strong emotions, yet balanced and dignified. Their

343

relationship, intimate yet distant, charms him at first, but when Elli, though deeply in love, keeps her distance and remains faithful to her dull husband, Olavi's pride is hurt; he begins to feel both jealous and ridiculous, and leaves. Elli remains, heartbroken, once again betrayed by life and the elusiveness of happiness. The last pages of the novel convey an undercurrent of speechless despair that recalls the end of Chekhov's *Three Sisters*. It is one of Aho's triumphs as an interpreter of moods.

The main drama is enacted in the minds of the protagonists and conveyed through direct and indirect inner monologues. The lively discussions on topical matters that interrupt the more dramatic happenings and descriptions of nature are matter-of-fact and bare of imagery. Elli's conservative attitudes are (it seems) successfully moulded by Olavi into more "advanced" views. Topicality and realism are balanced by moods. Landscapes are mostly seen through states of mind, and imagery is almost entirely connected with nature. Personification and animism are the dominant devices: the landscape is smiling, the corn whispering, the garden gate squeaking in a special manner when the mood is happy. Elli's dreams and hopes before Olavi's arrival are compared with a bunch of everlasting flowers that she has placed between the leaves of her book of life without ever dreaming that one day they might be taken out blooming and fragrant. But happiness is as short-lived as a Finnish summer night. Its long, lingering, pastel-coloured twilight is the dominating mood of the book.

Aho's year in Paris, 1889–90, was of decisive importance, for it was then that the rightness of combining realism and Romanticism became clear to him and formed the literary credo to which he was to remain faithful. *Yksin* (Alone) is a story of a middle-aged man's infatuation with a young girl, and of his struggle against unrequited love. Autobiographical elements derive from Aho's own growing attachment to Aino Järnefelt, who became Jean Sibelius's fiancée in 1890, but Aho retains the realist's detachment in telling the story. The sights and sounds of Paris are vivid in the background: the "real" action takes place within the mind. The scene shifts from Helsinki to Paris and then in retrospect, through flashbacks, to the Finnish countryside. The style is impressionistic; the varied settings offer a rich opportunity for visual and aural imagery. Realistic description has been used sparingly in this book, and is invariably linked with particular states of mind: it reflects the disillusioned moments of insight into bleak reality.

The impressionistic *plein-air* fashion in painting had by that time produced its best-known Finnish exponent, Albert Edelfelt, whose

Luxembourg Gardens was painted in 1887. *Yksin* abounds in open-air word pictures created by means of elliptical sentences that give a staccato, hammering effect. When the Great Exhibition in Paris is described, visual and aural images are massed together, often with onomatopoetic verbs and neologisms. The bustle and movement of street scenes are conveyed with verbs of motion and action, in short rhythmic sentences in which mainly substantives predominate. Inversion and accumulation are much-used devices; parallelism and hyperbole add to the effect of motion and flight; antithesis and contrast are used to give breadth and richness to both the stylistic patterns and the meanings they convey.

In all three of these novels Aho reviews the domestic values from a variety of angles. *Yksin* is a bitter self-analysis by its protagonist: a dissection of a mature and sensitive mind re-living its illusions and disappointments. Mood and setting, symbolism and impressionism, are interwoven. The lyrical mood in the retrospective chapters and the fluctuation of hope and despair in the passing moment are expressed through imagery in which pathetic fallacy is the dominating feature: the external world takes its colouring from the state of mind of the onlooker; the mind is an active projector rather than a passive mirror. Wordsworth, Coleridge, and the idealist doctrines come to mind, rather than Zola's "corner of reality seen through a temperament," unless one agrees with Brandes that Zola's *temperament* is really a synonym for what Coleridge, say, would have called "imagination."

Brandes' lecture on Zola was given in 1887: a landmark in the turmoil of a literature that was moving away from realism. Symbolism (or neo-Romanticism, as it is usually termed in Finland) overlapped the "frost years" and "Karelianism"—the return to idealization of the mythical past embodied in the *Kalevala*. (Remnants of the past were to be found in Karelia, where rune-singing could still be heard.) The idealized picture, created by Runeberg and Topelius, of the tough, brave, and long-suffering Finnish people had been shattered, bit by bit, by the social criticism of the 1880s, which had exposed the gap between the ideal and the real. Minna Canth had attacked social injustices: poverty, the lack of social welfare, women's helpless position as wives of drunkards and loafers. *Hårda tider* (1891; Hard Times), by K. A. Tavaststjerna (1860–98), is a vivid account of the contrast between the poor and the well-to-do gentry during the hungry years of the 1860s. Writers were opening people's eyes to glaring social grievances. Aho, always a student of values, had voiced the general feeling for the supreme value of national unity in his sketches. Perhaps it was a kind of self-protective gesture, during the years of political oppression and strain, to cherish a dream of a magnificent though mythical past.

Jean Sibelius wrote from Vienna on 15 April 1891 to his fiancée Aino Järnefelt:

> I am sure that the time is not far off when we shall begin to see what a rich store we have in our genuine folksongs. It will become obvious that the ancient Finns who created the *Kalevala* were also highly gifted musically. I am now struggling with a new symphony, Finnish through and through. This feeling of being utterly Finnish has taken possession of me body and soul. When I obey it, I succeed best.[11]

The symphony mentioned is *Kullervo*, first performed in 1892. Sibelius's period of Karelianism covered 10 years, 1892–1902, and also inspired the composition of *Satu* (1892; En Saga); *Tuonelan joutsen* (1893; The Swan of Tuonela); and the three other legends of the *Lemminkäinen Suite*, 1895; the *Karelia Suite*, 1893; and numerous pieces of vocal music. In 1892 Sibelius married Aino Järnefelt, and for their honeymoon they went on a walking tour of Karelia, the favourite pastime of Finnish artists in the 1890s. In the same year Aho travelled to eastern Karelia with his wife and Eero Järnefelt, both painters. While they were being rowed across one of the lakes, the oarsman began spinning a yarn about animals and fairies. The listeners were spell-bound—so Aho tells us—speechless with admiration of the man's imagination and the ease with which he expressed himself: the oral tradition was still evidently alive. The solemn stillness of the scenery and the feeling of being one with nature were powerfully experienced by all three. *Lastuja, Panu* and *Juha* (1911)—the last a triangle drama in poetic prose with a Karelian setting, usually considered Aho's finest achievement—all drew part of their inspiration from that journey.

Kasimir Leino had brought symbolist literature with him from Paris, where he had been collecting material for his doctoral thesis in 1890. His long article on "New Tendencies in French Literature" in the following year was influential in spreading information about the symbolists in Finland. A committed realist, Leino was not particularly enthusiastic about the new movement. He likened the decadents to degenerate cells in the organism of society, lacking positive, creative energy but having the asset of the unprejudiced minds of sceptics; he admitted, too, that theirs was a necessary reaction to the one-sidedness of Naturalism. Ferdinand Brunetière's article on symbolism in *Revue des Deux Mondes*, 1 April 1891, became well-known also in Finland, and the Paris correspondents of Finnish journals wrote articles on Péladan and Moréas. Baudelaire, Verlaine, and Mallarmé were discussed in articles and lectures by native and other Scandinavian critics.

It became obvious that realistic and naturalistic treatments of themes no longer satisfied the artistic *avant-garde*, which felt a need for something less earth-bound, more elevated, lyrical, and mystical. In an address in Stockholm, Ibsen himself had voiced the longing for something new, of which *The Master Builder* (1892) was a sign. By 1895 the era of symbolism had begun, and in the northern countries, too, the artist became a translator of universal analogies, a seer in the world of Platonic ideas, which were to be revealed and made sensuous by a new kind of imagery. There is perhaps an innate lyrical vein, both in the Finnish landscape and in the national temperament, that made the transition from realism to symbolism a fairly easy one.

Themes from the *Kalevala* had originally been considered to be artistically compatible with realism. Thus, for instance, Juhana Henrik Erkko (1849–1906) used them for social criticism in his three plays. *Aino* (1893) contains reminiscences from Ibsen's *Doll's House* and Minna Canth's *Työmiehen vaimo*, in that it is a contribution to the debate on the woman's cause, a defence of her right to decide for herself, to be independent both intellectually and financially. *Kullervo* (1895) presents different strata of society, including serfs, represented by Kullervo himself, who, born free, becomes a misanthrope. *Pohjolan häät* (1902; The Wedding of Pohjola) carries political implications: the sting of criticism is aimed at the policy of submissiveness to Russian demands of the conservative Old-Finnish wing. Juhani Aho thought realistic treatment possible and applied it in *Panu*. He advised painters to go and paint what they saw. Axel Gallén-Kallela's *Aino* triptych is one of the results.

But now democratic ideas and the love of the small man, cherished by realism, were giving way to a neo-romantic idealization of the superman, the genius. Brandes' lecture on Nietzsche in Copenhagen in 1888 had found a receptive audience also in Finland. Gallén-Kallela's Nietzsche cult was particularly strong in the 1890s, but as early as 1885 his painting *Excelsior Homo* had shown features of this new trend. Eino Leino's play *Tuonelan joutsen* (1898; The Swan of Tuonela) now combined Kalevala symbolism and the superman ideal in the strong-willed, knowledge-thirsty, truth-seeking Lemminkäinen. To his question: "Who am I?" the Maiden of Tuoni, who is washing her veils in the river Tuoni (i.e. Lethe), answers: "Man is as man wills." The swan of Tuonela, the symbol of truth, glides along the river, the object of Lemminkäinen's ambitious hunt. But truth

347

escapes human striving. In a letter to Dr and Mrs J. J. Mikkola (the novelist Maila Talvio), Leino explained the symbolism of his play, which he was working on at the time:

> Lemminkäinen has been made a titan, a seeker after truth. . . . The swan is the Queen of Death, the symbol of Tuoni's secret, which is to be caught by Lemminkäinen's arrow, that is, an Idea, bringing peace to himself and a message of joy to suffering mankind. . . . He is about to shoot when the shepherd of Pohjola's arrow, i.e. Lemminkäinen's own guilt, kills him. . . . The man who conquers death must be guiltless (Christ).[12]

The typical symbolist devices make the play representative of its kind: an evocative vocabulary, varying rhythms, alliteration and accumulation, the musicality and suggestiveness needed to convey the vanishing lyrical moment as contrasted with the metaphysical questioning of eternal truths.

Eino Leino (1878–1926) came to absorb *Kalevala* themes and to apply them to suit modern sensibility more thoroughly than any of his fellow-poets. He developed his characteristic rhythms and ornamental devices "after a long search for a genuinely Finnish style."[13] In 1903, when he was writing the first collection of *Helkavirsiä* (Whitsuntide Songs) in the country villa of a close friend, the poet Otto Manninen, he had a collection of old Finnish folk-tales and a copy of *Kanteletar* with him. In an article published in the summer of 1903 he explains his thoughts concerning so-called "national" art. Success in music and visual arts is, he thinks, to a great extent a result of their having a national basis.

> Now we are trying to create a national poetry. . . . We want to create our own art patterns of poetry as an art form, a genuinely Finnish style based on folklore, especially on its later, more highly developed forms that correspond to the present-day idiom, in order to make our poetry widely understood and accepted by the people. We want to carry out what has already been achieved in music and the visual arts.[14]

Leino's ambition (as L. Onerva, Leino's life-long friend and biographer, points out) was to bridge the gap between the ancient Finnish culture and the modern, individual philosophy of life, to combine European metric devices with the metres of the *Kalevala*, to create internationally acceptable Finnish poetry based on popular and national tradition. Writing about his metric experimentations Leino says:

> It is usually thought that the metre of the *Kalevala* is easy. In reality it is the most difficult of all forms. A great intensity and a large store of emotional experience are needed to infuse it with rich nuances of a personal tone. But it suits the Finnish language and the Finnish

temperament. The four-foot trochaic beat of the *Kalevala* is the polished outcome of the development and experimentation of thousands of years. It has also been a fine medium for interpreting a sensitively vibrating impression as the secret passion that dwells in the depth of the Finnish psyche. This passion has found an outlet in, for instance, the incantations with such force, with such shamanic fury, that it has no equal in the poetry of any other nation.[15]

Of Leino's skill in handling *Kalevala* metres, Otto Manninen (1872–1950), himself one of the foremost Finnish poets, says that Leino was the only one of his countrymen who really knew how to manipulate them at will for his own purposes.

Helkavirsiä (1903, 1916) are generally regarded as the peak of Leino's poetry. His inspired mood when writing them is reflected in a letter he wrote in German to his fiancée, Freya Schoultz, 18 July 1903:

> ... I have written some legends and ballads, which may turn out to be the best I have ever written. Wild poetry in the ancient Finnish style, with the rich colourfulness of the Middle Ages, in soft or harsh tones—it will be something new. I have never felt so independent, never been in such a mood, stood so utterly on my own ground.[16]

This propitious mood lasted to give us one of the great achievements in Finnish poetry. *Helkavirsiä* have been placed on the same high level as Runeberg's finest works and Kivi's *Kanervala*. Leino's metres are flexible, and his variations of the *Kalevala* and *Kanteletar* rhythms, enjambement, refrain, parallelism, imagery, and vocabulary, recall the ancient prosodic devices but give the poems new dimensions of metaphysical questioning mediated by modern sensibility. The archetypal themes of the ballads allow scope for ideological and philosophical attitudes. The hero in "Ylermi" is, like Lemminkäinen, a Nietzschean superman, related to Prometheus and Lucifer in his pride. He defies all natural as well as supernatural forces, and is severely punished for his defiance, but never cowed. He asserts his own value as a human being and places courageous rebellion higher than meek acceptance of help from others. In "Kouta" the hero is a shaman, the greatest of all in Lapland. The imagery used in describing him—vipers, bats, wolverines, weasels, ravens, vultures—suggests the "shamanic fury" of his extraordinary power. He knows everything except how to open magic treasure pits, how to defeat Maahinen, the *Erdgeist*, and how to get at the secrets of the goddess Ajatar (Time). He is ready to sacrifice everything to his Ideal—to give his blood, renounce joy, happiness, his own mother, his very life if necessary. Not even when he has to descend into Hades, to the Halls of Mana, does he waver. He acts as a free man, completely conscious of what he is risking, making free choices for what he considers to be—in today's jargon—existential, authentic life. In *Helkavirsiä* universally recognizable archetypal themes and figures are combined in a unique manner with the atmosphere of folklore; therein lies their extraordinary depth.

Not all the figures are supermen. "Tuuri" is about an ordinary human being, a farmer content with everyday human happiness, afraid of death, and asking for mercy when it is his turn to die. He is given respite, only to realize that years are for the gods what minutes or hours are for men. When he wakes up from what he believes to have been a night's sleep, he learns that his family have all died long ago and he alone has been left behind, more lonely than he has ever been. He comes to understand that man cannot bargain with the gods; it is best to obey them. The protagonist of "Tumma" (The Dark One) is a youngster, born a sick soul, a stranger to the world, seeing evil all around him. He asks only to be allowed to die. But when he learns from his parents in the underworld (Tuonela) that the after-life is nothing but everlasting tedium and monotony, he is cured of his illness. He lives on, neither rejoicing or sorrowing, content to take his days as they come. "Räikkö Räähkä" is about the revelation of values understood too late. Räikkö Räähkä, a traitor, despised by everybody, is on the point of leaving his homestead for ever. As he glances for the last time at what he holds most dear, he perceives the beauty of all its familiar sights and sounds: the cattle-bells, the creaking of the well-sweep and of the door, the blue smoke from the chimney of the sauna. Again, the simple emotions and the typical Finnish rural scenery are bound together in a manner that gives the story universal dimensions.

In the poems that tell a tale, archetypal elements are skilfully combined with the emotional content: jealousy in "Oterma ja Katerma," revenge on the seducer in "Kimmon kosto" (Kimmo's Revenge), love-hate ambivalence in "Pyhä Yrjänä" (St George). "Merenkylpijä-neidot" (The Bathing Maidens) is a Finnish version of the swan-maidens.[17] The legends centre mostly upon the Virgin Mary and the miracles of Christ. As the Eastern Karelian Church is Greek Orthodox, the religious references are more suggestive of the colourful symbols and rites of that religion than of the simple Lutheran Church. They serve both poetry and the truthfulness of the atmosphere, as in "Luojan leipä" (God's Bread), "Sininen risti" (A Blue Cross), "Ihalempi," "Tyyrin tytti". "Kaleva" is a variant of the Tannhäuser story, with the temptress seducing King Kaleva to stay with her in a mountain, Hiiden vuori (i.e. Venusberg). Kaleva is released from the magic love-spell through the help of Herra Kiesus (Christ), and starts out on a pilgrimage to Jordan to wash away his sins in the waters of the holy river.

The second series of *Helkavirsiä* (1916) relies strongly on myths with cosmic references. The nature myth based on the *Kalevala* has here gained new depth through its modern Freudian associations—for example in "Iku-Turso" (the name of a mythical sea monster in the *Kalevala*). Space with its constellations and nebulae, its cosmic dimensions, is now part of the background imagery. The poems are mostly allegorical, embodiments of Leino's religious, philosophical, and ideological visions. Ecstasy, a visionary quality, is the characteristic of this second series. There is more of the "shamanic fury" in these poems than in any other Finnish poetry.

It has been asked[18] whether the interest of artists and writers in the *Kalevala* at the turn of the century was primarily aroused by national enthusiasm and the feeling that they were guardians of a national legacy, or whether they were drawn to Karelianism by the necessity of finding new inspiration, new themes, in their search for new forms of expression. Research now in progress may answer the question. It seems likely that the second explanation was the decisive one, even though patriotism played its part in the quest for themes.

The social problems of mid-19th-century Finland had centred on such contrasts as urban versus rural population, the educated classes versus the peasants, the Swedish-speaking section versus the Finnish-speaking population. At the beginning of the 20th century the tension was concentrated less in these issues than in directly political and ideological ones that cut across social strata and created new antagonisms.

During the years of oppression from outside, the nation underwent an internal calamity as well: it split into two factions, into the so-called Constitutionalists, or Young Finns, who were prepared to disobey orders from the Russians if they were contrary to the established laws of the country, and the Compliers, or Old Finns, who "had no faith in the triumph of justice, and held that the ways of a great Power were inexorable."[19] The latter decided that they would not disobey regulations merely because they had been imposed unconstitutionally. The Constitutionalists began to be dismissed from their posts, and the Compliers often took their places. They defended themselves by saying that if they did not do so, Russians would. This is the issue in Juhani Aho's play *Tuomio* (1907; The Judgment), which was to have been performed at the Finnish National Theatre, but was stopped by official injunction while still in rehearsal. In the play, a

Finnish Provincial Governor, a Complier, is shot by the son of a Constitutionalist who has been expelled to Siberia. Although a Constitutionalist
himself, like most of his friends, Aho tried to be fair to the opposing party,
whose position was by no means easy, for they were accused by the Young
Finns of being traitors to their country. Indeed, many prominent and
respected national figures considered it their patriotic duty to comply as a
matter of principle. But circumstances like these are apt to bring forth
despicable features as well: there were people who turned informer to get
others dismissed from their jobs and themselves installed instead. Aho's
play deals with people of this kind. He wrote on 28 August, 1902:

> Blow after blow against us. The most deplorable thing is that Finns
> have not proved to be what I have always portrayed them to be
> like. . . . Of what use has it been to have worked for the Finnish
> people, of what use education and raising the standard of living, if it
> has not opened the eyes of a greater number of people.[20]

His disappointment was all the more profound because his illusions had
soared so high.

This intellectual disillusion changed the character of literature in
Finland: the popular image of the masses as well as of the gentry was
gradually found to have been false. The "melancholy idealism" of the
1890s, of which Jalmari Hahl spoke in an article in the daily newspaper
Uusi Suometar in 1900, changed to fierce national self-criticism and a
general feeling of helplessness. It was not the lower classes that were the
targets of criticism; it was felt that the intellectuals were to blame. Once
people's eyes were opened, a new sense of responsibility was born and a new
angle of vision was accepted, painful though it was. Perhaps a new sense of
humility came with it, too: it was not for the intellectuals to go and teach
the people; it was necessary for them to go and learn from the people. But
there, too, a shock was in store: the educated classes were no longer
accepted as purveyors of a higher kind of widsom. On the contrary, a deep
distrust of the upper classes emerged, a distrust directed particularly
toward the owners of the manor houses, who had been exploiting their
tenants for so long.

Arvid Järnefelt's *Maaemon lapsia* (1905; Children of the Earth) preached
Tolstoy's message, that the land belongs to all and that both the tenant and
the owner of the farm have the right to possess land. Järnefelt does not
idealize tenants any more than he denigrates the land-owning classes. He is
on the side of the weak, but takes an absolute stand against all violence.
His sympathy is with the honest farmer, whether an owner or a crofter, who
tills his land, faithful to his task. Järnefelt himself had given up a successful

career as a lawyer and, like his mother Elisabeth, had bought a plot of land in the country and lived there in utter simplicity. In *Veneh'ojalaiset* (1909; The Veneh'oja Tenants) Järnefelt defends tenants against landowners in a story based on a true and notorious case of 1906–7, in which the owners of Laukko Manor evicted their tenants, who had long taken care of their small farm. (In 1918, after Finland had become independent, a law was passed giving tenants the right to buy the land they had tilled as crofters.)

The relations between the Finnish-speaking rural population and the Swedish-speaking squirearchy, clergy, and civil servants were examined and criticized by Maila Talvio (1871–1951) in her early novels *Pimeän-pirttin hävitys* (1901; The Destruction of Pimeänpirtti Farm), *Juha Joutsia* (1903), and *Louhilinna* (1906). She sympathizes with the exploited tenants and their helpless position, but assesses also what is valuable in the traditional, sheltered upper-class modes of life. K. A. Tavaststjerna's *Kvinno-regemente* (1894; Regiment of Women) is a merciless attack on materialism and superstitious stupidity represented by a landowner and her son, a half-baked intellectual. The irony is brought out especially by the contrast between them and a young man, an intellectual idealist, who comes to teach the country people whom he has learnt to love through Runeberg's poetry, only to find that the reality is completely different. On the whole, Swedo-Finnish writers had remained immune to the national Romanticism of the 1890s. Tavaststjerna is their foremost representative, as poet, novelist, and dramatist; but there was a kind of hiatus in Swedish writing. Professor Yrjö Hirn (1870–1952) was fond of telling a revealing anecdote: when he was sitting with the poet Mikael Lybeck in a carriage in Tavast-stjerna's funeral cortège (1898), he had the feeling that he was riding in company with the whole of Swedo-Finnish literature.

Not surprisingly, the new political party, the Social Democrats, found support from rural as well as from urban workers in the early years of the new century. The aim of the new party was to effect a shift in power by means of a revolution of the proletariat. It was natural that both the Old Finns and the Young Finns should have tried to win over the working classes. The Young Finns were, at least at the start, in real sympathy with them and their legitimate demands. These political developments were, of course, bound to affect the literary climate (Social Democrats appeared in several novels published in this period). A new impetus was given to authors to re-evaluate the ways in which the Finnish character could be expressed in literary terms. Juhani Aho's *Kevät ja takatalvi* was published in May 1906, on the eve of the great celebrations in honour of

z

J. V. Snellman's centenary. Aho had begun writing it in the 1890s, when national Romanticism was still in vogue. By the time of its completion in Italy in 1903–4, a darkening political outlook coloured also the portrayal of characters and ideas. The main spokesman in the novel for Aho's growing disillusionment is the sceptical Jaakko Martin, A. I. Arwidsson's fellow-fighter in the 1820s.

At the time of Runeberg's centenary celebrations two years earlier, in 1904, debunking of his idealized picture of the Finns was already in progress, but sincere tribute was paid—by Eino Leino, for instance—to the artistic values of his work. The criticism was aimed not at the poet but at those who refused to see that Runeberg's idealism was no longer valid.

Leino and his friends were leaving behind their romantic-symbolist period and turning to national soul-searching. In 1895, when Leino had arrived in Helsinki as an undergraduate of 17, with a collection of poetry ready to be published the next year, he had found himself in the little world that had been immortalized in Axel Gallén-Kallela's *Symposion* (1894), a typically symbolistic presentation of a group of friends: the artist himself, Sibelius, and the orchestra-leader and composer Kajanus. By 1906 Leino was ready to satirize that world in his novel *Tuomas Vitikka*, lashing with bitter irony the naive belief in the great future of the Finnish nation: "The road towards Finland's might and glory seemed to everybody to be straight and uneventful. She was to become a wonderful civilized country, to conquer the world with her song and to defend her borders with the kantele. Her people was nothing short of divine in origin, a people tough and strong like juniper, unvanquished by any storms. . . . Truth, beauty, justice, and all those great golden eagles seemed to have been given as it were gratuitously to the ever-increasing legions of this marvellous people, guiding them straight to paradise."

Like most of his friends, Leino retained his illusions about the possibility of a "new" man emerging from the struggles, "a man of innate nobility, the future man, the optimistic dream of a human being who will reach a high level of maturity" (*Olli Suurpää*, 1908). Leino had passed through the inevitable influences of Ibsen and Nietzsche, arriving at mysticism of a theosophical brand, fashionable at that time in artistic circles in Helsinki. But he retained his critical faculty. In *Jaana Rönty* (1907), his analysis of the class hatred and vindictiveness that broke out at the beginning of the labour movement, Baron Manfeld and his daughter represent the upper classes, the latter being a Tolstoy-inspired theosophist. Despite Leino's own theosophist leanings, he makes the daughter illustrate the fact that, unless grounded in reality, such virtues as good will, philanthropy, and refinement of sensibility are likely to be useless in the flux of violent social change. Jaana Rönty, an anarchist, is an exponent of the hidden and repressed fury that Leino found deep in the Finnish soul, the Caliban quality he recognized in himself. Depth-psychology interested him, and he already knew some of Freud's works. In *Olli Suurpää* we find a description of Finns as a nation "with wide untilled areas, stony land where vipers hiss, and a quagmire never penetrated by the sun's rays."

The political unrest of those years led to bloodshed in the clash between the "reds" and the "white" guards in the summer of 1906. To his novel dealing with these events Ilmari Kianto gave a pertinent name: *Pyhä viha* (1908; Holy Hatred). As Annamari Sarajas has written, the struggle was

> between two dreams fostered throughout the 19th century, about the utopia of an ever-lasting happiness, a millennium. One side believed in a quick realization of that dream by anarchic measures, the other, that such anarchy meant a total collapse of the idealism that had been fostered for decades by an evolutionary optimism that put its faith in the gradual improvement of man and society.[21]

Leino and his friends considered it their duty to be exponents of national self-criticism, yet at the same time they felt attracted to, and found themselves in sympathy with, the new tendencies and modes in literary fashions elsewhere. In 1907, the Helsinki newspaper *Nya Pressen* found it necessary to underline that the dramatic period in progress should give ample material for writers to take up: ". . . the sterile sensuality and sentimental romancing must be wiped away to make way for healthier, purer, and more robust art, reflecting the raging battle in all its aspects and stages." In fact, in his "frost years" novels Leino was doing just that; but he took up arms at once to defend the freedom of the artist: "Literature in Finland, as indeed elsewhere, develops and succeeds best if its representatives are allowed latitude to feel and think freely, broadly, independently. Social problems must, naturally, be included. No mature artist can in the long run remain a stranger to the conditions around him, nor do circumstances fail to influence him." But, he argued later, circumstances may also discourage the examination of external reality, if they lay too heavy a burden on a sensitive mind. Leino was to find reality so oppressive that it drove artists to examine the abysses of their own hearts, forcing them to "think, dream, and forget." *Fin-de-siècle* moods and aestheticism helped in the process of forgetting.

The reference in *Nya Pressen* to "sterile sensuality" was probably addressed to Leino's *Kaunosielu* (1904; An Aesthete), a Finnish variety of continental decadence, with Poe, Baudelaire, Huysmans, and Wilde as progenitors. He

355

explored the theme further in four so-called "slave" novels—*Työn orja* (A Slave to Work), *Rahan orja* (A Slave to Money), *Naisen orja* (A Slave to Woman), *Onnen orja* (A Slave to Happiness)—between 1911 and 1913. Leino's versatility and his protean sensibility are without rival in Finland's literature; in no other Finnish writer do native tradition and foreign influences reinforce each other in so fruitful a manner. Between 1905 and 1911 he published six volumes of plays called *Naamioita* (Masks), including symbolist plays inspired by the *Kalevala*, and historical and topical plays of a polemical nature. The focus of his interest in Finnish history was now the Middle Ages, and not any longer "the mystical, blissful and legendary Kalevala period, which we so much like to imagine as the setting of our ancient past, no wild barbarian period, of which we know nothing definite, yet are so fond of embroidering with the rainbows of our imagination" (in the daily newspaper *Helsingin Sanomat*, 1907). He found "knights and squires," the Finnish nobles and historical personalities, "our only true renaissance figures—brilliant enough to throw at least some glory on our past, otherwise so poor and ascetic." The knights and squires he depicted had powerful bishops—Henrik, Tuomas, Maunu Tavast—to vie with for supremacy. And yet Leino never really escaped from the magic of the *Kalevala*: *Helkavirsiä II* was published in 1916, and a poetic play, *Karjalan kuningas* (The King of Karelia), in 1917.

Many Finnish literary historians consider the first and second decades of the 20th century to have been the most cosmopolitan in Finnish literature, although the "Tulenkantajat" (Torchbearers) in the 1920s prided themselves upon opening Finland's doors to the European literary scene. The group of artists and writers associated with Leino—L. Onerva (b. 1882) was their high-priestess—were all widely travelled and able to read continental literatures in their original languages. *Mirdja* (1908), Onerva's first novel, is a *roman à clef* and gives a vivid picture of what was discussed and read by that coterie of young intellectuals, who in many ways recall the young Bloomsbury set in contemporary London. All of them were intellectually alert, well-read (especially in French literature), open-minded, and sophisticated. They all shared the kind of cultural background and formative influences that had made them mediators between the native tradition and continental influences. Their interest in what was happening elsewhere was in some quarters considered excessive, but in fact their specifically Finnish gifts were nourished, rather than weakened, by foreign influences. Otto Manninen, like Eino Leino, dreamed of a genuinely original Finnish verbal art, in which the inheritance of folk poetry—on which the strength of Finnish lyrical poetry in the 19th century was based—the original Finnish cultural atmosphere, and European stimuli were to become fused in a richly flavoured artistic unity. Manninen's own poetry is an example of that combination.

Much earlier than the Finnish variety, Swedo-Finnish poetry had been in a position legitimately to claim credit for a high level of artistic achievement (especially in the work of Creutz, Franzén, Runeberg, and Topelius); it was natural enough, because they were working in an old cultural medium, whereas their Finnish contemporaries (Oksanen, Suonio, Jännes, and Cajander) were struggling to combine the old idiom inherited from the oral tradition with a new sensibility and metres. But once Finnish writers such as Aleksis Kivi had found their own idiom, the language gained new colour and new dimensions. Folk poetry and song became happily married to new metres and rhythms, while retaining a quality peculiarly their own. Modern poets such as Aaro Hellaakoski, P. Mustapää, Einari Vuorela, Helvi Juvonen, Marja-Liisa Vartio, Lauri Viita, Tuomas Anhava, Paavo Haavikko, and others have continued the experiments with traditional ingredients in modern idiom. The earthy freshness that the Swedish translator of the *Kalevala*, Björn Collinder, in his study *Finskan som kulturspråk* (1962; Finnish as a Language of Culture), believes to be characteristic of the Finnish language, is, according to him, to be attributed to its historical role as the voice of a unified rural culture.

The task of Swedish writers in Finland (as defined by Professor C. G. Estlander in a manifesto in 1887) was to form the vanguard of Western culture in Finland. Their mouthpiece was the magazine *Euterpe* (1902–5), followed by *Argus* (1907–11), and *Nya Argus* (1911–   ). The *Euterpe* group —including the poets Bertel Gripenberg, Hjalmar Procopé, and Arvid Mörne—called themselves "aristocratic radicals," and felt most at home with French culture. Many of them later had distinguished academic careers, notably Emil Zilliacus, Werner Söderhjelm, Yrjö Hirn, Rolf Lagerborg, Olaf Homén, Hans Ruin, and Gunnar Castrén. Another group called themselves the *dagdrivare* (idlers); they were in revolt against their wealthy homes and bourgeois modes of life. Disillusion, ennui, disappointment, and the rest of the *fin-de-siècle* fashions and moods were their battle-cry; pessimism, misanthropy, loneliness, and death, their *leit-motivs*.

The Swedish writer Edith Södergran (1892–1923) belonged to neither of these groups; the ideas of Nietzscheanism found a new voice in her poetry, which, though small in volume, was extremely influential. Her first collection of poetry, *Dikter*, in 1916, ushered in the era of modernism, Expressionism, and free verse; *Dikter* was soon followed by the first collection of essays by Hagar Olsson (b. 1893), *Lars Thorman och döden* (1916; Lars Thorman and Death), and by the appearance of Aaro Hellaakoski and Frans Emil Sillanpää, both to become prominent representatives of Finnish writing.

Swedish writing was entering a very productive, interesting, and varied phase, but the Finnish writers, too, were active. New styles and metres were experimented with: Leino's ballads, V. A. Koskenniemi's Parnassian sonnets, Grecian elegies, and *fin-de-siècle* moods, Onerva's and Manninen's symbolistic poems, Leino's and Joel Lehtonen's pre-expressionistic explorations of the human psyche. Larin-Kyösti's play *Ad astra* (1906), and Arvid Järnefelt's *Kuolema* (1903; Death), for which Sibelius composed the *Valse triste*, owed much to Strindberg's *Ett drömspel* (1903; A Dream Play). The poetic prose of Volter Kilpi (1874–1939) in *Bathseba* (1900), *Parsifal* (1902), and *Antinous* (1903) was reminiscent of the Bible in vocabulary, syntax, and rhythms; later, in the 1930s, Kilpi experimented with the stream-of-consciousness technique, which he had evolved independently of Joyce or Virginia Woolf. Johannes Linnankoski (1869–1913) dealt in archetypal themes: biblical ones in the plays *Ikuinen taistelu* (1903; The Eternal Struggle), *Simson ja Delila* (1911), and *Jeftan tytär* (1911); and the erotic in *Laulu tulipunaisesta kukkasta* (1905; Song of the Blood-red Flower), which gave the Finns a Don Juan of their very own. Aino Kallas (1888–1956) turned from poetry to archaic, stylized prose to suit Estonian themes.

Social criticism in the novels of the second decade of the 20th century found new targets in the *nouveaux riches* and half-baked intellectuals, in the profiteers of the war years, and in the crude "undeveloped hearts" and sensibilities of those who should have known better. Maria Jotuni (1880–1943) was their delineator *par excellence*: she was equally skilful in her pictures of common people, especially women, who have no pretensions to culture of any kind. She presented them in their basic humanity—or, more often, inhumanity—without sentimentality or contempt, and often with wry, sour humour.

A new burst of psycho-realism, inspired by Russian masters, emerged in Linnankoski's *Pakolaiset* (1908; The Fugitives) and *Taistelu Heikkilän talosta* (1907; The Struggle over Heikkilä Farm), and in such bitterly humorous studies of backwoods mentality as Ilmari Kianto's *Ryysyrannan Jooseppi* (1924; Joseph of the "Ragshore"), and *Putkinotko* by Joel Lehtonen (1881–1934), in which the author lashes with humour and satire both the poor Oblomovs and the wealthy profiteers. Humour has a prominent place in the Finnish novel, however grim the reality depicted: one need only think of Väinö Linna's *Tuntematon sotilas* (1954; The Unknown Soldier).

One of the greatest representatives of Finnish peasant realism is *Hurskas kurjuus* (1919; Meek Heritage) by F. E. Sillanpää. The "hero," a tenant farmer of the most inefficient kind, is poor, unimportant, and unlucky. He joins the Reds in the Civil War of 1918 and is killed, as if by mistake, still totally ignorant of what the war is about. The story sounds drab, yet the underlying current of tender humour and pity makes it memorable, a monument to the "little man," a very small cog in the big wheel of nature. In spite of his deterministic materialism, Sillanpää was a mystic, an admirer of Hamsun, with a vivid sense of the irrational in life. His stylistic range extends to the lyrical and the idyllic as well as the passionate and the tragic. Mysticism appeared late in the work of Toivo Pekkanen (1902–57), in the form of a kind of surrealism, in *Mies ja punapartaiset herrat* (1950; A Man and the Gentlemen with Red Beards). Pekkanen had grown up "in the shadow of a factory" (the title of his most important early novel, published in 1932). He is *the* novelist of the proletariat in Finland, but he ended his distinguished career as a member of the Finnish Academy. His book of memoirs, *Lapsuuteni* (1953; My Childhood), covers the socially important period up to the war of 1918, which coincided with his own formative years; outwardly it is full of great suffering and meagre joys, yet it subtly conveys the sense of an unusual human being's advance to a true maturity.

In a recent study of Finnish literature during its first 50 years of independence,[22] the *Kalevala*, Runeberg, and Kivi are called the three "prime movers," the seminal forces in the development of the general character of Finnish literature. It is characteristic that the heroes of the *Kalevala* are not, like those of the *Nibelungenlied* or the *Chanson de Roland*, mighty kings and warriors with their own courts and attendants. They are ordinary people living ordinary lives: smiths, fishermen, farmers. Väinämöinen the sage is no idle singer either; it was he who introduced agriculture into Finland. The "democratic" character of Finnish literature was established at that early stage. Runeberg added idealism and ethos, and Kivi humour; in all three, the love of nature is mixed with a strain of Romanticism.

In the process of establishing the national identity, Finnish literature has all along done its best to show the nation its true face—acting as the super-ego, lifting a warning finger when necessary, but also giving moral support in periods of national despair. The people of the *Kalevala* did not put much trust in the sword; they listened to the word, and practised the magic of singing. *Mythos* and *logos*, the irrational and the rational, acting together, have continued to mould the Finnish mind and their national literature.

References

1. J. V. SNELLMAN, "Inhemsk litteratur," in *Saima*, 1 March 1864.
2. For information on the *Kalevala, Kanteletar,* and Lönnrot, see articles by Väinö Kaukonen in *Penguin Companion to Literature,* II : *European* (Harmondsworth 1969). See also SUSANNE K. LANGER, *Philosophy in a New Key* (New York 1955), pp. 161 ff., and MARTTI HAAVIO, *Väinämöinen* (1950; trans. by H. Goldthwait-Väänänen as *Väinämöinen, Eternal Sage,* Helsinki 1952).
3. EINO LEINO, *Suomalaisia kirjailijoita* [On Finnish Writers] (Helsinki 1909).
4. *The Ballad of the Death of Bishop Henry,* discovered in 1852, is the oldest manuscript in the folklore archives of the Society of Finnish Literature. The manuscript has been dated to the end of the 17th century; the ballad is presumed to have been composed toward the end of the 13th century.
5. J. V. Snellman, still considered the greatest of Finnish statesmen, was a Hegelian philosopher. For him the concept of "state" was based upon a national spirit that sprang from the historical development of a nation. He travelled widely in Sweden, Germany, and France, dividing his time between philosophical studies and furthering the cause of Finnish nationalism. Later, he refused the Chair of History at Lund University (Sweden) because he considered it his duty to remain in Finland. In 1856 he was offered a professorship in ethics at Helsinki University. In 1863 he became a senator, and he was raised to the nobility in 1866.
6. SNELLMAN, *op. cit.*
7. Elisabeth Järnefelt's influence on Finnish literature is incalculable. She was born into a family with strong artistic leanings; her uncle was a sculptor, her brother, sister, and a cousin were painters. She and her husband Alexander (who became a provincial governor in Finland) were well-known as "Fennomaniacs." Elisabeth's influence was primarily upon younger contemporary writers, especially Juhani Aho, to whom she was both counsel and critic. Her children all became well known in the arts—Arvid and Kasper as writers, Armas as a composer and conductor, Eero as a painter, and Aino as the wife of Jean Sibelius. Arvid's novel *Vanhempieni romaani* (1928–30; The Story of My Parents) is largely a biography of his mother.
8. Russian influence on Finnish literature is the subject of ANNAMARI SARAJAS, *Tunnuskuvia* [Emblems] (Helsinki 1968). ARMO NOKKALA, *Tolstoilaisuus Suomessa* [Tolstoyism in Finland] (Helsinki 1958), considers the influence of Tolstoy in particular.
9. Shakespeare's plays and 30 sonnets were translated into Finnish by Paavo Cajander between 1879 and 1912.

10. JUHANI AHO, *Kirjeitä vuosilta 1877–1921* [Letters] (Helsinki 1961), p. 251.
11. ERIK TAVASTSTJERNA, *Jean Sibelius* (Helsinki-Keuruu 1965), Vol. I, p. 239.
12. EINO LEINO, *Runot* [Poems], ed. with notes by A. Peltonen (Helsinki-Keuruu 1961), Vol. I, p. 439.
13. *ibid.*, pp. 520 f.
14. *ibid.*
15. *ibid.*, pp. 524 f.
16. *ibid.*, p. 521.
17. ANNAMARI SARAJAS, *Elämän meri* [The Sea of Life] (Helsinki 1961), draws interesting parallels between the swan symbols of Leino and those of Yeats (who was familiar with the *Kalevala*).
18. RAFAEL KOSKIMIES, *Suomen kirjallisuus* [Finnish Literature] (Helsinki 1965), Vol. IV, pp. 304 f.
19. OLIVER WARNER, *Marshall Mannerheim and the Finns* (Helsinki 1967), p. 25.
20. AHO, *op. cit.*
21. *Viimeiset romantikot* [The Last Romantics] (Helsinki 1962), p. 179.
22. KAI LAITINEN, *Suomen kirjallisuus 1917–1967* [Finnish Literature, 1917–1967] (Helsinki 1967); German edition, *Finnlands moderne Literatur*, trans. by C.-A. von Willebrand (Hamburg 1969).

Bibliography

ANTTI AARNE and STITH THOMPSON, *The Types of the Folk-Tale* (Helsinki 1961).

MARTTI HAAVIO, *Väinämöinen, Eternal Sage*, trans. by H. Goldthwait-Väänänen (Helsinki 1952).

RAFAEL KOSKIMIES, *Elävä kansalliskirjallisuus* [Our Living National Literature], 3 vols (Helsinki 1944–9).

KAARLE KROHN, *Kalevalastudien* [*Kalevala* Studies], 4 vols (Helsinki 1924–8).

KAI LAITINEN, *Suomen, kirjallisuus 1917–1967* [Finnish Literature, 1917–1967] (Helsinki 1967).

SUSANNE K. LANGER, *Philosophy in a New Key* (New York 1955).

EINO LEINO, *Helkavirsiä*: German edition, *Finnische Balladen: Helkalieder*, trans. by H.-E. von Hausen and G. Otalampi (Helsinki 1943).

Penguin Companion to Literature, Vol. II (Harmondsworth 1969).

JEAN-LOUIS PERRET, *Littérature de Finlande* (Paris 1936).

MATTI SADENIEMI, *Die Metrik des Kalevala-Verses* (Helsinki 1951).

Suomen kirjallisuus [Finnish Literature], 8 vols (Helsinki 1963–70).

Suomen kirjallisuus antologia [Anthology of Finnish Literature], 5 vols (Keuruu 1963–   ).

ELLI TOMPURI (ed.), *Voices from Finland* (Helsinki 1947).

AIMO TURUNEN, *Lexique du Kalevala* (Helsinki 1949).

CHAPTER 12

The Emergence of Modern
Hebrew Literature

David Patterson*

Modern Hebrew literature is of more than parochial interest for a
number of reasons. Quite apart from its considerable literary worth,
the close links that it displays variously with Italian, French, German,
Yiddish, Russian, English, and American writing can prove highly
instructive to the student of comparative literature. Its vigorous search
for new modes of expression played a major role in the revival of Hebrew
as a living language. Hebrew appears to be the sole examples of an entirely
successful resurrection of a "dead" language, and thus the laboratory
situation it offers in the field of linguistics must be unique. Hebrew
literature, moreover, reflects the complex of social forces and pressures
that underlay European anti-Semitism and led to the horror of the
holocaust during World War II. That nightmare episode must be
regarded as a yardstick for European civilization, and any literature that
illuminates the background from which it evolved deserves the closest
scrutiny. No less importantly, Hebrew literature served as midwife to
the birth of modern Jewish nationalism, which in turn produced the
Zionist movement and culminated in the state of Israel.

The period covered by this essay extends roughly from the French
Revolution to World War I. Although it has been argued that modern
Hebrew literature may be traced back to the first half of the 18th century,
and indeed even earlier, in Italy and Holland, perhaps a better starting-
point is its appearance in Germany at the end of the 18th century.
But whichever view is held, the principal difference between modern
Hebrew literature and the Hebrew literature that preceded it is one of
spirit. The previous strata of Hebrew literature—namely the Bible,

* Cowley Lecturer in Post-Biblical Hebrew and Fellow of St Cross College, Oxford.

363

Mishnah, Talmud, Midrash, and the vast collection covered by the term "mediaeval"—reflect a mainly Jewish creativity. For the most part the literature serves as a medium for expressing and transmitting specifically Jewish values, and for that reason form and content appear welded together in harmony, with the language admirably suited to the themes. For modern Hebrew literature, particularly in the 100 years following the French Revolution, this is no longer true. For a century the literature is largely concerned with the expression of other values in Hebrew guise; the language and form remain the same, but the content is vastly different. Instead of suiting the content, the form is imposed upon it artificially, and attempts are made to cover a wide range of ideas in Hebrew before the language is properly able to express them. It is important to consider why this should have been so, because there can be few periods of literature when social motivations are more clearly discernible than during the century and a quarter under review. The historical processes may also help to explain the remarkable improvement in quality that characterizes Hebrew literature during the 25 years before World War I.

In Western Europe the Jewish people entered the modern world some 250 years late, although still well in advance of the Jewish communities in Eastern Europe. This painful retardation stems from the institution of the ghetto in the middle of the 16th century, first in Italy and then with great rapidity in many other parts of Europe. Before the ghetto period the Jews, although scattered throughout many lands and without title to any particular territory, had managed to maintain their integrity as a people: the nature of Judaism, which combined an element of nationalism sufficient to fashion a self-contained and self-sustaining pattern of life with an admixture of universality, accorded well with mediaeval concepts. Their confidence was buoyed, moreover, by a sincere and absolute belief in the imminent coming of the Messiah. The tenacity of that faith is witnessed by the succession of false "messiahs" throughout the mediaeval period, each of whom received enthusiastic support in spite of all previous disappointments. Glückel von Hameln relates, for example, how hard-headed Jewish businessmen sold their possessions and flocked to the Hanseatic ports waiting to be transferred to the Holy Land in the wake of Sabbatai Zevi, the most celebrated pretender to the messianic throne. Again, mediaeval Jewish communities drew comfort from a sense of cultural superiority, in keeping with the "chosen people" concept, that was nourished by a high level of literacy and by strict rules concerning hygiene and morality at a time when such practices were held in scant esteem within the host societies. Such feelings of pride, however, were due for a sobering reappraisal.

The period of the ghetto, which extends from the middle of the 16th to the end of the 18th century, is one of the most degrading in Jewish history, and one that led to a narrowing of intellectual horizons no less severe than the ugly limitations to physical freedom. Confined behind walls and gates in cramped and insalubrious quarters, securely insulated from the outside world, Jews suffered overcrowding, squalor, and occupational diseases of lung and eye, as well as intellectual atrophy. Even the ancient tradition of scholarship became increasingly geared to a barren casuistry concerned with peripheral and minor issues, while the real springs of intellectual activity ran dry. The ever-narrowing circle of ideas is reflected in the pettiness of what were considered issues. Toward the end of the period a dispute over the proper pronunciation of the half-vowels in Hebrew split the ghetto in Rome for almost 30 years!

It is important to recall that the two and a half centuries of ghetto life coincide with the great flowering of the spirit in Western Europe in almost every intellectual and artistic realm. In music and architecture, in art and literature, in mathematics, science, philosophy, and law, the Renaissance ushered in an era of splendid creativity, widening the intellectual horizons of Europe even as its physical horizons were being widened by the great voyages of discovery. Navigators and scientists, soldiers and philosophers, were pushing back frontiers, voyaging strange seas, and exploring unknown regions, both in the physical world and in the realm of the intellect. A revolution in economics went hand in hand with a change in the whole method of scholarship from mediaeval scholasticism to experimental science. And during the whole of this formative era, Jewish life was more and more turned in upon itself.

Thus, when the Napoleonic armies swept across Europe and broke down the ghetto gates, the Jews emerged into a world that had changed beyond all recognition. The bitter truth was all too evident. Far from occupying a comforting role of superiority, they had become cultural laggards. The relative positions had altered so drastically that if the glittering prizes of European culture were to be won, some radical adjustment was unavoidable. The impact of the outside world on the Jews released from the confines of the ghetto is one of the main formative factors in modern Jewish history. Within the space of a few years a generation attempted to catapult itself through a process of intellectual and cultural development that Western Europe had undergone slowly and painfully in no less than two and a half centuries. That Jewish life was thrown into confusion, that the task of grappling with the modern world and adapting the old beliefs to European concepts became the over-riding problem, need occasion little surprise. Indeed, the subsequent major movements within Judaism may largely be regarded as attempts to answer a single but compelling question: how to harmonize the old traditions with the newly discovered, enticing, but still elusive blandishments of Western European civilization.

The struggle for political emancipation and social acceptance gave rise to two far-reaching changes that permeated Jewish life in the course of the 19th century. It was also responsible for a monumental self-delusion that was finally shaken off only in the traumatic events of the 20th century. In the first place, the process of integration into the wider society seemed to be impeded by two important elements in Judaism. One was the still unimpaired strength of the belief in a messianic restoration of the people to its ancient homeland. The second lay in the great complex of Jewish law, which served as a barrier to participation of the Jew in the broad activities of the society in which he lived. Opponents of Jewish emancipation argued repeatedly that the Jews could scarcely claim the rights and duties of citizenship when they lived by different laws and deliberately fostered a sense of national unity with their brethren in other lands. To refute these charges a movement of religious reform arose, which attempted to purge Judaism of its national element, especially the belief in the coming of a personal messiah and the return of the exiles. At the same time, it called upon Jews to abrogate the injunctions and prohibitions that inhibited Jewish participation in wider society on equal terms.

The second major change arising from the attempt to forge an outlook compatible with contemporary European society, while still maintaining Jewish identity and the traditional values, was embodied in the Hebrew movement of enlightenment, known as *Haskalah*. The belief that a knowledge of at least the rudiments of European culture was an essential step toward social acceptance led to a radical modification of the patterns of Jewish education. For centuries the Jewish child had received a traditional Hebrew education devoted almost entirely to Rabbinical studies. But now a demand arose to widen the syllabus, to introduce, side by side with religious instruction, the elements of secular studies: a little geography, history, and mathematics, and even some knowledge of a European language. In Germany, for example, German was introduced into the syllabus of some Jewish schools, so that instead of being able to speak only Yiddish, the Jewish child began to make his first acquaintance with the language of the country in which he lived! The aim of education was focussed on enlightenment: the triumph of knowledge over ignorance, reason over superstition, modern light over mediaeval darkness.

Jewish self-delusion in the 19th century springs largely from the time-lag in the movement of formative ideas from the ouside world into Jewish thinking. The appeal to reason and enlightenment, which had so powerful an impact on Western European society in the 18th century, penetrated Jewish circles in full measure only in the 19th. By then, however, other powerful movements that were destined to play a decisive role in shaping the face of Europe, such as nationalism and socialism, were already gathering force in the outside world. But, again, a similar time-lag delayed any effective penetration by these two main currents of European thought into Jewish life until the last quarter of the 19th century. Hence the call for enlightenment—which exerted an almost hypnotic appeal in Jewish intellectual circles, first in Western Europe and later in the much more numerous settlements in Eastern Europe, for a century following the French Revolution—seems curiously unreal. Jews became persuaded of the efficacy of reason as a panacea for all their difficulties almost as Europe was becoming soberly aware of the limitations of reason as a guide to the understanding of human conduct. For most of the 19th century the Jews of Europe hitched their aspirations to an 18th-century star.

The yearning for equality of opportunity, intellectual excitement, and social acceptance persuaded many Jews to believe that with the spread of enlightenment prejudice would vanish, and all would be "sweetness and light." All the persecution and segregation, it was agreed, must surely have been some ghastly mistake. Once the peoples of Europe had been shown that hatred of the Jews was illogical, unfounded, and contrary to the principles of brotherly love, they would welcome them into their ranks, provided only—and the proviso was important—that the Jews could prove their readiness to appreciate the benefits of European culture. The spread of enlightenment demanded a process of self-enlightenment, which in turn required changes in education. The resulting shift in perspectives gave rise to a new kind of literature.

The growth of modern Hebrew literature clearly mirrors the broad aim of Jewish self-enlightenment, and was regarded as a major instrument for its fulfilment. Side by side with the attempt to widen the school syllabus, the exponents of the Hebrew movement of enlightenment, known as *Maskilim*, tried to expand the horizons of Jewish life by introducing a whole range of new ideas into Hebrew literature. Hebrew, after all, was then the only literary language at their disposal, because no other was taught in their schools. The *Maskilim's* new ideas required the translation of a large number of standard works into Hebrew—including textbooks on philosophy, mathematics, grammar, geography, and history—as well as the composition of comparable original works. Thus a wide range of knowledge was squeezed into linguistic moulds that were alien to its nature.

The *Maskilim* were convinced that one of the principal obstacles to the harmonization of Jewish life with the modern world arose from the fact that the Jews in the ghetto had been so cut off from the sources of nature that their aesthetic appreciation of the world had atrophied. The belief was bolstered by the prevailing concept of the link between aesthetics and ethics, so that any attempt to improve the ethical standards of the Jewish people seemed to demand a prior refinement of the aesthetic sense. An examination of the various strata of Hebrew that might prove most suitable for the achievement of such aims persuaded the *Maskilim* to concentrate upon the Hebrew of the Bible, first because the language of the Bible is full of simile and metaphor drawn from the springs of nature, and second because of the quality and quantity of biblical Hebrew poetry (which, it was felt, would help to awaken the aesthetic sense regarded as so important for Jewish regeneration).

The vocabulary of the Bible, however, contains less than 6000 words, and although it is admirably suited to certain categories of expression— such as historical narrative, wisdom literature, nature poetry, and especially prophecy—it remains a very clumsy instrument for the expression of modern concepts. For psychology, philology, mathematics, or any of the wide range of modern disciplines, its vocabulary is simply not adequate. Any attempt to express such concepts in biblical language must resort to circumlocution. The writer is forced to employ a biblical phrase that seems to approximate to the required meaning, and then try to foster a general convention among his readers that, when such and such a phrase is used, what is actually meant is something else. This proved to be one of the most serious difficulties encountered by early writers in modern Hebrew literature. Their very attempt to widen the scope of Jewish interests to include the range of modern knowledge conflicted with their second ideal, namely the expression of those ideas in a revived biblical Hebrew.

It was a fundamental dichotomy, and because of it the growth of Hebrew literature remained stunted for almost a century. With a few notable exceptions, the *Maskilim* deliberately avoided the vocabulary of the whole range of post-biblical Hebrew—the Mishnah, Talmud,

Midrash, and mediaeval Hebrew literature—in spite of its richness of vocabulary, its flexibility of syntax, and its much greater suitability, in many ways, for the expression of modern ideas; instead, they fixed their eyes firmly on the basic stratum of the language. It was a quixotic attitude to literature, a combination of idealism and naivety that, in spite of its quaintness, can still exert a certain fascination.

For almost 100 years, the character of modern Hebrew literature was mainly experimental. Although the regeneration of Hebrew was fostered in Königsberg (East Prussia) and Berlin in the last decades of the 18th century, the movement derived its impetus from Germany for no more than 20 or 30 years. During that time a modest quantity of interesting literature was produced by a group of writers who were the main contributors to a literary journal, *Ha-Meassef*; the best of them were Isaac Satnow, Judah Lev Ben-Zeev, Joel Brill, Baruch Lindau, and Isaac Eichel. The literature includes much high-flown poetry, wisdom literature, proverbs, fables, and the like, as well as numerous works on history, geography, natural science, education, ethics, grammar, and criticism.

The period also produced a poet of some stature, Naphtali Hartwig Wessely, who—convinced that it should be the task of poetry to elevate the spirit—devoted his energies to the search for lofty themes. He was particularly impressed by the German poet F. G. Klopstock's epic *Messias* (1748), and resolved to compose a Hebrew epic in a similar vein, using the story of the Exodus as his theme and Moses as his hero. The work was planned to extend to no less than 18 cantos divided into six parts, of which all but the final section were completed. The achievement remains impressive, mainly because of the author's skill in tackling the formidable linguistic problems arising from so grandiose a project. In its day Wessely's *Shirei tiferet* (the title means "Songs of Glory") was loudly acclaimed, but today it is regarded as a museum piece. Few readers will have the stamina to struggle through so lengthy and laboured a work. Yet Wessely's poetry exerted a dominating influence on his successors for more than half a century. He is also responsible for the fact that a large proportion of Hebrew poetry composed during the first 60 years of the 19th century was written in heavy six-line stanzas with the rhyme-scheme: a a b c c b. His influence may also be discerned in the reflective, philosophic themes favoured by his immediate successors.

But life ran ahead of the exponents of enlightenment. The *Maskilim* had undertaken the formidable task of producing a new kind of Hebrew literature in the firm belief that their labours would enable a rising generation to acquire at least a modicum of modern knowledge while remaining faithful to Hebrew. In practice, the young generation soon found that it was far easier to learn German and approach the sources in the original, rather than attempt to grasp their meaning through the veil of a stilted and artificial Hebrew. Within the space of one generation, Jewish youth in Germany largely abandoned Hebrew as a mode of obtaining the kinds of knowledge they felt they needed in the modern world, and turned to German as a much more flexible and satisfactory instrument for its acquisition. Indeed, had modern Hebrew literature been limited solely to Germany, it is likely that it would have been short-lived and without lasting importance.

Seeds of the new kind of Hebrew literature, however, were soon planted in the more fertile soil of Eastern Europe, where the great majority of Jews lived during the 19th century. The ideas were carried by wandering scholars, most of whom travelled from Galicia and the Russian "Pale of Settlement" (the area in which the Jews of Russia were compelled to reside) to Berlin or one of the other centres of enlightenment in Western Europe. There they would acquire the ideas of *Haskalah* before returning to propagate the new learning in the *Yeshivot*, the great centres of Jewish study in Eastern Europe. Because many of the new tenets seemed to conflict sharply with orthodox Judaism, the scholars frequently encountered vigorous opposition, and were compelled to spread their teachings by stealth. Henceforth, their disciples in the *Yeshivot* would often sit, ostensibly studying the Talmud, but actually reading some new Hebrew work on mathematics, philosophy, or grammar, or even some recent literary composition. Discovery often resulted in expulsion, which was a double misfortune, because not only the student's studies but also his source of livelihood was put in jeopardy.

Stealthily, from cellars and attics, the new learning gradually spread among the Jews of Eastern Europe, gaining a surer foothold than it had ever won in Germany. In the great Jewish preserve of Eastern Europe the real foundations of modern Hebrew literature were firmly established, and it was there that the main lines of its subsequent development were determined. In addition to the forms and themes that had appeared in Germany, new literary genres arose, reflecting an entirely different social and political situation. The Jewries of Eastern Europe were much more concentrated than was that of Germany, and they formed a more compact and self-contained stratum of the population. Russian Jewry, in particular, was far less able to channel its energies through the medium of a language other than Hebrew. In Eastern Europe generally, Hebrew continued for many decades to be the language through which Jews could hope to gain a knowledge of the modern world. For that reason it was cultivated far more seriously than in Germany. The number of translations increased dramatically, while the amount of original writing in Hebrew grew even more rapidly in the vigorous attempt to mirror the social struggles of the day.

The acute conflict between the Jews of Russia and the tsarist administration in the 19th century may be traced to the partitions of Poland at the end of the 18th century, when an area containing no less than one million Jews was absorbed into the Russian Empire. With their own customs, mores, modes of dress, and dietary laws, their own distinctive religion, language, and system of education, the Jews clearly constituted an alien element in Russia at a time when the government was attempting to weld the various elements in the population into a homogeneous nation. The resulting confrontation is one of the keys to the understanding of modern Jewish history. Indeed, the growth of Jewish nationalism in the second half of the 19th century may be viewed as a by-product of Russian nationalist policies.

The accession of Nicholas I marks the beginning of the struggle. Bigot, fanatic, and tyrant, Nicholas (1825–55) embarked upon a ruthless oppression of the Jews in an attempt to eradicate their alien identity. Economic pressure was applied by reducing the area of the Pale of Settlement at a time of population explosion. By the middle of the century the Jewish economic plight had become so acute that a man with a barrel of herrings was deemed a merchant! The misery was exacerbated by the introduction of military service for 25 years, with the recruits sent to areas remote from any Jewish contact. To ensure the necessary quota of conscripts, kidnappers were hired to impress mere children from the streets and schools and dispatch them to so-called pre-military training establishments, where they remained until they became old enough to begin their military service. Hebrew literature abounds with agonized descriptions of this reign of terror, which haunted Jewish life for more than a generation.

To wean the Jews from their ancestral faith, Nicholas established some 2000 elementary schools in the Pale of Settlement, and made attendance compulsory. In their anxiety to protect their young from missionary influences, Jewish parents resorted to every possible method to prevent their children attending government schools. Frequently they bribed the underpaid teachers to mark the registers as full while the classrooms remained empty.[1] The compulsory teaching of Russian in the *Yeshivot*, which the government intended as a means of undermining Jewish cultural insularity, was largely evaded by limiting the study of Russian to such pupils as were considered not bright enough to study the Talmud! This method ensured a number of pupils being able to answer the questions of government inspectors, so as to give the impression that Russian was being widely taught. (In many cases, the children who did learn Russian derived great benefit from it in later life, but that is by the way.)

The cultural divide between Jews and Gentiles in the reign of Nicholas I is sharply revealed in a snatch of conversation between two characters in a novel, who meet during a snowstorm at night and are able to see each other only on arriving at an inn:

> When he saw me at the inn, he called out in amazement: "Are you the man who was travelling with me?"
>
> "Yes! Why are you so surprised?"
>
> "A man like you, dressed in Hasidic clothes, speaking the language of the country fluently! That's something I never expected to see."
>
> "I know many Jews who speak it just as well," I replied.
>
> "I know that, too. I'm a Jew myself. But this is the first time I have seen a man dressed as a *Hasid* speaking it!"—But I was even more surprised to hear that he was a Jew, for I had never expected to find a Jew dressed like a Gentile in these parts. During the whole time I had spent with the *Mitnaggedim* I had never seen another instance of it.[2]

The communities suffered from internal strife no less than from outside pressure. For many decades, orthodox Jewry in Eastern Europe had been divided into two hostile camps: the old orthodox believers, known as *Mitnaggedim*, and the followers of a more recent religious movement, called *Hasidim*. So bitter was the factionalism that even intermarriage was rare and strenuously discouraged. Once the exponents of enlightenment entered the fray, a fierce three-cornered "free-for-all" ensued, with each of the factions bitterly denouncing (and even persecuting) the other two. The question of religious reform, which the *Maskilim* advocated, aroused much passion and personal animosity, even though the proposed reforms were mild compared with what had previously taken place in Germany.

The *Maskilim* aroused even greater resentment, however, for taking the educational experiments of the tsarist administration at their face value as a serious attempt to alleviate Jewish disabilities. Whereas the government was interested primarily in the disappearance of a specifically Jewish section of its population, the *Maskilim* were anxious to integrate the Jewish population into the broad framework of Russian society, without sacrificing its Jewish identity. Although fundamentally incompatible, the aims of both parties seemed initially to coincide. Indeed, the exponents of enlightenment scored some considerable success, not during the bitter years of Nicholas, but in the more enlightened early years of his successor, Alexander II (1855–81). Alexander's policies included alleviation of some of the severest hardships inflicted by his predecessor. Permission to attend high schools and universities, and even on certain terms to reside outside the Pale of Settlement, encouraged large numbers of Jewish students to avail themselves of the new educational and professional opportunities. They hoped that emancipation would follow hard upon the heels of education, and that real equality would ensue as soon as a sufficient number of Jews had reached the level of education enjoyed by cultivated Russian society. A wave of enthusiasm for secular learning, which the repressive measures of Nicholas I had been powerless to arouse, swept through the Jewish community following the more enlightened policies of his successor.

From about 1870, however, the Russian government became increasingly concerned with the growth of revolutionary movements, and embarked upon a policy of renewed oppression, which the Jews shared in full measure. As the dream of emancipation faded, the *Maskilim* discovered that they had helped to rear a generation of young Jews who were turning their backs on Judaism in search of success and satisfaction in wider Russian circles. No less than in Germany more than half a century previously, the sad equation governing Jewish life became only too clear, namely, that secular education without emancipation leads to apostasy. After decades of preaching the ideals of universalism and integration into Russian society, the *Maskilim* suddenly found their aspirations shattered, and a reverse process gradually set in, aimed at retrenchment. The problem now was how to strengthen Judaism internally and to create a renewed interest in specifically national ideals.

This new tendency received a sudden and dramatic spur from the wave of pogroms that swept over the Jewish communities of Russia following the assassination of Alexander II in 1881. The fact that the pogroms were deliberately fomented by the Russian government put an end, once and for all, to any Jewish hope of emancipation or equality of citizenship in tsarist Russia. The reality of the Jewish situation was suddenly revealed in all its horror. Mass emigration westward (and particularly to the United States), an uncritical adherence to the revolutionary movements, and the first trickle of Jewish pioneers to Palestine were three of the more important reactions to the catastrophe. By the end of the 1880s the naive and self-deluding ideology of enlightenment had largely vanished, to be replaced by a more sober, if unflattering, self-awareness.

It is against this background—of crushing poverty, communal strife, and government oppression, followed first by a short span of comparative alleviation and dawning hope, and then by a new and even more ferocious period of oppression—that the movement of *Haskalah* in Russia set the patterns of modern Hebrew literature. It was primarily polemical, engaged in a battle to change not only the course of Jewish education, but also, ultimately, the forms of Jewish life. It attempted not merely to broaden the scope of economic activity, but in addition to introduce new attitudes toward Judaism itself. Anxiously it sought solutions, ready to pounce upon scapegoats within the community who were considered to be the causes of the general distress. It was a highly motivated literature.

The literary forms used for the attainment of its ends include satire, story, novel, essay, and even poetry. The early satirists Joseph Perl (1773–1839) and Isaac Erter (1792–1851) had already proved the effectiveness of their weapons in Galicia, where the Jewish community— a prey to poverty, ignorance, and superstitition—seemed ripe for the introduction of social and educational reform. Joseph Perl had launched a devastating attack on what he regarded as a debased and degrading religiosity in two quasi-novels in epistolary form. *Megalleh temirin* (1819; The Revealer of Secrets) and *Bohan zaddic* (1838; The Test of the Righteous) employ the methods of Rubianus's *Epistolae obscurorum virorum* to expose the alleged abuses of Hasidism from within, while pretending that the writer's aim is to glorify the sect! At the same time the author indirectly attempts to advance the cause of *Haskalah* by pouring ridicule on its opponents.

Not only Hasidism, but the whole spectrum of Jewish society in Galicia, came under Erter's fire. A slender volume of his collected satires, *Ha-Zofeh le-Veit Yisrael* (1858; The Watchman of the House of Israel), although somewhat dated, represents a real contribution to literature in addition to having considerable historical interest. Erter's insight and passion for truth were combined with artistic economy and literary skill. In the realm of satire he was a master. But quite apart from their intrinsic worth, the writings of the Galician satirists served as a valuable pre- liminary exercise for the Hebrew novelists in Russia. The handling of plot, narrative, characterization, and dialogue together with the satirical and didactic elements proved very instructive for their successors. The constant resort to letters and dreams as major plot devices for nearly 40 years, which stems partly from the work of Perl and Erter, is a measure of their influence on the early Hebrew novel.

The novel proper, however, begins with the publication of *Ahavat*

Ziyyon (1853; The Love of Zion) by Abraham Mapu (1808–67), which is
the first novel in a biblical setting in any language, as far as the writer
is aware. Mapu also wrote a second novel depicting life in ancient Israel,
entitled *Ashmat Shomron* (1865–6; The Guilt of Samaria), and a third
novel, *Ayit zavu'a*[3] (The Hypocrite), that describes contemporary Jewish
life in Lithuania. The appearance of this third novel opened up a whole
new realm in Hebrew literature. Although poor in structure, rambling,
and inadequate, *Ayit zavu'a* became a literary signpost for no less than
a generation. This was due, at least in part, to the fact that the social
and didactic aspects of Mapu's work were regarded as most immediately
relevant to the Jewish situation in Russia. In any case they were more
susceptible to imitation than the impressive aesthetic qualities of his
historical novels.

Mapu's originality stems from overall conception rather than from
forms and details. Apart from the direct influence of the Bible and of
such Hebrew authors as Moses Chaim Luzzatto (1707–47) and the aforementioned Perl and Erter on his writings, Mapu leaned heavily on the
French Romantic novelists, particularly Dumas *père* and Eugène Sue.
His stories also reflect a more than passing acquaintance with German
literature and literary theory. His debt to European writing is most
obvious in plot, dramatic technique, and characterization, all of which
display serious limitations. As a story-teller Mapu resembles an apprentice
rather than a polished craftsman, and he never mastered the art of
weaving a successful plot. Nevertheless his writings contain elements of
freshness and originality that reveal a touch of genius.

Mapu possessed a power of imagination that could resurrect dead
bones. In his historical romances the Bible came to life, and the period
of Isaiah was depicted with vividness and freshness of appeal. His strength
lay in the portrayal of setting, in smoothness of style, and in an unrivalled
mastery of language. Above all, he opened a channel for the free expression
of emotion, transfusing a somewhat dry and intellectual literature with
feelings of heroism and love. By fostering a sense of pride in the national
past and focussing attention on ancient Israel, he played a considerable
part in preparing the ground for the nationalist movement from which
Zionism later emerged. His novels must be regarded as a factor in modern
Jewish history.

In this respect his instinct proved to be more soundly based than his
ideals. His adherence to enlightenment as the panacea for the Jewish
plight in Russia, and his self-deluding pursuit of emancipation, lend an
air of unreality to his novel of contemporary life. The heroes and heroines,

who combine a loyalty to their own tradition with the grace and culture of European society, remain curiously unconvincing within the brutal and bigoted framework of tsarist Russia. Yet a quarter of a century was to pass before the lingering traces of such wishful thinking largely disappeared from Hebrew literature. A similar inhibiting effect may be traced to his mastery of language. Mapu's writing represents the consummation of the neo-biblical style so warmly advocated by the *Maskilim*. The style is perhaps the most remarkable, attractive, and yet limiting feature of his novels. In the historical romances the suitability of form and content engenders a feeling of cohesion. But the social novel demonstrates the inadequacy of biblical Hebrew as a means of depicting the complex phenomena of the modern world. In spite of Mapu's own considered advice to his successors to utilize the rich linguistic resources of the later strata of Hebrew literature, the Hebrew novel continued to struggle inside a strait jacket of biblical vocabulary for another two decades.

The most illustrious of Mapu's immediate successors, Peretz Smolenskin (1842–85) and Reuben Asher Braudes (1851–1902), are interesting for other reasons. Both writers inherited Mapu's involvement with social problems and his reforming zeal, and both gave them expression in more telling and effective forms. Smolenskin was even more concerned than Mapu with Jewish disabilities, whether caused by external oppression or by communal strife. But his novels display a sober recognition of the absurdity of applying the kinds of remedy suggested for the Jewish communities of Western Europe at the end of the 18th century to alleviate the Jewish plight in Russia almost a century later. Whereas the Jewish community in Berlin had found a natural centre for imitation in the intellectual and cultural life of a capital city, the Russian Jewish communities were surrounded by illiterate peasants. The channels through which enlightenment was conveyed were so restricted that only a trickle of secular culture could be drawn through them. Hence sprang the gulf between the grandiose ideals of *Haskalah* and the pettiness of their application in practice. Again, Smolenskin demonstrates a healthy disdain for the stock proposals suggested by the *Maskilim* for the alleviation of the dire economic conditions; he argues conclusively that the changes in occupation that they advocate, far from improving the situation, would only aggravate it further. His penetrating analysis of the realities of Jewish life added a new and powerful dimension to the Hebrew novel, and some of his predictions proved chillingly accurate.

Yet side by side with serious purpose, cutting social satire, and reforming zeal, a persistent thread of melodrama runs through his novels, forming a strange juxtaposition of bitter realism and escapist phantasy. The influence of Dickens is clearly recognizable, although Smolenskin lacked the English novelist's ability to sustain a cohesive plot. But even the grotesque elements take on an entertaining and at times hilarious quality. However undisciplined, Smolenskin's talent was immense. Time and again he broke the fetters of a restricted vocabulary and contrived phraseology to fashion a powerful prose. It is the easier to forgive the artistic lapses, frequently caused by the exigencies of over-hasty composition, because of his sincerity and moral earnestness.

Hebrew fiction still required a more vigorous concern with artistry and detail, and the stories of Reuben Asher Braudes represent a step forward along the road to maturity. His novels display a restraint and self-control that compare favourably with the extravagance and phantasy of contemporary Hebrew fiction. But the didactic quality of his writing, and the strong flavour of Russian positivism (which first began to penetrate Hebrew literature at the end of the 1860s), can be seen in the following extract from an unfinished novel, *Ha-Dat-ve-ha-Hayyim* (Religion and Life):

> Rachel had brought her books with her from Naharayim, the latest Russian books at that time, devoted to questions of *community life*, a phrase then in vogue, and of reform of social life in general; questions of "bread and butter," work and money, the people and its rulers, men and women, and many similar matters. They also probed into the question of faith and religion in general, subjecting them to searching criticism in the light of natural science—"matter and force," Darwin's theory of the origin of species, the ideas of materialist philosophy, and the theories of determinism in nature and history. All such ideas were brought together and treated at length in these books, which aroused great interest among the young.[4]

Braudes' view of literature as a means of encouraging social and religious reform was counterbalanced by an instinctive artistry. A second novel, *Shete ha-Kezavot* (1888; The Two Extremes), enjoys a much improved structure, with social and religious criticism integrated into the mainstream of the story with considerable skill. In this respect the novel contrasts sharply with most of the Hebrew fiction produced in the period of *Haskalah*, in which the didactic elements obtrude painfully from the course of the narrative. Braudes deserves credit for demonstrating that hyperbole and exaggeration, whether in phraseology or in dramatic device, are by no means the most effective methods of sustaining interest. By avoiding the flamboyant tendencies of contemporary Hebrew writing and by subjecting his material to a more vigorous discipline, Braudes helped to stabilize the Hebrew novel.

It was with Mendele,[5] however, that modern Hebrew literature came of age. A virtuosity that spanned both Yiddish and Hebrew was responsible for his unusual distinction as the "grandfather" of two modern literatures. The translation, or rather transmutation, of his Yiddish novels into Hebrew in the early 1890s made Hebrew fiction aesthetically viable. The relationship between the two versions of each work is very complex, and serious investigation of the problem is still in its infancy. But there can be no doubt but that the experience of working in the rich and varied idiom of a spoken language made Mendele impatient with the artificial shackles that Hebrew writers had lovingly imposed upon themselves for more than a century.

The difference between Mendele and his predecessors lies in his power of exact expression. Determined to fashion an instrument sufficiently flexible and idiomatic to cope with the language requirements of the modern novel, Mendele utilized not only biblical Hebrew but the whole range of post-biblical vocabulary. Aramaic, too, was made to yield elements of racy dialogue. All the various strata were fused together to form a smooth and convincing idiom. For the first time in modern Hebrew literature the reader feels that the author is completely master of his material, and that he is making the language express exactly what he wishes to say, instead of having to confine his expression to the linguistic limitations of his medium. This rejection of an outworn and inhibiting theory of literature was crucial for the development of Hebrew literature. The benefit is most immediately recognizable in his descriptive passages, which are often touched with humour.

> Alter Yoknehaz is a plump, well-padded, pot-bellied Jew, with a face submerged in a sea of muddy yellow hair in sufficient profusion to supply beard, moustache and sidelocks for himself and any number of Jews besides. Out of this sea of hair a thick, broad nose protrudes like an island—an object worthy of respect, which for most of the year is stopped up and idle; but at the changing of the seasons, as for example with the approach of the Passover when the snows begin to melt, its owner grasps it firmly and blows it with enthusiasm, at which it emits a series of trumpet-like blasts, mingling its chorus with the swans being prepared for the festival—and the whole town of Bitalon is in uproar. The citizens offer him pinches of snuff amid cries of "Bless you! Bless you!"
>
> Alter Yoknehaz of Bitalon is a bookseller, too, and my acquaintance of many a year. He is not overbright nor given to conversation. But he is a character.[6]

Whereas the novels of Mendele's predecessors suffer from the uncomfortable juxtaposition of serious social criticism and widely improbable melodrama, Mendele's strength lies in the harmonization of his material. Although no less concerned with the misery and degradation of his environment, he approaches his subject with restraint. By means of carefully selected description, he enables the reader to glimpse the ghastly milieu without belabouring him with exhortations. By allowing the lessons to speak for themselves, Mendele lifted the Hebrew novel from the arena of polemics to the realm of artistry. He had grasped the basic truth that art itself is a most potent instrument of education, and in so doing he performed a service of prime importance for Hebrew writing. The ability to couch devastating satire in a light, bantering, matter-of-fact tone earns him a place among the masters.

His art stems partly from his ambivalent attitude toward his characters. Behind their unattractive and indeed grotesque façade, Mendele recognized a certain nobility and gentleness of spirit. The self-deprecating humour that derives from the absurdity of a God-intoxicated people wallowing in mire is delicately balanced by the shame of their constant subjection to humiliation and contempt. The warm attachment to a culture that sees a universe tinged with the divine, with all nature, animate and inanimate alike, endowed with Jewish characteristics, is tempered by the bitter recognition of its wretched plight. In contrast to the self-delusion of the exponents of enlightenment, Mendele's work is permeated with an artistic self-awareness. Jewish life is stripped of its pretensions, but the nakedness is clothed in a web of artistry. Art and reality had at last made contact, and Hebrew literature had come of age.

Although Mendele's world is largely self-contained and self-sustaining, much of the literature written during the 25 years before World War I is concerned with the disintegration of traditional Jewish life in Eastern Europe and the struggle of the individual to escape from the toils of a decaying society. As awareness ousted self-delusion, and artistry took the place of verbiage, the emergence of writers of real talent led to a dramatic improvement in the quality of Hebrew literature. The new trends reflect a period of bitter conflict. The crisis of faith that accompanied the disintegration of traditional Jewish life produced a number of "angry young men," in hot revolt against diaspora Judaism in all its manifestations. Whereas the traditionalist authors thought in reasoned terms of the continuity of the Jewish spirit, cultural evolution, and the regeneration of Jewish values, with a strong emphasis on the sense of community, their young opponents demanded revolution, a complete break with the past, and the right of the individual to lead a rich, unfettered emotional life. Despite their differences, however, the writers of the period demonstrated a remarkable loyalty to the Hebrew language and Hebrew literature in the face of all obstacles. Their insistence on the revival of Hebrew as the national language was largely responsible for its successful resurrection.

A dominant theme in the fiction of the period is the erosion of the close community life of the little Jewish townships in Poland, Lithuania, and the Ukraine. As the spiritual and psychological security that they afforded was gradually whittled away, a feeling of loneliness and isolation became increasingly apparent. In literature this was reflected in a longing for the certainties of the past counterbalanced by a yearning to escape into the wider world. This ambivalence tends to inhibit action, and the characters —many of them discontented intellectuals—yield more and more to introspection and self-analysis. A greater subtlety and depth of understanding distinguish the characterizations of such talented writers as M. J. Berdichevsky (1865–1921) and M. Z. Feierberg (1874–99), and later of U. N. Gnessin (1879–1913), G. Shofman (b. 1880), and particularly J. H. Brenner (1881–1921), from those of their predecessors. Individuation endows their work with greater conviction and intensity. They are concerned with the inner life and the dark recesses of the mind.

Their psychological probings and—for the first time in modern Hebrew literature—the inclusion of markedly erotic elements considerably strengthen the affinities with contemporary European writing. The time-lag separating Hebrew literature from the great literatures of Europe was rapidly closing. Far from trailing behind the movements in Russian, French, German, and English literature at the end of the 19th and the beginning of the 20th century, Hebrew writers demonstrate a close familiarity with contemporary literary tendencies and techniques, including stream-of-consciousness writing, even before World War I. The major writers had learnt the secret of artistic economy and the loading of sentences to convey different levels of meaning. The use of language is much more flexible, combining clarity with subtlety. Although still inhibited to some degree, Hebrew prose was gradually acquiring the power to come to terms with modern life. The process was accelerated particularly by Brenner, who broke away from the trammels of a stilted vocabulary and clumsy syntax by evolving a direct and uninhibited style. His frequent resort to European vocabulary and his dramatic use of punctuation irritated the purists beyond measure. But, however painful, the impact of his vivid, unconventional style on Hebrew literature was to prove highly salutory.

The sturdy growth of Hebrew prose from the last decade of the 19th century was matched by a parallel development in poetry. For much of the century the heavy hand of N. H. Wessely had been all too pervasive. Convinced of the importance of poetry as an instrument for raising the level of aesthetic appreciation and re-awakening the emotions, almost every Hebrew writer during the period of *Haskalah* considered the publication of at least one poem, if not a collection, as an essential pre-liminary to a literary career. Much of the Hebrew poetry of the period, therefore, appears the product more of a sense of duty than of inspiration. Its impact was limited to a self-conscious, intellectual appreciation of the aesthetic values of poetry, but it did little to evoke the serious deepening of awareness that stems from the real poet's attitude to his experience.

Apart from Wessely, Hebrew literature in the century following the French Revolution was graced with only three poets of any stature, two of whom—Solomon Löwisohn and M. J. Lebenson—suffered tragic early death. Their slender works are full of promise. The third, Jehuda Leib Gordon (1830–92), succeeded in weaning Hebrew poetry from its devo-tion to lofty and philosophical themes, and in forging it into an instrument for the expression of social and religious problems. But in spite of his reputation as the poet-champion of reform, Gordon wrote poetry that is sometimes wooden, often laboured, and lacks sensitivity; it is more convincing as social commentary than as art.

Gordon deserves credit, however, for one important contribution to modern Hebrew poetry. Far from confining his language to the vocabulary of the Bible, he utilized the whole range of biblical and later Hebrew for the exposition of his ideas. In so doing, he performed a service for Hebrew poetry not unlike Mendele's achievement in the realm of the novel. But although Gordon displayed considerable skill and ingenuity in the em-ployment of post-biblical idiom, he lacked Mendele's artistry. As a result, even his linguistic contribution must be regarded as experimental. The fusion of the various strata of Hebrew into a sufficiently flexible medium for the composition of great poetry was accomplished only by Gordon's more illustrious successor, Chaim Nachman Bialik (1873–1934), who was born in Russia but spent his last years in Palestine.

Prior to Bialik, then, modern Hebrew poetry lacked the originality of ideas and expression that can evoke a truly creative response in the reader. This inability to find the magic spring of language is partly accidental. In every literature there are periods that can boast of no great poet, and 19th-century Hebrew letters simply lacked a writer of sufficient talent. But the power to express truth springs from a different source. The inadequacy of Hebrew poetry in the 19th century is due at least partly to the fact that even the most ardent exponents of enlightenment lacked a sufficiently profound understanding of the values and ideals of the European civilization they were attempting to graft onto Hebrew culture. Time and again they stress that life must be felt as well as thought, that it is essential to develop the emotional aspect of personality in order to live richly and to the full, but they were themselves unable to do so. Whether they write of nature, therefore, or of love, or of any other of the great themes of lyric poetry, it is as if their feelings are experienced only at second hand, as though their inspiration arises from an intellectual conviction that such feelings *ought* to be expressed, rather than from an inner compulsion that *demands* expression of particular feelings in a particular way.

Bialik raised the level of Hebrew poetry to a new plane. He succeeded partly because he wrote from personal experience and an inner compulsion, and partly because he was able to lay his finger unerringly on the magic spring of language. This facility derived from a mastery of the range of Hebrew sources, together with a powerfully inventive imagination: he moulded his material into shapes of his own choosing, instead of limiting himself to artificial patterns laid down by others.

Bialik's inspiration draws continually on his childhood experience, and the impressions of his earliest years recur throughout his poetry. In his delightfully sensitive autobiography, *Safiah*, Bialik reveals an intense awareness of nature, and a sense of the closeness and intimacy of God, in his attempt to comprehend the essence of things in greater depth than is ever possible by the exercise of intellect.

> Hardly had I bared to the heavens the little windows of my soul, my two eyes, when the visions of God came streaming unsummoned from the four winds. Sometimes they would well up to me from the depth of silence, in shapes such as appear in dreams or in the waters of a clear pool. There was no speech and no words—only a vision. Such utterance as there was came without words or even sounds. It was a mystic utterance especially created, from which all sound had evaporated, yet which still remained. . . . And there were times when I heard the silence and saw the voices, for as yet my senses had neither bounds nor limits, but each encroached upon the other. Sound drew sight after it and sight sound, and scent—both of them. As yet I knew neither rhythm nor measure. The little mound in the field was a mountain, the pond—an ocean, the end of the village—the horizon of the earth.[7]

Over and above his personal experience, however, Bialik's poetry is a distillation of Jewish experience in Eastern Europe. By the end of the 19th century, external and internal pressures were causing a process of fragmentation and disintegration, with the erosion of ancient Hebrew traditions and institutions, mass emigration, and a wholesale flight from Judaism. Even more tragic for Bialik was the disintegration of the spirit, in which he saw the real pathos of the Jewish condition. He suggested no remedies, nor did he attempt to formulate a policy. All he did was to identify himself with the deepest sources of Jewish tradition, and to lament its fate. His creative strength derived from a combination of private and public experience. However individual, he was regarded as the mouthpiece of the people in all its moods: hope, aspiration, sorrow, disappointment, and defeat. His poetry reflects the nation's vicissitudes in a manner reminiscent of the Psalms: it is a fusion of national and individual emotion. He described a milieu that he had experienced to the core of his being; a society whose values he could appreciate at their highest level, but one that was rapidly crumbling for reasons he knew only too well. The intensity of his experience struck a new chord in Hebrew poetry. By liberating it from alien and artificial themes, and by restoring its ancient integrity, Bialik raised the stature of Hebrew poetry to a level scarcely equalled for almost a millennium.

The emancipation of Hebrew poetry, however, was not yet complete. The notion that the Jew was not merely a member of a religious or national group, but equally—if not primarily—a member of the commonwealth of mankind, a human being in the broadest sense, still required demonstration. An awareness that life must be enriched, that the emotions are something to be developed rather than stifled, that beauty and love are precious things rather than temptations to be thrust aside, needed a poet whose roots had drawn nourishment from a more promising soil and whose personality had flowered in a more liberal atmosphere. And in so far as the portrayal of love, beauty, and uninhibited emotion is a legitimate preserve of poetry, modern Hebrew literature owes much to Saul Tschernichowsky (1875–1943).

In his native village in the Crimea, the poet grew up close to nature, with Gentile urchins for companions. Third-generation village-dwellers, his parents were pious but not rigorously so, and the home atmosphere was happy. Hence his formative years differed greatly from those of most other Hebrew writers. His childhood memories were not clouded by the misery and fear—the dirty crooked streets, the squalid classrooms, and the beatings at the hands of despised, frustrated teachers—that were the normal lot of Jewish children in the towns. His first impressions were of golden fields, blue skies, and the joy of freedom. He combined a flair for languages and literature with a lifelong interest in science and medicine. At the same time his natural exuberance and zest for life were fed upon romantic love. One affair was followed by the next, as he found himself enchanted by a whole series of attractive maidens. The love lyrics that resulted form a striking contrast with the deliberate, self-conscious, and unconvincing presentations of love in the Hebrew literature preceding them. They are spontaneous, natural, and fresh, the genuine outpourings of an enraptured soul.

A passion for Greek literature turned natural inclination into an almost pagan worship of beauty for its own sake. His ideas unfolded in a series of poems decrying a Judaism that had emasculated the people and stifled their ability to live a full, rich life, and celebrating the springs of vitality and the pristine God of valour. Such notes had never been sounded in Hebrew poetry;* they were shocking and painful, but were also strangely compelling.

In spite of his awareness of tragedy and pathos, beauty remained the central pillar of his universe:

> The priests of beauty and the artists' throng
> followers of poesy who hold her dear
> will save the world with music and with song.[8]

Above all, he stressed man's unity with nature to the point of pantheism, an approach that endowed his poetry with a broad humanism of a kind that modern Hebrew literature had sought but never found before. Both in form and in content his contribution to Hebrew poetry was profound. The wide variety of metres he employed is equalled only by the range of daring linguistic coinages.

Any appreciation of the striking improvement in the quality of Hebrew literature in the quarter of a century before World War I would be incomplete unless it mentioned, however briefly, the work of the literary critics. Throughout most of the period of *Haskalah*, writers indulged heavily in mutual admiration or resorted to self-praise for daring to compose in Hebrew at all. From the 1860s onward, however, the rapid spread of Hebrew periodicals, together with the appearance of a number of talented critics, such as S. J. Abramovitch (Mendele), U. Z. Kovner, A. J. Papirno, and M. L. Lilienblum, exerted a salutary influence.

---

* They had, of course, been sounded elsewhere in European literature. See the discussion of "The Two Traditions: the Hebraic and the Hellenic" (Vol. I). For the revival of the question in 19th-century literature by Heine, Matthew Arnold, and Nietzsche, see Ch. 2, "Poetry and Ideology," and Ch. 4, "Irrationalism."

Condemning the amateur quality of Hebrew writing, the hollow phraseology, its inconsistencies, its displays of ignorance and smugness, critics demanded more content, a more positive and practical spirit, a greater depth of feeling, and felicity of expression. Once the initial wave of outraged indignation in the wake of this critical onslaught had subsided, vapid writings gradually gave way to compositions of greater substance, and artistry began to take the place of verbiage.

It is curious, however, that in the period extending from 1890 to 1914—which is marked by the emergence of a galaxy of talented writers, and which witnessed a veritable renaissance in Hebrew literature—literary criticism was plunged into despair. Most critics were themselves creative writers, and almost all regarded their colleagues as worthless scribblers. They accused each other of plagiarism, hypocrisy, insincerity, and self-aggrandizement. The literature was dubbed artificial, exaggerated, stupid, empty, and unreal. Writers were blamed for jumbling various styles into an unpalatable mess. Criticism itself was regarded as deplorable, and personal abuse went hand in hand with literary denigration. Criticism was likened to a broomstick, whose task was to sweep Hebrew literature clean, regardless of the casualties *en route*. Amid this welter of attack and counter-attack, a certain stability was finally achieved through the efforts of Asher Ginsburg (1856–1927)—known by his pseudonym Ahad Ha-Am—in his capacity as the first editor of the important literary journal *Ha-Shiloah*. By sheer determination and personal authority, he was able to raise the sights and standards of Hebrew literature, and to banish many of the meretricious literary habits that still lingered on from the previous era. His refusal to countenance any contribution to his journal that failed to satisfy his own rigorous standards helped to raise the Hebrew essay to a higher level of craftsmanship.

World War I is a watershed in modern Hebrew literature. After 1918 the main literary centre shifted from Eastern Europe to Palestine, where Hebrew writers were faced with a new environment and the formidable problems of adaptation to a very different social setting. In Palestine between the two World Wars, a very considerable body of literature that reflects the process of transition appeared in Hebrew. Since the creation of the State of Israel in 1948, a new kind of Hebrew literature has emerged, written by native-born authors whose mother tongue is Hebrew. At its best, the range and quality of their work is striking and worthy of detailed study.

References

1. The procedure is described in a novel by S. J. ABRAMOVITCH, *Ha-avot-veha-banim* (1868; Fathers and Sons). For an English translation of the passage, see D. PATTERSON, *The Hebrew Novel in Czarist Russia* (Edinburgh 1964), pp. 111 f.
2. P. SMOLENSKIN, *Ha-to'eh be-darekhe ha-hayyim* (1905; The Wanderer in the Paths of Life), Pt III, pp. 95 f. See PATTERSON, *op. cit.*, pp. 167 f. The novel first appeared in instalments in Smolenskin's journal *Ha-Shahar* in 1868–70.
3. Vilna: Pt I, 1858; Pt II, 1861; Pt III, 1864. A second edition containing all five parts appeared posthumously in 1869.
4. First published Lemberg 1876–7. The translation is from the second enlarged edition, Lemberg 1885, Pt III, pp. 155 f. Cf. PATTERSON, *op. cit.*, pp. 117 f.
5. MENDELE MOKHER SEFORIM (Mendele the Bookseller) was the pen-name of Shalom Jacob Abramovitch (1835–1917).
6. From the novel *Sefer ha-kabzanim* (The Book of the Beggars), *Kol Kitve Mendele Mokher Seforim* (Tel-Aviv 1958), p. 92.
7. H. N. BIALIK, *Sippurim* (Tel-Aviv 1950), pp. 200 f.
8. From a sonnet-cycle, "On the Blood," translated by L. Bernard in E. SILBERSCHLAG, *Saul Tschernichowsky* (London and Ithaca, N.Y. 1968).

Bibliography

S. HALKIN, *Modern Hebrew Literature: Trends and Values*, rev. edn (New York 1970).

J. KLAUSNER, *A History of Modern Hebrew Literature* (London 1932).

D. PATTERSON, *The Hebrew Novel in Czarist Russia* (Edinburgh 1964); *Abraham Mapu* (London 1964; Ithaca, N.Y. 1968).

I. RABINOVICH, *Major Trends in Modern Hebrew Fiction* (Chicago and London 1968).

M. RIBALOW, *The Flowering of Modern Hebrew Literature* (New York and London 1959).

E. SILBERSCHLAG, *Saul Tschernichowsky* (London and Ithaca, N.Y. 1968).

S. SPIEGEL, *Hebrew Reborn* (London 1931).

R. WALLENROD, *The Literature of Modern Israel* (New York and London 1956).

M. WAXMAN, *A History of Jewish Literature*, Vols. III and IV, rev. edn (New York 1960).

CHAPTER 13

The Development of Yiddish Literature

Jacob Sonntag[*]

The Yiddish Language

Throughout their long history of dispersion, Jews have as a rule acquired the language of their new environment, while for a time retaining basic elements of speech and writing of their own original language—for the most part Hebrew or Aramaic, with an admixture of other linguistic elements. However, this process of assimilation has not been complete, owing to external pressures and internal resistance. As a result, they developed a new language, different from their own original language and from that of their new environment, with elements of both, and with its own grammar and specific character. Thus the Sephardim (Jews who lived in Spain and Portugal until their expulsion, 1492–7) developed Ladino, based on Spanish; the Ashkenazim (Jews who settled in Germany, whence they later emigrated in great numbers to the Slavic countries) created Yiddish; and scattered Jewish communities in other parts of the world acquired other local dialects with an admixture of Hebrew and Aramaic elements (Judaeo-Tati in the Caucasus, Judaeo-Arabic in North Africa, and so on). Significantly, in all these cases they retained the Hebrew script, although Hebrew ceased to be their language for daily use.

Linguistically, Yiddish presents a unique and most interesting phenomenon. In the first place, we are dealing with the case of an Oriental language (Hebrew/Aramaic) assimilating, and incorporating into its own structure, a European language (German). It is generally accepted that Yiddish originated in the northern and southern regions of the Rhineland, where the first Jewish settlements in Germany were established. There is

* Editor, *The Jewish Quarterly* (London).

some uncertainty about the time when this happened: according to some philologists, Yiddish dates back to the 10th century; according to others, to an even earlier date. But in any case a language develops over a period of time, and it seems irrelevant to fix an exact date when Yiddish ceased to be a local dialect (from which it undoubtedly derived) and started to become a fully fledged language for both daily use and literary creation. (Ignorance and prejudice persisted for a long time in regarding Yiddish as a mere "jargon," a corrupt German dialect, a mixture of various other linguistic elements—anything but a true language.)

The Jews who settled in the Rhineland had come from Italy and northern France about the beginning of the 10th century. They not only brought with them the relics of an ancient civilization, embodied in the Hebrew Bible and the Talmud, but probably still spoke Hebrew or Aramaic with an admixture of Romanic elements (Old Italian and Old French) that they called *loez*, which means a foreign language. In their new environment they began to acquire the local dialect, while to a large extent continuing to use their own vocabulary among themselves in the home, the synagogue, and the house of study.

Significantly, the Jews themselves referred to early Yiddish as "Ivri-Taitch" or "Yiddish-Taitch" (Hebrew-German or Judaeo-German), the term *taitch* (*Deutsch* = German) assuming in time the wider meaning of "making clear," "translating," "interpreting," in the same way that Aramaic, the spoken language of post-biblical times, was called *targum-loshn* (the language of translation). This is an indication of how the Jews maintained their association with their original language, Hebrew, at a time when the latter was no longer in daily use. Another example of this is the fact that the weekly portion of the Bible, which was required reading on the Sabbath for an orthodox Jew, had to be read aloud three times: twice in the original Hebrew, and once in Aramaic, accompanying the Hebrew text. In this way the Hebrew tradition was kept alive long after Hebrew had ceased to be a living language. Yiddish helped to maintain that tradition by preserving some basic Hebrew features and a good deal of Hebrew in its vocabulary. According to various estimates, present-day Yiddish contains about 30 per cent of Hebrew words, or words derived from Hebrew, in its total vocabulary.

A few examples may illustrate how German words were assimilated into Yiddish. The masculine plural ending in Hebrew is *-im*, and this is probably why many Yiddish expressions derived from German words have this ending, whether in the singular or in the plural, where the end syllable in the German would be *-en*. In some cases German and

Hebrew words would be used synonymously, though with a slightly different connotation. For instance, *bukh* (from the German for book) is used for ordinary, non-secular books, whereas *sefer* (the Hebrew word) is used for religious books (written mostly in Hebrew). Similarly, *tisch* (German for table) stands for an ordinary table, whereas *shulkhan* (the Hebrew word) is used for the table on which the Scroll of the Torah is unfolded. In general, anything to do with spiritual matters—not only in a strictly religious sense—is designated by a Hebrew term, or by terms derived from the Hebrew, e.g. *makhshove* (thought), *meyashev zayn* (to consider or re-consider). Often German words were taken over because they sounded similar to Hebrew words, but they were given a different meaning from the original; on the other hand, many German words have no equivalents in Yiddish, but were for some reason not admitted into the Yiddish vocabulary, or were subsequently rejected as "superfluous Germanism" (as were also some Hebraisms), for which other, more expressive terms were employed.

During the 12th- and 13th-century migrations of the Jews from western Germany across central Europe to Poland, Russia, and the Baltic countries, Yiddish acquired and adapted in the same or a similar way many Slavonic elements. These, in turn, greatly influenced the syntax and structure of the written language as we know it today, although the German-originating vocabulary remained the dominant feature. Western Yiddish in Holland, northern Italy, and central Europe was of course unaffected by this later process. Being more exposed to environmental influences, it proved much less enduring than eastern European Yiddish. (Relics of western Yiddish were to be found quite recently in parts of Hungary and Slovakia.)

Yiddish, although written uniformly, is spoken differently in specific areas (Lithuania, southern Russia, Poland, and so on). One explanation for this is that the original German dialect spoken in the northern and southern regions of the Rhineland showed a similar differentiation. Accordingly, the Jews who came from the northern region and settled in the Baltic countries, and those who came from the southern region and settled in Poland and Russia, reflected these differences in pronunciation in addition to acquiring some local idioms in their new environment. Thus geography and political frontiers had something to do with the different developments of Yiddish in different areas. But because Yiddish was written in Hebrew script without vowels (before modern spelling was introduced), the different pronunciations did not affect the written language.

The history and development of Yiddish reflect 1000 years of Jewish migration, first from the west to the east, and then back again from the east across Europe to the American continent, to South Africa (mainly from Lithuania), and to Australia (mainly from Poland). At one time it was the *lingua franca* among Jews throughout the world. Before the outbreak of World War II various estimates gave the number of Jews able to speak, or at least to understand, Yiddish as about 13 million (out of the world's Jewish population at the time of about 16 million). Today the number may be no more than perhaps 4 to 5 million, or even less.

Several factors favoured the growth and unique development of Yiddish into the most enduring and most important language of the Jews, except Hebrew, right up to modern times. In the first place, early Jewish settlers in Germany continued for a long time to lead a separate existence, different from that of non-Jewish Germans by virtue of their religion and way of life. Moreover, throughout the Middle Ages they were confined to ghettos, which kept them apart from the majority population and reduced their social contacts with the latter to trading of a limited character. This apartheid continued in eastern Europe until the downfall of the Tsarist regime in 1917. Even where legal restrictions of residence did not apply directly, or were gradually removed, the Jews tended to concentrate in specific urban districts, for reasons of kinship and self-protection. (In eastern Europe they formed the majority of inhabitants of small towns that became known as *shtetls*.)

Another factor that worked against linguistic and cultural assimilation in the earlier periods in western as well as in eastern Europe was that, at the time the Jews appeared on the scene there, they were surrounded by a largely illiterate and culturally underdeveloped population, while they themselves had an ancient cultural tradition going back to biblical times. Religious practices required of the ordinary Jew that he be able at least to read the Hebrew Bible and Hebrew prayers, and the more educated among them were constantly engaged in the study and interpretation of the sacred texts, which included a considerable body of post-biblical literature, such as the Talmud and its numerous commentaries. In these circumstances cultural assimilation was impractical. In the 18th and 19th century the picture changed drastically, when the enlightment movement spread from the west to the east and finally reached the ghettos and *shtetls* of Russia and Poland.

By the time this happened, several centuries of organic growth had already produced a great body of literature in Yiddish. This literature, drawing on national memories and morals and biblical lore, and still very much alive, received a new impetus from the wave of enlightenment (or *Haskalah*, as it was called in Hebrew). Its preachers and practitioners, who started out with the idea of abolishing separateness and advocated secularism and acculturization, became themselves the forerunners and founders of modern Yiddish literature, against their own original intentions, with startling results. Not only has modern Yiddish literature, at the peak of its achievement, made a great contribution to the European and world literature of the 20th century, but it has also revolutionized Jewish life in eastern Europe, where it originated and whence it spread to other parts of the world, particularly the Americas.

It happened in a curious way. The protagonists of the *Haskalah*, in their effort to spread the new ideas of modernism, addressed themselves at first to educated Jews in the language understood by them, which was Hebrew. But these were a minority among the population—the religious leaders of the community, the holders of communal offices, the well-to-do merchants, and so on. They were not interested in social changes, seeing in the new ideas an inherent danger to their old, accepted way of life. The mass of the population lived in poverty and ignorance, accepting their status in life as God-given and unalterable. They had been brought up on popular stories and folk-tales in Yiddish that circulated in great numbers and were read particularly by the womenfolk. These included compilations of the Bible that were not just translations into Yiddish of the Hebrew texts, but popular presentations interspersed with commentaries and popular legends. There was also a considerable oral tradition of Khassidic tales, attributed to the founder of the Khassidic sect, Israel Baal Shem Tov (often abbreviated as *Besht*—"the Master of the Good Name"), and to his early successors such as Nakhman of Bratzlav ("the Bratzlaver") and Itzhak Levi of Berdichev. There is much to be said about the influence this movement has had as an expression of social tension and of messianic hopes in the eastern European ghettos; here it should be noted that, in order to reach out to the masses, its leaders resorted to the use of the Yiddish language in their writings and their speeches.

This is exactly what the men of the *Haskalah* did. Realizing that the audiences at which they were aiming must be addressed in the only language understood by them, the popularizers of the new ideas began to write in Yiddish. In the process they discovered the language anew, and adapted it to their own requirements. Having themselves acquired a secular education, and influenced by the current literary trends, they employed a Yiddish that included Germanisms, by which they thought to refine the language and to give it greater respectability. Underlying this tendency was, of course, an intention to educate their readers, making them aware of life outside the "Pale of Settlement," and counteracting the influence of the clergy and its rigid orthodoxy. "Those who will read these books, while amused, will at the same time learn something about morals and etiquette and indeed all useful sciences, too," wrote Israel Aksenfeld, one of these writers, the author of some 30 works.

Aksenfeld was one of several writers of the middle of the 19th century who wrote in Yiddish, some of them writing also in Hebrew. Among these were Solomon Ettinger (1801–56), author of the first full-length play in Yiddish (*Serkele*), Avroom Ben Gottlober, a contemporary and friend of Aksenfeld, and Isaac Meir Dick (1814–93), whose literary output was considerable, and who, more than any of his predecessors, developed a personal style, and made use of the rich Yiddish folklore and of Yiddish idiomatic expressions.

But Yiddish literature of this period, although it represented an advance on the prevailing popular religious literature, did not reach beyond its didactic purpose. The first great writer in modern Yiddish literature is Sholem Jacob Abramovitch (1835–1917), known by his pen-name, Mendele Mokher Seforim (Mendele the Bookseller). Like contemporaries of his, and some other Yiddish writers after him, he began writing in Hebrew, but soon changed to Yiddish, in which language he wrote his major works, and he was henceforth to become known as the "grandfather of modern Yiddish literature." Literary historians generally refer to the year 1856, in which his first story in Yiddish appeared in print, as the beginning of modern Yiddish literature. At about the same time, two other writers emerged: Yitzhok Leibush Peretz (1852–1915) and Sholem Aleichem (Sholem Rabinowitch, 1859–1916). Though different in their styles and, in some ways, in their philosophy and outlook on life, these three men comprise the celebrated trio of the Yiddish classics.

Before discussing the work of each of the three it should be noted that the case of Mendele is significant in another respect. Although all three wrote in Hebrew (and Peretz in Polish, too) before turning to Yiddish, Mendele continued writing in both languages, and at a later stage of his long literary career he rewrote his Yiddish works in Hebrew, not because he considered Hebrew to be the more literary or superior of the two languages, but because he attached importance to the revival of the Hebrew language as a medium of modern literary expression. He is, indeed, the pioneer of modern Hebrew prose writing, which, at the time of his death in 1916, was still in its infancy, and developed fully only with the revival of the Hebrew language in what was to become the state of Israel. Thus he is an illustration of the thesis advanced by some linguists that Yiddish embodied the Hebrew literary tradition, which would have vanished otherwise, and that the Hebrew element in the language accounts for the structure of Yiddish speech. Conversely, the Yiddish literary tradition, established over the centuries, exerted a major influence on modern Hebrew and, in the opinion of some literary critics, is increasingly being absorbed by it. If this thesis is correct, it explains some of the peculiarities of Yiddish, and its importance both for national-cultural survival throughout the history of Jewish dispersion and, in modern times, as a contributory factor to the revival of Hebrew culture.

Modern Yiddish Literature

As we have shown, modern Yiddish literature is quite new, although a literature in Yiddish has existed since the 16th century at least, and the Yiddish language itself dates back to the 10th century. (The usual dating is "Initial" Yiddish 1000–1250, Old Yiddish 1250–1500, Middle Yiddish 1500–1750, and Modern Yiddish from 1750 onward). Chronological divisions are not necessarily exact, of course, but we speak of modern Yiddish literature as having begun with Mendele Mokher Seforim on account of his status and achievements, and his new approach to language, which set him apart from his predecessors.

Earlier writers merely told a story, for amusement or enlightenment, or both. Mendele was the first to consider content and language as inseparable. Earlier writers tried to improve the language, but Mendele made the spoken word, the living idiom, his tool. In giving it shape, however, he did not distort it: he listened to the speech of the ordinary people and recreated it on the page, always improving and revising his works when they appeared in new editions. Language, to him, was a living thing, not an artificial creation. It is said that when he was in search of a suitable expression he simply went out into the street, asking any passers-by to tell him how they would say it. It should be remembered that at this time there was no academic institution for the scientific study of the Yiddish language; the first of its kind—YIVO, the Yiddish Vissenshaftlekher Institut—was founded only in 1925, at Vilno, Lithuania, at about the same time as a Yiddish Linguistic Department was established in Kiev, Ukraine, within the Ukrainian Academy of Sciences. (YIVO was later transplanted to the United States, where it still flourishes; but the Yiddish Linguistic Department at Kiev was closed down, together with other Yiddish institutions, following the Stalinist purges in the late 1940s.) In Mendele's day there was not even a unified spelling system for Yiddish. The northern dialect of Yiddish, centred in Lithuania, and the southern dialect, extending from Poland to the Ukraine, differed both in spelling and in pronunciation. Mendele became the first writer in Yiddish with a style of his own that was both personal and indigenous, and he contributed greatly to the development of the unified literary style that marked the beginning of a new era in Yiddish literature.

Although Mendele, too, started out in the spirit of the enlightenment, aiming at educating his readers, he departed from his predecessors by making his immediate environment the source from which he drew his themes and characters, and not, as had been the case with earlier Yiddish writers, copying European models of plot and narrative and transferring them into a Jewish environment. Mendele made the poor and dispossessed the heroes of his stories. Cripples, beggars—the outcasts of society—appear frequently in his novels and narrative tales. In describing their lives and thoughts, their worries and despair, he was concerned with more than arousing pity and sympathy: by attacking the corrupt practices and merciless exploitation by the self-appointed leaders of the community, he showed up the evils of society, as no Jewish writer had done before him. Mendele employs both satire and humour, and with his acute gift for observation he provides realistic, detailed descriptions of the life of his time, so that his works can be studied both as literature and as documentaries of Jewish life in the first half of the 19th century in Tsarist Russia. Kabtsansk, the imaginary town in several of his stories (derived from *kabtsan*, the poor and destitute), stands for all the little *shtetls* of the Russian Pale of Settlement, and the muddy, rickety streets of Glupsk (another of his imaginary towns) stand for the dirt and mud and misery not of a single place but of all the places where poverty and ugliness reign supreme.

Yiddish and Hebrew literary critics have sometimes denigrated Mendele's writings as one-sided and negative, even calling him "anti-Semitic"—a practice often used by apologists when dismissing social criticism that might seem to be against the national interest.

Among Mendele's major works are *Fishke the Lame; The Travels of Binyomin the Third; The Nag;* and *The Tax, or the Gang of the Town's Charity Dispensers. Fishke* and *The Travels* have also been successfully dramatized and presented on the stage.

Sholem Aleichem, the second great Yiddish writer of this period, followed the tradition established by Mendele, but exceeded him as the greatest humorist Yiddish literature has so far produced. He, too, was a great explorer who gave voice to the speech of ordinary, simple people. His concern, too, is with the poor, the suffering, the dispossessed. As distinct from Mendele, he does not sit in judgment; he simply identifies himself with the victims, speaking their language, dreaming their dreams, and sharing their hopes. For him there is nothing so sad that you cannot laugh about it, and there is always the hope that things will get better. "Laughter is healthy, it is what the doctor ordered," goes one of his sayings.

Sholem Aleichem is unique not only in Yiddish but in world literature. He is certainly the most popular of Yiddish writers, and not only of his own time; others followed his style, Yiddish writers of great talent and originality, but he was surpassed by none. His humour and wit are of a kind that is both national and universal, and he seems to confirm the view that the universality of an artist depends on his genuineness and originality as an artist of his own people. In the case of Sholem Aleichem this is the more surprising when we consider that his humour rests entirely on his Jewish characters and types, and to a large extent on the language they use and the way they use it. And although it is true that a full appreciation of his art depends on the knowledge of the time and place to which it relates—and this is necessarily limited in many of his readers— he can be read with pleasure by non-Jewish readers.

Take the character of *Tevye the Milkman*, one of Sholem Aleichem's most famous creations. He is a simple villager who ekes out a living selling milk in the nearby town. He has a large family, and is beset by worries of having to provide dowries for his daughters, one of whom follows her revolutionary lover into Siberian exile, and another runs off with a local gentile. Finally, he is himself driven from his home by a government decree. A moving, though not unusual, story, but the character of Tevye raises it to the level of the universal human condition, reflecting man's struggle with a hostile world. He would like to understand the world but he cannot; instead, he creates another, imaginary world, where he is at home and from which no one can remove him. He is comforted by his faith, unshaken by the grave doubts that he expresses in lengthy monologues, addressing himself to the people around him, to his horse (which he treats as his companion), and to God himself (with whom he is on familiar terms, as if He were a next-door neighbour). He provides his own answers to his many questions, using holy scripture and twisting the text to suit his thoughts. He radiates a humour that is as irresistible as it is deadly serious. This, the most Jewish of Sholem

Aleichem's characters, conquered the world's stage in *Fiddler on the Roof*. The immense success of this musical cannot be explained simply by its value as pure entertainment, but must be seen as a popular response to the warmth and humanity of its chief character.

Other Sholem Aleichem characters are Menachem Mendel, the *luftmensch* (the man who lives on thin air), who faces the world with an indomitable optimism in spite of his constant failures; and Shimele Soroker, the one-day millionaire who is cheated of his fortune because his lottery win turns out to be an unfortunate mistake. Although Sholem Aleichem wrote a great deal, including short stories, novels, and plays, his greatest accomplishment was his perfection of the monologue as an art form. In it he presents life in the raw, extracting from the spoken word the subtlest meanings and finest nuances. The liveliness of his writings emerges most effectively in public readings and performances. Not surprisingly, during his lifetime Sholem Aleichem was much sought after as a reader of his own works to mass audiences.

The third of the great trio of Yiddish classics, Yitzhok Leibush Peretz, is properly regarded as the father of modern Yiddish literature inasmuch as he is looked upon as a source of ideas as well as a major artist. A poet, playwright, and writer of short stories, Peretz also wrote philosophical essays on literature, history, and the task and function of the writer. Yiddish literature, at its best, has always been one of commitment, but of all Yiddish writers, past and present, Peretz has been the most committed. He addressed himself not only to the reading public but also to his fellow writers, to his contemporaries as well as to the writers of the future. He saw the function of the writer as being a spokesman for his people, a mentor, guide, and representative.

Before discussing Peretz's work in some detail, a word or two should be said about Khassidism, a religious reform movement that flourished among eastern European Jews during the 18th century, to which we referred briefly earlier, in pointing out its oral tradition in Yiddish. By the middle of the 19th century the movement had already deteriorated, becoming indistinguishable from rigid orthodoxy. Nevertheless, in the intellectual sphere its leaders were still engaged in their dispute with the so-called *mitnagdim* (the Hebrew word for "opponents"). The *mitnagdim* attacked the Khassidic rabbis, who had assumed the role of popular leaders, accusing them of maintaining and spreading superstitious obscurantism. In this dispute, the *mitnagdim*, stressing the need for study and learning (necessarily confined to the chosen few), acted as conservatives, while the Khassidim, less concerned with either, continued in their rôle as reformers. In the Khassidim's concept of Judaism the ordinary people, ignorant though they might be of the finer points in the sacred texts, were equal partners in the service of God and man, and emotional involvement and practical deeds counted more than social status and depth of knowledge. The conservatives, on the other hand, appeared to defend social privilege and to look down on the mass of the people and their "uncultured" language, Yiddish, the "language of carters and maidservants." To the extent to which Khassidism, as a mass movement, revealed social tensions and threatened to undermine the basis of society, the conservatives acted as the upholders of the law of the land.

Peretz rediscovered the original basic elements in Khassidism and made them the themes of some of his finest creations. In his *Khassidic Tales* he was not out to glorify the myths of the Cabbala or the miraculous works of the Khassidic rabbis. Khassidism, to Peretz, was not the unthinking and unquestioning code of conduct to which its latter-day adherents had reduced it; nor was it the mystical dialogue to which Martin Buber elevated it. He saw in it the poetic expression of a people's longing for joy and happiness, the humble messianic idea of world redemption putting an end to suffering and opening up a new era for all mankind, including the Jewish people.

This idea of universal redemption found its finest artistic expression in the verse play *Di goldene keyt* (The Golden Chain), in which Rabbi Shlomo, who refuses to say the prayer marking the end of the Sabbath Day in order to prolong it, calls out: "Redeemed from horror and pain must be—the world!" While Jews are suffering "death and disease and evil decrees" and "Jewish blood is flowing like water," he looks upon it all as part of a world that is "tottering between death and life." He is not afraid of that world perishing, for on its ruins will rise a new world that is one with its God, one with itself. In such a world "we do not ask favours nor charity—great and proud people—Jews are we."

Whereas Mendele satirized his environment, attacking parochialism and corruption in spirit and body, and Sholem Aleichem brought healing laughter into otherwise unbearable misery, Peretz introduced into the life of his time and generation a new concept of living; rooted in the past, it is also linked with the new ideas in the world of today and tomorrow.

His concern with universal ideas is also reflected in the *Popular Stories* for which he is best known. These are short stories, founded not so much on subtleties of individual characters as on general themes with a social

397

content. One of the best-known is "Bontche Shweig" (Bontche the Silent). It tells of an unknown, silently suffering carrier of heavy loads, with no friends, no sympathy, and no home of his own in his earthly life. When, in heaven, his life story is being retold, he listens to it as if it were that of a third person. He recognizes himself in every detail, but he still does not think that it is himself the heavenly advocate is talking about: it *could* be him, but it could equally be someone else. When, in the end, as a reward for his earthly suffering he is offered all the riches on earth— "it's all yours"—his choice is a fresh roll with butter every morning.

Peretz's influence on his own generation of Jews far exceeded that of any other public figure of his time. His home in Warsaw became the Mecca of every young aspiring writer, and the great names in Yiddish literature of a later generation—such as Sholem Asch, David Bergelson, David Pinski, and many others—acknowledged their debt to him as the man who inspired and guided them. His philosophy (by no means a clearly defined system) may be termed "Jewish secularism," with equal stress on its national (Jewish) and universal (secular) aspects. "Peretzism," as an idea, won adherents and admirers among Jewish intellectuals far beyond literary circles. It was sufficiently broad and all-embracing to appeal to the emerging Jewish labour movement—both the anti-Zionist *Bund* and the socialist *Poale Zion*—as well as to various Zionist groups (Peretz found himself imprisoned for a time as a socialist agitator), and left its mark on Jewish visual art, the theatre, the press, and cultural life in general. It is said that when Peretz died, the whole Jewish population of Warsaw followed his hearse.

Modern Yiddish literature was born in the process of secularization of Jewish life and of the gradual emancipation of Jews in the eastern European ghettos that went hand in hand with it. In turn, that literature played an important part in the process, as can be seen in the impact the three Yiddish authors discussed here had on the reading public. There were of course other writers of lesser significance who wrote at the same time. There existed a widespread Yiddish literary press, including literary annuals that published the works of young, aspiring writers. Sholem Aleichem and Peretz themselves founded and edited such periodicals and occasional literary collections. Generally the Yiddish press made a decisive contribution to the dissemination of literature through regular literary supplements, and most of the works of contemporary Yiddish writers—not only short stories, but instalment novels— appeared in the press before they were published in book form.

By 1917, the year of Mendele's death, there had already developed a new centre of Yiddish literature on the other side of the Atlantic, following the mass emigration of Jews from eastern Europe to the United States, which began in the 1880s and continued on an increasing scale right up to the beginning of World War I. All the new writers came from eastern Europe, and most of them had begun their literary careers while still in their native Poland or Russia.

The year 1917 also marked the beginning of a new era in Yiddish writing in eastern Europe itself; it was the year of the Russian Revolution, which split the old Russian Empire, leaving roughly equal numbers of Jews on both sides of the new frontiers, with the Yiddish literary centres of Kiev and Odessa remaining in the Soviet orbit, and those of Warsaw and Vilna, in the newly formed independent states of Poland and Lithuania respectively, falling outside it. From now on there existed three major centres of Yiddish literature: Poland and Lithuania, with their fringe outlets in Romania and Austria; the Soviet Union; and the United States. In time, each of these centres, although seeing itself as continuing a common literary tradition, developed independently, and reflected in various ways the influences and trends of their different environments. The inter-war years provided other shifts. For a time a number of important Yiddish writers lived and published in Berlin; others settled in Paris. A considerable Jewish emigration to South Africa led to the establishment of a Yiddish press and publishing house there. During the 1930s a similar development took place in Australia. Throughout that period these centres were linked by constant exchanges, and influenced each other. Even the Soviet-Yiddish centres, which flourished and attained their peak of achievement in the 1930s in spite of enforced or self-imposed isolation, were not completely cut off from the rest of the world: each new book and each new author emerging there was widely read and discussed in the Yiddish literary press throughout the world.

This period of Yiddish literature may be said to extend to the eve of World War II. It produced a steadily growing number of writers in every genre in the three major centres; the number of Yiddish readers increased, too, although it should be added that, with the advance of general education, Yiddish literature now had to compete with the literatures of the majority cultures (Polish, Russian, English) if it was to keep its younger readers. During this period, too, a vast amount of great European literature was translated into Yiddish and made accessible to the culture-hungry masses of Jewish workers and artisans. It was the time when a Jewish proletariat came into being, with the beginning of industrialization in Poland, and after the Russian Revolution of 1917 the small-town

Jewish traders, having lost their traditional occupations, were increasingly absorbed by the industrial transformation of the country. On the other side of the Atlantic, new Jewish immigrants—Yiddish-speaking, poor, and looking for jobs—swelled the ranks of the sweat-shop industries. Jewish life was undergoing a profound transformation.

Yiddish literature of this period faithfully reflects the transition from the *shtetl* to the big city, and the transformation in the outlook and aspirations of the masses that resulted. Already Sholem Aleichem had depicted the changing scene; Menachem Mendel, in letters to his wife at home, tells her about his dealings at the stock exchange, and his other adventures in fictional Yehupetz. Peretz looked at the life of Jewish weavers in the developing textile workshops and factories. I. M. Wajsenberg (1881–1937), the first writer to emerge from such poverty himself, and considered by contemporary critics to have great talent, wrote of the life of the shoemakers, tailors, carpenters, and hatters among whom he had grown up, seeing and experiencing exploitation and the first signs of rebellion against it. Poverty and suffering, the gulf between the generations, and the political struggles all became dominant features in Yiddish literature of the time. Naturally, it found its most responsive audiences in the poorer sections of the population. In general the Yiddishist movement and Yiddish cultural tradition were linked with, and maintained by, the organized Jewish labour movement, which placed opportunity for education on a par with improving material conditions. It was not unusual for political meetings to open or close with readings from the newest works of Yiddish writers, or for public readings and lectures to assume the character of political manifestations.

It is neither possible nor desirable in this general survey to discuss all the major writers of this period. The outstanding among them are Sholem Asch (1880–1957), David Bergelson (1884–1952), Der Nister (Pinhas Kahanowicz, 1884–1950), Abraham Reizen (1875–1953), David Pinski (1872–1960), Josef Opatoshu (1887–1954), Leon Kobrin (1872–1946), and Zalman Libin (1872–1955). Of these writers the best-known outside his native Poland is Sholem Asch. His works have been translated into most European languages, with the result that they have had a much wider circulation among non-Jewish readers than among the Yiddish reading public. In some cases the translations were made from the manuscript and appeared in print before the original Yiddish editions.

He wrote short stories, plays, and novels set in the *shtetls* and the great cities. (*Three Cities* [1933], a three-novel cycle, is about the Russian Revolution and its effects on life in Warsaw, Moscow, and St Petersburg.)

He follows his characters across countries and continents, showing them in their new surroundings, in their struggles to adjust and make new roots. He was already an established writer when he emigrated to New York, where he lived for many years, although he frequently visited Europe. He finally settled in London, where he spent the last years of his life.

Early in his literary career he became the subject of a heated controversy when his play *God of Vengeance* (1907) was presented on the stage. Its chief character is the owner of a brothel, a pious Jew who is anxious for his daughter to retain her chastity; he arranges for a Torah scroll to be placed in her room, as a kind of guardian angel to watch over her. When she nevertheless becomes a victim of seduction, her father, in his rage, desecrates the holy scroll in public. Because of the unusual theme and its dramatic force, the play was taken up by the European theatre and earned fame and success for its author. The ensuing controversy centred on whether it was permissible to present on stage what appeared to many an unlikely and purely fictional character. In this case critics and attackers were concerned not with literary merit but with morals, and with the effect the play might have on Jewish and non-Jewish audiences. The controversy merely added to Asch's popularity. He soon branched out into wider fields, writing a series of novels with historical and contemporary settings. In his later period, however, Asch was once again exposed to abuse and personal attack when he embarked on his so-called Christological novels—*The Nazarene* (1929), *Mary* (1949), and *The Apostle* (1943)—dealing with the life of Jesus and his time. He was even accused (wrongly) of missionary ideas and of undergoing conversion. On the other hand, he undoubtedly enhanced his reputation with this series of novels, which in a way represented his answer to Hitler's persecution of the Jews. By reminding Christians of the Jewish association with Christianity, he hoped to awaken their conscience in the face of Nazi crimes.

Equal in status to Asch, and in some respects superior to him both technically and artistically, are Bergelson and Opatoshu. The former is considered by some critics to be the best prose writer in Yiddish of his generation. What distinguishes him from Asch is his greater understanding of the motivations of his characters as well as of the social forces at work in shaping them. Bergelson witnessed the transformation of Jewish life in the last stages of the Tsarist regime in Russia, the process of economic displacement of the Jews after the Bolshevik Revolution, and their gradual integration into the new economy. In his novels he represents the various stages as they affected the lives of individuals and of whole families. He lived to witness the destruction of Jewish communal life and the murder of his people during the German invasion of Russia in World War II, and he wrote several moving stories during this period. Also at this time he wrote two plays, one of which, *Prince Reubeni* (1946), with a historical setting, was published in the Soviet Union in a cut version but not performed there. A Hebrew version was staged by Habimah in Tel Aviv, and in the original Yiddish it was performed in America and in Romania. Bergelson's collected works appeared in several volumes, both in the Soviet Union and abroad (Berlin 1922–3, 6 vols.; Vilna 1928–30, 8 vols.; Buenos Aires 1961–8, 10 vols.). His major works include the triology *Baym Dniepr* (By the River Dnieper) and *Nokh alemen* (1913; After Everything). Very few of his works appeared in translation, except in Hebrew, although several of his short stories were published in English translations in American periodicals.

Bergelson shared the fate of other leading Soviet-Yiddish writers who were arrested in 1949 and, after spending some time in forced-labour camps, were tried on false charges and executed. His, and the others', rehabilitation after Stalin's death cannot remove the stains that remain of the black years of Stalinist terror, and emphasizes the immense and tragic losses that Yiddish literature has suffered.

Another of these victims was Der Nister, the pen-name of Pinhas Kahanowicz. He represents a different trend in modern Yiddish literature. In a way he continued the tradition of the Khassidic folk-tales, using the cabbalistic imagery with its mystery and symbolism rather than the more earth-bound elements in Khassidism. The very name he assumed as a writer (*der Nister* means "the hidden one") indicates the direction he intended to follow. Together with a number of other writers (Bergelson, Hofsteyn, Halkin, Markish, Kvitko) he left the Soviet Union in the 1920s, only to return in the early 1930s, as did the others, convinced that here was the most promising centre for the development of a Jewish national culture in the Yiddish language. Yiddish having been officially recognized as the national language of the Russian Jews, the government at the time appeared to do everything to encourage Yiddish publishing, the Yiddish theatre, a widespread net of Yiddish schools, and other educational institutions. It is understandable that these writers should have been attracted by the promise of an almost messianic age for the much-abused and neglected Yiddish culture to which, they felt, they had to make their own contribution. But it soon became clear that, whatever may have been in the minds of the theoreticians, in practice accepted principles were sacrified to expediency, and the principles themselves modified to fit the frequent changes in the party line. Thus, not surprisingly, the early works of Der Nister were hotly debated and criticized in the Soviet-Yiddish literary press, notwithstanding this author's individual style and his search for a synthesis between the old and the new, between tradition and revolution, in which other writers were also engaged. There is tragic irony in the fact that both the critics and their targets shared the same fate, in the end. Like Bergelson, Der Nister wrote a trilogy, *The Family Mashber*, of which only the first part was published in the Soviet Union; the second part found its way abroad and appeared in New York in 1948; of the third part, only fragments survive.

Opatoshu was the first major Yiddish writer to emerge in the United States, where he arrived in 1907 from Poland, as a young man of 20. He had participated in the Russian Revolution of 1905, after which he went to France and studied engineering. He continued his studies at evening classes in New York, attaining a degree in civil engineering in 1914. His multilingualism and general education are reflected in his short stories and novels, which embrace both Europe and America, setting against it Jewish life of a particular period in history. His major work is the historical novel *In Polish Woods* (1921), with its sequel *1863*, which presents the Polish uprising against Tsarist rule, the part Jews played in it, and the effect it had on Polish-Jewish relations then and later. Continuing his series of historical novels, he wrote *A Day in Regensburg* (1933), dealing with Jewish life in mediaeval Germany, and *Rabbi Akiba* (1948) and *Bar Kochba* (1955), depicting the Jewish uprising against Rome.

Of the other writers mentioned, Abraham Reizen wrote mainly poetry (which became very popular) and hundreds of short stories, whereas Pinski, Kobrin, and Libin wrote mainly for the stage, the last two being among the pioneers of Yiddish literature in the United States. Pinski, closely associated with the Jewish labour movement, spent the last years of his life in Israel.

Drama and Poetry

The inter-war years saw a steady growth of Yiddish literature in every field, with the three major centres of Yiddish developing independently and competing for hegemony. Romania and Lithuania (Vilna) made significant contributions, particularly in the fields of poetry and drama, producing a number of outstandingly original talents.

The Yiddish theatre, as a permanent institution, originated in Romania.

It came into being in Jassy, where in 1876 Abraham Goldfaden (1840–1908) presented his first theatrical troupe at a local tavern. Goldfaden began his literary career as a writer of popular poetry and as an editor of various short-lived journals, before turning his attention to the theatre, combining the roles of librettist, composer, producer, and manager. With his troupe he toured the major cities of Romania and Russia, and later moved to the United States. Long after Yiddish art theatres were functioning in all these countries, the Goldfaden repertoire of light operettas and comic operas based on historical themes was continuously performed in revised versions and expensive new productions, but essentially in the spirit of the original, which is an indication of the impact they had on both audiences and producers.

Yiddish verbal and musical entertainment has long traditions outside the theatre. The professional preacher, or *maggid*, wandering from town to town, partly fulfilled this role, and there were often competing preachers who clamoured for attention at synagogue gatherings. Then there was the wedding jester, or *badchen*, who improvised in words and music at the ceremony itself and at the festive meal following it. And finally, and nearest to theatrical performances, there were the so-called *Purim-shpieler*, who enacted biblical episodes (such as the story of Esther, or the "sacrifice" of Isaac) in masks and costumes during the festival of Purim. These seasonal presentations were not performed on a stage; the players went from door to door, enacting their scenes in family circles. There was no theatrical tradition as such before Goldfaden appeared on the scene.

Like Yiddish literature in general, Yiddish drama was regarded as educational; it exerted a considerable influence on its audiences, and most of the important Yiddish authors, beginning with Peretz and Sholem Aleichem, also wrote for the stage. By the 1920s, Yiddish art theatres had already reached a standard comparable in every respect with the national theatres in their countries of adoption.

The foremost Yiddish theatre at the time was the Moscow State Jewish Theatre under the direction of Solomon Mikhoels, who was an outstanding actor and producer. It was established during the early 1920s and continued until the end of 1948, when it was forced to close, together with all other Yiddish cultural institutions (Mikhoels himself having been killed by agents of the Soviet secret service at the beginning of 1947). Several other Yiddish national theatres had flourished in various Soviet regions, including Kiev, Odessa, and Birobidjan, each under its own artistic direction.

Established earlier and continuing longer was the Warsaw Yiddish Art Theatre under Esther Rahel Kaminska; her daughter, Ida Kaminska, has carried on the tradition with great success. Another outstanding theatre was the Vilna Troupe; after a few years of dazzling international success, however, the troupe split up, its leading members either joining other theatrical groups or establishing groups on their own. In the United States, Maurice Schwartz founded his successful Yiddish Art Theatre, with which he toured Europe. For a time, London had its Yiddish People's Theatre, as had Paris and Vienna. A flourishing Yiddish theatre is functioning to this day in Romania.

As mentioned earlier, many leading Yiddish writers were attracted by the theatre; so, too, were leading painters (notably Marc Chagall) and composers. Others wrote exclusively for the stage. Among these were Peretz Hirshbein, David Pinski (referred to earlier), Jacob Gordin (who wrote more than 60 plays), and B. Gordin (who is also the author of the first history of the Yiddish theatre).

The Yiddish theatre did not confine itself to original plays in Yiddish, but used plays from the world repertoire, either in adaptations (one of Gordin's plays, for example, is entitled *The Jewish King Lear*) or in straight translation (Ibsen, Gorki, Rolland, and so on). Moreover, works by earlier Yiddish writers, as well as those by contemporary writers, have been dramatized for the stage (including *Three Cities* and *Salvation* by Asch, *Yashe Kalb* by I. J. Singer, and many others). In style and method of production the Yiddish theatre was greatly influenced by the Russian theatre, and in turn it influenced the American theatre. To the few great Yiddish plays originally written for the stage belong Peretz's *Di goldene keyt* (referred to earlier) and *The Night in the old Market Place* (both only rarely performed), Pinski's *The Treasure*, and An-ski's *The Dybbuk* (1916). The last-named acquired a significance beyond its purely literary merits because of its spectacular presentation by the Vilna Troupe in the original Yiddish in 1920, and by the Moscow Habimah Theatre in a Hebrew version in the same year. It has since been performed many times in many languages all over the world. One reason for its popularity is that it lends itself to various interpretations. On one level it is purely a mystery play, exotic and tense; on another its richness in folklore elements has a unique charm; and on yet another it reveals the world of Khassidism with all its social and psychological undertones. It is not without interest that the Moscow production was directed by the Armenian Vachtangoff, an inspired pupil of Stanislavsky.

Modern Yiddish poetry properly dates from the beginning of this century. To be sure, Peretz started his literary career in Yiddish with the balladic poem *Monish* in 1888 (before that, he wrote in Hebrew and Polish), and some of his plays were written in verse, but he did not establish a style of his own as a poet. He himself admitted being influenced by Heine (as were other Yiddish poets) in his verses for children, which were of a sentimental and didactic character.

Earlier Yiddish poetry was formal, rhetorical, and (at its best) motivated by social and national sentiments. At the same time it was imitative of the prevailing tendencies in Russian and German poetry. This applies in particular to the four pioneers of proletarian poetry in Yiddish: Morris Rosenfeld (1862–1923), David Edelshtat (1866–92), Josef Bovshover (1872–1915), and Morris Wintshevsky (1856–1932). Their lyrics are concerned with the plight of the working-man in American sweat-shops, with calls for revolutionary action, and with outcries against poverty and injustice. The most important of the four is Morris Rosenfeld, who became widely known through translations into English and German, and whose poetry is strongest in imagery.

The breakthrough came in 1907, when, in a revolt against the literary establishment (which, by then, was already flourishing) and in search of individual expression, there emerged in the United States a group of Yiddish poets calling itself *Di Younge* (The Young Ones). In their journal *Literatur und lebn* (Literature and Life) they rejected old conventions of style and subject-matter, proceeding from the assumption that the poet is writing for himself in the first place, and for the reader only incidentally. ("As to why we publish—well, that is a contradiction, neither the first nor the last," to quote one of their spokesmen.) To this group belonged Halper Leiwick, M. L. Halpern, I. J. Schwartz, A. Glanz-Leyeles, Menachem Boraisha, Zishe Landau, Mani Leib, and several others. They were by no means a united group; on the contrary, following their individualistic tendencies, some of them broke away very soon. Out of this group developed (a few years later) another group, calling itself *In-zikh-istn* (Introspectives), also with a literary journal of its own, led by the aforementioned Glanz-Leyeles, and joined by the poet and essayist Jacob Glatshteyn. This new group no longer subscribed to the extreme nihilism fostered by *Di Younge*, but insisted on poetry of a personal and reflective nature. The whole trend was unmistakably influenced by similar trends in European poetry of the time; besides breaking new ground in the handling of the Yiddish language, it was also a reaction against the mechanization of American life.

An older poet, Yehoash Solomon Blumgarten, or Yehoash for short

(1871–1927)—who by his earlier achievements inspired *Di Younge* and encouraged them in their endeavours—set himself the immsense task of rendering the Hebrew Bible into poetic Yiddish. His *Collected Poems*, published in 1907, established him as an original poet, reflective and intellectual rather than lyrical. He also pioneered the first Yiddish translations of American poetry by his translation of Longfellow's *Hiawatha*. In spite of ill-health, which caused his early death, he accomplished his life's ambition, but only parts of his translation of the Bible were published during his lifetime. (The full translation, in several volumes, appeared years later.)

Similar developments, but with more far-reaching results, occurred in Europe after World War I, at a time when the *Di Younge* movement in America had come to an end. Disillusioned and embittered by the course and outcome of the war, three Yiddish poets in Poland began publishing a literary journal that bore the eccentric name *Khalastrie* (The Gang). The three were Uri Zvi Greenberg, Moishe Broderson, and Melech Ravich. They were joined for a time by Peretz Markish, after he had left the Soviet Union and before he returned there to become one of the leading Soviet-Yiddish poets and novelists of his generation. Different in temperament and outlook though they were, they were nevertheless united in their rebellion against accepted forms and values. Disregarding traditional imagery, they experimented with the language itself in the manner of the Expressionism prevalent in German and Russian poetry of the post-war period. In their outbursts against violence they often used language bordering on blasphemy. A good example of this trend is Greenberg's long poem *Mephisto*, which appeared in a large album format and with a cover of cubist design. (Innovations in typography and design were another departure reflecting the new trend, in which the artists Lissitzky and Chagall played an important part.)

The *Khalastrie* group left its mark long after it had ceased to be a distinct literary movement. Greenberg, emigrating to Palestine, reverted to Hebrew poetry, and became one of the leading Hebrew poets of his generation, although he occupied a somewhat isolated position because of his extreme nationalism and right-wing political views. Ravich, after years of travelling and spending some time in South Africa and Australia, finally settled in America, where his pantheistic-Spinozist outlook brought him closest to the introspective group of Yiddish poets. Only Broderson remained in Poland, where he established his own small-stage satirical theatre, in which he continued experimenting with language and new styles.

Yiddish poetry found particularly fertile soil in neighbouring Romania, within the extended frontiers resulting from the political changes after World War I. Bucovina, formerly a province of Austria, and Bessarabia, both now incorporated into Romania, had large and culturally active Jewish communities. Here Jacob Sternberg and Eliezer Steinbarg were outstanding as Yiddish poets, the former being also a dramatist and theatrical producer, and the latter reviving the art of poetic fables, in which he excelled in highly sophisticated inventiveness. Here, too, one of the finest Yiddish poets of the century, Itzik Manger (1901–69), began his literary career.

In many respects Manger's poetry represents a unique blend of Europeanism with a deep-rooted Yiddish folk tradition that forms an essential element in his work. In his tuneful, easy-flowing verse he combines a refined Heine-like lyricism with biblical simplicity and an ever-present humour, sometimes sad or tragic, but more often of a boisterous kind. For instance, in *Khumash-lieder* (1936) he recreates biblical characters in a modern idiom, placing the familiar figures in an unfamiliar yet homely setting, as in "Mother Sarah's Lullaby to Father Isaac." He does the same, with even greater effect, in his *Megillah-lieder* by adding new characters and a new plot. (Recently, this has been set to music and presented as a musical, which rivals *Fiddler on the Roof* in popularity.) In his ballads he occasionally employs an Old Yiddish style reminiscent of the *Bible for Women*. In his *Hotsmach-spiel* (1947) he transforms the familiar types of the Goldfaden operettas into grotesque mystery plays of great poetic charm. Manger spent the war years in London, as a refugee; later he went to the United States, and finally settled in Israel, where he has become very popular even with the young generation who do not know Yiddish.

In quantity, no less than in quality, Yiddish poetry flourished in the Soviet Union, reaching its climax in the mid-1930s, when a whole group of Yiddish writers and intellectuals became victims of the first round of Stalin's purges. Although Yiddish publishing continued for a time, political pressure intensified and led to a further decline in output. During World War II, with the entry of the Soviet Union into the war, Yiddish literature received a new lease of life, and was even permitted to stress the unity of Jewish people throughout the world. Unfortunately, it proved to be only a passing phase. During the 30 years from 1917 to 1948, the Soviet Union was undoubtedly the largest and most prolific centre of Yiddish writing in the world. A study of Yiddish publications in the Soviet Union during that period, published under the auspices of the Israel Historical Society (Jerusalem 1961), lists some 3500 books in the category of *belles-lettres* alone; although the list (which the editors say is not complete) includes re-issues of the Yiddish classics and works by a number of non-Russian Yiddish authors, it excludes translations into Yiddish from Russian and other European languages, as well as technical books and textbooks for schools. This extraordinarily large output came to an abrupt end in November 1948.

Like any other national literature in the Soviet Union, and like Russian literature itself, Soviet-Yiddish literature in all its forms faithfully reflected the changing trends dictated by the cultural policies of the Soviet government, from the proletarian-revolutionary phase to the "socialist realism" of the Stalin era, with the intervening period of Soviet patriotism during World War II. The dogmatic application of the principle "national in form and socialist in content" to Yiddish literature meant, in practice, abandoning any attempt at presenting artistically the inner world of the Jew (which is bound up with historical associations and his often isolated position in society), and ignored the fact that content and form are closely linked in any field of art. In this context, the individuality and originality of a writer made him an easy target for the professional critics who saw themselves as guardians of the party line. Nevertheless, within the official conformity imposed from above, the stronger the individuality of the writer the more it asserted itself against all pressures.

It is impossible, within this brief survey, to single out individual writers. An anthology entitled *A shpigel oif a shteyn* (As a Mirror on a Stone)—a title taken from a line in a poem by Markish—published in Tel Aviv in 1964, contains a representative selection of prose and verse by 12 Soviet-Yiddish writers, including Bergelson, Der Nister, and Peretz Markish. The others are David Hofshteyn (1889–1952), Shmuel Persoff (1890–1952), Aron Kushniroff (1890–1949), Leib Kvitko (1890–1952), Moishe Kulbak (1896–1940), Shmuel Halkin (1897–1960), Izi Charik (1898–1937), Itzik Feffer (1900–52), and Selig Akselrod (1904–41). Of these only three died a natural death. Most of the 12 are poets, which is an indication of the important position poetry occupies in the Soviet Union in general. Some of the poets, such as Kulbak and Markish, also wrote novels and plays, and the latter, in particular, was a writer of great versatility. His long poem of 660 pages, *Milkhome* (War), published in 1948, is a forceful narrative of suffering and heroism during World War II. His last long novel, *Trot fun doires* (March of Generations), set in Nazi-occupied Poland and culminating in the Warsaw ghetto uprising, was published posthumously in 1963.

In spite of the political barriers, Soviet-Yiddish literature exerted a considerable influence on Yiddish writing outside the Soviet Union, particularly on neighbouring Poland and Lithuania. This accounts for the left-wing tendencies in a great deal of Yiddish literature in these countries during the 1930s, which were also reflected in the controversies and polemics in literary journals of the time. In Poland a new generation of poets and novelists followed more or less in the footsteps of the Yiddish post-classicists mentioned earlier, notably Isaac Bashevis Singer, his older brother I. J. Singer, Alter Katzisno, Israel Stern, and Yehoshua Perle.

A new literary movement started in Lithuania, known as "Young Vilna," and led by the poets Abraham Sutzkever, Chaim Grade, Leizer Wolf, Elchonon Wogler, and a few others. Their influence was rather more sustained than that of the *Khalastrie* group of the 1920s. Of the four poets named, Sutzkever became a central figure in Yiddish writing during the post-war years after he settled in Israel, where since 1949 he has edited the literary quarterly *Di goldene keyt* (The Golden Chain), to which Yiddish writers of many countries contribute regularly. Of the others, Grade, now in New York, and Wogler, in Paris, continue to write poetry of merit.

Yiddish Literature in Perspective

The decline in the use of the Yiddish language, and the reduction in the number of Yiddish readers, had begun before World War II, but the war itself delivered the hardest blow yet to Yiddish literature. Not only were many Yiddish writers killed, but more than half the six million Jews killed by the Nazis were Yiddish speakers. Moreover, the great eastern European centres of Yiddish have become practically extinct. An attempted revival in Poland, which looked promising for a time, failed in the end: the small remnant of what was once the largest Jewish community in Europe is being driven out of the country by the anti-Jewish policies of the government, following the Arab-Israeli war of June 1967. In the Soviet Union, where there are still some three million Jews (of whom about half a million declared Yiddish as their mother tongue) and where a considerable number of Yiddish writers are still at work, there are no signs of a real revival, because Yiddish schools are not permitted and the general tendency is toward growing Russification. The literary monthly *Sovietish Heymland* continues to publish the work of the hundred or so surviving Yiddish writers, but only a handful of Yiddish books are published every year.

The war also brought about a further shift in the centres of Yiddish writing, with South America and Israel developing as two new centres; but the prospect of these holding out against the pressures of assimilation is poor, to say the least. On the other hand, we have the paradoxical situation that the number of Yiddish writers today is greater than at the time, say, when the Yiddish classics were being written. The scientific study of Yiddish has also progressed beyond all expectations: several American universities maintain chairs of Yiddish studies, and the Hebrew University in Jerusalem has a Yiddish Department that is engaged in teaching and research. A lively Yiddish press still flourishes in several countries, and book publishing is continuing, though on a diminishing scale.

We have, then, a body of writing that has accumulated over the last 150 years or so (taking into account only modern Yiddish literature), some of it of the highest standard, and an integral part of European literature of the 19th and 20th centuries. This literature, influenced as it was by the literary trends of the time, has in turn influenced Jewish writing in other languages. As far as Yiddish literature embodies and reflects a cultural tradition of its own, it is important beyond its linguistic aspect. Some of its traditions can certainly be seen in contemporary American Jewish novels. Certain stylistic elements of Yiddish have found their way into modern Hebrew literature, and are being absorbed by it. In this context the work of translation, important for an appreciation of minority literatures in general, assumes an even greater significance in the case of Yiddish literature, which is in danger of being overlooked and finally forgotten.

Translations from the Yiddish present certain difficulties that other minority literatures do not, at any rate to the same extent. Apart from the mere technique of finding suitable equivalents in diction and terminology, there is the additional problem of conveying emotive associations bound up with certain expressions and situations that serve in the original as a kind of shorthand, but that in translation require further explanation. These difficulties can be overcome, as is proved by the high quality of some recent translations.

On account of both its wealth and variety and its tragic fate, Yiddish literature deserves to be studied, not as some literature of antiquity, but as one of significant contemporaneity. Moreover, no student of the history of the Nazi holocaust can ignore the large body of so-called *khurban* (holocaust) literature, which was written mostly in Yiddish by survivors or by writers who perished but whose work survived—a testimony to their faith and courage. Outstanding among the latter is the work of

Yitzhak Katzenelson, who died in Auschwitz, and whose long poem *Des lid fun oisgehargerten yiddishen folk* (The Song of the Murdered Jewish People), written in the style of the biblical Book of Lamentations, will remain one of the most moving documents of all time, an outcry and accusation against inhumanity.

Conclusion

Modern Yiddish literature shares with other minority literatures some of their aspirations—among others, to attain the standard and standing of the "host" culture, by which it is influenced in many ways.

In the case of the best Yiddish writers of the 19th and 20th centuries, we note their pronounced commitment as writers and spokesmen of their people. They did not have a ready-made public, but had to create it from among the ordinary people, the heroes of their stories. It was this sense of mutual recognition that created a close link between writers and readers, the latter seeing themselves, for the first time, as if in a mirror: it was of themselves, their lives, their needs and worries, their hopes and dreams, that their writers told them, not of remote figures in history or of people in high places. Even where historical subjects were treated, based on familiar traditional tales, the characters were presented as ordinary human beings: their sufferings and struggles, their oppression and persecution, were of the kind that contemporary readers experienced in everyday life.

The best and most effective medium of this kind of popular literature is the short story, and the Yiddish classics are mostly of this genre. The accent here is not so much on the individual psychology of the hero as on the type he personifies, and the art rests less on the content of the story than on the manner of its telling. This is why it was common practice for Yiddish writers to read their stories in public. These public recitals became virtual festivals in big and small towns, and attracted huge audiences (there are vivid accounts of public recitals by Sholem Aleichem and Peretz).

Drawing from the living source of daily speech, modern Yiddish literature made full use of the great expressiveness of the language. In contrast with other European literatures—in which literary activity and literary appreciation were for centuries confined to an educated élite and remained outside the experience of the broad mass of the uneducated ordinary people—Yiddish literature was directed toward the mass reader from its beginning. True, most of the early writers had come from the wealthier classes, and had received a good Jewish and general education; but it was the poorer and less-articulate section of the population to whom they appealed and who, in their turn, became the real torch-bearers of Yiddish culture. The class gap that existed in other European literatures of an earlier period, and that narrowed only with the advent of general, compulsory education, contrasts strongly with the homogeneity of the audience for Yiddish literature. That literature advanced hand in hand with the social awakening of the lower classes, which it greatly influenced and was in turn nourished by; whence comes its generally progressive character.

Although mainly secular in content and character, Yiddish literature has nevertheless preserved something of the spiritual Hebrew tradition of Jewish writing. This is why one often finds among older Yiddish readers the kind of reverence for the printed word that is evident among readers of Hebrew, irrespective of subject-matter and literary merit. This attitude helps to explain the existence of a great deal of writing by many people of little talent; but there is another side to it. Thanks to this general urge to chronicle events, we know so much more than we should otherwise of what happened to Jews at various periods of history, including the Nazi holocaust. There is a remarkable story by David Bergelson, called "The Witness," about an elderly Jew returning from a German death camp and relating his experiences to a young woman, who writes it all down in Russian. From time to time she stops to re-read a passage in order to make sure that she is translating correctly. The Jew eventually grows impatient and shouts: "How should I know? What we have suffered, we suffered in Yiddish!"

Bibliography

History: in Yiddish or Hebrew

s. l. CITRON, *History of the Yiddish Press* (Vilna 1923).

Lexicon of Contemporary Yiddish Literature (New York 1956–), a multi-volume series of which several volumes have already been published.

BER MARK, *Yiddish Writers Who Perished in the Ghettos and Camps* (Warsaw 1954).

ZALMAN REIZEN, *Lexicon of Yiddish Literature, Press, and Philology*, 4 vols. (Warsaw 1926–30).

H. SHMERUK, "Yiddish Literature," *Hebrew Encyclopaedia* (Jerusalem 1968), Vol. 15, Cols. 794–810.

H. SHMERUK (ed.), *Yiddish Publishing in the Soviet Union, 1917–1960* (Jerusalem 1961), contains introductions in Hebrew, Yiddish, and English.

History: in English

H. BLANC, "Some Yiddish Influences in Israeli Hebrew," *The Field of Yiddish*, Vol. II (New York 1965).

J. JOFEN, *A Linguistic Atlas of Eastern European Yiddish* (New York 1964).

S. LIPTZIN, *The Flowering of Yiddish Literature* (New York 1963).

A. A. ROBACK, *Contemporary Yiddish Literature* (London 1957); *The Story of Yiddish Literature* (Cambridge, Mass. 1940).

L. WIENER, *The History of Yiddish Literature in the 19th Century* (New York 1899).

Anthologies in Yiddish or Hebrew

M. BASSOK (ed.), *A Selection of Yiddish Poetry in Hebrew Translation* (Tel Aviv 1963), from Peretz to the present.

Dos lid is gebliben [The Song Remained] (Warsaw 1947), selected from Yiddish poets who died in World War II.

B. MINKOFF (ed.), *Pioneers of Yiddish Poetry in America*, 3 vols. (New York 1956).

M. RAVICH (ed.), *Des amolike Warshe* [Jewish Warsaw That Was] (Montreal 1966), a selection of poetry and prose by 130 Yiddish writers.

A. SHAMRI, *Anthology of Yiddish Writing in Israel* (Tel Aviv 1966).

H. SHMERUK (ed.), *A shpigel oif a shteyn* (Tel Aviv 1964), prose and poetry by 12 Russo-Yiddish writers who died in the Stalinist purges, with biographical and bibliographical notes.

J. TRUNK and A. TZAITLIN (ed.), *Anthology of Yiddish Prose in Poland, 1914–1939* (New York 1946).

English Translations

The list of Yiddish authors in English translation is too extensive to give here; more important, perhaps, is to note the shortage of translations of major writers such as Bergelson, Der Nister, Markish, and Opatoshu. The stories and poetry listed below are particularly recommended.

SHOLEM ALEICHEM, *Stories and Satires*, trans. by Curt Leviant (New York and London 1959); *The Old Country*, 22 stories trans. by Julius and Frances Butwin (London 1958).

SHOLEM ASCH, *From Many Countries* (London 1958), a collection of 31 short stories.

Caravan, ed. by Jacob Sonntag (London and New York 1962), a selection of verse and prose by Peretz, Reizen, Manger, Sholem Aleichem, and others.

IRVING HOWE and ELIEZER GREENBERG (ed.), *A Treasury of Yiddish Stories* (London 1955), a selection of works by 24 writers, with an introduction and notes; *A Treasury of Yiddish Poetry* (New York 1962), contains a valuable introduction.

JOSEPH LEFTWICH (ed.), *The Golden Peacock* (London 1939; New York 1961), a selection of works by more than 140 Yiddish poets; *The Way We Think*, 2 vols. (New York 1969), a collection of essays from the Yiddish.

DAVID S. LIFSON, *The Yiddish Theatre in America* (New York 1965).

SUTZKEVER, *Siberia*, trans. by Jacob Sonntag (London and New York 1964).

The New Country, trans. by Henry Goodman (New York 1961), contains 60 short stories by 24 Yiddish writers about life in America; with an introduction and biographical notes.

CHAPTER 14

Ideas of Innocence in American Literature

Tony Tanner*

> The American is a new man who acts on new principles: he must therefore entertain new ideas and form new opinions.[1]
>
> J. HECTOR ST JOHN DE CRÈVECOEUR (1782)

> That is the true myth of America. She starts old, old, wrinkled and writhing in an old skin. And there is a gradual sloughing off of the old skin, towards a new youth. It is the myth of America.[2]
>
> D. H. LAWRENCE (1922)

> England? A dry skin to be cast off, an itch, that's all. There was a deeper matter, a yeast in the sap, an untracked force that might lead anywhere; it was spring time in a new world when all things were possible.[3]
>
> WILLIAM CARLOS WILLIAMS (1925)

A new man, a new youth, a new world: the echoing phrases in these three representative quotations taken variously from a French immigrant who farmed in America before the Revolution, a European visitor, and a doctor-poet who lived until recently in New Jersey, suggest how potent and prevalent the idea of new beginnings has been in all thinking, and myth-making, about America. In seeking appropriate imagery to convey this sense of the new American man in the new American world, and all the promise and possibility generated by this confrontation, American writers often had recourse to the oldest story they knew. "Here's for the plain old Adam, the simple genuine self against the whole world,"[4] wrote Emerson in his journals; and this was not only a literary convention. We can find many non-professional writers turning back to Genesis to communicate their response to America. "Here, as in Eden, man feels alone with the God of Nature and seems in a peculiar manner to enjoy

* Lecturer in English at the University of Cambridge and Director of English Studies at King's College, Cambridge.

the rich bounties of heaven, in common with all created things"[5] (Mary Austin Holley). Adam's innocence, and his wonder at the paradise surrounding him, have provided abiding metaphors for American writers. In the 19th century, many American commentators felt that America was indeed a second paradise; that it had escaped the centuries of bloodshed and corruption that made up the history of the rest of the world. Being outside the gravitational field of history, the continent of America had somehow avoided the Fall with which history elsewhere began. To leave Europe for America was to slough off history, to re-enter the Garden of Eden. It meant a second chance, a new youth, a move from the sullying accretions of experience to the primal freshness of innocence and the clean spaces of a New World. So much is, indeed, mythology, but it is often in mythology that we can detect a nation's most searching attempts to give outline to its experience and to apprehend the meaning of the conditions of its existence.

This Adamic imagery permeated 19th-century American writing, as has been well documented by R. W. B. Lewis in his admirable book *The American Adam*. If American literature was to have a distinctive theme, it was to be the recovered innocence of man in the New World. The first major American poet, Walt Whitman, identified himself with Adam quite consciously:

> As Adam, early in the morning,
> Walking forth from the bower refreshed with sleep,
> Behold me where I pass. . . .[6]

Emerson celebrated the divine, unfallen innocence of man, and denied the need of any institutionalized religion to mediate between man and God. Thoreau affirmed that "the impression made on a wise man is that of universal innocence,"[7] and by going to live alone in the woods by Walden pond he made a gesture of disengagement from the clouded complexities of social living that was to be emulated in innumerable subsequent American works.

The first major American novelist, James Fenimore Cooper, in his most influential and popular series of novels, *Leatherstocking Tales* (1823–41), focusses on the innocent figure of Natty Bumppo, who also moves constantly away from the settlements and society, preferring the natural freedom of the woods. In the first novel, *The Pioneers*, he innocently breaks one of society's laws and leaves the town for the country out west, a move that many more American heroes are to make after him. In the last of the series, *The Deerslayer*, Cooper goes back to the youth of Natty

Bumppo, effectively celebrating his "birth" (as Lewis points out) by killing his first Indian. It is an initiation—but an initiation into the ways of the forest, not the *mores* of the town. It was D. H. Lawrence who noticed an interesting aspect of the whole sequence: "The Leatherstocking novels . . . go backwards from old age to golden youth."[8] It is as though as he grew more pessimistic about the actual state of contemporary America Cooper returned in his imagination to the moment of greatest promise and innocence—youth. In this he anticipates the concentration on the child or adolescent that has marked out American fiction ever since. Thoreau's sentiments suggest some of the reasons for this preoccupation with youth. "In youth, before I lost any of my senses, I can remember that I was all alive, and inhabited my body with inexpressible satisfaction."[9] More importantly, perhaps, youth is the period before the onset of unavoidable knowledge and all the bruising and wasteful entanglements with the world. In youth, it was felt, man lived as Adam did in an Eden of unconscious innocence. No other literature has produced so many books with a child or adolescent as the central figure. And no other literature has gone to such pains to develop a sort of innocent style that could evoke and convey youth's innocent perspectives on the world.

But there were many American writers who also realized that an essential part of the Adamic myth was that Adam fell, and *had to fall* to become fully human. As Henry James Senior firmly put it:

> Nothing can indeed be more remote . . . from distinctively human attributes, or from the spontaneous life of man, than this sleek and comely Adamic condition, provided it should turn out an abiding one: because man in that case would prove a mere dimpled nursling of the skies . . . without ever realizing a truly divine manhood and dignity. . . . Any one with half an eye can see . . . that Adam's "fall," as it is called, was not that stupid lapse from the divine favour which it has vulgarly been reputed to have been, but an actual rise to the normal human level.[10]

This feeling that man *must* fall—into knowledge, into time, even into sin—before he can become fully human, challenges that nostalgia for pure innocence so prevalent in American literature, and is responsible for much of the tension and drama in the greatest American writers. It is a feeling everywhere to be found in the work of Nathaniel Hawthorne, particularly in his last book, *The Marble Faun* (1860). The plot is complicated and scarcely summarizable, but the basic "action" is clear. To Rome, the domain of History and Time *par excellence*, comes an "Arcadian simpleton" called Donatello. He is a complete innocent, totally unaware of time and all it means. But when he gets involved with a woman and kills a man, he becomes aware that his own ancestry goes far back in time; it is as though he is discovering that to be human is to be involved in history. After his crime he flees to the woods outside Rome (in American terms an oft-repeated flight from society to the forest), but returns to Rome to face his punishment (as Hester Prynne returns from the forest to society to face her punishment in *The Scarlet Letter* [1850]). The attempted move back toward nature and innocence is reversed, and the hero submits himself to the forms and laws and exigencies of society and history. Donatello ends up in Rome, imprisoned but a full human being. His story, as Miriam perceives, is "the story of the fall of man!" and the American, Kenyon, wonders: "Did Adam fall, that we might ultimately rise to a far loftier paradise than his?"[11] It is Kenyon who compares his feelings in the scenery around Donatello's home to those "of an adventurer who should find his way to the site of ancient Eden, and behold its loveliness through the transparency of gloom which has been brooding over these haunts of innocence ever since the fall."[12] The gloom makes it more beautiful, thinks Kenyon. "Adam saw it in a brighter sunshine, but never knew the shade of pensive beauty which Eden won from his expulsion."[13] The sense that the bright unrefracted light of innocence might take on new beauties and new meanings when it encountered the shadows and shapes of time is one that is responsible for the sombre richness of many of the more searching works of the American imagination.

Another story by Hawthorne is worth bringing forward at this point because of its parabolic clarity. It is entitled, obviously enough, "The New Adam and Eve." Hawthorne starts by pointing out how man's arts superimpose an "artificial system" on nature, and then he imagines how this man-made world would appear to Adam and Eve if all life was suddenly banished from the earth and they returned as solitary human witnesses. Among the massed buildings of the now deserted town they feel desolate and uneasy: "Evidently we have strayed away from our home; for I see nothing hereabouts that seems to belong to us,"[14] says Adam. The most significant of their reactions is their sense of constriction and contamination among the buildings of the town. Indeed at first they yearn to go and live in the "blue depths" of the sky (they would *like* to be "dimpled nurslings of the skies"), but "they acknowledge the necessity of keeping to the beaten track of earth." So they explore all the confining structures that man erects in nature's spaces—church, house, library, prison, hospital. Hawthorne's comment as they enter a leper house is typical:

> Man never had attempted to cure sin by LOVE! Had he but once made the effort it might well have happened that there would have been no need of the dark lazar house into which Adam and Eve have wandered. Hasten forth with your native innocence, lest the damps of these still conscious walls infect you likewise, and thus another fallen race be propagated.[15]

Here is a deeply American feeling. The buildings and towns of man are infected; society is like a vast "prison house," history is a disease, knowledge is sickness. The best thing for innocence is flight and retreat. At one point Adam enters a library and nearly gets involved in reading the old books: "Had he then and there become a student . . . the fatal apple of another Tree of Knowledge would have been eaten."[16] Let the edifice collapse and bury the rubbish it contains, says Hawthorne. Adam has no need to take on the burden of knowledge of human history: "Blessed in his ignorance, he may still enjoy a new world in our wornout one."[17] The parabolic simplicity of the tale only serves to throw the attitudes that inform it into sharper focus, and the picture of the figure of Adam reluctantly and confusedly exploring the stained and corrupting architecture of the man-made environment—all the time longing to escape into free clean space—is a crucial one for American literature. It is a picture of innocence tentatively encountering the periphery of knowledge, and it is a picture also of contrary compulsions: a move toward initiation into the world of experience countered by a yearning for flight from it. This figure of the reluctant initiate, resisting the very experience he is drawn to, is one to which we shall return.

One other aspect of Hawthorne's story deserves mention. Adam is still Adam, but he is no longer in the conventional paradise. Clearly Hawthorne's little parable is not to be confused with an accurate picture of contemporary America, but it is only one of many documents that testify to some uncertainty as to the nature of the American Eden. One of the first great American landscape painters, Thomas Cole, reveals this dilemma in his "Essay on American Scenery" (1835). First he celebrates the untouched American wildness with religious fervour. "You see no ruined tower to tell of outrage—no gorgeous temple to speak of ostentation," and "the wilderness is YET a fitting place to speak of God." But then he is forced to add, "yet I cannot but express my sorrow that the beauty of such landscapes is quickly passing away—the ravages of the axe are daily increasing—the most noble scenes are made desolate and oftentimes with a wantonness and barbarism scarcely credible in a civilized nation."[18] The myth of the American Eden was not easily reconciled with the visible facts of its ruthless exploitation. In American fiction America does not retain its paradisal status for very long, and the confusing man-made territories into which the innocent hero falls, or from which he flees, are as often American as they are European. The attempt to "enjoy a new world in our wornout one," as Hawthorne aptly puts it, often turns out to be a search for an ever-receding dream.

Hawthorne's picture of the new Adam puzzling himself in the library of books from the past brings out another important issue we should consider here. The American might well feel himself to be a new man in a new world, but how was he to write about this newness, this escape to a historic innocence? He could leave England behind, but he brought the English language—and all its literature—with him, and a language is as saturated with history as the country that evolved it. A language is a way of organizing one's perceptions of reality; its vocabulary, syntax, and habitual forms contain the attitudes, values, prejudices, and pre-occupations of the people who speak it. To invent an absolutely new language with which to speak of the New World was impossible; and yet to impose European forms on American realities—to look at the New World with old eyes—inevitably involved distortion and violation. The Indians, of course, were at home in the American terrain and had a unique language—but the Indians were regarded with hostility and continually slaughtered out of fear and greed. The need to develop new literary forms and styles that would be true and adequate to the New World experience preoccupied many American writers and inspired many of their greatest works. But it was a struggle, because the temptation was always to impose old *schemata* on the unknown novelty of the American landscape. The art critic Harold Rosenberg makes this point by citing the defeat of the English soldiers under Edward Braddock by Indians and trappers. The reason for their defeat is that they treat the American "wilderness, with its disorder of rocks, underbrush and sharp-shooters, as if they were on a parade ground or on the meadows of a classical battlefield and one by one they fall and die." The Redcoats simply could not see the American landscape as it was, because of all the European preoccupations that had shaped their vision.

> The difficulty of the Redcoats was that they were in the wrong place. The dream-world of a style always moves ahead of the actual world and overlays it; unless one is of the unblinking wilderness like those Coonskinners behind the trees.[19]

How to *see* the new world, how to be in it, how to write of it—these were problems that nearly all the important American writers confronted and grappled with.

These problems provoked one of the most interesting books written by an American writer in the 20th century, *In the American Grain* by William Carlos Williams (1925). Neither a novel nor history, it is his own unique compilation of selections from old documents concerning the discovery and settling of America, woven together by his own contemporary prose. The theme of the book is "the New World," so constantly reiterated in a variety of contexts that it acquires spiritual as well as geographical force. And Williams sets out to show how explorers such as Columbus and Cortez and De Soto, and colonists such as the Puritans, treated this New World, and how often they savaged it. Unable to appreciate and assimilate the wonder of the New World, they imposed their own emptiness on it, trying to reshape and distort it into Old-World moulds, releasing into it the inherited evil of the race. What they should have loved they raped; what they could not appreciate they exploited.

> For the problem of the New World was, as every new comer soon found out, an awkward one, on all sides the same: how to replace from the wild land that which, at home, they had scarcely known the Old World meant to them; through difficulty and even brutal hardship to find a ground to take the place of England. They could not do it. They clung, one way or another, to the old, striving the while to pull off pieces to themselves from the fat of the new bounty.[20]

It is the rigid failure of the Puritans to open themselves to the sensuous beauty and generous promise of the New World that angers Williams. "They must have closed all the world out . . . having in themselves nothing of curiosity, no wonder, for the New World."[21] With that new world blossoming all around them they merely raided and looted it, and set about recreating the old world. And, as Williams sees it, the consequences have been dire.

> If the Puritans have damned us with their abstinence, removal from the world, denial, slowly we are forced within ourselves upon an emptiness which cannot be supplied,—this is the soul, according to their tenets.[22]

But there were some who came to America who had the right spirit. For instance Père Rasles—"a new spirit in the New World." He "recognized" the wonder of this new world; unlike the Protestant priests, this Catholic was happy to touch the Indians he met. His attitude was "nothing shall be ignored. All shall be included."[23] Williams uses him as an example of the correct moral response to the New World.

> This is a moral source not reckoned with, peculiarly sensitive and daring in its close embrace of native things. . . . For everything his fine sense, blossoming, thriving, opening, reviving—not shutting out—was tuned.[24]

Even more passionately, Williams celebrates Daniel Boone, who "lived to enjoy ecstasy through his single devotion to the wilderness with which he was surrounded."[25] Unlike the majority of the settlers, he did not try to "own" the land: "he avoided the half logic of stealing from the immense profusion." Instead:

> Boone's genius was to recognize the difficulty as neither material nor political but one purely moral and aesthetic. Filled with the wild beauty of the New World to overbrimming so long as he had what he desired, to bathe in, to explore always more deeply, to see, to feel, to touch—his instincts were contented. Sensing a limitless fortune which daring could make his own, he sought only with primal lust to grow close to it, to understand it and to be part of its mysterious movements—like an Indian.[26]

The greatness of Boone, for Williams, was that he sought "to be *himself* in a new world . . . he offered himself to his world." Typically, Williams often refers to the American continent as a waiting female, subjected to repeated and dreadful violations. His own feeling is that "there must be a new wedding." Men such as Rasles and Boone are examples of those rare but essential few who were "inspired by the new QUALITY about them to yield to loveliness in a fresh spirit."[27] But in place of their reverent openness, the majority of those who settled America practised exclusion and severe domination. Instead of embracing the New World they held it by the neck in a "frightened grip" in case it proved them empty. It is significant, says Williams, "how nearly all our national heroes have been . . . praised by reason of their shrewdness in making walls: not in bursting into flower."[28]

I have stressed Williams' book because it seems to me to make clear one very important contradiction in the cherished notion of the new American man as Adam. Adam in Eden is an essentially static picture; yet the whole history of America is one of ferocious activity and movement. Men who arrived in America had to do things: to do nothing was to die. Poets such as Emerson and Thoreau and Whitman might celebrate a passive, still communion with nature, but the actual experience for most Americans was one of necessary locomotion and activity. Many

American heroes have a dream of stillness, and seek a secure and pure immobility, but it is fair to say that nearly all major American novels are novels of movement. The nature and direction of that movement, and the exigencies and opportunities to which it is related, often turn out to be the organizing subject of the book. And many of those innocent heroes find themselves building walls instead of bursting into flower, as Williams so perceptively noted. Such a hero is Colonel Sutpen, the dominant figure in William Faulkner's *Absalom, Absalom!* (1936), and one of the nost notable "innocents" in 20th-century American literature.

In this sombre novel about the concealed and guilt-ridden "family" relations between black and white in the South, Sutpen is an archetypal American figure "who came out of nowhere and without warning upon the land with a band of strange niggers and built a plantation."[29] He is pre-eminently a man of will, a builder who imposes his determined shapes on the quiescent land, and along with Quentin—the young boy who is learning about him—we watch him "drag house and formal gardens violently out of the soundless Nothing and clap them down like cards upon a table . . . creating the Sutpen's Hundred."[30] Significantly, after two years of "unflagging fury" while building the house, for a period he goes "completely static," an alternation between energy and inertia that I think can be detected at the heart of American literature. But Sutpen has a "design"—a desire to create a fine house, become a respected citizen, and found a noble lineage. The design, like the house, finally founders. He has an illegitimate part-Negro son whom he will not acknowledge (Charles Bon), who returns to court Sutpen's legitimate daughter. This act of incest and miscegenation is prevented by Sutpen's legitimate son, Henry, who shoots Bon and goes into hiding inside the house, which finally burns to the ground. Sutpen himself is ignominiously killed by a poor white for maltreating the latter's daughter because she does not provide him with another male heir. A grandiose dream; fierce energy; ultimate disaster:

> "You see, I had a design in my mind. Whether it was a good or a bad design is beside the point; the question is, Where did I make the mistake in it. . . ."[31]

This is Sutpen's question when faced by the dreadful ruin he himself brings about. Faulkner shows how the dream and the disaster are connected, and his most important insight is that Sutpen is not the figure of deliberate evil others think him; on the contrary, he has not attained the ability to make moral evaluations of his own desires and deeds. He follows his dream, his plan, never asking "whether it was a good or a bad design." As Quentin's grandfather tells him, "Sutpen's trouble was innocence."[32]

In the long section that recounts Sutpen's childhood we find Faulkner's analysis of that innocence. Sutpen was born in a wild part of the country where nobody bothered to fence off private property. He had no experience of a world of divided land, rank, authority, and social hierarchy: "he had hardly heard of such a world until he fell into it." The echo of the first Fall is deliberate. The Sutpen family travels east in "a sort of dreamy and destinationless locomotion," and "falls" into the social world of the South. "Sutpen knew neither where he had come from nor where he was nor why." He is sent to deliver a message at one of the big houses of a rich plantation owner and is unceremoniously told to leave even before he opens his mouth.

> He didn't even remember leaving. All of a sudden he found himself running and already some distance from the house, and not toward home. . . . He went into the woods . . . he couldn't get it straight yet. He couldn't even realize yet that his trouble, his impediment, was innocence, because he would not be able to realize that until he got it straight.[33]

The house stands for the whole world of human exploitation, rank, and vicious prejudice that is society. Sutpen is the innocent coming from some timeless pre-social vacuum to knock on the door of the house. His reaction to his reception is to flee to the woods, to that natural wildness where society as yet has no hold. This move toward the house, then away from it into the woods, is a compact version of a classic American fictional pattern. But the story does not end there, for as a child Sutpen decides "you got to have land and niggers and a fine house to combat them with." And at this moment of decision his state of mind is described as "a limitless flat plain with the severe shape of his intact innocence rising from it like a monument; that innocence instructing him. . . ."[34] With ruthless determination he erects his own fine house; and when in due course his own natural son comes to his house craving only a single gesture of recognition from his father, Sutpen sends him away unacknowledged. In his lethal innocence he cannot see that he is repeating even more cruelly the pattern of which he was at first a victim, when he too was banished from a house where he had wanted to be recognized as a human being. It is only a matter of time before Bon returns and effectively precipitates the ruin of the house that Sutpen built. In this novel William Faulkner has undertaken an important exploration of the possibly inhuman and destructive aspects of "innocence."

Another American innocent who acquires a house is Jay Gatsby in F. Scott Fitzgerald's *The Great Gatsby* (1925), certainly one of the major American novels written this century. Like Sutpen, Gatsby is of vague origin, the son of shiftless farm people out west; like Sutpen he "invents" himself by wedding himself to a great design.

> The truth was that Jay Gatsby of West Egg, Long Island, sprang from his Platonic conception of himself. He was a son of God—a phrase which, if it means anything, means just that—and he must be about His Father's business, the service of a vast, vulgar, and meretricious beauty.[35]

Coming from nowhere into the rich materialistic society of his time, he forms his visions and aspirations accordingly. From the outside his actions and achievements look "vulgar and meretricious." Involved in shady business enterprises he amasses great wealth, purchases a vast house on Long Island, and gives the most lavish parties imaginable. But these are the clumsy outward manifestations of a dream of singular, and vulnerable, innocence and purity. As a young soldier in World War I he had met a girl, Daisy, and fallen in love with her. When he returned from the war she had married Tom Buchanan, a man with an established social position, great wealth, and a brutal, insensitive power. Gatsby's life from then on is devoted to his dream of regaining Daisy. He acquires his wealth to build the sort of house he thinks she might like (for he had been overwhelmed by the beauty of *her* house when he first entered it as a penniless soldier); he gives his vast parties in the hope that one day she will turn up at one of them. Despite its sordid contacts and connections, his life is compared to "the following of a grail." The narrator of the story, Nick Carraway, says of him, "there was something gorgeous about him, some heightened sensitivity to the promises of life."[36] He is surrounded by spoilt, self-indulgent, appetitive parasites, but he is not of them. As Nick spontaneously says to him shortly before his death: "They're a rotten crowd. . . . You're worth the whole damn bunch put together."[37] He tells us at the start: "Gatsby turned out all right in the end; it is what preyed on Gatsby, what foul dust floated in the wake of his dreams,"[38] that really depressed and disillusioned him. For Gatsby is effectively destroyed by the Buchanans (he allows it to be thought that he ran over and killed Tom's mistress, and the woman's husband shoots him—but in fact Daisy was driving): "they were careless people, Tom and Daisy—they smashed up things and creatures and then retreated back into their money or their vast carelessness, or whatever it was that kept them together, and let other people clean up the mess they had made. . . ."[39] At Gatsby's funeral, "nobody came." Society conspires to abuse, destroy, and forget the innocent visionary.

What is the nature of his dream? At one point Nick tells him, hoping to prepare him for possible disappointments, "You can't repeat the past," but Gatsby answers incredulously, "Can't repeat the past? . . . Why of course you can!"[40] The irreversible movement of time means nothing to him. In his youth, we read, "a universe of ineffable gaudiness spun itself out in his brain while the clock ticked on the washstand."[41] It is the glory and the weakness of the innocent dreamer that he cannot hear that clock. When Gatsby does finally meet Daisy again, he clumsily almost knocks a clock off the mantelpiece; a Freudian slip, if you like, that nicely indicates his deep instinct to deny time. (The destruction of clocks is something of a pastime in American fiction!) Characteristically, Gatsby is always "restless. He was never quite still." He loves cars, hydroplanes, all forms of speed, for he has "that resourcefulness of movement that is so peculiarly American."[42] (It is a car accident that precipitates the tragedy.) What this surface nervousness or agitation conceals is the more profound restlessness of the quest: Gatsby moves forever after his dream, unaware that time is taking it ever farther away from him, just as he seeks his dream-love Daisy in the future, although in fact he has already lost her in the past. Nick muses at the end:

> . . . his dream must have seemed so close that he could hardly fail to grasp it. He did not know that it was already behind him, somewhere back in that vast obscurity beyond the city, where the dark fields of the republic rolled on under the night. Gatsby believed in the green light, the orgiastic future that year by year recedes before us. It eluded us then, but that's no matter—to-morrow we will run faster, stretch out our arms further. . . . And one fine morning—So we beat on, boats against the current, borne back ceaselessly into the past.[43]

Gatsby acquired his big ostentatious house to no end; there was never a chance that Daisy would come and live in it with him. But Fitzgerald makes us feel that what really matters, underneath Gatsby's sentimental day-dreams, is the generous sense of wonder, the visionary response to the rich promise of America, that Fitzgerald elsewhere described as "a willingness of the heart." Gatsby's pride in his house when he persuades Daisy to visit it is naive: "My house looks well, doesn't it? . . . See how the whole front of it catches the light."[44] But in contrast to the insincere, dead-hearted worldliness of the rest of society, this naivety is pure poetry that transforms what it touches. Yet Fitzgerald can see that Gatsby's inchoate poetic visions cannot be realized in this material world (hence the Platonic echoes). When Gatsby finally attempts to force his dream into reality and to marry the actual Daisy instead of worshipping his ideal image of her, the dream is bound to shatter. This leaves him in a raw and frightening world bereft of all poetry and wonder, "material without being real," as Fitzgerald says, picking up the Platonic distinction. One feels that it is almost with relief that Gatsby watches his approaching death.

After Gatsby has been killed, Nick makes a final pilgrimage and goes over to look "at that huge incoherent failure of a house once more." Gatsby's house is a failure, but as Nick continues his meditation by the beach he comes to perceive the relative triviality of all man-made edifices.

> And as the moon rose higher the inessential houses began to melt away until gradually I became aware of the old island here that flowered once for Dutch sailors' eyes—a fresh, green breast of the new world. Its vanished trees, the trees that had made way for Gatsby's house, had once pandered in whispers to the last and greatest of all human dreams; for a transitory enchanted moment man must have held his breath in the presence of this continent, compelled into an aesthetic contemplation he neither understood nor desired, face to face for the last time in history with something commensurate to his capacity for wonder.[45]

The houses that man builds are not of the essence of America, and all houses are bound to fail, Sutpen's and Gatsby's alike. The crucial difference is that Sutpen's house represented a vengeful effort of will, whereas Gatsby's is in part an imaginative gesture of wonder, a wonder as vast as the continent that inspired it. Both these builders were "innocent," but Gatsby's innocence contained an element of awkward aesthetic response absent from Sutpen's grim act of appropriation. And it should be stressed that although both are innocent, both have been remarkably successful in exploiting the American landscape: these "Adams" have been very active in acquiring the wealth to expedite their dreams. The fact that they are both murdered suggests not only that society is hostile to innocence, but also that innocence carries within it the seeds of its own vulnerability and self-destruction.

These innocents are nominally adults, who enter society to their ultimate doom. But there is another figure of abiding importance for American literature, and that is the child or adolescent caught at the moment when he refuses to be initiated, when he attempts to deny or avoid the whole world of experience ahead of him. A typical example of this gesture is to be found in a short story by Sherwood Anderson called "I Want to Know Why" (from *The Triumph of the Egg*, 1921). The adolescent narrator of this story (a very important development in American fiction) tells how he and some friends who are mad about horses run away from home to see the races at Saratoga. The boy is full of wonder and happiness at the spectacle of one superb horse, Sunstreak, winning the race and breaking all records. As a result of his deep contentment he feels himself loving the trainer of the horse, Jerry Tillford. "I liked him that afternoon even more than I ever liked my own father."[46] In his excitement he wants to stay near Jerry Tillford and so he follows him in the evening. Tillford goes to a brothel at the edge of the town and, watching through the window, the boy is horrified to see him looking at the ugly, unclean women in the same way he had looked at his wonderful horse earlier in the day. "I stood there by the window—gee!—but I wished I hadn't gone away from the tracks, but had stayed with the boys and the niggers and the horses. . . . Then all of a sudden I began to hate that man."[47] The brothel is an image of the world of depraved adult experience, and the track (with the "boys . . . niggers and . . . horses") is a realm of clean air and rural innocence. The boy looking through the window and recoiling in horror from what he sees is innocence in outrage at the soiling betrayals of experience. And once he has looked through that window, things can never be quite the same.

> At the tracks the air don't taste as good or smell as good. It's because a man like Jerry Tillford, who knows what he does, could see a horse like Sunstreak run, and kiss a woman like that the same day. I can't make it out. Darn him, what did he want to do like that for? I keep thinking about it and it spoils looking at horses and smelling things and hearing niggers laugh and everything. Sometimes I'm so mad about it I want to fight someone. It gives me the fantods. What did he do it for? I want to know why.[48]

This is one of the perennial questions that the American innocent asks—why must youth give way to age, why does life betray our fondest expectations, why is the adult world so given over to ugly appetites? (Most American heroes and heroines are curiously sexless.) Ultimately the question is—why was I born into time, why must I encounter knowledge, why is all movement toward darkness and death? This boy's hurt and horrified recoil and flight from what he sees of the adult world is, of course, naive; but it is one of the most recurrent gestures in American fiction, which more than any other fiction has preoccupied itself with the values and virtues of innocence and naivety. At its best it also explores their vulnerabilities and limitations, even their dangers.

To suggest how deep this theme of the fate of innocence—be it flight or death—penetrates American literature, it will be enough to cite some representative works of the major 19th-century American writers. Mark Twain's *Huckleberry Finn* (1884) is one of the great creations of American literature, one of the most convincing and attractive innocents of all literature. He is an outcast, the town pariah, a lonely self-communing figure, who can find comfort only in the company of the runaway slave Jim (Negroes and Indians, being unassimilated into the dominant society, are often companions of the American hero). The Southern society in which he finds himself is violent, hypocritical, and cruel—a place where people indulge in fraudulent pretensions to elegance and gentility, and in bloodthirsty feuds; where sanctimonious piety and the vicious practice of slave-owning go together. Huck is brought up to think of this brutal and corrupt society as being the true and the good. All the more remarkable, therefore, is his instinctive disaffiliation (with attendant guilt) from its values, as when he defends the slave Jim from his would-be recapturers. It is as though his particular kind of being, no matter how coerced and trained by society, is bound to take flight from it. This is a radical innocence of the heart that will have recourse to every strategy of evasion and flight rather than be trapped in the corrupting confines of adult society. As Huck makes his escape with Jim down the river we notice a distinct opposition is set up. When he and Jim are alone on their raft in the middle of the river, they can relax, take their clothes off, and passively commune with nature (the Adamic state). But there are constant intrusions from the society of the river bank. Criminals invade the raft, a ship smashes it: constantly Huck finds himself unwillingly back on the shore. And when he does get involved with the communities on the river banks, the behaviour of people so sickens and saddens him that he longs only to move on, to get away. He is constantly adopting false identities, changing names and clothes, in his efforts to avoid being trapped; and this is entirely appropriate, because a true innocent like Huck has no authentic social identity, no role in the adult world. He is a true outlaw because of his instinctive egalitarianism, his longing for peace and quiet, his indifference to profitable labour, his non-acceptance or non-comprehension of all the paraphernalia of social hierarchy. He is an outcast because of what Mark Twain called his "sound heart," and his desire for an unconstricted freedom of consciousness goes against all the confining structures and arresting rules of "civilization."

Huck doesn't build houses, he leaves them.

> The Widow Douglas, she took me for her son, and allowed she would civilise me; but it was rough living in the house all the time, considering how dismal regular and decent the widow was in all her ways; and so when I couldn't stand it no longer, I lit out.[49]

So the book starts—and so, after many abrasive and threatening encounters with society, it ends:

> But I reckon I got to light out for the Territory ahead of the rest, because Aunt Sally she's going to adopt me and civilise me and I can't stand it. I been there before.[50]

This gesture of repudiation and disengagement has recurred constantly in American fiction (often in stories purportedly narrated by adolescents, it being another of Mark Twain's achievements that he first perfected the use of the vernacular youthful narrator, and showed the rich possibilities of using this strategy of deliberately adopting an "innocent" point of view when telling a story). As long as there was still unpopulated territory out in the west, Huck's flight could seem to have a real destination. But in the same decade as the book was published, the Frontier was declared closed (*c.* 1890), and since then the innocent in recoil from society has had problems of where to direct his retreat. As a character says in another of Sherwood Anderson's stories: "I wanted to run away from everything but I wanted to run towards something too."[51]

Huckleberry Finn is the classic example of those American works that propose, in R. W. B. Lewis's words, "that the valid rite of initiation for the individual in the new world is not an initiation *into* society, but, given the character of society, an initiation *away from it.*"[52] Melville's *Billy Budd* (written in 1890 but not published until 1924) is perhaps the most profound of those American works that dramatize the unavoidable involvement of the innocent hero in a fallen society and his inevitable consequent destruction or sacrifice. What the world did to the venturing innocents who inquiringly entered it was a theme that Melville explored in book after book, and although Billy Budd is nominally an Englishman he features in Melville's final, and perhaps finest, version of a distinctly American fable. Like so many other American heroes, Billy seems to have no parentage ("his entire family was practically invested in himself") and he is specifically described as being "as Adam presumably might have been ere the urbane Serpent wriggled himself into his company."[53] The action takes place at sea during the wars between England and France at the end of the 18th century. Billy, a handsome good-natured

432

sailor, is forced to leave a peaceful ship called *The Rights-of-Man* and serve on a warship called *The Indomitable*. It is like a sudden birth into a darker world—"the abrupt transition from his former simpler sphere to the ampler and more knowing world of a great warship";[54] the pacific Billy seems incongruous amid all the cannons around the ship, which sufficiently indicate that he is now forced to live in a world where man is set against man, and deadly opposition and hostility is the order of the day.

Because he is "one to whom not yet has been proffered the questionable apple of knowledge,"[55] he is quite unprepared for the fact of evil, here centred in Claggart, a complex figure of "natural depravity" who conspires to destroy Billy out of feelings of spontaneous antipathy. Claggart, in his cool yet irrational malice, has a "disdain of innocence. To be nothing more than innocent!"[56] and, using false evidence, levels charges of mutiny against Billy. Captain Vere calls Billy to defend himself, but Billy is so appalled at Claggart's gratuitously evil lies that he is unable to speak, for the one defect in this modern Adam is a speech impediment that becomes acute in moments of stress. (Claggart is a smooth manipulator of words; Billy, in his innocence, has not yet mastered the deceptive symbols with which men impose their forms on experience, often in order to deceive. It is quite common in the American novel to find inarticulateness a measure of sincerity.) By way of dumb protest, Billy strikes Claggart a fatal blow. The captain knows Billy is innocent, but—fearing indiscipline on the ship if Billy is acquitted—he instructs the court to find him guilty, and Billy is subsequently hanged. He cannot compete with the complex sophistries and exigencies urged at the trial, and he goes willingly to his death, bestowing a blessing on Captain Vere with his last words. Melville invites us to feel this death as another crucifixion. For the first (but not the last) time, the innocent victim is discernible as a Christ-figure.

What makes this story more than a melodrama of the victimization of innocence is Melville's comprehension of the complexities of the case. Billy is invested with the most attractive human qualities, which man indeed needs if he is to be saved. And yet he remains a "child-man." The most vivid picture of him is as he sleeps the night before his hanging, "lying between the two guns"; he looks like "a slumbering child in the cradle." The guns symbolize all that dark human aggressiveness that has brought him to the rope; yet even at the moment when he is about to be destroyed he remains curiously unaware of the evil amidst which he rests like a sleeping child. His main reaction to the presence of anything that seems less direct and innocent than himself is "disgustful recoil," a fine instinct that nevertheless indicates an inability or an unwillingness to develop any knowledge or comprehension of the darker, more complex areas of human nature. He doesn't want to know, as the colloquialism so exactly puts it. The problem is whether such simple-mindedness can live in the far-from-simple world. Billy accepts the surface of things as the total truth, takes appearance for reality, and is unaware that every "form of life has its secret mines and dubious side,"[57] and Melville can see that such refusal to "look behind" must inevitably prove fatal. If the world were a better place . . . but Melville could see that the world was what it was, and not to confront it in its full complications and ambiguities he considered an evasion or a failure of moral energy.

Captain Vere is a fine example of Melville's understanding of the case. The Captain says, "with mankind . . . forms, measured forms, are everything," and it is to the maintenance of these forms that he reluctantly sacrifices Billy. Similarly he sympathizes with those of the tribunal who want at first to acquit Billy.

> It is Nature. But do these buttons that we wear attest that our allegiance is to Nature? No, to the King. Though the ocean, which is inviolate Nature primeval, though this be the element where we move and have our being as sailors, yet as the King's officers lies our duty in a sphere correspondingly natural? So little is that true, that in receiving our commissions we in the most important regards ceased to be natural free agents.[58]

This remark embraces far more than the rights and wrongs in a naval legal problem. It suggests that to be born as a man is to receive a commission; human beings cannot be as free and natural as the shapeless sea from which no doubt they once came, but over which they now sail in deliberately shaped forms. Man makes structures—be they ships or laws—and imposes these on the undifferentiated continuum of nature. Melville is making the profound point that innocence has to encounter form if it is to take on a defining contour and achieve an identity. That forms are also constructions and often involve the falsification of nature is part of the tragically paradoxical knowledge with which Captain Vere wrestles while Billy sleeps like a child among the guns. Captain Vere's heart goes out to Billy; his allegiance stays with the man-made structures he serves. Man's position in existence is full of potentially tragic contradictions—between Nature and society, between innocence and knowledge, between the ocean that spawned us and the ship on which we are forced to serve—and it was part of Melville's greatness to arrive at a vision that could comprehend such tragic contraries and oppositions, and even

434

transcend them, so that we feel the virtue and validity of both Billy Budd and Captain Vere. We feel that taken together they somehow make up a human whole, yet we are brought to see how it is inevitable that after a loving embrace one must send the other to his doom. We can even dimly apprehend how the necessary death of innocence may yet be turned into a sacrifice that will bestow a blessing.

At one point in *Billy Budd*, an experienced old sailor looks speculatively at the innocent Billy, wondering

> what might eventually befall a nature like that, dropped into a world not without some mantraps and against whose subtleties simple courage lacking experience and address and without any touch of defensive ugliness, is of little avail; and where such innocence as man is capable of does yet in a moral emergency not always sharpen the faculties or enlighten the will.[59]

It was precisely such a speculation that dominated the fiction of Henry James from the outset: from his first hero, called Newman, to almost his last, called Adam, James subjected the progress and fate of innocence to its most profound and thoroughgoing scrutiny and assessment. (As in the works of Hawthorne and Melville, the innocent protagonists are often, but not always, American.) In the preface for his early novel called simply *The American* (1877), James describes how he first envisaged the character for his novel—"some robust but insidiously beguiled and betrayed, some cruelly wronged, compatriot"—and then the situation that would provide the drama: "Great and gilded the whole trap set, in fine, for his wary freshness and into which it would blunder upon its fate."[60] Here in perfectly clear outline is the shape, the action, that has dominated American fiction since Charles Brockden Brown's *Arthur Mervyn* (1799), whom R. W. B. Lewis calls "the first of our Adams."

We first see Christopher Newman as it were prior to experience, with a "look of being committed to nothing in particular, of standing in an attitude of general hospitality to the chances of life," but we note that he has "an eye in which innocence and experience were singularly blended."[61] This is James's perceptiveness. Newman has made a lot of money out of America—he has had *that* kind of experience, just as Sutpen and Gatsby have. It is in the more complex realm of values and relationships that he is innocent. Sensing this loss or incompletion, Newman gives up business: "I seemed to feel a new man inside my old skin, and I longed for a new world."[62] Very American words, as we have seen; but Newman's search for a "new world" takes him *away* from America. "As soon as I could get out of the game I sailed for Europe."[63] It is

435

there that he has his somewhat Gothic adventures with an old aristocratic European family, who bewilder and deceive him with their duplicities and designs. Finally abandoning his marriage plans, he repudiates the family and the whole European experience and returns to America.

In bringing an innocent figure over from America to explore the dazzling and bewildering territories of Europe, James had found the theme that was to shape his major works. James is too fine an artist to permit schematization, but roughly we can say that he sees America as a country that produces a variety of vital, innocent, wondering consciousnesses, but is too empty to nourish and stimulate those consciousnesses into full growth. This is what brings them to Europe, seeking among the time-drenched accumulations of its ancient societies something that the "juvenile" landscapes of American apparently could not offer them—a destiny. Unlike Huck Finn, they move resolutely *toward* society. Sometimes these innocent venturers die, as Daisy Miller dies in the mephitic air of Rome, and as Milly Theale dies amid treachery in Venice in *The Wings of the Dove* (1902); sometimes they make bad errors of judgment and find themselves trapped where they had expected to feel themselves free (Isabel Archer in *The Portrait of a Lady* [1881] is the finest example); sometimes they turn their backs on labyrinthine difficulties and disturbingly unreliable appearances, and return to the assuring simplicities of America, as Newman does, and Laura Wing (in *A London Life* [1888]) and even Strether (in *The Ambassadors* [1901])—though James makes us feel that the initially innocent Strether ends up with such an inclusive and comprehensive vision and appreciation of the virtues and limitations of both American and European life that he will never again be at home in any one country unless it be the trans-geographic realm of art.

In his last complete novel, *The Golden Bowl* (1905), James even shows us innocence triumphing over the world of European experience, as Maggie and Adam Verver effectively dominate and dictate the lives of the Prince and Charlotte Stant (their respective husband and wife), who at first seem to be exploiting the Americans' innocence to pursue an adulterous relationship. The symbolism of the books is very complex, and James may be suggesting that American wealth and innocence will eventually take over and sustain the flawed but valuable European past, picking up the pieces of the "broken bowl" to make a new society. On the other hand he also makes it clear that there is an element of revenge in the way the innocents ring the changes on their worldly, knowing partners, finally controlling all their movements while they flounder in impotent ignorance. There is cruelty and appropriation, for by the end the Americans seem almost to regard their two Europeans as acquisitions, fine bits of human furniture. At first Adam is described in terms that echo those used of Billy Budd: he is often compared to a child or a baby, and is "natural" and has "no form." Europe is the realm of forms. But what happens in this book is that the innocent Americans finally appropriate those forms (including the masters of those forms, the Prince and Charlotte) on their own terms: literally so, for Adam builds a great museum in America, which is to be a triumph of "acquisition on the highest terms," full of European objects; and also, more subtly, for Maggie, who starts with the traditional refusal of initiation ("I don't *want* to know"), ends up by knowing more than anyone and exercising a corresponding control over the involved characters. "There was no limit to her conceived design of not letting them escape."[64] Her realization that "I make them do what I like"[65] is indeed the moment of triumph for an innocence that has learnt to control the world of experience and forms without succumbing to it. James was perceptive enough to discern that American innocence combined with American wealth might be capable of a disturbing exercise of power. Having previously explored the renunciation, the flight, the imprisonment, the death, the sacrifice of innocence, in this extraordinary book he dramatized the triumph of innocence. Whether that triumph takes the form of vengeance on the world of experience or of redeeming it is an unresolvable ambiguity that testifies to the profundity of James's understanding of his theme, which, I have tried to suggest, is really *the* American theme—the fate of innocence.

References

1. J. HECTOR ST JOHN DE CRÈVECOEUR, *Letters from an American Farmer* [1782] (New York 1957), p. 40.
2. D. H. LAWRENCE, *Studies in Classical American Literature* [1922] (New York 1955), p. 64.
3. WILLIAM CARLOS WILLIAMS, *In the American Grain* [1925] (paperback: Harmondsworth 1971), "The Virtue of History."
4. Quoted in R. W. B. LEWIS, *The American Adam* (Chicago 1955), opp. p. 1. Professor Lewis's seminal work is a pioneer study in this field, and I have inevitably had to cover ground already charted by him.
5. REBECCA SMITH LEE, *Mary Austin Holley* (Austin 1967), p. 133.
6. Quoted in LEWIS, *op. cit.*, p. 43.
7. *ibid.*, p. 29.

8. LAWRENCE, *op. cit.*, p. 64.
9. HENRY THOREAU, *Complete Works* (Boston and New York 1906), Vol. VIII, pp. 306–7.
10. Quoted in LEWIS, *op. cit.*, p. 59.
11. *ibid.*, p. 125.
12. *ibid.*, p. 126.
13. *ibid.*, p. 126.
14. NATHANIEL HAWTHORNE, "The New Adam and Eve" (*c.* 1844).
15. *ibid.*
16. *ibid.*
17. *ibid.*
18. JOHN W. MCCOUBREY (ed.), *American Art 1700–1960* (Englewood Cliffs, N.J. 1965), p. 109.
19. HAROLD ROSENBERG, *The Tradition of the New* (London 1962), p. 14.
20. WILLIAMS, *op. cit.*, "The Discovery of Kentucky."
21. *ibid.*, "Père Sebastian Rasles."
22. *ibid.*
23. *ibid.*
24. *ibid.*
25. *ibid.*, "The Discovery of Kentucky."
26. *ibid.*
27. *ibid.*, "Voyage of the Mayflower'."
28. *ibid.*, "Poor Richard."
29. WILLIAM FAULKNER, *Absalom, Absalom!* (paperback: Harmondsworth 1971), Ch. I.
30. *ibid.*
31. *ibid.*, Ch. II.
32. *ibid.*, Ch. VII.
33. *ibid.*
34. *ibid.*
35. F. SCOTT FITZGERALD, *The Great Gatsby* (paperback: Harmondsworth 1954), p. 105.
36. *ibid.*, p. 8.
37. *ibid.*, p. 160.
38. *ibid.*, p. 8.
39. *ibid.*, p. 186.
40. *ibid.*, p. 117.
41. *ibid.*, p. 105.
42. *ibid.*, p. 70.
43. *ibid.*, p. 187.
44. *ibid.*, p. 96.
45. *ibid.*, pp. 187–8.
46. SHERWOOD ANDERSON, *Short Stories*, ed. by Maxwell Geismar (New York 1962), p. 11.
47. *ibid.*, p. 12.
48. *ibid.*, p. 13.

49. MARK TWAIN, *The Adventures of Huckleberry Finn* (paperback: Harmondsworth 1966), Ch. I.
50. *ibid.*, "Chapter the Last."
51. SHERWOOD ANDERSON, *Winesburg, Ohio* (London 1968), "Death."
52. LEWIS, *op. cit.*, p. 115.
53. HERMAN MELVILLE, *Billy Budd* (paperback: Harmondsworth 1968), Ch. I.
54. *ibid.*, Ch. II.
55. *ibid.*
56. *ibid.*
57. *ibid.*, Ch. XVI.
58. *ibid.*, Ch. XVII.
59. *ibid.*, Ch. VIII.
60. HENRY JAMES, *The Art of the Novel: Critical Prefaces*, ed. by R. P. Blackmur (New York 1934), p. 24.
61. HENRY JAMES, *The American* (paperback: London 1964), Ch. I.
62. *ibid.*, Ch. II.
63. *ibid.*
64. HENRY JAMES, *The Golden Bowl* (paperback: Harmondsworth 1966), Ch. XXVII.
65. *ibid.*, Ch. XXX.

CHAPTER 15

Literature and Science in 19th-Century England

David Daiches*

Early in the 17th century the English poet John Donne had expressed his unease about new scientific ideas:

> The new Philosophy calls all in doubt,
> The Element of fire is quite put out.

Over 100 years later Alexander Pope made it clear that the doubts had been dispelled:

> Nature and Nature's Laws lay hid in Night.
> God said, *Let Newton be!* and All was *Light*.

The English poets welcomed Newton with alacrity.[1] James Thomson's "A Poem Sacred to the Memory of Sir Isaac Newton" (1727) makes it clear how Newton had assisted the poet's contemplation of Nature:

> All-intellectual eye, our solar round
> First gazing through, he by the blended power
> Of *gravitation* and *projection* saw
> The whole in silent harmony revolve.
> From unassisted vision hid, the moons
> To cheer remoter planets numerous form'd,
> By him in all their mingled tracts were seen.

And again, in the same poem:

> Even Light itself, which every thing displays,
> Shone undiscover'd, till his brighter mind
> Untwisted all the shining robe of day;
> And, from the whitening undistinguish'd blaze,
> Collecting every ray unto his kind,
> To the charm'd eye educed the gorgeous train

* Professor of English, University of Sussex.

> Of parent colours. First the flaming Red
> Sprung vivid forth; the tawny Orange next;
> And next delicious Yellow; by whose side
> Fell the kind beams of all-refreshing Green:
> Then the pure Blue, that swells autumnal skies,
> Ethereal play'd; and then, of sadder hue,
> Emerged the deepen'd Indico, as when
> The heavy-skirted evening droops with frost;
> While the last gleamings of refracted light
> Died in the fainting Violet away.

And once again:

> Even now the setting sun and shifting clouds,
> Seen, Greenwich, from thy lovely heights, declare,
> How just, how beauteous, the *refractive law*.

The "laws" revealed by Newton gave a new beauty to the universe, and also gave those who contemplated them a renewed confidence in the existence of a Great Designer whose skill is revealed in his creation. Francis Bacon had distinguished between "God's word" and "God's work,"[2] insisting that the study of the latter—what we should call the natural sciences—is at least as proper for man as the study of the former. After Newton, defence of the study of God's work became easier. Although both speculative and experimental science were attacked in the early 18th century—by Swift among others—the deistic implications of order in nature were developed on all sides. Indeed, Deism, so important in English thought of the 18th century, was intimately connected with a confidence in the ordered government of the natural world. As Addison put it, in a poem that remained popular throughout the century and was to haunt the mind of Robert Burns:

> The spacious firmament on high,
> With all the blue ethereal sky,
> And spangled heavens, a shining frame,
> Their great Original proclaim.
> Th' unwearied Sun from day to day
> Does his Creator's power display;
> And publishes to every land
> The work of an Almighty hand. . . .
>
> What though in solemn silence all
> Move round the dark terrestrial ball;
> What though no real voice nor sound
> Amidst their radiant orbs be found?
> In Reason's ear they all rejoice,
> And utter forth a glorious Voice;
> For ever singing as they shine,
> "The Hand that made us is Divine."

John Ray's *The Wisdom of God Manifested in the Works of Creation*, though published as early as 1691, remained in use as a science text-book throughout the 18th century, and, together with William Derham's *Physico-Theology* (1713; significantly, originally given as Boyle Lectures, that is, lectures in natural theology endowed by the scientist Robert Boyle) and *Astro-Theology* (1715), provided the total scientific education of the young Robert Burns. Well into the 19th century, science continued to be taught to young people as part of the "argument from design" for the existence of God. And it was Newton who had restored Nature to God.

The effects of Newton's demonstration that the world of nature is governed by mathematical laws worked side by side with John Locke's view of the functioning of the mind as analogous to the workings of matter. But, as Donald Davie has pointed out,[3] the Lockean analogies could be made to work both ways, either "to bring over into ethics and psychology the terminology of natural science," or ironically, to degrade pretentious spiritual terms into mechanical ones (as Swift did with "inspiration"). "If words from physics, chemistry and physiology can be dignified from having a merely material reference into having an immaterial one, words from religion and ethics and aesthetics can be deflated from having a spiritual reference into having a grossly corporeal one."[4] "Gravity" had a primarily psychological meaning when Newton first used it; by restoring its root meaning in denoting a physical law, Newton made it possible for poets to be witty in new ways. Thus Pope could write in Book IV of *The Dunciad* (1742):

> None need a guide, by sure Attraction led,
> And strong impulsive gravity of Head:
> None want a place, for all their Centre found,
> Hung to the Goddess, and coher'd around.
> Not closer, orb in orb, conglob'd are seen
> The buzzing Bees about their dusky Queen.

The Newtonian pun thus enriches the English poetic language.

Whether the Augustan writers used such language satirically, to imply their suspicion of mechanical philosophy, or seriously, to suggest their approval of the new science, or humorously and punningly, exploiting the situation without committing themselves—Swift, Thomson, and Pope respectively are examples of the three categories—the reader gets the feeling that science is working *with* literature. There is certainly no suggestion of the man of letters being blankly hostile to the scientist, or of the literary imagination feeling the scientific mode of apprehension as a threat and a menace. But it is precisely this kind of hostility, this feeling of threat, that develops later in the 18th century, to become an important current in the Romantic movement. Even before this there were signs of a developing feeling that the literary imagination preferred to roam

> Where Superstition with capricious hand
> In many a maze the wreathèd window planned,
> With hues romantic tinged the gorgeous pane,
> To fill with holy light the wondrous fane.[5]

Bishop Hurd's *Letters on Chivalry and Romance* (1762) suggested that a pre-scientific age might foster the literary imagination more than an age of reason. "What we have gotten by this revolution . . . is a great deal of good sense. What we have lost, is a world of fine fabling." Here lies the germ of a rift between science and the literary imagination that was to provoke much discussion in the 19th and 20th centuries. Nevertheless, the point as expressed by Hurd and Warton did not seem to represent a frontal attack on established ways of thinking; it was nothing more than a mild suggestion. But when William Blake takes up the cry (in "The Song of Los"), the discussion is on a quite different level:

> Thus the terrible race of Los & Enitharmon gave
> Laws & Religions to the sons of Har, binding them more
> And more to Earth, closing and restraining,
> Till a Philosophy of Five Senses was complete.
> Urizen wept & gave it into the hands of Newton & Locke.

Blake's attack on the whole tradition of Western thought since the 17th century was open and radical. "Bacon's Philosophy has Destroy'd Art & Science." And, most succinctly of all:

> May God us keep
> From Single vision & Newton's sleep![6]

Newton and Locke are the villains of the piece for Blake, as they were to be more than a century later for W. B. Yeats:

> Locke sank into a swoon;
> The Garden died;
> God took the spinning-jenny
> Out of his side.

A "Philosophy of Five Senses," an industrial, materialist society, and middle-class Philistinism were, on this view, equated or closely related. And though one current in the Romantic movement was in fact pro-scientific—as we see clearly in Shelley (whose poem "The Cloud" is meteorologically exact, and who combined a high neo-Platonic idealism with the traditional Platonic interest in the mathematical sciences) and, in a different way, later in Tennyson—the anti-scientific current was strong enough to reach into the next century. The lines on Newton that Wordsworth added after 1830 to Book III of *The Prelude* (lines 61–3) show Newton as a hero:

> Newton with his prism and silent face,
> The marble index of a mind for ever
> Voyaging through strange seas of Thought, alone.

Wordsworth had not immediately joined in drinking a famous toast proposed by Keats many years earlier. "And don't you remember," Haydon wrote years later to Wordsworth, "Keats proposing 'Confusion to the memory of Newton,' and upon your insisting on an explanation before you drank it, his saying: 'Because he destroyed the poetry of the rainbow by reducing it to a prism.' "[7]

Wordsworth was in fact notable among the Romantic poets in agreeing with the late 17th- and early 18th-century writers who believed that poetry could be enriched by science; he went further, and argued that poetry could and should *absorb* science. "Poetry is the breath and finer spirit of all Science. . . . If the labours of Men of science should ever create any material revolution, direct or indirect, in our condition, and in the impressions which we habitually receive, the Poet will sleep then no more than at present: he will be ready to follow the steps of the Man of science, not only in those general indirect effects, but he will be at his side, carrying sensation into the midst of the objects of the science itself."[8] And Wordsworth specifically names "the remotest discoveries of the Chemist, the Botanist, or Mineralogist" as proper objects of the Poet's art "if the time should ever come when these things shall be familiar to us as enjoying and suffering beings."[8] The poet, to Wordsworth, brings out the human relevance of scientific knowledge. So we understand why he was reluctant to join Keats in denouncing Newton. Nor would he have agreed with Keats's famous lines in *Lamia*:

> Do not all charms fly
> At the mere touch of cold philosophy?
> There was an awful rainbow once in heaven:
> We know her woof, her texture; she is given
> In the dull catalogue of common things.
> Philosophy will clip an Angel's wings,
> Conquer all mysteries by rule and line,
> Empty the haunted air, and gnomèd mine—
> Unweave a rainbow, as it erewhile made
> The tender-person'd Lamia melt into a shade.

Keats is radically opposed to Thomson here. "In maintaining, with Lamb, that Newton 'had destroyed all the poetry of the rainbow by *reducing* it to the prismatic colours,' Keats accedes to the fallacy (in which he has been joined by numerous professional philosophers) that, when a perceptual phenomenon is explained by correlating it with something more elementary than itself, the explanation discredits and replaces the perception—that only the explanation is real, and the perception illusory. And to Keats, if not to Thomson, the ability to versify and dramatize the new scientific 'truths' was no adequate payment for the 'life of sensations,' and the 'indolent' surrender to the sensuous concrete which is integral to his characteristic poetry."[9] Neither Wordsworth nor Shelley, for different reasons, would have agreed. Wordsworth himself asserted quite specifically that "the beauty in form of a plant or an animal is made not less but more apparent as a whole by more accurate insight into its constituent properties and powers."[10] Shelley, who classed Francis Bacon with Dante, Shakespeare, and Milton as ideally a "poet," and who firmly believed that poetry and science should go hand in hand, only criticized the effects of a science unaccompanied by "the poetical faculty." In *A Defence of Poetry* he conceded that the Baconian aim of dominating nature could have bad results: "The cultivation of those sciences which have enlarged the limits of the empire of men over the external world, has, for want of the poetical faculty, proportionately circumscribed those of the internal world; and man, having enslaved the elements, remains himself a slave. To what but a cultivation of the mechanical arts in a degree disproportioned to the presence of the creative faculty, which is the basis of all knowledge, is to be attributed the abuse of all inventions for abridging and combining labour, to the exasperation of the inequality of mankind." This side of Shelley's thought brings him close to the Victorian "prophets" Carlyle and Ruskin, with their suspicion of mechanism, where they were at one with Blake and with Coleridge. But theirs was not, as Blake's was, a fundamental suspicion of the whole basis of modern science. Coleridge objected to what Abrams has conveniently called "the mistaken and unbounded metaphysical pretensions of atomism and mechanism—in Coleridge's view, a useful working hypothesis for physical research which had been illicitly converted first into fact, and then into a total world-view."[11] The suspicion of science and the suspicion of a mechanistic philosophy, though they sometimes went together, were far from being the same thing.

In his notes on Joshua Reynolds' *Discourses* (*c.* 1808), Blake had written: "To Generalize is to be an Idiot. To Particularize is the Alone

Distinction of Merit. General Knowledges are those Knowledges that Idiots possess." This is a virulent version of a long tradition, which goes back at least to Joseph Warton's *Essay on the Writings and Genius of Pope* (1756). Warton saw the selection and description of minute particulars as characteristic of poetry as distinct from history, and thus flatly contradicted both Aristotle (who saw poetry as more universal than history) and Dr Johnson (who objected to the poet's numbering "the streaks of the tulip" because his business was "to remark general properties and large appearances"). That poetry is concrete and science general became more and more accepted as the 19th century progressed. "Generalization is necessary to the advancement of knowledge, but particularity is indispensable to the creatures of imagination," wrote Macaulay in his essay on Milton (1825). This tradition was given a new lease of life in the 20th century by the Imagist movement, and has entered into modern critical theory as a fairly central and orthodox view. For John Crowe Ransom in 1934, "pure poetry" was "a kind of Physical Poetry" that is "the basic constituent of any poetry." And "its visible content is a thing-content." What is called "Platonic poetry" only pretended to deal in things; it really dealt with general ideas, and was therefore bad.[12]

Another distinction that came to be made more and more as the 19th century advanced concerned the role of poetry and of imaginative literature in general in the education of the feelings. It is what things are to human sensibility, not to the analysing instruments and classifying mind of the scientist, that matters in man's emotional life, and the emotional life is the true inner life. "The difference between the mere botanist's knowledge of plants, and the great poet's or painter's knowledge of them," wrote Ruskin in the Preface to *Modern Painters* (1843), is that "the one notes their distinctions for the sake of swelling his herbarium, the other, that he may render them vehicles of expression and emotion." Abrams has set beside this quotation Matthew Arnold's remark in his essay "Maurice de Guérin" (in *Essays in Criticism,* 1865):

> It is not Linnaeus or Cavendish or Cuvier who gives us the true
> sense of animals, or water, or plants, who seizes their secret for us,
> who makes us participate in their life; it is Shakespeare, with his
> "daffodils
> That come before the swallow dares, and take
> The winds of March with beauty. . . ."

The distinction between science (which addresses itself to the individual's belief) and poetry (which addresses itself to his feelings) is closely related to the distinction between scientific and poetic truth, about which critics have argued since Aristotle. Coleridge's famous remark about the "willing suspension of disbelief" that poetry produces in us is only one, rather faint, shot in a long battle. The general lines on which the idea of poetic truth was developed are indicated partly by J. S. Mill's view that the poet's duty is to feel and communicate feeling, whereas the scientist's is to know and communicate truth (in a letter to G. H. Lewes he defined poetry as "feeling expressing itself in the forms of thought"[13]), and partly by Matthew Arnold's argument in trying to rescue religion from its dependence on the literal historicity of the Bible:

> Our religion has materialised itself in the fact, in the supposed fact; it has attached its emotion to the fact, and now the fact is failing it. But for poetry the idea is everything; the rest is a world of illusion, of divine illusion. Poetry attaches its emotion to the idea; the idea *is* the fact. The strongest part of our religion to-day is its unconscious poetry.[14]

In spite of his somewhat misleading emphasis on "the idea," Arnold is not here pleading for poetry as primarily a philosophical or intellectual activity; he is trying to differentiate the kind of meaning that language bears in poetry from that which it bears in history or science. I. A. Richards quoted with approval this passage of Arnold's, 46 years later, when, in his book *Science and Poetry* (1926), he made distinctions between the poetic and the scientific use of language. Richards had already—with C. K. Ogden, in *The Meaning of Meaning* (1923)—differentiated between "emotive" meaning (which "tells us, or should tell us, nothing") and "scientific" or "referential" meaning. In *Science and Poetry* he developed this point further. "In its use of words poetry is just the reverse of science. Very definite thoughts do occur, but not because the words are so chosen as logically to bar all possibilities but one. No. But because the manner, the tone of voice, the cadence and the rhythm play upon our interests and make *them* pick out from among an indefinite number of possibilities the precise particular thought which they need."[15] Ultimately, this line of argument goes right back to Sir Philip Sidney, who in his *Apologie for Poetrie* (first published posthumously in 1595) had argued that the poet "nothing affirmes, and therefore never lyeth." But the concern of both Arnold and Richards was not to defend poets against the ancient charge of being liars: it was, for Arnold, to defend and define the central value to civilization of a kind of discourse that was not necessarily (or even preferably) true in any historical or scientific way; and, for Richards, to define as scientifically as possible the non-scientific use of language in poetry, and to show the psychological value to the reader of reading and responding to works written in that non-scientific kind of language. Arnold was also concerned to save religion from biblical fundamentalism, because the higher criticism of the Bible was daily making a literal-historical reading of some parts of the Bible more difficult. If there is a truth of the imagination, a truth of feeling, a religious truth—and these terms were increasingly being associated—then the Bible can be saved as poetry, to rank with the *Iliad* as a work in which "perfect plainness of speech is allied with perfect nobleness" (*On Translating Homer*, 1861), and religion can be re-defined as "morality touched by emotion" (*Literature and Dogma*, 1873).

The higher criticism of the Bible, no less than new ideas in geology and biology, represented a threat from science to fundamentalist religion; and in subsuming religion in poetry, Arnold was extending to it the kind of protection that critics had for some time been developing for imaginative literature. The "argument from design" had enabled 18th-century thinkers to reconcile science and religion, although at the cost of trans-forming the latter from a dogmatic Christianity into a generalized Deism. But the evangelical movements of the late 18th and early 19th century and the increasing commitment, when challenged, not only of Nonconformism but also of a considerable section of the Church of England to a biblical fundamentalism, and indeed the new interest in dogma, ritual, and theology illustrated by the Oxford Movement, now made the simple equation of religion with belief in the existence of a Great Designer impossible. It was not, in Baconian terms, God's Work but God's Word that was the subject of debate. If what the scientist told us about the age and the development of the natural world (including man) contradicted what was told in holy writ, then arguments about a Great Designer were beside the point. The question was whether the ways of discovering truth open to the natural scientist represented the only ways; and if they did not, what kind of insights, discovered in what way, communicated in what kind of language, were represented by the "truths" of religion—and poetry. There is an interesting corollary here. If religion is saved as poetry, and is still seen as representing something central in civilization, then poetry too must take on the prestige of religion and be valued as something central in civilization, and the task of defining what Arnold called "the best" poetry becomes the high function of the priest-critic. The distinction of the literary canon from the apocrypha, the selection of the best, the tracing of the "great tradition" in a national literature, becomes, in a line of thought that extends from Arnold to F. R. Leavis (who coined the phrase "great tradition"), the critic's function. And so the function of the critic becomes exalted: he is now, as it were, an interpreter of holy writ. This is one reason why the 20th century has become a great age of criticism.

The impact on Victorian thought of the work of geologists and biologists—notably of Sir Charles Lyell (*Principles of Geology*, 1830–4; *The Geological Evidences of the Antiquity of Man*, 1863) and Sir Charles Darwin (*On the Origin of Species*, 1859; *The Descent of Man*, 1871)—led to a new kind of conflict between science and religious orthodoxy that is a familiar aspect of late Victorian thought. Edmund Gosse, in his *Father and Son* (1907), gives an account of his father P. H. Gosse, a distinguished biologist, who was at the same time a member of the Plymouth Brethren and an uncompromising biblical fundamentalist. This conflict between the scientist and the man of religion within the same person is a classic case. P. H. Gosse's book *Omphalos* (1857) is an ingenious but basically preposterous attempt to reconcile geological evidence with the biblical account of the Creation. Even where there was no direct conflict there were varieties of doubt and even anguish that are reflected in literature. Tennyson, who had read Lyell's *Principles of Geology* in 1837, worried about evolution years before Darwin presented his views on natural selection and the survival of the fittest:

> Are God and Nature then at strife,
> > That Nature lends such evil dreams?
> > So careful of the type she seems,
> So careless of the single life;
>
> That I, considering everywhere
> > Her secret meaning in her deeds,
> > And finding that of fifty seeds
> She often brings but one to bear,
>
> I falter where I firmly trod. . . .

And in the next section of "In Memoriam" he talked of "Nature, red in tooth and claw." But he willed himself to believe optimistically in evolution and in progress, in spite of doubts. In the poem "By an Evolutionist," written in old age, we see this willed belief at work:

> If my body come from brutes, though somewhat finer than their own,
> > I am heir, and this my kingdom. Shall the royal voice be mute?
> No, but if the rebel subject seek to drag me from the throne,
> > Hold the sceptre, Human Soul, and rule thy Province of the brute.
>
> I have climbed to the snows of Age, and I gaze at a field in the Past,
> > Where I sank with the body at times in the sloughs of a low desire,
> But I hear no yelp of the beast, and the Man is quiet at last
> > As he stands on the heights of his life with a glimpse of a height
> > > that is higher.

Nevertheless, the shaking of traditional beliefs by the joint forces of biblical criticism, geology, and biology lay behind the sense of loss that we find echoed in so many ways in Victorian poetry. "There is not a creed which is not shaken, not an accredited dogma which is not shown to be questionable, not a received tradition which does not threaten to dissolve," wrote Arnold at the beginning of his essay on "The Study of Poetry," and in "Dover Beach," a central poem in the Victorian elegiac mode, he gave classic expression to the mid-century sense of loss:

> The Sea of Faith
> Was once, too, at the full, and round earth's shore
> Lay like the folds of a bright girdle furled.
> But now I only hear
> Its melancholy, long, withdrawing roar,
> Retreating, to the breath
> Of the night-wind, down the vast edges drear
> And naked shingles of the world.

This is the Victorian version of Donne's line, "The new Philosophy calls all in doubt." In "Stanzas from the Grande Chartreuse" Arnold spoke of himself as

> Wandering between two worlds, one dead,
> The other powerless to be born. . . .

His friend A. H. Clough faced the question more directly:

> Matthew and Mark and Luke and holy John
> Evanished all and gone!

And sometimes with genuine anguish (in "Easter Day, Naples, 1849"):

> Where they have laid Him is there none to say!
> No sound, nor in, nor out; no word
> Of where to seek the dead or meet the living Lord;
> There is no glistering of an angel's wings,
> There is no voice of heavenly clear behest:
> Let us go hence, and think upon these things
> In silence, which is best.
> > Is He not risen? No—
> > But lies and moulders low—
> > > Christ is not risen.

It is true that Clough answers this with a counter-poem, also called "Easter Day," in which he asserts

> In the great Gospel, and true Creed,
> He is yet risen indeed;
> > Christ is yet risen.

Clough interspersed his sceptical or anguished or ironical poems with such cries of willed optimistic belief, as in the famous "Say not the struggle nought availeth" (which may have been written as a reply to Arnold's "Dover Beach"), but it is the former note that is sounded more memorably. Sometimes he is the most explicit of all the Victorian poets on the science-religion theme, as in "When Israel Came Out of Egypt":

> And as of old from Sinai's top
>   God said that God is one,
> By Science strict so speaks He now
>   To tell us, There is None!
> Earth goes by chemic forces; Heaven's
>   A Mécanique Céleste!
> And heart and mind of human kind
>   A watch-work as the rest!

Yet this might almost have been written in the 18th century: it does not touch on any of the specifically Victorian reasons for doubt.

The writer in whom the currents of Victorian thought moved to deepest scepticism was Thomas Hardy, for whom the part played by chance in Darwinian natural selection coincided with his own view (as in "Nature's Questioning") that human life was governed by "purblind Doomsters":

> Has some Vast Imbecility,
>   Mighty to build and blend,
>   But impotent to tend,
> Framed us in jest, and left us now to hazardry?

Of course it was not only, or even mainly, modern science that influenced Hardy here: he had read and been influenced by J. S. Mill, Herbert Spencer, Leslie Stephen, and probably also Schopenhauer. And he was less worried by Arnold's problem of the loss of traditional faith than by the way the world was governed with respect to human existence. "It was as though he said: 'Never mind about Arnold's Sea of Faith retreating: what about the paradoxes, ironies, frustrations and contradictions in the lives of ordinary people?' He changed the terms of the question, which was no more either 'What can I believe?' or even 'What should I do?' but 'What are the true conditions of ordinary human existence?' "[16] And that is what his novels are about.

Darwinism had other effects on literature apart from inducing worry. What has been called "social Darwinism," emphasizing the Malthusian element in Darwin and the implications of the "struggle for existence" and "the survival of the fittest," had an effect on the naturalistic novel

452

on both sides of the Atlantic, strengthening the tendency to show environment rather than individual character as the main determinant of man's fate.[17] In many ways the most interesting response to Darwin on the part of a man of letters was that of Samuel Butler. Butler objected to the non-teleological nature of Darwin's theory of natural selection, to the assumption that no active intelligence was at work in the evolutionary process, and though he rejected a divine intelligence designing from without, he accepted and developed Lamarck's view that evolutionary changes occurred because of the design and purpose of the creatures involved. According to Lamarck, new surroundings (*circonstances*) gave rise to new wants (*besoins*), and these produced new habits and new organs; "new parts . . . become insensibly evolved in the creature by its own efforts from within."[18] Thus there was a purposive "life force" at work, and natural selection was not an automatic process. There are evolutionary ideas in Butler's novels, from *Erewhon* (1872) to *The Way of All Flesh* (1903), but it is in such works as *Life and Habit* (1877–8), *Evolution Old and New* (1879), and *Luck, or Cunning?* (1886–7) that he develops his ideas on evolution directly and at length.

Bernard Shaw took over with enthusiasm Butler's view of evolution (as of certain other matters), and his most ambitious play, *Back to Methuselah* (1921), which he considered his masterpiece, is wholly based on this view. That Shaw rejected Darwin and accepted Lamarck and Butler, where the latter two differed from the former, he makes abundantly clear in the belligerent preface to this play. Shaw held that the Darwinian theory held out no hope of human improvement. "According to the Neo-Darwinists, to the Mechanists, there is no hope whatever, because improvement can come only through some senseless accident which must, on the statistical average of accidents, be presently wiped out by some other equally senseless accident." In opposition to this "dismal creed" Shaw put what he called "creative evolution," whose advocates "have observed the simple fact that the will to do anything can and does, at a certain pitch of intensity set up by the conviction of its necessity, create and organize new tissue to do it with." The duration of individual life could, he maintained, be changed in this way. "If Man now fixes the term of his life at three score and ten years he can fix it at three hundred or three thousand. . . . This is not fantastic speculation: it is deductive biology, if there is such a science as biology." Shaw wanted an enormous increase in human longevity because he believed that "even our oldest men do not live long enough: they are, for all the purposes of high civilization, mere children when they die." He wanted an increase in

453

human wisdom far beyond anything that could be acquired in the present term of an individual human life. But more than that, he wanted assurance that will and intelligence counted for something in the evolutionary process. "If you like eating the tender tops of trees enough to make you concentrate all your energies on the stretching of your neck, you will finally get a long neck, like the giraffe." At bottom, this represented a very Victorian belief in will-power, and it sounds a bit like Samuel Smiles. Shaw was responding, as Butler had done, from a standpoint that could in the most general sense be called religious, to the casualness, the "chapter of accidents" as he called it, involved in the Darwinian process. "There is a hideous fatalism about it, a ghastly and damnable reduction of beauty and intelligence, of strength and purpose, of honour and aspiration, to such casually picturesque changes as an avalanche may make in a mountain landscape, or a railway accident in a human figure." It is interesting that Shaw, the iconoclast, the scourge of the respectable and the traditional, should in the work that he considered his masterpiece have struck a blow for the traditional religious view of man against the popular scientific view.

Meanwhile, an important debate on the conflicting claims of science and literature had been going on in the field of education, notably between T. H. Huxley and Matthew Arnold. The key documents here are, on the one side, Huxley's essays *A Liberal Education and Where to Find It*, originally delivered at the South London Workingmen's College in 1868, and *Science and Culture*, originally an address delivered at the opening of Sir Josiah Mason's Science College, Birmingham, in 1880; and, on the other side, Arnold's *Literature and Science*, originally the Rede Lecture at Cambridge, 1882, and later published in *Discourses in America* (1885). Huxley makes an eloquent plea for Nature as the true educator:

> To every one of us the world was once as fresh and new as to Adam. And then, long before we were susceptible of any other mode of instruction, Nature took us in hand, and every minute of waking life brought its educational influence, shaping our actions into rough accordance with Nature's laws, so that we might not be ended untimely by too gross disobedience. . . . Those who take honours in Nature's university, who learn the laws which govern men and things and obey them, are the really great and successful men in this world. . . .

Nature, however, is a harsh teacher. "Nature's discipline is not even a word and a blow, and the blow first; but the blow without the word. It is left to you to find out why your ears are boxed."

454

The object of what we commonly call education—that education in which man intervenes which I shall distinguish as artificial education—is to make good these defects in Nature's methods; to prepare the child to receive Nature's education, neither incapably nor ignorantly, nor with wilful disobedience; and to understand the preliminary symptoms of her pleasure, without waiting for the box on the ear. . . .

He goes on to give a damning description of conventional English education, with a great deal of ironical wit. Not that he is by any means against literature and the study of the classics:

But if the classics were taught as they might be taught—if boys and girls were instructed in Greek and Latin, not merely as languages, but as illustrations of philological science; if a vivid picture of life on the shores of the Mediterranean two thousand years ago were imprinted on the minds of scholars; if ancient history were taught, not as a weary series of feuds and fights, but traced to its causes in such men placed under such conditions; if, lastly, the study of the classical books were followed in such a manner as to impress boys with their beauties, and with the grand simplicity of their statement of the everlasting problems of human life, instead of with their verbal and grammatical peculiarities—I still think it as little proper that they should form the basis of a liberal education for our contemporaries, as I should think it fitting to make that sort of palaeontology with which I am familiar the backbone of modern education.

It is wonderful how close a parallel to classical training could be made out of that palaeontology to which I refer. In the first place I could get up an osteological primer so arid, so pedantic in its terminology, so altogether distasteful to the youthful mind, as to beat the recent famous production of the headmasters out of the field in all these excellences. Next, I could exercise my boys upon easy fossils, and bring out all their powers of memory and all their ingenuity in the application of my osteo-grammatical rules to the interpretation, or the construing, of those fragments. To those who had reached the higher classes, I might supply odd bones to be built up into animals, giving great honour and reward to him who succeeded in fabricating monsters most entirely in accordance with the rules. That would answer to verse-making and essay-writing in the dead languages.

Huxley goes on to re-assert his belief in "the beauty, and the human interest, which appertain to classical studies," but points out that most schoolboys never reach the stage of proficiency that allows them to appreciate these. He compares English university education unfavourably with German, mocking the limitations of the former:

Imagine the success of the attempt to still the intellectual hunger of any of the men I have mentioned by putting before him, as the

> object of existence, the successful mimicry of the measure of a Greek
> song, or the role of Ciceronian prose! Imagine how much success
> would be likely to attend the attempt to persuade such men that
> the education which leads to perfection in such elegances is alone
> to be called culture, while the facts of history, the process of thought,
> the conditions of moral and social existence, and the laws of physical
> nature are left to be dealt with as they may by outside barbarians![19]

Huxley's plea is for a more inclusive education, not for a purely
scientific one:

> Thus I venture to think that the pretensions of our modern Humanists
> to the possession of the monopoly of culture and to the exclusive
> inheritance of the spirit of antiquity must be abated, if not abandoned.
> But I should be very sorry that anything I have said should be taken
> to imply a desire on my part to depreciate the value of classical
> education, as it might be, and as it sometimes is.[20]

He pleads also for a knowledge of French and German, the latter being
"absolutely indispensable to those who desire full knowledge in any
department of science," and for a proper grounding in the student's own
native English literature. "If an Englishman cannot get literary culture
out of his Bible, his Shakespeare, his Milton, neither, in my belief, will
the profoundest study of Homer and Sophocles, Virgil and Horace, give
it to him." He argues for the study of the history of science as well as of
science itself, and he adds that students "must learn that social phenomena
are as much the expression of natural laws as any others" and that knowledge of them "is only to be obtained by the application of the methods
of investigation adopted in physical researches to the investigation of the
phenomena of society." And therefore he advocates sociology as part of
the curriculum. He gives, in short, a radically new view of the nature of
a liberal education, with the natural and biological sciences playing their
full part alongside the study of society and the properly humane study of
literature.

Huxley was answered by Arnold in *Literature and Science*. He begins by
correcting what he considers a misapprehension on Huxley's part of the
nature of classical studies and of literary studies in general. "I mean
more than a knowledge of so much vocabulary, so much grammar, so
many portions of authors in the Greek and Latin languages. I mean
knowing the Greeks and Romans, and their life and genius, and what
they were and did in the world; what we get from them and what is its
value." And by literature Arnold does not mean merely *belles lettres*: his
definition would include Euclid's *Elements* and Newton's *Principia*, and
"by knowing modern nations, I mean not merely knowing their *belles*

lettres, but knowing also what has been done by such men as Copernicus, Galileo, Newton, Darwin." So far, then, there is no real disagreement between them. But although admitting the interest and importance of the natural sciences, Arnold insists that they belong to what he calls "the sphere of intellect and knowledge." "It will be knowledge only which [the natural scientists] give us; knowledge not put for us into relation with our sense of conduct, our sense of beauty, and touched with emotion by being so put; not thus put for us, and therefore, to the majority of mankind, after a certain while, unsatisfying, wearying." This knowledge will not, of course, be unsatisfying "to the born naturalist," such as Darwin, "but then Darwins are extremely rare."

The greater the advance of modern science, Arnold argues, the greater "the need of humane letters":

> The need of humane letters, as they are truly called, because they serve the paramount desire in men that good should be for ever present to them,—the need of humane letters, to establish a relation between the new conceptions [in science, which have ousted "the notions held by our forefathers"], and our instinct for beauty, our instinct for conduct, is only the more visible. The Middle Ages could do without humane letters, as it could do without the study of nature, because its supposed knowledge was made to engage its emotions so powerfully. Grant that the supposed knowledge disappears, its power of being made to engage the emotions will of course disappear along with it,—but the emotions themselves, and their claim to be engaged and satisfied, will remain. Now if we find by experience that humane letters have an undeniable power of engaging the emotions, the importance of humane letters in a man's training becomes not less, but greater, in proportion to the success of modern science in extirpating what it calls "mediaeval thinking". . . .
>
> And the more that men's minds are cleared, the more that the results of science are frankly accepted, the more that poetry and eloquence come to be received and studied as what in truth they really are,—criticism of life by gifted men, alive and active with extraordinary power at an unusual number of points;—so much the more will the value of humane letters, and of art also, which is an utterance having a like kind of power with theirs, be felt and acknowledged, and their place in education be secured.[21]

Turning to the classics, Arnold goes on to plead for the extended study of Greek, because Greek literature and art serve "the instinct for beauty . . . as it is served by no other literature and art." He stresses Greek rather than Latin here because it was Greek that had come under heaviest attack (and it has been declining in English education ever since). He agrees that Greek, "with letters generally," should be "studied more rationally." But humane letters in general must hold their place in education "so long as human nature is what it is." The implication is clearly that literature serves a timeless aesthetic and moral need in a way that natural knowledge, for all its importance, does not.

The first stage in the conflict between literature and science in England was less a direct conflict between these than a larger debate between those who believed in the decline of the world and those who believed in progress—a debate that was conducted on large theological, philosophical, and historical grounds in the 17th century, and attenuated down by the end of the century to become the Battle of the Books between the Ancients, who defended the supremacy of the classics, and the Moderns, who defended modern writing (which included scientific writing). The second stage emerged in the 19th century, and is clearly shown in the debate between Huxley and Arnold. The third stage emerged with unusual virulence in the 1960s, in F. R. Leavis's attack on C. P. Snow's view of the "two cultures." Snow's essay *The Two Cultures and the Scientific Revolution* (1959) was the Rede Lecture at Cambridge 77 years after Arnold's Rede Lecture, *Literature and Science*, and Leavis's attack on it was the Richmond Lecture at Downing College, Cambridge, in 1962. Snow's position was in favour of the emergent scientific culture as against traditional literary culture in the interests of survival: it is neither as clearheaded nor as thoughtful as Huxley's. And Leavis's attack had nothing of the courtesy and humanity of Arnold's reply to Huxley, and was full of irrelevant arguments *ad hominem*. But at least this confused and ill-argued controversy showed that the problem of the relation between science and literature was still exercising intelligent people in the second half of the 20th century.[22]

References

1. See MARJORIE NICOLSON, *Newton Demands the Muse* (Princeton 1946), which deals particularly with the influence of the *Opticks* (1704) on 18th-century English poetry; and DONALD DAVIE, *The Language of Science and the Language of Literature, 1700–1740* (London 1963), which considers the effects of Newtonian theories on literary language.
2. FRANCIS BACON, *The Advancement of Learning* (1605).
3. DAVIE, *op. cit.*, pp. 23 ff.
4. *ibid.*, p. 27.
5. THOMAS WARTON, "Verses on Sir Joshua Reynolds' Painted Window at New College, Oxford" (1782).

6. In G. KEYNES (ed.), *The Poetry and Prose of William Blake* (London 1932). The remark about Bacon (pp. 1002–3) is in Blake's "Marginalia" to Reynolds' *Discourses*; the lines of verse (p. 1068) are the conclusion of some verses he copies out for his friend Thomas Butts.

7. Quoted in M. H. ABRAMS, *The Mirror and the Lamp* (New York 1953), p. 309. Ch. 11 of Abrams' book, "Science and Poetry in Romantic Criticism," is very relevant to this whole subject.

8. Preface to 2nd edn of *Lyrical Ballads*, in *The Poetical Works of William Wordsworth*, ed. by T. Hutchinson, rev. by E. de Selincourt (London 1950), p. 738.

9. ABRAMS, *op. cit.*, p. 307.

10. Notes dictated to Isabella Fenwick, on "This Lawn, a carpet all alive"; in *The Poetical Works of William Wordsworth*, ed. by E. de Selincourt and H. Darbishire (Oxford 1940–9), Vol. IV, p. 425.

11. ABRAMS, *op. cit.*, p. 310.

12. JOHN CROWE RANSOM, "Pure and Impure Poetry," in *Critiques and Essays in Criticism*, ed. by R. W. Stallman (New York 1949).

13. *The Earlier Letters of John Stuart Mill, 1812–1848*, ed. by F. E. Mineka (Toronto and London 1963), Vol. II, pp. 470–1.

14. Introduction to *The English Poets*, selected and ed. by T. H. Ward (London 1880), Vol. I, p. xvii. Arnold quoted this passage from himself at the beginning of his essay "The Study of Poetry," in *Essays in Criticism*, 2nd series (1888).

15. Quoted and discussed in DAVID DAICHES, *Critical Approaches to Literature* (New York 1956), pp. 129–42.

16. DAVID DAICHES, *Some Late Victorian Attitudes* (London 1969), p. 75.

17. See LEO J. HENKIN, *Darwinism in the English Novel: 1860–1910* (New York 1940); MALCOLM COWLEY, "Naturalism in America," in *Evolutionary Thought in America*, ed. by S. Persons (New York 1956); L. STEVENSON, *Darwin Among the Poets* (Chicago 1932); GEORG ROPPEN, *Evolution and Poetic Belief* (Oslo 1956).

18. See B. WILLEY, *Darwin and Butler: Two Versions of Evolution* (London 1960), pp. 76–7 *et passim*.

19. T. H. HUXLEY, *A Liberal Education and Where to Find It*. This was published in *Macmillan's Magazine* in 1868. Reprinted in F. W. ROE (ed.), *Victorian Prose* (New York 1947), pp. 487–97.

20. *Science and Culture*. Published in T. H. HUXLEY, *Science and Culture and Other Essays* (1881). Reprinted in ROE (ed.), *op. cit.*, pp. 497–505.

21. MATTHEW ARNOLD, *Literature and Science*. Reprinted in *Matthew Arnold: Poetry and Prose*, ed. by John Bryson (London 1954), pp. 642–66.

22. The sanest and most thoughtful account of the controversy is LIONEL TRILLING, "The Leavis-Snow Controversy," in *Beyond Culture: Essays on Literature and Learning* (London 1966).

CHAPTER 16

The Cult of Art

Anthony Thorlby*

> Social rules are made by normal people for normal people, and the man of genius is fundamentally abnormal. It is the poet against society, society against the poet, a direct antagonism.[1]
>
> ARTHUR SYMONS

> Outside the hive the bee sickens and dies; when man is cut off from society, or takes an inadequate part in its communal efforts, he suffers perhaps from a similar disease, which has hitherto not been properly studied: it is called *ennui*.[2]
>
> HENRI BERGSON

The doctrine of Art for Art's Sake rests upon a distinction between what is useful and what is beautiful, between all that serves merely to perpetuate the life process, and art, which transcends it. From this point of view, art can be regarded as perfectly useless; its ultimate perfection coincides with its utter uselessness. During the 19th century a growing number of artists and writers throughout Europe came to accept as self-evident the basic premise of this doctrine, even though there was no general acceptance of any single theory based upon it. In fact, by the beginning of the present century there was rather a variety of doctrines, some of them of great imaginative subtlety, concerning the autonomy and absoluteness of art. Although it would be inadequate to consider the work of, say, Yeats or Joyce, Proust or Valéry, Rilke or George, in terms of so simple an axiom, their achievement may be said to exploit possibilities of vision and language made available by the earlier, prolonged tendency toward Art for Art's Sake. The European imagination owed this new creative opportunity largely to France. There the doctrine first began to take shape in such writings as Gautier's preface to *Mademoiselle de Maupin* (1835), in similar prefaces by Leconte de Lisle, in the essays of Baudelaire, the letters of Flaubert, and the journal of the

* Professor of Comparative Literature, University of Sussex.

brothers Goncourt. It was fulfilled above all in *Les fleurs du mal* (1857) and in *Madame Bovary* (1857), and in less memorable manner in the poetry of Gautier and Théodore de Banville.

No development in literature, of course, is entirely without precedents. The autonomy of art had been adumbrated in much 18th-century aesthetic theory; it was a basic principle of Kant's *Kritik der Urteilskraft* (1790; The Critique of Judgment) and contributed to the high position enjoyed by art in the speculative metaphysics of the Romantic period. But simply to trace back the doctrine of Art for Art's Sake through, say, Schiller to Kant would be misleading, even though various points of contact might be found. (For instance, it was after reading Kant that Benjamin Constant first coined the phrase *l'art pour l'art* in his *Journal intime* (1804), and it was also used, in his Sorbonne courses of 1818, by the philosopher V. Cousin, who was also much influenced by German philosophy.) What separates German idealist thought from the more nihilistic-sounding pronouncements of the French aesthetes is not so much any intellectual incompatibility: indeed, the ready acceptance of German philosophical ideas by French writers in the later 19th century is well known.* There remains, however, a difference of mood, of ambience. The ideas that writers hold are not timeless theoretical propositions, but responses to concrete historical and social circumstances that colour those ideas. The idea of *l'art pour l'art* is coloured by the kind of experience that was typically the lot of a French poet or artist or intellectual living in the bohemian circles of Paris during the 19th century.

One important factor, which tends to be either understated or melo-dramatized, was the very existence of such intellectual circles in numbers large enough to constitute a society within a society, or rather—to use a preposition more appropriate to their mood—"outside" it. To Gautier, looking back on the first golden years of French Romanticism, it seemed like a second Renaissance; and there may well not have been since 15th-century Italy a community of intellectually and artistically gifted men either as extensive or as lasting as that which established Paris as the mecca of modern art in Europe for over 100 years. But the new Renaissance differed strikingly from the old, above all because of the antagonism that the artist began to feel toward his public. This helped to foster a sense of solidarity among all kinds of poets and painters, who

---

* Most influential were Schopenhauer and von Hartmann. The question is well documented by C. DIGEON, *La crise allemande de la pensée française 1870–1914* (Paris 1959). The irrationalistic tendencies of Schopenhauer's thought, and of the "cult of art" generally, are discussed in Ch. 4, "Irrationalism."

felt they belonged to a special spiritual caste or class—or, as Catulle Mendès described it, "a bizarre, morbid, and charming aristocracy." (The only disqualification was sympathy for any official organ or canon of bourgeois taste; teachers and scholars were also generally excluded, i.e. people connected with what Ezra Pound, echoing their century-old contempt, called "learneries.")

Thackeray, writing from Paris in 1839, satirized "the beggarly beardless scribbler . . . [who] tells you in his preface of the *sainteté* of the *sacerdoce littéraire.*"[3] Baudelaire, by contrast, idealized the true representative of this class in the dandy, the founder of this "new sort of aristocracy, which will be especially difficult to destroy because it is based upon the most precious and indestructible of endowments, and upon the heavenly gifts that neither labour nor money can confer."[4] This drawing together of all more or less "artistic" persons was accompanied by a growing interest in creativity as a principle superior to any particular form of talent. The importance of this idea, and of the admiration that poets felt for painting and music (supposedly purer forms of beauty), will be discussed later.

A negative attitude toward contemporary bourgeois society was in the end the only article of faith common to all members and all generations of this intellectual élite. It is not altogether easy to explain it, perhaps least so by simply assuming that bourgeois society was a spiritually negative phenomenon in every part. To the poetic imagination of the time, bourgeois life symbolized the denial of poetry; more generally, the bourgeois preoccupation with the manufacture of material things, with progressive prosperity, and with whatever rules and institutions might be conducive to these utilitarian goals, appeared as the death of the spirit. It is arguable that one element that entered into the formation of this generalized attitude was the kind of religious disorientation decried by anti-democratic thinkers such as Joseph de Maistre or Félicité de Lamennais. They diagnosed a spiritual malaise in modern society due to the loss of any organic sense of community such as religion had formerly provided. In its place democracy had created only "an edifice of illusions and follies," the optimistic and superficially respectable way of life that masked the underlying materialism, venality, and corruption of bourgeois society. Even left-wing diagnoses were likely to strike the imagination just as negatively. Fourrier, too, attacked the disintegrating effect on social relationships produced by modern capitalism. Because few poets were actively interested in the kinds of reform proposed by either catholicism or socialism, they were left passively at the mercy of a mood of cultural pessimism, in which they could feel no spiritual significance in the "normal" activities of the world about them.

One aspect of those activities that particularly disgusted the aesthete was their supposed contribution to progress. This fundamental, though ill-defined, value of bourgeois society was an amalgam of assumptions about industrial expansion, scientific advance, personal enrichment, and political improvement. Baudelaire considered it "a grotesque idea which has blossomed on the rotten soil of modern weakmindedness."[5] The simple absence of any sympathy for it constituted a positive quality of Baudelaire's poetry in Swinburne's eyes, when he first presented the French poet's work to the English public in an article in the *Spectator* (1862). He welcomed Baudelaire as an ally in the struggle against the conventional view that poetry must have a moral purpose and "lend a shove forward to some theory of progress." What the average English response may have been to such pernicious foreign influences may be judged from Tennyson's diatribe against the new doctrine in connection with painting:

> Art for Art's sake! Hail, truest Lord of Hell!
> Hail, Genius, Master of the Moral Will!
> "The filthiest of all paintings painted well
> Is mightier than the purest painted ill!"
> Yes, mightier than the purest painted well,
> So prone are we toward the broad way to Hell.[6]

Faith in progress was a moral touchstone to the active, entrepreneurial spirit of the middle classes; it signified faith in man's moral capacity to strive for the better. It was because Hugo struggled to preserve and voice this faith that he enjoyed such immense success. Contemporary reports show that the first of his *Légende des siècles* sold thousands of copies in a few days in 1859, at a time when Baudelaire's *Fleurs du mal* had been censored (1857) and he himself was known chiefly as a translator of Poe. Interestingly, Hugo's success was matched in the same year by that of Tennyson's "Idylls of the King"; although they might seem to be pandering to a kind of aesthetic escapism, Tennyson's phantasies are not indulged simply for phantasy's sake but also voice a strain of moral idealism.

That there is an element of escapism in the cult of art can scarcely be denied. In France, disillusion with the world was exacerbated by—some even said caused by—the upheavals and defeats suffered by the nation since 1789. Chateaubriand, Musset, and Stendhal have all variously borne witness to the frustrated longings for greatness and adventure that lingered on after the downfall of Napoleon. In 1830 Charles Nodier found society to be so corrupt and mediocre that an artistic soul could, he believed, only escape into a world of phantasy. Some 20 years later, Flaubert declared in a letter: "Let the Empire go its own way, and let us close our door, and go to the top of our ivory tower, to the highest step, the one nearest the sky."[7] And at the end of the century the symbolist magazine *Mercure de France* told its readers: "We belong to a world that is on its way out and it is only fitting that we should go with it. . . . The only appropriate thing to do is to stay more than ever in our ivory towers, while they are still standing."

The increasingly materialistic and hedonistic outlook of French bourgeois society after the middle of the century was attacked by Taine in his *Vie et opinions de M. Frédéric Thomas Graindorge* (1867) and contrasted with the idealism of an earlier generation. This darkening of mood among French intellectuals after the outcome of the 1848 revolution and again after the defeat of 1870 is reflected in the development of Ernest Renan, who was disappointed in his messianic (and personal) hopes that the intellectuals would take over from the revolution, regenerate the nation, and achieve cultural unity with Germany. Faced with a condition of society that he characterized as *à l'américaine*, he too began to consider how "in such a world, one will be able to create entirely quiet places of retreat." He defines the age as a whole by quoting a phrase from the French Swiss writer, Henri-Frederic Amiel: "The era of mediocrity in everything is beginning."[8]

This was the French intellectual cliché of the 19th century. It is worth quoting again only in order to remark that it passes *aesthetic*, rather than moral, judgment on society. Renan stresses that the century "is going neither to the bad nor to the good; it is heading for mediocrity." The high and difficult art to which the aesthetes aspired was itself a kind of protest against the facile products and cheap pleasures of the time. But the absence of positive moral power in the aesthete's attitude gave to much of his writing a decadent quality that often seemed more corrupt than the simple citizens he despised. The corruption of the moral will was diagnosed in France by Paul Bourget in his *Essais de psychologie contemporaine* (1880–6), and in comparable terms by Nietzsche in Germany and by Dostoyevsky and Turgenev in Russia. The term they all used in connection with the intellectual's exultant attack on the mediocrity of others was the *nihilism* of his own position.

Art, then, did not simply offer the consolation of a timeless value at the moment when so many other forms of value—religious, moral, political, and others—had fallen victim to the evil hour: art positively flourished, so it was believed, when other values decayed. In support of this view, interest revived in the decadent period of Roman culture and in the flamboyant licence, even corruption, of the most artistic society in recent European history, that of the Renaissance. (That the Renaissance had been a period of "aesthetic immorality" was an idea already familiar to some much earlier writers; the phrase actually occurs in Wilhelm Heinse's *Ardinghello*, for instance, published in 1787.) It did not matter whether moralists claimed that European society had progressed or declined. The aesthete enjoyed a profounder view, which accepted that time destroyed a large part of every civilization; all the greater glory attached to those works of art that survived.

The aesthetic interest in history went still further. Huysmans believed that the aesthete could also recreate for himself in his imagination "all the passions and moods of thought that belonged to every century except his own."[9] Pater's aesthete hero aspires, as he says, "to fill up the measure of the present with vivid sensations and such intellectual apprehensions as . . . are most like sensations."[10] (But Marius is, of course, doing this very much in the past. He is a historical personage, and the real aesthete is Pater himself, savouring these sensations from the retreat of his Oxford study.) Closely related to this donnish aestheticism was the speculation whether the "spirit" of former times might not be resurrected through the historian's art. Some such saving vision seems to have obsessed that most artistic of all historians, Michelet. Perhaps life had to become the past, "to die, in order to be resurrected in song," as Schiller had written. Unfortunately, most of the actual poems about the dead past—written by poets such as Leconte de Lisle, who composed a vast panorama of vanished civilizations, mythologies, and religions, from ancient Greek to Polynesian—turned out to be pretty dull. Equally unacceptable to modern readers is the fascination felt by many aesthetes for the vigorous barbarian, the blond beast, half feared and half invoked as the necessary vital force that must come to reinvigorate the exhausted stock of the European races.

It is with regard not so much to what was felt to be wrong with contemporary society as to what ought to be done about it, that it is possible to distinguish fairly clearly between the Romantic generation and that of the aesthetes. Mallarmé may also have thought that "the world will be saved by better literature," but for him the poet's task was purely to make his own writing as beautiful as possible. Hugo's response was very different, with his notion of poetry as prophecy, the theatre as a pulpit, and the poet as a hero. This difference is reflected in the rhetorical and polemical atmosphere of Hugo's *cénacle*, the rallying point of his Romantic contemporaries, whose literary cause was being fought out as a public issue, in newspapers and journals, and in that centre of social life, the theatre. How unlike the gatherings at Mallarmé's house, in the years when he was the most influential but far from the most popular poet in Paris; here the talk was literary, theoretical, and *recherché*. The visitors, who at different times included Valéry and Yeats, were united only by a most impersonal passion for art. It seems as much in keeping with Hugo's circle that Sainte-Beuve should there fall in love with Mme Hugo, as it is inconceivable that anything of the kind should happen at Mallarmé's formal gatherings. Love was as uninteresting as politics to the true aesthete.

No Romantic poet ever quite gave up hope that the world could really be as beautiful as his poetic vision, and that the poet might be acclaimed as the philosopher king. It was this expectation in particular that struck the new aesthetic generation as absurd. In spite of all they owed to their Romantic forebears, they could not accept any tendency toward social or moral commitment in art. The younger Hugo of 1830 was still admired, but *Les misérables* (1862) was regarded by Baudelaire as "his dishonour," and Flaubert called it a "childish book." The difference between the generations is symbolized on the one hand by Hugo's real exile from a regime he considered wrong, and on the other by Flaubert's inner withdrawal from a society he considered vulgar. "We are going to become one big, flat, industrial country like Belgium," Flaubert wrote with regard to the new democracy of the Third Republic, which depressed him even more than the Second Empire had done. He, too, incurred the displeasure of the state for the alleged immorality of *Madame Bovary*, thereby establishing a characteristic mode of passive resistance to society that was to become almost the only "positive" social ideal of which the purer forms of modern art would be capable for nearly a century. Flaubert's defence counsel could point to the fact that, after all, Emma Bovary's adultery ended in suffering and suicide. The prosecution obscurely felt, but could not prove, that this was not the point of the book. And indeed, morally speaking, the book has no point: it is purely a work of art. Precisely this aestheticism was what made it look so "dangerous."

Although the new aesthetes appear at first to have renounced the temptation to dream romantically of the poet's mission, it would be wrong to suppose that either their belief in art or their social isolation was in any way diminished. On the contrary, both tended to increase. When Théodore de Banville published *Les cariatides* in 1842, he associated himself with those for whom "art is an intolerant, jealous religion"; the phrase is suggestive, almost prophetic: how many of the new believers were to discover that indeed they could have no other god but art. Moreover, the god demanded nothing less than the sacrifice of the artist's personal life. The pain and paradox of this experience are recorded in Flaubert's letters, which reveal the true meaning of his hard-won ideal of impersonality in art. The artist can "depict wine, love, women, glory, on condition that [he] does not become a drunkard, a lover, a husband, a soldier"[11]—provided, in fact, that he does not participate in life at all, except as an exercise in art. And art, as these letters make clear, does not mean the exercise of generous emotions, or an expression of moral sympathy, or any attempt at spiritual justification. It means the search for a style that should be as completely purified of any such personal contamination as possible. It was in solitary pursuit of this ultimately impossible ideal that Flaubert lived with his "hair shirt" in his "cell" (as he called the work in his study), meditating for years on a story and a setting that were the antithesis of everything he admired, and that bored and disgusted him, until, impersonally void of anything but this alien subject, which he had transmuted into a pure work of art, and which had taken the place of any life of his own, he could pronounce the paradox: "*Madame Bovary, c'est moi.*"

More significant than their occasional urge to escape into some luxurious world of phantasy is the consuming "passion for reality," as Yeats called it, that many of the aesthetes felt. The condition is always the same: for the sake of this one passion, the artist must deny all other passions, must "deny" the world, and even (in a sense) deny himself as any kind of real person in society. It is easy to liken this to a religious calling, though probably the points of similarity are less precise than the points of difference. (It is doubtful whether Christian self-denial is the same virtue, and certain that the Gospels teach a message of moral concern for the world.) The wisest view of this artistic spirituality is probably that offered by Thomas Mann, who has exposed its ambiguity, its "sympathy with the abyss," as he describes it in *Death in Venice* (1911). Kafka, who admired Mann's portrayal of the artist, expresses in his diaries and letters a similar sense of the ambiguity in artistic inspiration: was it a communion with daemonic powers or a form of prayer? In an aphorism dated 1922 he defined the artist as follows: "He has found the Archimedean point [Kafka means of absolute intellectual detachment]; but he has turned it against himself; evidently this is the condition that has enabled him to find it."[12]

468

Of course, many factors of cultural background, social situation, and personal temperament affect the appearance of this basic aesthetic experience, which we are assuming to be nevertheless essentially similar in all instances. It is important to notice that Thomas Mann, who is morally critical of the artist's alienation from society, belonged to the first generation of Germans to grow up in a completely modern society, i.e. one that was centralized, urbanized, industrialized. He resisted the bohemian and revolutionary tendencies of the expressionist poets of that generation, preserving always a feeling for what was ideally the due of social life, as hallowed by still-recent tradition. No less an authority than Goethe had blessed that tradition by holding, in his life and in his work, the balance between poetry and the social order. It was owing to his influence, as well as to the relatively unmodern state of society throughout the German-speaking world, that Gottfried Keller strove to make himself, and the artistic hero of his *Bildungsroman, Der grüne Heinrich* (1853, revised 1880; Green Heinrich), accept their place in Swiss provincial society, though in his heart he knew its limitations. Similarly, in the very same years when Flaubert was working on *Madame Bovary*, Adalbert Stifter in Austria was also devoting all his artistic talent to a largely aesthetic ideal, to a novel of initiation into the mystery of beauty and indeed of self-denial; but this he saw as the moral key to experience, as the basis of a true human relationship. *Der Nachsommer* (1857; The Indian Summer) is set not in Vienna, where Stifter's unpolitical imagination had been terrified by the violence of the 1848 disturbances, but in the timeless country of a small estate, where the educated man and the peasant still shared a common faith. Not that Stifter personally believed in it: he took his life in pain and melancholy; but ideally he could still imagine the world to which he wanted, as artist, to belong.

The modifying effect of cultural background is particularly obvious in the case of Kafka; in him, the pursuit of pure art assumed a desperate quality, partly because the dilemma of being an enlightened Jew exacerbated that of being an alienated intellectual, and this in Prague, where he was a German in a Czech city! Another striking example may be found by considering Gottfried Keller's compatriot and contemporary, H.-F. Amiel, quoted above. Like Keller, he held a public appointment (in his case, a professorship) in an uncongenial social ambience. But because he was a native of Geneva and therefore culturally French, he felt his situation in terms borrowed from the French Romantics, and he frequently expressed states of mind characteristic of the later aesthetic generation. Thus, he describes the experience, already familiar in Paris, of having no personal identity as a writer: "If to other people I seem to be someone, to myself I am but a shadow without substance."[13] Over half a century was to elapse before any Italian poet, for instance, experienced this, as eventually Montale did in 1920:

> Se un'ombra scorgete, non è
> un'ombra, ma quella io sono,
> potessi spiccarla da me
> offrirvela in dono.[14]
>
> (If you notice a shadow, it is not a shadow, it is me; I could detach
> it from myself and offer it to you as a gift.)

Again, the reason is not hard to find. The greatest contemporary of Mallarmé in Italy was Giosuè Carducci, who wrote in conditions quite unlike those in Paris. That he was not devoid of modern impulses is evident from his hymn "To Satan," the patron of what is in effect an aesthete's idea of beauty; but Carducci invokes Satan mainly as an ally in the democratic struggle against popes and kings—the struggle in which Italy herself was then engaged, and that was the real object of the poet's interest. When he looked for poetic models it was to the pre-eminently public tradition of the classics; he might praise the glory of art, but what he wanted was a culture that he could share with his emerging nation.

When, in 1917, we hear W. B. Yeats declare that poetry is written not by the socially recognizable person of the poet but by "the anti-self or the antithetical self,"[15] then the echo of French aesthetic doctrine seems clear. "*Je,*" Rimbaud had exclaimed, "*est un autre.*"[16] Moreover, Yeats goes on to draw the familiar contrast between the passion proper to poetry and the mere feelings involved in social existence. "The sentimentalists are practical men who believe in money, in position, in a marriage bell, and whose understanding of happiness is to be so busy, whether at work or at play, that all is forgotten but the momentary aim." Yet in his case the aesthetic psychology derives a distinctive colouring from his position as an Irishman in the years of the Celtic revival and the independence movement (the scale and mood of which was very different from that in Italy, being—among other things—separatist rather than unionist). The relationship of the "anti-self" to the self, of the poet to the man of action, is for Yeats not a straight social severance but part of a larger world order, whose operation gives a mythological meaning to history and a mystical quality to art. It is usually said that Yeats achieved his true stature as a modern or symbolist poet only when he had put aside Romantic daydreams about old Ireland, together with any political illusions about its restoration. But seen in a European perspective, his aestheticism continues to be involved in myth and ancestral feeling in a way that would have been unthinkable in France.

Comparable conditions to those in Ireland might be found perhaps in Russia, where there was also no native philosophical tradition of any substance, but a still vital one of popular religious feeling, which was shaped by myth rather than by theology. To this the Russian intellectual was still receptive, just as the ideas he was most inclined to accept from abroad were generally of a mystical character. Thus, for the Russian symbolist poets the cult of art, which they associated indiscriminately with Goethe and Schiller, with Mallarmé and Verlaine, had a diffusely religious significance. Their leader, Aleksandr Blok, was at first fascinated by a mystical idea of beauty as Divine Wisdom, which offers a parallel to the theosophy of Yeats's early interest. When Blok also was forced out of such Romantic notions, and then discovered his mature style as a symbolist, the mythological element still persisted in his work, though more discreetly. The power he invoked now was more irrational, immanent—the spirit of creativity, or (as he called it) of music. His poem *The Artist* (1913) describes how this power transforms the world in a moment of timeless, visionary joy. The other parts of the poem show more familiar aspects of the aesthetic mood: scorn for the ordinary life of others, who merely marry and amuse themselves, and the poet's *ennui* when the spirit does not move him, and again when it is afterwards destroyed by dull reason. One of the puzzles of Blok's symbolism was his ability (shared to some extent by other mystical aesthetes in Russia) to see the 1917 revolution as an outbreak of the same spirit. There is, in this respect, a further parallel to be drawn between Blok's "The Twelve," in which Christ is represented as the leader of a band of trigger-happy, ex-convict revolutionaries, and Yeats's poem "The Second Coming," which heralds a "rough beast," "a shape with lion body and the head of a man," about to be born in Bethlehem.*

To return to France: it should not, of course, be supposed that there no cultural conditions modified the development of aestheticism. Whatever freedoms Paris offered, no French poet could be unaware of the long tradition behind him. Indeed, one explanation of why the aesthetes wrote such daring things is simply that they were bored with writing conventional things; the explanation is banal only because it scratches at

---

* For a fuller discussion of Blok's poetry, see Vol. VI, "Literature and Revolution in the U.S.S.R."

the surface of the much profounder, though almost inscrutable, truth that every artistic style becomes exhausted. A more specifically French characteristic in the influence exerted by tradition may be glimpsed in the way Flaubert insists on the separation of the poet from "life." At first sight, he seems to be labouring the obvious: writing cannot be the same kind of thing as doing. His comment derives its force, however, from the absoluteness of his passion for observation, and in particular for self-observation. It is his mind that imagines itself lucidly separate from experience, and not just the man who studies his separateness from society. There is a rationalistic dualism here—a fascination with the nature of the passions and appetites, as if they were always deluded, and reason were always right—that is in many ways characteristic of the French intellectual tradition. This moral scrutiny of the self, as of society, from an absolute, metaphysical vantage point is devastating: it can only discover its opposite, murky self-deception, wherever it looks. Something of the atmosphere of Jansenism clings to Baudelaire's and Flaubert's sense of life's universal evil; and there is the echo of old theological debates in the doubts felt by Mallarmé and Valéry about the possibility of achieving pure poetry. Its achievement becomes as absolutely desirable and as impossibly difficult as the achievement of divine grace; the only certainty that remains is the reality of doubt and damnation.

In retrospect it looks like a privileged age, rather than a disturbed one. The ideal of moral non-commitment, the concentration on aesthetic sensation, the freedom to play with the medium of art, all imply a reliance on the protective framework of bourgeois society, a reliance that goes deeper psychologically than any stated rejection. By comparison with the violent physical and moral challenges that 20th-century Europe has presented to the poet, the elected isolation of the 19th-century aesthetes appears quite idyllic. There was a sense in which Murger's *Scènes de la vie de bohème* (1851), and later Puccini's opera based upon it, were true: the freedom enjoyed by those young writers and painters to develop their talents and thoughts and feelings as they would was a very real one. Censorship might occasionally result in the withdrawal of a book, as in the case of *Les fleurs du mal*; but Baudelaire had no difficulty in publishing his poems in journals.* The little magazine, which played an important part in the growth of the aesthetic movement, flourished in the social and economic circumstances of a bourgeois capital city. Literary magazines proliferated in Paris, particularly toward the end of the century, and the

---

* An expurgated edition, containing also new poems, appeared in 1881. The offending poems themselves were published as *Les épaves* in Brussels (1866).

phenomenon was repeated in most European countries.* Stefan George lamented in an early number of his *Blätter für die Kunst* (1890 ff.; Papers for Art), a journal founded in 1890 in emulation of the French school, that Germany had no journals in which poets interested only in works of pure beauty could publish what they wrote; and he attributed the backwardness of German poetry to this fact. But by 1914 both Berlin and Munich were supporting several comparable periodicals (which were still more revolutionary in style). Low costs of printing and distribution helped to make this form of publication possible, just as they allowed a publisher to recover his costs on a collection of poems from the sale of only 100 or so copies. From this the author earned very little, of course, and many poets were at some time obliged to take jobs: Verlaine as a clerk, Mallarmé as a teacher, and so on. A lucky few, including Henri de Régnier (a minor disciple of Mallarmé), not only made a living from poetry but also possessed private means. It is one of the paradoxes of the aesthete's position that he was far from indifferent to literary fame, although he affected to despise the public that ultimately granted such fame.

The aesthetic movement among English writers is distinguished less by their dissociation from middle-class society than by their association with Oxford University. Among the comparable English contemporaries of the French aesthetes, and later on of the symbolists, we find Swinburne and Hopkins, Wilde and Beerbohm, at Oxford as students, and Pater as a life fellow of Brasenose College. The list might be extended by including poets whose work exemplifies aesthetic attitudes only in some minor way, such as Bridges, Lionel Johnson, and Dowson (though he never graduated). Whether Ruskin and Arnold could be added to the list is more doubtful; yet they certainly contributed something to the quality of English aestheticism by giving art such a conspicuous place in their struggle against the ugliness, degradation, and doubts of the age.

Even if the association with Oxford cannot be shown to have caused, it might be said to symbolize, the kind of modifications that the cult of art variously displayed in England. It remained more nearly associated with a sense of social commitment, of a cause to be championed; it remained more concerned about the place of art in an ideal hierarchy of moral and intellectual values, of whose continuity Oxford itself seemed to constitute a guarantee. Thus, Pater's aestheticism lacks the metaphysical tension, the solitary confrontation with the void, that is a recurrent

---

* The importance of this phenomenon in Spain is discussed in Ch. 9, "Naturalism and the Spanish Novel."

experience in France. Admittedly, he sounds a little like Mallarmé when he speculates about "ideal types of poetry" in which a purely artistic principle, which he likened to music, would triumph over all lesser forms of interest in mere content or subject-matter. But the conventional element in his aestheticism comes out in the famous conclusion to *Studies in the History of the Renaissance* (1873), where it is evident that the actual content of experience is really of fundamental value. His aesthete looks to the world and to common living for moments of perfect beauty, and he has no more absolute goal than to experience as *many* of these moments, and as *much* of life, as he can. When Pater writes in this way in praise of "the greatest number of vital forces," he betrays a side of his thinking that is only a more cultured version of the conventional British philosophy of Jeremy Bentham.

A similar absence of any significant sense of tension within experience, particularly as regards the relationship between art and life, constitutes the essential weakness of Swinburne's poetry. His aestheticism is all phantasy, his radicalism largely rhetoric, often modelled on the poet he most truly admired, who was not Baudelaire but Hugo. His call to us to feel that all life is ah! so poetic, relies on his gifted ear for what sounds poetic and on his deficient understanding of what life is actually like. His paganism has been decently schooled in the classics, and his songs of satiety suggest nothing that might not be enjoyed, in comfortable reverie, in the privileged seclusion of the family estate on the Isle of Wight or in the respectable London suburb of Putney. We sense the same kind of artificiality in the sensual and sexual experience of Swinburne as we do, for instance, in the mystical experience of Rossetti. In both cases there is a self-conscious, almost missionary, enthusiasm for beauty as the key to the essential meaning of these experiences. In neither case were the implications of a shift of emphasis toward a more purely aesthetic treatment (and hence away from any serious moral or religious consideration of the subject-matter) at all understood or developed, any more than they were in the pre-Raphaelite movement of English aestheticism generally. As we shall see, the profounder developments of aestheticism in Europe as a whole came from exploring what art meant on its own, as a principle independent of, even alien to, the common substance of life. Any aesthete who seeks to persuade us that all things in life—history, nature, human relationships—are to be enjoyed simply for their beauty, as though this were in fact all that their existence amounted to, is liable to strike us as superficial.

Keats's "Ode on a Grecian Urn" (1820) is exceptional. It may be considered as an early poem in praise of aestheticism, long before any comparable thoughts were current in France. Its claim to greatness in this respect does not rest on the famous conclusion that "Beauty is truth, truth beauty," for this is suggestive of only the more superficial kind of aestheticism (though it was probably just this kind that Keats's poetry generally did suggest to his Victorian followers). The decisive inspiration of the poem lies in the thought that there is *no* sensual fulfilment in the world of art. However beautiful the figures represented on the urn may be, they have no life and cannot move. "Bold lover, never, never canst thou kiss. . . ." Keats here expresses his awareness of that metaphysical tension that gives aestheticism its profounder interest. The urn becomes for him the symbol of a dilemma, a rivalry between art and life, that only an aesthete would find comprehensible. To a more conventional mind, used to considering art merely as a pleasing reflection of the natural order, Keats's thought is absurd, or at best a playful whim that need scarcely have been voiced in such solemn language. The thought makes sense only to someone who can imagine entering into the "world" of art, and thus can draw comparisons between the state of people in that world and the state of people in life. If the conclusion of the poem is not to contradict this insight, it ought presumably to be addressed to the figures on the urn: that is certainly all *they* need to know on earth, simply because they are not alive. That Keats would have liked to know no other truth but art, which he regarded desperately as his only salvation, there is no doubt. But that his yearning for this ideal sprang from a very different kind of knowledge, from a deeply negative kind of awareness of the difference between life and art, must be no less evident from the power of his poetry and the tragedy of his life.

It is this ambivalence between the positive and negative aspects of art, rather than any more traditional belief in transcendental ideas (such as Shelley had, for instance, in Platonism), that gives Keats a place in the mainstream of European aestheticism. His sense of "negative capability," which was grounded in a feeling of having no real social self or role, is psychologically more akin to the aesthetic experience of Flaubert, or even Kafka, than to the Romantic loneliness of Byron, which was still something of a social pose. Byron and Shelley, it should be remembered, enjoyed the university education appropriate to their position as gentlemen. It is significant that the only other Romantic poet to have a more modern, more absolute, and more daemonic feeling for art was Blake (who has been heralded as the first symbolist), and, like Keats, he also escaped the influence of university.

Many of the most interesting departures in English poetry, in matters both of diction and of sensibility, were made during the symbolist period by those outside the university tradition: Browning, Francis Thompson, Kipling, and Wilfrid Owen (whose letters reveal how deeply he regretted the lack of it). But, of course, these departures were not all in the direction of aestheticism.

The decisive break with the traditionalism that clung to English literature, and its eventual *rapprochement* with the French movement, were brought about largely by American and Irish writers: James, Pound, and Eliot; Moore, Joyce, and Yeats. (The first critic to show genuine understanding of Baudelaire and his followers was Arthur Symons—an Englishman who had been educated abroad.) When Pound came to London in 1908 and made his stand against "literariness" in poetic style, he acknowledged one ally, a foreigner like himself:

> It should be realized that Ford Madox Ford had been hammering this point of view into me from the time I first met him (1908 or 1909) and that I owe him anything that I don't owe myself for having saved me from the academic influences then raging in London.[17]

The other aspect of English literary life that struck Pound was no less associated with the influence of university: it was amateurism, the wearing of culture lightly, as though literature were a thing a gentleman might turn his hand to, among other things. Oxford had preserved this gentlemanly ideal from an earlier century: an education in the classics was equally appropriate for poets and for prime ministers. Pound's ideal of professionalism—one independent of "learneries," needless to say—was frustrated by this "country in love with amateurs . . . where the incompetent have such beautiful manners and personalities so fragile and charming that one cannot bear to injure their feelings by the introduction of competent criticism."[18] What Pound meant by "competent" was, in fact, the reverse of academic. The contrast may be glimpsed in the faces that Housman and W. P. Ker are reported to have made to one another as they sat listening to Pound lecturing on mediaeval poetry. They doubtless knew more *about* the past; but what Pound was really trying to learn from it was a purely artistic secret for his own use, a fresh way of handling rhythm and imagery. In much of his subsequent work, and most obviously in his translations, the truth about a text—as about the culture from which it sprang—lay for him in the verbal opportunities it presented. The direction of his development as a poet is the same as that of Joyce.

Although their association with Oxford helped to make the English aesthetes feel a high-minded sense of superiority not *to* their society but *within* it, it also helped to make aestheticism appear, in its more colourful aspects, to be a youthful pose, an extravagance of the upper-class young. "His humour of being carried in a sedan chair, swathed in blankets and reading a Latin poet, from his rooms to the Turkish bath, is still remembered in college," wrote G. S. Street, in his popular satire, *The Autobiography of a Boy*. There were others in the same vein, all suggesting that aestheticism was not about anything more serious than it had been for W. S. Gilbert, who in *Patience* made it look like one of the more pleasing occasions of London life to "walk down Piccadilly / with a poppy or a lily / in your mediaeval hand." Pleasing, that is, until May 1895, when Wilde was convicted of homosexuality (then a criminal offence) and sent to prison for two years. Nowadays, publishers flourish when scandals befall their authors; then, Wilde's books were allowed to go out of print. The extravagance could not be tolerated, once it presented a serious moral challenge. The society that had been charmed by Oscar's wit no longer wished to hear of him. Moreover, unlike other writers condemned for legal offences (Dostoyevsky, for political intrigue, for instance, or Verlaine, for shooting at Rimbaud), Wilde was broken by this experience. Partly perhaps because he was a dramatist, and drama is a more public art than poetry, but mainly because his brilliant perversity of mind had been no more than a daring play with the spiritual furniture of a society that he basically enjoyed, he could not survive social ostracism. "To dominate a London dinner table" had been for him "to dominate the world."

It has often been remarked that Wilde seems to have insisted on his own downfall, not staying in France till gossip tired (though he often lived there with evident pleasure), but returning to England against the advice of his friends to initiate libel proceedings that could end only in disaster. A theory of aesthetic psychology might suggest that he sensed the superficiality to which his aestheticism was doomed so long as it remained associated with social wit and elegance. Perhaps only Reading gaol could lend depth to his view that nothing in life mattered except beauty. Certainly he uttered there one paradox more profound than the rest, when his feeling of kinship with a murderer about to be hanged inspired him to declare that "each man kills the thing he loves." It is still the saying of an aesthete, but it carries more conviction in Wilde's poem than his rather vague expressions of religious sentiment. The paradox is as telling as his identification with the murderer's state of mind, which has moments of Flaubertian intensity (mixed also with some Victorian rhetoric). As a moral explanation of why evil things are done, it is very confusing; but it is uncannily precise as an aesthetic observation of how life itself must be sacrificed through man's effort to possess it: not *any* man's effort, perhaps, but quite often that of the modern artist. The aesthete is particularly prone to discover this fatal relationship in *his* dealings with reality; trooper C. T. W. has become a symbol of Wilde's artistic soul.

The destruction of the heart's ideal was a theme that echoed in much poetry of the period. The experience where beauty most readily met her death was in sex. Dowson owes his fame largely to the popularity of one poem that epitomized the mood, well-bred even in its debauch, of the English "decadence."

> Surely the kisses of her bought red mouth were sweet;
> But I was desolate and sick of an old passion,
>   When I awoke and found the dawn was grey:
> I have been faithful to thee, Cynara! in my fashion. . . .
>
> I cried for madder music and for stronger wine,
> But when the feast is finished and the lamps expire,
>   Then falls thy shadow, Cynara! the night is thine. . . . [19]

How faint these echoes sound beside the theme as it has been played by numerous French poets since Baudelaire: the imagination's ancient passion for beauty betrayed by the evil substance of the world. "*O fangeuse grandeur! sublime ignominie!*" [20] That French poets had dared to find beauty in the confessed wickedness of sex made them, of course, particularly notorious in late Victorian England. T. S. Eliot has commented on the over-insistence during the 1890s on Baudelaire's perversity, and he tried to correct the balance by suggesting that "his prostitutes, mulattoes, Jewesses, serpents, cats, corpses" are really no more than a kind of poetic "machinery which has not worn very well." This over-states the case, but it may be necessary to do so where there exist philistine tendencies to overlook the *metaphysical* passion that enters into all Baudelaire's greatest work. His defence of Art for Art's Sake (which he derived not from Gautier but from Edgar Allan Poe's essay on the *Poetic Principle*) stresses that a poem should be written "solely for the pleasure of writing a poem." [21] Because this pleasure is evidently distinct from moral purpose, the confusion may arise that such pleasure is in fact immoral, at least to the extent that it finds attractive any immoralities that the poem contemplates. But Baudelaire understands this aesthetic pleasure in a more absolute sense. In a world where moral ideas appeared to be merely hypocritical delusions (and love the foremost of them) the pleasure of art is alone incorruptible, impersonal (that is, above all personal weakness), perhaps even eternal. He writes not "for the sake of" the evil, the sensuality, the sordidness *of his material*, although this was often drawn from real experience. The evil is there solely for the sake of his art, for the sake of that "unique pleasure" that is not like any other. This may still be a morally paradoxical position, but at least it is not as simple as common opinion in England sometimes supposed. French art was not a pretext for French vice; the aesthete's pleasure did not lie there, nor in any affectation of indifference to good and evil. Therein lay mostly suffering, both spiritual and physical, degradation, defiance, and despair, all of which were endured, and doubtless in a sense "indulged in" and desired, for the sake of Art—for the beautiful word, image, or line that would redeem it all. For some of these writers the process assumed a religious aspect, and even ended in a more or less explicit Christian acceptance: only to arouse still further scandalized doubts whether this too was "for the sake of Art."

In a brilliant essay on *Baudelaire* (1947), Sartre has rejected the notion that Baudelaire's wretched life was simply a misfortune, thrust on him by an alien society, which he did not deserve. In a very real sense Baudelaire chose his misfortune, as Verlaine and Rimbaud also chose their own forms of suffering and degradation. The crux of their choice lay in the strange new poetic possibilities that were revealed by a heightened feeling of personal otherness; thus, they induced in themselves a sense of alienation not only from society but, to an ever more extreme degree of estrangement, from the very process of life itself. The pursuit of this spiritual sensation was the paradoxical purpose of much determined debauch, derangement of the dull senses, and other desperate demonstrations that the artist's soul was not contaminated by the moral delusions of decent living. To insist on lying in the gutter was, as a famous quip of Oscar Wilde's suggests, to give a new significance to "looking at the stars."

The portrait of the writer as a fallen angel, or social outcast, or *poète maudit*, must not be exaggerated. It belongs to the Romantic rather than to the aesthetic period, and although it never entirely disappeared later, it was frequently modified by a sharper focus on the artist's role as craftsman and connoisseur. Indeed, a growing preoccupation with the artistic medium is a common strand that runs through many different

479

styles of 19th-century art. For instance, although it is customary to treat Naturalism under a different heading from aestheticism, the two tendencies were not in fact always so distinct. "The pursuit of truth in literature," which the brothers Goncourt claimed they had initiated, was inspired in part by the characteristic suspicion of French aesthetes that truth is essentially something morally and materially repulsive. The challenge was to make this material into art. Because moralizing was forbidden, one solution was to render it as exactly as possible in terms of nervous sensations and visual impressions. The technique adopted by the Goncourts, for instance, was to write that "the cabman's back was surprised [at the conversation of his passengers]"; the back becomes more vivid, the person of the cabman less important. This gradual dissolution of objects into impressions characterizes also the contemporary school of painting, and the aim of Jules and Edmond de Goncourt to "describe exactly indescribable sensations," by means of what they called an *écriture artiste*, resembles the desire of Monet or Turner to capture the fleeting effects of light. Their ideal can easily be represented in a quasi-scientific fashion, as an objective study of reality; but it would be as true to say that their real object of study was the aesthetic effect that could be achieved on the canvas or the page, the "pure" possibilities to be discovered by a new attention to vocabulary and the resources of the palette.

Artists, of course, have always been concerned with their medium. The quality of their concern varies in character, however, according to the context in which they experience it. For instance, G. M. Hopkins, like the Goncourts, kept notebooks to record his sensations and impressions (in Hopkins' case, mostly of nature) and to make experiments with words. He was certainly influenced in this as an undergraduate by Pater, who was his tutor. But Hopkins is generally not regarded as an aesthete. He was ordained a priest and became a Jesuit: he intended his poetry to be as much an act of praise and service as his life. In some of his poems the sheer excitement of sound and sight seems in danger of breaking away from the controlling context of thought, but it is doubtful if his aestheticism would have been much more fruitful had this tension been lacking and he had been free to become a pure poet (as some critics have wished). His concern with poetic craftsmanship preserves, at all events, a more obviously traditional quality, as a result of being subordinate to his religious convictions.

The notion of craftsmanship suggests an artist working within a convention and with some solid, fairly hard material. The associations of the word are not with originality of conception, but with skill in execution; the craftsman makes objects that are in demand in the society he inhabits, and that may well be useful. The word seems, therefore, thoroughly inappropriate to modern aestheticism. If an ideal of craftsmanship is reverted to by a modern poet, who neither stands in this kind of relationship to his society nor works with anything like the same kind of public material, then it will mean something rather different in this altered context. The hardness of the work itself becomes one of its chief attractions to a poet disillusioned with the softness of his mere emotions; the impersonality of the form also becomes interesting in a new way: not as a means for the poet to communicate with others, but for him to escape from himself. Herein lies the reason for the success of Gautier's poem, which was widely admired by the Parnassian devotees of art:

> Oui, l'œuvre sort plus belle
> D'une forme au travail
> > Rebelle,
> Vers, marbre, onyx, émail.[22]

(Yes, the work of art emerges more beautiful from a form that is hard to work with—poetry, marble, onyx, enamel.)

The theme is developed again by Rilke, who makes explicit its psychological significance:

> > Wie die Kranken
> gebrauchen sie die Sprache voller Wehleid,
> um zu beschreiben, wo es ihnen wehtut,
> statt hart sich in die Worte zu verwandeln,
> wie sich der Steinmetz einer Kathedrale
> verbissen umsetzt in des Steines Gleichmut.
>
> > Dies war die Rettung. Hättest du nur *ein* Mal
> gesehn, wie Schicksal in die Verse eingeht
> und nicht zurückkommt, wie es drinnen Bild wird
> und nichts als Bild . . .[23]

(They use language the way sick people do—full of misery, to describe where they are in pain; instead of turning themselves firmly into words, as a stonemason at work on a cathedral grimly cuts his image into the serene, hard stone.

This was the salvation. If you had only *once* seen how fate passes into the lines of poetry and does not come back out again, how it becomes there an image and nothing but an image . . .).

Many other variations could be quoted, from Mallarmé's idealization of the Chinese porcelain painter to Yeats's famous goldsmiths in Byzantium. One further thought by Pound may be added:

> His true Penelope
> Was Flaubert
> And his tool
> The engraver's
>
> Firmness,
> Not the full smile,
> His art, but an art
> In profile.

These lines from *Mauberley* (1920)—a figure who may be said loosely to stand for Pound himself—nicely imply the position of the artist *vis-à-vis* his material: not full-faced participation, not the partner in a smile, but firmly to one side, apart in aesthetic contemplation. Though the warmth of the smile is lost, the engraved line of the profile will remain forever. Gautier again:

> Tout passe.—L'art robuste
> Seul a l'éternité:
>   Le buste
> Survit à la cité.[24]
>
> (Everything passes.—Only robust art has eternity: the bust outlives the city.)

A significant aspect of the aesthetic desire for impersonality, and of the kindred wish to become absorbed into the work of art itself, was defined by Baudelaire. "For what is pure art according to the modern idea?" he asked. "It aims to create a suggestive magic which contains within itself both the object and the subject, the world outside the artist and the artist himself."[25] Whether or not Baudelaire's definition always explains what the best modern art achieves, it suggests the terms in which two of its characteristic kinds of failure can be understood. Attempts at a poetry of pure, perfect images have not always had the magical effect of combining subjective and objective interest into one. There has been a tendency, on the one hand, to produce colourful but flat descriptions that arouse no feeling of personal involvement, and, on the other, to discover inner, visionary shows that seem to have no objective relevance to the world at all. The first danger might be said to characterize the Parnassian school of French poets, against whose inhuman literature even Baudelaire protested, despite his admiration for Gautier and his own preoccupation with the "plasticity" of his poetic images. Mallarmé also criticized the Parnassians as being "deficient in mystery: they deprive the mind of the delicious joy of believing that it is creating. To name an object is to do away with three quarters of the enjoyment of the poem, which is derived from the satisfaction of guessing little by little."[26] But the prolongation of this play of the mind is liable, of course, to become equally sterile. Sterility was the spectre that haunted Mallarmé's imagination. Pure inwardness proved in the end as impossible a poetic ideal as pure outwardness.

The Parnassian experiment was not only a literary protest against the confessional style of the Romantics. It was also a social protest against bourgeois expectations that poetry should provide some fine sentiment, and more generally against sentimental notions about the facts of natural life. Hence the Parnassian predeliction for savage subjects, a new kind of primitive exoticism designed to shock sensibilities brought up on the edifying and picturesque primitivism of Bernardin de St Pierre and Chateaubriand. No work of this type was designed more deliberately to "shock the bourgeois" than Flaubert's prose epic *Salammbô* (1862). Here he employed all the resources of a highly sophisticated—not to say decadent—sensitivity to language to render the "pure image" of crude and brutal experiences. The result is a kind of soundless scream, silent violence, sensations burningly intense yet quite abstract. The intelligent perspective that the style seems to offer, in fact establishes no relationship between the reader and the "reality" represented before him, and the latter consequently begins to assume the quality of pure fantasy—if the word "pure" can be used of such ghastly orgies. A recent critic has stressed the immobility of Flaubert's epic. Because it does not move us in any human—let alone humane—fashion, all its violent action seems not to move at all; it is all aimless, except as aesthetic spectacle. There can indeed be no significant connection between one moment and the next, when all moments in the process of existence express only its permanent, unchanging tedium. Then no motives matter; they are merely more or less strong. Flaubert's heroic desire for a style that should simply be as powerful as possible is entirely appropriate to a spiritually senseless condition of life, an appropriateness that he recognized in the observation: "Art is the search for the useless. It is in the field of speculation what heroism is in ethics."

The unconnected image, the static moment, the unmotivated vision become the hallmarks of much of the purest aesthetic writing. It would be difficult to name a modern poet who has not made some use of techniques of this kind. The bewildering variety of new schools and styles of poetry throughout Europe appears in retrospect to have been united chiefly in the search for fresh sources of poetic imagery: Anglo-American Imagism and Vorticism, French Symbolism and Surrealism, Hermeticism in Italy and Expressionism in Germany, Acmeism in Russia, and so on. To understand the character of this phenomenon we shall have to extend our inquiry into the relationship of artistic gifts to the context in which they are employed.

The search for new imagery was once likened (by a critic writing in 1913) to the mood of imperialism, to a desire to conquer new imaginative territory. It would seem now to be more appropriate to liken it to much deeper tendencies toward social decadence and disruption. The new vitality in poetry is a sympton of weariness with the norm, of social and cultural *ennui*, through which the beginnings of a new chaos are released: "the chaos you must have within you to be able to give birth to a dancing star,"[27] as Nietzsche formulated it. The aesthetic intensity of experience, its strength as sensation, tends to increase in proportion as it is no longer related to familiar, conventional ways of understanding. This experience has been described by many different kinds of writer. In *La nausée* (1939), Sartre shows the surrealist visions of his outsider hero, who is losing his grip on the meaningfulness of any form of bourgeois existence. In his *Brief an Lord Chandos* (1902), Hofmannsthal recounts the visionary consequences when a man finds he no longer sees any sense in the simplest statements about the world. In *The Doors of Perception* (1954), Aldous Huxley reports the intensification of instantaneous perception brought about by mescalin. And for the same reason all men, no doubt, feel the greater memorableness of childhood experience, the power of dreams, the romance of foreign places, and the temptation to use stimulants to escape the dull familiarity of things. But just as it is obvious that this does not make all men poets, so it is clear that something else must enter into the making of a poem besides the purely vivid image.

This "something" is, of course, language, a medium serving the practical purposes of communication, and therefore always a little inimical to the purity of the aesthete's ideal. Nietzsche, the philosopher who contributed most to the aesthetic philosophy—beginning from the premise that "the only justification of life is to be found in art," and criticising this view also as a kind of decadence—considered the question of language to be fundamental. For language, he discovered, is essentially a *social* product, embodying those conventions of subject and object, substance and quality, action and responsibility, that make possible a purposeful human community. Through the centuries every word and phrase has become encrusted with the rhetoric of man's ordered expectations. Nietzsche's philosophy is not a system, but an imaginative experiment to release the mind from this dead crust and make it creative again. To this end he turns the devices of language and thought against themselves, and often appears in the process to be turning civilization against itself. What he hoped to attain thereby was new purity of vision, a new *style*, as he sometimes called it, beyond the exhausted rhetoric of past values, beyond "good" and "evil." The paradox of his task resembles that of many a modern aesthete: for how can a poet preserve the "uselessness" of his vision, when language is so unavoidably useful? The techniques adopted by modern poets in order to "purify the language of the tribe" (in Mallarmé's and Eliot's phrase) are familiar: sentences without verbs, unexplained changes of subject, the absence of explanatory conjunctions, pronouns, or articles, the disruption through syntactical inconsistency of any recognizable point of view—all to the accompaniment sometimes of typographical experiments, and ultimately even of the horseplay that the Dada movement inspired.

The paradox of the modern poet's position is evident in the admiring allusions that the exponents of Art for Art's Sake and of Symbolism make to the other arts, most frequently to music and sculpture, but also to painting, architecture, and the dance. It is toward the non-literary beauty that these other arts achieve that the poet paradoxically aspires. Pater declares that "all art aspires towards the condition of music," whereas Flaubert insists rather that "the primary quality of art is plastic beauty," but the difference of opinion is no more than superficial. In practice there may be a difference between the *vague littérature* of poets such as Verlaine or Mallarmé, whose preference is for musicality, and the brilliant visual effects achieved by Rimbaud or Valéry; but there can be no doubt that in all these cases there is a common impulse *away* from a rational, rhetorical, or even ideational principle of poetic organization. For "poems are not written with ideas, they are written with words." Mallarmé's famous remark leaves it open whether a word that is not an idea should ideally be experienced as a pure sound or as a pure image: it is the non-conceptual purity that counts.

Perhaps the ideal response to pure art should rather be the total synaesthetic one that was a favourite subject of speculation at the time. Wagner's operas represent perhaps the most grandiose attempt to achieve a fusion of this kind, binding spectacle, poetry, and music in a pseudo-religious festival. The Bayreuth performances pandered to a longing, characteristic of the aesthetic movement, for total absorption, for a rapture of all the senses, of which it is impossible to say whether it constitutes sensual abandon or ascetic inwardness—"the spiritual ecstasies of some mediaeval saint or the morbid confessions of a modern sinner," as Wilde's Dorian Gray phrases it after reading Huysmans' *À rebours* (1884). And it is very much the same kind of problem that is raised by the refinements of Des Esseintes, Huysmans' hero and the prototype of the dandy, who celebrated aesthetic sensations as though they constituted a mystical cult. The ambiguous spirituality of aestheticism found many deliberate exponents besides. Edmund Wilson makes a brilliant case for Axel, the hero of Villiers de l'Isle-Adam's strange, dramatic poem in prose by that name, as the "type of all the heroes of the Symbolists." A more plausible relative of this aesthetic family is depicted by d'Annunzio in *Trionfo della morte* (1894), in which Giorgio Aurispa pursues his worship of sensation to the limit of sensual exhaustion, only to recognize (with the help of Nietzsche's philosophy and Wagner's *Tristan*) that there can be no fulfilment short of death.

We have already referred to Thomas Mann's lifelong preoccupation with the spiritual ambiguity of modern art. In connection with Wagner's music he wrote: "There was something primitive and crude in it, as well as something ascetically religious" (*Buddenbrooks*, 1898). In *Doktor Faustus* (1945) he draws once more the two sides of the artist's nature: looked at in one way, it shows selfless dedication to craftsmanship and control; looked at in another, it shows self-abandonment to darker, daemonic sources of inspiration. He suggests that an imbalance of these forces is not only capable of producing tragedy in a man's life, but on a larger scale can destroy a whole society. And indeed the ambiguity in modern aesthetics can be related to a more general uncertainty in European society about just how much genuine spirit there is in traditional spiritual values. The terms used by Thomas Mann and Nietzsche to construct their aesthetic philosophies have become more widely familiar in the scientific guise that Freud put on them. No ambiguity is more widespread or more characteristic of the period than that arising from Freud's association of social and religious values with repression and of art with substitute liberation. As a result, Freud has been invoked both by surrealist poets eager to dredge their dreams for the stuff of poetry and by critics eager to diagnose some form of sickness in poetic phantasies. (It is interesting that Freud himself did not like most of what little modern art he encountered, evidently sensing that what he called the "preconscious elaboration" of the unconscious material was not as unambiguously beautiful as his rather conventional taste demanded.)

The ambiguity of the aesthete's attempts to reach new sources of poetic insight is reflected in one of the favourite stylistic devices of the period: an alternation in style between irony and lyricism. Such perverse productions as Lautréamont's *Chants de Maldoror* (1869) and Rimbaud's *Saison en enfer* (1873) seem to have been written in obedience to Nietzsche's dictum that to create one must destroy:

> Enfin, ô bonheur, ô raison, j'écartai du ciel l'azur, qui est du noir, et je vécus, étincelle d'or de la lumière nature. De joie, je prenais une expression bouffonne et égarée au possible:
>
> > Elle est retrouvée!
> > Quoi? l'éternité.
> > C'est la mer mêlée
> > Au soleil. . . .
>
> Je devins un opéra fabuleux; je vis que tous les êtres ont une fatalité de bonheur: l'action n'est pas la vie, mais une façon de gâcher quelque force, un énervement. La morale est la faiblesse de la cervelle.
>
> A chaque être, plusieurs autres vies me semblaient dues. Ce monsieur ne sait ce qu'il fait: il est un ange. Cette famille est une nichée de chiens. Devant plusieurs hommes, je causerai tout haut avec un moment d'une de leurs autres vies.—Ainsi, j'ai aimé un porc.[28]

> (At last, O happiness, O reason, I removed the azure from the sky, which is all blackness, and I lived, a gleam of gold from the light of nature. For joy, I assumed the most clownish and wild expression possible. //It is found again! /What? Eternity. / It is the sea mixed / with the sun. . . .// I became a legendary opera: I saw that there is a fatality in the happiness of every being: action is not life, but a way of spoiling a certain force, a producing of nervous tension. Morality is the weakness of the brain.
>
> It seems to me that several other lives are the due of every being. This gentleman does not know what he is doing: he is an angel. This family is a litter of dogs. Before several people, I will talk out loud with a moment of one of their other lives. And so I have loved a pig.)

Again, in the more violent imagery employed by German expressionist poets, such as Georg Heym or Gottfried Benn, an exultantly aggressive tone is inseparable from their sensational displays of vision. A deliberate playing with the level of the reader's response—so that he can reach beauty only at the price of enduring blasphemies, and taste tragedy only by contrast with farce—is a technique that can be observed in wider reaches of modern literature than can be surveyed here: for instance, in the drama of Jarry or Brecht. Or again, it may sometimes be discovered in what would otherwise appear to be quite dissimilar kinds of writing:

in the largely inward-looking, word-conscious, self-absorbed, "craft" literature of Joyce or Beckett, as well as in the tough, terse, outward-looking fiction of Hemingway and of his European imitators, such as Pavese.

If, in the future, cultural historians come to see a unity in the literature of the later 19th century and earlier 20th century—so that, like other periods, such as the Enlightenment and the Romantic movement, it can be given a name—then it is possible that Baudelaire's conception of poetry as "flowers of evil" will provide the clue to its unity, and that some more abstract way of formulating the idea of ambiguous aestheticism (to which his title points) will provide scholars with their still-missing label. Such a characterization of the period would suggest that the alienation of the artist from society was due not simply to a particular historical situation or to unfavourable circumstances, but just as much to a psychological necessity of the creative mind.

In conclusion we may cite one or two further examples, which remind us again of how the poetic imagination has repeatedly felt itself compelled to sin against the established order for the sake of its art. At the end of his thinly veiled autobiography, *Die Aufzeichnungen des Malte Laurids Brigge* (1910; The Notebook of Malte Laurids Brigge), Rilke retells the story of the prodigal son in such a way as to justify not the son's return, but his going away. It is to escape the constriction of being loved, of being the person that those who love him want him to be, that he goes. In his days as a swineherd he comes closest to *his* God, to the solitude from any social relationship that alone could open his eyes and heart to the impersonal mystery of things. Gide makes use of the parable in a very similar way in *Le retour de l'enfant prodigue* (1912), although he understands the personal and more conventionally human aspect of the story (which Rilke neglects) better than he knows how to express the poetry of any deeper experience of life beyond good and evil. (The same is generally true of his other aesthetic works, such as *Les nourritures terrestres* [1903; Fruits of the Earth] and *L'immoraliste* [1910].) Just how deep a hold this problem could take on a poet's imagination can be seen from the lines Apollinaire wrote about it during World War I. He has served at the front and been severely wounded, but despite all he has suffered and lost (which he begins by describing) he will talk with his remaining friends now about the aesthetic problem that concerns them most. These friends, we may conveniently remind ourselves, included Picasso and other cubist painters, the members of that artistic bohemia that had flourished in Paris then for nearly a century.

... sans m'inquiéter aujourd'hui de cette guerre
Entre nous et pour nous mes amis
Je juge cette longue querelle de la tradition et de l'invention
        De l'Ordre et de l'Aventure

Vous dont la bouche est faite à l'image de celle de Dieu
Bouche qui est l'ordre même
Soyez indulgents quand vous nous comparez
A ceux qui furent la perfection de l'ordre
Nous qui quêtons partout l'aventure

Nous ne sommes pas vos ennemis
Nous voulons vous donner de vastes et d'étranges domaines
Où le mystère en fleurs s'offre à qui veut le cueillir
Il y a là des feux nouveaux des couleurs jamais vues
Mille phantasmes impondérables
Auxquels il faut donner de la réalité
Nous voulons explorer la bonté contrée énorme où tout se tait
Il y a aussi le temps qu'on peut chasser ou faire revenir
Pitié pour nous qui combattons toujours aux frontières
De l'illimité et de l'avenir
Pitié pour nos erreurs pitié pour nos péchés ...

(. . . without troubling now about this war / Between ourselves and for our own sakes my friends / I sit in judgment on this long quarrel between tradition and invention / Between Order and Adventure /

You whose mouths are fashioned in the image of God's mouth / Mouth which is order itself / Be lenient when you compare us / With those who were perfect order / Us who seek adventure everywhere /

We are not enemies / We want to bequeath to you vast and strange domains / Where the flower of mystery offers itself to anyone who wishes to pluck it / There there are unknown fires and colours never before seen / A thousand unknowable phantasms / Which must be given reality / We wish to explore kindness the vast and peaceful country / There is also Time which can either be banished or else retrieved / Pity on us who are always fighting at the frontiers / Of limitlessness and the future / Pity for our mistakes pity for our sins . . .).[29]

References

1. ARTHUR SYMONS, *Confessions: a Study in Pathology* (New York 1930), p. 5.
2. HENRI BERGSON, *Oeuvres* (Paris 1959), p. 1065.
3. W. M. THACKERAY, "Mme Sand and the New Apocalypse," *The Paris Sketch Book* (1840).
4. C.-P. BAUDELAIRE, "Le dandy," *Le peintre de la vie moderne* (1863).
5. In an article entitled "Exposition Universelle—Beaux Arts," in *Le*

Pays (26 May 1855). (*Curiosités esthétiques*, p. 227, in *Oeuvres complètes*, ed. by J. Crépet [Paris 1923].)

6. Quoted by Hallam Lord Tennyson in *Alfred Lord Tennyson, a Memoir* (1897), Vol. II, p. 92.

7. Letter to Louise Colet, 22 November 1852.

8. ERNEST RENAN, Preface to *Souvenirs d'enfance et de jeunesse* (Paris 1883).

9. J. K. HUYSMANS, *À rebours*, Ch. xiv.

10. WALTER PATER, *Marius the Epicurean*, Ch. ix.

11. Letter to his mother, 15 December 1850.

12. FRANZ KAFKA, *Hochzeitsvorbereitungen auf dem Lande* (New York and Frankfurt 1953), p. 418.

13. *Amiel's Journal*, trans. by Mrs H. Ward (London 1933); see pp. 49 f.

14. EUGENIO MONTALE, *Ossi di seppia* (1925).

15. W. B. YEATS, "Per Amica Silentia Lunae" (1917), in *Mythologies* (1959).

16. ARTHUR RIMBAUD, "Lettre d'un voyant."

17. Footnote by Ezra Pound in HARRIET MONROE, *A Poet's Life* (New York 1938).

18. Quoted by C. NORMAN in *Ezra Pound* (New York 1960), p. 170.

19. ERNEST DOWSON, "Cynara."

20. C.-P. BAUDELAIRE, "Tu mettrais l'univers entier dans ta ruelle," *Les fleurs du mal*.

21. Baudelaire stressed this point particularly when he repeated it in "Théophile Gautier," *L'art romantique* (1869). He first made it in "Notes nouvelles sur Edgar Poe" (1857).

22. THÉOPHILE GAUTIER, "L'art," *Emaux et camées* (1852).

23. RAINER MARIA RILKE, "Requiem für Graf von Kalckreuth" (1909).

24. GAUTIER, *op. cit.*

25. C.-P. BAUDELAIRE, "L'art philosophique," *L'art romantique*.

26. STÉPHANE MALLARMÉ, *Divagations* (1897). See especially "Crise de vers" and "Le mystère dans les lettres."

27. FRIEDRICH NIETZSCHE, *Thus Spake Zarathustra* (1883–92), Pt I, Prologue, Section 5.

28. ARTHUR RIMBAUD, *Une saison en enfer* (1873).

29. GUILLAUME APOLLINAIRE, "La jolie rousse," *Calligrammes* (Paris 1925).

CHAPTER 17

Writer and Reader: a New Relationship

Robert M. Adams*

Earlier chapters have referred to the beginnings of a change, which became more marked as the 19th century wore on, in traditional assumptions about how a work of literature relates to reality. It is a change that may have begun already in the 18th century, as aesthetic theory began to lay more stress on the emotional response aroused by art in the spectator, and less on the imitation by art of reality. Inevitably, the implication grew stronger that the work, or at least the experience, of literature constituted some sort of reality in its own right. One of the earliest writers in Europe to play with the reader's response to a book as an artificial structure was Laurence Sterne. In Germany, where Sterne's writing was known and admired, various sophisticated and philosophically sometimes pretentious attempts to play with the level at which a text was meant to be read have been dignified by critics with the name of "Romantic irony." Kierkegaard, who was steeped in German literature, published all his "aesthetical writings" under pseudonyms, because it seemed to him that any claim by an author to be communicating directly a truth about existence must be suspect. A "true" response might be elicited from a reader, however, by some more or less provocative type of "indirect communication." Baudelaire assaulted his readers with many more obviously scandalous thoughts in *Les fleurs du mal* (1857), pointing the way toward new relationships of reader to author, and of literature to reality, even though he preserved a conventional outward form for his poetry (except for the so-called *poèmes en prose*). The line that may be said to proclaim formally this new state of affairs is the celebrated:

* Professor of English, University of California at Los Angeles.

Hypocrite lecteur,—mon semblable,—mon frère!
(Hypocrite reader—my kin—my brother!)

The theme of "Au lecteur" (1855) is a moral one, an attack by Baudelaire on the vice he considered to be the curse not only of his own life but of the modern age altogether: *ennui*. It is the vice that leads men to literature —that is, to the strange pleasure of making and unmaking the world in one's own and, worst of all, in someone else's imagination. Whether or not we share Baudelaire's complex indignation with the cannibalistic reader, there can be no doubt that, by defining a new relation between reader and writer, he released a new source of inspiration in modern poets. Baudelaire's influence on the poets who came after him was primarily linguistic, only secondarily moral: he had shown that words might be used in a new way, to involve the reader in the scrimmage of the poet's attitudes, to force upon him an act of self-definition. Words used thus could open up *in* the reader (and *to* the reader) a world of symbolic associations in no way congruent with those that common sense conventionally calls "real." The poets who went farthest

Au ciel antérieur où fleurit la Beauté
(Toward the threshold heaven where beauty flowers)

were Mallarmé and Rimbaud; in their wake came a whole generation of French symbolist poets, both minor and major; and the symbolist "movement" was not long in spreading throughout Europe. This story is told elsewhere;* but because writers in English resisted the tendency for so long, we must reach forward into the 20th century to examine its culmination in the work of James Joyce, who deliberately turned away from the English tradition in favour of one that he traced from Flaubert to Huysmans, J. P. Jacobsen, and Gabriele d'Annunzio. In combining the peculiar but extended demands of the prose epic with those no less strenuous and intricate exercises of the symbolist lyric, *Ulysses* (1922) and even more strikingly *Finnegans Wake* (1939) strive toward the status of the Mallarméan *livre*—the ultimate "book" in which the whole cosmos inscribes itself.

One way of recognizing the shift in the relation of reader to writer that was becoming widespread by the turn of the century would be to define it as the decision of authors to tantalize in order to entertain their readers. Put like this it sounds, at first hearing, like a relatively unimportant

* See, for instance, Ch. 16, "The Cult of Art," and, in Volume VI, "Experiments in Language" and "Poetry after Eliot in the English-speaking World."

and not particularly original option, going at least as far back as the deliberate obscurities of the 12th-century Provençal *trobar clus*. Later mediaeval allegorists, including Dante, knew perfectly well the advantages of intriguing the reader's curiosity and challenging his powers of interpretation; the humble detective story, the *roman à clef*, the ever-present charade and riddle, remind us of the continuing appeal of the literary puzzle. But in the historical context of English fiction and poetry, as one looks back from Eliot and Joyce through the 19th century toward the remote eminences of Milton and Defoe, the turn-about was startling enough. Essentially it involved a reversal in the priority assigned to two different orders of "plot."

Most traditional literary works achieve two different orders of continuity. There is a sequence of events, assertions, or attitudes, taking place within a fictive world, and describing by means of words on a page; there is also a cycle of sympathetic emotional responses that constitutes, for the reader, the reactive "content" of the work. Ordinarily, traditionally, these two levels of continuity do not diverge very sharply. In reading Matthew Arnold's poem "The Forsaken Merman," for example, one follows the external action of the merman calling his children away from their mother, recalling their last separation, and then surrendering to fresh waves of nostalgic resignation; and simultaneously one is moved through a cycle of sympathetic response, tempered perhaps by a slight sense of distancing caused by our awareness of an unfamiliar perspective. But the primary continuity of the poem is the discourse of the merman, which controls the secondary continuity, the emotional response of the reader, via the nexus of imaginative sympathy. And anyone will no doubt be able to apply this same, very commonplace formula to the analysis of most conventional novels of the 19th century. We are familiar enough with the exaggerated responses to which this good understanding between reader and writer sometimes gave rise: the floods of tears shed over the death of Little Nell and the generous impulses to social reform stirred by the literary sufferings of Uncle Tom were spectacular exaggerations of an imaginative process that had a perfectly respectable normal character, from which, however, Joyce and Eliot departed, with consequences I shall discuss.

They departed, primarily, by fracturing or frustrating that continuity on the printed page once considered basic to the work of literary art, and by challenging the reader to construct, on the other level of psychological understanding and sympathetic response, a relationship across the gap. This shift, in the first place, does odd things to one's notion of

493

reading a book or a poem consecutively, from beginning to end. A constellation does not have a beginning, a middle, and an end. There is no way of crossing an imaginative gap except retrospectively, when you know where you have to get from and where you have to get to. So the practice of reading a book or a poem as a series of cross-connected points of energy that are experienced more or less simultaneously (as one sees a physical pattern), rather than consecutively (as one tells a story), is a direct consequence of the new technique. Another resource tapped by the new technique is the anxiety of a responsible reader confronting an incomplete pattern: he can be trusted to reach across immense distances and search out remote possibilities. Other consequences involve diminished emphasis on impetus, consecutive narration, rendering and other forms of author-control, and psychological depth. Stories stop still ("nothing happens" is the reader's usual complaint), or repeat themselves, or refuse to "get anywhere"; sympathy, in the sense of identification with a character, is discouraged or made impossible; chronological con-secutivity is violated, so that one sequence of events breaks off in the middle (a middle that the reader is trusted to fill in for himself), or two sequences are run together (and the reader is trusted to formulate a relation between them). The reader is not invited to be "caught up in a situation" by adopting a single point of view, he is not allowed to forget that he is a reader; rather, he is consciously engaged in the verbal structure and invited to contrast several different points of view within it or toward it. At the same time, he is deprived of that measure of assurance that readers of conventional fiction generally enjoy. For example, a reader of Dickens can be fairly sure that the intrigue will be resolved one way or another, that the author will not bring either himself or his trusting reader up against insoluble difficulties. Such a reader can count on the fact that a novel that begins in one tonality will not modulate arbitrarily every 30 pages into another; he can define, after the first few pages, the range of emotional reaction that will be expected of him, the level on which he should "take" the characters set before him. Mr Pumblechook, Mr Wopsle, and good old Peggotty are not going to turn—perhaps only momentarily, but all the more unnervingly, if so—into wandering stars, Irish mountains, Agamemnon, the spinning earth, or the human kidney. Above all, the reader of a conventional novel does not have to fear that, if he misses an allusion or commits the oversight of reading a symbol in its literal sense, he has lost a major element of the fiction. No doubt there are a good many patterns of incidental and decorative symbolism in *Great Expectations*, for example; but a reader can feel he has got a satisfying measure of the novelistic experience without any but the most available of these. For he can still have experienced what is clearly the main continuum of the novel, the social and sentimental career of Pip, his tests, triumphs, and failures, the working-out of his destiny.

But the reader of Joyce, aware that the narrative he is reading has several dimensions, and vaguely suspicious that a superficial reading feels somehow incomplete, is driven to grope amid, and extrapolate from, the clustered symbols in search of a pattern that will bring order out of the shadows and hints in which he has been wandering. His energies are engaged in the ordering and integrating of the work of art, as surely as if he had been given a group of episodes written on a pack of cards, and invited to arrange them. Finally, as the artifice of artistic creation and arrangement is transferred, as a moral burden, to the reader, the possibility of inwardness, the importance of sympathy, and the concern with psychology, all diminish in importance as elements of reader response. In the foreground, formal pattern becomes more important than psychological analysis; in the background, symbolism tends to render character translucent. From both directions, therefore, the authenticity of "character" is squeezed by competing levels of significance, and the reader is required to adjust and readjust his focus with an agility that the earlier novel never demanded of him.

To assert that all these consequences flowed from a single basic decision to tantalize the reader is surely to oversimplify a complicated process; yet the issue does seem to be one essentially of authority. Traditional novelists had assumed that the reader's sensibility was in some degree a measure to which the work of art must, in prudence, be tailored. Joyce follows rather the dogmatic formulation of Oscar Wilde in "The Soul of Man under Socialism" (1891):

> The work of art is to dominate the spectator: the spectator is not to dominate the work of art.

He takes for granted that the work of art is a rack on which the reader's sensibility must, with his active consent and even complicity, be stretched. As it happens, the process has revealed unexpected resiliencies and elasticities in modern readers; perhaps it has even created them. But the turnabout pivoted on the simple question of whose mind was the measure of whose.

Primary responsibility for the changeover doubtless belongs to Joyce's glacial, imperious power of will. For years he had to fight—legally, logically, socially, financially—with every weapon at his command

495

against what amounted to the world of culture, with its arsenal of timidities, conventions, and vetoes. Had he not been a fighter he must surely have succumbed. But he was supported, in addition to his own intuitions, by a curious collection of precedents and sympathetic spiritual ancestors. From the start, he identified himself with Parnell as a lone, inflexible (and alien) spokesman for Ireland's spiritual integrity against England's materially minded and hypocritical social order. He drew spiritual strength from the thought of artists such as Flaubert and Ibsen, James Clarence Mangan and W. B. Yeats, who had stood out, as he saw it, against commercial and provincial values. The idea that art must provide a substitute for the gradually fading values of religion was prevalent, in many different tonalities, throughout the late 19th century. Joyce took the new role, not as a *faute-de-mieux* solution, but as a real foundation for a priesthood of the imagination, within which he himself would naturally be a hierophant. Deep in his Irish background may have survived almost superstitious feelings about the independence and dignity of the artist—no mere paid entertainer, but a priest, a trusted adviser to kings, a diviner entrusted with the spiritual health of the whole society. With a curious kind of inverted pride, too, he thought of himself, and of artists generally as a public sewer through which the filth and guilt of the whole community found an outlet and was purged away. On all these scores Joyce was emboldened, by a logic grounded in the past and a shaping vision of the present, to push forward with a literary mode that, as he soon learned, not only entangled but terrified and infuriated readers. The protracted intermittent struggles over *Dubliners* (eventually published in 1914), the suppression of *Ulysses*, the unrelenting stream of criticism levelled at *Work in Progress*, must surely have broken the will of a man less surely grounded and less inflexibly motivated.

But the story of Joyce's triumph over his opposition is less interesting as melodrama than as strategy; it is extraordinary, for one thing, to sense how deeply laid Joyce's plans were. Many themes, later to become dominant, appear in the early fiction with so little emphasis, and imply a perspective so remote from anything else that appears in the story, that the suspicion of their presence (which is all we can have within the framework of the story) seems deliberately intended to tantalize and disquiet. In the first story of *Dubliners*, for example, the sisters of the title are seen waking a dead priest, Father Flynn. Three words have a particular fascination for the boy who acts as narrator: the words *simony*, *paralysis*, and *gnomon*. They are all related to the dead priest, to the Dublin scene of which he was a part, or to the method of the story; but these relations the reader is required to work out for himself; they are not handed to him. And there is not only little help for him in constructing these relations, but also some deliberate, built-in confusion. For the priest is referred to as an actual simoniac, which in its catechetical sense implies that his sin was the selling of the gifts of the Holy Spirit for money. But there are other and conflicting suggestions: in his dream, the boy encounters the old priest in "some pleasant and vicious region," whereas in Eliza's account of her brother's misfortune it is simply the dropping and breaking of a chalice that caused his downfall. None of these hints is quite congruent with the others: dropping a chalice is neither pleasant nor is it simony; and simony is not particularly pleasant. The chalice is perhaps the most capacious of these three indications: it might be the metaphorical vessel of the priest's talents, which he spilled and spoiled. And we recall that the boy in "Araby" bears his imaginary chalice, his private dream, through a throng of foes in the sordid Dublin streets. In this sense, dropping a chalice could be metaphorical "simony," i.e. misapplication of talents.*

This notion is greatly reinforced by the uncanonical detail that Father Flynn as he lies in his coffin bears an "idle chalice" on his breast, as a sort of emblem of his life. But Eliza now tells us, as if in afterthought, that "they say it was all right, that it contained nothing, I mean." Of course, if it had contained something, a real chalice would have contained communion wine, the blood of Christ, and its emptiness when dropped would be a good thing. But, supposing it was metaphorical, then we must read the phrase, "they say it was all right, that it contained nothing," as bitterly ironical. "They," who are Dubliners such as Old Cotter, always find that things are at their best when there's nothing in the chalice, when any gift that might distinguish a man is proved illusory. But perhaps, too, there is an insinuation here that the church in which Father Flynn served, and against whose canons he thought he had sinned, was no true church: his chalice was empty, his service, like his sin, was merely superstitious. And similarly, in that phrase "they say it was the boy's fault," there may be more than an attempt to spread the guilt to a

---

* Secondary connotations are sometimes traced out, by uneasy critics, through corresponding names; thus the "simony" of the priest may be related to the figure of Simon Moonan in the *Portrait*, about whom we know chiefly that he took a (presumably degrading) job in a brewery, and to Simon Dedalus, who wasted his gifts at the other end of the brewery. To be sure, these parallels fly in the face of our very different feelings about these different faces of "simony"; if there is a moral parallel, it works directly against the pattern of our literary responses; but this is no evidence that it was not intended. A stronger case might be made that Joyce's world contains so much simony, in the sense of mere human wastage, that he cannot be understood as making a distinct moral point about it.

II

long-forgotten acolyte; because symbols are a-chronological, one may see the speech as (perhaps unconsciously) prophetic: the broken chalice that doomed the priest was the fault of one boy, and will in due course be the fault of this present boy, his sin. Boys are not only guilty in Dublin, but the occasions of guilt in others; how much of the mistrust expressed by the uncle and Old Cotter concerning the boy's association with Father Flynn represents covert suspicion of homosexuality? No wonder that George Roberts, of Maunsell & Co., faced with all these multiplying and sinister possibilities in one word of one story, demanded a dictionary definition of "simony" before he would consent to publish.[1] He would have been even more disturbed could he have imagined that dead Father James Flynn of "The Sister" foreshadowed, implied, and in some sense included, the legendary Finn MacCool, Bygmester Solness, Daniel O'Connell, Adam, a giant salmon in the Liffey, the Duke of Wellington, and Humpty Dumpty. Father Flynn "is" all these characters, of course, only in retrospect from *Finnegans Wake*; yet there is reason, as the story is written, to feel the pressure of these presences. By contrast with the ignoble Dublin background, Father Flynn has been a giant consciousness; he has dealt with issues of heroic import, issues of salvation, damnation, and ultimate legality, issues too great for him to resolve and too vague for the reader to define precisely. His fate therefore spreads out through the mediating mind of the curiously, the tacitly fatherless narrator; his death is a death of many ancestors to whom narrator and reader are mysteriously bound by a link of undefined guilt and shame. There is, in this little story, an almost limitless empty space around the dead enigma of the priest; idle talk and formal observances do a little to fill it, but not much, and the reader is invited to do the rest by multiplying symbolic significances.

That Joyce should have invoked, in "The Sisters," a theme that he would exploit again in *Finnegans Wake*, is a little more than odd, but not really startling. Artists who work in recurrent forms, playing many variations on a single theme and ending where they began, are not uncommon, and apart from the habit of mind itself, there is not a great deal to be remarked about them. Ibsen is one immediate predecessor of Joyce whose work, from *Catilina* to *When We Dead Awaken*, can be seen to follow the single thematic line of ethical versus aesthetic personalities. So too, in lesser measure, with Flaubert, whom Joyce also revered; a seeker-out of parallels between *La tentation de St Antoine* (1874) and *Bouvard et Pécuchet* (1881) could undoubtedly find them. Joyce carried consistency a little farther, perhaps, than either of his predecessors; one can see, in the sequence of *Dubliners*, *A Portrait of the Artist as a Young Man* (1916),

Ulysses, and *Finnegans Wake*, an increasing fascination with the concept of eternal return, an increasing emphasis on the presence of the dead or dying past and its power to compel the living present into ancient forms. A notable peculiarity in the case of Joyce seems to be the subsurface character of so much of the development. It is true that from the hindsight vantage point of the *Wake* one can see why the note struck in "The Sisters" has deeper and more resonant overtones than the story itself dramatizes. The unexplained gravity of the story's issues, the remarkable excess of its moody atmosphere over its episodic structure, are understood—placed in context—when one reads the career backward. But we look in vain for outward signs of the hidden intent in the story itself. The chief effect of the muted allusions and portents of the story is of something mysterious, something operative yet withheld.

A second, and more disturbing, instance of buried import has to do with a passage in the *Portrait of the Artist* (Compass edition [New York 1965], p. 95) that has not, to my knowledge, been supposed to shelter any particular profundities. Mr Simon Dedalus, drinking with a couple of his cronies at a bar in Cork, calls out to the bartender, "Here, Tim or Tom or whatever your name is, give us the same again." Now, obviously, this passage does not cry aloud for symbolic interpretation. Quite the contrary, it makes obvious "sense" when viewed as a piece of surface realism; Mr Dedalus knows what he wants, the bartender understands him perfectly well; and we may seem to be simply borrowing trouble when we point out that *Finnegans Wake*,* which stands at a considerable distance, both temporally and stylistically, from the *Portrait*, makes much play with the names Tim and Tom—to which, at the risk of compounding the confusion, I will add Tum. Mrs Glasheen has pointed out, in the *Second Census*,[2] that there is something going on with these vocables, though she doesn't say very convincingly what, and the Tim-Tom arrangement can be illustrated by the following passages chosen more or less at random:

> Allfor the books and never pegging smashers after Tom Bowe Glassarse or Timmy the Tosser (p. 27).

> 'Twas two pisononse Timcoves . . . of the name of Treacle Tom . . . and his own blood and milk brother Frisky Shorty (p. 39).

> But, of course, he could call himself Tem, too, if he had time to? You butt he could anytom (p. 88).

> Drop me the sound of the findhorn's name, Mtu or Mti, sombogger was wisness (p. 204).

---

* All editions of *Finnegans Wake* so far published are page-for-page identical.

> For the Clearer of the Air from on high has spoken in tumbuldum tambaldam to his tembledim tombaldoom worrild (p. 258).

> . . . and thou hast set thy guards thereby, even Garda Didymus and Garda Domas . . . the cherryboyum chirryboth with the kerrybommers in their krubeems, Pray-your-Prayers Timothy and Back-to-Bunk Tom (p. 258).

> . . . when they were all four collegians on the nod, neer the Nodderlands Nurskery, whiteboys and oakboys, peep of tim boys and piping tom boys (p. 385).

> This is his largos life, this is me timtomtum and this is her two peekweeny ones (p. 519).

On pages 597 and 598, "Tom" and "Tim" stand as separate lines of text, evidently representing dialectically opposed habits of mind; their conjunction is memorialized on the next page in the phrase, "Tip. Take Tamotimo's topical. Tip. Browne yet Noland. Tip. Advert" (p. 599). And finally (though one could go on), on p. 617 we find the following bit of compressed ecclesiastical history:

> Timothy and Lorcan, the bucket Toolers, both are Timsons now they've changed their characticuls during their blackout.

A first and relatively obvious comment would place Tim and Tom among the Brunonian opposites with which the book is crowded: Shem and Shaun, Mutt and Jute, Justius and Mercius, Browne and Nolan, Thomas à Becket and Lorcan O'Toole. Like these other paired figures, they often coalesce (into Tamotimos or Timsons); or as Anna Livia says, "I seen the likes in the twinngling of an aye. Som. So oft. Sim. Time after time. The sehm asnuh" (p. 620). Tim would seem to be singular, Tom his double; Thomas is Aramaic for "twin," and Saint Thomas the apostle is often referred to in the Greek Testament by the Greek form of his name, Didymus, i.e. "twin." Combining Tim and Tom gives us the total value of the father, "this is me timtomtum" (his "largos life" is, via Cockney rhyming slang, his wife, and with the two peekweeny ones we have very nearly the whole family). Father's connection with the "tumbuldum" thunder brings to mind the Viconian giant who creates civilization as a response to the terror of the thunderclap; and the vocable "Tum" clusters thick about the father under this aspect. He is "Tumult son of Thunder" (p. 184); he is "tumulous under his chthonic exterior, but plain Mr Tumulty in muftilife" (p. 261). When he lies buried under the Dublin landscape, his "tumptytum toes" stick up near the Phoenix Park (p. 3); and some sort of bellringer or accountant is invited to "tal the tem of the tumulum" (p. 56). (The phrase implies that he will tell or toll the time or tally the tempo or cut out a trench through the teeming of the tumulus or burial-mound.) Thus the cycle tim-tom-tum as it progresses through the vowels chronicles the cycle of mankind through time, its rise and fall. And, given the prominence of Egyptian themes in the *Wake*, we are probably justified in seeing, in the last of these names, an identification of the aging father HCE with the Egyptian god of the setting sun, Tem, Tum, or Atum. Michelet, who probably introduced Joyce to Vico in the first place, would have provided him, through *La Bible de l'humanité* (1884), with ample material on the great god Tum, even if the rest of the *Wake* did not provide copious evidence of Joyce's close acquaintance with *The Book of the Dead*.*

In the world of the *Wake* these things are accepted readily enough. But now what about Mr Dedalus's convivial words to that faraway bartender in Cork? We don't need a connection with the *Wake*'s Tim-Tom syndrome to redeem the *Portrait*'s phrase from any glaring deficiencies. But the thematic correspondences are striking indeed. Time is of the essence of the scene; Mr Dedalus's fortunes are on the decline, and he has been discussing, with some bravado, his own reluctance to "take a back seat" in the face of his (rising) son. Talk about his former sexual prowess is already counterpointed by his son's discovery of precocious sexual appetites in himself; that son will be found meditating, in the immediate context, on vast cycles of meaningless repetition. Mr Dedalus's hesitation over the barman's name, so close to his own mythological one (Tum), the circularity of his sentence (which begins and ends with the same word), and the crucial phrase, "the same again" (cf. the *Wake*, p. 215 "the seim anew"; p. 620 "the sehm asnuh"), all tease us with the suspicion that concepts subtly operative in the *Wake* may have been present in Joyce's mind as early as the *Portrait*. It is not, as in the instance of "The Sisters," that *Wake*-elements of a very general nature are present in rudimentary form in the earlier work. The sentence in the *Portrait* could not have been written at all if the cyclical theory of history—a parallel between Ireland and Egypt as lands of the living dead, and the conception of Tim and Tom as rising sons of the setting Tum—had not been firmly established in the author's mind. He did not stumble upon such rudiments as a Cork bar-

---

* At least one of the passages quoted above occurs in close conjunction with Egyptian themes. See, on p. 385, "Two-tongue common" = Tut-ankh-amun, and "Nush the carrier of the word and . . . Mesh the cutter of the reed" are Shaun and Shem reversed and thinly disguised as Egyptian-style deities. The same god whom Michelet calls "Tum," E. A. W. Budge, in his translation of *The Book of the Dead* (London 1898), calls "Tem"; he is the sun, who is Ra when he rises, and Tem or Tum when he sets.

tender named Tim or Tom, and then later discover, in *The Book of the Dead*, or Michelet, or wherever, the existence of the God Tem/Tum. The whole complex must have been present in his mind as early as 1908, when there is every evidence that the first three chapters of the *Portrait* were more or less complete in substantially their present form. Neither in the letters of this period, nor in the other writings, nor anywhere in the canon, do we find the slightest positive evidence that Joyce was thinking in Egyptian terms, that he saw Simon Dedalus under the aspect of a sun-god, or that Tim and Tom meant anything more to him than ordinary nicknames for Timothy and Thomas, two perfectly ordinary Irish names. Yet the presence of all these occult implications is unmistakable. It is a little bit like finding a single, fully formed neolithic artefact in the middle of some unmistakably palaeolithic strata. The solution to the problem is not to fudge the evidence or dismiss the find as a mere "accident," but to redefine what we mean by "palaeolithic" and perhaps to rethink our conceptions of stratum formation. Redefining the periods of Joyce's life is a less than presumptuous undertaking, because the categories so far applied to it are so patently provisional and perfunctory. And both "concealment" and "creation" have special meanings in a Joycean context that should make us hesitant about invoking capsule formulas to describe the way in which his mind grew.

"Concealment," for example, is often a special form of revelation—a way, indeed, of requiring discovery; it may be a way of conveying, in addition to information, an insider's complicity; it may suggest a construct in which not everything is arranged for the reader's comprehension, hence a construct more like life than like conventional art and less subservient to an established social function; or it may assert a special power of arbitrary dominion in the artist, who can give light to his universe or withhold it as he chooses. Similarly, "creation" for Joyce is often a plunge out of sterile logic into the dark sphere of appetite; it may be a widening of the mind to embrace all sorts of subliminal verbal scraps, garbage, and litter (yet, at the same time, it includes an intricate process of highly conscious mosaic-work). Finally, it may be the laying bare of immense substructures in the mind—constructs not so much built as found and used in the work as needed. If we combine a couple of these concepts appropriately, we may get a notion of Joyce's creative process that will make the flash of an Egyptian perspective in the *Portrait* seem less anomalous. For example, a scene that juxtaposed beery sentiment about young and old with a sense of cyclical continuity might well need the touch of a remote perspective to reassure the author of his own authenticity. And the substructure half-revealed here could have been built on a schoolboy's knowledge of Egyptology by anyone playful enough about vocables to connect Tem/Tum with time and tomb, which, with a bit of bobtailing, become Tim and Tom.

Thus, it is not impossible to form some conjectures as to why Joyce did the remarkable thing he did on p. 95 of the *Portrait* and in the *Wake*. But seeing this connection, whether we think we understand it or not, effects curious changes in a reader's definition of himself as a responsive agent. The traditional reader's reward for successfully completing a pattern deliberately left incomplete is a better understanding of the work's dynamic relations, its completed structure of energies. One's "ratification" of the work, long suspended and withheld, is at last released when one sees it as a whole. Instead of sitting, as it were, before the screen of a work and submitting passively to the pre-programmed flow of its surface impressions, the man who experiences fiction as pattern-to-be-completed must create for himself what Mr Kernan, of *Ulysses*, is fond of calling a "retrospective rearrangement." But in all this the basic premise is that our framework of attention is the work of art itself, as an arranged structure of impressions. That is how the reader recognizes an incompletion in the first place, which he is impelled to fill in the second. But the sort of connecting lines we have drawn between the *Portrait* and the *Wake* do not tell us so much about either work as about the mind that created them in such a strange relationship. In a word, our interest in the observation of this particular parallel is an analyst's interest in a surprising and important symptom, not a reader's interest in a moving insight or a fine structural effect. Fair enough to say that if reading Joyce in a non-literary way repels us, we need only read him in a literary way; the point is simply that the texts themselves invite us to read actively, investigatively, with an almost unlimited attention to minor verbal details that recur, seemingly at random, throughout Joyce's work. And this comes close to making us analysts, not simply of the text, but of the world implied by the text, and of the mind that conceived the world and the text.

Thus the reader is involved in reading not just the books of Joyce, but Joyce himself as well; his books are not merely spectacles arranged on a discreetly lit stage by an invisible artist to delight and instruct (and, above all, to entertain) a paying audience. We must enter into them to complete the patterns and make the connections they imply, bringing with us whatever knowledge seems useful. Sometimes the path into them is through Joyce the biographical person; at other times, this same person is the terminus to which that path leads. That is why there is some point to saying that Joyce himself imposed on us the task of reading him like a case history. But it is a case history that claims, in pride, disgust, terror, and anguish, to be nothing less than a window upon the cosmos. In the cycle of his own death and resurrection, Joyce proposed to all men and civilizations a paradigm of their own spiritual history. Shem the Penman, cowering in his pitchblack house O'Shame, writes world history in ink of his own excrement on paper of his own integument (the *Wake*, pp. 185–6):

> with this double due, brought to blood heat, gallic acid on iron ore, through the bowels of his misery, flashly, faithly, nastily, appropriately, this Esuan Menschavik and the first till last alshemist wrote over every square inch of the only foolscap available, his own body, till by its corrosive sublimation one continuous present tense integument slowly unfolded all marryvoising moodmoulded cyclewheeling history (thereby, he said, reflecting from his own individual person life unlivable, transaccidentated through the slow fires of consciousness into a dividual chaos, perilous, potent, common to allflesh, human only, mortal). . . .

Evidently, for a writer who defines himself and his task in this way, there is not much distinction between reading the man and reading the book. Nor is it easy to imagine a relationship in which the reader's mind could be more fully and complexly engaged with that of the writer, on more different and demanding levels. But we had better beware of saying that Joyce found a primitive idea in Oscar Wilde and developed it into something complex. Probably what he found simple in Wilde was for him, from the beginning, complex. It was the idea of shaking the reader out of his complacency—his institutional complacency as a reader confronting a book—by making him aware initially of his inferiority. By setting him on the track of ever more elusive and tantalizing clues, Joyce enticed the reader from his secure study and settled linguistic-literary habits into the depths of the haunted artist's mind and personality, and at last, via inconceivable elaborations of development, back into the presence of his own universal, buried, moral darkness. The reader's putting-down was thus a preliminary to his rising anew. The title, *Finnegans Wake*, is an imperative as well as the name of a social occasion.

Joyce's multiple meanings, the punning echoes and re-echoes that run right through his work and culminate in the sustained, reverberative paranomasia of *Finnegans Wake*, represent much more than an arrogant writer's imperious demands on the reader. They are bound up with late-

19th-century aestheticism, as we observed at the start, in that they are designed to prevent the emergence of a point of view relevant to decision and action in the ordinary world. The autonomy of the world of art can be defined in many different ways. One definition would emphasize the artist's refusal to commit himself to any public attitude—as Joyce refused to abandon a total neutrality about politics and public affairs, even though he had begun as a rebel, had supported Ibsen's anti-bourgeois attitudes as a young man, and had defined the purpose of *Dubliners* as "to write a chapter in the moral history of my country" with Dublin as the "centre of paralysis." Joyce's presentation, in the *Portrait*, of growing up to be an artist as inevitably involving growing up to be an exile, and his own voluntary exile from Ireland, were his ways of acting out the withdrawal of the artist from bourgeois society that was so much a part of the late-19th-century literary scene. (It must be remembered that Joyce's basic attitudes were formed in the 19th century, though his work belongs to the 20th.) The continuous expansion of meaning is a means of disengagement from the problem of deciding whether he would accept the public valuation of what was significant in experience or whether (as other late 19th- and early 20th-century poets and novelists did) he would fall back on his own personally intuited sense. In fact, what Joyce came to recognize, as Ibsen did before him, was that only the deep and private values gave him any access whatever to the public consciousness. In spite of his early doctrine of the "epiphany"—the suddenly and inexplicably revealed sense of significance in an incident or scene or situation that would be trivial or meaningless by any public standard—Joyce never used it to force a private vision on his public. His vision transcended privacy by its all-inclusiveness. Leopold Bloom in *Ulysses* is both coward and hero, both trivial and important, both a petty, unsuccessful advertisement canvasser and a fabulous voyager, and the style of the book is continually altered so as to keep changing the valuation given to him. In the "Cyclops" episode, when Bloom's courageous behaviour in the face of the Citizen's bigoted attack seems to be leading him to a clear heroic role, Joyce neatly turns the tables by a richly comic mock-heroic account of the ending of the episode, as indeed he punctuates it throughout with comic parody. Joyce told the painter Frank Budgen that he took Ulysses as the central figure and title of his novel because Homer's Ulysses is the most complete man in literature. "Ulysses is son to Laertes, but he is father to Telemachus, husband to Penelope, lover of Calypso, companion in arms of the Greek warriors around Troy, and King of Ithaca. . . . Don't forget that he was a war dodger who tried to evade military service by simulating madness. . . . But once at the war the conscientious objector became a jusqu'auboutist."[3]

Thus Joyce confronts the dilemma of the artist living at a time when agreement between reader and writer on what is significant in experience can no longer be taken for granted, by creating a kind of comedy whose essence is multiple correspondence, infinite transparency. Everything is significant, everything is insignificant; what doesn't make sense in one context may do so in another, and to see the biggest pattern possible as resourcefully as possible is the responsibility of the reader. Everything can be seen as everything else, mutating continuously as it changes character by being presented in different contexts, through different styles. But the process is not really a chronological one, with something being first this and then that. The search for simultaneity of expression that has already been noted as characteristic of Joyce was a search for ways of expressing the simultaneous—not the developing or successive— identity of everything with everything else. Joyce's ideal work of art would have been a massive and infinitely reverberating pun, echoing away for ever to include everything in everything. In *Ulysses* the process of multiple identification is limited, and takes place within a chronological sequence. But in *Finnegans Wake* the obsessive punning orchestrates the work so as to expand the meaning independently of chronology. Naturally, language being what it is, Joyce could not do without time and space: he needed over 600 pages to say his piece in the *Wake*. Yet its movement is circular and its meaning can be grasped (or glimpsed: perhaps it is impossible for any individual to grasp completely the meaning of this astonishing work) only by a reader who knows the book well enough to have it all lying in his mind at once—and who knows his own mind well enough to see all its potential relations to the book.

The puzzles that Joyce's work sets us are thus radically different from those set by the poets of the *trobar clus,* by the allegorizing and symbolizing mind of Dante, by the mystical poets of the 17th century, by the *roman à clef,* or by the personal association of ideas found in the French Symbolist poets (as in Rimbaud's "A noir, E blanc, I rouge, U vert, O bleu"). Joyce was indeed much interested in symbolism, but for him symbolism was but one of many means of achieving multiple statement, and thus of defining the mind forced to choose for itself among the multiple statements. His aim was to re-create the world with the word with impartial totality, refusing commitment to any attitude other than that of satisfaction with the comprehensiveness of the creation. It is true that other attitudes can sometimes be found in Joyce—moral preferences, disgust, even righteous indignation—but the attitude that lies behind his most characteristic work, in particular behind the continuous fading of names into other names and the infinite expansion of meaning that this suggests, is one of accepting the universe because of its kaleidoscopic interchangeability. The pun is the last refuge of relativism, and Joyce was a relativist because he wilfully decided to see any given person or thing as expansible by language into an enormous range of other persons or things with quite different kinds of significance. In doing this he found a unique way of solving a problem posed by the relation of the writer to society in his time.

References

1. *The Letters of James Joyce*, Vol. II, ed. by Richard Ellman (New York 1966), pp. 304–6.
2. ADALINE GLASHEEN, *A Second Census of "Finnegans Wake,"* rev. edn (Evanston, Ill. 1963), pp. 252, 258.
3. FRANK BUDGEN, *James Joyce and the Making of "Ulysses"* (London 1934), p. 16.

CHAPTER 18

Book Production and Distribution

The late S. H. Steinberg*

Seen through the foreshortening telescope of historical hindsight, the increase of the reading public and the production and distribution of its reading matter during the 19th century may appear as a social and intellectual "explosion" not dissimilar from the social and biological population explosion of our own days.

The motive forces that impelled this movement were as diverse as they were interpenetrating. There was, first of all, the long-term effect of the Enlightenment, which had questioned all traditional values in every sphere and continued to stimulate the inquiring mind. There was the immediate shock of the American and French revolutions, which aroused an irrepressible and widespread interest in public affairs—political as well as social and economic—that had hitherto been the preserve of the chancelleries and a handful of theorists. There was the spread of the industrial and agricultural revolutions, which forced the established and (even more) the aspiring owners of factories and landed estates to make themselves familiar with technical innovations, with the prospects of expanding markets, and with the fluctuations of prices and currencies. Philosophy, politics, and economics worked hand in hand in asking for a better-educated public, responsive to new ideas and able to cope with the complexities of the modern age: educationalists demanded a broadening of the curricula of the ossified universities and the stagnant grammar schools, a determined fight against the illiteracy of the masses, consideration of the neglected female half of the population, and the application of psychological criteria to books for children and young people.

The response of the book trade—in its widest sense—was instant. Like their ancestors in the incunabula period, printers, publishers, typefounders, paper-makers, booksellers, publicists, and the rest at once scented the immense possibilities that the spirit of the age offered them. They quickly

* Former Editor, *The Statesman's Yearbook* (London).

adopted technical innovations that both increased output and lowered production costs. They created the trade organizations, of masters as well as of men, to improve the standard of production and the living standard of the operatives, to increase the flow of books from the producer to the customer, and to protect themselves against piracy and the lack of copyright protection on the one hand and against censorship and government interference on the other.

By looking at the printing trade from the point of view of the social historian, we avoid the pit into which the historian of literature is prone to fall. Histories of literature deal, understandably, with the peaks of literature, disregarding the lowlands. A detailed study of, for instance, the *Goethezeit* has made it clear that it was not Goethe, Schiller, Kleist, and the like who were most highly esteemed and most avidly read by their contemporaries, but a host of minor writers now known only to specialists; not to mention the masses of horror stories, pornography and near-pornography, ephemeral political pamphlets, and the periodicals and newspapers of the period. But it was these sub-literary productions that provided bread and butter for their authors and publishers, made profitable the book-shops and lending libraries, and provided a livelihood to compositors, printers, binders, salesmen, and their families.

For three and a half centuries after Gutenberg the trade underwent virtually no change. The production of types, the setting-up of copy, the printing process, paper-making, binding, publishing, and selling, as practised at the end of the 18th century, were almost indistinguishable from what they had been like in the incunabula period. Then, within a few decades, everything changed.

The Third Earl of Stanhope (1753–1816) deserves a place among the great inventors. In 1804 he constructed the first iron printing-press, which, superseding the old wooden press, allowed a considerable increase in the size of the printed sheet and halved the labour involved. Stanhope's second claim to fame is his perfection of the stereotyping process, originally invented by the Scotsman William Ged, and improved by the Frenchman Firmin Didot, but only now, in 1805, made a business proposition. Stereotyping became the basis of the mass-production and reprinting of books, especially when, 25 years later, French, Italian, and English technicians, independently of one another, replaced the plaster and metal matrices by papier mâché, thus reducing weight, bulk, labour, and cost.

Stanhope's iron press was the necessary antecedent of the steam-press, which the German Friedrich König invented in 1811. It proved its superiority over the hand-press when it was adopted by *The Times* newspaper in 1814 and by the Leipzig printing and publishing house of Brockhaus in 1826. The steam-press at once more than doubled the output, and multiplied it 12-fold when Applegath and Cowper invented the four-cylinder press in 1828. Further improvements eventually reduced the hand-press to a hobby or a museum-piece.

König's steam-press lowered the production cost by 25 per cent, and thus made possible larger as well as cheaper editions. This, in turn, required the production of more and cheaper paper. Here, too, a beginning was made by the invention of machines to replace the ancient technique of making paper by hand. The invention was made in France in 1798 at the Essonnes paper-mill of the firm of Didot. The mechanical technique became economic after it had been adopted and patented by the English firms of Fourdrinier and Gamble in 1803. The output of machine-made paper at once increased 10-fold; its price dropped from 1s. 6d. to 1d. between 1800 and 1900, by which time the production of hand-made paper had dwindled to insignificance.

Experiments in making paper from raw materials other than rags, first undertaken by the biologist René de Réaumur, were intensified during the Napoleonic wars, when the need for bandages caused an acute shortage of linen and lint, and again when the steam-presses clamoured for more and more paper. In 1843 a Saxon weaver, Friedrich Gottlob Keller, succeeded in producing paper from wood-pulp. At first quickly "foxed" (discoloured) and apt to disintegrate, pulp-paper gradually acquired greater durability and better quality by the admixture of various chemical compounds, and has since become an important industry in well-forested countries such as Canada and Finland. All ephemeral reading-matter as well as not-so-ephemeral books have for the past 100 years been printed on pulp-paper, pure rag-paper today being reserved for *de luxe* editions.

A corollary of the ever-increasing speed and volume of printing was the demand for composing machines that would eventually supersede slow and expensive hand-setting. The first practical step was taken by William Church: his letter-founding machine of 1822 quadrupled the number of letters that could be cast by hand in a working day. Of more than 1500 composing machines that had been patented by the end of the 19th century, only a few had more than passing success (one, invented in 1869 by Charles Kastenbein, was used by *The Times* newspaper until 1908); only two have survived to the present. These, too, were preceded by a mechanical device simplifying and multiplying the production of punches: Linton Boyd Benton's punch-cutting machine (1885). It guaranteed the success of the Linotype and Monotype composing machines, the first invented in 1884 by Ottmar Mergenthaler, a German immigrant to the United States, the second in 1887 by the American Tolbert Lanston. On either of these the output of the average compositor rose from 2000 letters an hour to 6000 or more, and the quality of his work was not impaired, but rather improved upon that of a hand-compositor.

This steady acceleration in the output of printed texts was accompanied by a steady growth of processes revolutionizing the illustration of these texts. Woodcuts and copper-engravings had been used from the 15th century; at the end of the 18th century, Thomas Bewick added to them the technique of wood-engraving, which was rapidly applied to the illustration of books, magazines, and even newspapers, and from about 1800 visual representation began to be considered an essential adjunct of the printed word. More important from both the artistic and the technical point of view was the invention in 1796–9, by the Munich playwright Alois Senefelder, of the lithographic process. It allowed an artist to transfer his original design immediately onto the stone (originally slate, later various synthetic stones and metal plates) from which it was printed, thus eliminating its deterioration at the hands of successive draughtsmen of varying skill and accuracy. Senefelder had his invention patented in England in 1800. From 1805 he experimented with substitutes of slate—which 100 years later resulted in offset printing, i.e. the replacement of stone or metal by rubber. Delacroix, Daumier, Goya, and Menzel were among the first great artists to make extensive use of lithography.

The invention of photography and its adaptation to printing was a revolutionary step. Half-tone engraving (in 1847), photogravure (1852), collotype (1854), and three-colour printing (1880, with earlier experiments from 1835) extended the usefulness of photography to every branch of the sciences and humanities, supplying faithful reproductions of anatomical and pathological, geographical and artistic objects with the help of the camera.

The printing and publishing trade has always required from its practitioners a combination of idealism and business acumen; the excess of either aspect has usually meant commercial failure, sometimes recompensed posthumously by the admiration of posterity, or a spurious reputation among envious contemporaries, followed by the obloquy of later generations. A healthy balance between public service and self-interest, characteristic of all great publishers, makes their biographies or autobiographies fascinating reading.

One feature common to nearly every printer and publisher during the greater part of the 19th century is their indifference to, amounting to contempt for, fine or even decent presentation of their commodity. At the beginning of the century every country could boast of type-faces comparable with the best products of earlier periods; by 1890 typography had reached its lowest level ever. France withstood longest this universal deterioration. The elegant type-faces of the Didot family—whose head was appointed manager of the imperial type-foundry in 1811—held sway over French printing until the end of the Second Empire. Italy, once the home of the best European printing, owed its downfall—strange to say—to the opposition to her last great printer of international fame, Giovanni Battista Bodoni. His beautiful books were designed for a small aristocratic clientele, but the leaders of the Risorgimento despised them as offending the popular ideals of the democratic age, and Italian printing became as bad as that of the rest of Europe. In Germany, Justus Erich Walbaum designed some very good roman and gothic founts for the publisher Göschen, but they were ousted by the spindly and anaemic "new German letters" produced by the type-foundry of Unger; this lamentable type-face dominated German printing for 100 years. Similarly, in England, William Bulmer, the friend and champion of Thomas Bewick, made a gallant attempt to uphold the tradition of Baskerville and Caslon. But although Bulmer was supported by the printer Charles Whittingham and the publisher William Pickering, his pleasant types were completely superseded by what became known as "modern face" and its offshoot "Scotch modern face." Thanks to its technical perfection, best shown in the specimen (1833) of the Edinburgh foundry of A. & P. Wilson, this dreary fount not only corrupted British printing but was accepted as a standard throughout Europe; in Germany "modern face" was known as "Englische Antiqua."

The revival of good printing began in Oxford, where in 1876 the Provost of Worcester College rediscovered the splendid 16th- and 17th-century Fell types, and Horace Hart (Printer to the University) employed them from 1883. However, the real breakthrough was accomplished by Emery Walker and William Morris in 1888. Morris had learnt printing at Whittingham's Chiswick Press; his Kelmscott Press, which issued some 50 books between 1890 and 1898, became the inspiration of typographical reformers throughout the world. This is the more surprising because we can now see that, however seminal and sound Morris's theory was, his practical application of that theory was all wrong. For his type-face, Morris went back to the best models of the incunabula period; like the early printers, he insisted on painstaking workmanship, correct inking,

KK

attention to imposition and impression, careful choice of paper, and the opening (i.e. two opposite pages) as the unit of typographical design—all matters neglected by 19th-century printers. However, Morris was quite blind to the needs of the contemporary world: although he was a socialist, Morris's books were designed (and priced) for a limited circle of wealthy aesthetes, and his romantic misapplication of mediaeval craftsmanship took no notice of what modern craftsmen could achieve or what the modern mass public needed.

Fortunately Morris's followers abandoned the master's velleities and took over only his precepts. Not only was he the godfather of a series of outstanding private presses in England, America, and Germany, but he also influenced commercial printers everywhere. The greatest advance of Morris's successors was the abandonment of the belief in the superiority of handicraft in favour of the application of mechanical processes to every stage of book production.

The professional organization of the book trade started, and later attained its highest development, in the German-speaking countries of central Europe. The reason for this is twofold. From about 1750 Leipzig was the indisputable centre of the German book trade, and its fairs attracted publishers, booksellers, and ancillary businessmen from all over Europe. At the same time the multiplicity and confusion of currencies was nowhere worse than in Germany and its neighbours. The settling of accounts between the creditors and debtors of talers, guilders, marks, and their innumerable varieties led in 1797 to the establishment of a central clearing-house in Leipzig. From it developed the Association of German Booksellers, founded in 1825; its very name, *Börsenverein* (Exchange Association), has kept alive its original main purpose. The idealistic aspect of the book trade and the proud claims that the best of its members made for their profession were succinctly expressed in the title of a pamphlet published in 1816 by one of the founders of the *Börsenverein*, Friedrich Perthes: *Der deutsche Buchhandel als Bedingung des Daseins einer deutschen Literatur* (The German Book Trade as the Pre-requisite for the Existence of a German Literature).

The statutes of the *Börsenverein* did not, however, exclude foreigners and, from 1826, English, Russian, Danish, Norwegian, Swedish, Romanian, and American firms appear among its members. No other country in the world has succeeded in establishing a comparable organization, and the annual book fairs at Leipzig (and, from 1949, at Frankfurt) have been international meeting places of publishers, booksellers, printers, papermakers, and binders.

The organization of the book trade extended also to the organization of workers within the "printing and kindred trades," as their English Federation, founded in 1890, comprehensively described them. Their beginnings lay under the shadow of the fear of the working class felt by many governments after the French Revolution, and intensified by the post-Napoleonic restoration. The British "Act for the More Effectual Suppression of Societies Established for Seditious and Treasonable Purposes" (1799) was directed expressly against the budding associations of printers and letter-founders. The celebration in 1840 of the fourth centenary of Gutenberg's invention, which German printers hoped might inaugurate a liberalization of their status, was forbidden in Prussia, Austria, and Bavaria; and in the same year the German Confederation banned all coalitions of journeymen. Although the growth of trade unions could be impeded by the hostility of governments and employers, it could not be stopped. From about 1800, workers' trade associations began to appear and (when suppressed) to re-appear all over Europe. Thus, the first union of the London compositors was founded in 1801; it was dissolved in 1810, reorganized in 1834, and in 1845 extended to the provinces as the National Typographical Association.

Recognition of printers' organizations was granted first by some Swiss cantons: Zürich (1819), Berne (1824), St Gallen (1832). Here German journeymen received the impetus to organize themselves after their return home. But it was 40 years after the foundation of the first German trade union (in Brunswick, 1827) before the *Deutscher Buchdruckerverband* could be established in 1866. Even then, the police continued to harass the trade unions, and in 1878 Bismarck's anti-socialist legislation was used to dissolve the associations of lithographers, bookbinders, and printers. The position gradually improved, however, and after the lapse of the anti-socialist laws in 1890, the German printers' union was described by their English fellow-workers as "the vanguard of the European working class." At this time, the printers were the highest-paid workers in Germany; their wages were below those paid in England and the United States, but greatly exceeded those of French printers—a contributory factor to the international competitiveness of French and German books compared with English and American ones.

The German *Börsenverein*, supported by the trade everywhere, led a successful fight against two evils that had dogged publishers and authors from the days of Gutenberg: censorship and piracy. Piracy (the unauthorized reprinting of other publishers' productions) was as old as printing itself. Its cause was the absence of copyright protection of the original author and publisher. Even the governmental grant of privileges was not only ineffective outside the borders of the issuing authority: it actually stimulated piracy. Both piracy and privilege had their good as well as bad aspects. Privileges secured the quality of the text and guaranteed the publisher the recovery of his expenses; but, at the same time, it raised the price to the sole advantage of the publisher, and thereby limited the circulation to the wealthier book-buyers. Piracy might deprive the respectable publisher of his deserved recompense, and damage an author's reputation by mutilated or faulty texts, but it considerably lowered the price of books—often by half or more—and thus spread literature among a wider public.

England (by the Copyright Act of 1709) and France (by a copyright law of 1793) were the first countries to protect authors and publishers within large territories. But before the Union of 1801, Irish printers violated the act with impunity and smuggled their reprints into the United Kingdom. Even worse, publishers in New York, Boston, and Philadelphia shamelessly exploited the situation by re-printing English books as the first copies or (preferably) advance sheets of potentially profitable titles arrived in America. Walter Scott's *Waverley* novels were in greatest demand in the 1820s; about 20 American publishers reprinted them, and German translations appeared by the dozen—five complete editions, for instance, in 1825.

French publishers suffered particularly by the *contrefaçon* (counterfeit) editions of Belgian printers. It seems certain that the world-wide dissemination of French literature after 1815 was mainly due to these Belgian reprints. In fact, the *contrefaçons* were usually superior, at least textually, because they contained all the passages that French censorship had suppressed in the original editions. In 1852 the *contrefaçon* business was terminated by mutual agreement between publishers.

The political jealousy of the member states of the German Confederation prevented any common regulation of copyright matters, and publishers, printers, and authors had to rely on the privileges that individual states (Prussia, Austria, Saxony, and so on) might grant. Goethe, a shrewd businessman, obtained almost complete protection of his writings throughout the Confederation.

An international regulation was achieved only by the Berne "Convention for the Protection of Literary and Artistic Works," adopted in 1886 by the majority of civilized countries, with the deplorable exception of the United States of America. There, piracy continued to flourish until 1952, when at last Washington adhered to the "Universal Copyright

Convention" sponsored by UNESCO. In view of the chaotic state of the business before 1886, the more honour is due to those publishers who paid royalties to authors unprotected by international law, notably Harper & Brothers in New York, and Tauchnitz in Leipzig.

The 1842 revision of the English Copyright Act, and the expiration in 1867 of the privileges granted by the German Confederation, had a tremendous influence upon the spread and pricing of high-class literature. The English act laid down that the privileged copyright should cease seven years after an author's death or 42 years after the first publication of a book. In Germany, the exclusive copyright based on specific privileges was terminated forthwith. The result was that in Germany from 1867 and in England from about 1900 the writings of every major 19th-century author became available for cheap reprints. It was the natal hour of the popular series, which opened the treasures of literature to the poor.

Censorship of the printed word is virtually coincidental in time and place with the invention of printing itself. Every spiritual or temporal power tried to suppress what it considered dangerous publications— dangerous to theological doctrines, to established authorities, to public and private morals. The chief instrument of Roman Catholic censorship, the *Index librorum prohibitorum* (codified in the 16th century) is the outstanding example of a self-defeating attempt to curb intellectual freedom. Disregarded by non-Catholics from the very beginning, the *Index* was soon scrutinized by Catholic readers in search of forbidden fruits, and from about 1800 it was almost completely ignored because it continued to list the greater part of standard literature. The decision of the Second Vatican Council to discontinue the *Index* was welcomed by almost every literate member of the Roman Church.

Political censorship saw its widest and strictest application during the first half of the 19th century, owing to the fear that the French Revolution had struck into the statesmen of Europe—not least those of France after 1815. In fact the French Revolution nipped in the bud the first attempts in continental Europe to liberalize, or even abolish, political censorship. Scandinavia was in the van of this movement. In 1766 the Swedish Diet passed the first "decree on the freedom of printing." It was confirmed by the first written Swedish constitution of 1809. In 1770, Struensee, the virtual dictator of Denmark-Norway, abolished censorship altogether, and his successor confirmed and reinforced this measure in 1790; however, under Russian pressure, Denmark had to reintroduce censorship in 1799.

Germany, the nearest and most vulnerable target of French revolutionary propaganda, reacted most violently. In 1790 the Emperor Leopold II tightened censorship regulations for the whole empire, although the execution of imperial decrees depended entirely on the concurrence of the individual member states.

Nowhere was the gulf between theory and practice wider than in France. The Rights of Man of 1789 included the clause: *tout citoyen peut parler, écrire, imprimer librement* (every citizen may speak, write, and publish freely), but after the blissful dawn of revolutionary fervour was over, French censorship—soon extended over the whole Napoleonic empire—was more ruthless than any previous supervision of press and literature had been. (Events in Soviet Russia after 1917 offer an almost exact parallel.) The Bourbons, Orleans, and Napoleon III maintained this attitude, although the Charte of 1830 included the noble clause that *la censure ne pourra jamais être rétablie* (censorship will never be able to be restored)—a sentiment repeated, but in practice disregarded, by every written constitution.

After 1815 censorship was particularly severe in Austria, the Papal States, and the Bourbon countries of Italy and Spain, whereas the notorious Karlsbad decrees of 1819, which reintroduced strict censorship in the German Confederation, remained to a large extent a dead letter: the particularism of the 30-odd member states defied uniform application, and the highly developed German book trade found enough secret and open ways to stultify the censors and magistrates. Heinrich Heine and his publisher Campe, of Hamburg, were experts at this game. The formal abolition of censorship was achieved in Germany in 1848 and in France in 1872, but the judicial and administrative persecution of journalists and authors and their publishers continued, nowhere perhaps more ruthlessly than in Bismarck's Prussia between 1862 and 1890.

After the demise of ecclesiastical censorship and the abolition of political censorship (now openly exercised in Europe only by Spain and the communist countries), moral censorship remained the last standby of the "fugitive and cloistered virtue" that Milton's *Areopagitica* had pilloried. The problem has always revolved around the definition of obscenity. In Britain, the Obscene Publications Act of 1857 remained in force for over 100 years, until it was superseded by the act of 1959, which took into consideration "the interests of science, literature, art, or learning" as established by "expert opinion." The complete abolition of every kind of literary censorship in Denmark in 1967 had a surprising effect: the sales of pornographic books dropped immediately by half, and booksellers now stock them mainly for foreign customers.

Moral censorship has been most active in the United States of America.

There, pressure has been exerted not by any governmental department, but by private organizations of vigilantes, chiefly women. If the muted complaints of authors, publishers, booksellers, and librarians can be accepted, it would seem to a European observer that no pope or emperor has ever been as prudish and powerful as these pressure groups.

The reading matter in greatest demand by the public, and therefore most liberally supplied by the publishers, reflects the desire of the middle class during the first half of the 19th century, and of the rising working class later, to underpin its social position by acquiring the knowledge that had hitherto been the preserve of the gentry.* Francis Bacon's maxim that "knowledge is power" became a generally accepted slogan; and the motto *Bildung macht frei* (education liberates), under which Joseph Meyer launched the first cheap paperback series in 1826, might have been adopted by the majority of 19th-century publishers. However, the characteristic types of "new" reading matter were, without exception, developments of established patterns adapted to the needs of different classes of consumers. Thus, the encyclopaedia ceased to be a product designed by and for a society of men of letters (as was Diderot and d'Alembert's *Encyclopédie* of 1751) or for "a society of gentlemen" (as was the original *Encyclopaedia Britannica* of 1771) and became a dictionary for the educated classes (*für die gebildeten Stände*), as the Leipzig publisher F. A. Brockhaus proclaimed his *Conversations-Lexicon* (1812) to be.

In fact, the educational function of the Brockhaus encyclopaedia corresponded so closely with the spirit of the age that Brockhaus had to issue a reprint, a new edition, and a supplement in quick succession, and several other German publishers brought out rival encyclopaedias that proved equally successful. Of these, Joseph Meyer's *Conversations-Lexicon* (1840) deliberately deviated from the predominantly "arts" flavour of most previous encyclopaedias, and gave prominence to scientific and technical subjects. Some leading non-German publishers acquired translation rights from Brockhaus, and issued licensed editions that attained a similar popularity. These encyclopaedias started with an unauthorized Dutch encyclopaedia (1820), followed by the "popular dictionary" of the *Encyclopaedia Americana* (1829), Ambroise Firmin Didot's *Dictionnaire de la conversation* (1833), and Polish, Czech, Swedish, and Greek encyclopaedias, and they culminated in the 43-volume Russian encyclopaedia of 1890.

Parallel with these Brockhaus imitations there appeared numerous English, Scottish, and American encyclopaedias modelled on the *Encyclo-*

* See also the discussion of this subject in Vol. IV, "The Sociology of the Enlightenment," and "Literature and the Education of the Middle Classes."

paedia Britannica. They were surpassed in size and permanency by the *Grand dictionnaire universel,* begun by P.-A. Larousse in 1865 and intended to be the 19th-century equivalent of the *Encyclopédie;* owing to the then un-assailed international prestige of the French language, it was found on the shelves of the intelligentsia throughout the world.

Although a number of these encyclopaedias emphasized in their titles or subtitles their "popular" character, they were bought mainly by the prosperous middle classes who could afford the comparatively high price. It is significant that two early attempts to reach a less-well-off public proved costly failures: *The Penny Encyclopaedia,* published by Charles Knight for the Society for the Diffusion of Useful Knowledge (1833), and the *Pfennig-Encyklopädie* (1834) did not survive their first editions. The *Harmsworth Encyclopaedia* (1905) was the first of its kind to reach the masses whom Alfred Harmsworth (later Lord Northcliffe) had previously won over to his "new journalism."

Newspapers and periodicals are another kind of reading matter that came into its own in the 19th century. Newspapers had established themselves by the middle of the 17th century (superseding the newsbooks of the preceding age, which in turn made obsolete the earlier handwritten newsletters). At about the same time there began to appear periodicals—weeklies, monthlies, quarterlies—of which Addison and Steele's *Tatler* and *Spectator* achieved a sensational success and became the prototype on which were modelled some 800 magazines throughout Europe.

The impact of the French Revolution on the growth of newspapers all over Europe can hardly be over-estimated. In France itself, some 350 newspapers came into existence during the first years of the revolution; their number declined to four, however, under the rigorous supervision of the Napoleonic dictatorship, when the *Moniteur* (1799–1869) became the model of governmental gazettes that tried, more or less successfully, to combat revolutionary, nationalist, liberal, and democratic tendencies, and to inculcate the proper submissiveness toward the established powers.

The unprecedented upheaval in France excited the curiosity of all classes everywhere, stimulated demands for change among the intelligentsia, and stirred up those groups that had hitherto been excluded from any participation in public life. Opposition newspapers sprang up where there had been at most one official or semi-official gazette; "subversive" pamphlets, broadsheets, and ballads were disseminated among the urban and rural working classes. The reaction of the established authorities showed their helplessness and lack of any effective counter-ideology. Strict application of censorship regulations, a ban on the importation of printed matter, and the rigorous supervision of bookshops and lending libraries were the usual, and usually futile, means of preventing the spread of revolutionary ideas. A plaintive article in *Magazin*, the only licensed newspaper of the Electorate of Hanover, is illuminating. It asked (October 1795): "How can the widespread mania for reading be stopped?" and mourned that even women and children had been infected by a "love of reading," and that the "perniciousness of reading journals" distracted students and professors from the pursuit of learning. Political apathy was replaced by a hectic craving for political information, and news-sheets, pamphlets, and manifestos poured from the presses as soon as the slightest breach appeared in the walls of paternalism. The flood of anti-government publications that swept Prussia after the crushing defeats of Jena and Auerstädt in 1806 was particularly significant, because supervision of public opinion had been most repressive in Prussia. But similar manifestations of unrest among the hitherto silenced middle classes—the *bourgeoisie*, as they were now termed—were prevalent wherever the old order collapsed or was shaken.

Even in the reaction that characterized the period of 1815–48, the thirst for political and intellectual—though not yet economic—information created by the French Revolution could not be repressed permanently. Up to about 1880, however, the solid, stolid "quality" newspapers satisfied the needs of the politically awakened middle classes: the London *Times* (appearing under this name in 1788), Cotta's *Allgemeine Zeitung* (1799), the *Kölnische Zeitung* (1798), the *Journal des Débats* (1789), were the early leaders; later, they were equalled in influence by the *Neue Zürcher Zeitung* (1821), the *Vossische Zeitung* (1824), the *Journal de Genève* (1826), the *Aftonbladet* (1830), the *Algemeen Handelsblad* (1838), and the Basel *National-zeitung* (1842). All of them were politically liberal; all cultivated the literary *feuilleton* (Heinrich Heine was Cotta's Paris correspondent); all enjoyed a reputation far beyond their countries of origin, especially because (following the example of *The Times*) they were building up an extensive foreign service.

The first paper deliberately aimed at a mass readership was *La Presse*, which Émile de Girardin brought out in 1836 at the price of one *sou*. It was the prototype of the "faceless" metropolitan press that toward the end of the century swamped all large European cities. The "new journalism" of American origin reached England in 1883; the halfpenny *Daily Mail*, founded by Alfred Harmsworth in 1896, was the first popular morning paper of this type.

For a century and a half the circulation of British newspapers had been restricted to the well-to-do middle class, because the stamp duty kept the price artificially high. When it was abolished in 1855, the *Daily Telegraph*, the *Liverpool Post*, the *Scotsman*, and the *Manchester Guardian* at once lowered the price per copy to 1*d*. The abolition of the duty on paper in 1861 allowed the owners to maintain this low price in spite of steadily increasing size and circulation. More important, from the public's point of view, the removal of these "taxes on knowledge" permitted editors to be more adventurous in their use of space: headlines in bold display types broke up the solid columns and made possible rapid reading, which the papers written by gentlemen for gentlemen had scorned. The papers brought out by the press magnates with both eyes on making money catered for a public that preferred "personal journalism," "human interest," and light entertainment.

This development was accelerated by the competition to which the daily newspapers, and even more the weekly Sunday papers, were exposed by the popularity that all types of magazines enjoyed during the preceding 50 or 60 years.* Scotland was the birthplace of the "serious" periodical that addressed itself to students of politics, philosophy, literature, and the arts. The Liberal *Edinburgh Review* (1802) and the Conservative *Quarterly Review* (1809) were the forerunners of numerous weeklies, monthlies, and quarterlies in England, France, Italy, and Germany. Most of them attracted leading men of letters as contributors. Carlyle, Hazlitt, and Macaulay wrote for the *Edinburgh Review;* Scott, Canning, and Southey for the *Quarterly;* George Eliot and Lord Lytton for Blackwood's *Edinburgh Magazine* (1817). The *Revue des deux mondes* (1829), with Balzac, Victor Hugo, Taine, Renan, and Sainte-Beuve among its contributors, the *Nuova antologia* (1866), Brockhaus's *Literarisches Wochenblatt* (1820–98), and other continental periodicals were influential sponsors of literary and cultural movements. The *Preussische Jahrbücher* (1858)—in fact, a monthly, not yearly, magazine—came nearest to the *Edinburgh Review* in that it espoused a definite political line, that of the National Liberal Party, following its downward course from mild liberalism to fierce nationalism.

The growth of the literate public was reflected in the appearance of a less austere category of periodicals known as "family magazines." They started almost simultaneously in England, France, and Germany in the early 1830s. The brothers R. and W. Chambers launched the *Edinburgh Journal* in 1832, and it continued until 1956. The *Penny Magazine* (1832–

* More information on this subject may be found in Chapter 19, "Working-class Literature in England."

45), published by Charles Knight for the Society for the Diffusion of Useful Knowledge, was aimed at instructing the lower middle classes; although at one time its circulation reached 200,000, its impact was not lasting. The *Magasin pittoresque* (1833) was inspired by the positivist philosophers. The *Illustrated London News* (1842), the Paris *Illustration* (1843), and the *Leipziger illustrierte Zeitung* (1843) were the first weeklies to base their appeal mainly on pictures. The Leipzig *Gartenlaube* (1853–1943) was perhaps the most influential of all the "family magazines"; at its height in the 1870s it had some 400,000 subscribers. The *Gartenlaube* strengthened the apolitical tendencies of the Bismarckian pseudo-liberal bourgeoisie by supporting the literary and domestic aspects of German *Kultur* and by avoiding disturbing social features. In this it contrasted vividly with *Household Words* (1850–9) and *All the Year Round* (1859–70), in which Charles Dickens tried to stir the social conscience of Victorian England. Dickens also created a kind of book-periodical hybrid, when in 1836 he brought out *The Pickwick Papers* in weekly instalments. The spreading of the price over a long period anticipated the hire-purchase principle. The notion was taken up by the so-called "slum publishers" and their weekly "penny dreadfuls," the precursors of the tabloids.

After about 1880 the influence of the family magazines declined. They were superseded by papers such as George Newnes' *Tit-Bits* (1881) and Alfred Harmsworth's *Answers* (1888); they addressed themselves to the new public that the Elementary Education Act of 1870 was raising to a rudimentary literacy. These papers professed to impart instruction and information, but this had to be without mental effort, and thus did little to prepare the mass readership for the dawning age of technology—a task that the earlier magazines had at least attempted.

The great technical advances in book production during the first third of the 19th century made possible the mass production of cheap editions manufactured in a uniform style and at a uniform price—a consideration that Aldus Manutius had made the basis of his octavo classics 300 years earlier.

Joseph Meyer's *Groschen-Bibliotek der deutschen Klassiker für alle Stände* (Penny Library of German Standard Authors for all Classes), launched in 1826, may be considered the ancestor of what, 100 years later, became known as paperbacks. An interesting feature of this popular series, as of all its continental successors, is the inclusion of Shakespeare and Walter Scott in translations that have made these British authors part and parcel of every European literature.

In England, the first popular series came out about 1830: Archibald

Constable's *Miscellany* (1827–35), John Murray's *Family Library* (1829–34) —both of which comprised mainly instructive writings on history and travel—and Colburn & Bentley's *Standard Novels* (1831–54), which at 6*s.* each were a real bargain compared with the usual price of 31*s.* 6*d.* for a novel. In 1848 the growth of travelling by railway inspired George Routledge to start his *Railway Library*, sold at 1*s.* per volume through the railway book stalls that W. H. Smith opened in the same year; by 1898 the series comprised 1300 volumes. Of greater impact upon a public eager for self-improvement were the nine series that the enterprising and scholarly Henry George Bohn produced between 1846 and 1853; their titles—"Scientific Library," "Classical Library," "Ecclesiastical Library," and so on—show the wide range of interests Bohn catered for; and these excellent series were sold at the low price of 1*s.* per volume.

An indirect effect of the railway age may be seen in two remarkable German series. In the early 1830s the Frankfurt publisher Carl Jügel issued his *Pocket Novelists*, for the benefit of the English travellers flocking to the romantic Rhine valley and to the spas of the Frankfurt region. However, Jügel's series was completely overshadowed by the *Collection of British* (later: *and American*) *Authors* started in 1841 by the 24-year-old Leipzig printer-publisher Christian Bernhard Tauchnitz. Its immediate success was partly due to a shrewd and unprecedented step taken by the young German: despite the absence of any international copyright obligation, he obtained for his reprints the authorization of both the English authors and the English publishers. The former received outright payments, ranging from £20 for *Treasure Island* by the then little-known R. L. Stevenson to £225 for *Frederick the Great* by Carlyle. The publishers were won over by Tauchnitz's pledge not to sell his collection anywhere in the British Empire, although Tauchnitz did not object to the sale of the original issues in Germany. The price for each volume of 1.60 marks in Germany and 2 francs in France (equivalent to 1*s.* 6*d.*) helped the Tauchnitz paperbacks—eventually some 5400 titles—to find their way into the luggage of tens of thousands of English and American travellers and on to the shelves of continental students of English literature.

A by-product of the Tauchnitz collection was its effect, though long delayed, upon English book production. English readers began to realize that good literature could be presented in paperbacks—already a common feature of German and French publishing, but hitherto abhorred by the English book-buyer, who had insisted on hard covers for any book above the level of penny dreadfuls. Almost 100 years were to pass before Sir

Allen Lane succeeded in accustoming the English public to his version of the Tauchnitz principle: Penguin Books, launched in 1935.

Shakespeare, the eternal money-spinner for printers, publishers, editors, and booksellers, enabled Anton Philip Reclam to produce the most successful and most enduring of all popular paperback series. The tremendous success of his Shakespeare editions—the first, in 1858, in 12 volumes for $1\frac{1}{2}$ talers (4s. 6d.) the set, and then, in 1865, in 25 fascicles at 2 groschen (3d.) each—encouraged Reclam to start the *Universal-Bibliothek* in 1867, when the privileges that the German Confederation had granted to authors and publishers expired. Until 1917 Reclam maintained the original price of 2 groschen for the series, which by 1942, when the Leipzig premises were destroyed in a bombing raid, included some 7600 titles, with Ibsen as the most successful non-German author next to Shakespeare.

The British Copyright Act of 1842 had a similar effect: toward the end of the century the writings of nearly all the great Victorian authors became available for unprotected reprints. Cassell's *National Library* (1886; 3d. paperback, 6d. in hard cover), Nelson's *New Century Library* (1900: in 1905 renamed *Classics*), the *World's Classics* (1901: acquired by the Oxford University Press in 1905), Collins' *Pocket Classics* (1903), and (the most popular of all) Dent's *Everyman's Library* (1906) competed side by side for the ever-increasing market.

The success of these series was due partly to their literary and editorial quality and partly to the world-wide expansion of English as the *lingua franca*. This place had been occupied throughout the 19th century by the French language, and the cheap editions of French writers, poured out by half a dozen Paris publishing houses—and the Belgian pirated editions—supplied millions of francophile readers throughout the world. Garnier's *Collection des grands écrivains classiques*, Calman Lévy's promotion of Balzac, Dumas *père* and *fils*, and George Sand, Carpentier's editions of Zola, and Hetzel's editions of Victor Hugo and Jules Verne, may be mentioned as typical. All these series had in common their cheapness in the worst sense of the term: careless editing, poor printing on quickly disintegrating paper, and gaudy yellow paper covers. But their low price (and the fame of their authors) had ensured sales running into millions by the beginning of the 20th century.

Books especially designed for the entertainment of children originated in 18th-century France, when a diversity of works originally written for adults began to be read by (or to) children. The sophisticated fairy-tales of Charles Perrault and Madame d'Aulnoy, the often-lascivious *Arabian Nights*, the religious and anthropological adventure stories of

Pilgrim's Progress and *Robinson Crusoe*, and the political and social satire of *Gulliver's Travels*, were among the first to be adapted for youthful readers. The English publisher John Newbery (1713–67) seems to have been the first to realize that children's books offered an unexploited market of great promise. Of his numerous publications, mostly well illustrated, at least the title of *Little Goody Two-Shoes* has survived. The London bookseller Tabart, early in the 19th century, reserved a department of his shop and his lending library for juvenile browsers and buyers.

The growth of specifically juvenile reading matter is bound up with the spread of elementary education. The pedagogical ideas of the Enlightenment came to fruition in the reorganization of the French school system under the consulate of Napoleon, and were imitated in the Napoleonic satellite states. The theory and practice of the Swiss educationalist Johann Heinrich Pestalozzi (1746–1827) influenced the whole of Europe. By 1830 every European country had introduced, at least in theory, compulsory primary schooling—with the exception of England, which followed as late as 1870. Here, however, the gap was at least partly filled by the flourishing Sunday School Movement, initiated by the Gloucester printer Robert Raikes, which soon spread all over England, Ireland, Scotland, and especially Wales.

The influence of the ever-growing class of juvenile readers made itself felt in a vast expansion of juvenile literature. The fairy-tale tradition produced some masterpieces of international fame, such as the *Kinder- und Hausmärchen* of the brothers Grimm (1812–22), and Hans Christian Andersen's *Eventyr* (1835–72), and culminating in Selma Lagerlöf's *Nils Holgerssons underbara resa* (1906–7), which was commissioned by the Swedish government for use in schools, and was probably the most enjoyable "compulsory" schoolbook of all time.

On the other hand, the wish to spread "useful knowledge," characteristic of so much adult reading matter in the first half of the century, blighted much juvenile literature of the period with obtrusive didacticism and dreary lessons in morality—as in such pseudo-classics as *Tom Brown's School Days* (1857) and *Eric, or Little by Little* (1858). Captain (Frederick) Marryat's adventure stories, published between 1834 and 1847, mark a turning-point. From the mid-century onward, many respectable (and some great) authors began to write expressly for a juvenile public. The works include Charles Kingsley's *Westward Ho!* (1856), Wilhelm Busch's *Max und Moritz* (1858), R. D. Blackmore's *Lorna Doone* (1869), Johanna Spyri's *Heidi* (1880), Rudyard Kipling's *Jungle Books* (1894–5), and, greatest of all, Lewis Carroll's *Alice* books (1865, 1871). It is noteworthy that not a few of these books have found as much, if not more, favour with adults as with youthful readers; and also that the best children's books have enjoyed an international circulation paralleled by comparatively few books for adults.

One of the beneficial results of the Education Act of 1870 was the appearance of a number of good magazines for young readers, of which *The Boys' Own Paper*, launched in 1879 by the Religious Tract Society, was on a par with the best of the contemporary "family magazines." Like these, the children's periodicals fell into a sad decline after World War I, when they were ousted by the brasher "comics" of transatlantic origin.

By the end of the 18th century, lending libraries had become a common feature of every European town with even modest intellectual aspirations. They were mostly run as a profitable side-line by book-shops or by literary societies on a subscription basis. Both types incurred the suspicion of the authorities after the outbreak of the French Revolution, and in many countries had to submit lists of their members and the titles of their stock for approval.

In view of the high prices of books, the circulating libraries fulfilled an important role in making contemporary literature available to the majority, who could not afford the arbitrary and artificial price of 31s. 6d. for the "three-decker" novel that dominated the English market between 1820 and 1890. For about 50 years Mudie's Lending Library, opened in London in 1842, occupied a near-monopoly position. This may have been justified by the moderate annual subscription of one guinea, but was vitiated by the ruthless dictatorship that Charles Edward Mudie imposed upon authors and publishers, who were at the mercy of what Mudie thought suitable or unsuitable for his public. A good deal of the bigotry, prudery, and insularity of Victorian fiction must be laid at Mudie's door; he banned Meredith and George Moore from his shelves, while boosting the sales of Ouida and Marie Corelli.

Mudie's death in 1890 was followed by the virtual collapse of his empire, although the firm lingered on until 1937. The replacement of the three-decker by the one-volume novel and the rise of the popular series, both within the reach of people of modest means, made the lending library less necessary for access to good literature. In addition, the lending libraries had to face growing competition from free public libraries, especially in urban areas. These, in their modern guise, owed their origin to American enterprise. The city of Boston opened the first public library as early as 1653, and in 1798 the Commonwealth of Massachusetts consolidated its public libraries by state legislation. The bill that William Ewart piloted through the British Parliament in 1850 secured financial support for a comprehensive system of public libraries throughout the country, maintained as a public utility and supervised by local authorities. Special children's departments and a number of libraries exclusively for children were later added.

The nation-wide free libraries and their use by all social classes of readers is characteristic of the English-speaking countries and those with a similar cultural outlook: Scandinavia, Switzerland, and the Netherlands. The public, but not always free, libraries in (for instance) a highly literate country such as Germany cannot bear comparison with these achievements.

CHAPTER 19

Working-class Literature in England

Louis James*

Three broad eras of popular literature can be distinguished since 1800. At the opening of the 19th century, England was still predominantly an agricultural nation with a largely non-literate folk culture centred on traditional rituals and superstitions. The common people were called not "the working classes" but "the lower orders." This term covered a broad spectrum of occupations, reaching from the poorest labourers through skilled artisans to what was already becoming known as "the middle classes."[1] The literature of this group, where it existed, consisted mainly of sheet almanacks, broadsheets, and chapbooks, and to a lesser extent, books sold in cheap parts by itinerant "number men." These books were generally religious, the most common being the Bible and Bunyan's *Pilgrim's Progress*, but there was also some fiction.[2] From 1791, when Tom Paine's *The Rights of Man* sold a reputed 200,000 copies in two years,[3] radical literature increasingly emerged, but this was to become a major feature only in the next era.

Thirty years later the changes at work in nearly all aspects of society were becoming more evident. Although "the lower orders" were still highly diverse, there was a growing sense of class solidarity, in particular in opposition to the capitalist factory employers of the expanding northern industrial cities. In 1813 we find the term "working class" used. An important factor in the emergence of a new class consciousness was increased literacy. Between 1780 and 1830, on a conservative estimate, the reading public increased from one and a half to between seven and eight million.[4] Although, with an average schooling of one year, literacy among the poor remained low, an observer in 1832 could declare, "the

* Senior Lecturer in English, University of Kent at Canterbury.

population of this country is for the first time becoming a reading population, actuated by tastes and habits unknown to preceding generations."[5] Print broke down the old localized and remembered traditions, and fostered a new consciousness both of society and of oneself. It also provided the way in which the nascent working class could educate and organize itself. At the same time advances in papermaking and printing drastically cheapened and extended the range of popular literature. In 1800 a typical cheap publication would cost sixpence: in 1840 a comparable amount of material was available for a penny. Cheapness and content make it possible to distinguish the wide variety of literature provided for the working classes during much of the 19th century. But the demarcation, never precise, becomes increasingly hard to define as we move into the third phase of popular publishing. Standards of living improved, and with first the 1870 Education Act providing universal elementary education, and later the media of broadcasting bringing standardized entertainment to all, there is a movement from "working class" into "mass culture."

This brief essay deals with the period that begins with the expansion of literacy and literature at the beginning of the 19th century. Both increases are related to each other and to the social background. At this time, learning to read was a social act. It was often part of the adaptation from rural to urban life. It was also part of the movement toward self-improvement and class organization. Much of the cheap literature available had social intentions behind it, especially in the early decades of the century. The various religious bodies dominated elementary education, for they believed that ability to read the Bible was part of the road to salvation. Their interest in providing religious reading was spurred by the dramatic spread of Paine's work and other radical and irreligious material among the very labourers their Sunday schools were training in Christian piety. In counter-attack they built up religious tract societies, which distributed literally millions of tracts annually: in 1849 the Religious Tract Society alone published over 18 million.[6] The secular Utilitarians also intervened. They were the moving force behind the formation of the Society for the Diffusion of Useful Knowledge in 1826. Its cheap publications tried to provide a non-political and non-religious education in largely scientific information. Its works, such as *The Penny Magazine* (1832–46), which reached a peak circulation of 200,000, missed the working-class audience it was seeking both because it misjudged popular taste and because many saw it as an attempted diversion from the more important education into social injustice. More successful in this field were Robert and William Chambers, who sold some 170,000 sets of *Chambers' Information for the People* (1833–72), besides much similar material. John Cassell in 1850 began publishing *The Working Man's Friend*, and by 1862 was selling from 25 to 30 million educational publications annually.

There was also a movement among working-class writers and publishers to control the newly influential medium of print, an action bitterly fought not only by the middle-class tract- and pamphlet-publishing bodies, but also by the government, which attempted, in particular through the 1819 Seditious Publications Act, to tax cheap publications out of existence. The pioneer here was William Cobbett, who in 1816 lowered the cost of his *Political Register* from just over a shilling to twopence, using a pamphlet format. It sold 200,000 in two months, and was bought by a public that had had to borrow papers, if they could get hold of them, in such places as the public house. When Cobbett bowed to restrictive legislation and raised the cost of the *Register* by paying tax on it, more fiercely radical cheap journals, such as Jonathan Wooler's *The Black Dwarf* (1817–23), took its place.

Radical journals, together with pamphlets and tracts (*The Political House that Jack Built* sold 250,000 copies between 1819 and 1822), had an erratic sale through the first half of the 19th century, dependent on the political interest of the time. Cumulatively, however, they have an essential role in a wide variety of social movements. Henry Hetherington's unstamped paper, *The Poor Man's Guardian* (1831–6, circulation up to 20,000 per week), played its part in the agitation for the first Reform Bill, in trade-union organization, and, most notably, in the abolition of stamp duty on cheap newspapers. The most important periodical behind the Chartist movement was *The Northern Star* (1837–52), a stamped newspaper, which in 1839 reached a circulation of 50,000. But to select even the most important examples is to distort. The field is huge. Although most of them were short-lived, more than 560 unstamped periodicals alone—political, religious, educational, and entertaining— were recorded during the period of feverish publishing activity, 1830–6.[7] The radical segment of this was a forum in which the ideology and organization of a key phase of working-class movements were worked out. The press continued to play this role: an important later example is *The Beehive Newspaper* (1861–76).[8]

This literature also had an artistic contribution to make. In his highly popular *Grammar of the English Language* (over 100,000 sold, 1818–34), Cobbett argued for an unambiguous style and the expression of spontaneous feelings, based not on a classical education but on the best of the vernacular idiom. Worked out in the vivid prose of his journalism, Cobbett's vitalizing influence runs wide, although the vigour of his style could degenerate into bombast, as it tended to do, for instance, in the Chartist journalism of Feargus O'Connor. One should also mention verse. Out of scores of published poets with a working-class background, two of the best-known are Thomas Cooper (1805–92), a model for the hero of Charles Kingsley's *Alton Locke* (1850), and Gerald Massey (1828–1907), at one time an operative in a silk factory, who lies behind the radical poet in George Eliot's *Felix Holt* (1866). Their work could be ambitious. Cooper's *Purgatory of Suicides* (1845), for instance, is an erudite epic in 12 books about the self-destruction of tyranny down the ages. Dialect popular verse appeared in the 1850s and 1860s with the development of northern music-hall, but in general these poets did not use the rich folk traditions, which continued largely unrecorded. For political verse the strongest influence was the hymn book; for the rest, poets with a labouring-class background tended to emulate the models of Pope, Wordsworth, and Tennyson. Popular taste for poetry is shown by the large sales of cheap editions of verse, although particular fashions could change. In the 1820s the radical atmosphere helped sales of Shelley's *Queen Mab* (1821) and Southey's *Wat Tyler* (1817). In the latter half of the century William Milner in Halifax found a huge market for cheap editions of Burns, Byron, Milton, and Pope.[9]

The "serious" working-class element was to form the basis of the Workers' Educational Association in 1903, and of the British Labour Party in 1906. But from the 1830s onward it was in conflict, even within the working-class movement itself, with other literary tastes. This was the same public that devoured Gothic chapbooks, "Newgate Calendars" of criminal stories; and the ballad broadsheets (survivors of the age when Autolycus undid his pack) attained a new popularity in the years following the Napoleonic wars. Published by James Catnach and some 30 other printers, broadsheets flourished beyond the mid-century. In 1848–9, 2·5 million broadsheets about the Rush murders were sold.[10] They catered for the semi-literate masses. Moreover, as the first Reform Act of 1832 failed to relieve the sufferings of economic depression, many workers turned to literature not for political guidance, but for escape. In the years 1837–9, Edward Lloyd published *The Penny Pickwick* by "Bos" (Thomas Peckett Prest). This was a working-class version of Dickens' *Pickwick Papers*, exploiting the popular traditions (present in Dickens' work itself) of melodrama, slapstick humour, and caricature. Its considerable success—its claimed circulation of 50,000 is quite believable—led to further plagiarisms of Dickens and W. H. Ainsworth, then to original romances published by themselves as weekly serials or in magazines such as *Lloyd's Penny Weekly Miscellany* (1843–5) and its rivals.[11] They reinterpreted old popular themes for the urban reader: the Gothic story; honest "Jack Tar" of the Napoleonic wars; the domestic story that offered the reader identification with "life as it is," then romanticized it; and the crime that was flourishing with new vigour in the overcrowded cities. Two of the most popular were T. P. Prest's *Ela the Outcast* (1840) and J. M. Rymer's *Ada the Betrayed* (1845), whose heroines, of unknown backgrounds, in conflict with vice and crime, must have had a particular appeal to those lost in the new industrial towns, with little chance of preserving moral innocence.

Working-class fiction cannot be examined against the standards of criticism of the literary élite; they were not written in terms of these standards, nor would their readers have enjoyed them if they had been. But how can one discover a working-class aesthetic? In *The Unsophisticated Arts* (1951)[12] Barbara Jones has suggested that the popular mind is complex yet unsubtle. Uncluttered by formal education, it can hold the complexity of a smocking pattern, a long ballad, or the formidably involved plots of these penny-issue romances. At the same time it does not see life in terms of the fine shades of moral issues and significance explored by works of "high" culture. The plots of these stories, however complex, are built on simple emotive conflicts between heroine and villain, between absolute goodness and absolute evil. This conflict serves a dramatic purpose, but it also shows a strong moral and religious sentiment existing, often in a secular context, in the popular mind. Religion is strongly present in the radical "hymns" of the time, and it is unlikely that the millions of tracts distributed among the workers went entirely disregarded. There is a distinct link between the Reverend Legh Richmond's account of a country girl showing her purity and courage in the face of death in *The Dairy-Man's Daughter* (2 million sold, 1814–32), and Rymer's secular but also triumphantly pure heroine in *Ada the Betrayed*. In 1897 *The Publisher's Circular* could still announce, "of all forms of fiction the semi-religious is the most popular."[13]

Barbara Jones also notes the popular taste for horror. This runs in a line from the old Gothic chapbooks, through 19th-century popular novels such as Rymer's *Varney the Vampire* (1846), to the modern horror film, which can chill better than print. This taste is related both to a religious sense of the numinous, and to a stress on emotion, a stress that spread across a wide spectrum of Victorian society, although, at the top, the public schools were inculcating emotional self-restraint, and Trollope sneered at Dickens as "Mr Popular Sentiment." The arousing of emotion is the chief aim of melodrama and the penny-issue novel. This does not mean that there was no stylistic control. As a perceptive commentator noted in 1859, "Diction is part of the thought. . . . Manner is as essential as matter in these cases. The mind of the narrator dwells in an atmosphere of melodramatic traditions; to ascertain whether these traditions are probable, or even possible, is none of his business. . . ."[14] The language used ("By Lucifer, my mark this time has proved sure"), the description of action and person ("her beautiful flaxen hair fell over a neck and shoulders as fair as alabaster"), have a baroque stylization. Today one has only to examine the curiously old-fashioned format of *The Red Letter* or *The People's Friend* to realize how important style and presentation remain to some working-class tastes.

By 1850 the "adult" penny-issue novel was beginning to change into the "juvenile" penny-issue fiction published in the 1850s and 1860s by such houses as George Purkess Jr and The Newsagent's Company, under such titles as *The Skeleton Crew*, *Spring-Heeled Jack*, and *The Wild Boys of London* (suppressed by the police in 1865). This does not mean that they were read only by children. Helen Bosanquet noted of "juvenile" publications in a north-country manufacturing village, "there are probably as many adults as juveniles among its readers, and, indeed, 'The Girl's Friend' is careful to state in its title that it is a paper for readers of all ages."[15] We may compare this with Geoffrey Wagner's estimate that 41 per cent of American male adults read "children's" comics.[16] Whereas in the middle class there is a tendency for "classics," such as Defoe, Swift, and Dickens, to become children's reading, in the working class the opposite is generally true. In "juvenile" reading the working-class reader may enjoy a spontaneity and level of phantasy that "adult" literature represses.

The penny-issue "adult" novel lost its appeal for many reasons. The years from 1850 to 1875 saw a rapid and nearly continuous economic advance. Workers' real wages rose by at least a third. There is a corresponding change of tone from Lloyd's publications to the more "respectable" format of the dominant working-class periodicals of the time, *The London Journal* (1845–1942), and *Reynolds' Miscellany* (1846–69), which cost 1*d.*, with magazines such as *The Family Herald* (1843–1939) and *Household Words* (1850–9), costing 1½*d.*, appealing to the upper fringe of the group. Their fiction could still be melodramatic and violent, however.

The appearance of fiction mainly in periodical form has another significance. In spite of its crudity, Lloyd's penny-issue fiction included a frontispiece and title-page for possible binding. In the first volume of *The London Journal*, however, John Wilson Ross greeted the "new era" of "economic literature,"[17] a literature designed not to be kept and lived with, but to be bought and "consumed" like any other transient, expendable commodity. Although hack writers have existed since the dawn of publishing, the profits of the new mass market attracted a new type of professional popular writer, whose names go unmentioned in literary histories, but who enjoyed immense sales. They included J. M. Rymer, Pierce Egan Sr, and George William MacArthur Reynolds, called at his death "the most popular writer in England," including Dickens.[18]

Reynolds's first major success, *The Mysteries of London* (1846–8), followed Pierce Egan Sr's earlier *Life in London* (1820) in moving the concern of popular fiction from the country to the life of the city, exploring the drama of its smoky atmosphere, crime, social variety, and class conflict. He portrayed the town as sharply divided between the corrupt rich and the oppressed poor, and presented class resentments and social issues in a dramatic form that appealed to the least politically minded workers. By way of "revelations" of intimate life in the Court of George IV, he attacked royalty in *The Mysteries of the Court of London* (1849–56). Although he capitalized on the taste for fashionable romance typified by the novels of Mrs Gore and Bulwer Lytton, he broke away from middle-class conventions of respectability with uninhibited portrayal of sexual themes. His exploration of feminine emotions shows certain insights beyond the range of many of the more highly regarded Victorian novelists.

Reynolds' journalistic flair enabled *Reynolds' Weekly Newspaper* (1850–1962) to become the one national Sunday paper with extreme radical views to survive in the second half of the 19th century. The Sunday newspaper demands particular attention here. Resented by the middle class as contravening the third commandment, it catered for the worker who could not afford time or money for a daily paper. Its dominant features are an index of popular tastes. Sport always received good coverage, and was the speciality of certain Sunday papers, such as *Bell's Life in London* (1822–86). It had its own jargon, and Pierce Egan Sr in particular, in his journalism and his annals of the ring, *Boxiana* (1812–24), expressed a ritual stylization of brutal emotions that is a paradigm of one aspect of working-class sensibility. Crime was another central feature of the Sunday papers; in this way they were the most sophisticated successors of the broadsheet. Crime reports catapulted the *News of the World* (1843) to its immediate success, although its genius was to give the details without varying the emotionally neutral tone of "respectable" journalism. In 8 months its circulation reached 86,050; and in 1896 sensational reports of the Jack the Ripper murders helped its rival, *Lloyd's Weekly Newspaper*, to become the first newspaper to sell one million copies a week. In the 1930s Lord Southwood exploited another broadsheet feature, when he used sensational "confessions" to raise the circulation of *The People* (1881).

Throughout the second half of the 19th century, education steadily widened, culminating in Forster's Education Act of 1870, which made elementary education available to all, and in 1876 compulsory education was provided up to the age of 12. By the 1850 Public Libraries Act, local authorities could use rates to set up free libraries: after a slow beginning, these also spread rapidly in the 1870s. At this time John Dicks began a "paperback revolution," publishing a wide range of major English poetry, drama, and fiction at prices between one shilling (for a complete edition of Shakespeare) and one halfpenny. In 1883 Percy B. St-John introduced Dicks's English Library of Standard Works, optimistically noting that "with the spread of education and of knowledge, a sudden and general demand arose for the works of our great masters of English." Henceforward it became more difficult to demarcate between working-class and middle-class popular fiction. Richard Hoggart has written that Mrs Henry Wood, Florence Barclay, and Marie Corelli were popular in north-country working homes,[19] and Florence Barclay's *The Rosary* (1909) was said to cheer the life of London slum-dwellers.[20] Their sensationalism and sentiment made them attractive to working-class tastes.

On the other hand, the 1870s and 1880s were a period of severe depression and of setbacks for the trade unions, culminating in the dock strike of 1889. The low ebb of workers' movements was an ominous backcloth to the success of a periodical that *The History of The Times* (1947) declared was "destined to modify, in a most profound degree, the intellectual, social and political tone of the press as a whole."[21] This was George Newnes' *Tit-Bits from all the most Interesting Books, Periodicals, and Newspapers of the World* (1881). Newnes built his success upon the belief that the educational revolution had produced a public that, though able to read, had little interest in good literature or the world of the mind. His medley of information, news, and jokes was offered without any regard to their importance, or even to their accuracy. A prize-winning "tit-bit" in the first volume, backed with a "medical man's" assurance that it was "quite possible," told of a woman who drank impure water and grew a live crab in her stomach. In three months *Tit-Bits* had a circulation of 900,000 and was soon to attract rivals such as *Answers* (1888). The new journalism of T. P. O'Connor's *The Star* (1888–1960) and Lord Northcliffe's *Daily Mail* (1896), which were written for a more middle-class reader, drew on American journalistic styles, but owed much more to Newnes' use of short, easy-to-understand items and a boisterously informal style. Serious radical journals, such as Robert Blatchford's *The Clarion* (1891–1934) and *The Daily Herald* (1912–66), the solid attractions of Workers' Educational Association and University Extension courses, and series such as Watts' Thinkers' Library (1929) had to compete with the commercial journalism of *Tit-Bits* and the popular press. *The Daily Mirror* (1903)—under the aggressive guidance of Harry Bartholomew, who joined its staff in 1904 and edited it from 1934 to 1951—was to take the tabloid format to its extreme form and to establish itself as the most popular working-class paper (its circulation in 1965 was five million). Although its concern with "human interest" stories often made news out of trivia, it also had the gift of making important matters exciting: it vigorously backed many specifically working-class interests and often took a courageously responsible stand on issues such as fascism and race relations.

In 1914, all social and literary developments were cut across by the outbreak of World War I. The war itself curtailed publishing, and it altered the family reading public on which journals such as *The London Journal* and *The Family Herald* depended. Three quarters of a million men in their prime were killed, and, after the initial post-war "baby-boom," families became smaller. Working-class fiction split, more obviously than before, into two distinct genres, one catering for male readers, the other (and dominating one) for female readers.

At the height of the war, in 1916, Miss N. W. Kennedy had launched *Peg's Paper*. It aimed, with unprecedented audience selection (the editor spent three years researching in Wigan), at the young north-country millgirl. It introduced future romantic best-sellers such as Denise Robins, Maisie Grieg, and Hermina Black, and quickly achieved the then formidable circulation of one quarter of a million. From *The London Journal* onward, 19th-century magazines had catered for the failure of social and religious guidance in the towns with their correspondence columns, which offered an incredible range of information from how to apply for a job to how to make ink from soot and gum. Miss Kennedy, looking forward to the specialist services of later women's magazines, went further. "Not long ago I was a millgirl too," declared "Peg" in the first number; "I want you to come to me with your joys and sorrows. . . ." Her "Private Post-bag" gave advice on a new level of intimacy. She paid careful attention to the dreams and superstitions of her readers. At the same time there was a down-to-earth quality in this and other working-class journals, as opposed to those of the middle class, noticed in America by Mary McCarthy in her essay "Up the Ladder from Charm to Vogue."[22] They would discuss details of mouth ulcers or of "itching bumps"; in fiction, they would cope with the problems of living with an unpleasant mother-in-law, and a recurrent theme in the stories was that the ordinary "boy next door" is best. In a typical story in *Red Letter*, "She wanted a Picture Hero," for instance, Netta, after a moment of dreaming of a film star, settles happily for a life with Bert, with his "familiar old pipe." At the same time, although they may start in realistic working-class situations, the stories might move, as did Cinderella from the cinders to the royal ball, into greater extremes of phantasy than do middle-class women's stories. In an early *Peg's Paper* story, for instance, Joan, a poor seamstress, faints with fatigue and hunger while modelling a wedding dress for the haughty rich girl Poppy Andrews. Poppy's fiancé falls in love with Joan and marries her instead. In these stories, too, the emotive element is always strong. It was still possible to find dialogue that might have come out of a Lloyd romance, and as late as 1940 a heroine in a *True Romances* story snarls, "Get out of here before I put a bullet in your vile heart."

It would require a separate study to examine the ways in which the treatment of romantic themes in women's popular fiction has changed during the 20th century;[23] we can make here only the most perfunctory suggestions of lines to be explored. The 1930s were years of depression and unemployment. There was a population drift, still continuing, from the industrial north to the south, and from the old manufacturing trades to distribution, commerce, and transport. The old working-class community life was being eroded by expansion into the suburbs and by the removal of neighbourhood populations into new towns. In the 1920s the heroines in *Peg's Paper* had often escaped from their millgirl status upward within the north-country social structure. In the next decade we see the popularity of this industrial fictional world giving way before the more generalized romantic worlds offered, alongside "homely" stories, by such periodicals as D. C. Thomson's *Red Letter*, *Red Star*, *Family Star*, *The People's Friend*, and *Secrets*. A leading popular writer was Ruby M. Ayres, with her phantasies of a "Southern" world of high society. The influence of Hollywood also began to make itself felt in such publications as the

Argus Press's *True Story* (1922) and *True Romances* (1934), both of which featured photographs of dramatic episodes in their stories. The effects of both television (especially of serials such as *Dr Kildare* and *Emergency Ward 10*) and the emergence of a meritocracy to challenge the values of an older society based on class, are evident in the popularity of the doctor hero in romance stories of the 1960s: there is at least one series of novelettes devoted to nothing else, Newnes' *Hospital Nurse Romances* (1967).

Since the depression of the 1890s, which accelerated the centralization of industries, with brand names sold on a national scale and backed by massive advertising, commerce has played an increasingly important part in journalism. *Woman's Own* (1932) and its rival *Woman* (1937) were launched as "shop windows" for female readers of all ages and social groups. Colour advertisements, and even strip cartoons selling soap or beverages, equated personal and commercial values. These periodicals rapidly came to dominate the women's magazine market in all class groups. In 1955 *Woman* was read by 26·9 per cent of the working-class female reading population. We see here two paradoxical movements. On the one hand, an increasingly monopolistic magazine press and the mass production of commodities do, at least superficially, create a mass culture. On the other hand, the five Thomson periodicals, old-fashioned in style and content, have continued to hold their ground, and in 1967 were indeed gaining readers, with a combined sale of nearly one million. The whole field is further complicated by the increasing split between the reading habits of different age groups, and by the greatly increased purchasing power of teen-agers since the war. *Marilyn* (1955) was the first of a mass of teen-age magazines, and in 1968 Connie Alderson estimated that such magazines had a combined circulation of 3 million.[24] The teen-age subculture is an important feature of English society since the war, not least because in many respects it cuts right across class barriers.

There has been less specialized development in the area of working-class men's literature. Here a major feature has been the influence of America. During the 19th century there was a considerable influx of American literature at all levels, from the novels of James Fenimore Cooper and Jack London to the "dime novels" of men such as J. H. Ingraham; but after World War I it became more pervasive and influential. The cowboy story, backed by the cinema, became a staple working-class genre. As is evident from the continuing popularity (since the appearance of his most successful work, *Riders of the Purple Sage*, 1912) of stories by Zane Grey ("clean as an ocean breeze," enthused his biographer),[25] cowboy stories have based their appeal on violent action in wide-open spaces. An even more violent American influence appeared in the crime story. From his first success (about 1893) in Alfred Harmsworth's *Marvel*, the great English working-class detective hero was Sexton Blake who, adventuring through some 250 million words, has some claim to be considered a modern folk hero.[26] Blake made an unequivocal stand for Right against Wrong, and his bizarre antagonists—who included the Brotherhood of the Yellow Beetle, and King Karl II of Serbovia with his Double-Four Gang including a circus strong-man and a baby-faced midget—appealed to imaginations that earlier would have read Gothic tales or bought penny-issues of Eugène Sue's *The Wandering Jew* (1844). In matters of sex the tone was impeccable, and the fights were upright "desperate combats." In his essay "Raffles and Miss Blandish,"[27] George Orwell compared the casual but "sporting" morality of E. W. Hornung's crime novels at the beginning of this century with the calculated sadism and power worship of James Hadley Chase's *No Orchids for Miss Blandish* (1939), in which an English writer deliberately recreated the American crime world. Between the wars Sexton Blake held his ground against a more violent American-style tale that first appeared in such periodicals as *The Thriller* (1929). The violence of World War II, which probably aided the success of Chase's novel, helped further to transform popular tastes, and between 1948 and 1963 "Hank Janson" emerged as perhaps the most popular English crime writer for the lower classes, issuing some 187 titles. The original "Janson" was Stephen D. Frances. Although his early novels were comparatively innocuous, he was successfully prosecuted for obscenity in 1954. His work thereafter not only continued, but became more violent, a crude *mélange* of sex and sadism. This is particularly true since 1960, when the novels have been produced by a syndicate. Titles change from *Gun Moll for Hire* (1948) and the like to such innuendoes as *She Sleeps to Conquer* (1961) and *Visit from A Broad* (1963). Frances, an Englishman, assumed the persona of a tough American crime reporter. He created a world where the only moral code is individual strength, and the only course of justice is through violence. Although the crudity of story-telling and book production suggest that they are read by a semi-literate public, it is difficult to delimit thriller literature today by class. The novels of the American Mickey Spillane, which sold over 5 million copies in England between 1963 and 1968 in paperbacks alone, are probably read by both middle- and lower-class readers, although no statistical evidence is available. Spillane's hero, Mike Hammer, exhibits many of the traits of Janson heroes, but because he is a more coherent and credible character, he may throw some light on the connection between the growing violence and amorality in crime fiction and in society since the war. Hammer is turned to compulsive violence by his experience of brutality and killing during the war. Society offers no tenable moral code. In *I, the Jury* (1952), for instance, Hammer races to catch the murderer of his friend before he can be given up to the "injustices" of the law. "He" turns out to be a beautiful girl. Whereas women's fiction is typically about winning a man's love, in male fiction women are either objects of sexual pleasure or dangerous deceivers. Attempting to seduce Hammer, the girl undresses, and Hammer, in a perfect paradigm of sex turned to sadism, shoots her in the stomach. This brutality has spread from pulp fiction into weekly working-class journals. Two successive issues of *Reveille* in 1960, for instance, included stories of a man being slowly dismembered alive while struggling in the water, and of a man having his face slowly shot away with an airgun.

Reveille (1940) leads us on to another area in which American influence has been marked: the "pin-up." The pin-up is by no means exclusively working class, but its place in working-class culture is evident enough to merit particular notice. For obvious reasons, the form flourished with the troops during both world wars. In World War I they were most popularly French, with the "naughty" designs of the artist Kirschner. In the United States, however, they were also part of the mechanization of human response in advertising techniques, and they inspired Marshall McLuhan's celebrated title essay in *The Mechanical Bride* (1951). The female figure, he noted, intimate and anonymous, was reduced to mandatory, uniform "vital statistics." Her legs became "date-baited power levers for the management of her male audience," dulling discrimination, selling the magazine and her products. During World War II, the dominant pin-up image was not French but American, and, in subdued form, they were a regular feature of *Reveille*, which was to continue after the war and, exploiting pin-ups, was to become the most popular of all weekly magazines with the working-class readership, read in 1955 by over one quarter of all this group. This was more than twice as many as read *Tit-Bits*, although the latter also tried to follow the pin-up-centred style of *Reveille* and its competitor, *Weekend Mail*.[28] In *The Uses of Literacy* (1957) Richard Hoggart declared that pin-ups had become "the most striking features of mid-twentieth-century mass-art; we are a democracy whose working-people are exchanging their birthright for a mass of pin-ups." He also noted cruder monthly versions of these "sex-and-bittiness" journals, consisting almost entirely of coarse jokes and suggestive hand-drawn pin-ups, appearing in the north of England with circulations of up to one third of a million. Imported American pornographic magazines, with titles such as *Figure*, *Blaze*, and *Bachelor*, also enjoyed a steady sale in the 1960s. Pin-ups are the product of a culture split and alienated in its imagination: a survey of pin-ups during the war showed the most popular to be a sexual phantasy of a naked girl hugging a rock face, and a "nice" girl, primly dressed, "the girl one would like to come home to."[29] The pin-up also shows the ultimate in the commercialization of literature: it produces an automatic stimulus bypassing all issues of art and human involvement. Although the pin-up is an American influence, however, there are national differences. The coy "naughtiness" of the English lower-class versions still tends to imply certain moral standards that are being contravened, and during World War II the most popular pin-up strip with the British forces, "Jane" (*Daily Mirror*, 1932–59), lost more and more of her clothes with an innocence that fascinated American readers.

Comics also show a divergence between English and American working-class cultures. The influx of American horror comics, introduced by G.I.s during the war, was halted by the Children's and Young Persons' Publications Act of 1955. But few American comic strips have had an extensive run in English newspapers and no English paper has found it profitable to follow the American practice of issuing comic supplements. There is a difference in sensibility. The English comic *Chips* (1896–1953), featuring Weary Willy and Tired Tim, reached a circulation of half a million. Yet it lacked the imaginative exuberance of its American counterparts, such as the Yellow Kid, the Katzenjammer Kids, and Ignatz Kat, appearing in comic supplements to papers such as *The New York World*. In the contemporary scene, the American *Marvel* and *Superman* comics are in colour; the English reprints, and indigenous comic series such as Fleetway "Battle Picture Library," are in black-and-white. The American comics use colour contrasts, distorted perspectives, stress and speed lines, to give a sense of movement and force: they are a genuine folk art, read by academics in search of "camp," and a source of inspiration to painters such as Roy Lichtenstein.[30] The English working-class culture's visual-art traditions began to deteriorate, in literature, a century ago, with the disappearance of Lloyd's woodcut illustrations to the penny-issue novel.

If the British working class has a "comic" tradition, it is more typically the cartoon joke, single or a short series of frames, that looks back to the music-hall comedian's patter, and to the postcard art of Donald MacGill.[31] American strip series show a variety of social and cultural experience:

"Dick Tracy," the German-Jewish "Katzenjammer Kids," the pseudo-Walter-Scott "Prince Valiant," and "Peanuts" are characteristic examples. The English cartoon emphasizes stereotyped traditional situations and characters such as the mother-in-law, or the marooned man on a desert island.[32] The best-known working-class series, "Andy Capp" in the *Daily Mirror*, has established itself on the affirmation of a predictable class image, all the sharper in that Capp's world is passing. Their popularity in newspapers has forced them to become a little more topical since the war, but they have never become the medium of social comment we see in the middle-class Giles in *The Daily Express*, Jak in the *Evening Standard*, and in "Flook" by Trog in *The Daily Mail*.[33]

This picture of working-class reading, which in part provoked Richard Hoggart to write *The Uses of Literacy*, can be modified. The paperback revolution started by Allen Lane's Penguin Books in 1935, with the commissioning of original titles for paperback publication two years later, was not the first venture into mass-produced paperbound books, but it was unique in extent. In 1960 some 70 million paperbacks a year were published in Britain, and the number increases annually. They bring literature of good, as well as poor, quality to a mass readership, and the quality of their design and typography is often high. Series such as Pelican Books, begun in 1955, have brought serious non-fiction to many working-class readers, while radio and television offer major opportunities for developing popular taste. A sample of popular fiction taken from present-day women's magazines shows a marked improvement in "literary" quality over that of previous decades.

But the situation is extremely difficult to analyse. This essay began by suggesting that the emergence of a distinctive working-class readership created a new phase of popular literature. Today, the identity of the working class itself is increasingly difficult to define: Raymond Williams has pointed out that "working class" and "middle class" are no longer mutually exclusive terms.[34] One refers to occupation, the other to social and economic status, and the two overlap. Yet, in spite of mass literacy, mass media, and universal suffrage, England has not yet fully reached the state of "mass society" that we see in the United States. Accent, dress, and a complex of personal attitudes still determine the type of public house, restaurant, or shop one patronizes; background and educational opportunity remain rigidly stratified by class, as *Education and the Working Class* (1962) by Brian Jackson and Dennis Marsden illustrates. The research of Basil Berstein[35] has confirmed how one's social group determines one's patterns of apprehension and expression;

because of this, however complex the problems of exploring literature against the class that reads it may be, the venture remains valuable. It offers ways of understanding elements in the total society that may otherwise be classified as undesirable because they do not correspond with the predominantly middle- and upper-class sensibilities of literary critics or social pundits. These elements may not only be valuable in themselves; the meeting of "high" and "popular" traditions in writers as diverse as Shakespeare, Dickens, and D. H. Lawrence has invigorated, not corrupted, their work. But that is matter for another study.

References

1. ASA BRIGGS, "The Language of 'Class' in Nineteenth-century England," *Essays in Labour History*, ed. by Asa Briggs and John Saville (London 1960), pp. 43–73.
2. See J. M. S. TOMPKINS, *The Popular Novel in England 1770–1800* (London 1932).
3. For these and many of the following statistics of circulation, see RICHARD ALTICK, *The English Common Reader* (Chicago 1957), pp. 379–90.
4. M. J. QUINLAN, *Victorian Prelude* (New York 1941), p. 160; for a later and more thorough study, which gives a higher estimate, see R. K. WEBB, *The British Working Class Reader, 1790–1848* (London 1955), *passim*.
5. *S.P.C.K. Minutes* (S.P.C.K. House, London, manuscript), 21 May 1832, pp. 284–5.
6. S. G. GREEN, *The Story of the Religious Tract Society* (London 1899), p. 57.
7. JOEL H. WEINER, *A Descriptive Finding List of Unstamped British Periodicals 1830–1836* (London 1970).
8. WILLIAM H. WICKWAR, *The Struggle for the Freedom of the Press* (London 1828), pp. 259–73.
9. W. E. WROOT, "William Milner of Halifax," *The Bookman* (March 1897), pp. 169–75.
10. CHARLES HINDLEY, *The History of the Catnach Press* (London 1886), p. 92.
11. LOUIS JAMES, *Fiction for the Working Man 1830–1850* (London 1963), especially pp. 45–71.
12. BARBARA JONES, *The Unsophisticated Arts* (London 1951), pp. 10–1.
13. 2 January 1897, p. 5.
14. *British Quarterly Review* LVIII (London 1859), p. 333.
15. "Cheap Literature," *Contemporary Review* LXXIX (London 1901), p. 673.
16. *Parade of Pleasure* (London 1954), p. 71.

17. "The Influence of Cheap Literature," *The London Journal* I (London 1845), p. 115.
18. *The Bookseller* (3 July 1879), pp. 600–1.
19. *The Uses of Literacy* (paperback: Harmondsworth 1958), p. 103.
20. *The Life of Florence Barclay by "One of her Daughters"* (London 1921), p. 215.
21. STANLEY MORISON, *The History of The Times, 1884–1912* (London 1935–52), Vol. III, p. 95.
22. In *On the Contrary* (New York 1962).
23. See, for example, B. BERELSON, "Content Analysis," *Handbook of Social Psychology*, ed. by G. Lindzey (Reading, Mass. 1954); CAROL OWEN, "Feminine Roles and Social Mobility in Women's Weekly Magazines," *Sociological Review* X (London 1962), pp. 283–96.
24. *Magazines Teenagers Read* (Oxford 1968), p. 5.
25. JEAN KARR, *Zane Grey, Man of the West* (Kingswood 1951), p. xvi.
26. E. S. TURNER, *Boys Will Be Boys*, rev. edn (London 1957), p. 118.
27. In *Critical Essays* (London 1951).
28. *Hulton Readership Survey* (London 1955), Table 9.
29. Mass Observation, "What is a Pin-up Girl?", *Picture Post* (23 September 1944), pp. 14, 15, 25.
30. See, for example, SUSAN SONTAG, "Notes on Camp," *Against Interpretation* (New York 1966), Ch. V.
31. See GEORGE ORWELL, "The Art of Donald McGill," *Critical Essays* (London 1951).
32. On humour in Sunday newspaper cartoons, see GEORGE MELLY, "Humour," in *Your Sunday Paper*, ed. by Richard Hoggart (London 1967).
33. On comic strips, see GEORGE PERRY and ALAN ALDRIDGE, *The Penguin Book of Comics* (Harmondsworth 1967).
34. RAYMOND WILLIAMS, *The Long Revolution* (London 1961), Pt III, iii.
35. See, for example, "Social Structure, Language, and Learning," *Educational Research* 3 (Birmingham 1961), pp. 163–76.

Bibliography

The following works, in addition to those cited in the References, are recommended.

KINGSLEY AMIS, *New Maps of Hell* (London 1961), on science fiction.
Daedalus 89 (Richmond, Va. 1960), No. 2: a special issue on "Mass Culture and the Mass Media," with articles by Hannah Arendt, James Baldwin, Ernest Schils, and others.
MARGARET DALZIEL, *Popular Fiction a Hundred Years Ago* (London 1957).
STUART HALL and PADDY WHANNEL, *The Popular Arts* (London 1964).
JOHN F. C. HARRISON, *Learning and Living, 1790–1960* (London 1961).
PATRICIA HOLLIS, *The Pauper Press* (London 1970).

Hulton Readership Survey, 1947–55.

M. LAMBERT and ENID MARX, *English Popular Art* (London 1951).

F. R. LEAVIS and DENYS THOMPSON, *Culture and Environment* (London 1933).

Q. D. LEAVIS, *Fiction and the Reading Public* (London 1932).

LEO LOWENTHAL, *Literature, Popular Culture, and Society* (New York 1961).

MARSHALL MCLUHAN, *The Mechanical Bride* (New York 1951).

National Readership Survey, Society of Incorporated Practitioners in Advertising, 1965 onward.

JAMES REEVES, *The Idiom of the People* (London 1958), on ballads.

BERNARD ROSENBERG and DAVID MANNING WHITE, *Mass Culture* (New York 1957).

DENYS THOMPSON (ed.), *Discrimination and Popular Culture* (London 1964).

W. LLOYD WARNER, *American Life, Dream and Reality*, rev. edn (Chicago 1962).

JOEL H. WEINER, *War of the Unstamped* (Ithaca 1969).

FREDERICK WERTHAM, *The Seduction of the Innocent* (London 1956).

FRANCIS WILLIAMS, *Dangerous Estate* (London 1957).

RAYMOND WILLIAMS, *Communications* (London 1962).

Author's note: I am grateful to Miss Patricia Lamburn and other editors in the magazine world for their generous help and information.

CHAPTER 20

The Reading Public in England and America in 1900

Richard D. Altick*

At the turn of the century, more people were reading, and a larger quantity
of printed matter was being produced, than ever before in the history of
the English-speaking world. In Lord Salisbury's Britain and President
McKinley's America, the continuing steady growth of the mass reading
audience and the refinement of the various instruments designed to serve
it were witness to the power the printed word had acquired in the course
of the 19th century. In terms of popular culture, if not of politics, the dictum of Finley Peter Dunne's Chicago saloon-keeper, Mr Dooley, was
wholly accurate: "Yes, sir, th' hand that rocks th' fountain pen is th' hand
that rules th' wurruld."

The similarities between the British mass audience and that of the
United States in 1900 were more numerous than the differences: a circum-
stance the more striking because they were the products of quite dissimilar
developments. In Britain, the existence of millions of habitual readers
represented the long-delayed triumph of the idea of social and cultural
democracy over the many religious and political forces that for centuries
had opposed the spread of reading for any but narrowly religious purposes
throughout the lower stratum of the enlarging middle class and into the
very ranks of the workers.† It had been a hard-won victory, with effects
on the national culture that were then, as they have remained, the topic
of endless controversy and concern. In America there had been no such
struggle. The "right to read" had always been implicit in the premises of
American society; no body of clergy, no aristocracy, no political faction,

* Regents' Professor of English, The Ohio State University.

† The development of working-class reading habits and tastes in the 19th century is discussed
in Ch. 19, "Working-class Literature in England."

had ever, in any important way, ventured to deny it. In the one nation, therefore, the reading public owed its being to many decades of social friction, anxiety, and attempted repression; in the other, it was the unscarred fruit of social evolution.

Britons of the era agreed that the state of reading in the United States was markedly superior to that at home. The historian E. A. Freeman, writing in 1883, called America "the land of the 'general reader' "; five years later James Bryce, the political scientist, in his classic work *The American Commonwealth*, declared that "Nowhere in the world is there growing up such a vast multitude of intelligent, cultivated, and curious readers." Most Americans were of the same mind. One, writing in the *Forum* for December 1894, enumerated the various factors that, he believed, made his nation more of a reading race than the English, and concluded that "the great bulk of the English read nothing, literally nothing." That this was mere exuberant American hyperbole is proved by sales figures of the sort that will occur on later pages. But it is probably true that, relative to the total population, America had a larger body of readers than did Britain. It may also be true that, as Freeman maintained, "the class of those who read widely, who read, as far as they go, intelligently, but who do not read deeply—the class of those who, without being professed scholars, read enough and know enough to be quite worth talking to—form a larger proportion of mankind in America than they do in England."

According to the same *Forum* writer, the reason for England's inferiority in this respect was that "a very large number of intelligent people . . . are altogether opposed to free general education . . . . [They] hold that the children, as of old, in each parish, should be taught to read and write and to say their catechism in the schools under the supervision of the clergy, and then earn a living as did their forefathers." Here he was clearly misinformed: in the 1890s nobody, except perhaps the few extreme reactionaries who survive in every age, held such opinions. But in the earlier part of the century they had been influential enough, and popular education was still paying the price at its end. As national life had been transformed by the simultaneous shift from an agrarian to an industrial economy and from a rural to a predominantly urban population, the practical necessity of literacy had steadily increased. In factories and mills, in city shops and streets, illiterate men and women were at an ever greater disadvantage both in their occupation and in the everyday routine of living. In the earlier part of the century these pressures had been met by equally strong counterforces, chiefly stemming from the fear of a potentially revolutionary populace (a chronic English anxiety from the time of the French Revolution to the Chartist fiasco of 1848), that opposed any but the most rudimentary education for the masses. Responsibility for providing this had been assumed by the rival educational organizations of Church and dissent, whose "voluntary" schools did their best within the stringent limitations of their funds and of their aims, which remained prudently modest. Successive attempts to shift a major portion of the financing and management of elementary schools to the state had foundered on the venerable and still formidable religious issue: Church and dissent, though they agreed on nothing else in connection with their educational mission, concurred in resisting any inroads of secularization. Until 1870, the state's role in education had been confined to small annual grants made to the voluntary schools, a loose system of inspection that had been imposed as a condition of the grants, and a much deplored scheme of "payment by results," which determined the annual amount of a school's subsidy on the basis of the number of pupils who passed the standards set in the various subjects. As a result, the schools attended by working-class children were poorly housed and equipped, incompetently taught, and generally so inefficient that the millions who—to use a grossly inapplicable word—enjoyed such education were hardly better off than the thousands who never went to school at all, as was the case in some parts of the countryside and in the terrible slums of the new mill and factory cities.

While it is true, therefore, that in absolute terms educational opportunity did spread throughout the century, it lagged far behind the need, in respect both to the numbers to be taught and to the changing conditions that made literacy increasingly indispensable. Only in 1870 did an act of Parliament provide for the state education of children unreached by voluntary schools. Only in 1880 did another law make attendance compulsory for children between the ages of 5 and 10. But the law was full of loopholes and unevenly enforced, and in any case the quality of instruction remained very poor. Not until the very last years of the century, moreover, were there enough places for all the children who by law should have been in school. Thus, although the reading public of 1900 was swelled by hundreds of thousands of young men and women who owed their literacy to the recent advent of government in a field hitherto sacred to private enterprise, they had left school at so early an age, and had received so meagre an introduction to the art of reading while at school, as to constitute an audience for only the simplest kind of printed matter—a fact that proved the fortune of more than one shrewd publishing entrepreneur.

On the whole, America was better off, but such superiority as it possessed should not be exaggerated. The principle of tax-supported education had been accepted in the North as early as the middle of the century, but the schools made available on this principle had been slow in appearing, and in the South, whose school system was shattered by the Civil War, they were almost non-existent. By 1900, some 30 states had enacted compulsory laws, typically requiring children between 8 and 14 to attend school from 12 to 16 weeks a year. As in England, however, the degree of enforcement varied from place to place, and children in the country attended school for much shorter periods than did their city cousins. Although the nation was experiencing what one historian would later call "the educational revival" at the turn of the century, the marked improvements in American elementary education—longer terms of attendance, provision of free textbooks in a score of states, gradual substitution of consolidated rural schools for the picturesque but primitive one-room establishments—had come too late to affect the millions who comprised the adult audience of 1900. The average adult American of that year had had the equivalent of no more than four or five years of formal schooling.

Literacy figures, inseparable though they are from any discussion of the reading public, are (here as always) undependable indexes of size or quality. On the English side one thing, at least, is certain: despite the common assumption that persists even today, the Forster Education Act of 1870 did not dramatically hasten the spread of literacy. In the two preceding decades, the literacy rate for males had increased by 11·3 per cent and for females by 18·4; in the next two decades, the rate of increase was 13·0 and 19·5 respectively. The chief effect of the 1870 law was that it underwrote elementary education in those areas of the nation that had previously been the most neglected; it was there, supposedly, that the greatest gains in literacy occurred between 1871 and 1891, the year of the first census that fully reflected the results of the state's decisive intervention in educational affairs.

In 1900 the literacy rate in England and Wales was approximately 97 per cent. This figure, however, represents only those young men and women who, upon being married in that year, were able to sign their names. It does not reveal how many could actually read—a quite different accomplishment from the mechanical one of scrawling a signature—and it is useless as an indication of the understanding with which the brides and grooms could read, if they read at all. Moreover, it takes no account of the millions of older persons who, having had less chance to learn to read in their own youth, greatly reduced the real percentage of literacy in the population as a whole. These older persons formed no market whatever for reading matter, a fact too often obscured by the size of the population that did, but one that must be remembered if the mass reading public is to be seen in its proper perspective.

No simple comparison is possible with America, whose own literacy rate—a little above 89 per cent in the census of 1900—was based on the ability of persons 10 years of age or older to read their own language. The greatest incidence of illiteracy was found, expectedly enough, among the large immigrant population and in the South. If the American criterion had been applied in Britain, it is likely that the British literacy rate would have proved to be no higher than the American one, if indeed as high. However that may be, the nature of the reading material that sold in greatest quantities, both in England and in America, makes it plain that the possession of what might be called statistical literacy, doubtfully enriched by the educational experience that produced it, did not encourage the average working-class reader to aspire beyond the magazines and newspapers that were carefully designed for his limited comprehension.

America had at least this one clear-cut educational advantage over Britain: the abler or more fortunate children, mainly in the cities, could continue beyond the elementary grades. In 20 years (1878–98) the number of high schools in the country had risen from fewer than 800 to 5500, and the number of pupils from fewer than 100,000 to more than half a million. The products of this system might reasonably have been expected to constitute an audience for a somewhat higher level of reading matter than that to which those who had had no more than an elementary education were normally limited. In England, however, no laws as yet provided for state-supported schooling beyond the first few years—a small beginning was to be made with Balfour's Act in 1902—and the existing provision for secondary education was decidedly inadequate. It is true that toward the end of the century, in belated response to Germany's well-attested superiority in scientific and engineering training that enabled her to surpass Britain in the competition for world markets, a certain amount of technical instruction had been made available in the manufacturing centres. Otherwise conditions had not improved markedly since 1868, when the Taunton Commission declared that two thirds of English towns entirely lacked schools above the primary level and most of the remaining one third had schools whose advanced level was noticeable only in name. Analysis of the figures collected at the time that the Bryce Commission inquired into secondary education (1895) has led recent historians to hazard the guess that there were then about 75,000 pupils in the 621 endowed secondary schools reporting; but of these, no more than 30,000 to 40,000 (including the boys in the ancient public schools, which always made some pretence, however anachronistic, of preparing their students for intellectual maturity) were receiving what would be regarded in the 20th century as a satisfactory secondary education. Altogether, enrolment in secondary schools of all kinds, including non-profit-making schools of varying merit, did not exceed 2·5 per thousand of the population. Education beyond the twelfth or thirteenth year was still widely regarded as a privilege of the middle class, to which only the most exceptional child from the working class was entitled. Inherited notions of class structure and prerogatives thus continued to govern educational thinking, which for the most part was considerably in arrears of the actual social situation.

In Scotland, however, the story was different, as indeed it had been ever since the nation's ideal of schooling for all had been formulated in John Knox's *First Book of Discipline* (1559). During the intervening period, though with a decided lapse in the 18th century, an unco-ordinated but effective combination of parish and burgh (municipal) effort had made elementary schooling accessible to virtually every Scots child, and secondary education, even university training, to all boys who were qualified, regardless of social class. The universal democratic education toward which England groped throughout the 19th century had long since been an established fact north of the Tweed. It was no accident that some of the most influential contributions toward a mass British reading public had originated in Scotland, with Lord Brougham (the advocate of popular education), George Birkbeck (the originator of the Mechanics' Institutes), Archibald Constable and the brothers William and Robert Chambers (pioneers of cheap books and periodicals), and Samuel Brown (founder of the "itinerating libraries" in East Lothian, which helped to prepare the way for public libraries). In 1872, the Education (Scotland) Act—which, significantly, omitted the word "elementary" from its description of the education aimed for, and specified "the children of the *whole* people of Scotland" as the intended beneficiaries—took over the chaotic patchwork of Scottish schools from the church, the burghs, sectarian bodies, and private societies and individuals, and brought them together under elected school boards. Although the new necessity for uniform quality led to a temporary concentration of national educational energies upon improving the teaching of the "ordinary branches," higher education remained available to the most promising of the young, thanks partly to the opportune channelling of income from obsolete charitable endowments into foundations (scholarships) and bursaries.

To make good the general lack of formal educational opportunity beyond the elementary level, England adopted various schemes. In the period 1825–75, Mechanics' Institutes had provided courses of evening lectures, libraries, and in some cases classes for the ambitious working-men, artisans, and clerks of many hundreds of towns. In the last quarter of the century, the movement lost its momentum and such social homogeneity as it had earlier possessed. In the north of England it continued to serve primarily craftsmen, operatives, and other members of the labouring class and lower middle class. In 1891 the Yorkshire Union of 280 institutes had some 60,000 members, most of whom belonged for the sake of acquiring a certain amount of technical knowledge. A number of institutes in Yorkshire and elsewhere had, as a matter of fact, already been transformed into technical schools, supported in part by local grants. But at the same time, the Yorkshire Union continued the Mechanics' Institutes' long-standing practice of circulating books to its members. It maintained a library of 30,000 volumes, which were distributed to 200 remote villages as yet untouched by the public-library movement. In the south of England, meanwhile, the clientele of the institutes was predominantly middle-class and the emphasis was on general "literary and philosophical" lectures and lighter entertainment. In some instances they, too, continued to maintain their libraries, although in others the Mechanics' Institute buildings and book stocks had been taken over as the nucleus of a rate-supported public library.

A second important means of providing education beyond the elementary level in England was university extension. Originating in the desire to make university training available to poor students, and given additional impetus by one of the questions left unanswered by the Forster Act—what shall be done with those whose hunger for learning is only sharpened, not satisfied, by compulsory elementary schooling?—the movement got under way in the 1870s. Despite many disappointments and generally slow progress, in the last 15 years of the century and the first decade of the new, extension courses offered in various towns by Oxford, Cambridge, and London universities attracted some 50,000 men and women each year. These adult seekers after knowledge, however, were chiefly of the middle class. Only between one quarter and one fifth of them, and these mainly in the north, were from the ranks of the workers. University extension as originally constituted failed in its aim of bringing a liberal education to the labouring class, partly because the local sponsoring committees were middle-class and therefore (as had also been too often the case with sponsors of the Mechanics' Institutes) suspected of ulterior motives, and partly because of difficulties in financing. Not until 1905 did the universities and the organized working-class movement join in a successful concerted effort to provide part-time continued education to the workers, principally in the form of tutorial classes. It was then that Albert Mansbridge saw a proposal he had made two years earlier flower into the Workers' Educational Association, a federation of the educational arms of numerous co-operative societies and trade unions that was to be the most successful and influential adult-education agency in the new century.

Toward the end of the 1880s, attempts had been made to introduce university extension on the English model into the United States. But the courses organized by a few universities—notably that of Chicago, under its vigorous president, William Rainey Harper—had but a brief success, and only in 1906 was the extension scheme to be revitalized under the leadership of the University of Wisconsin. Meanwhile, its purposes were served in two other, characteristically American ways. The public libraries of some larger cities, obedient to the wider conception of community service through adult education that distinguished the American library movement from the British, sponsored courses of university-level lectures. And, more important, the well-established and popular Chautauqua programme was enlarged to include a Literary and Scientific Circle that during the 1890s enrolled some 100,000 Americans, half of whom were between 30 and 40 years of age, in courses of home reading. By 1900, some 50,000 such students had "graduated" after four years of directed reading. The British equivalent of this institution was the Home Reading Union, founded in 1889 by James Bryce, the philologist Max Müller, Archdeacon Farrar, the philosopher Frederic Harrison, and others, which sought the same end—education through purposeful fireside reading—by the same means: reading lists, monthly magazines, neighbourhood discussion circles, and summer assemblies.

In both Britain and the United States, the tendency in these various instruments of adult education that had the most pronounced effect on the tone of the reading public was the increasing presence of women. Like their transatlantic cousins who had long attended the lyceums (the venerable and influential counterpart of the Mechanics' Institutes, devoted especially to lectures and libraries), English women had long been active in the cultural and social programmes of the Mechanics' Institutes, especially in those towns where the middle class, rather than the workers, dominated the organization. But now women began to swell the audiences for the afternoon series of university extension lectures and classes, and were the majority in the home reading circles; and in America they organized the innumerable clubs, dedicated to the more or less earnest study of art and

554

literature, that soon became a familiar and, to some observers, perennially risible part of the social scene. In the United States, where female higher education had met considerably less resistance than in Britain, young women remained at school beyond the elementary grades in ever-growing numbers; in 1900, indeed, 37,000 had gone beyond high school to become students in normal (teacher-training) colleges, and 25,000 more were in regular colleges and universities. On both sides of the ocean, women had generally greater educational opportunities, possessed a larger portion of leisure (thanks to labour-saving appliances and similar blessings), and enjoyed a many-sided "emancipation" that was a widely publicized social phenomenon of the 1890s. All these factors combined to increase the woman reader's consumption of print. And, as a consumer, she acquired greater power over what was produced for popular consumption than had been wielded even by the middle-class women of previous generations under whose ever-present threat of disfavour such writers as Dickens and Thackeray—to say nothing of all publishers, and the submissive Mr Mudie of the circulating library—had laboured. To adapt Mr Dooley's dictum to a new use, the hand that rocked the cradle was the hand that ruled the pens of popular authors and commanded the consciences of editors. No analysis of contemporary literary taste and taboo can overlook the numerous and assertive presence of women as wives, mothers, and guardians of morality and decorum.

On balance, the conditions of everyday life around 1900 favoured the cultivation of the reading habit. Because of the gradual increase of real income and the fall of prices, including that of printed matter, the ordinary man, earning say 38 shillings a week, could afford sixpennyworth of reading matter oftener than had been possible for his father. Although the crowding that had made private reading so impracticable a recreation in countless Victorian households was not noticeably lessened, another requisite for comfortable application to a book or paper—adequate illumination—had become more available. In the country, to be sure, the dim old stand-bys, candles and paraffin lamps, persisted; but in town and city, gas lighting (greatly improved by the invention of the Welsbach mantle in 1885), and in the most favoured households the incandescent electric lamp had eliminated what had been, in the earlier part of the century, one of the gravest obstacles to the free indulgence of the reading habit. On the other hand, except for the fortunate few who belonged to the "leisured class," during six days of the week the time for reading was severely limited. In the great majority of occupations one of the classic goals of the labour movement, the 8-hour day and 40-hour week, was nowhere in sight. As late as 1913, the standard working week in Britain was to range from 46 to 56 hours, and in the United States from 44 to 66.

The small additions to leisure time that changing conditions provided in 1900 had many claimants. Outdoor sports, both participant and spectator, were increasingly popular: the football and the cricket or baseball bat competed with the book for attention. In 1900, furthermore, the bicycle craze that had been one of the great international social phenomena of the 1890s was far from over. In America, where it was estimated that one million bicycles were in use, the rivalry of the pneumatic tyre with the printed word was so strenuous that book-sellers, it was reported, proposed to fight impending losses by adding cycles to their wares.

Fifty years earlier, in Britain and America, the principle that libraries open to all might be supported from tax funds had won formal acceptance. Parliament's passage of Ewart's bill (1850), which enabled local authorities to levy rates for building libraries, was a landmark in the history of mid-Victorian social improvement, the latest in a series of panaceas that, it was hoped, would ease social tensions and remove the ever-present threat of unruliness (or worse) on the part of the working population. If religion had proved ineffective as the opiate of the people, wholesome reading matter, made freely available in libraries, would succeed; the printed word would also prove a beneficent substitute for the public house. Such hopes, expressed by orators at the dedication of scores of libraries built under Ewart's Act, epitomized the widespread Victorian faith in the power of print. Unfortunately, however, these high expectations had not been fulfilled. The pace of library building, slow in the first decades after the enabling legislation was passed, was still hobbled at the end of the century by various difficulties, such as the statutory provision that no more than a penny in the pound could be levied for library purposes. Once the buildings were erected, further difficulties presented themselves: the selection of books was often grotesquely inappropriate for a lower-middle- and working-class clientele; the atmosphere in some libraries was not conducive to quiet reading; and librarians and the local "friends of the library" were too often censorious and patronizing in their relations with readers and borrowers and in their supervision of clients' tastes.

Nevertheless, by the time of the queen's Golden Jubilee in 1887 the public library movement had gathered momentum. The inadequate financial support derived from the rates was handsomely supplemented by philanthropists such as J. Passmore Edwards, the millionaire newspaper proprietor, who endowed numerous London libraries, and above all by Andrew Carnegie, whose benefactions, starting in his native Dunfermline in 1881, extended to England in 1897 and were to reach their peak in 1900–5. Assisted by new legislation (1893 in England, 1894 in Scotland) that allowed local authorities to "adopt the acts" by resolution rather than rely on the problematic success of a popular referendum, many communities that had hitherto been without public libraries now acquired them. Between 1880 and 1889, some 65 rate-supported libraries were founded; in the next decade 153 more were built. The total number of such libraries in 1900 was approximately 500. Even so, in England there was only one municipal library for every 88,943 of population (in Scotland 93,619), and it was asserted that in every community that *did* possess a library—a number of populous towns were still without one—95 per cent of the people were indifferent to its presence. As a self-styled "Working Woman" candidly put it in *Chambers' Journal* in 1899, the working class, for whom the libraries had been established, had found little use for them. "In spite of modern civilization and modern education, working men, but more especially working women, have . . . 'as much use for learning as a cow has for clogs.' . . . There is absolutely nothing in the home life to encourage a taste for literary pursuits." It is true that a certain number of working-class children used the libraries, but their choice of books merely swelled the total of fiction circulated—which constituted about 80 per cent of all books issued, a figure that persistently disturbed librarians and their local sponsors—and in mature life they ceased to borrow books of any kind.

Here again the United States was more fortunate. Public libraries had sprung up in most cities and towns following the establishment of the first major tax-supported library, the Boston Public Library, at mid-century. By 1900 most of the states has passed legislation permitting (and in New Hampshire, requiring) the use of tax funds to establish and maintain such facilities, as well as setting up centralized libraries to serve the whole state. In addition to tax revenues, some 36 million dollars in private benefactions (including Carnegie's) had flowed to libraries in the two decades preceding 1900. In that year there were over 1700 free circulating libraries that possessed book stocks of more than 5000 volumes, and the total number of volumes owned by American public libraries was about 47 million, compared with 5 million in Britain.

A comparison of the British and American library situations is incomplete and misleading without mention of the English commercial libraries, which had no really important counterpart in America. During the high Victorian era, Mudie's Select Circulating Library had had a central, indeed crucial, role in supplying books to the middle class. When it declined in prosperity at the turn of the century, its place was taken by a host of cheaper rental- and subscription-libraries, the most famous of which, begun in 1900, were those of Boots, the retail chemist chain. Meanwhile the firm of W. H. Smith and Son, which half a century earlier had taken its stand on railway platforms throughout England, was doing a thriving rental business in addition to selling huge quantities of newspapers, magazines, and cheap books to the traveller. It was reported about 1900 that, of the 50,000 copies initially printed of a new novel by, say, Marie Corelli, no fewer than 10,000 were earmarked for the circulating libraries. These commercial outlets catered to a major portion of the book-borrowing public, which in America, by contrast, tended to rely on municipal libraries.

The fading of Mudie's library was the direct result of a long-overdue event that occurred in 1894: the demise of the expensive three-decker novel, costing more than 30 shillings, whose survival, sustained by the self-interested collaboration of publishers and circulating libraries, had kept the price of all original editions artificially high throughout the century, despite the many successful experiments with cheap reprints that had enlivened British publishing since before Victoria came to the throne. Now, finally, the price of books could (in theory at least) find its natural level. All technical barriers to cheapness had been overcome. Chemistry had made paper far less costly; a series of inventions had made possible the swift setting of type, the mechanized printing, folding, and gathering of sheets, and the quantity prefabrication of casings.

To some extent counterbalancing this tendency toward cheapness, however, were two new developments. One was the increased proportion of the total expense of producing a new book that was devoted to advertising and to paying authors. By 1900 the old system of buying a literary property outright from the author had been almost entirely replaced by the royalty arrangement, which meant that in the case of any moderately successful book, payment to the author continued to be a running charge against profits throughout the book's life instead of being written off, as before, after a relatively short period. Aware, moreover, of the great profits that publishers made with popular books, and stirred (by Sir Walter Besant and his Society of Authors) to demanding what they deemed their fair share of those profits, writers for both book-publishers and periodicals were receiving better pay for their commodity than ever before.

Missing from the Anglo-American publishing scene in 1900, also, was one potent element that throughout the century had kept a certain large category of books in each country artificially cheap, so to speak, and their authors unwarrantedly poor. This was the lack of international copyright, an omission of justice finally remedied in 1891. Because of it, American works had been pirated at will by British publishers, the retail prices being far below those of comparable books that bore British copyrights. American publishers returned the compliment with great enthusiasm and gain. In 1886, for example, Hardy's *The Mayor of Casterbridge* had appeared in seven American editions, only two of which were authorized, ranging in price from one dollar to 20 cents. The books of Robert Louis Stevenson and such individual titles as Mrs Humphry Ward's *Robert Elsmere* (1888) and Haggard's *Cleopatra* (1889), which had at least 10 American editions, were appropriated with similar freedom, the result being so many competing editions that often nobody—author, designated publisher, or pirate—made any money. With the introduction of international copyright, the proportion of American to British works on American publishers' lists sharply increased, with an inverted effect, of course, in Britain. Although the impecunious book-lover who had bought cheap pirated editions was temporarily the loser, the new agreement had the salutary effect of stabilizing a trade hitherto afflicted with cut-throat competition and of making possible the production and sale of equally cheap books on a legitimate basis.

In 1900 the average English price of a novel in its original edition was 6s.—a welcome decline from the old three-decker price of 31s. 6d. Original non-fiction ranged from 7s. 6d. to 21s. Cloth-bound reprints of original fiction cost 2s. 6d. or 3s. 6d., and a wide variety of books by recent or currently popular novelists (Reade, Collins, Hall Caine, Marion Crawford, Clark Russell, William Black, Stevenson) could be bought in paper covers for only 6d. These sold in vast quantities: a sixpenny *Lorna Doone* (1869), for example, had an advance order of 100,000 copies. But even these bargains were not the cheapest books on the market. Non-copyright reprints of older romances and sensational novels were priced at 3d., and below them were abridgments of standard fiction (such as W. T. Stead's Penny Novelist series), more or less complete texts of tales and novels (Newnes' Penny Library of Famous Books), and collections of poetry (Stead's Penny Poets). By 1900, as has been observed elsewhere, "books had become so cheap that seemingly the only step remaining was to give them away. But these paperbacks were a credit to the bookmaker only in a strictly technological sense. Aesthetic appeal and durability had been almost wholly sacrificed to economy." The reader who liked his books to be comely was not overlooked, however. In the mid-1890s J. M. Dent had introduced his Temple Shakespeare, one play per shilling volume, in well-designed, convenient, and durable format. This and the immediately following Temple Classics series were the precursors of the immensely successful and influential Everyman's Library, which began in 1906, and of the World's Classics series, initiated by Grant Richards in 1901 but soon transferred to the Oxford University Press. Such series of classic reprints proved that cheap books could also be physically attractive.

The result of all this activity was that books, whether bound in cloth or in perishable paper, were now familiar objects in hundreds of thousands of British homes that earlier had known only the Bible, perhaps a few tracts or other examples of gratuitously distributed religious literature, and cheap weekly papers. This was the case also in America, where the flood of cheap books had begun in the 1870s, partly as a consequence of providing paperbacks (especially dime novels) for the soldiers in the Civil War. Where England had, for instance, the remarkably prolific and long-lived Railway Library (Routledge), which by 1898 had reprinted 1300 novels in 2s., 1s. 6d., and 1s. formats, the United States had its Lakeside, Fireside, Seaside, Franklin Square, and similar "libraries." Some of these cheap series, such as Street and Smith's Log Cabin series, were composed of old but still-popular dime novels; others, as in England, were reprints of uncopyrighted current literature.

American prices of new books were roughly equivalent to those in Britain. New novels could be bought for $1.00 or $1.25 in cloth and for 50 cents in paper. Serious non-fiction cost somewhat more. Hardbound reprints were about to appear: shortly after 1900, the firm of A. L. Burt was to reprint many copyright editions by arrangement with the original publishers, soon to be followed and surpassed by Grosset and Dunlap, whose first reprinted title, Paul Leicester Ford's *Janice Meredith* (1903), sold several hundred thousand copies after sales of the original edition had begun to decline.

On both sides of the Atlantic, regular bookshops were out-flanked and out-sold by newer agencies of distribution. It is true that the bookselling business has at least as much claim to the sobriquet of "the fabulous invalid" as the Broadway theatre, but about the turn of the century the perennial complaints of retailers had more substance than usual. The multitude of paperback volumes that flowed from the high-speed presses could be bought at stalls operated at every railway station by the great wholesaling and retailing firms, W. H. Smith and Son in Britain, the American News Company in the United States. In addition, British drapers' shops and American department stores sold books at prices below those asked by booksellers. In the former, the buyer could expect a discount of as much as 15 per cent; in the latter, he could benefit not only by the reduced prices of the department stores' "book bazaars" but also by what are now called "tie-in deals": with the purchase of, say, a pair of gloves, he was entitled to buy any book in the store for only 25 cents. The Net Book Agreement negotiated by British publishers and booksellers in 1899 largely (but not entirely) ended price cutting on books bearing a catalogue price of 6s. or more, but it did not affect cheaper publications. In America, a similar arrangement put a stop to discounts on non-fiction books by most department stores (Macy's, the great New York store, continued to offer discounts for many years) but another decade was to pass before fiction was price-fixed.

Americans could also buy books through subscription schemes peddled by door-to-door salesmen. Their portable "lists" included reference works, sets of poets and novelists, and individual titles by such celebrities as Horace Greeley, P. T. Barnum, Henry Ward Beecher, and President Grant (whose memoirs, published and distributed in this fashion by Mark Twain in a short-lived and disastrous venture in get-rich-quick publishing, sold 312,000 in the first 30 months). In the 1890s the subscription book business had an annual volume of 12 million dollars. Publishers specializing in such books were said to turn a cold eye upon any book offered them that could not be depended upon to sell 100,000 copies.

A third means of American book distribution, which in 1900 was said to be as important as that of regular book-shops and subscription selling in a land where only two or three per cent of the people lived near book-shops, was the mail-order service available from every publisher. Thanks to this, and with the aid of the Rural Free Delivery postal routes inaugurated in 1897, books conquered the vast distances that had been one of the chief barriers to the dissemination of culture on the American continent.

Although normally the stream of commercial aggressiveness ran the other way, at the turn of the century it was British publishers who set the Americans an example in advertising and general promotion. The American publishing industry had a long tradition of "respectability" and conservatism. Only toward 1900 had it adopted the policy, cultivated for some years past by the livelier sections of the British trade, of lavish advertising and the use of publicity campaigns specially tailored to sell individual titles for which great hopes were entertained. Once roused from their gentlemanly lethargy, the leading American publishers outdid their British colleagues in promotional activity. In 1900 most houses had an annual advertising budget of $50,000 or more, and one was reported to spend a quarter of a million dollars a year. In 1900 the first full-page newspaper advertisement in trade history started Maurice Thompson's historical novel, *Alice of Old Vincennes*, on its highly prosperous career. If people still did not buy books on the scale publishers dreamed of—though one hears little complaint on that score from the successful firms of the period—it was not for lack of encouragement. Provocative advertising, the hustling salesmanship of department-store book sections, the cajolery of canvassers, the economic attractiveness of premium arrangements such as that which included a free book with every purchase of a quantity of soap (in the mid-1880s the publisher of the Seaside Library had sold 3 million unsold books to soap companies), and the well-publicized presence of mail-order desks within reach of everyone with a postage stamp—all these devices thrust books into the consciousness of every American.

It is only fitting, therefore, that these years should have witnessed the birth of the word "best-seller": an example of language promptly filling an urgent new need. Although the *Dictionary of Americanisms* dates the word only from 1905, it was actually in use as early as 1897, in connection with the list of "the most popular new books" that the New York *Bookman* had been running since its first issue, two years earlier. The periodical's London namesake had been featuring a similar monthly list since it began in 1891. This was, in truth, the great age of the best-seller. Records were set during these years that were to stand for a long time. Between 1900 and 1915 no fewer than 19 books sold over one million copies each in America; in the next 15 years, only three books did so (Edith M. Hull's *The Sheik*, H. G. Wells's *Outline of History*, and Will Durant's *Story of Philosophy*). Nearly all of those 19, in contrast to one of the subsequent three, were fiction. In 1901, six novels sold 150,000 each in the United States, and nine more exceeded 100,000. A book about a shrewd Yankee horse dealer, Edward Noyes Westcott's *David Harum* (1898), had sold more than 400,000 copies by early 1901, and 750,000 by 1904; riding the wave of its popularity, in a pattern often noticed during the period, a novel with a similar appeal, Irving Bacheller's *Eben Holden*, sold 300,000 copies in 1900 between July and Christmas. A sentimental little book set in the Louisville factory slums, Alice Hegan Rice's *Mrs Wiggs of the Cabbage Patch* (1901), was on the best-seller lists for two years, in the course of which the printers had to supply 40,000 copies a month. American historical romances were especially in demand. In 1899 the genre was represented by *Janice Meredith*, which had sold 275,000 copies by the end of 1902, and by Winston Churchill's *Richard Carvel*, whose record was 420,000 copies in two years; in 1900 Mary Johnston's *To Have and To Hold* sold 200,000 copies within two months of publication.

Such novels, of course, appealed principally to American tastes. But otherwise, the colour of English and American best-seller lists in this epoch was strikingly homogeneous. The historical romance with an American setting was merely one variety of a larger genre that dominated popular literature for at least a decade: the romance of sword-play and high adventure, whether set in historical times or with a contemporary but exotic setting, or having its *mise en scène* in a fictitious realm (such as George Barr McCutcheon's Graustark). Authors such as Rider Haggard, Anthony Hope, Stanley Weyman, and F. Marion Crawford—three Britons, one American—won success after writing this kind of fiction. One particular type of historical novel that was equally popular in both countries was that set in early Christian times, preferably the decadent age of Nero, when religion could be mixed with a faint suggestion of sex—a sure-fire formula for a best-seller then as (occasionally) now. In the wake of Henryk Sienkiewicz's *Quo Vadis?*, which had swept the Anglo-American world in the mid-1890s, came such hits as Hall Caine's *The Eternal City* (1901), which had an American first printing of 200,000 copies, and *The Christian*, which sold 50,000 in the first month of English publication; and Marie Corelli's *The Master Christian* (1900), which had a pre-publication printing of 75,000—the largest on record, according to its London publishers.

Tastes in these "fat years of fiction," as they were later to be called, were nothing if not catholic. For a while there was a vogue for *Gemütlichkeit* of the "kailyard school" exemplified by J. M. Barrie's *Auld Licht Idylls* (1888) and *A Window in Thrums* (1889) and by "Ian Maclaren's" *Beside the Bonnie Brier Bush* (1894), which, assisted (as was Barrie's *The Little Minister*) by a defective copyright, sold nearly one million copies in America in a few years. If a reader preferred contemporary theological quandaries wrapped up in fiction, he could select *Robert Elsmere*, whose success in America was even greater than in England; or if he wanted religion tinged with social criticism there was the Rev. Charles M. Sheldon's *In His Steps*, a moral romance that first appeared, without benefit of copyright, in a denominational paper in Topeka, Kansas, was quickly discovered by 10 publishers, and ultimately sold (according to conservative estimates) a world total of 6 million copies, one third of them in the United States.

Notwithstanding the impression conveyed by these sample sales figures, which certify beyond a doubt that more people were buying more books than ever before, it remains true that in both Britain and America the majority of literate men and women, whether by choice or by necessity, never opened a book. Their experience of print, and therefore, in those pre-cinema, pre-radio, pre-television days, their only experience of the world beyond the narrow sphere of their daily lives, was confined to magazines and newspapers. In Britain, where experiments in suiting periodicals to the tastes and capacities of the semi-literate masses had been going on ever since the 1830s, dramatic breakthroughs occurred in the last years of the century. Among them, the three titans of late-Victorian journalism, George Newnes (*Tit-Bits*, 1881), Alfred Harmsworth (*Answers to Correspondents*, 1888), and Cyril Pearson (*Pearson's Weekly*, 1890), developed a formula of anecdotes, jokes, excerpts, riddles—everything simple, nothing profound, something for everyone, and no long attention-span required—that won millions of new readers who lacked the education, the intellectual interest, the time, or the money to read anything more substantial. By the end of the 1890s, each of these magazines was selling between 400,000 and 600,000 copies a week, and a prize contest—a much-employed circulation-building device in the journalism of this fiercely competitive epoch—once sent *Pearson's Weekly* sales up to a million and a quarter. On a somewhat higher level, meanwhile, the most popular magazines—the *Strand*, *Windsor*, and *Pearson's*, priced at between 3*d*. and 6*d*.—had circulations of between 200,000 and 400,000. But even these unprecedented figures were soon surpassed by newcomers: in 1898 *Harmsworth's Magazine* started at 500,000 and approached one million, and in the same year Pearson's *Royal Magazine* started at one million and immediately trained its sights on a second. In addition to its nice balance of fiction and deftly written topical articles, this class of periodicals exploited the newly perfected technique of photo-engraving, which, by replacing the expensive and laborious woodcut with the cheap half-tone, permitted a freer and more flexible use of illustrations. In 1890 there had been five illustrated papers on the English bookstalls; in 1899 there were 13.

Similar prosperity visited other segments of this feverishly expanding mass journalism. Women and children, if not the prime targets, were certainly not neglected. *Woman's Life*, a Newnes inspiration, sold 200,000 copies a week in 1896; in the same field, competing with a more or less standard assortment of fiction, needlework patterns, domestic hints, and fragments of easily assimilable general information, were such papers as *Home Chat*, *Our Home*, *The Happy Home*, and *Home Notes*. For the factory girl there was *Forget-Me-Not*, and for the errand boy, *Chips*; Harmsworth, whose properties these were, had a special Midas touch with papers for the child and adolescent. Building energetically on the foundations laid long before by Reynolds and Lloyd, the early Victorian penny-dreadful magnates, he established or revived during the 1890s a whole galaxy of sensational fiction papers for boys—*Union Jack*, the *Halfpenny Wonder*, the *Halfpenny Marvel*, and the *Boys' Friend*—some of which flourished as late as World War II. Only a few older juvenile papers, notably the Religious Tract Society's *Boy's Own Paper*, survived their keen competition. It was Harmsworth's periodicals, after all, not the more decorous Tract Society's, that year after year featured the detective hero Sexton Blake.

The same ferment and spectacular expansion characterized the American magazine world, which had long profited by the lack of an international copyright law, by an efficient and cheap postal system, and by its ability to command the nation's best writing and editorial talent. The inventive editors of Fleet Street had their counterparts in such figures as S. S. McClure and Edward Bok, a young Dutch immigrant whose innovations (among them a zeal for public-spirited crusades on behalf of causes especially meaningful to the housewife and mother) made his *Ladies' Home Journal* the most popular of all the magazines for the middle-class American home. Priced at 10 cents, the *Journal* was typical of the meaty, well-illustrated general periodicals—*McClure's*, *Munsey's*, and *Cosmopolitan* were others—that gave better value for the money than had their predecessors selling for 25 or 30 cents a copy. The audience discovered and served by these magazines—a substantial part of whose success was due to their use of timely articles and short stories in place of the polite essays and travel sketches that had been the staple of their genteel forebears—was immense. In 1885, the only four American magazines with circulations of over 100,000 had sold an aggregate of 600,000 a month; by 1905, there were five times as many, and their total sale was more than 5,500,000 copies. One by one, the chief mass periodicals had arrived at circulations of over half a million: the *Ladies' Home Journal* in 1891, the *Youth's Companion* about 1894, the *Delineator* in 1895, *Munsey's* in 1897. In 1903 the *Ladies' Home Journal* was to pass one million. As in Britain, such records were achieved not only through the expert selection, editing, and arrangement of the magazines' contents, but also by constant advertising and schemes of rewards by which readers who collected groups of new subscriptions were entitled to premiums such as books, sewing machines, jewellery, clothing, and portfolios of views of the Chicago Columbian Exposition.

Meanwhile, certain older institutions continued to flourish. One was the weekly story paper, exemplified in Britain by the *Family Herald*, which had been among the first in the field and was still bought by countless maidservants, and in America by Beadle's *Banner Weekly* and George Munro's *Fireside Companion*. Another was the weekly novelette, complete in one issue, with an indispensable picture of dramatic action on the front page to attract the purchaser's eye. In Britain the Heartsease Library, the Duchess Novelettes, Horner's Penny Stories, and others sold huge quantities of tales with titles such as *The Voice of Blood*, *The Kiss of Judas*, *The Bracelet of Death*, *Betrayed at the Altar*, *Betrothed to a Brigand*, and *The Phantom Boatman*. These, presumably, were the kind of papers favoured by the barmaid of William Ernest Henley's sonnet, who "tries / From penny novels to amend her taste."

However mightily they prospered at the turn of the century, these were instruments of mass culture that looked backward rather than forward, and the future belonged to the innovators. While Newnes and Bok and their rivals were transforming their respective nations' weekly papers and magazines, the Harmsworths and the Pulitzers were presiding over a concurrent revolution in daily journalism. The technique of presenting the news—or the most vivid items of news—in short, snappy form, with frequent sub-headings and other editorial and typographical aids to easy reading, was mastered. "Scoops," sensational crusades, signed articles, and interviews proved time and again to sell more papers. Politics, the chief concern of the established dailies, had given way to entertainment, sport, and crime news—hitherto generally the special province of the Sunday press—in the halfpenny evening papers (the *Star*, the *Echo*, the *Evening News*) of the late 1880s. But the big break with the past came in 1896 with the establishment of the *Daily Mail*, the first halfpenny morning paper. Launched, typically, with an extravagant publicity campaign, Harmsworth's paper—"written by office-boys for office-boys," as Lord Salisbury observed—quickly eclipsed all existing circulation records. Figures of 1901 eloquently tell the story: the *Times* (3*d.*) sold 37,900 copies a day, the *Manchester Guardian* (1*d.*) sold 44,300, and the *Daily Mail* ($\frac{1}{2}$*d.*) sold 836,000. The day of the press lords, building journalistic empires with the coppers of millions of readers, had arrived. There could have been no more pregnant symbol of this revolution in journalism—the new domination of mass-circulation papers over the old-established, august journals of opinion—than Harmsworth's (by now Lord Northcliffe's) saving of the ailing *Times* from extinction, in 1908, with the profits from the *Daily Mail*.

In the United States, as in Britain, newspaper proprietors and editors fought to increase circulation, not for the sake of the money brought in by actual sales but to attract the more profitable custom of advertisers.

Advertising, instead of being merely a welcome incidental source of revenue, became the very life-blood of modern journalism as viewed from the increasingly potent business office. W. T. Stead's campaigns in Britain for social and political reform (motivated, it is true, as much by altruism as by the hope of increased sales—which did not materialize) were matched in America by those of Joseph Pulitzer, whose transformation of the moribund *New York World* into a paper with a circulation of one million copies by 1898 marked the birth of modern American journalism. The *Daily Mail*'s violent xenophobia, served by carefree doctoring of the news to suit the paper's policy, stirred aggressive British feelings against the Transvaal, and during the Boer War that ensued the paper's circulation rose to almost one million. At almost the same moment, the American William Randolph Hearst, in similarly reckless fashion, propelled his nation into a circulation-boosting war with Spain. The yellow press had acquired the fearsome power of committing a whole people to war.

One American newspaper development, however, did not have its ready analogue in Great Britain. Faced with the competition of the new cheap general magazines, with their brightly written topical articles and pictures, newspapers turned more and more to the production of Sunday supplements, whose *mélange* of "fact, fiction, fun and folly," as the historian Arthur Schlesinger Sr once put it, rivalled that of the magazines. In 1890 there had been about 400 Sunday papers, two thirds of which were Sunday editions of dailies; in 1900 there were 639. In Britain the somewhat increased topicality of the general magazines neither reflected nor spurred any noteworthy expansion of the scope of the Sunday papers— among them *Reynolds' News, Lloyd's Weekly News*, the *News of the World*, and the *Weekly Dispatch*, veterans of more than 60 years' service to the working-man's sabbath—which remained dedicated for the most part to their traditional fare of sensation, scandal, sport, and radical politics.

Quietly persisting in the midst of the hurly-burly of cheap best-sellers and mass-circulation newspapers and magazines was the small but discriminating reading audience of the élite. Far more influential in proportion to its size than it would sometimes concede itself to be, it provided a steady and critical body of readers for the work of those gifted contemporary writers who had neither the skill nor the luck (nor, possibly, the desire) to attract the vast new public. In a world of mass readership, the literary establishment was at pains to uphold critical standards, to condemn not only the cynical greed of the commercial interests that provided the masses with their reading matter but also what seemed to them the irremediably crude tastes of working-class readers.

There is, of course, another side to the picture. In the time-scale of cultural movements, England and America acquired a mass reading public almost overnight. For the first time, millions of people in both countries had both the ability and the leisure to read; it was naive to have expected the newly literate to emerge with highly developed critical standards. To some extent, at least, public taste is formed by the quality of the material that is most readily available or most persuasively offered. With the sudden increase in literacy, reading matter became a commodity that could be sold on an industrial scale, and commercial interests responded with the undiscriminating zeal that mass marketing of almost any commodity demands.

The acute problem faced by a society that has acquired more leisure than it is readily equipped to use in any profitable way is not a new one. Its existence was recognized a century ago, not only by thoughtful social observers but even by American presidents not ordinarily given to cultural analysis or prophecy. Addressing the educational summer school at Chautauqua in 1880, James A. Garfield observed that "We may divide the whole struggle of the human race into two chapters: first, the fight to get leisure; and then the second fight of civilization—what we shall do with our leisure when we get it." The place of the printed word in that leisure remains unsettled, as disturbing to the guardians of quality in our own day as it was in Garfield's.

CHAPTER 21

Drama as Social Criticism: Ibsen, Shaw, and Brecht

Eric Bentley*

Matthew Arnold expected from poets in general a "criticism of life," and many today would not only agree but would add that this criticism should be a social one. Some will even argue that it *must* be a social one, because literature, in their view, is by nature social. Society, that is, can be regarded as providing both the source and the substance of literature. It can also be maintained that to communicate a thought to another person—even more, to a group of other persons—is to socialize it.

As for the drama, it has often been regarded as, in several senses, yet more social than other kinds of literature. In sense one, the theatre appeals most strongly and helpfully *to* society:

> The theatre is the most potent and direct means of strengthening human reason and enlightening the whole nation.[1]

In sense two, the theatre has an especially close connection with the social conditions of the moment:

> No portion of literature is connected by closer or more numerous ties with the present condition of society than the drama.[2]

In sense three, drama is pre-eminently the genre in which what is currently the characteristic type of relation of man to man is represented:

> Thus investigation as to which type of man is suited to dramatic art coincides with the investigation of the problem of man's relation to other men.[3]

* Former Brander Matthews Professor of Dramatic Literature, Columbia University; former Charles Eliot Norton Professor of Poetry, Harvard University.

Finally, drama since Ibsen has frequently been regarded as even more social than earlier drama, as peculiarly concerned with social problems: a thesis that can best be documented in the lives of the three dramatists to be commented on here.

Although Henrik Ibsen would seem to us today to have been concerned with modern social problems from the very beginning, he did not seem so in his early works to the leading Scandinavian critic of the time, Georg Brandes, who criticized *Brand* (1865) as reactionary and read the playwright (as well as the rest of the world) this lesson:

> What keeps a literature alive in our day is that it submits problems for debate. Thus, for example, George Sand debates the problem of the relations between the sexes, Byron and Feuerbach religion, John Stuart Mill and Proudhon property, Turgenev, Spielhagen, and Emile Augier social conditions. . . .[4]

To which Ibsen replied: ". . . your work is a great, shattering, and emancipating outbreak of genius," and: "what cannot withstand the ideas of the times must succumb." Undoubtedly Brandes' writings, which, as Ibsen said, disturbed his sleep, also led him toward his great "modern period." Some 15 years after Brandes' Inaugural Lecture, Ibsen's plays disturbed the sleep of George Bernard Shaw and led him to modernism and to the theatre. In 1886 he took the part of Krogstad in a reading of *A Doll's House* (1879) staged by Karl Marx's daughter Eleanor. In 1890 he gave a Fabian lecture about that play. In the next year appeared the first book on Ibsen in English: Shaw's *Quintessence of Ibsenism*. One year later Shaw's first play, *Widowers' Houses*, was ready. "It deals," Shaw said in a preface, "with a burning social question, and is deliberately intended to induce people to vote on the Progressive side at the next County Council election in London." It will be noted that Shaw is pushing the idea of problem literature further than Brandes had. Not debate now, but political pressure, though on a local, municipal scale. The scale would be enlarged later. In May 1895 a magazine called *The Humanitarian* asked a number of public men to answer the question: "Should social problems be freely dealt with in the drama?" Shaw answered:

> We are . . . witnessing a steady intensification in the hold of social questions on the larger poetic imagination. . . . If people are rotting and starving in all directions, and nobody else has the heart or brains to make a disturbance about it, the great writers must. In short, what is forcing our poets to follow Shelley in becoming political and social agitators, and to turn the theatre into a platform for propaganda

and an arena for discussion, is that whilst social questions are being thrown up for solution almost daily by the fierce rapidity with which industrial processes change and supersede one another . . . the political machinery by which alone our institutions can be kept abreast of these changes is so old-fashioned . . . that social questions never get solved until the pressure becomes so desperate that even governments recognize the necessity for moving. And to bring the pressure to this point, the poets must lend a hand. . . .

Shaw pushed the idea of problem drama further than Ibsen, but Bertolt Brecht pushed it further than Shaw. The changes correspond, of course, to stages of history—and of disillusionment. In 1871 there still seemed time for debate. In the 1890s it still seemed worthwhile to put pressure on governments, local and national. All Brecht's playwriting came after the definitive collapse of 19th-century civilization in World War I. By that token, it also came after a crucial attempt to build a new civilization by means other than parliamentary debate and propagandist pressure, namely, by revolution. The question that arose now was whether the theatre could be of any use at all. Could the modern world even be portrayed in it? Brecht answered that it could, if it was portrayed as alterable. And for him, to portray it as alterable was to help to alter it, beginning with an alteration of the means of portrayal, an alteration of the theatre itself:

> . . . half a century's experiments . . . had won the theatre brand new fields of subject matter and types of problem, and made it a factor of marked social importance. At the same time they had brought the theatre to a point where any further development of the intellectual, social (political) experience must wreck the artistic experience.[5]

> . . . *The Mother* is a piece of anti-metaphysical, materialistic, non-Aristotelian drama. This makes nothing like such a free use as the Aristotelian theatre does of the passive empathy of the spectator; it also relates differently to certain psychological effects, such as catharsis. Just as it refrains from handing its hero over to the world as if it were his inescapable fate, so it would not dream of handing over the spectator to an inspiring theatrical experience. Anxious to teach the spectator a quite different practical attitude, directed towards changing the world, it must begin by making him adopt in the theatre a quite different attitude from what he is used to.[6]

By means of a new kind of theatre, Brecht would work on audiences in a new way and, by changing them, would help to change the world.

So far, so good. These quotations from our three authors are unequivocal, and suggest accurately enough three clear phases of recent history. What they hardly begin to suggest is the actual tenor of the three writers' creative work. I have only been citing, really, the official stance of each man: the quotations are all from theoretical works, not from plays. If one wanted to document from actual theatre what has been cited here as principle, it would be easier to document the Brandes-Ibsen position from plays by Alexandre Dumas *fils*; the Shaw position from plays by Eugène Brieux; and the Brecht position either from Erwin Piscator's production experiments or from Brecht plays that most critics would regard as his weakest efforts. Here, for example, are the first and last speeches of Brieux's *Les avariés* (1901; Damaged Goods) cited in the translation (1909) for which Shaw wrote a preface:

> I. Before the play begins, the manager appears upon the stage and says:
> Ladies and Gentlemen, I beg leave to inform you, on behalf of the author and of the management, that the object of this play is a study of the disease of syphilis in its bearing on marriage.

> II. DOCTOR: This poor girl is typical. The whole problem is summed up in her: she is at once the product and the cause. We set the ball rolling, others keep it up, and it runs back to bruise our own shins. I have nothing more to say. [*He shakes hands with Loches as he conducts him to the door, and adds in a lighter tone*] But if you give a thought or two to what you have just seen when you are sitting in the Chamber [of Deputies], we shall not have wasted our time.

These passages correspond exactly to the young Shaw's belief that drama should put pressure on the people's parliamentary representatives. The significant thing is that no such passages occur in any play by Shaw. Even if they did, we could be sure that they would have an entirely different tone. Even where the theoretical remarks of our three authors are consistent with their respective practice, they really give no idea what that practice is. Were the plays to disappear and the prefatory remarks to survive, posterity would receive a wholly misleading impression of what the plays had been like. This ought not to amaze us: an author's official positions are one thing; his creative achievements are another. It is minor authors who make movements and are content to exemplify their principles. Major authors may start movements or join them, but they do not become submerged in them. To read Zola's proclamations, you would gather that novel-writing was a science, and that once you had mastered the latest teaching on heredity and environment you could put a novel together. Perhaps. But it would not be a Zola novel, which is a remarkably "unscientific" work, compounded of Gothic imagination, great human warmth, and even a macabre sense of humour. . . .

It need not be argued that Ibsen, Shaw, and Brecht are *not* social dramatists, only that the definition of the word *social* may need enlargement if it is to fit them, and that, in any case, each must be regarded not as a member of a school or as an example of a trend, but as an individual genius, making his own peculiar and wondrous explorations. Although all three have had imitators, the results do not show that any of the qualities for which we value them are imitable. Their criticisms of social phenomena may not be unique in the form in which we can abstract them from the work, but they *are* unique in the emphasis and colour given to them in the setting of the work. Which is why it is to that setting that we must pursue them.

"The object of this play is a study of the disease of syphilis in its bearing on marriage." Nine out of 10 students, questioned about this sentence, would guess that it referred to Ibsen's *Ghosts* (1881). Captain Alving had syphilis, and as a result his son Oswald becomes an idiot in front of our eyes. Brieux would use this story as a pretext for urging us to take all possible measures to combat venereal disease. We get no hint as to whether Ibsen would urge anything of this kind. What is *his* interest in the story? To be sure, Oswald's collapse is the central happening. But what does Ibsen do with it?

The question can be answered only in terms of the whole play, a fact that is in itself significant and, as it turns out, a tribute to Ibsen's genius. Oswald is an Orestes for whom the Furies (Erinyes) do not turn into Wellwishers (Eumenides) in accord with a poet's desire to affirm life and, by implication, the phase of life that his culture is passing through. He is irreclaimably doomed by "ghosts." Ibsen generally knew what he was doing, and never more so than in his choice of title for this play. Not *The House of Alving*, not *Mrs Alving*, not *Oswald*, although any of these titles would have been in the classical tradition. Rather, he chose a title in the tradition of *The Eumenides* and *The Bacchae*. In ancient literature these are unusual titles because they stress extra-human forces normally left in the background. Such forces come into the foreground at certain crises of history: Aeschylus celebrated the creation of the democratic city-state; Euripides pronounced a doom upon the whole Hellenic experiment. (I leave aside the question of how far back in history the accepted titles of Greek plays go. Suffice it here that they *are* the accepted titles.) Ibsen is a Euripidean playwright dramatizing the crisis of middle-class culture in his own day and somewhat beyond. Accordingly, his "ghosts" are neither furies nor bacchantes. What they *are* is very precisely, though complexly, worked out. To begin with, they are ghosts in the most ordinary sense, that of superstition. Overheard in the next room by Mrs Alving, Oswald and Regina sound like the ghosts (*revenants*, returned spirits, spooks) of Captain Alving and Regina's mother. *Sound like*—the word "ghosts" is in the first instance a simile. In the second, it is a metaphor.

Captain Alving's legacy of disease: this is how syphilis enters into Ibsen's scheme of things. But it is not where he leaves his presentation of ghosts. They are more than superstition, and more than physiology. They are cultural and social: they are a matter of the characters' beliefs and attitudes, their decisive and therefore dramatic beliefs and attitudes.

When Mrs Alving hears the "ghosts" in the next room, she is brought that much nearer to telling Oswald what she (at that point) believes to be the whole truth about his father. The simile drives her to explain the metaphor. And that would be where a conventional 19th-century play would have ended. But Ibsen's last and greatest act is still to come. In the process of telling this truth, Mrs Alving finds that it is not the whole truth. Under the traumatic influence of those events or discoveries that are Ibsen's plot, she finds herself telling a different story and realizing a different truth: that not only Alving, but she herself, was responsible for the *débâcle*. For she was a victim of the third kind of ghost, the ideological ghost. When she had tried, as a young wife, to flee from her husband to Parson Manders, who loved her, Manders had turned her away from the door, and she had consented to be turned away and to return to Alving. Not all the reading she then did in modern literature could erase the facts of her non-modern actions. In her phantasy life, she wants liberation from bourgeois culture. In actuality, she cannot defy the marriage laws; cannot contemplate the incestuous union of her son with his half-sister; cannot practise mercy killing.

Corresponding to this double twist whereby Mrs Alving's narrative turns from husband-denunciation to self-discovery, there is duality, too, in the main narrative line. Oswald's collapse, it has been ventured, is the central happening. One could even say it is the *only* thing that happens on this stage, and that once it *has* happened the play is over— the play of the superstition simile and the physiological metaphor. But this is to overlook the happenings within the breast of Mrs Alving. *Ghosts*, finally, is the story of Oswald *as witnessed by his mother*. The final effect is the effect upon her. She is the on-stage audience: such has been her fate from the beginning. What she now does, or fails to do, with her son, she had previously done, or failed to do, with her husband: she reduces herself to the position of helpless, agonized onlooker. Oswald's paralysis—physical, unaccompanied by suffering, and exceptional—is as nothing to hers as she stands there holding the lethal pills and not using them: with a life still to live, in unbearable agony, and typical of a whole class of people, a whole phase of history. At this point we see how different from furies or bacchantes, and how much more modern, Ibsenian ghosts are. Pale as they are by comparison, they are far more negative because they have no possibility of being transformed into Eumenides. They are inertia, where what is needed is movement. They are regression, where what is called for is progress. They are imprisonment and death, where what is "desired" is liberation and life. (I put the word "desired" in quotation marks because the authenticity of the desire is in question.) In the situation depicted, hope is mere cultured phantasy and modish liberalism. Wherever the seeds of life are shown to be still faintly alive, as in Oswald's hankering after joy *and after his half-sister*, they are precipitately, hysterically exterminated by Ibsen's enlightened abortionists.

It is tempting to call Ibsen the most ironical dramatist since Sophocles; for him, nothing that glitters is gold. Now such irony is not interesting if it merely has the impact of a trick or mannerism. It is interesting only (a) if it seems the author's authentic mode of vision, and (b) if it succeeds in redefining the author's subject for us. To establish that it is indeed Ibsen's authentic mode of vision, one can only refer people to his work. On the redefinition of subject, one might cite yet again the notion of ghosts. Those who have noticed that Ibsen's ghosts are not furies have perhaps not noticed that they are also not a curse rooted in real crimes (as in Greek drama and the mythology on which it is based), or in original sin (as in much Christian literature down to, say, T. S. Eliot's *Family Reunion*, based as it is on the Orestes legend). In *Ghosts*, there is a clear reference to the Old Testament idea of the sins of the fathers being visited upon the children, yet it would be disingenuous to cite this idea without noting that Ibsen exactly inverts it. The idea that emerges from *Ghosts* is that what Alving did was not sin after all, but was the unfortunate result of his legitimate joy in life. Can we conclude then that Mrs Alving was the sinner? Not that either. What was wrong was that she *believed* that Alving had sinned. What was wrong was what gave her this belief: her education, her culture, her background, her epoch, and her class—in a word, her society.

Here we have the deeper sense in which Ibsen's drama may truly be called social. Not to harp too long on one string, it can equally well be illustrated from *Hedda Gabler* (1890). One need only cite the ending. Hedda shoots herself to avoid being in Judge Brack's power. But Brack himself indicated that she had other alternatives. The relevant passage is worth quoting at some length. Brack knows that Løvborg shot himself with Hedda's pistol.

> BRACK: No, the police have it.
>
> HEDDA: What will the police do with the pistol?
>
> BRACK: Search till they find the owner.
>
> HEDDA: Do you think they will succeed?
>
> BRACK [*bending over her and whispering*]: No, Hedda Gabler, not so long as I keep silent.
>
> HEDDA [*looking askance at him*]: And if you do not keep silent, what then?
>
> BRACK [*shrugging his shoulders*]: One could always declare the pistol was stolen.
>
> HEDDA [*firmly*]: It would be better to die.
>
> BRACK [*smiling*]: One says such things; one doesn't do them.
>
> HEDDA [*without answering*]: And if the pistol were not stolen and the police find the owner, what then?
>
> BRACK: Well, Hedda, then, think of the scandal.
>
> HEDDA: The scandal?
>
> BRACK: The scandal, yes, which you are terrified of. You'd naturally have to appear in court, both you and Mademoiselle Diana. She would have to explain how the thing happened, whether it was accident or murder. Did he threaten to shoot her, and did the pistol go off then, or did she grab the pistol, shoot him, afterwards putting it back into his pocket? She might have done that, for she is a hefty woman, this—Mademoiselle Diana.
>
> HEDDA: What have I to do with all this repulsive business?
>
> BRACK: Nothing. But you will have to answer the question: why did you give Løvborg the pistol? And what conclusion will people draw from the fact that you did give it to him?
>
> HEDDA [*dropping her head*]: That is true. I didn't think of that.
>
> BRACK: Well, fortunately, there is no danger as long as I keep silent.
>
> HEDDA [*looking up at him*]: That means you have me in your power. . . .
>
> BRACK [*whispering softly*]: Dearest Hedda, believe me, I shall not abuse the position.
>
> HEDDA: In your power, all the same. At the mercy of your will and demands. And so a slave! [*Getting up impatiently*] No! I won't endure that thought, never!
>
> BRACK [*looking at her half mockingly*]: People manage to get used to the inevitable.

Why could Hedda not tell the police the pistol had been stolen, as Brack suggested? In her own mind, the answer is that she could not tell such a lie. Why not, considering that she is quite a fluent liar? Because this lie would hurt her image of herself as an aristocrat. It would be petty. Hara-kiri would be indicated. Nonsense, says Brack, such suicides have been abolished by bourgeois respectability. In any event, Brack is toying with Hedda. He himself would no doubt publicly deny that the pistol was stolen. He moves on to his principal threat. Unless he keeps his peace, there will be a scandal. What is a scandal? It is not wrongdoing itself: Løvborg is not being accused of iniquity and, if Mademoiselle Diana shot him, it was in self-defence. Hedda's response is all the more ironic because *she* really is the sinner in this whole affair. It is not sin or wrong-doing that Hedda finds repellent, but talk about it, being talked about, having her "name dragged through the mud." True, she will be accused of a wrong, placing a pistol in the hands of an unbalanced man, but to most people the man would remain the responsible party. She will be just a dubious character who was implicated—an object of scandal. In short, she will have a bad reputation.

Reputation is the social value *par excellence*. It is the equivalent of credit in financial matters: if people think you have it, you have it, for it is only what people think that counts. If, therefore, "people"—that is, a given social system—are given a positive valuation by the dramatist, then reputation will also be seen positively. It will be seen as honour and, despite its basis in opinion, will be regarded as the rock on which civilization rests, as it is in the classic drama of Spain. Now Hedda, as a character, has some vestige of feeling for genuine honour. This is one component of her statement that rather than lie she would kill herself. And it is a component of her actual suicide. It is seen in a corrupted, sick form in her phantasies of a heroic death for Løvborg, and it is because *he* didn't "do it beautifully" that *she* has to do it beautifully. What, then, prevents her suicide from being truly beautiful? The fact that it is only a transcendence in one aspect while being mainly an evasion of responsibility, an enactment of defeat, the expression of a simple death wish. Hedda has vaguely wished for death from the outset and accordingly was shown toying with her pistols in the first scene. Now she finds the energy to use them in what had all along been the "logical" way. Prodded by fear: and not of God, but of scandal; not of wrong, but of talk about wrong and about her.

"One says such things; one doesn't do them." "People manage to get used to the inevitable." "People don't do such things." So says Judge Brack in the last couple of minutes of the play. The idea was stated earlier by Hedda herself, when Mrs Elvsted spoke of the shadow of a woman standing between herself and Løvborg. (We sense that it is Hedda herself.)

> HEDDA: Has he told you anything about her?
> MRS ELVSTED: He spoke of her once—vaguely.
> HEDDA: What did he say?

> MRS ELVSTED: He said that when they parted she threatened to shoot him.
>
> HEDDA [*with cold composure*]: What nonsense! No one does that sort of thing here.

"Here" is bourgeois society, Brack's society. Brack's calculations are exactly as dependable as the social order itself. In this society, a woman will take an uncongenial lover, and even let a man have a blackmailer's power over her, rather than create a scandal. Brack does not misunderstand the social system, except in assuming that it has completely assimilated everyone. He is fooled by a vestige of aristocracy, however decadent, in Hedda. Adultery would have been all right. As for dishonour, if she had been Hedda Tesman through and through, even in this there would have been no problem. But she was Hedda Gabler, the general's daughter.

If the play had been written, not by Ibsen, but by Judge Brack, or even by an enemy of Brack who belonged to Brack's milieu—that is, by someone who lived wholly within the bourgeois scheme of things—then it would have been social drama on a familiar pattern, and would have ended with Hedda as Brack's mistress and victim. The "social drama" of Ibsen gains another dimension from his own ending and all that goes with it. Because the values of his society are not the values of the play, but only the rejected values *in* the play, the vision of the whole is a much broader one. In other words, Ibsen presupposes alternatives to his society.

One need not be surprised that he has generally been regarded as a pessimist. Clearly, his spirit, like the spirit of tragic artists in the past, is shot through with a sense of *curse* and *doom*—a curse upon the life he sees around him, the doom of his fellow-men and the form of non-community they have wrought. That the Judge Bracks in his audience find him totally negative is entirely correct from where they sit, and not entirely incorrect from where anyone else sits, because Ibsen put down on paper what he saw, not what he would have liked to see. Nonetheless, what he would have liked to see is present as something more than a phantasy of the impossible. The "ghosts" that in fact doom Mrs Alving, and the fear of scandal that in fact dooms Hedda Gabler, are not divine or diabolical, nor do they partake of any necessity other than the historical— which is to say, they are necessary only for a time. They have their day and cease to be. They become unnecessary.

Napoleon said: "Politics is fate." The view that permeates the modern epoch after Napoleon is that *history* is fate, and although history has been seen in various ways, there is one characteristically modern way: history as evolution. This implies a possible, if not an inevitable, progression. That Ibsen was captivated by this vision is very explicit in his letters and speeches, and was dramatized in an early play, *Emperor and Galilean* (1873), which as an older man he still made a point of endorsing (in an after-dinner speech in Stockholm, 1887). Now, because drama deals with collisions, it may be natural that what preoccupied the playwrights, when they were inspired by the modern historical outlook, was a single factor: the collision of two epochs. Friedrich Hebbel stressed this in the 1840s. Ibsen wrote of Brandes' Inaugural Lecture of 1871 (already cited):

> No more dangerous book could fall into the hands of a pregnant writer. It is one of those works which place a yawning gap between yesterday and today. . . . What will be the outcome of this mortal combat between two epochs I do not know, but anything rather than the existing state of affairs, say I.

Emperor and Galilean presents the clash of the pagan and Christian epochs. Christianity wins, but is not seen by the young (or old) Ibsen as the solution. As a guideline for such positive solutions as may be worked for, there hovers the vision of a Third Kingdom. So in the modern plays of Ibsen, there is a break with the past, but it is not a liberation from the past: for that we must wait long after the fall of the final curtain. Even some final curtains that at first seem optimistic prove not to be so under further examination. *Little Eyolf* (1894) is a clear instance, and *When We Dead Awaken* (1899) a more debatable one. Ibsen had no optimism about optimists: he depicts them as weaklings (Rosmer being the classic case) who fall headlong into pessimism. And optimism is probably not the best word to describe the positive conviction that underlies the critical thought and negative emotion of Ibsen himself. One can only say he withstands the luxury of pessimism; shows the evils depicted to be unnecessary; and therefore entitles us to retain an irreducible minimum of hope—not of Heaven, and not for oneself alone, but for human society, for civilization.

Ibsen made tragedy modern by infusing it with his sense that society is fate. In comedy, society has always been fate; and Ibsen can also be seen as fusing the tragic and comic traditions in his own essentially tragi-comic vision. But the "society" of older comedy had been as immutable as the fate of older tragedy. Shaw and Brecht followed Ibsen in presenting an evolving, historical fate, of which the theatrical form might best be expressed in some words by Chekhov: "You live badly, my friends. It is shameful to live like that." For people do not have to live like that. It need not be necessary for people to live like that.

But how will it come about that they *won't* live like that? Shaw's simplest (but by no means only) answer is that he will talk them out of it. "I write plays with the deliberate object of converting the nation to my opinion. . ." (Preface to *Blanco Posnet*). And Shaw was also inclined to see Ibsen as engaged in that kind of effort. As he says in the same preface: "Every one of Ibsen's plays is a deliberate act of war on society as at present constituted. . . . [Ibsen undertook] a task of no less magnitude than changing the mind of Europe with a view to changing its morals." Brecht once said that for Shaw a man's most precious possession was his opinions, and it should be added that part of Shaw remained ever hopeful of robbing people of their most precious possession, offering them his own by way of reparation. Behind Shaw's remarks in this vein is the Victorian liberal tradition that sees culture as the final locus of free trade. Presupposed are open ears and sympathetic souls. Not presupposed are conflicts of interest along class lines or "false consciousness" as a mode of intelligently deceiving oneself. Shaw himself learned to be highly critical of this liberalism, but it played a part in putting together his own conception of a drama in which all characters can genuinely claim to have something to offer. "They are all right from their several points of view; and their points of view are, for the dramatic moment, mine also. This may puzzle the people who believe there is such a thing as an absolutely right point of view . . . nobody who agrees with them can possibly be a dramatist . . ." (Epistle Dedicatory to *Man and Superman*). One need not be scornful of Shaw's wish to "convert the nation." During the first half of the 20th century the English nation was converted to many socialistic ideas, and Shaw could take some credit for this. But another conception of drama is implicit in this description of the several points of view that all embody part of the truth. Also there is hyperbole as well as humour in the idea that the whole nation was Shaw's audience. In fact, his plays were addressed to the educated bourgeoisie of all nations and were about that class, whether his characters wore tailcoat or toga, pinstripe trousers or doublet and hose. Shaw came to manhood in the century of the second great wave of *philosophes*, and, with the others, he helped the educated middle class to criticize itself. Ibsen had touched their guilt feelings; Shaw touched their funny bone. This is to say that Ibsen showed their complicity in crime, whereas Shaw showed incongruities, inconsistencies, and absurdities, both in the crimes and in the complicity. What comedy may lack in depth, it can make up in scope. The subject-matter of Ibsen's tragic plays is for ever the same. In his comedies, on the other hand, Shaw would "cover the field": war and peace, the capitalist system, education, biology, religion, metaphysics, penal law, the Irish Question, the family, the various professions (medical, martial, clerical) . . . anything and everything.

More precisely speaking it is in the prefaces and attendant pamphlets, articles, and treatises that the field was covered *in extenso*. The plays did what plays more characteristically do: they brought certain crucial conflicts into sharp focus. Indeed one might well say that it was in the prefaces and the like that Shaw did his best to convert a nation, whereas in the plays he provided comic relief. But it was comic relief of a highly ironical kind, because in it the subjects of the prefaces are seen, not in a simpler form, but in a form that is even more complex, being more human and concrete. The difference between preface and play has sometimes been viewed as one between the propagandist and the artist, the latter being considered "universally human." Shaw's critics are free to choose their terms, and even to invoke shibboleths. To the present writer, however, it seems mistaken to think of the plays as any less social in their commentary than the prefaces. Surely comedy was always the principal vehicle of sociological thought until academic men had the unhappy idea that the comic sense was not necessary in this field, and founded the science of sociology. In any event, Shaw's comedies bring social principles to the final test, asking what they mean in the lives of human beings. Some critics will perhaps see a claim to the "universally human"—a claim to be asocial, parasocial, metasocial—in Shaw's own statement that his plays present a conflict of free vitality with various abstract principles and impersonal institutions. Yet just as the principles and institutions are specific ones, and Shaw's satirical thrusts are directed at them, so the free vitality is seldom merely the Life Force in the abstract, but is to be found in the actual life generated in a character by Shaw the comic artist.

A recurring type in Shaw's comedies is what, with apologies to Nietzsche, we may call the superman: a human who is not divided against himself but is all of a piece and lives directly and happily from the primal vital spring. Caesar, Undershaft, and Joan are examples. There are no such people in the comedies of Aristophanes or Plautus, Machiavelli or Jonson, Shakespeare or Molière. Superior people stem from the epic and tragic tradition: and so, if Ibsen can be said to have given tragedy a comic twist, Shaw can be said to have given comedy a tragic one. Yet even tragic heroes are traditionally supposed to have a flaw, whereas the Shavian superman is flawless, an Achilles invulnerable even in the heel. Perhaps only one great tragic writer regularly risked such protagonists:

Corneille. And the result is that his tragedies verge upon comic effects, including some that were not intended.

Invulnerable in himself, as a dramatic creation the Shavian superman has not proved invulnerable to dramatic criticism. There are obvious dangers to the comic art in the presence, at its centre, of a man who (like Undershaft) knows all the answers, especially because it is not just verbal answers that he knows but practical ones. For drama is *praxis*. The plot of *Saint Joan* is not helped by the fact that the heroine could not do wrong if she tried. That she pleads guilty at one point in the trial is only a momentary hesitation that makes her final position the more heroic. Similarly the Shavian Caesar's vanity is only the charming humanizing foible of a great man, not a flaw undermining his greatness.

But has criticism been as ready to see why Shaw created this sort of hero as it has to note the reasons why he should not have done so? Such a "why" might not be especially significant if it were explored in biographical, psychological terms, citing factors in Shaw's life that impelled him to seek flawless heroes, but it surely has much interest in relation to modern social drama. It relates to what Ernst Bloch has called *das Prinzip Hoffnung*—the principle of hope as the very foundation of the modern radical outlook, as it was of the religions and mythologies in the eras of their full vitality. And, just as the religions and mythologies had a golden age in the past that one could hope for the return of, or a heaven in the sky that was eternally there, so modern radical philosophy has a future in which this earth is a home for men.

When society is fate, a historical fate, the dialectic of drama will be found in an interplay between epochs. One sees this first, as Ibsen did, as an interplay between past and present: the theatre exhibits a present into which the past ("ghosts") erupts. But, as Ibsen also knew, this is a simplification. There is a third factor: the future. And if art has a normative function—" it is always a writer's duty to make the world better" (Samuel Johnson)—the future is suffused by a definite sentiment, namely, hope. Indeed, one must perhaps say that, in the modern situation, if art is to have something positive about it, the most likely locus of the positive will be the future, for golden ages in the past have become as inconceivable as heavens in the skies. The past, far from being golden, hangs like lead around the necks of modern characters. The past is the dead weight of failure pressing upon the present and tending to kill the future. Such is the modern view of the past, personal and neurotic, social and historical. Thus, unless the modern artist is to acquiesce in a blank future, a future murdered by the past, he has to postulate and imagine a positive future: he has to work directly with his hopes; he has to build directly with such actual and vital hope as he can find within himself.

Ibsen the thinker certainly believed this. Ibsen the artist felt on firmer ground with the past and present, hence the fact that most of his plays provide a far more desolate image of life than his proclaimed philosophy. Shaw and Brecht, although they lived in a time of yet greater public catastrophes, by that very token felt themselves close to whatever positive solutions were to be found. They clearly resolved, at whatever cost to their art as art, to inject a far larger positive element into their work than Ibsen had usually done. For them, even more than for him, art was not for its own sake, but for the sake of the future. Like Ibsen's, their art would help to exorcise the ghosts of the past—"let the dead bury their dead"—and help to terminate the life-in-death of the present. Less ambiguously than Ibsen's, their art would help "us dead" to "awaken."

In itself this would have been sufficient reason for them to discontinue Ibsen's investigations of neurotic weakness. If they can be meaningfully referred back to him at all, it would be to his one or two attempts at a simply positive hero, notably Dr Stockmann in *An Enemy of the People* (1882). Such a superman was to find a place in both Shavian and Brechtian drama, though in different guises, corresponding to different nationalities and generations. Shaw's most characteristic and impressive superman is Undershaft, a radical critic of normal bourgeois procedures and shibboleths, yet himself a hero of bourgeois civilization—and a scintillating bourgeois intellectual too. If we look in the plays of Brecht for characters who are solid and all of a piece, who are always right and always do what is right, we shall find them only in the guise of the rebel as revolutionary: examples are Pavel in *The Mother* (1932), and several of the Communards in *Days of the Commune* (1949).

There are not many such supermen in Brecht or even in Shaw. Both playwrights remained Ibsenites to the extent that they dealt primarily with divided characters, if not with neurotic weakness. Pavel is a revolutionary from the outset, but the protagonist is his mother, who is not a revolutionary until near the end: meanwhile the play has shown her inner divisions. Particularly the Brecht characters who have universally been found most human and interesting—Mother Courage, Galileo, Azdak—are divided people, brave and cowardly, passive and active, good and bad. Even in Shaw, the superman did not always have to be protagonist. He could fill a character role such as that of General Burgoyne in *The Devil's Disciple* (1897) or Sergeant Meek in *Too True to be Good* (1931).

Shaw generally placed his supermen over against men who were all too human—the typical products of a given epoch and class. In these encounters he was able to give the age-old contrast of ironist and impostor a thoroughly actual and relevant treatment. And his own divided nature preserved him from supermanic dramaturgy on the scale of Corneille: the ironist did not defeat the impostor too easily. Some plays, such as *Heartbreak House* (1919), are principally about impostors and contain no outright supermen. In some, such as *John Bull's Other Island* (1904), the emphasis is strongly on a single impostor (Broadbent). Again, a favourite Shavian device and achievement is the ironist-superman who ironically turns out not to be a superman after all, but only too human. Such are Bluntschli (*Arms and the Man*, 1894) and Tanner (*Man and Superman*, 1903). Nor is it true that a Shavian character who embodies free vitality must have superhuman capabilities. He may be an impotent priest such as Father Keegan (*John Bull's Other Island*), or a senile crackpot such as Captain Shotover (*Heartbreak House*).

He may be a she. Shaw was a feminist, not only after the more political and abstract fashion, but in his human and artistic instincts. He tended to identify both himself and free vitality with the Eternal Feminine, and to identify the enemy with the society-ridden male. Hence, if we are looking for the positive element, for bridges to the future, for foundations of a socialist humanism, his women are just as important as his supermen. And this can be true in the least political of his comedies. *Pygmalion* (1913), for instance, is the tale of the incubation and liberation of a woman. With Tanner and the rest, Henry Higgins is a superman *manqué*, a clever ironist who proves to be an impostor, a Pygmalion who is only a Frankenstein.

A woman is the key to a Shaw play that has been widely misunderstood, *The Doctor's Dilemma* (1906), a play that will also permit us to illustrate another fact about Shaw the social dramatist: namely, that he delights to drive his critique beyond its ostensible main point to another point that is its dialectical opposite. Sometimes the very topic is not the ostensible one but another and contrary one. So with the "dilemma" represented by the choice between saving the life of an immoral genius or that of a moral mediocrity. This dilemma itself is thoroughly immoral. Only God can rightly assume such powers of life and death. A mere man can only plunge into folly or worse. The mere man in Shaw's play chooses to believe that his hand is pushed toward sacrificing the immoral genius by a solicitude for the latter's wife, who can thus be kept ignorant of her genius's immorality and so preserve her romantic image of him. However, we the audience know that it is not solicitude but desire that is forcing the man's hand: he wants to marry the widow. The "dilemma" is a false one, and its falsity is brought home to him in dramatic action. When he meets the now-widowed lady, he finds that she has already remarried. He is amazed, because it has never occurred to him that she might have found him resistible. "Other people" are a somewhat unreal category to him, pieces on a chess-board. His error over the widow springs from the same complex as his error in setting up a false dilemma.

Would it be fair to conclude that the social drama of the medical profession became a "universally human," or at least wholly psychological, drama? No. In drama, every subject must be humanized, must be steeped, as it were, in the essence of humanity; but surely "social" and "human" are not opposites? The topic here is private enterprise in medicine. The author's view is that medicine should be socialized. He is discreet enough not to state this view in the play. His play will show— in the flesh, as it were—private medicine as its exists. At one pole there are the more obvious impostors, the outright fools, who are lined up at the outset. The doctor-dramatist James Bridie complained that they are *too* foolish (in *Shaw at 90*, edited by S. Winsten [London 1946]), but then Shaw exhibits the less foolish kind of impostor in the protagonist, the man of the dilemma, Sir Colenso Ridgeon, a superman who, like Tanner and Higgins, is not a superman at all.

Sir Colenso is less of a superman than he supposes, but Jennifer Dubedat (the widow) is more fully human than she has seemed. She does not really need an inspiring, mendacious image to live by, after all; nor can she consent to be a marionette on Ridgeon's string. In counting on his idea of the inevitable female reaction, Ridgeon leaves out of account the woman, the human being. And so the parable remains political. Medicine should be socialized to free us from the caprices and phantasies of the Ridgeons, and all the more so if they can disguise their self-centred wishful thinking as objectivity and generosity. Second proposition: there exists a counter-force to Ridgeonism, namely, free vitality, that is sometimes (and not at all accidentally) embodied in women. Paradox: precisely where Ridgeon looked for compliance as the feminine contribution, he met with resistance and indeed with his come-uppance.

The social drama, as practised by non-geniuses such as Brieux, ran into fatal clichés. That Shaw just did not notice the limitations of Brieux is an index of his missionary zeal and of the strength of his commitment to a social criterion in drama. "Incomparably the greatest writer France has produced since Molière" (as Shaw calls him in the Preface to *Three Plays by Brieux*, 1909), Brieux was the kind of playwright that the propagandist-in-a-hurry in Shaw could not help envying, yet some deep intuition as to where his own calling lay prevented the envy from growing into emulation. Let those who once considered that Brieux rather than Shaw really came to grips with social problems take note that today Brieux cannot be seen as coming to grips with anything, whereas the playful Shaw must be seen to have tackled, in play as well as preface, the main problems of the era.

"We are coming fast," Shaw wrote in one of his 1896 theatre reviews, "to a melodramatic formula in which the villain shall be a bad employer and the hero a Socialist." In his first and third plays, completed in the early 1890s, he had provided a socialist critique of capitalism without recourse to this formula. In the first, *Widowers' Houses*, it was as if he set out to make the bad employer his hero, and the rebel against capitalism his villain. Yet that, though it "sounds like Shaw," is not exactly it, either. The capitalist Sartorius is a scoundrel who knows he is a scoundrel, whereas his adversary Trench is an exploiter who thinks he is outside the whole process of exploitation. Comedy has always been less inclined to scowl at iniquity than to laugh at a lack of self-knowledge, and so it is in this comedy of 19th-century capitalism, as in all the rest of its author's work.

Shaw's third play, *Mrs Warren's Profession* (1894), is founded on an innocent girl's discovery that her mother is a procuress and ex-whore. This would make mother a villainess and daughter a heroine if melodrama were true to life, but actually—and comedy has as its yardstick the actuality of society, of life as people live it—innocence is not of itself heroic, nor is membership of an anti-social profession (and for Shaw all professions are conspiracies against the public) an act of personal iniquity. If Mrs Warren has a sin, it consists only in a belief she shares with most of mankind, namely, that you can't buck the system: if you can't lick 'em, you join 'em, and she has joined 'em. In the end, her daughter, for her part, really *is* a heroine, to the extent that she is trying to buck the system: she has taken that first step, which nowadays would be called "dropping out." But she has also ceased to regard her mother as a villainess or herself as more wronged than others who are living on tainted money. For what money is *not* tainted? Under capitalism, you can either (as worker) have your earnings stolen or (as capitalist) do the stealing and live on the proceeds.

These two early plays are socialist not only in implying that socialism would be the remedy but also in their rendering of the *comédie humaine* generally. Just as the ultimate source of trouble in *Ghosts* and *Hedda*

Gabler is both social and unnecessary, so the ultimate source of trouble in *Widowers' Houses* and *Mrs Warren's Profession* is social and unnecessary. When the Mrs Alvings are truly liberated, when the Heddas don't give a damn about scandal, life will be different. When there are no landlords to exploit slum-dwellers, when there are no white-slavers to buy and sell sex, life can be better. Meanwhile it is ridiculous to condemn the individual landlord, pimp, or whore: ridiculous, deserving of ridicule, a proper object of laughter, a proper subject for comedy. What is needed, then, for the comic play on these themes is the plausible capitalist, the worshipper of the god of Things As They Are, and, opposing him, the idealistic rebel against capitalism who does not even know that the stocks and shares he lives off are investments in the same shabby business as the landlord he denounces. Or a procuress and ex-whore who is a very honest, agreeable, intelligent woman utterly devoted to a daughter who, well brought up as she is, will undergo a trauma when she finds out what money she has been well brought up on. . . .

The two plays present capitalism in miniature, and in this could be regarded as models for Brecht's *Threepenny Opera* (1928) and *The Rise and Fall of the City of Mahagonny* (1930). The perspective of all four comedies is suggested in some lines of Simon O. Lesser:

> The attitude of most comedies is that of an urbane and tolerant friend, amused rather than censorious about that blonde he saw us out with the night before. . . . Other comedies are caustic and the reverse of indulgent, but they suggest a scale of values against which the shortcomings and misdeeds of the characters seem trivial . . . granted that the little people [this kind of comedy] set before us are far from admirable, they, and by inference we ourselves, are no worse than anyone else.[7]

Shaw called the two types here adumbrated *Plays: Pleasant and Unpleasant*, a phrase that he used as the title for all his early plays (1892–8). The "unpleasant" play—exemplified by *Widowers' Houses* and *Mrs Warren's Profession*—was certainly a precision tool in social criticism, a dialectical tool for which their author has scarcely yet received due credit. You can smile all evening at the amusing crimes of Sartorius and Mrs Warren; but if, on your way home, you realize that the whole social order is run in this way, you may smile on the other side of your face.

Shaw, for his part, seems to have found the "unpleasant" mode constricting. Like Swift, he "served human liberty," and the schematic early plays afforded his enterprise far too little elbow-room. They had, for example, no room for his supermen and, although they had room for rebellious women such as Blanche Sartorius and Vivie Warren, they kept the rebellion within too narrow bounds. Even the impostors were miniatures compared with those to follow. Shaw once spoke of the need a dramatist has to let his characters rip. That is what he was not able to do in the earliest plays; the mould in which the plays were cast seemed to forbid it. There is far more freedom later, in two respects: first, there is the growing freedom of the playwright as he learns his craft and gives his genius its head; second, characters are placed in situations in which *they* have freedom in its ultimate form: real freedom of choice on crucial issues. Both kinds of freedom had been lacking in *Widowers' Houses.* Not only had the journeyman playwright acquired no kind of ease or daring in handling the structure, but inside the box of his plot, and in the box (with one side missing) of the Victorian stage-scene, he presented a version of humanity hemmed in by the capitalist system. It was cutting, even devastating, writing, but no wind of freedom blew from that stage to that audience. One thing needed was that characters should not just be worked upon by circumstances, but should themselves work on the circumstances. History, by all means, can determine their mode of existence; but they in turn must work upon history.

Saint Joan (1923) could not have been written by the Shaw of the early 1890s. He would not have known how to let Joan rip. In this play we breathe the air of human freedom, and again this is both an artistic, technical matter and a matter of the outlook defined by the art and the technique. The closed, box-like form of the 19th-century well-made play was progressively abandoned by Shaw. As a chronicle, *Saint Joan* is rather compact, but that it *is* a chronicle at all means open windows, fresh air, amplitude.

Half-a-dozen years after the première of *Saint Joan*, Bertolt Brecht wrote *Happy End,** which a couple of years later had grown into *Saint Joan of the Stockyards*. It can serve here as a cue for continued analysis of *Saint Joan* itself and for an exploration of the difference between Shaw and Brecht. The relation between the two dramatists was never closer than here, because *Saint Joan of the Stockyards* owes much, not only to *Saint Joan*, but also to *Major Barbara*.

As usual with Brecht, one can begin with surprise at how much he saw fit to borrow. "A Salvation Army officer forsaken by God" could be

---

* Actually, he disowned the play. The title page carries the name Dorothy Lane. Some have said it was written by Elisabeth Hauptman. Yet the present author's attribution seems also very plausible.

considered the central image of *Major Barbara*, and Brecht appropriated it. That the officer is a girl, with all that femininity connotes of delicacy in feeling and ardour in aspiration, is not lost on Brecht, either. And the general reason for the loss of God is the same in both authors: the dependence of the other-worldly institution upon a capitalistic world. However, although both authors rely upon a materialist analysis of the Salvation Army, they approach the subject from opposite ends. Shaw shows that the teetotalism of the Army, being promoted by brewers' money, is compromised at the start: the "idealism" of an Army officer has to be either ignorant or corrupt. Realizing this, Major Barbara feels drained, devastated, abandoned, by her God. She will remain in this state of mind and heart until a niche is found for her within the existing social order. The finding of such a niche is the psycho-spiritual solution to what Shaw has ironically portrayed as a psycho-spiritual problem. Brecht, on the other hand, is little concerned with the usefulness of capitalism to the Salvation Army. He is concerned with the usefulness of the Salvation Army to capitalism. If his Joan, too, suffers a psycho-spiritual crisis (and she does, though the phrase itself begins to let us down in a Brechtian context) it is from the sensation, not of being deserted, but of being cheated. God has not gone: he was never there. Joan discovers not a void of unbelief, but an active atheism that offers an alternative to deity in the idea of Man On His Own—man's fate is man himself. It is at this point that one can imagine the playwright Brecht asking whether, if one Shaw play wouldn't do his job for him, another might serve the purpose. Although *Saint Joan of the Stockyards* is mostly a *Major Barbara*, ultimately it is indeed a *Saint Joan*: for Barbara turns into Joan when Brecht's protagonist moves from false to true consciousness and from passivity disguised as action to action that is positive and revolutionary.

Brecht probably noted what most of Shaw's critics have missed: that Shaw himself goes part of the way toward making Joan a revolutionary leader whose final support comes from the people. She is his only non-bourgeois superman (even his Caesar is bourgeois in spirit, as is his super-king Magnus), and this fact yields much more broadly conceived political drama than Shaw was wont to attempt. In the great scene that is the turning-point of the story, Joan stands forth as the patron saint of all future National Liberation Fronts:

> Common folks understand . . . they follow me half naked into the
> moat and up the ladder and over the wall. . . . You locked the gates
> to keep me in; and it was the townsfolk and the common people

> that followed me, and forced the gate. . . . I will go out now to the
> common people, and let the love in their eyes comfort me for the
> hate in yours. You will all be glad to see me burnt; but if I go
> through the fire, I shall go through it to their hearts for ever and ever.

Unlike Shaw's Major Barbara, Brecht's Joan Dark has, in the Communist Party, an alternative to both the Salvation Army and big business.
However, she is not permitted a true martyrdom, like Shaw's Joan, but
only a fake one: her death is a "set-up," and so she remains in death
what she has been in life: a victim. The politics of *Saint Joan* and *Saint
Joan of the Stockyards* are thus revealed, in their respective endings, to be
diametrically opposite. Shaw calls for a democracy of supermen that shall
be worthy of his democratic superwoman. Brecht appeals for solidarity
among those people (the working class, the victims) by whom the myths
of sainthood will be shattered along with the social order that the myths
serve to flatter and conceal.

In nothing is the difference between Shaw and Brecht more marked
than in their presentation of the capitalist villain. Both authors are at the
top of their form: Undershaft is one of Shaw's most telling stage creations,
and Pierpont Mauler is one of Brecht's. Underlying both creations is the
Marxist principle that the individual capitalist is not to be equated with
the system. To Shaw, this means that whereas the system may be
rationally flimsy and morally outrageous, the individual capitalist may
be rational, plausible, intelligent, and charming. To Brecht, it means
that, although the system may be omnipotent and devoid of conscience,
the individual capitalist may well have a sense of guilt but that, sensing
also his own powerlessness, he will hold on to his position, anyway, seeing
no alternative:

> . . . Just think, if I—who have much against [the system], and sleep
> badly—were to desert it, I would be like a fly ceasing to hold back
> a landslide.

Thus Mauler in *Saint Joan of the Stockyards* (Scene VIII). Therefore,
although he does not feel sorry for mankind, because "mankind is evil,"
he is distinctly sorry for himself as the presumably non-evil exception.
He pities himself as he pities slaughtered cattle: both are true victims.
The alleged victims—members of the working class—are just those who,
being bad, meet with a bad fate.

One could elaborate indefinitely the different *schemata* behind Undershaft and Mauler respectively. The artistic result is two characters
who stand at opposite poles of comedy. Undershaft is a maker of

comedy—of amusing speeches and of dramas that will have a chilling comedic effect to begin with and a happy ending later. He is an entertainer, entertaining his workers in a model factory; entertaining Shaw's spectators whenever he comes on stage. Even in his family's home, he is the Father as Entertainer. If Undershaft represents comedy as the highest possible degree of *charm*, Mauler's effect is so close to the opposite pole of *nausea* that some will want to deny him the epithet "comic" altogether. What also may strike some people as uncomic is that he is so emotional; whereas Undershaft is cool, keeping his head in every crisis, Mauler loses his head throughout, suffering vociferously—the aggrieved victim of a social system in crisis. And what a system! Brecht reported that when he first studied capitalist economics, his reaction was not: "How unjust!" but: "It will never work!" To the extent that it did work, it kept its helpers and servers at fever pitch watching the fluctuations of the market. Thus the Pierpont Maulers experience the extreme tensions of the roulette player.

If we think such painful tensions out of place in comedy, we are forgetting the sufferings of, say, Jonson's Morose or Molière's Harpagon. But comedy, to use Brecht's word, "alienates" the emotions so that we feel no sympathy. And alienating the emotions so that we feel no sympathy, comedy is the exactly correct vehicle of this author's intention and philosophy. We are to recoil from Mauler and his colleagues in horror and disgust, and we do so because they are made ridiculous, that is, because they are seen through the eyes of comedy. Thus, to those who would assume that comedy might somehow make such figures pleasant and therefore acceptable, there would be several answers. One is: no, this is "unpleasant" comedy. A second is: no, the danger would lie in the more direct portrayal of gangsters as villains, whereby their villainy, conveying emotional intensity, gains a fascination by no means reduced in being called "evil" fascination. One could see a Hollywood movie of that era, such as *Scarface*, and draw the conclusion: "Scarface's life was good while it lasted. And how can one be upset by a premature death in a society that offers such empty living? Better to live dangerously. Gangsterism has glamour." Conclusions of this sort can be blocked by such "alienation" of the action as we see in Brecht's gangster play *The Resistible Rise of Arturo Ui* (1941), or in *Saint Joan of the Stockyards*.

In Andrew Undershaft and Pierpont Mauler we find our socialist playwrights equally determined to remove a mote from the public's eye— but not the same mote. For Shaw, the target is the audience who will exonerate the system by characterizing the businessman as bad. For

Brecht, the target is the audience who will exonerate the system by characterizing the businessman as "human." Shaw is portraying a businessman who is not merely human but *super*human. Brecht is portraying one whom the folklore of capitalism will see as a superman (man of distinction, VIP, member of the power élite) but who is actually subhuman, a worm. The difference, here, between Shaw and Brecht reflects the passage of time between the writing of *Major Barbara* and the writing of *Saint Joan of the Stockyards*, yet not so much the steady ticking of the clock, as the gigantic happening of World War I, a dual happening that consisted of the destruction of one world and the boldest attempt since the French Revolution to bring a new world into existence. Although he is an orphan and a rebel, Undershaft still very much belongs to the Victorian salons he despises. There still *exists* a world of salons in which his brilliant repartee is not really unwelcome. Mauler, on the other hand, is truly homeless, has nowhere nice to go, is trapped between the stock exchange and the stockyards. Whatever Undershaft's objections to the upper-class London of his wife and son, he actually enhances its claims on our respect by adding to the formal elegance of its furniture, dress, and accent his own elegance of word and thought. He is its crowning adornment; so that, from the vantage point of the 1970s although we may cry: "Obsolete!" we cannot restrain a sigh of longing for the snows of yesteryear. But Mauler's world has no more aesthetic appeal than the slums where his class-enemies live. Like the slums, it is ugly, nasty, stifling, and macabre—a kind of Inferno.

Saint Joan of the Stockyards is not just a play that happens to be different in kind from *Major Barbara* because time has passed, nor even because in that time a war and a revolution occurred. It also reflects deliberate conclusions on the subject of social theatre that Brecht reached during the 1920s. That was the decade in which he put together his theory of an Epic Theatre—"epic" in the sense of "narrative," as opposed to lyric or dramatic. Richard Wagner had perfected a lyric theatre, and in this had been echoed even by poets who did not need music, from Yeats to Maeterlinck. Ibsen had perfected the modern "dramatic" theatre—"dramatic" in the classic, Sophoclean-Racinian tradition, with its unity of time, place, and action; "modern" in its psychological, indeed psycho-analytical, emphasis. Brecht's scheme of things began with the rejection of Wagnerism and Ibsenism. As for Shavianism, he would not so much reject it as develop it—to an extent that would have made it unrecognizable to Shaw.

The essence of Shavianism in dramaturgy was the assumption that the modern world could best be placed on stage in the form of serious parody—a double form of parody, as it turned out, because Shaw consistently parodied both the behaviour of men and the patterns of dramatic art. In his mind, the two were so closely related as to be at essential points identical:

> The truth is that dramatic invention is the first effort of man to become intellectually conscious. No frontier can be marked between drama and history or religion, or between acting and conduct.[8]

Just as Marx proposed to stand Hegel on his feet, so Shaw proposed to stand all the 19th century's idealisms on their feet. Hence, notably, his subjection of melodrama, in theatre or in life, to the test of reality. For such purposes, already in the 1890s, he was demanding a non-illusionistic stage:

> For him [William Archer] there is illusion in the theatre: for me there is none. . . . To me the play is only the means, the end being the expression of feeling by the arts of the actor, the poet, the musician. Anything that makes this expression more vivid, whether it be versification, or an orchestra, or a deliberately artificial delivery of the lines, is so much to the good for me, even though it may destroy all the verisimilitude of the scene.[9]

Now what has just been called the essence of Shavianism was never challenged by Brecht. On the contrary, his plays, like Shaw's, are to a very large extent parodies both of conventional plays and of conventional behaviour. In the passage just quoted, Brecht would no doubt have been dissatisfied with the phrase "expression of feeling," but at the same time he would have enthusiastically accepted Shaw's invitation to a non-illusionistic theatre in which "versification, or an orchestra, or a deliberately artificial delivery" would not be out of place.

Perhaps the most damaging thing ever said about Shavian theatre was Egon Friedell's remark to the effect that Shaw's message was like a pill that he had covered with the sugar of entertainment, and the nice thing was that you could suck off the sugar and put the pill back on the plate. Seeing how much truth there was to this, Brecht resolved to write "Shavian" comedies that could not be disposed of in this way. Such are the theory and practice known as Epic Theatre. Brecht once said his efforts could all be summed up as an attempt to re-state in theatrical terms the famous thesis of Marx: "The philosophers have only *interpreted* the world in various ways: the point, however, is to *change* it." Shaw had of course wanted exactly the same thing but (as the young Brecht would see it) had been too nice to his audience, who took from his plays merely what they wished to take. The early theoretical work of Brecht is taken up with a condemnation of "culinary" theatre—theatre in which you just enjoy eating, as in a restaurant. It seemed to him almost as if the guests in the modern theatre-restaurant swallowed all their food without chewing it. Perhaps the answer was to serve them crunchy solids instead of smooth fluids? Certainly one must not, as Wagner had done, melt down the whole meal into a single smooth liquid, but, rather, break it up into dishes of various and contrasting kinds.

Brecht was aware of a cultural situation that was being discussed in his time and has been discussed since, particularly by writers of German background, from Herbert Marcuse to Hannah Arendt. Modern bourgeois civilization—to use the food metaphor in another way—*devours* everything, good or bad. It not only pours forth musical rubbish in the elevator or supermarket in the form of Muzak: it is equally capable of serving up the Ode of Joy from Beethoven's Ninth Symphony in a radio or television commercial and at the same time claiming to be spreading "culture" around. Against this kind of exploitation the music of Beethoven is as helpless as Mrs Warren before the white-slaver or a coolie before a colonialist. Being dead, Beethoven can do little about it; but what of the living artist?

Brecht's answer was that he can make his art less fluid and saccharine by means of crunchy and pungent ingredients known as alienation devices. The German for alien is *fremd*. Marx had seen the worker under capitalism as *entfremdet* (alienated). Brecht proposed actually to make alien (*verfremden*) the familiar elements of the theatre experience. A paradox, yes, because alienation is the problem and the antagonist, and communism will mark the end of alienation. But communism is a good way off, even in socialist countries. Meanwhile the artist can resist being consumed, can help to prevent the whole inherited culture from being trapped between the Leviathan's jaws and gobbled up. Brecht's theatre is an attempt at a different kind of communication. The result would inevitably be that some would not receive any message at all; but those who did receive one would know that they had. It would not be lost in the fine print. It would stand out. It would command attention, and perhaps even incite to action.

It was with such ends in view that Brecht discarded so many of the treasured devices of traditional theatre. The lighting was to be plain white and diffused over the whole stage. In this way the cult of *Stimmung* (mood) would be countered. To the same end, illusionistic scenery must go, for the paradox of scenery that "looked like the real thing" was that it induced dream-states in the audience. What was needed, instead of a hypnotic trance, was alertness. Actors would have to change their ways. Instead of attempting a hallucination of unrealities suddenly present ("I am Dracula"), they must exhibit realities that can be recognized as such and have thus belonged to our past ("This was a man"). Instead of the Stanislavsky actor who spoke in the first person and the present tense and absorbed all stage directions into a living illusion of the actual thing, Brecht proposed an Epic actor who seemed to be using the third person and the past tense; as for the stage directions, they could be read aloud, at least as an exercise.

This is not the place to itemize every feature of Brechtian theatre, either in its early (Epic) phase or in the final phase, when Brecht was beginning to substitute the term Dialectical Theatre. Too much theory would be misleading, at least if accompanied by too few looks at the practice. One must take care, as was suggested above, not to assume that Brecht's theories correspond exactly and in all ways to his practices. Even if they did, practice is no more deducible from theory than the beauty of a landscape is deducible from a map. Just as the Ibsenite drama could never be deduced from existing notions of social theatre, and Shavian comedy could never be deduced from free-floating notions such as discussion plays and propaganda, nor yet from Shaw's own prefaces, so Brecht's achievement as a playwright, even as a social playwright, could not be deduced from theoretical writings, even his own. On the contrary, it is possible to make bad mistakes about the plays by assuming that they conform exactly to what the theories prescribe.

Whenever active artistry is at work, many concrete elements come into being that escape the net of general ideas. You may read in Ibsen's workbooks that "marriage for external reasons . . . brings a nemesis upon the offspring," and this idea is obviously in *Ghosts*: yet it neither makes *Ghosts* a good play nor gives it its particular tone, style, and character, its mode of being. This latter stems (if the source can be isolated in a single phrase) from Ibsen's *ironical use* of the idea and of all his other materials. So, too, with Shaw: many of the ideas of, say, *The Intelligent Woman's Guide to Socialism* (1928) are also found in the plays, sometimes in similar phrasing, but they neither constitute the merit of the plays nor give them their life as theatre, as art. *A dramatic context ironizes*: and to say "dramatic irony" is often a little like saying "dramatic drama." A Shavian dramatic context sometimes ironizes to the point of conflict with the presumably intended idea. Thus it is not clear whether Shaw solved all his problems in the final act of *Major Barbara*. One may feel that Undershaft is so strong a character that an intended balance is upset and a desired synthesis is missed.

One would like to turn the attention of critics exercised by Shaw's opinions to something far more pervasive in his work than any particular opinion, and far more likely to endear him to some, while deterring others: namely, his habit of teasing. His opinions come from here, there, and everywhere, but his teasing tone is, somehow, his very self: it is present throughout his plays and his other writings. Shall we ask what his various avowals signify, and not ask what this central fact about him signifies? That would be like being seduced, and not asking who seduced us.

Teasing is a complex phenomenon, but it is easy to see at least two ingredients as it applies to Shaw: humorous acceptance of failure to persuade, and a degree of aggression toward the unpersuaded. On the few occasions when Shaw did not tease, he expressed complete exasperation. Teasing may be regarded as indicating either a disguised acceptance of defeat or a good-natured refusal to accept it, and it is not surprising that some have seen Shaw's humour as just another weapon of an optimistic fighter, while others have found in it a tacit admission of both defeat and defeatism. But these are not the only possible explanations. It is also possible for a man to be thinking "*Even if* we fail, *even if* we are mistaken. . . ." When Tolstoy expressed disapproval of Shaw's humorous approach to religion, Shaw replied: "Suppose the world were only one of God's jokes, would you work any the less to make it a good joke instead of a bad one?" That a man allows for failure does not mean that he thinks it is inevitable; and both Shaw's teasing and his humour in general, it appears to the present writer, serve to communicate neither optimism nor pessimism, but rather to *ironize* whatever topic *arises*, and so serve to make the thought dialectical and the form dramatic. The pessimist can surely find in much of the teasing an admission of difficulty—of possible impossibility, as it were. The optimist can congratulate the teaser on his admirable poise, the confident way in which he gets on top of his subject, but the shrewd psychologist will want to stress that, by teasing, Shaw ensures that he is always in an active relation to his audience: whenever he is not pushing, he is pulling. To be sure, what those who reject Shavian theatre reject it for is commonly what those who relish it relish it for. Here is an author who "never lets you alone." You are either stimulated and delighted, or provoked and disconcerted.

Such is the concrete Shaw, as opposed to the ideological Shaw. Of Brecht, it has been said that, although his views were communist, his concrete existence contradicted those views. Even if this formulation is correct, it need not be taken to be as damaging (either to Brecht or to communism) as has been assumed. Some tension between existence and idea is surely inevitable. No Christian is merely an embodiment of Christianity. If such a person existed, he would not, in any case, turn out to be a Christian *artist*. Always more concrete than theory, art must give a different account of the world, unless by sheer lack of merit (as with Brieux) it fails to be art. To the political artist, art presents a particular opportunity, which is not—as is commonly thought—simply to re-state his political views and thus to extend the political battle to another front, but, instead, *to test abstract principles in concrete situations*, to show what politics means in the lives of people. Contradictions enter the picture automatically: because the concretely human is the writer's special field, when he brings it into play, it brings with it the contradictoriness of people. Bertolt Brecht was a contradictory man, so is the present writer, and so are you, dear reader. Why not, also, Brecht's Galileo?

> . . . ich bin kein ausgeklügelt Buch,
> Ich bin ein Mensch mit seinem Widerspruch.[10]
>
> (. . . I am no clearly thought-out book, I am a man with his contradiction.)

It should, therefore, come as no surprise that the socialist humanism of Brecht is more adequately rendered in a many-sided and problematic work such as *The Caucasian Chalk Circle* (1945) than in the more explicit presentations, closer to Marx and Lenin, such as *The Mother* or *Days of the Commune*. Again the author's sense of humour—and specifically his ironizing of everything—is our best clue. When, as in the two plays just mentioned, Brecht writes of class-comrades, he abandons this irony—understandably, to be sure, as it was likely to turn against them. Yet it was evidently hard to find anything to take its place: a friendly attitude, however commendable morally and politically, has no particular aesthetic merit, no energy as art. Another author might perhaps have found another solution. Brecht the artist, like Shaw the artist, cannot be severed from his sense of humour. By his lyric gift, eked out by Hanns Eisler's musical genius, Brecht was able to raise both *The Mother* and *Days of the Commune* well above the common level of political plays, but to see what he can really do—even when he is writing about socialism itself—one must turn to works that have been steeped in his irony.

Ernst Bloch has written that, in the work of all the great poets and philosophers, there is a window that opens upon Utopia. One might add that sometimes (as in Shaw's *Back to Methuselah*, 1921) it is open too wide. What is engaging about *The Caucasian Chalk Circle* is the irony in the Utopianism, particularly in the wake of a prologue that presents the Soviet Union as much closer to Utopia than it actually was. In this play Brecht used the idea of the Lord of Misrule, who for a brief interregnum turns the existing society and its values upside down. If the existing society is an anti-human one, this would mean substituting a genuine humanism. To be human for a day: that is the formula. There is a catch in it. What we are likely to get is a flat, unbelievable virtuousness. Brecht does not give us this, arguing that if the whole society was monstrous, then even the misrule would be grotesque: in its origin a fluke, it is by nature a freak. The fact that by definition it will have no future affects its character: it is only a truancy, not a liberation. All of this would have remained so much theorizing, except that Brecht was able to write the poetry and the comedy, the narrative and the character, by which the word became flesh— by which the Lord of Misrule became *ein Mensch mit seinem Widerspruch* (a man with his contradiction): Azdak, the disenchanted philosopher as quasi-revolutionary activist.

Does the irony undercut the author's activism? As with Shaw, there will be those who think that it does, with the justification that, as they read or see the play, they find themselves responding more fully to the despair than to the hope, and it is always likely, *a priori*, that despair will outweigh hope in a work of art, because despair is an established fact that tends to pervade the past and the present, whereas hope tends to be just a project, located as it is, in that frail, as yet merely imagined, spot, the future. But it seems to the present writer that Brecht has linked despair and hope in lively dialectical interplay; and that although there are many moments when despair predominates, hope remains at the end: which is all that hope need do. It need not bring in the kingdom. It need only survive. The question is whether the good society is felt, nostalgically, to be in the past (that is, to be over), or whether it is felt, hopefully, to be in the future (that is, in the making), felt to be a possibility and "up to us," something we can work on, a matter of *praxis*. The old notion of the golden age has little meaning in *The Caucasian Chalk Circle* until it is inverted. We, the audience, return to the golden age when we see Azdak inverting our rules and laws. In thought, Azdak returns to a golden age when he nostalgically recalls the popular revolt of a former generation. On the other hand, the age of Azdak is no golden age, but an age of war and oppression in which, by a fluke, a little justice may be done. That, for Azdak himself, revolutions are identified with the past, is what is wrong with him. The era of Azdak itself has the transitory character of the Saturnalia, in which, after the brief interregnum, a Mock King goes back into anonymity, but the important Prologue suggests a *regnum* that is not *inter*. The ultimate ironic inversion (among many in the play) is that a golden age should be envisaged not in Arcadia, but in the state of Georgia. In this way, what is planted in the minds of at least a sympathetic audience is not a memory, a phantasy, or a dream, but a possibility. That this should be open to doubt, and that certain audiences can respond differently, is a tribute to the dialectical complexity of the piece, the subtlety of Brecht's method.

"What is a modern problem play but a clinical lecture on society?" Bernard Shaw asked in 1901.[11] If the works of Ibsen, Shaw, and Brecht may fairly be described as modern problem plays, then our answer must be that they are much else besides clinical lectures on society. They are tragedies, or comedies, or tragi-comedies of so special a kind that only close analysis can reveal their peculiarity, let alone their merit. They are dramatic art, and they are dramatic art in motion: we see the "problem play" developing from one Ibsen play to another, from one Shaw play to another, from one Brecht play to another. There is also development from one *author* to another. And because people are individuals and unique, geniuses (if an Irishism may be permitted) are even more individual and unique. The problem play, ultimately, was what Ibsen or Shaw or Brecht made of it; yet there is reason to say that it remained the problem play. Although it has been the aim of this essay, on the one hand, to suggest that far more art and artifice went into this form of play than has sometimes been assumed, it has equally been its aim to demonstrate that the social drama was indeed social, from *Ghosts* and *Hedda Gabler* to *Widowers' Houses* and *Mrs Warren's Profession*, and from *Major Barbara* and *Saint Joan* to *Saint Joan of the Stockyards* and *The Caucasian Chalk Circle*.

References

1. SEBASTIEN MERCIER, *Du théâtre* (1773), as cited in ROMAIN ROLLAND, *The People's Theatre*, trans. by Barrett H. Clark (London 1919).
2. ALEXIS DE TOCQUEVILLE, *Democracy in America*, Part II (1840).
3. GEORG LUKÁCS, *The Sociology of Modern Drama* (Budapest 1909).
4. Inaugural Lecture, Copenhagen (1871).

5. BERTOLT BRECHT, *On Experimental Theatre*, trans. by John Willett (Stockholm 1939).
6. BERTOLT BRECHT, Notes to *The Mother* (1933), trans. by Lee Baxendall (New York 1965).
7. *Fiction and the Unconscious* (London 1960).
8. BERNARD SHAW, Preface to the Pleasant Plays, in *Plays: Pleasant and Unpleasant* (1898).
9. BERNARD SHAW, in *The Saturday Review* (13 April 1895).
10. C. F. MEYER, *Huttens letzte Tage* (1871).
11. BERNARD SHAW, "Who I Am and What I Think," *The Candid Friend* (London, May 1901).

Bibliography

This chapter is based mainly on the published works of Ibsen, Shaw, and Brecht. There has never, in fact, been an absolutely complete English-language edition of any of these writers.

Ibsen

The standard British edition, edited by J. W. McFarlane, is published by Oxford University Press (London 1960 ff). Recommended translations in paperback include those of Rolf Fjelde published by New English Library: *Peer Gynt; Four Major Plays*, Vol. I (*A Doll's House, The Wild Duck, Hedda Gabler*, and *The Master Builder*); Vol. II (*Ghosts, An Enemy of the People, The Lady from the Sea*, and *John Gabriel Borkman*). Penguin has published five paperback volumes: *A Doll's House and Other Plays* (incl. *The Lady from the Sea* and *The League of Youth*); *Ghosts and Other Plays* (incl. *A Public Enemy* and *When We Dead Wake*); *Peer Gynt; Hedda Gabler and Other Plays* (incl. *The Pillars of the Community* and *The Wild Duck*); and *The Master Builder and Other Plays* (incl. *Rosmersholm, Little Eyolf*, and *John Gabriel Borkman*). The plays in the first three books are translated by Peter Watts, those in the last two by Una Ellis-Fermor.

Shaw

The most extensive is Constable's Standard Edition of 36 volumes (London 1931–50). Hamlyn has published all of Shaw's prefaces (London 1965). Odhams Press has published his complete plays in one volume (London 1934); a number of the plays are also available in paperbacks.

Brecht

His plays and other works have been published piecemeal since the early 1960s, notably by Methuen in Britain and Grove Press in the United States; but these editions are by no means identical. The quotations from Brecht plays in the text are taken from the Grove Press edition.

General

Most of the quotations on dramatic theory in the first part of the chapter are in ERIC BENTLEY (ed.), *The Theory of the Modern Stage* (paperback: Harmondsworth 1968). Later sections of the chapter draw on Eric Bentley's Introduction to the Grove Press edition of *The Caucasian Chalk Circle* (New York 1967). Some general ideas in the chapter draw on ERNST BLOCH, *Das Prinzip Hoffnung*, 3 vols. (Frankfurt 1954–9). The ideas discussed about all three authors are expounded at greater length in ERIC BENTLEY, *The Modern Theatre* (London 1948); *Bernard Shaw* (London 1950); *The Life of the Drama* (London 1965); *The Theatre of Commitment* (London 1968); and various prefaces to Brecht in the Grove Press edition.

Index

Page numbers in *italics* refer to footnotes.

613